MADE IN JAPAN

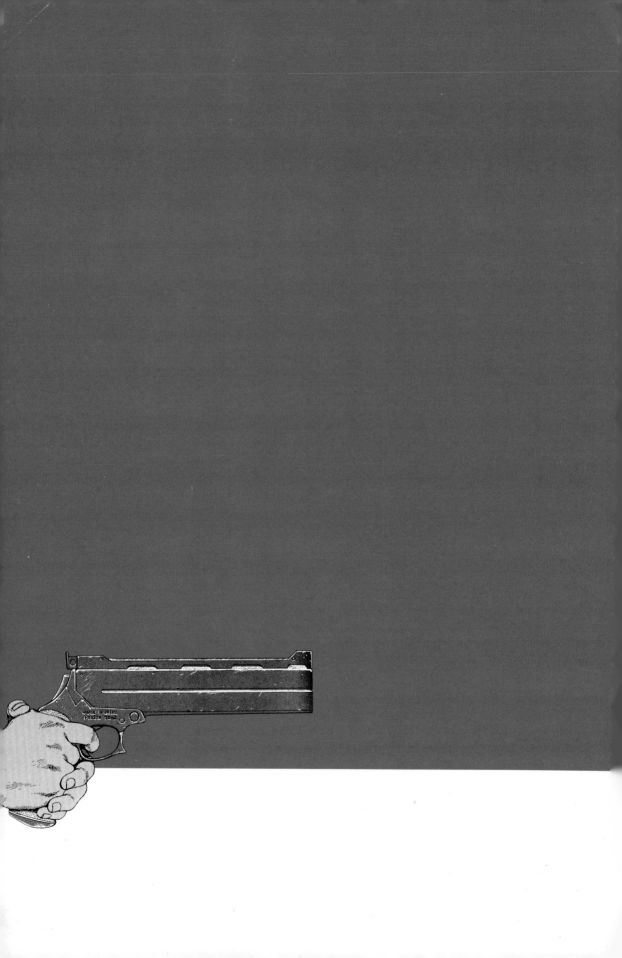

# AKIRA

## KATSUHIRO OTOMO

**BOOK
TWO**

A Kodansha Comics Trade Paperback Original

AKIRA Volume 2 © 1985 MASH•ROOM. All rights reserved.
English translation copyright © 1985 MASH•ROOM /Kodansha Ltd.
First published in Japan in 1985 by Kodansha Ltd., Tokyo.
Publication rights for this English edition arranged through Kodansha Ltd., Tokyo.

Published in the United States by Kodansha Comics, an imprint of Kodansha USA Publishing, New York.

Kodansha Comics is a registered trademark of Kodansha Ltd.

ISBN 978-1-935429-02-9

First edition: June 2010
Printed in the United States of America

10 9 8 7 6 5 4 3

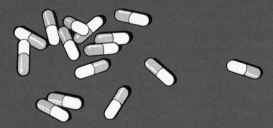

Translation and English-language adaptation:Yoko Umezawa, Linda M. York, Jo Duffy.
Graphics adaptation and sound effects lettering: David Schmit/ Digibox, Editions Glénat
Digital lettering and additional graphics adaptation: Digital Chameleon, Dark Horse Comics
English edition cover design and art direction: Lia Ribacchi, Mark Cox

MASH•ROOM staff: Makoto Shiosaki, Yasumitsu Suetake
Original series editor: Koichi Yuri
Original cover design: Akira Saito/Veia
Editor for this edition: Naoto Yasunaga, Takeshi Katsurada

# AKIRA

## PART 2

# アキラ I

## Akira I

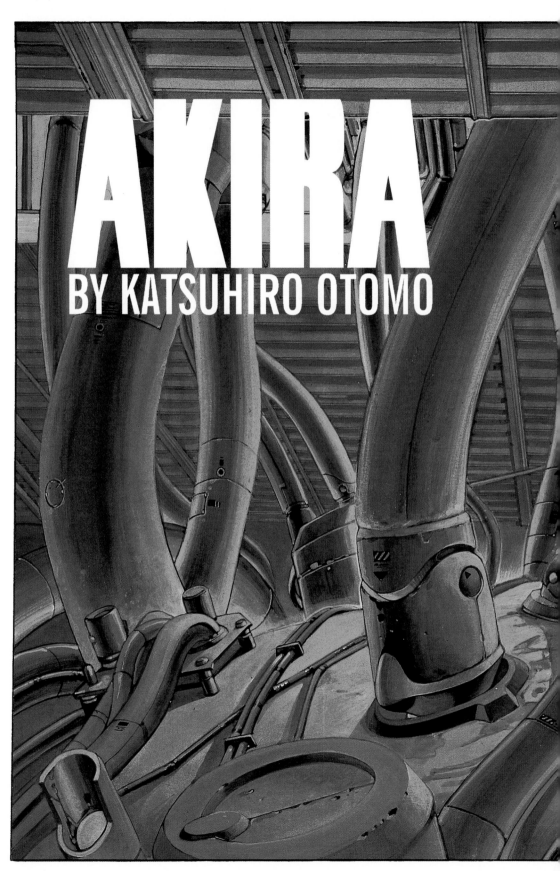

AKIRA

BY KATSUHIRO OTOMO

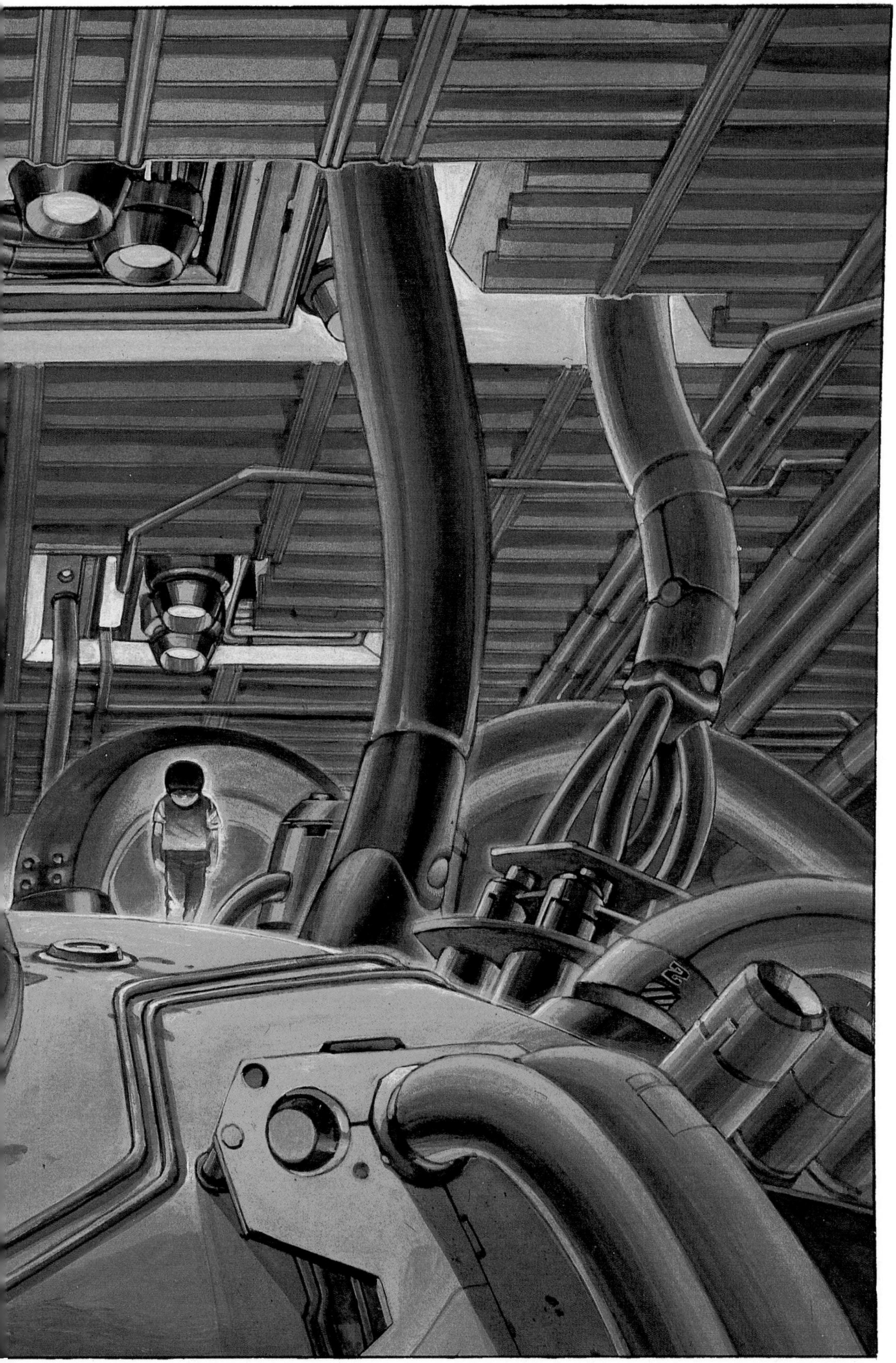

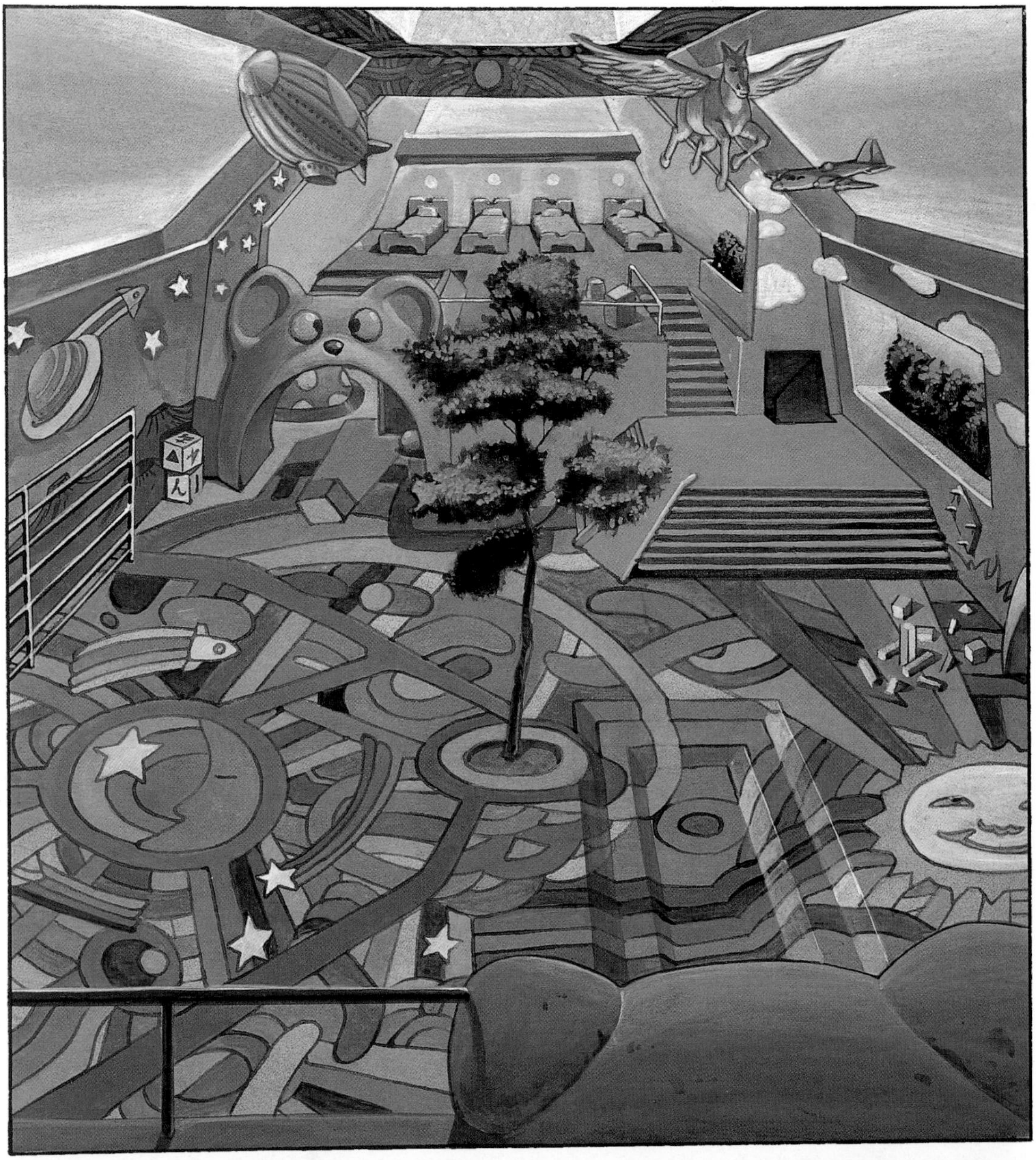

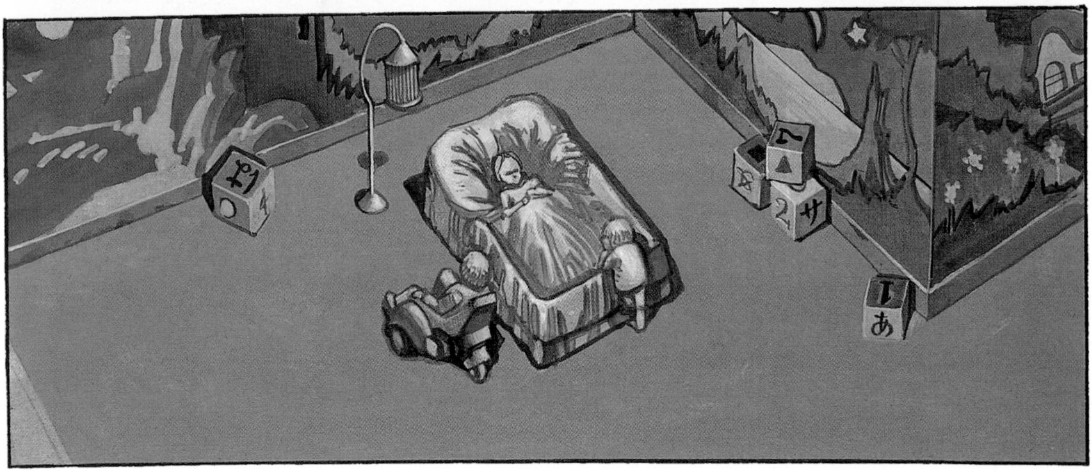

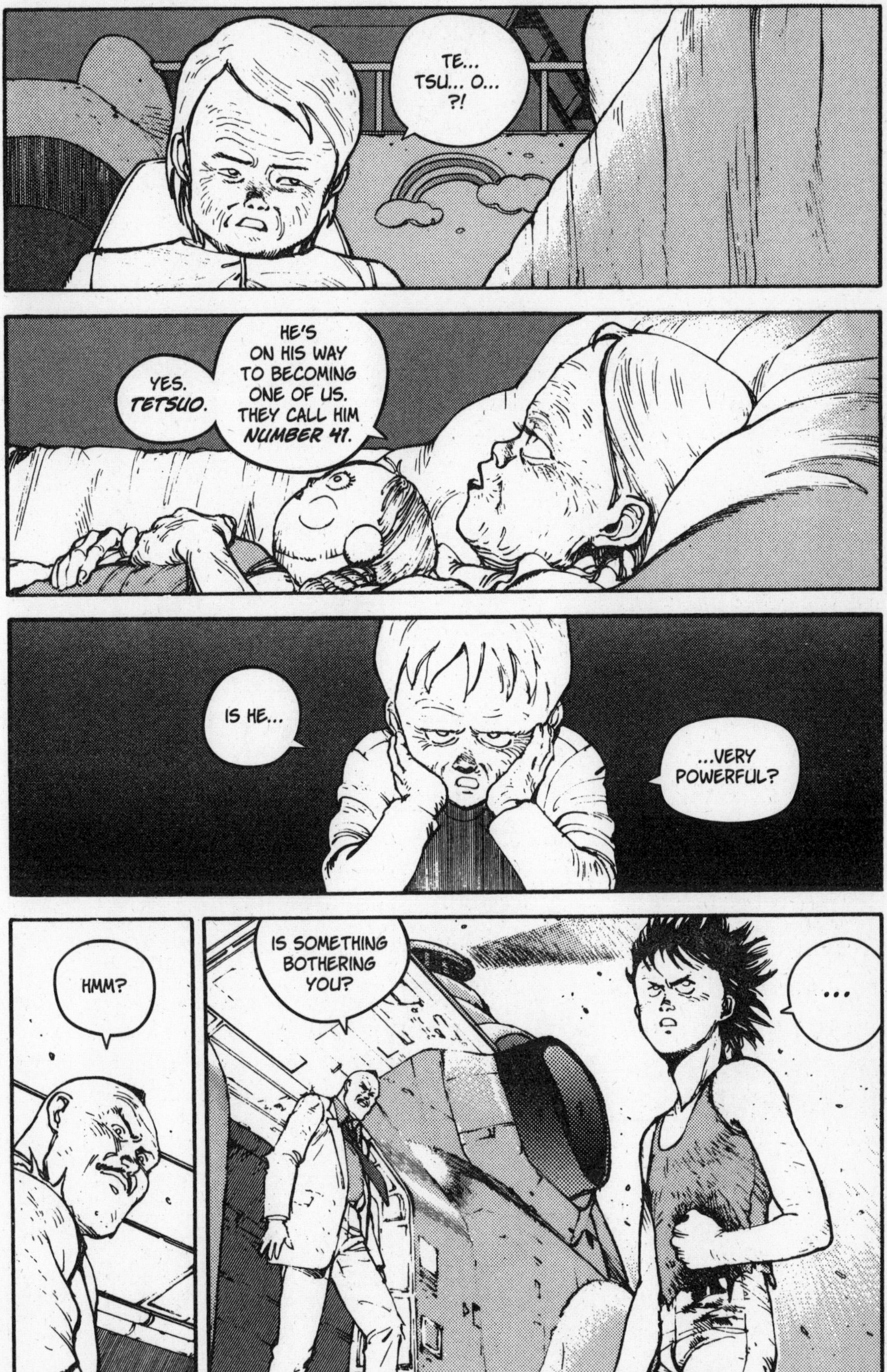
TE... TSU... O... ?!
YES. TETSUO.
HE'S ON HIS WAY TO BECOMING ONE OF US. THEY CALL HIM NUMBER 41.
IS HE...
...VERY POWERFUL?
HMM?
IS SOMETHING BOTHERING YOU?
...

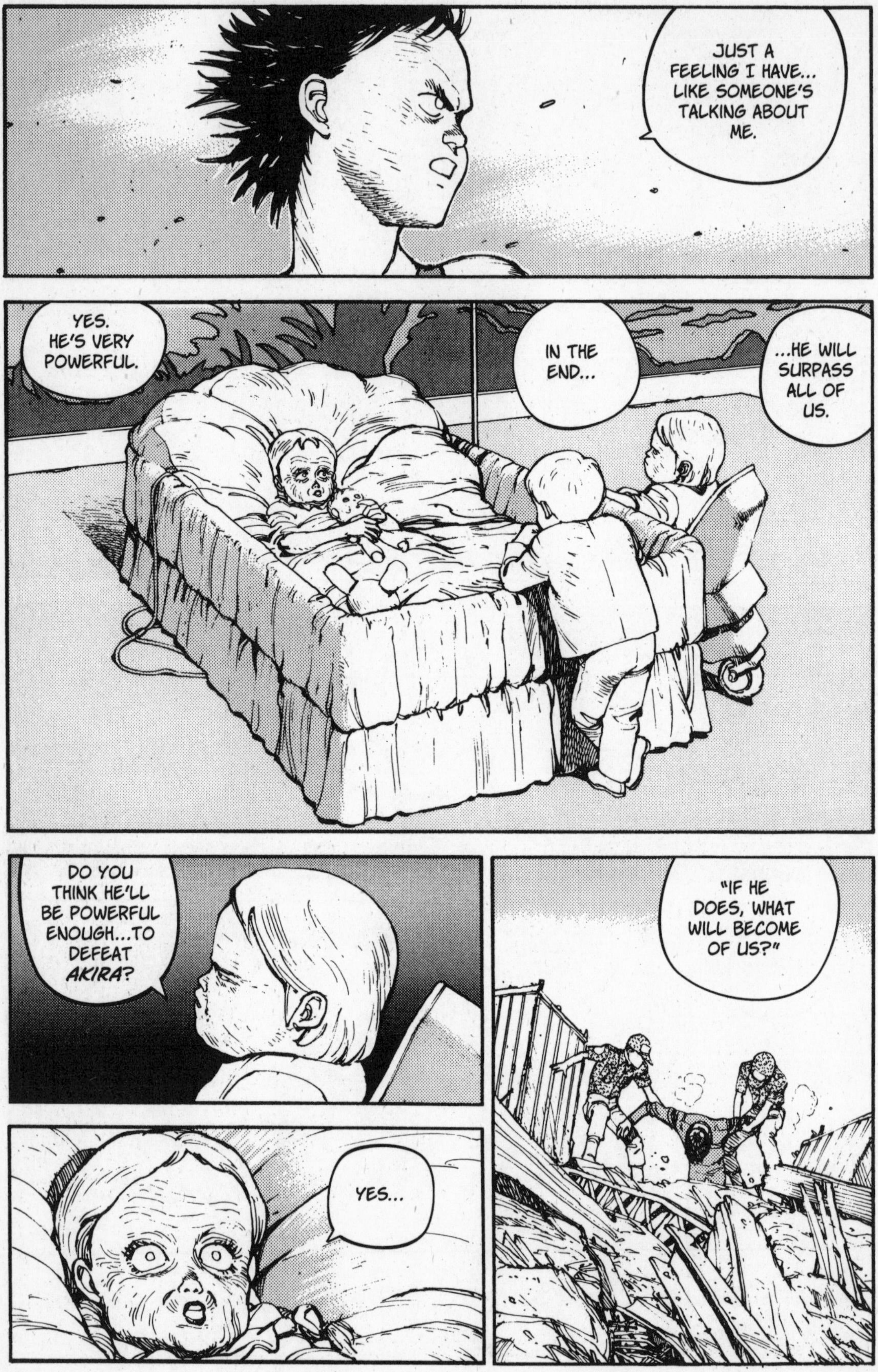
JUST A FEELING I HAVE... LIKE SOMEONE'S TALKING ABOUT ME.
YES. HE'S VERY POWERFUL.
IN THE END...
...HE WILL SURPASS ALL OF US.
DO YOU THINK HE'LL BE POWERFUL ENOUGH...TO DEFEAT *AKIRA*?
YES...
"IF HE DOES, WHAT WILL BECOME OF US?"

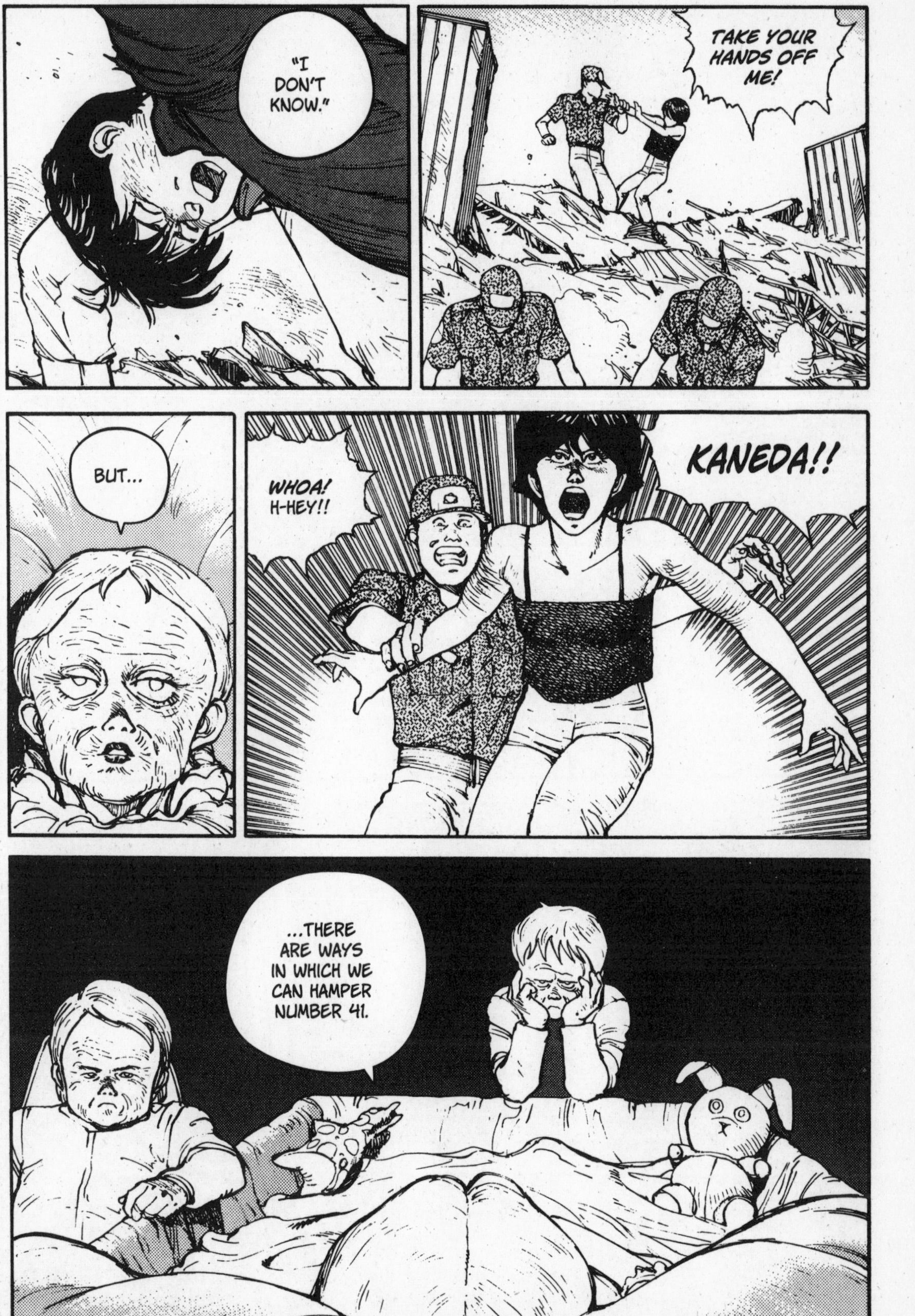
"I DON'T KNOW."
TAKE YOUR HANDS OFF ME!
BUT...
WHOA! H-HEY!!
KANEDA!!
...THERE ARE WAYS IN WHICH WE CAN HAMPER NUMBER 41.

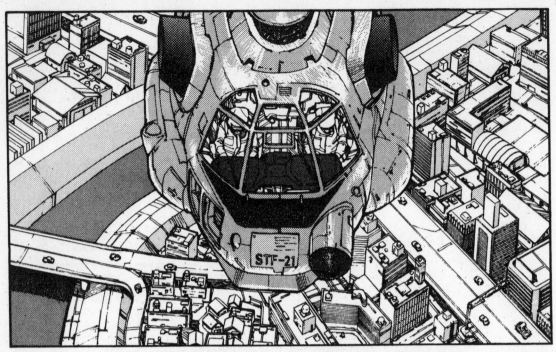

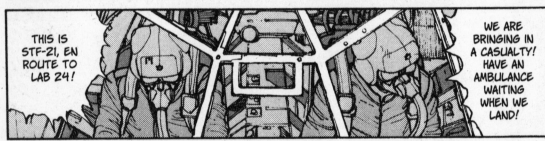

THIS IS STF-21, EN ROUTE TO LAB 24!

WE ARE BRINGING IN A CASUALTY! HAVE AN AMBULANCE WAITING WHEN WE LAND!

THIS IS TOP PRIORITY!

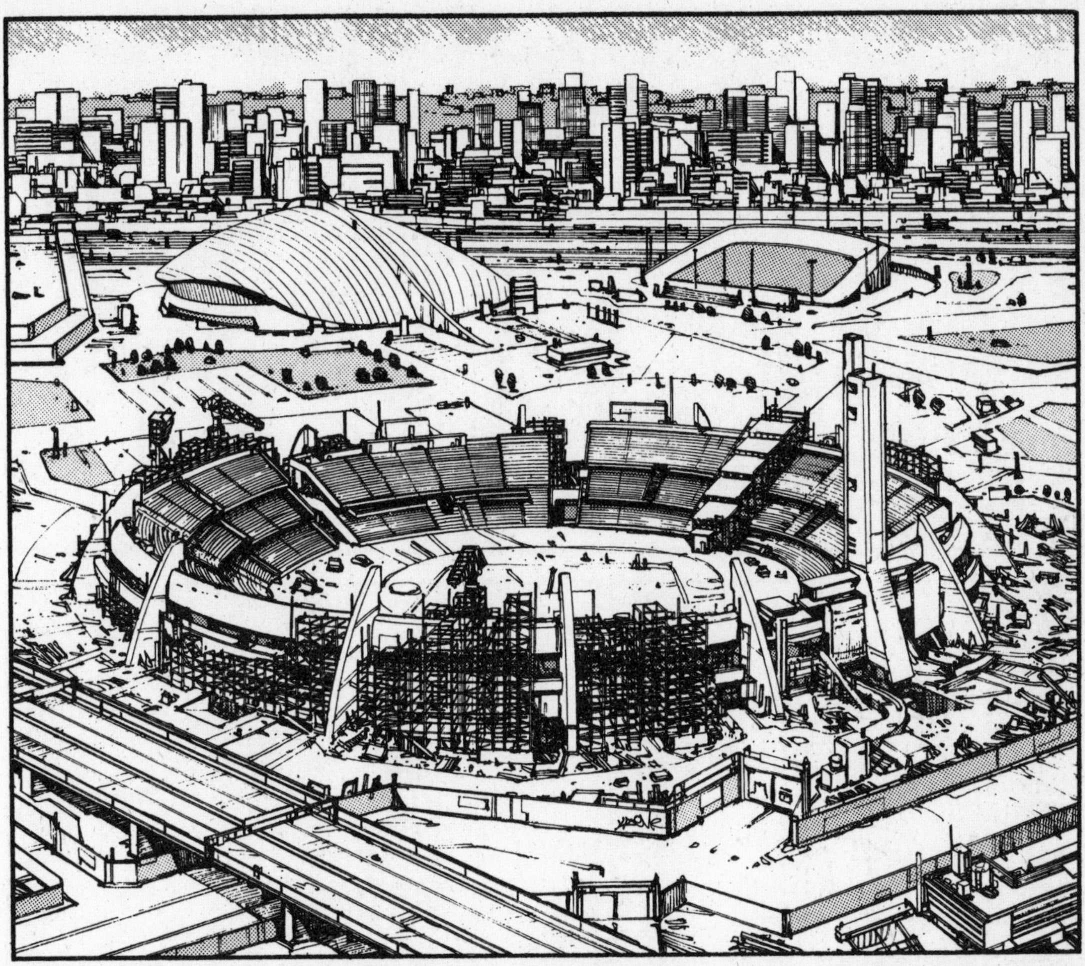

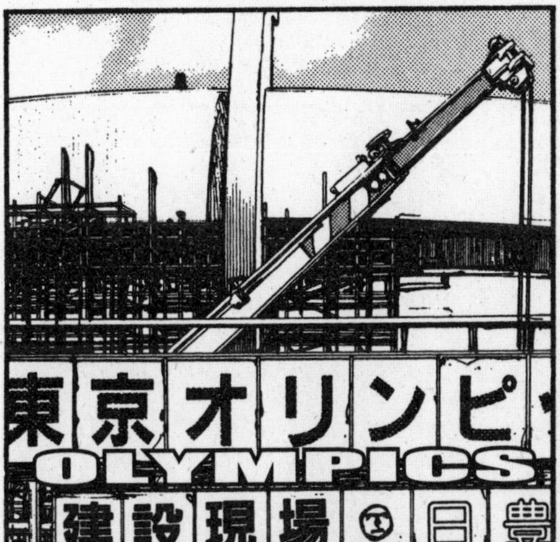
東京オリンピ
OLYMPICS
建設現場
日 豊
413 DAYS
UNTIL THE GAMES BEGIN!
安
TEAR IT DOWN

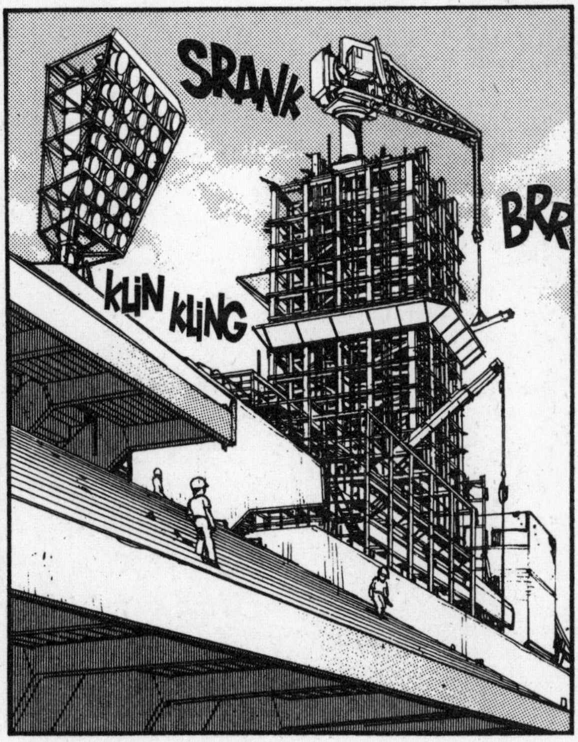
SRANK
BRR
KLIN KLING

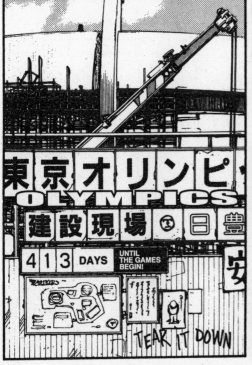

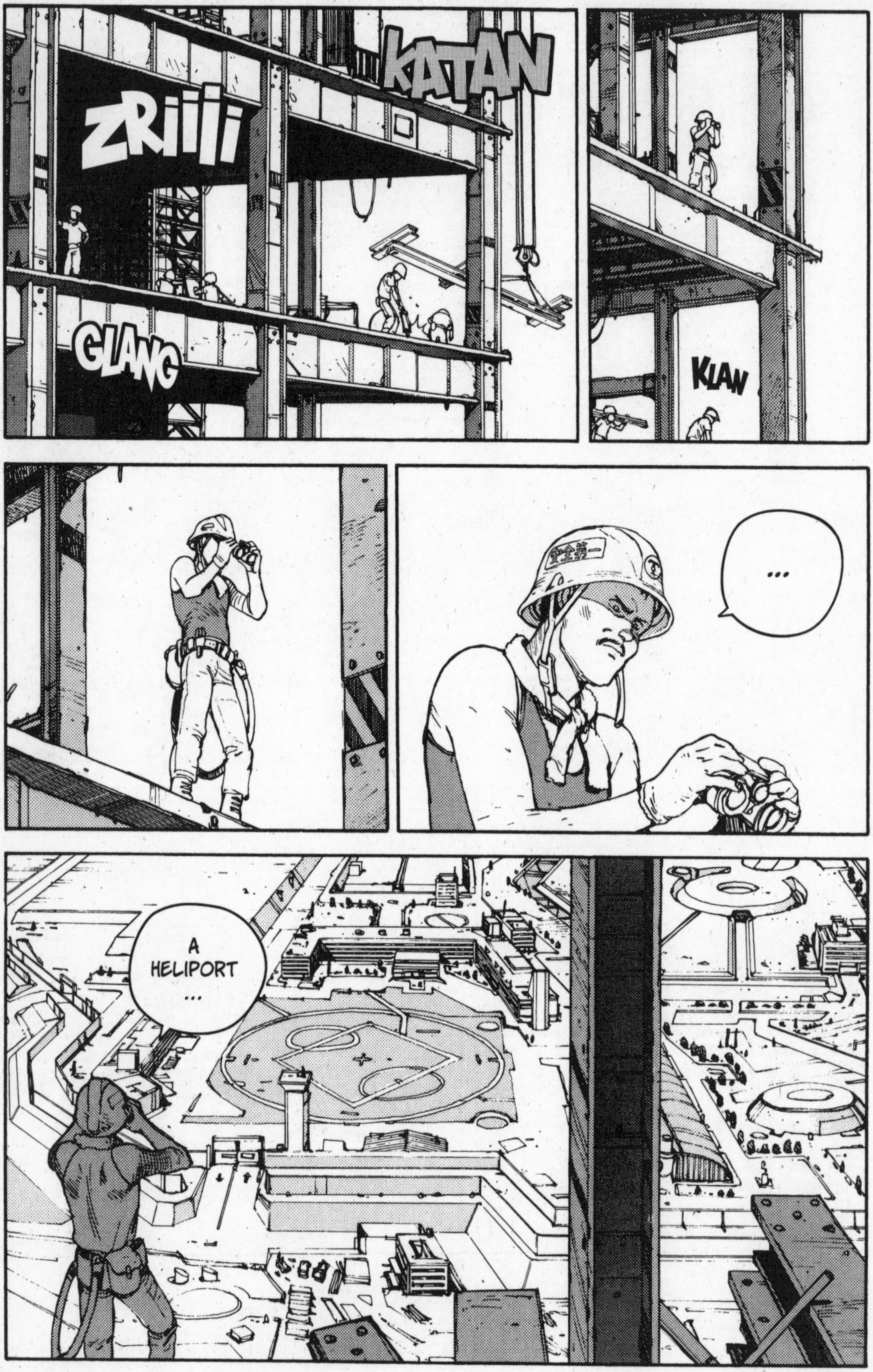
KATAN
ZRiiii
GLANG
KLAN
...
A HELIPORT ...

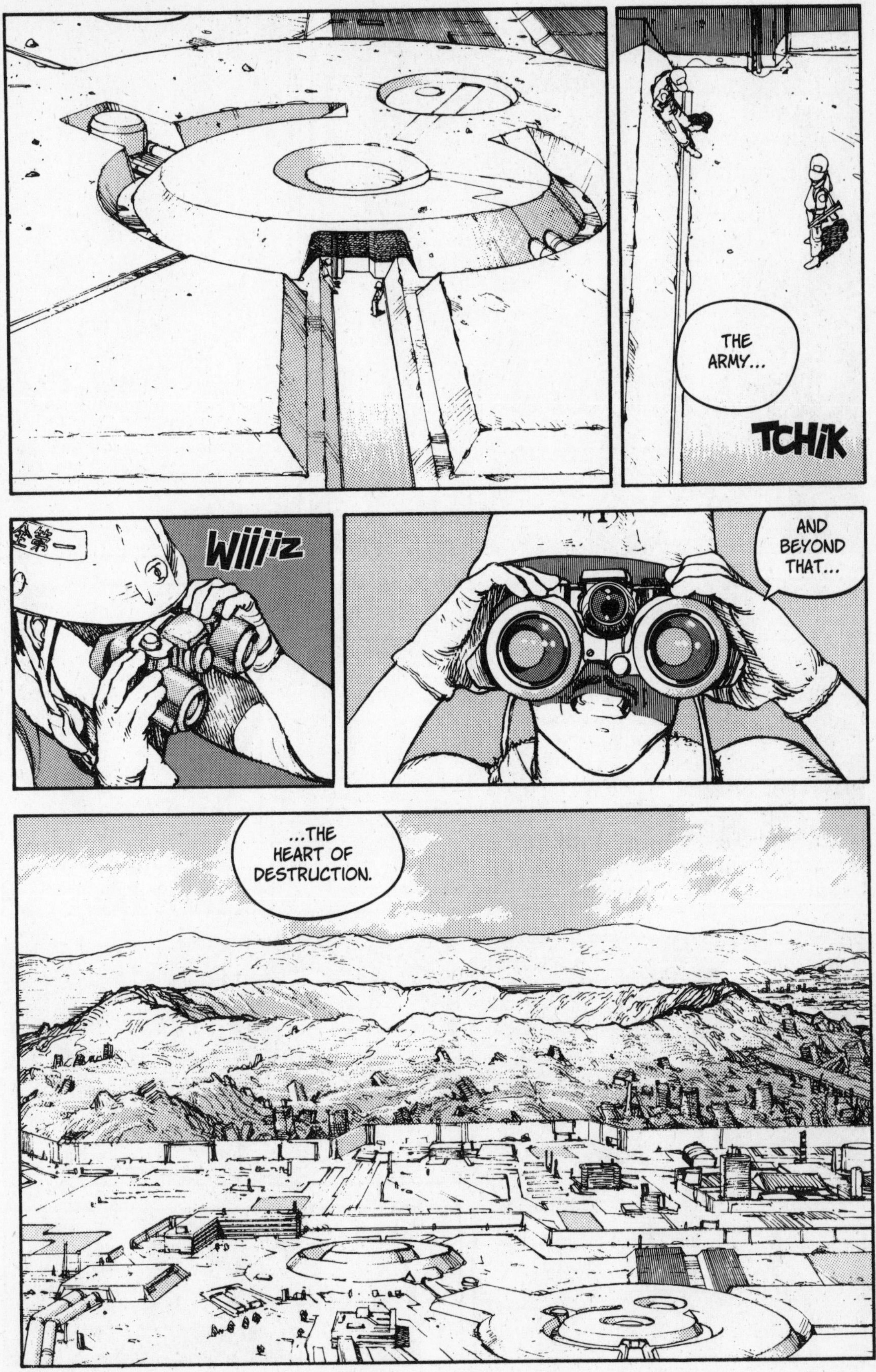
THE ARMY...
TCHIK
全第一
WIIIIZ
AND BEYOND THAT...
...THE HEART OF DESTRUCTION.

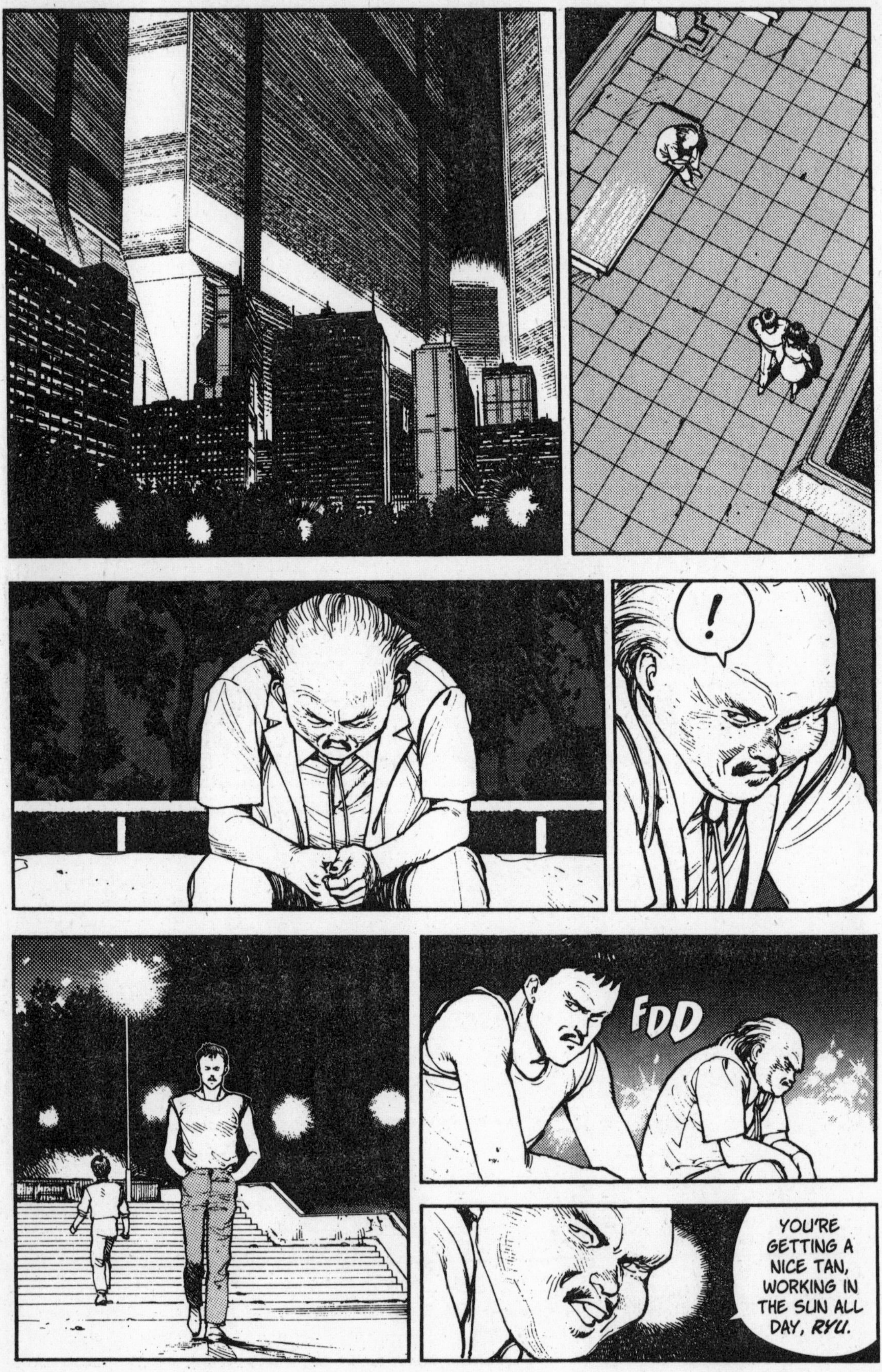
!
FDD
YOU'RE GETTING A NICE TAN, WORKING IN THE SUN ALL DAY, RYU.

HAVE YOU BEEN IN TOUCH WITH... *KEI*...? YOUR SISTER?

ANY LUCK AT THE OLYMPIC SITE? HAVE YOU ACQUIRED ANY USEABLE INFORMATION?

NOT YET.

TAK

DEVELOP THOSE. THEY'RE OF THE SEWAGE DISPOSAL PLANT NEXT TO THE SITE.

I FAIL TO SEE WHAT--

INTERESTING PLACE.

DUE SOUTH OF THE SITE, AND CRAWLING WITH SOLDIERS. OFF-LIMITS TO CONSTRUCTION WORKERS...

...AND TOO HEAVILY GUARDED FOR ME TO GET ANYWHERE NEAR IT.

DO WHAT YOU CAN--WE DESPERATELY NEED MORE INFORMATION!

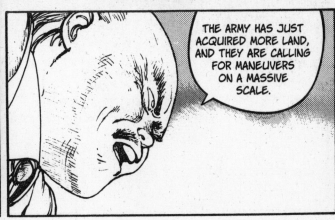

THE ARMY HAS JUST ACQUIRED MORE LAND, AND THEY ARE CALLING FOR MANEUVERS ON A MASSIVE SCALE.

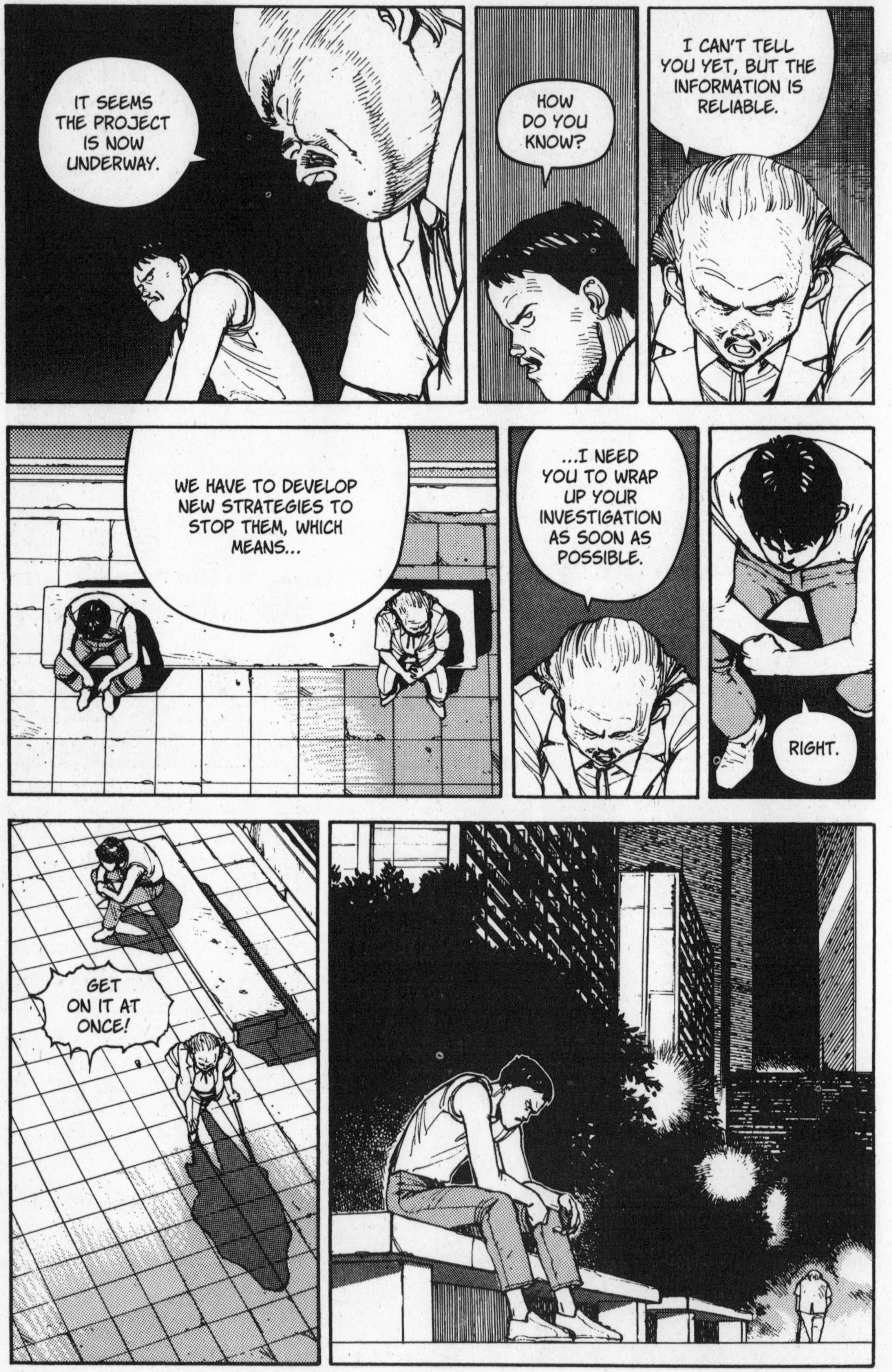
IT SEEMS THE PROJECT IS NOW UNDERWAY.
HOW DO YOU KNOW?
I CAN'T TELL YOU YET, BUT THE INFORMATION IS RELIABLE.
WE HAVE TO DEVELOP NEW STRATEGIES TO STOP THEM, WHICH MEANS...
...I NEED YOU TO WRAP UP YOUR INVESTIGATION AS SOON AS POSSIBLE.
RIGHT.
GET ON IT AT ONCE!

A MESSAGE CAME IN FROM H.Q., MR. NEZU.

LADY MIYAKO WANTS TO SEE YOU AS SOON AS POSSIBLE.

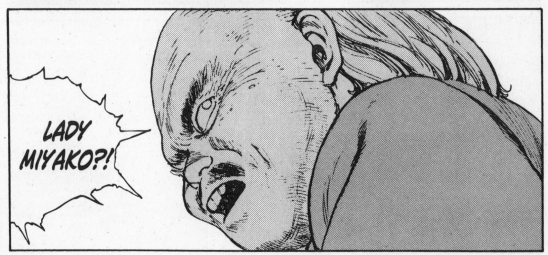

LADY MIYAKO?!

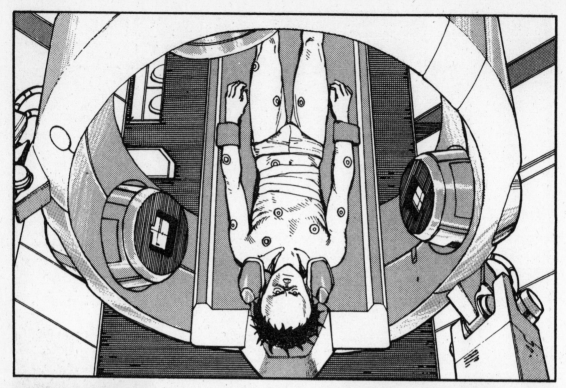

 HOW ARE YOU FEELING, *TETSUO*?

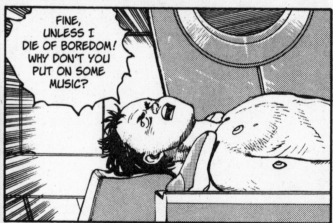 FINE, UNLESS I DIE OF BOREDOM! WHY DON'T YOU PUT ON SOME MUSIC?

 HIS INJURIES, DOCTOR?

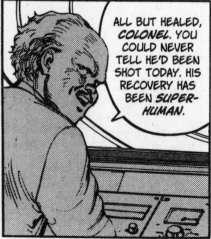 ALL BUT HEALED, *COLONEL.* YOU COULD NEVER TELL HE'D BEEN SHOT TODAY. HIS RECOVERY HAS BEEN *SUPER-HUMAN.*

WHAT IS HIS PRESENT LEVEL?

SOMEWHERE ABOVE *LEVEL 70*...

...AS YOU CAN SEE.

HE'S FANTASTIC!

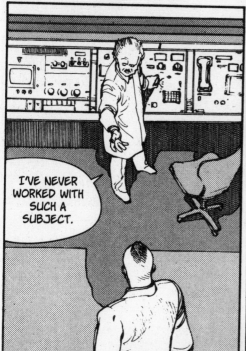

I'VE NEVER WORKED WITH SUCH A SUBJECT.

WHAT ABOUT HIS *ATTITUDE*, DOCTOR?

...

ATTITUDE?

NO AMOUNT OF POWER IS OF ANY USE TO US UNLESS WE CAN CONTROL THE SUBJECT.

WE CANNOT AFFORD...

...THE RISK OF CREATING A SECOND *AKIRA!*

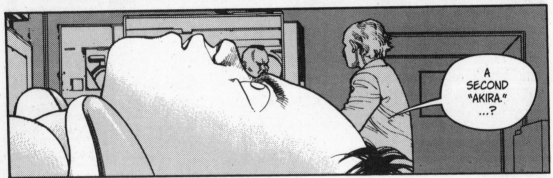

A SECOND "AKIRA." ...?

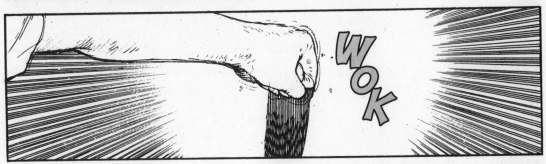

WOK

...SHIT.

GOD *DAMN* IT...

*LEMME OUT,* YOU BASTARDS!!

23

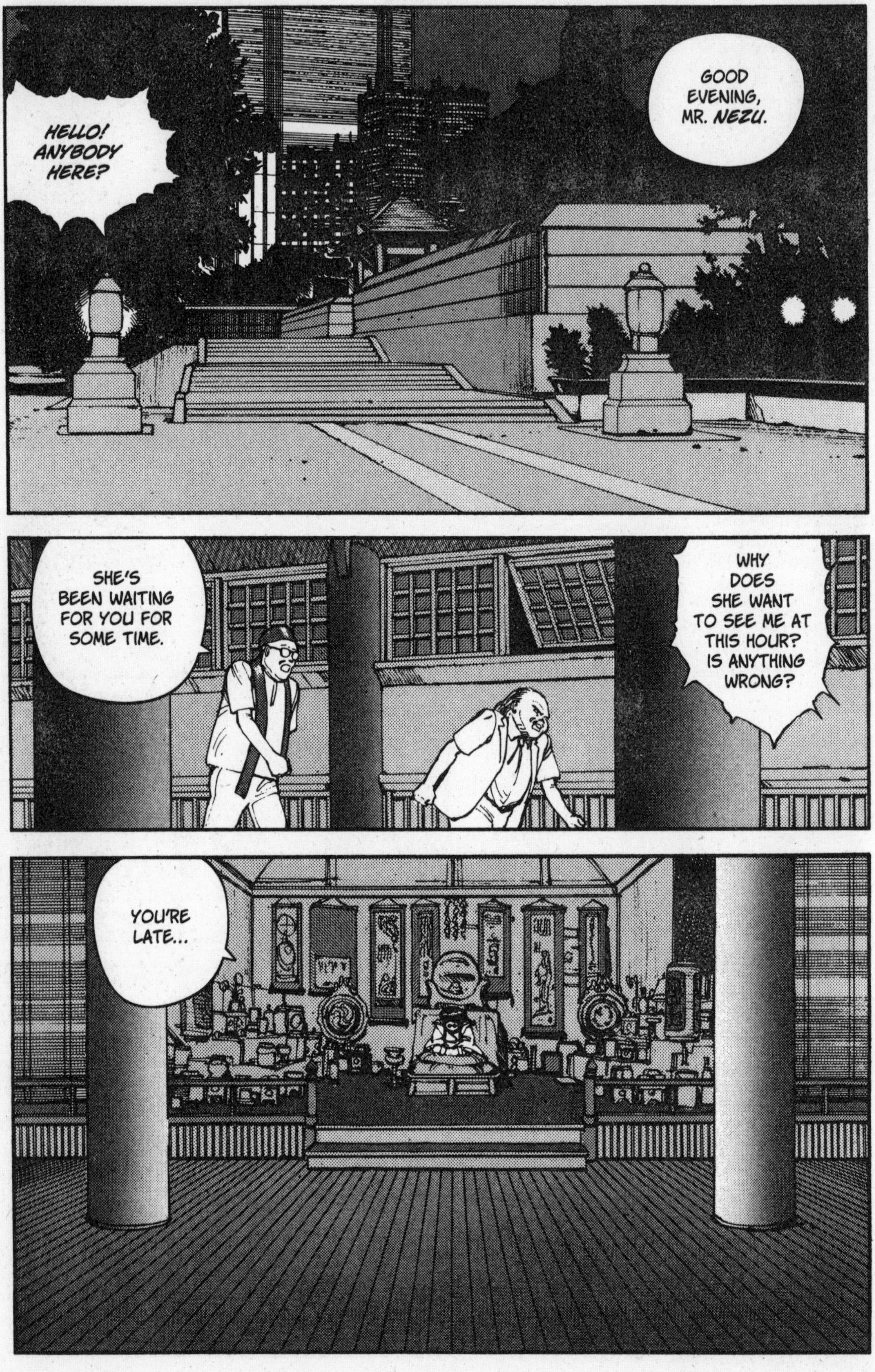
HELLO! ANYBODY HERE?
GOOD EVENING, MR. NEZU.
SHE'S BEEN WAITING FOR YOU FOR SOME TIME.
WHY DOES SHE WANT TO SEE ME AT THIS HOUR? IS ANYTHING WRONG?
YOU'RE LATE...

PLEASE ACCEPT MY APOLOGIES, LADY MIYAKO. WHY DID YOU SUMMON ME?

AH... NEZU... MY LITTLE RODENT...

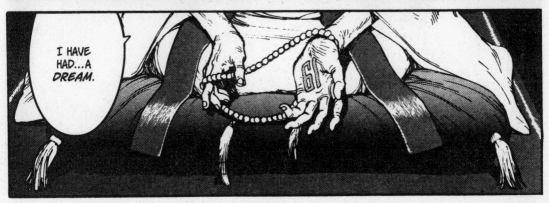

I HAVE HAD...A DREAM.

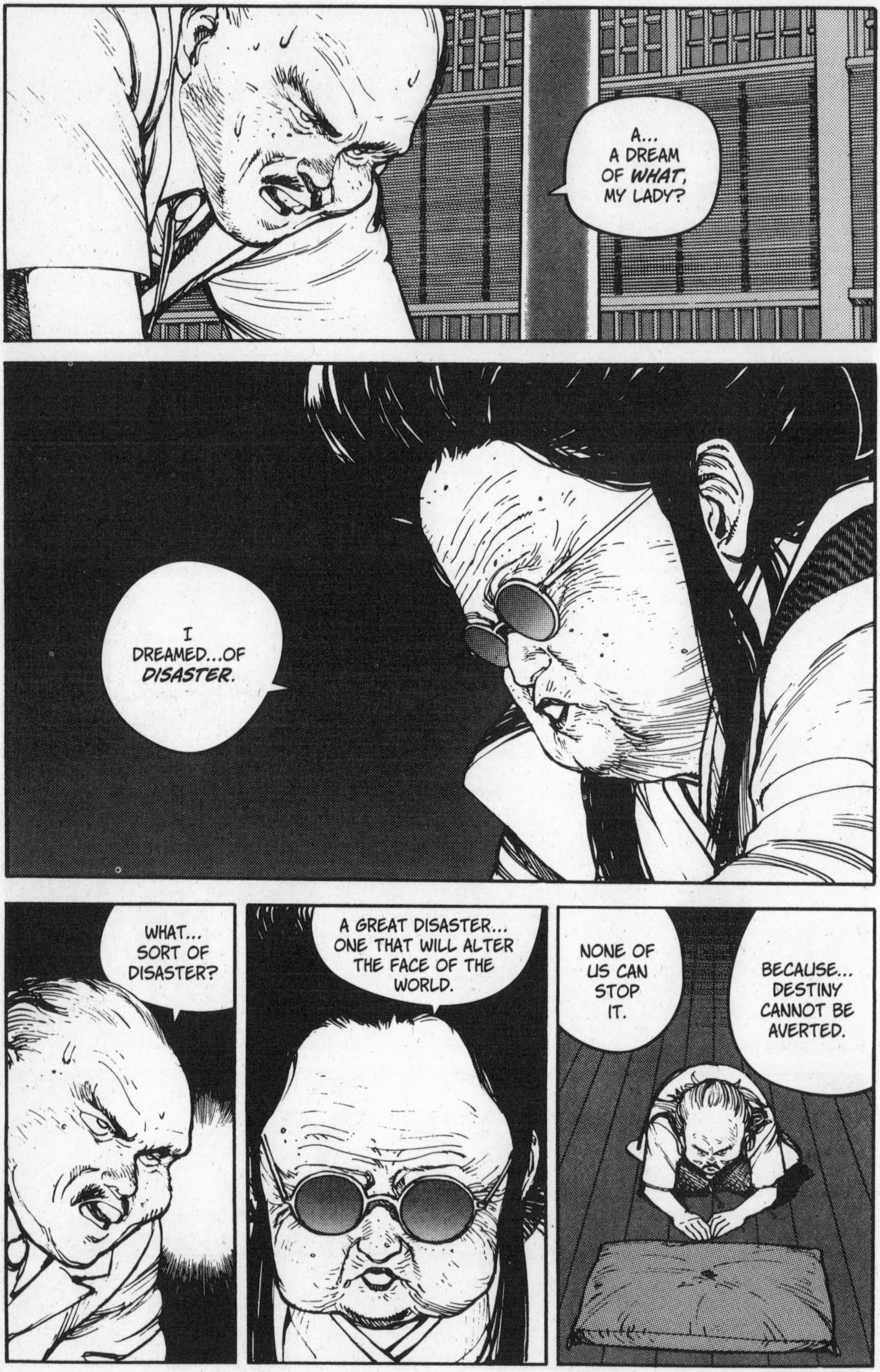
A... A DREAM OF WHAT, MY LADY?
I DREAMED...OF DISASTER.
WHAT... SORT OF DISASTER?
A GREAT DISASTER... ONE THAT WILL ALTER THE FACE OF THE WORLD.
NONE OF US CAN STOP IT.
BECAUSE... DESTINY CANNOT BE AVERTED.

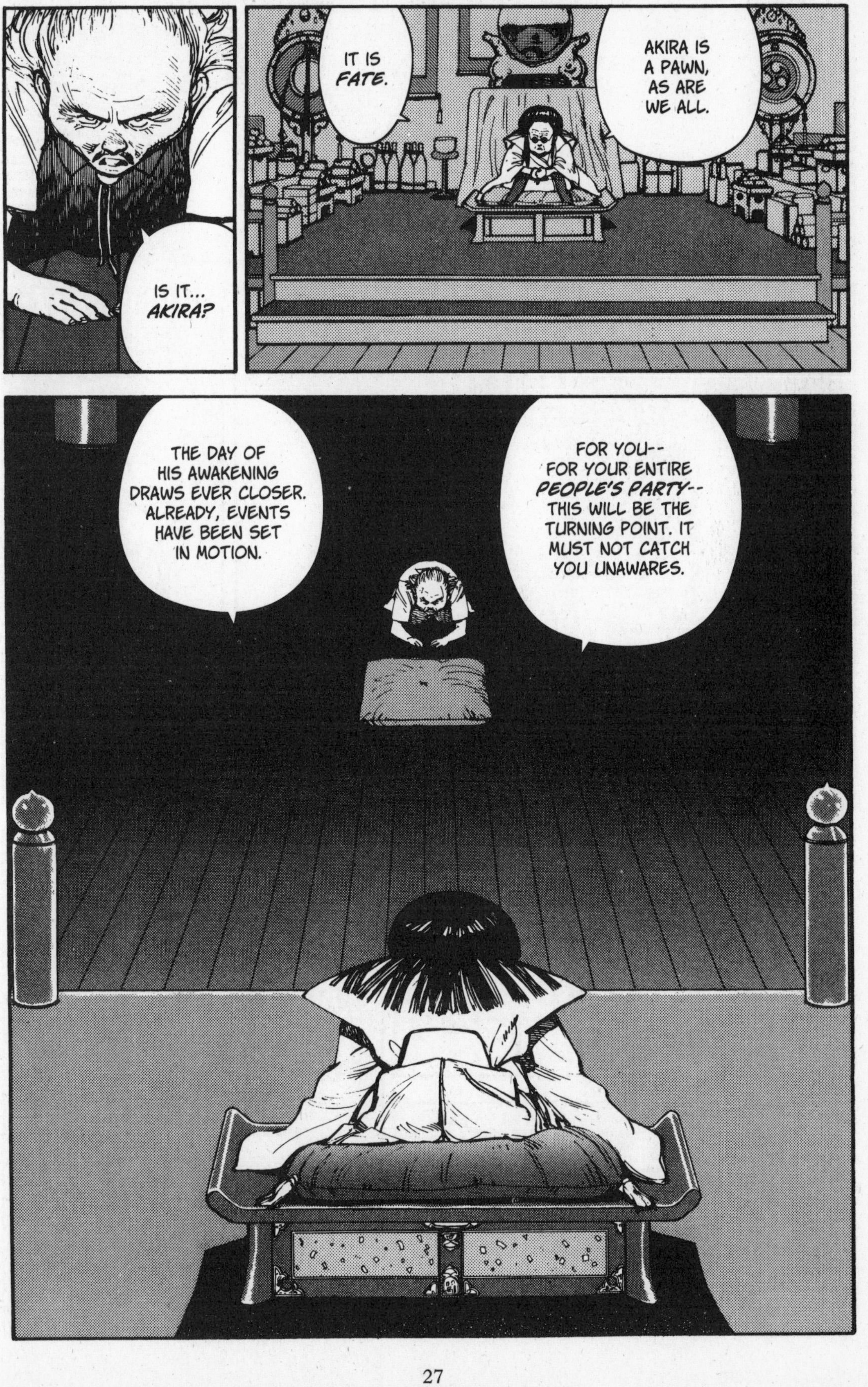
IS IT... AKIRA?
IT IS FATE.
AKIRA IS A PAWN, AS ARE WE ALL.
THE DAY OF HIS AWAKENING DRAWS EVER CLOSER. ALREADY, EVENTS HAVE BEEN SET IN MOTION.
FOR YOU-- FOR YOUR ENTIRE PEOPLE'S PARTY-- THIS WILL BE THE TURNING POINT. IT MUST NOT CATCH YOU UNAWARES.

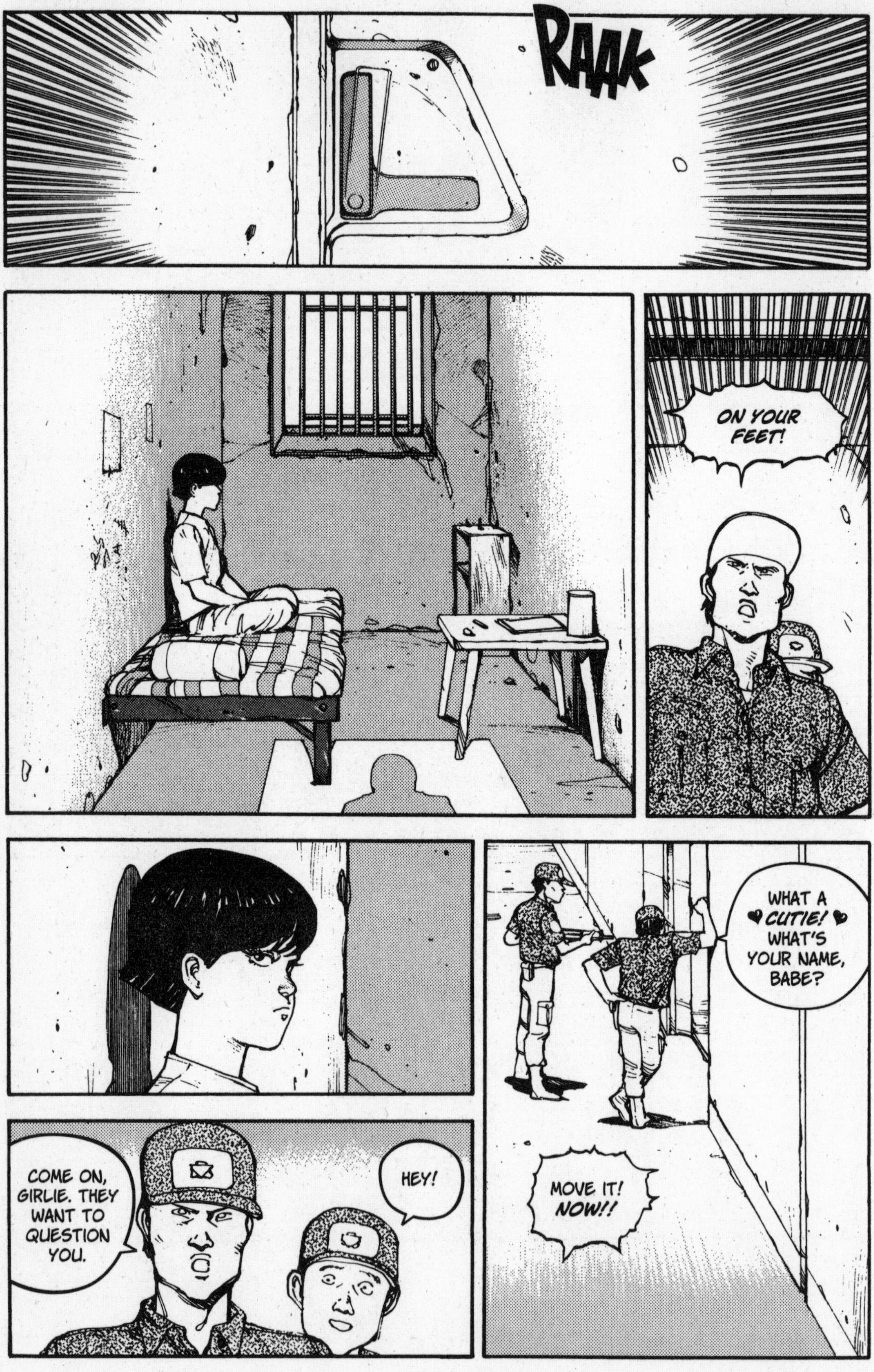
RAAK
ON YOUR FEET!
COME ON, GIRLIE. THEY WANT TO QUESTION YOU.
HEY!
WHAT A ♥ *CUTIE!* ♥ WHAT'S YOUR NAME, BABE?
MOVE IT! *NOW!!*

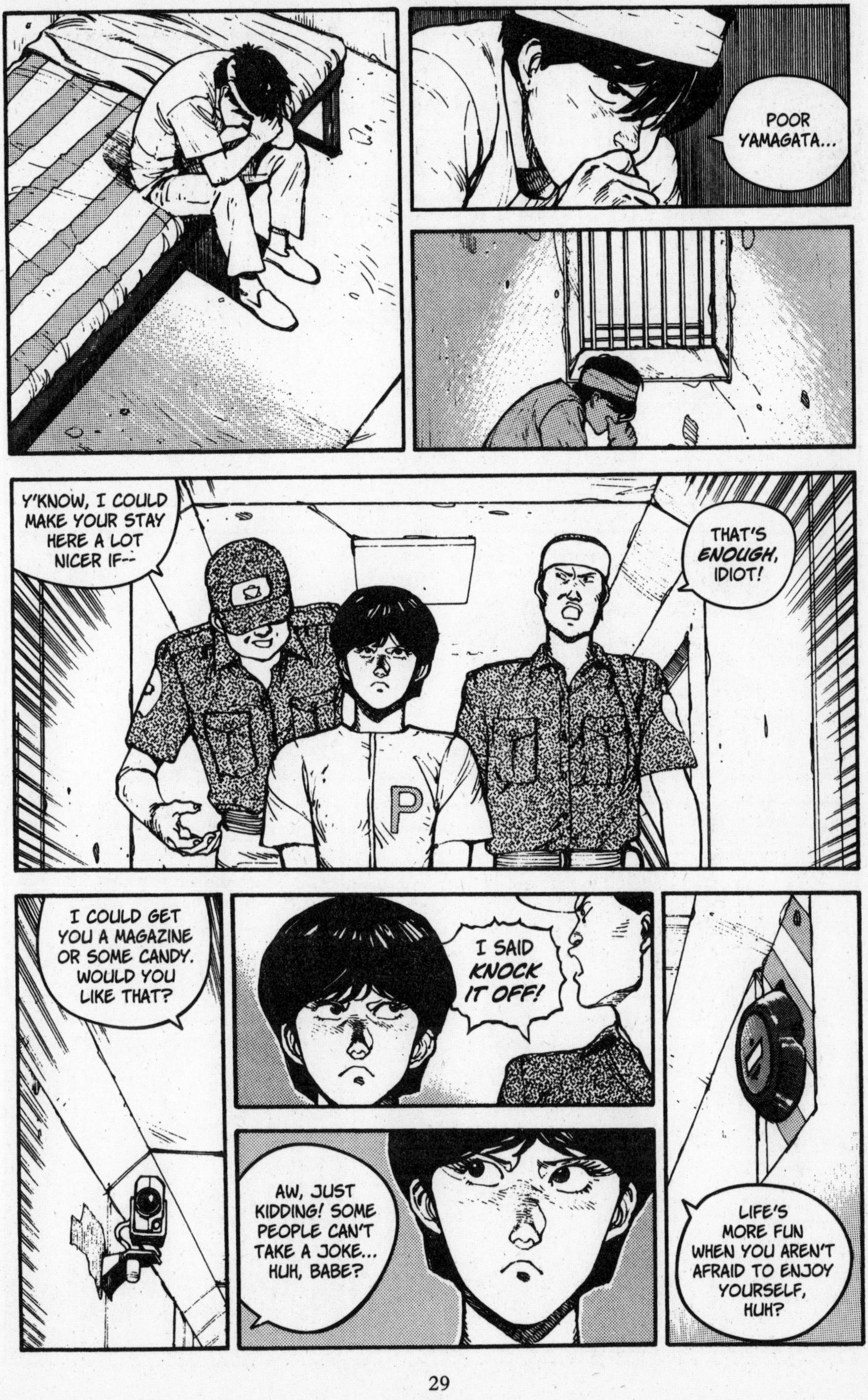
POOR YAMAGATA...
Y'KNOW, I COULD MAKE YOUR STAY HERE A LOT NICER IF--
THAT'S *ENOUGH*, IDIOT!
I COULD GET YOU A MAGAZINE OR SOME CANDY. WOULD YOU LIKE THAT?
I SAID *KNOCK IT OFF!*
AW, JUST KIDDING! SOME PEOPLE CAN'T TAKE A JOKE... HUH, BABE?
LIFE'S MORE FUN WHEN YOU AREN'T AFRAID TO ENJOY YOURSELF, HUH?

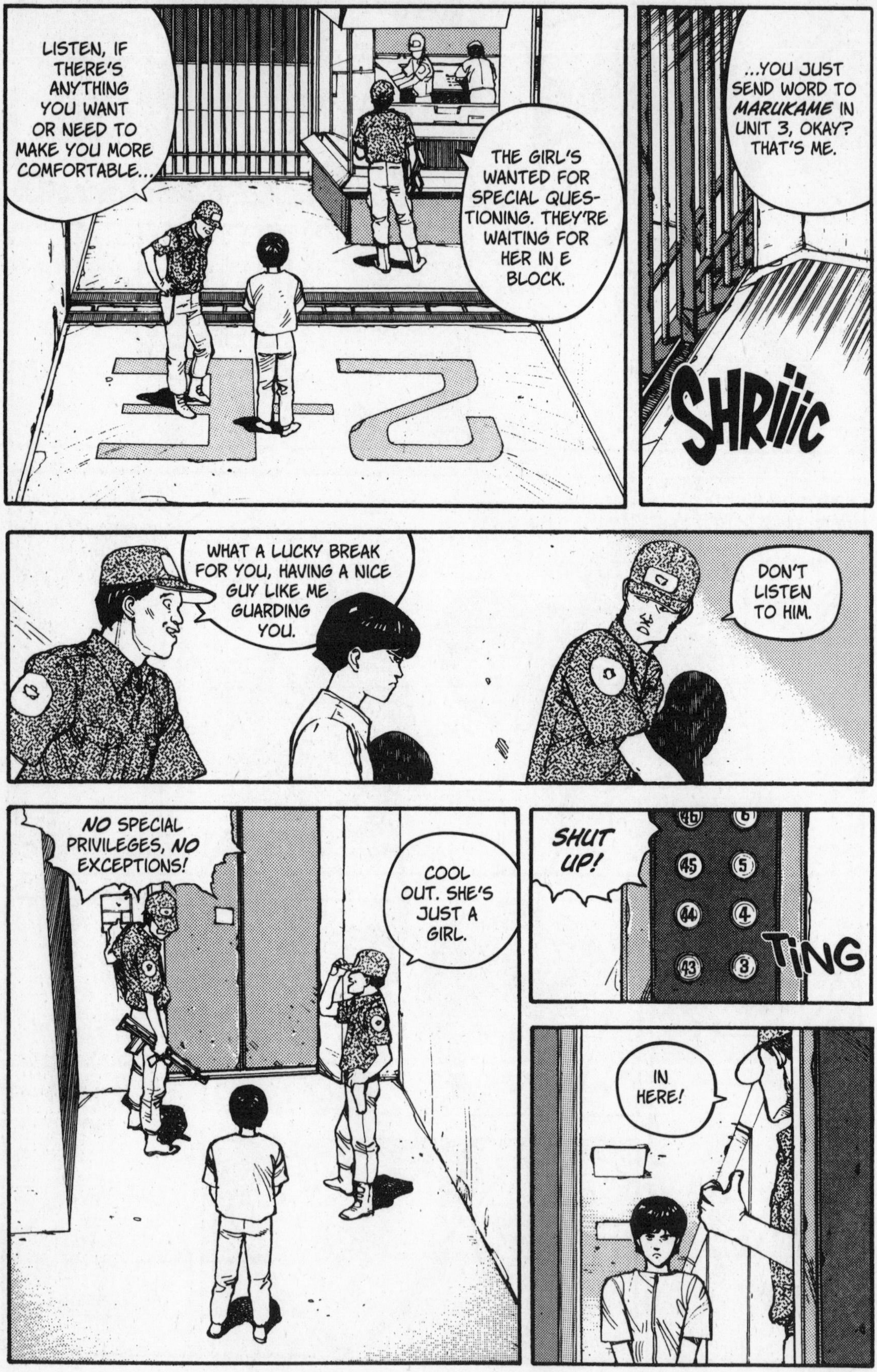
LISTEN, IF THERE'S ANYTHING YOU WANT OR NEED TO MAKE YOU MORE COMFORTABLE...
THE GIRL'S WANTED FOR SPECIAL QUESTIONING. THEY'RE WAITING FOR HER IN E BLOCK.
...YOU JUST SEND WORD TO MARUKAME IN UNIT 3, OKAY? THAT'S ME.
SHRIIIC
WHAT A LUCKY BREAK FOR YOU, HAVING A NICE GUY LIKE ME GUARDING YOU.
DON'T LISTEN TO HIM.
NO SPECIAL PRIVILEGES, NO EXCEPTIONS!
COOL OUT. SHE'S JUST A GIRL.
SHUT UP!
46
6
45
5
44
4
43
3
TING
IN HERE!

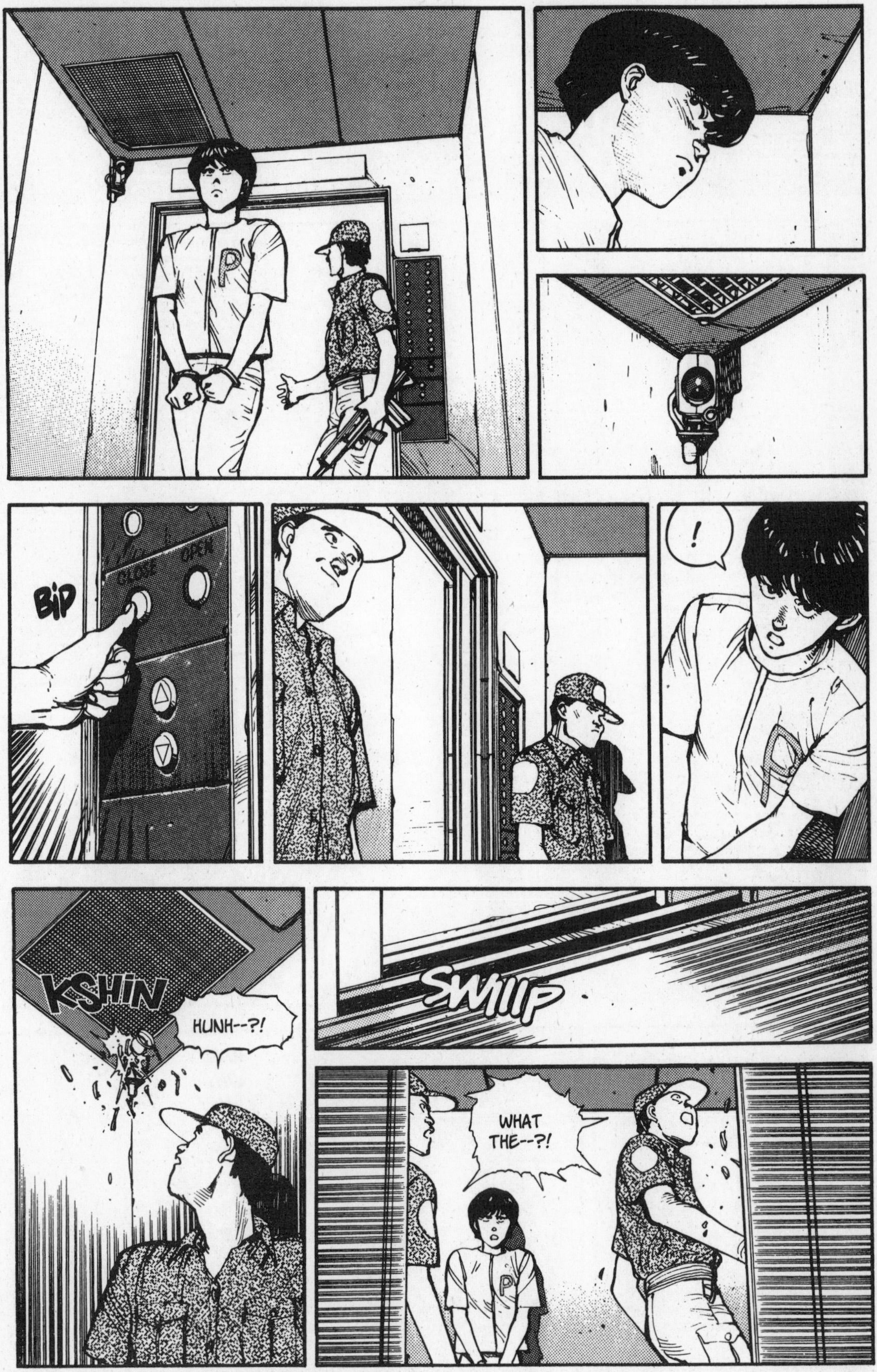
CLOSE
OPEN
BIP
!
KSHIN
HUNH--?!
SWIIIP
WHAT THE--?!

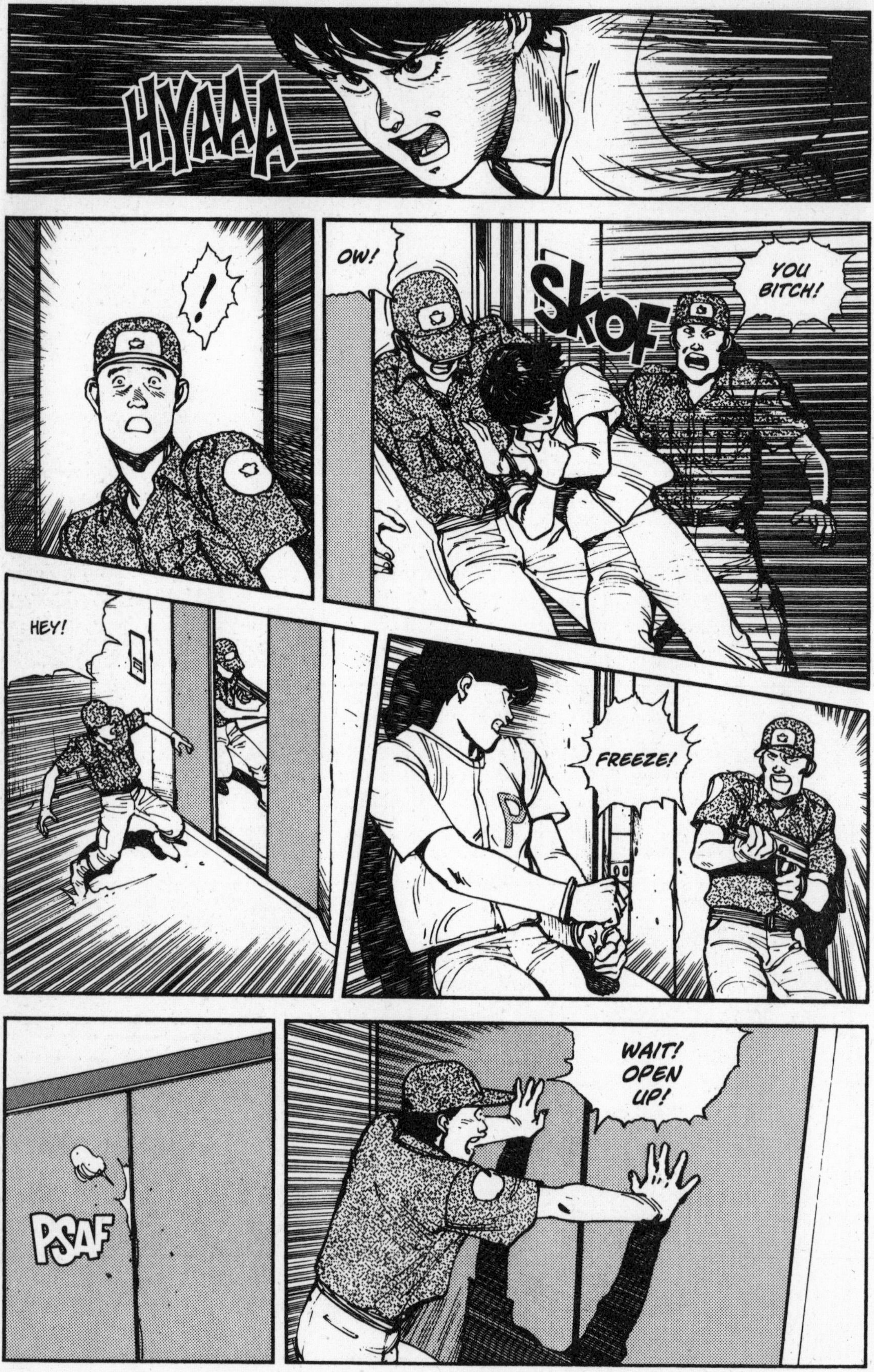
HYAAA
!
OW!
SKOF
YOU BITCH!
HEY!
FREEZE!
PSAF
WAIT! OPEN UP!

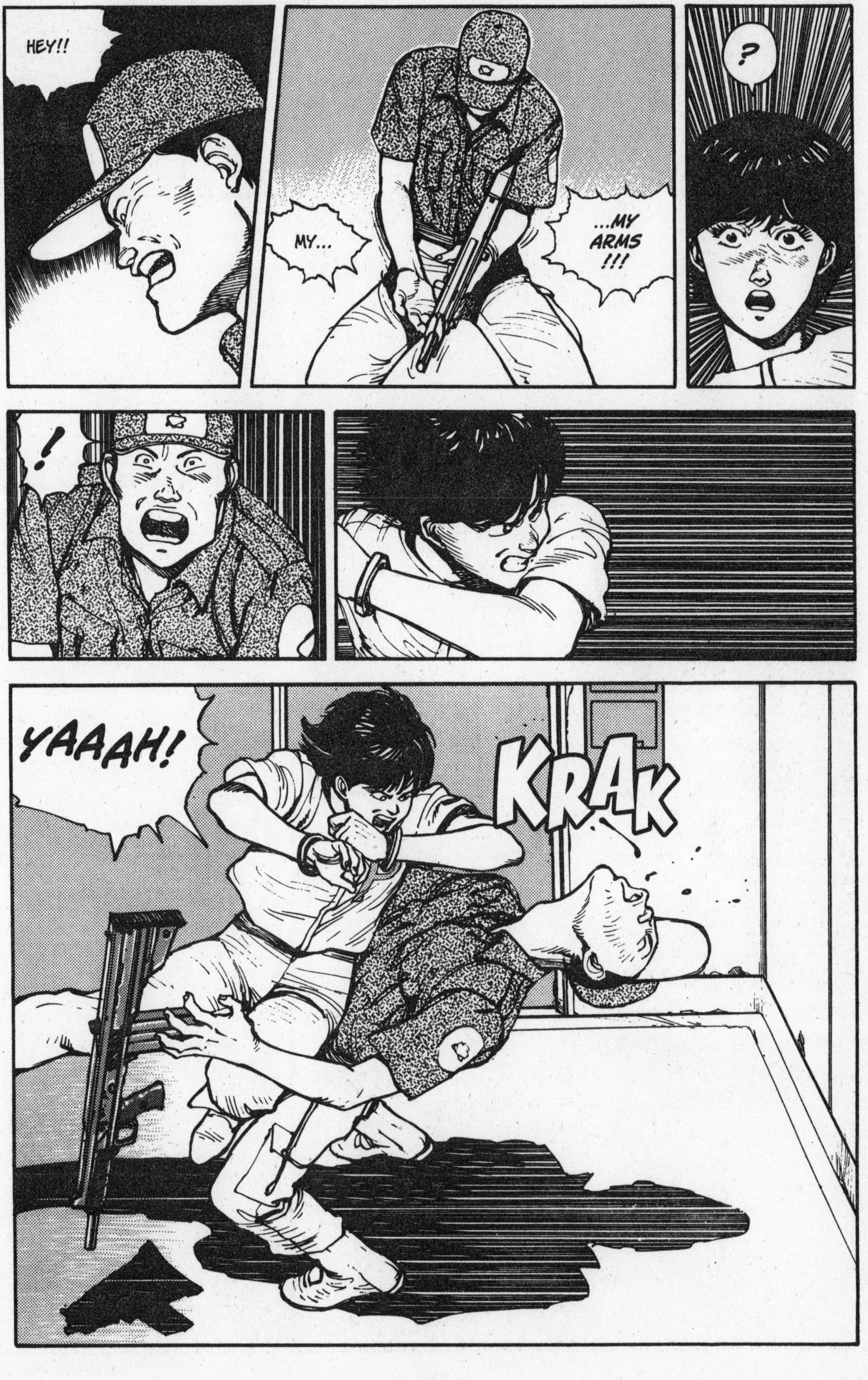
HEY!!
MY...
...MY ARMS !!!
?
!
YAAAH!
KRAK

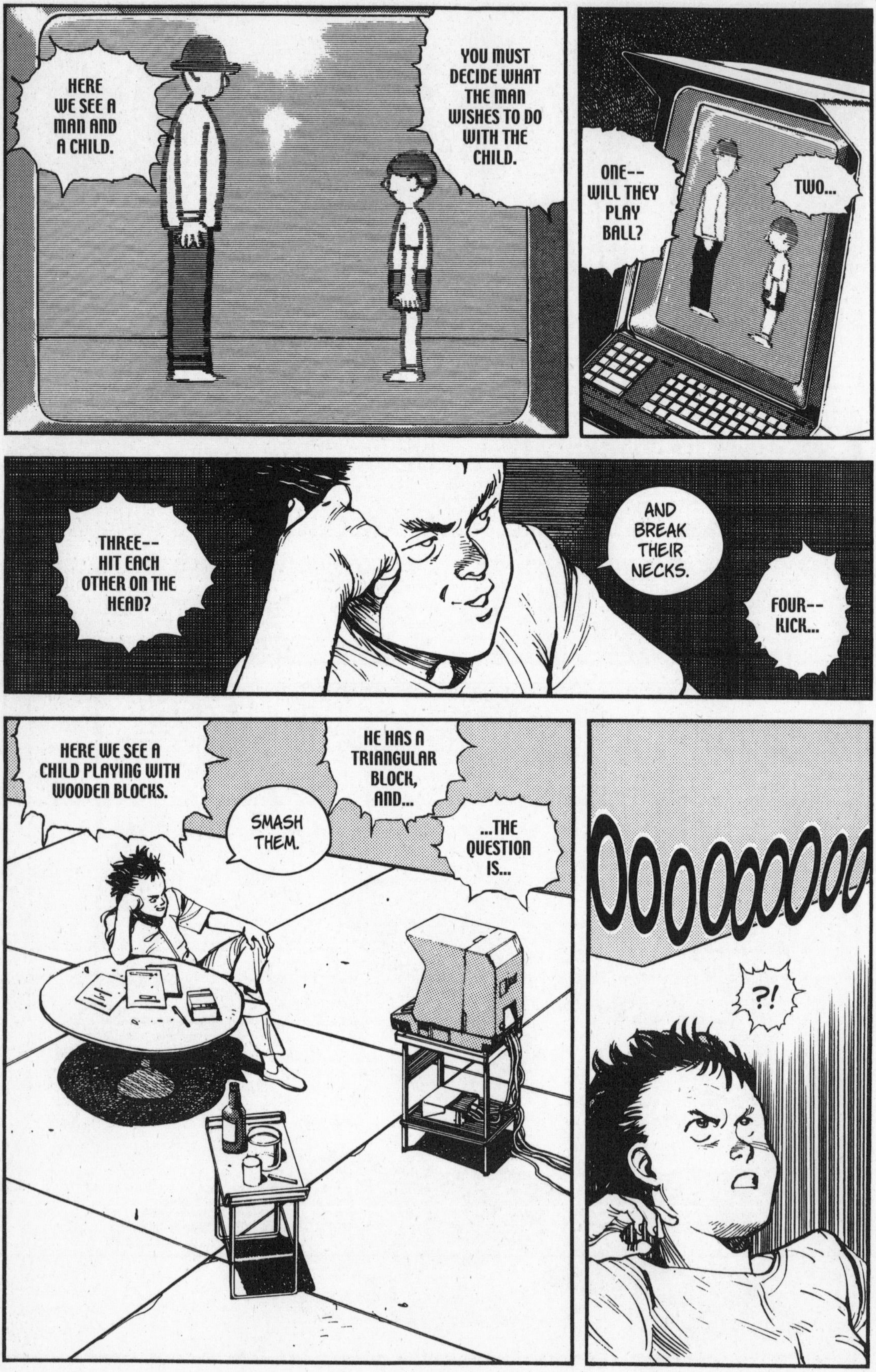
HERE WE SEE A MAN AND A CHILD.
YOU MUST DECIDE WHAT THE MAN WISHES TO DO WITH THE CHILD.
ONE-- WILL THEY PLAY BALL?
TWO...
THREE-- HIT EACH OTHER ON THE HEAD?
AND BREAK THEIR NECKS.
FOUR-- KICK...
HERE WE SEE A CHILD PLAYING WITH WOODEN BLOCKS.
SMASH THEM.
HE HAS A TRIANGULAR BLOCK, AND...
...THE QUESTION IS...
OOOOOOOOO
?!

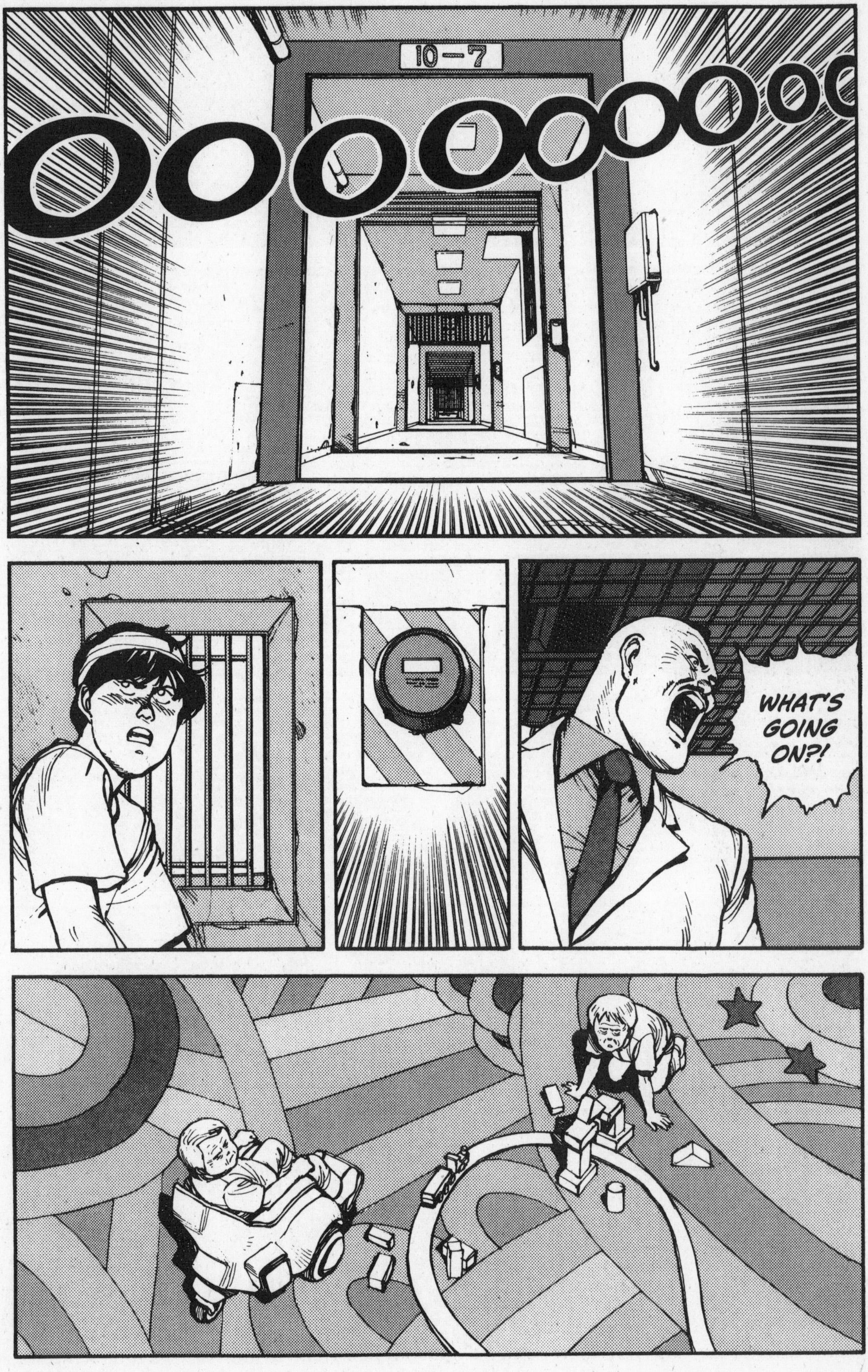
10-7
OOOOOOOOOOO
WHAT'S GOING ON?!

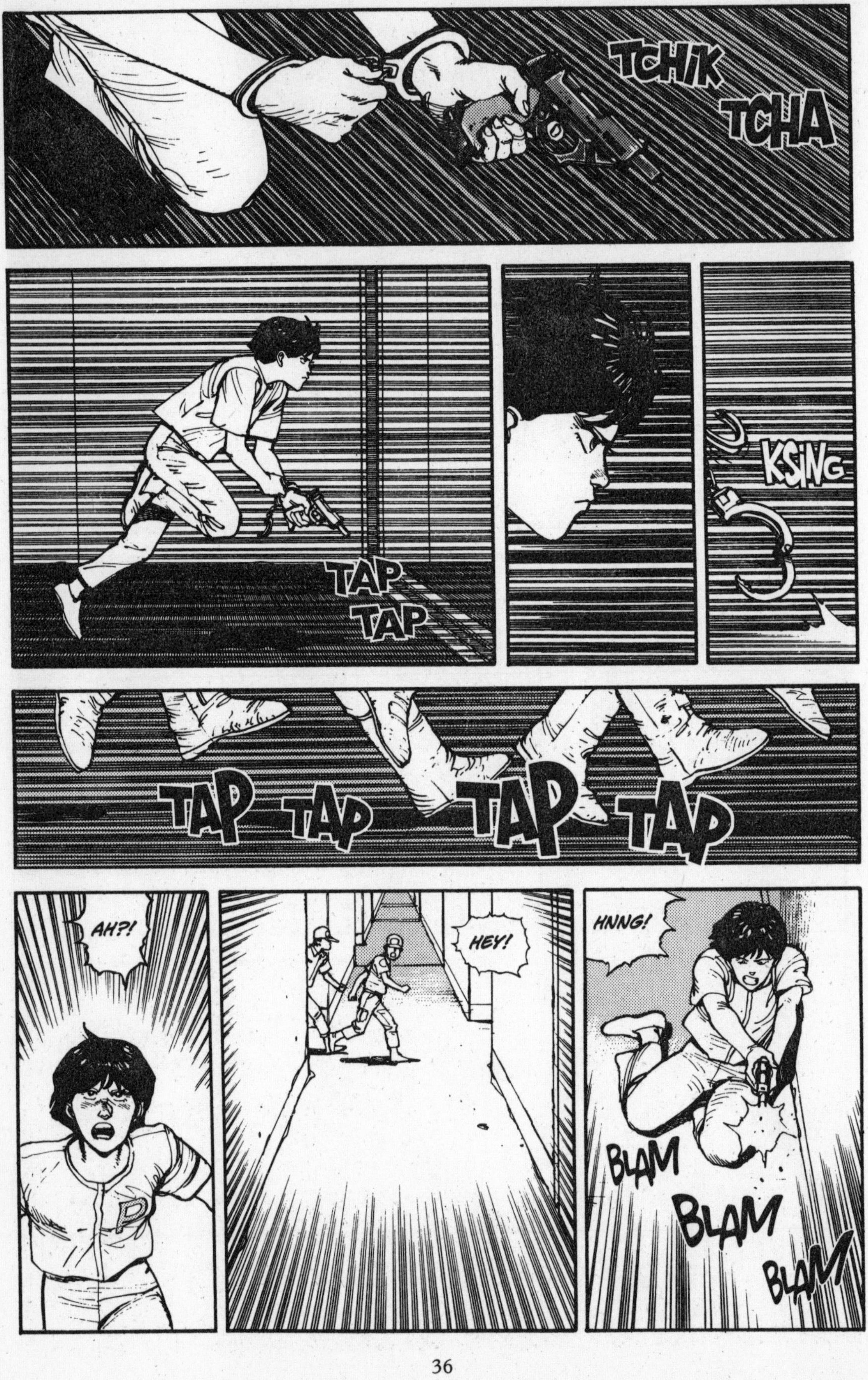
TCHIK
TCHA
TAP
TAP
KSING
TAP
TAP
TAP
TAP
AH?!
HEY!
HNNG!
BLAM
BLAM
BLAM

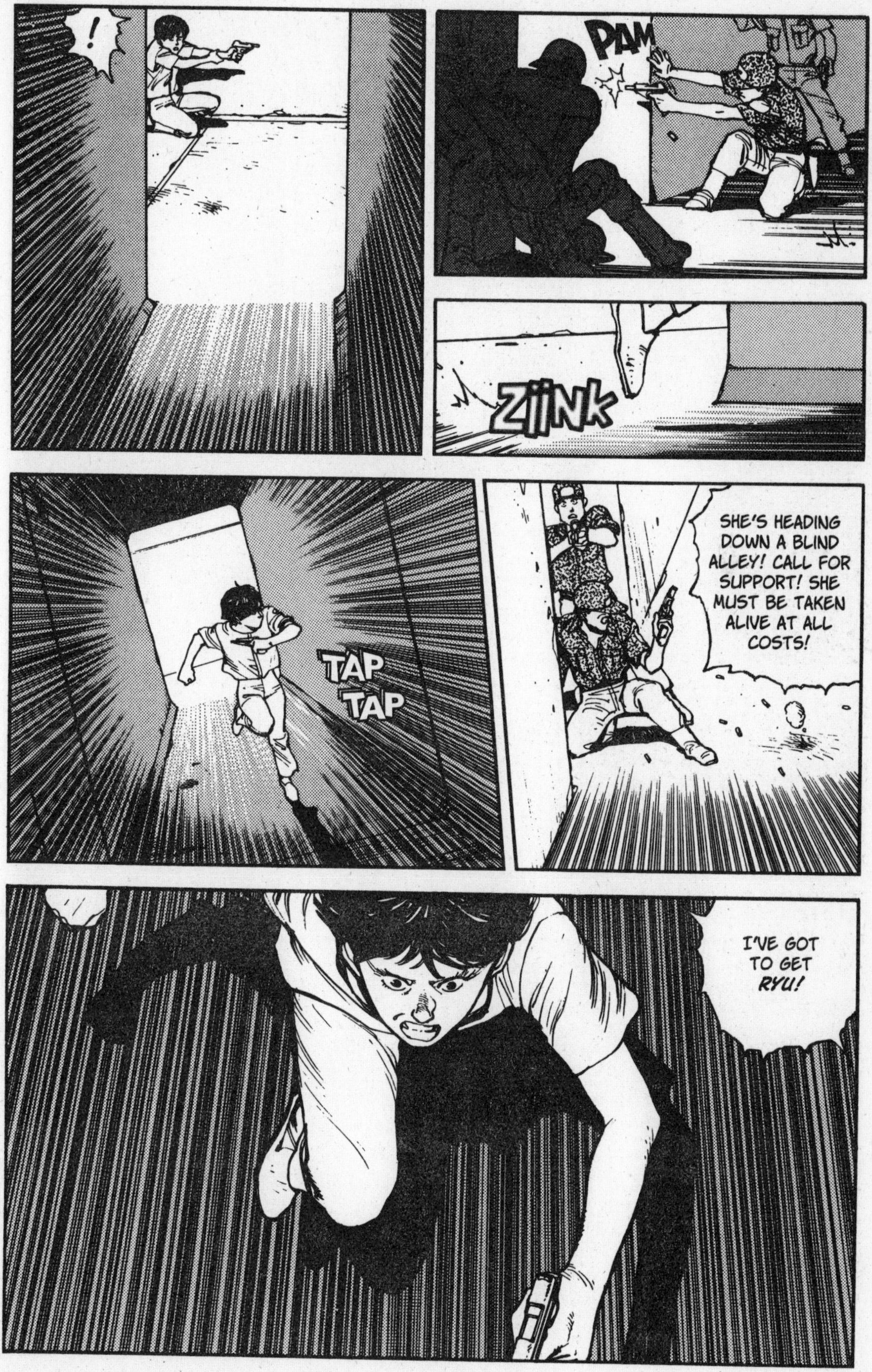
!
PAM
ZIINK
TAP
TAP
SHE'S HEADING DOWN A BLIND ALLEY! CALL FOR SUPPORT! SHE MUST BE TAKEN ALIVE AT ALL COSTS!
I'VE GOT TO GET RYU!

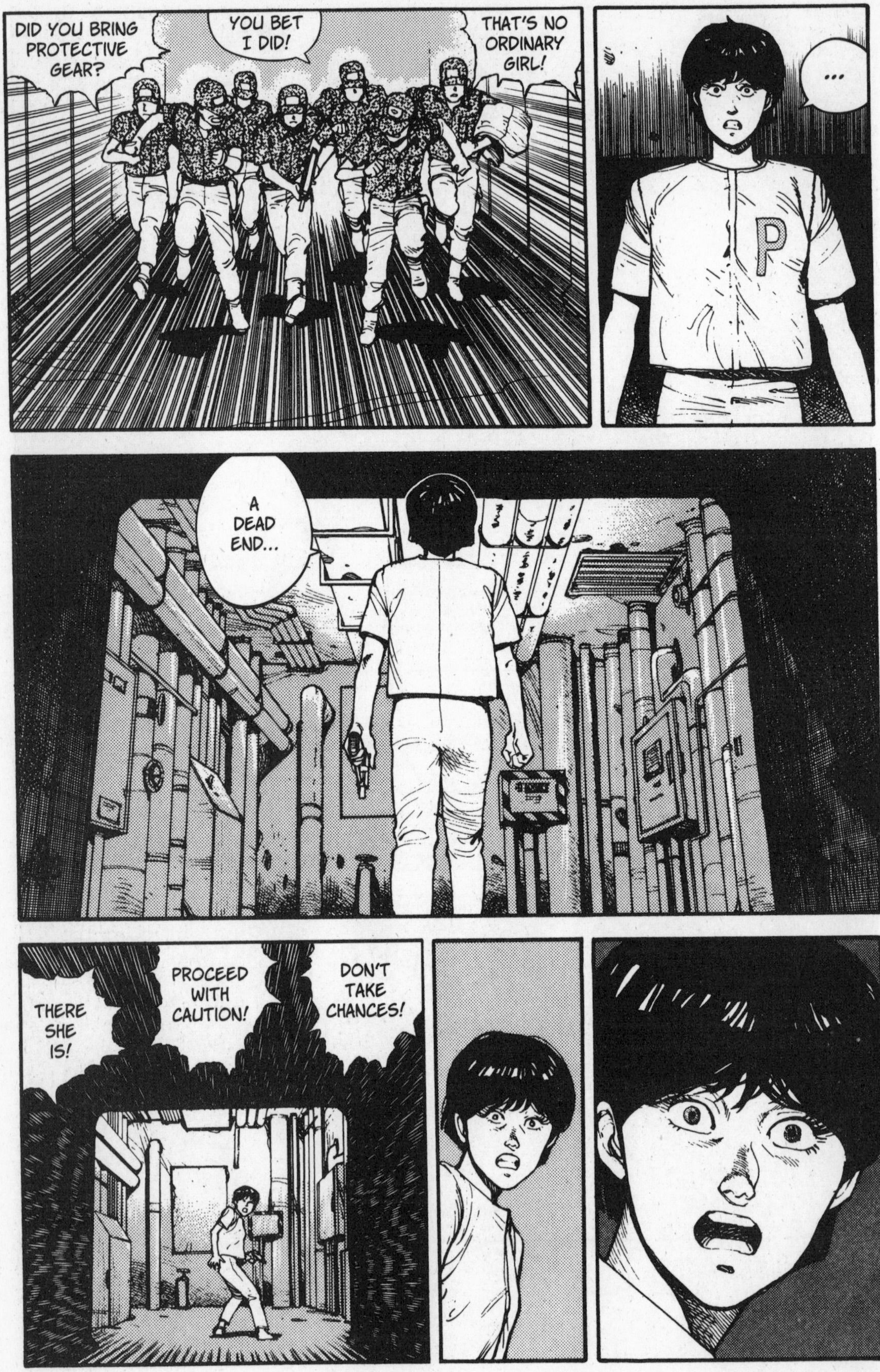
DID YOU BRING PROTECTIVE GEAR?
YOU BET I DID!
THAT'S NO ORDINARY GIRL!
...
A DEAD END...
THERE SHE IS!
PROCEED WITH CAUTION!
DON'T TAKE CHANCES!

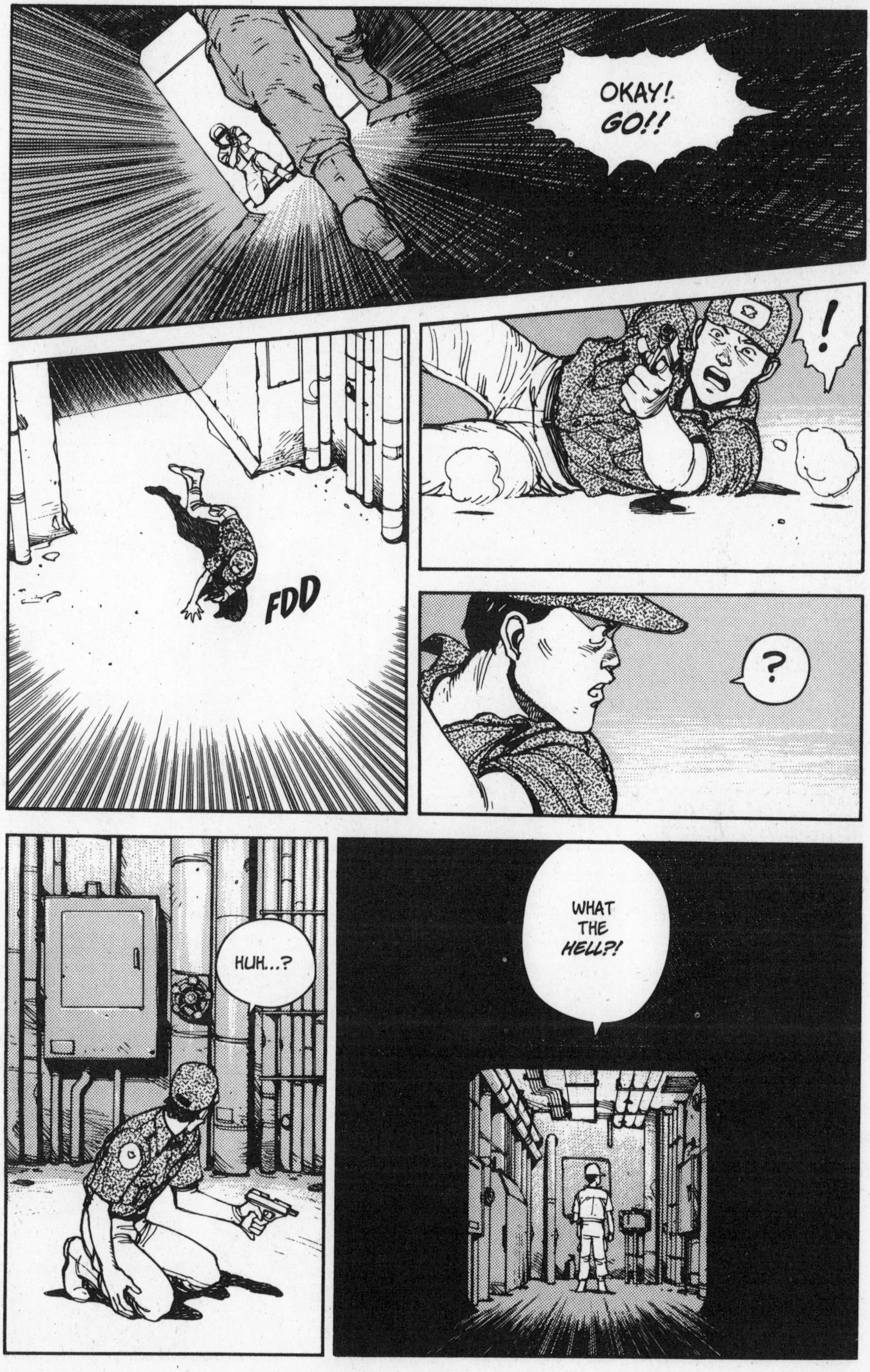
OKAY! GO!!
FDD
!
?
HUH...?
WHAT THE HELL?!

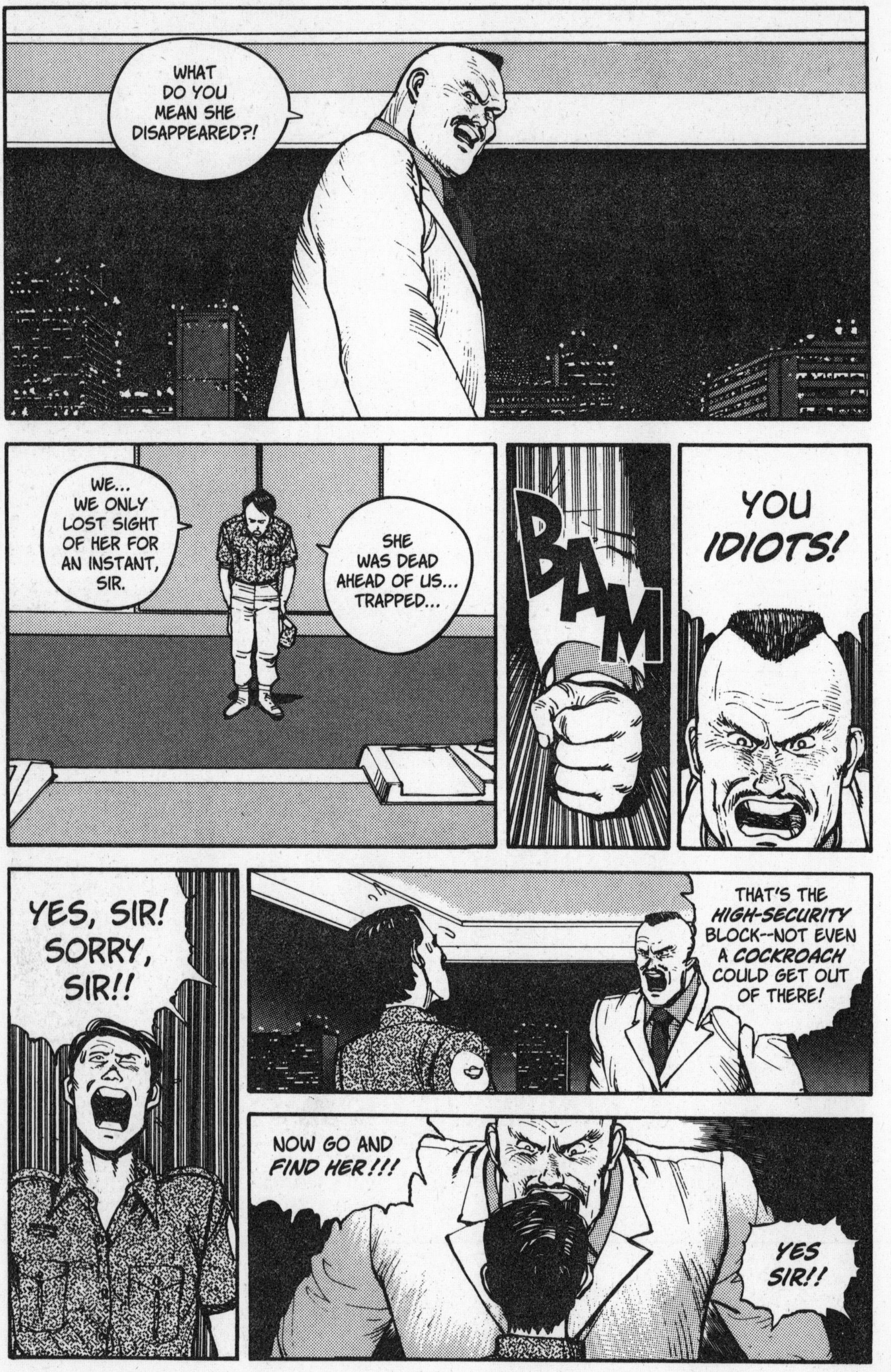
WHAT DO YOU MEAN SHE DISAPPEARED?!
WE... WE ONLY LOST SIGHT OF HER FOR AN INSTANT, SIR.
SHE WAS DEAD AHEAD OF US... TRAPPED...
BAM
YOU *IDIOTS!*
YES, SIR! SORRY, SIR!!
THAT'S THE *HIGH-SECURITY* BLOCK--NOT EVEN A *COCKROACH* COULD GET OUT OF THERE!
NOW GO AND *FIND HER!!!*
*YES SIR!!*

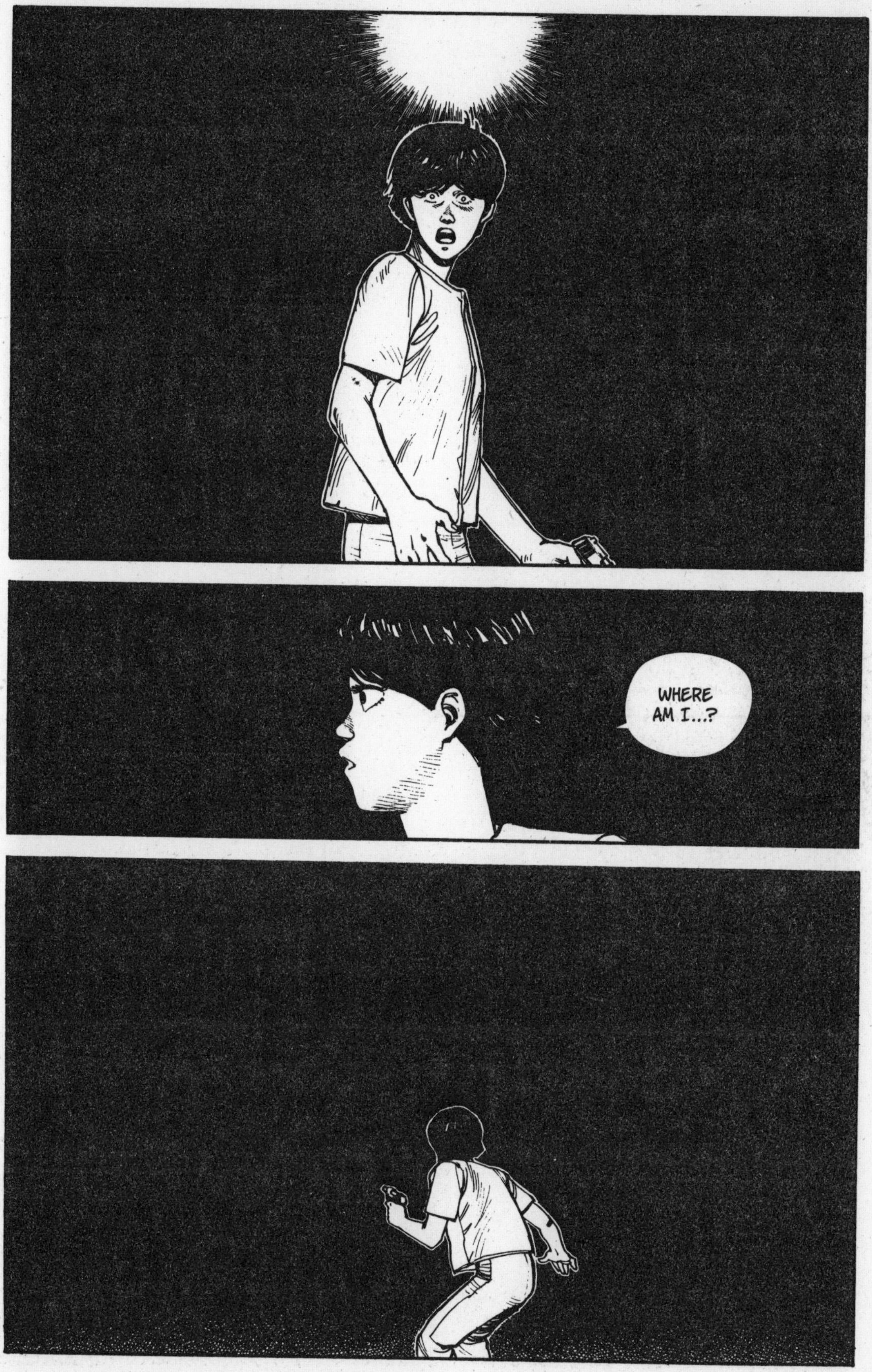
WHERE AM I...?

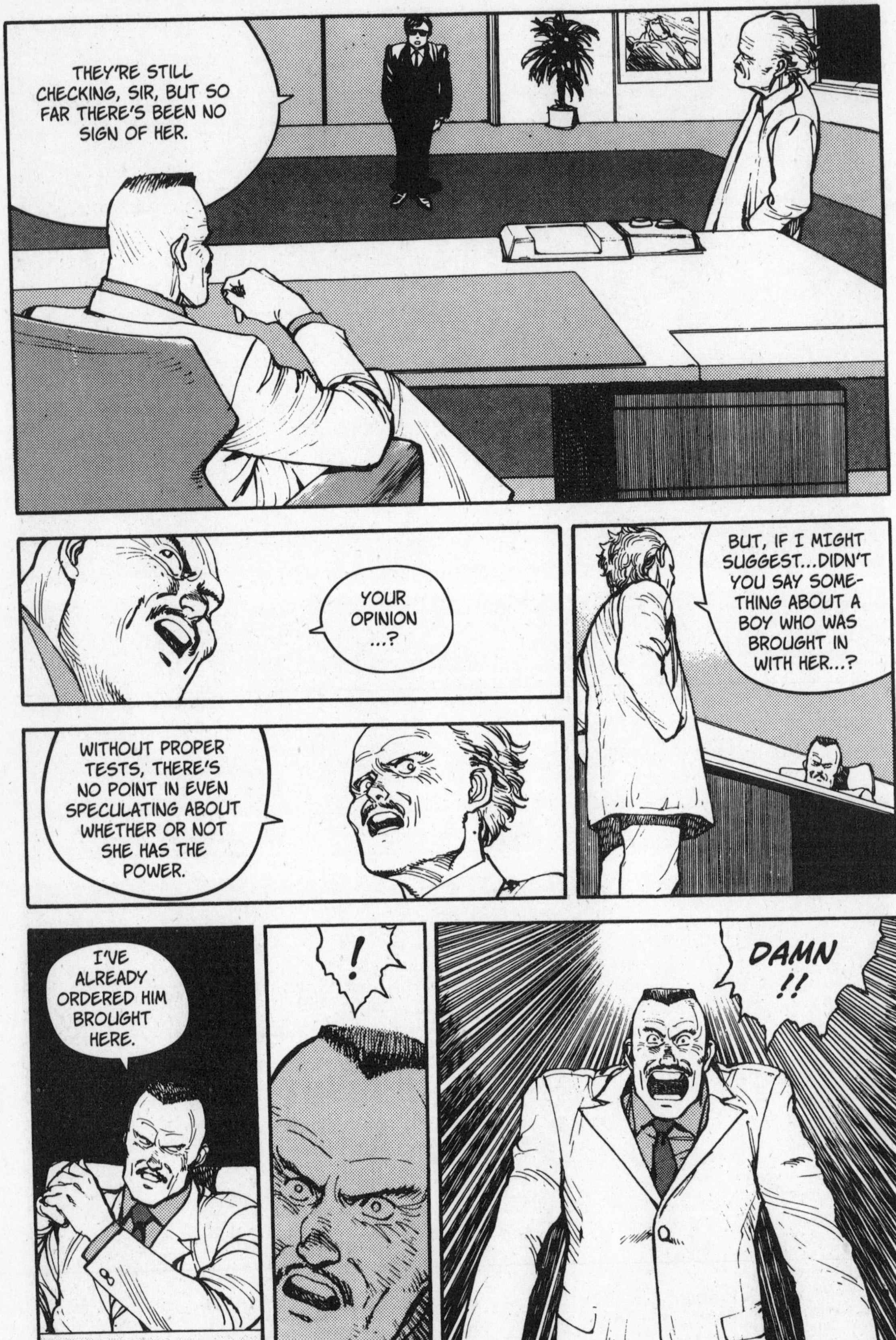
THEY'RE STILL CHECKING, SIR, BUT SO FAR THERE'S BEEN NO SIGN OF HER.
YOUR OPINION ...?
BUT, IF I MIGHT SUGGEST...DIDN'T YOU SAY SOME-THING ABOUT A BOY WHO WAS BROUGHT IN WITH HER...?
WITHOUT PROPER TESTS, THERE'S NO POINT IN EVEN SPECULATING ABOUT WHETHER OR NOT SHE HAS THE POWER.
I'VE ALREADY ORDERED HIM BROUGHT HERE.
!
DAMN !!

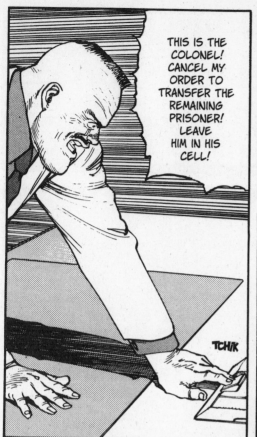

THIS IS THE COLONEL! CANCEL MY ORDER TO TRANSFER THE REMAINING PRISONER! LEAVE HIM IN HIS CELL!

B-BUT, SIR...

TCHIK

WHAT DO YOU MEAN HE'S ON HIS WAY HERE?!

WHAT IS THIS MAN DOING?

ONE-- IS HE TRYING TO HITCH A RIDE?

TWO-- IS HE WAVING GOODBYE TO SOMEONE?

THREE...

NEXT QUESTION...

A MAN IS STANDING IN FRONT OF A HOUSE WITH A RED ROOF...

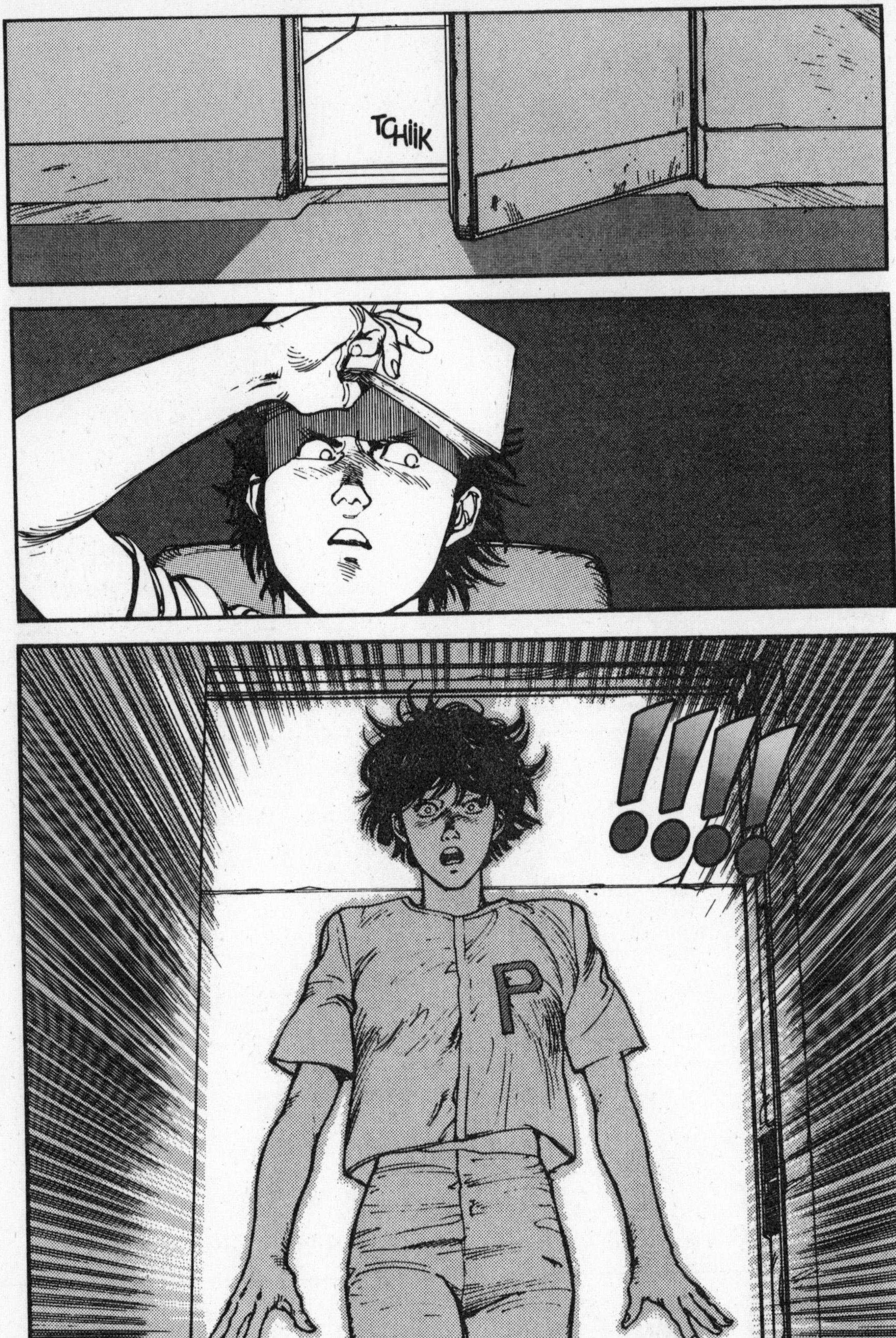
TCHIIK
!!!!

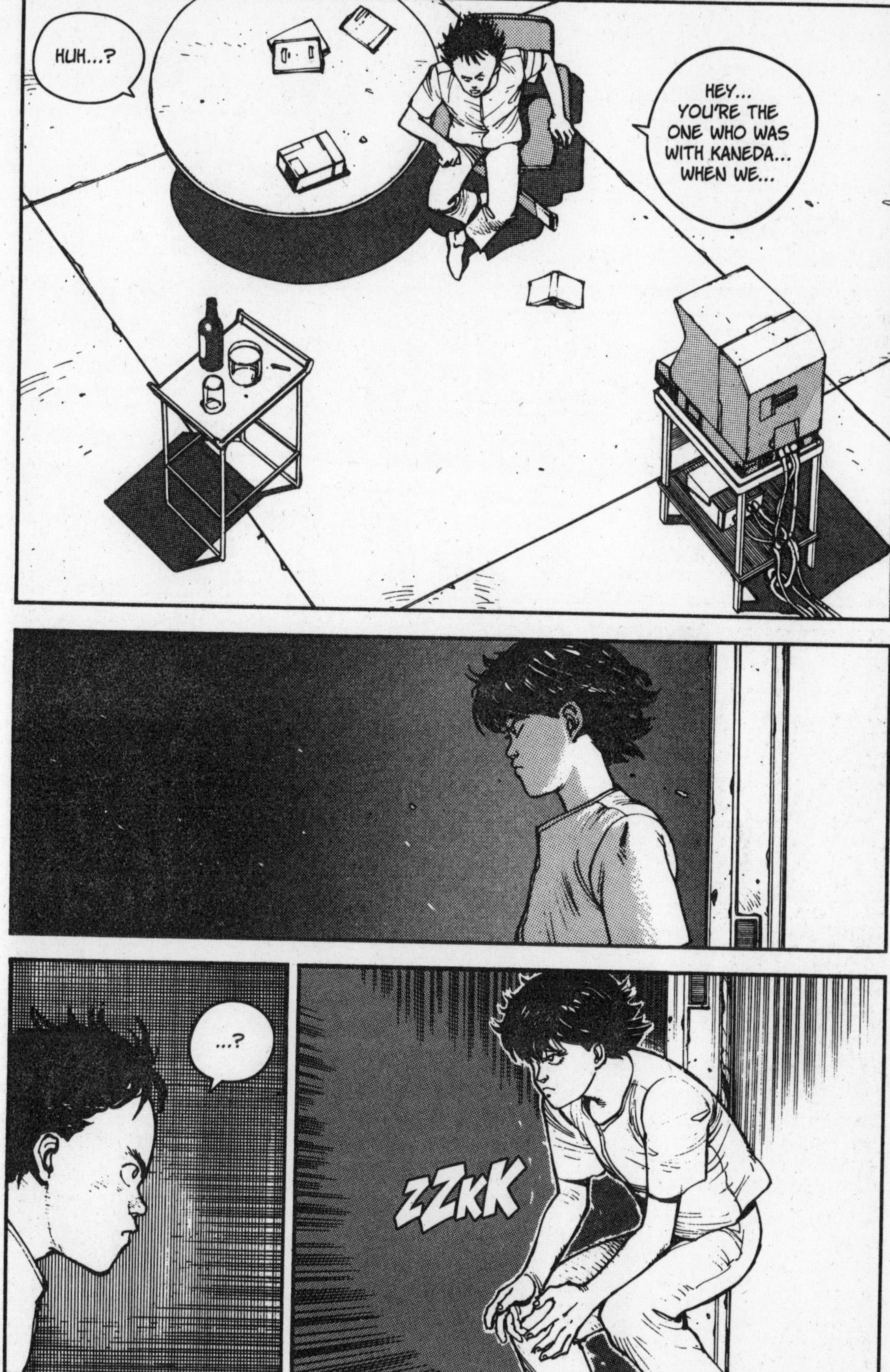
HUH...?
HEY... YOU'RE THE ONE WHO WAS WITH KANEDA... WHEN WE...
...?
ZZKK

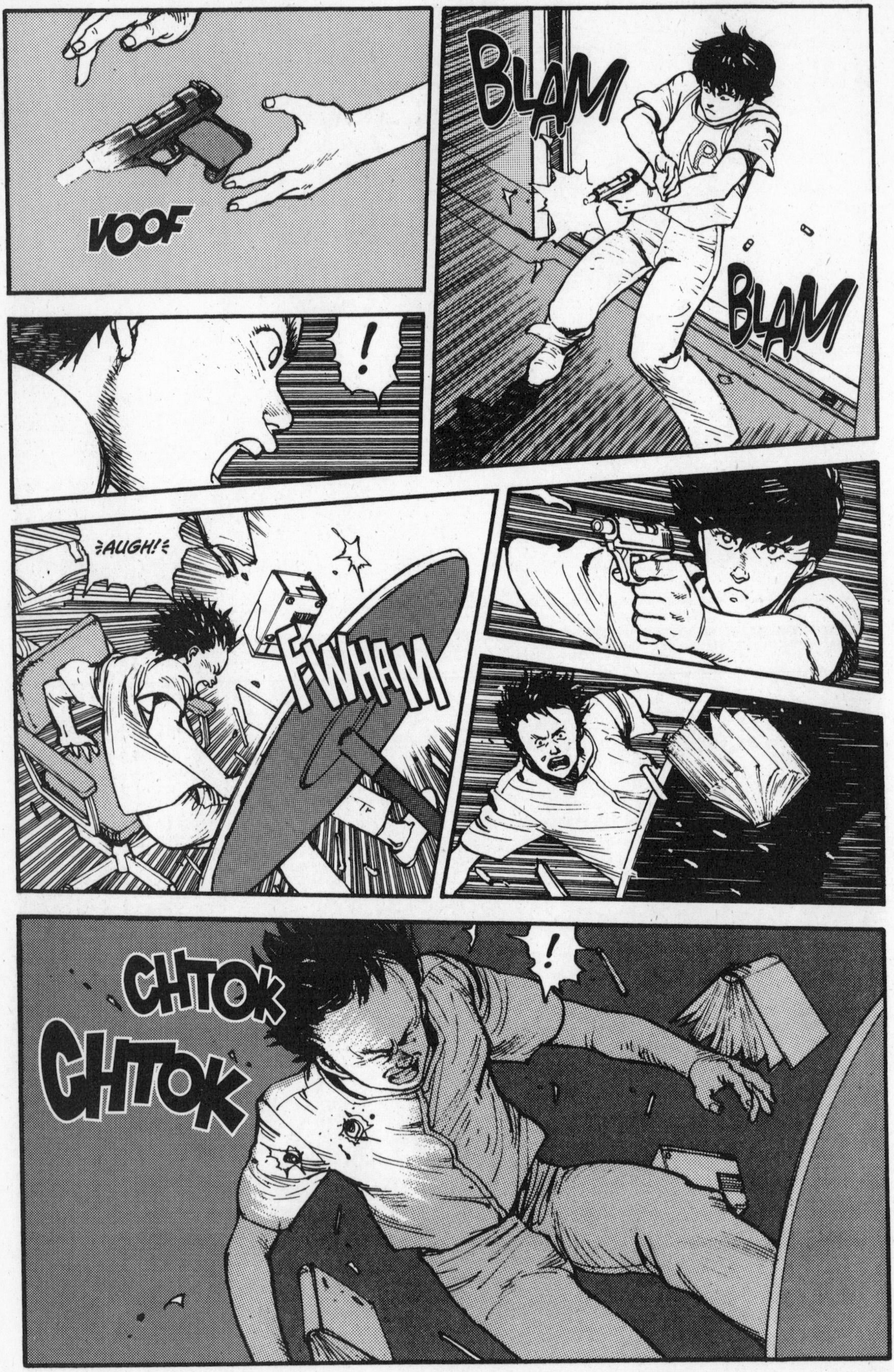
VOOF
BLAM
BLAM
!
AUGH!
FWHAM
CHTOK
CHTOK
!

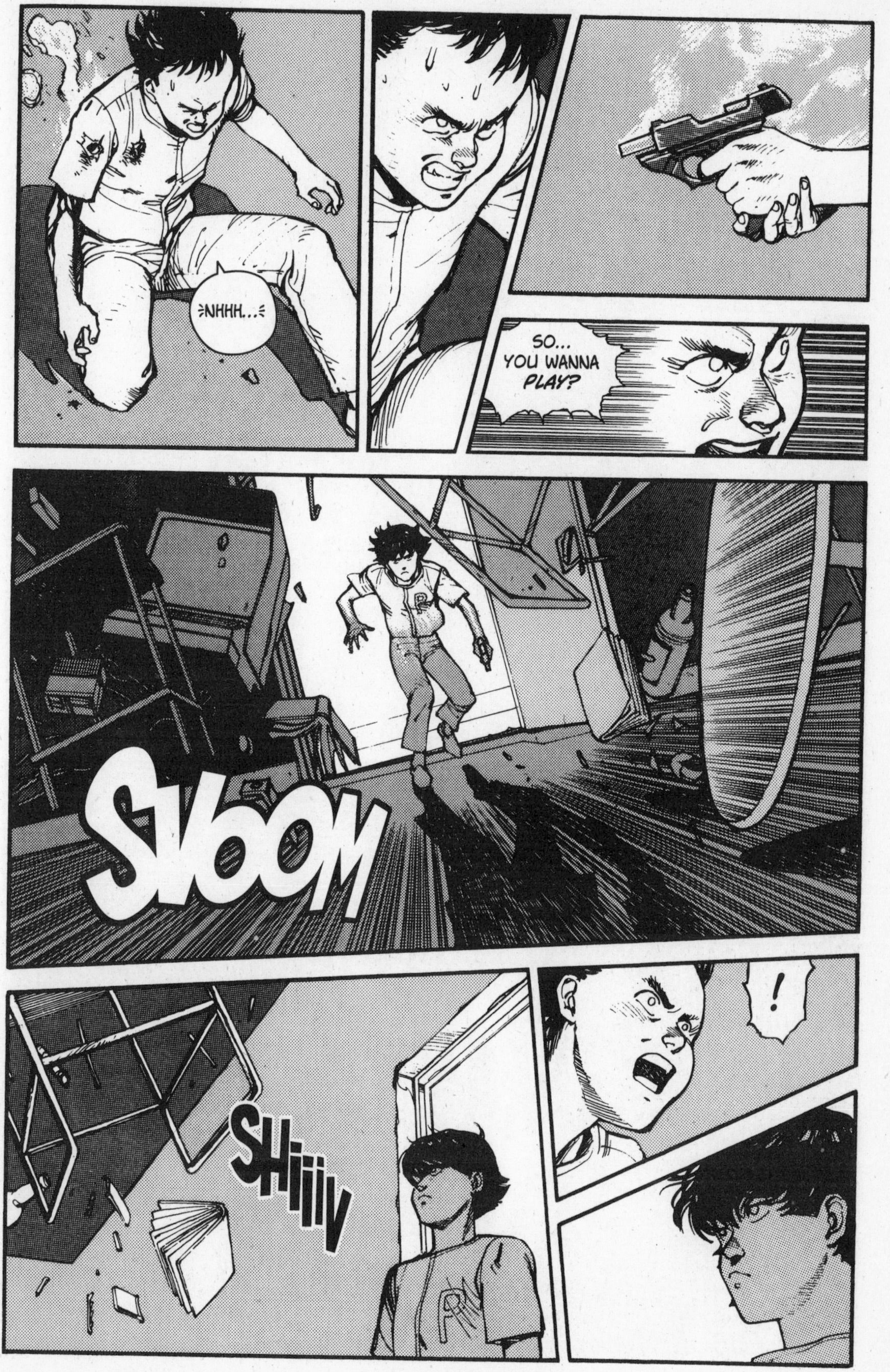
NHHH...
SO... YOU WANNA PLAY?
SVOOM
SHIIIV
!

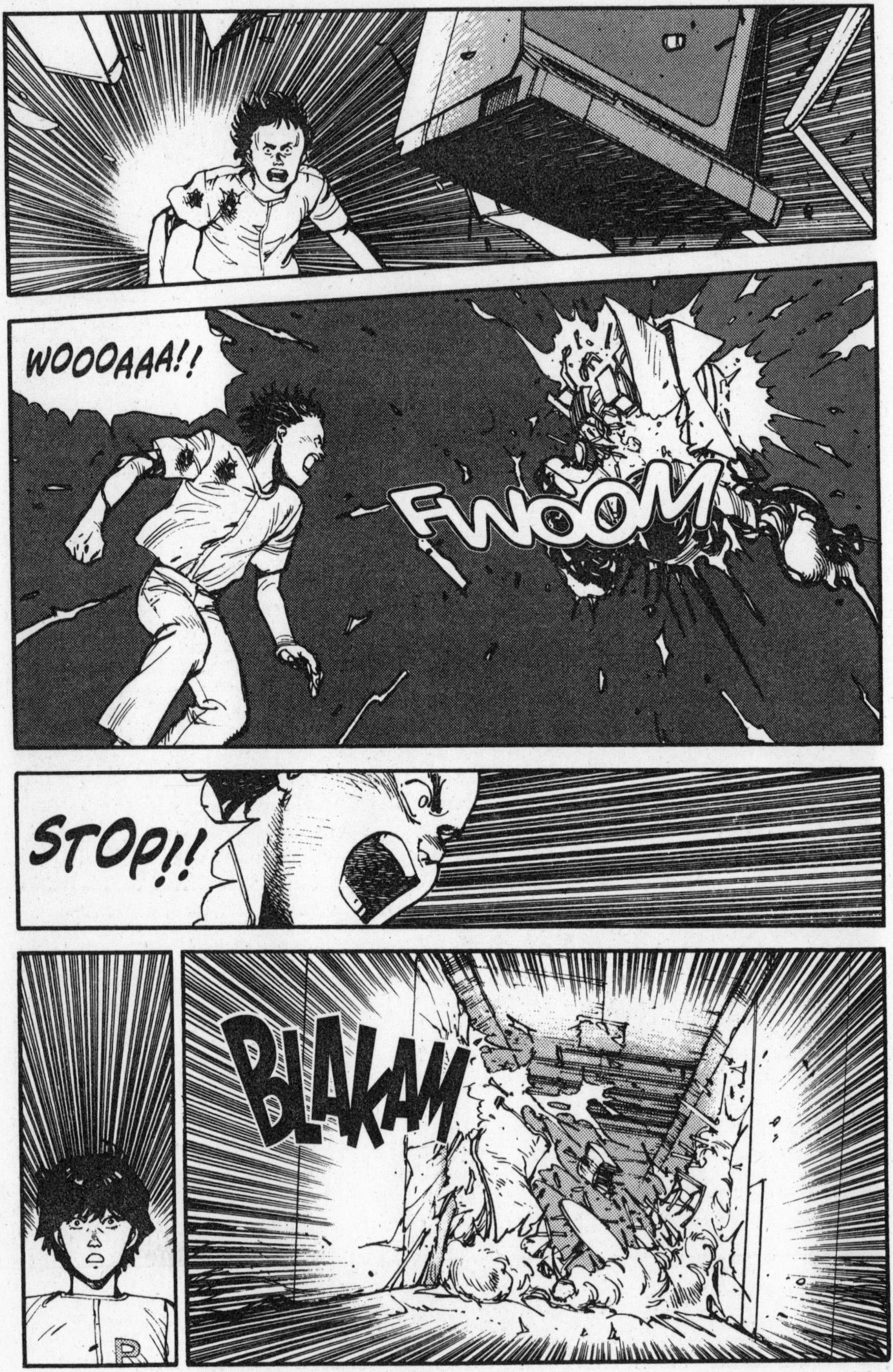
WOOOAAA!!
FWOOM
STOP!!
BLAKAM

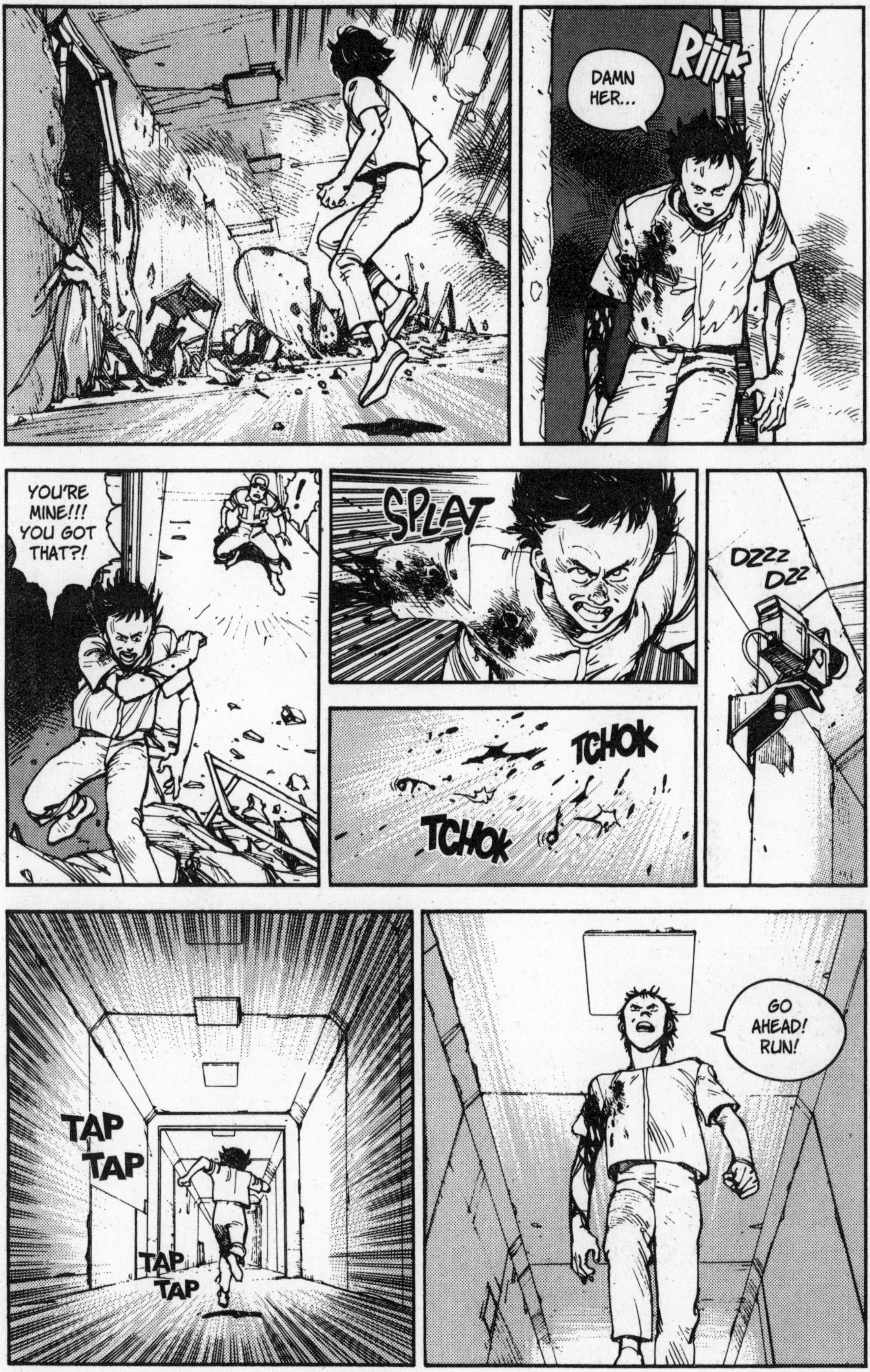
Riiik
DAMN HER...
YOU'RE MINE!!! YOU GOT THAT?!
!
SPLAT
DZZZ DZZ
TCHOK
TCHOK
TAP TAP
TAP TAP
GO AHEAD! RUN!

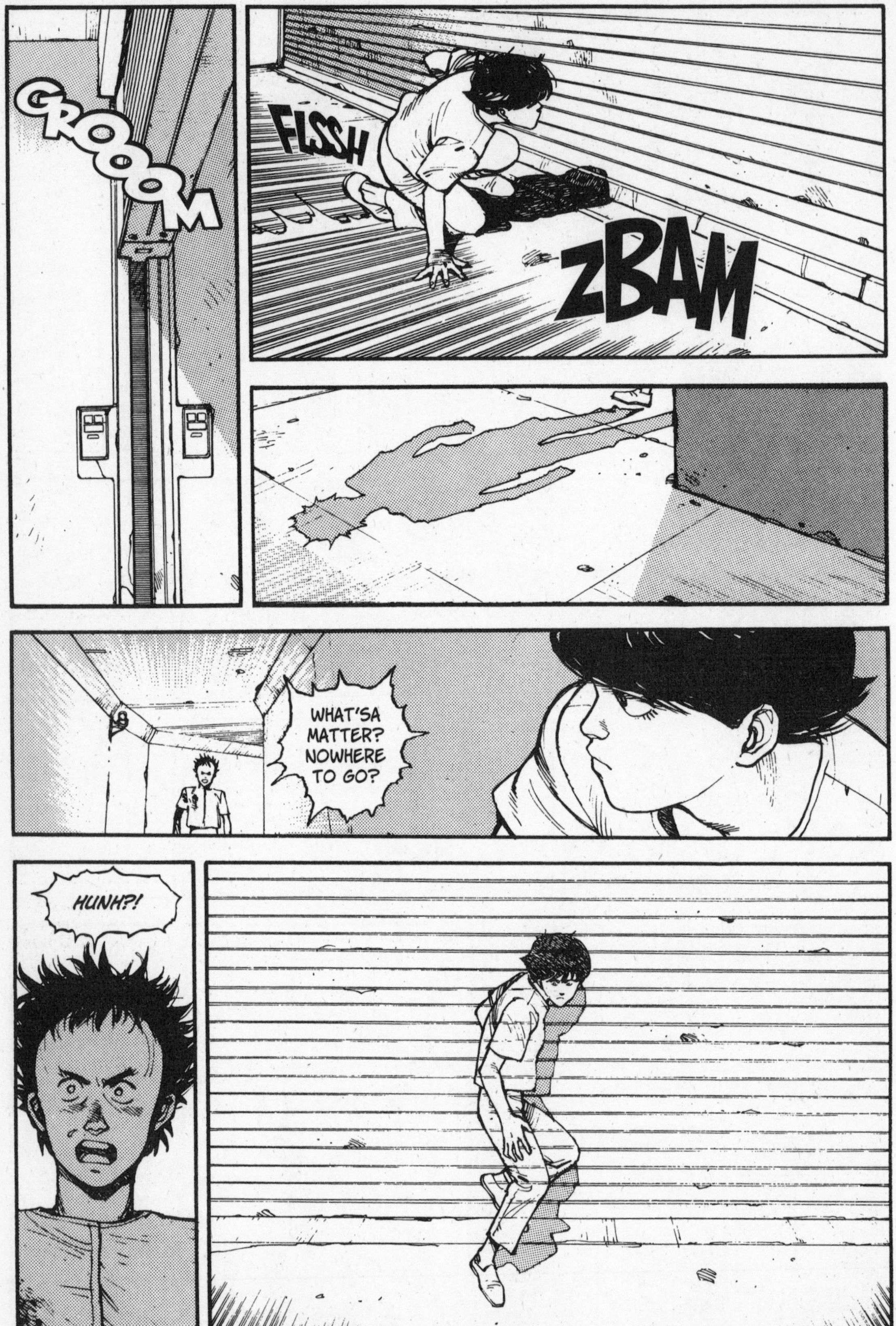
GROOOOM
FLSSH
ZBAM
WHAT'SA MATTER? NOWHERE TO GO?
HUNH?!

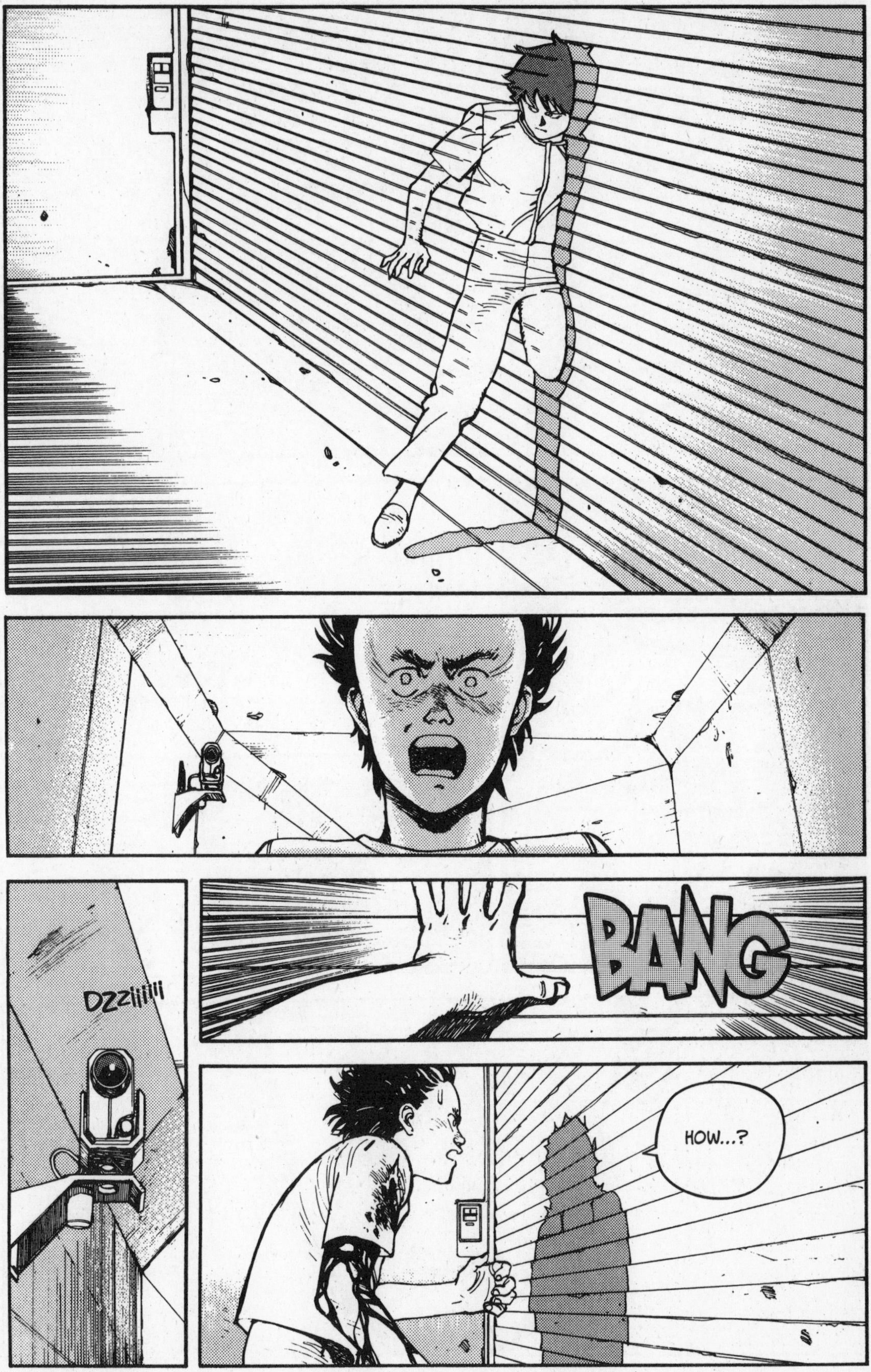
DZZIIIIII
BANG
HOW...?

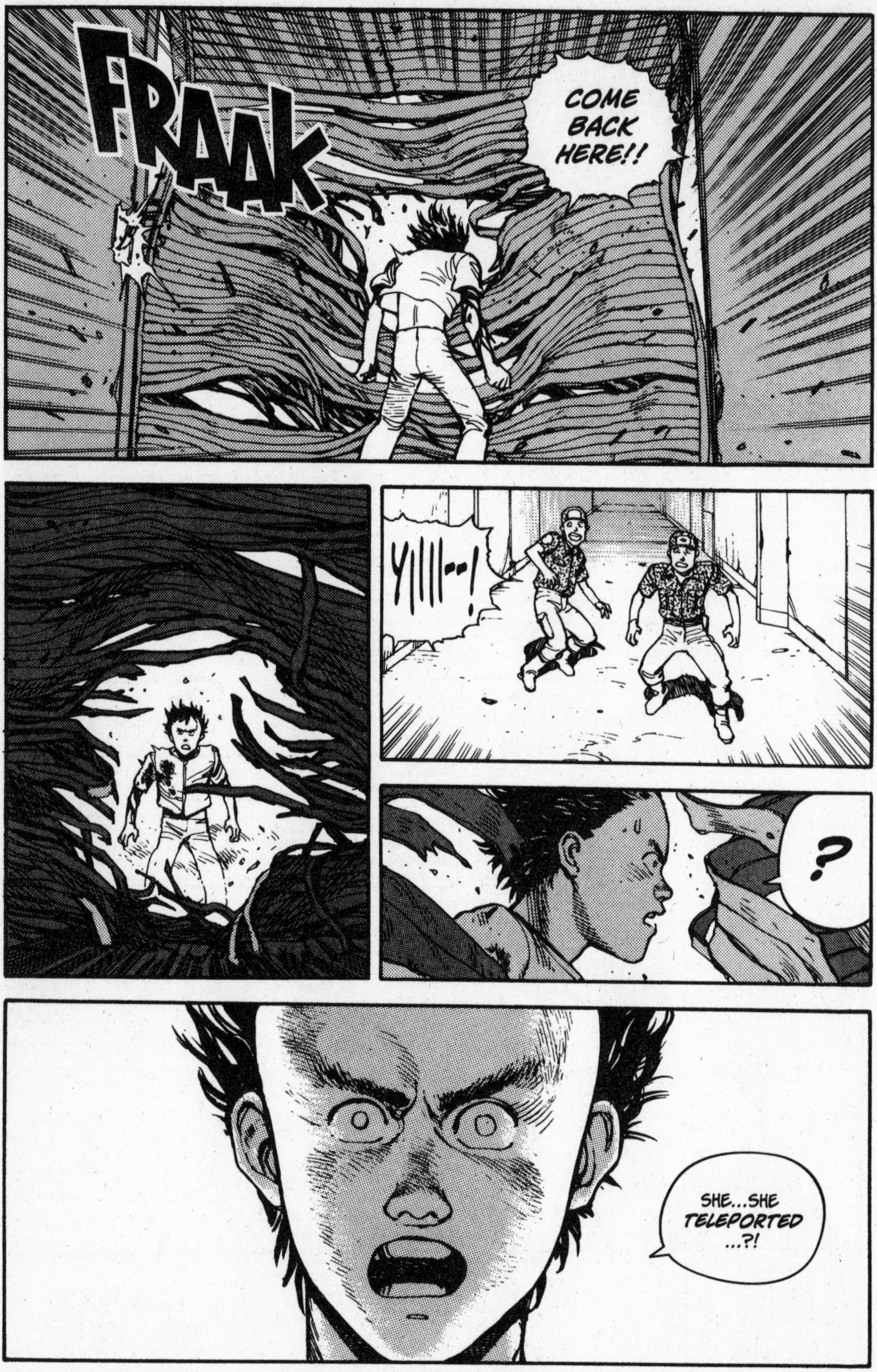
FRAAK
COME BACK HERE!!
YIIII--!
?
SHE...SHE TELEPORTED ...?!

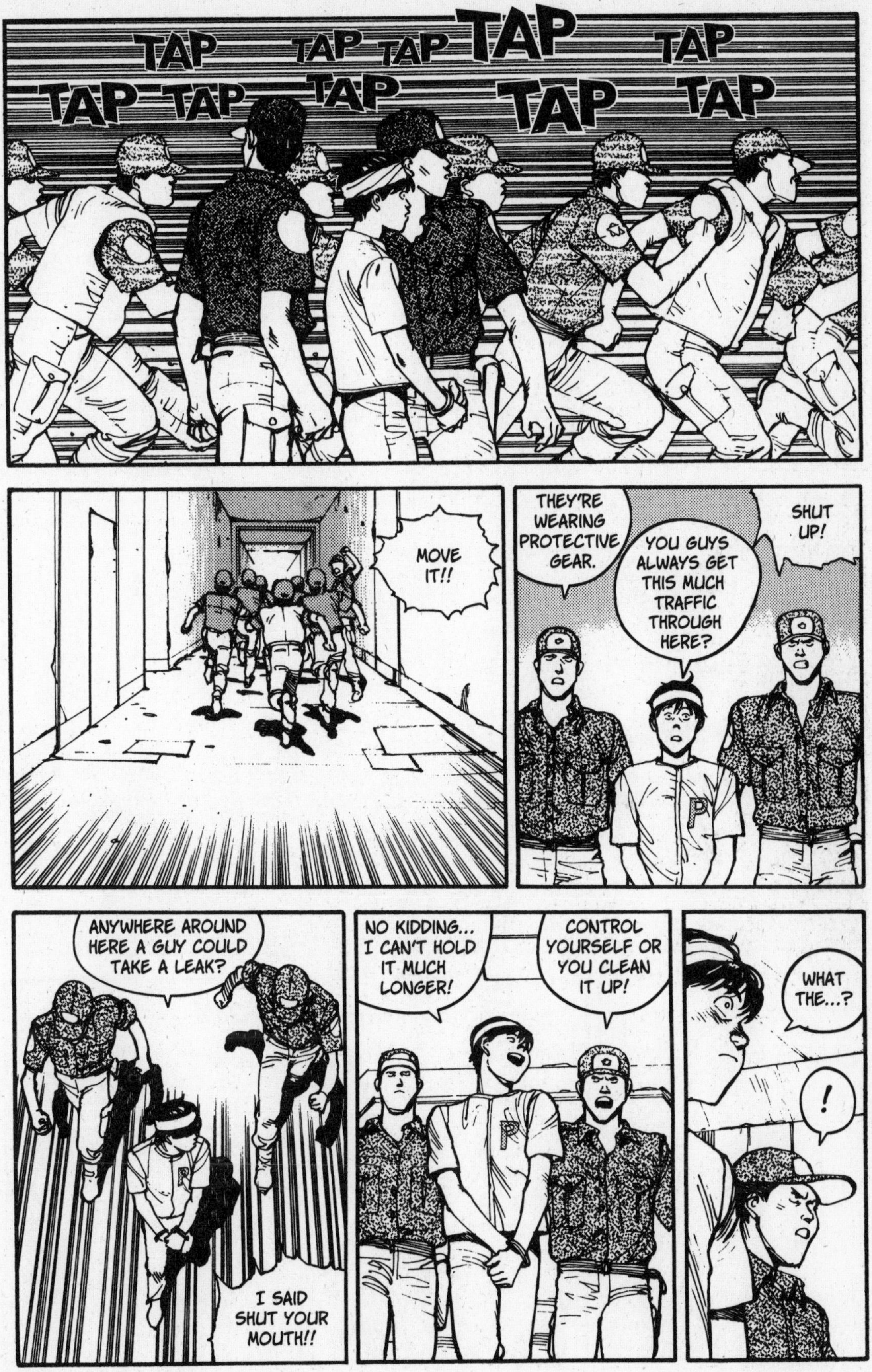
TAP
TAP TAP
TAP TAP TAP
TAP
TAP
TAP
TAP
TAP
TAP
MOVE IT!!
THEY'RE WEARING PROTECTIVE GEAR.
YOU GUYS ALWAYS GET THIS MUCH TRAFFIC THROUGH HERE?
SHUT UP!
ANYWHERE AROUND HERE A GUY COULD TAKE A LEAK?
I SAID SHUT YOUR MOUTH!!
NO KIDDING... I CAN'T HOLD IT MUCH LONGER!
CONTROL YOURSELF OR YOU CLEAN IT UP!
WHAT THE...?
!

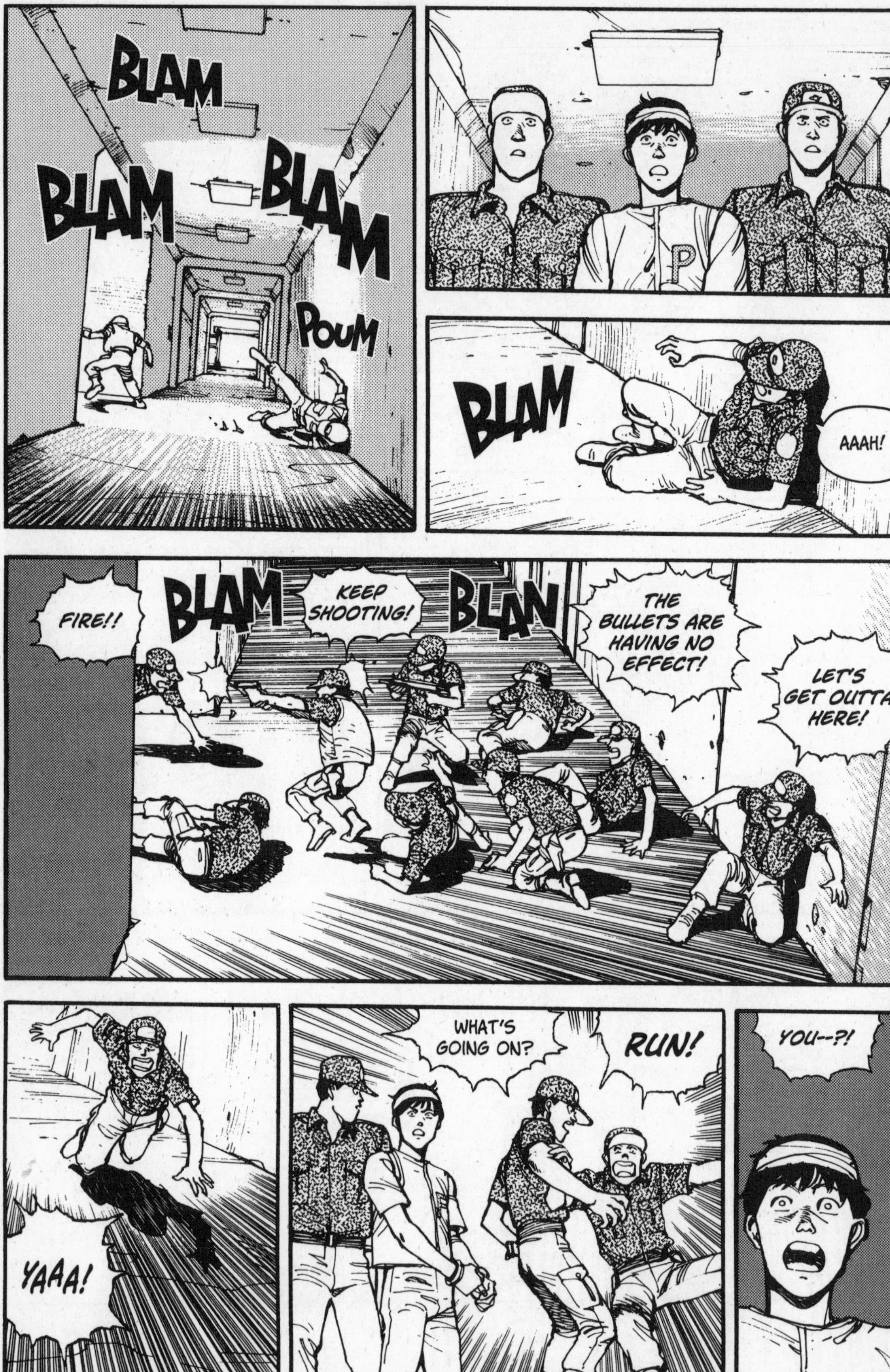
BLAM
BLAM
BLAM
POUM
BLAM
AAAH!
FIRE!!
BLAM
KEEP SHOOTING!
BLAN
THE BULLETS ARE HAVING NO EFFECT!
LET'S GET OUTTA HERE!
YAAA!
WHAT'S GOING ON?
RUN!
YOU--?!

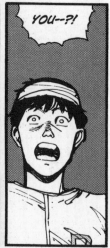

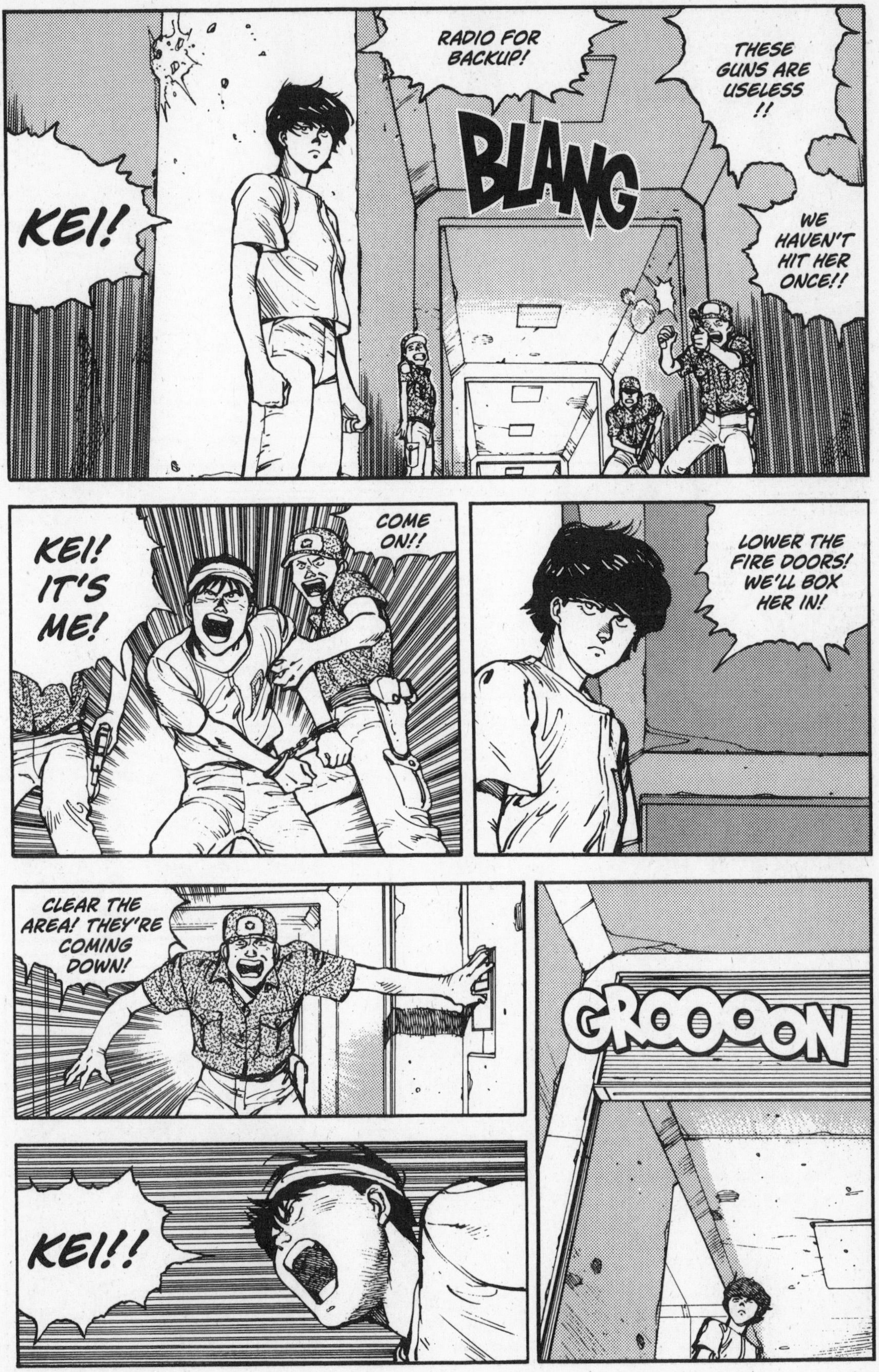
KEI!
RADIO FOR BACKUP!
BLANG
THESE GUNS ARE USELESS !!
WE HAVEN'T HIT HER ONCE!!
KEI! IT'S ME!
COME ON!!
LOWER THE FIRE DOORS! WE'LL BOX HER IN!
CLEAR THE AREA! THEY'RE COMING DOWN!
KEI!!
GROOOON

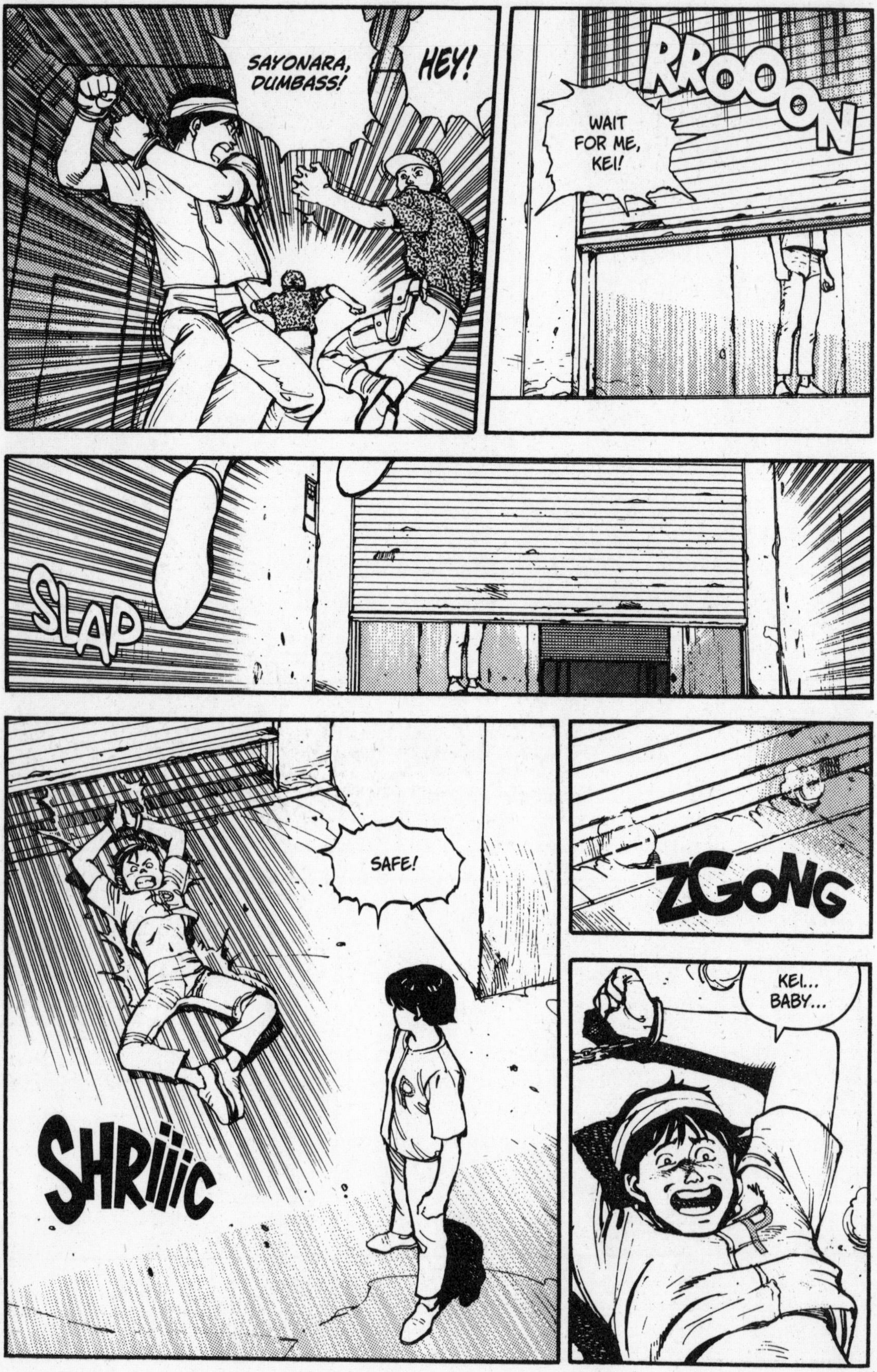
SAYONARA, DUMBASS!
HEY!
WAIT FOR ME, KEI!
RROOON
SLAP
SAFE!
SHRIiiC
ZGONG
KEI... BABY...

I GUESS I MISSED A LOT...BEING KNOCKED OUT AND ALL. I'M CLUELESS AS TO WHAT'S GOING ON HERE.

UH...HAVE I TOLD YOU HOW GREAT IT IS TO SEE YOU?

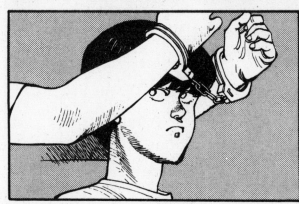

NO KIDDING, BABY... I WAS REALLY WORRIED ABOUT YOU...

MAN, THIS IS *GREAT*, HUH?

BACK TOGETHER AGAIN...

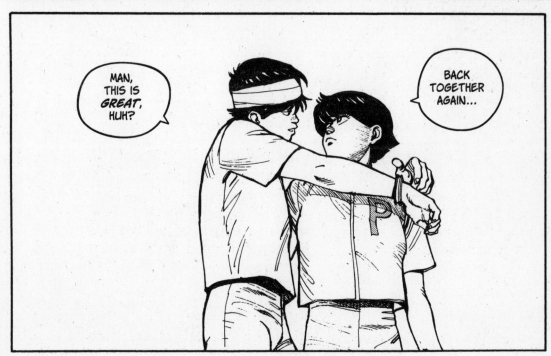

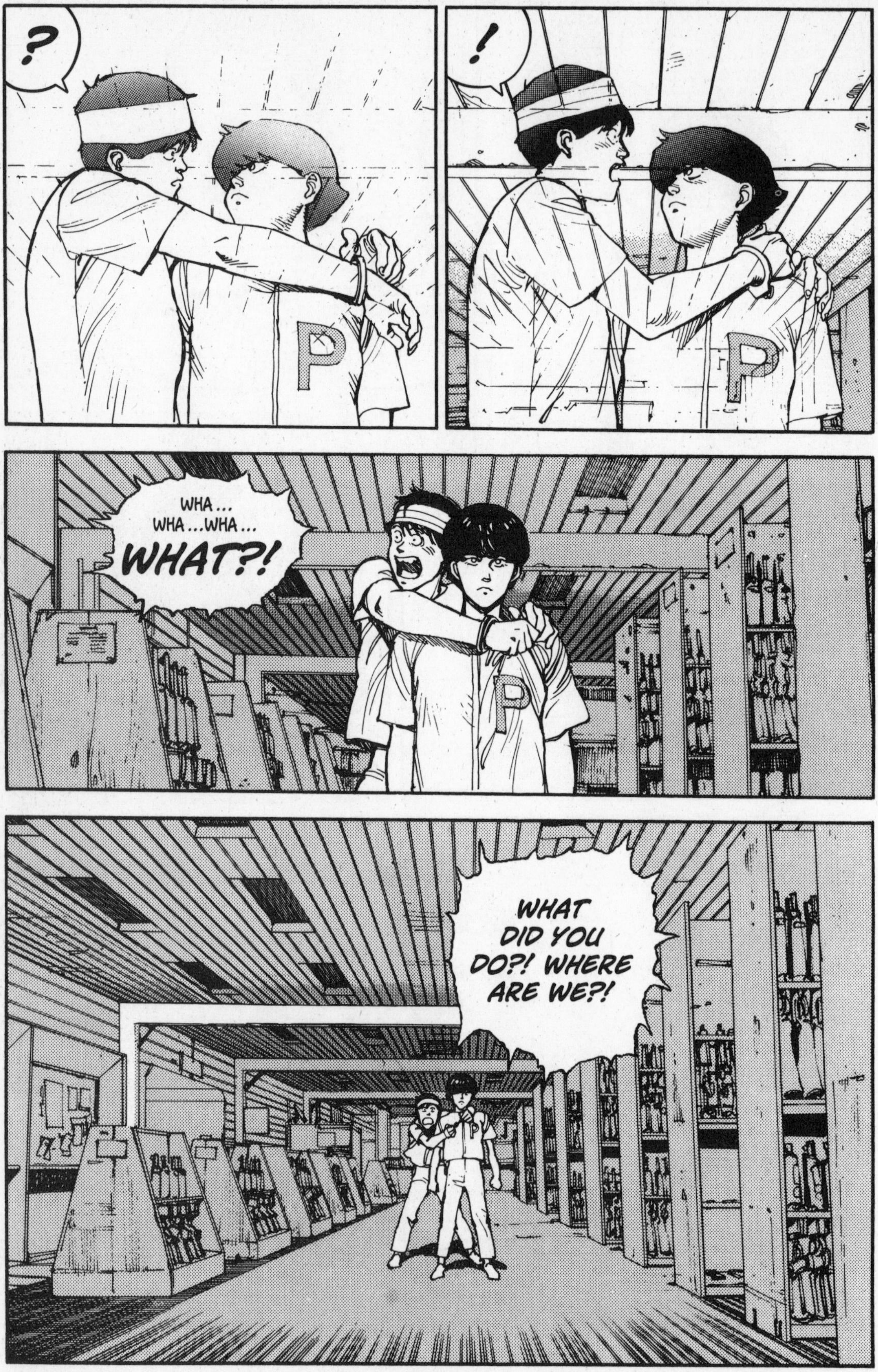
?
!
WHA... WHA...WHA... WHAT?!
WHAT DID YOU DO?! WHERE ARE WE?!

HERE IT COMES...

...NOW!!

SHE DISAPPEARED!

I...I DON'T KNOW WHAT TO SAY.

HMMM...

RUN THE TAPE AGAIN!

TOTAL INSTANTANEOUS MATTER TRANSFER...

...

A CLASSIC D-15 STYLE *TELEPORTER*... EXHIBITING THE SAME ABILITY AS NUMBER 26...

I DISAGREE. SHE IS CLEARLY A C-20...

TAP TAP

59

YES, COLONEL?

IT'S ME. IS THE DOCTOR THERE?

WHAT IS NUMBER 41'S CONDITION?

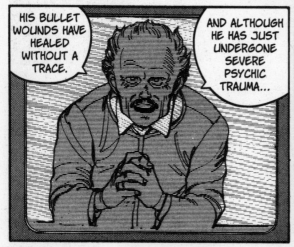

HIS BULLET WOUNDS HAVE HEALED WITHOUT A TRACE.

AND ALTHOUGH HE HAS JUST UNDERGONE SEVERE PSYCHIC TRAUMA...

...HE HAS ALREADY FULLY RECOVERED.

THIS IS *UNPRECEDENTED*, COLONEL!!

WHEN YOU'RE THROUGH THERE, COME TO MY OFFICE. THERE'S A TAPE I WANT YOU TO SEE.

VERY GOOD, SIR. IN HALF AN HOUR.

I'LL BE WAITING.

60

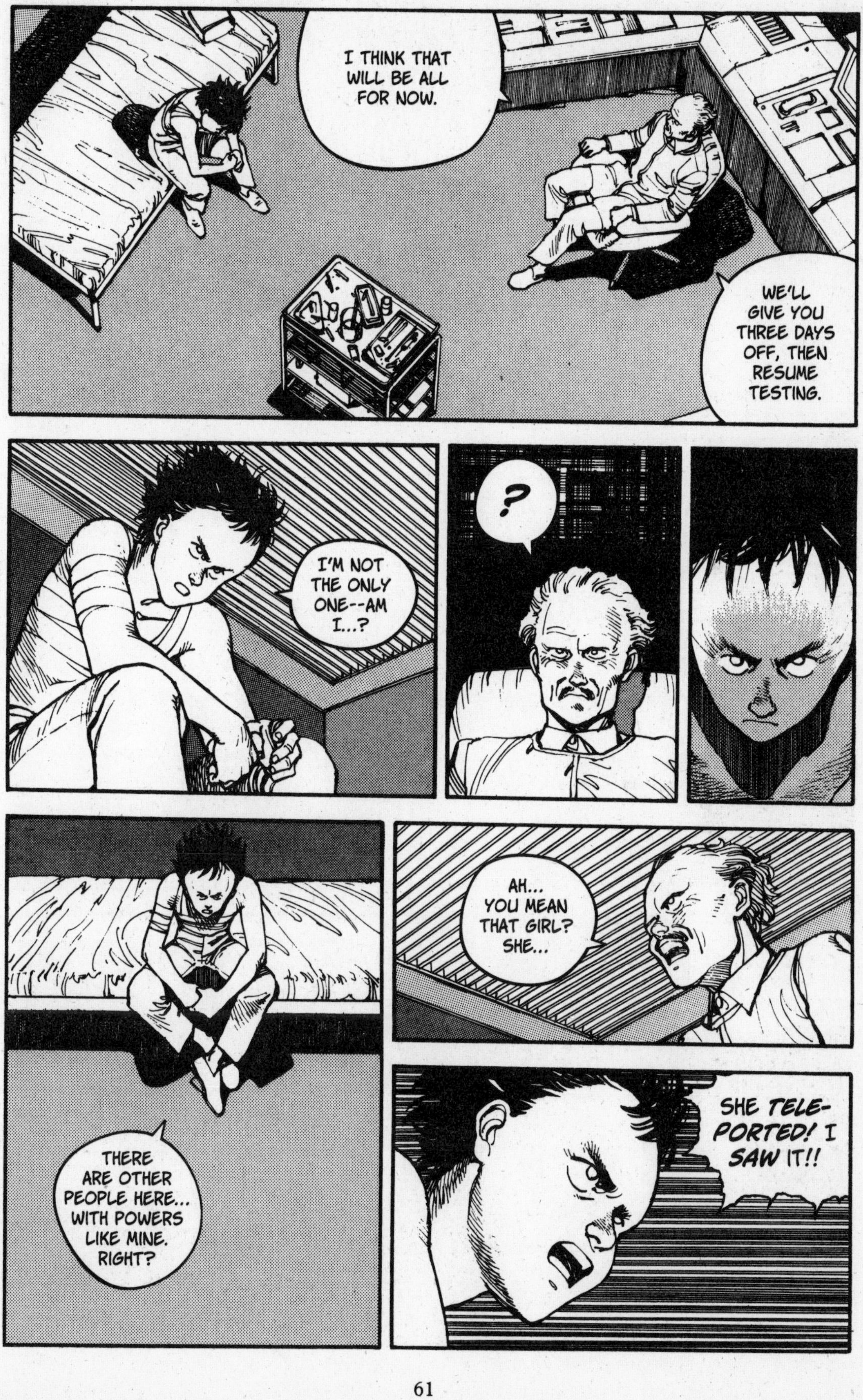
I THINK THAT WILL BE ALL FOR NOW.
WE'LL GIVE YOU THREE DAYS OFF, THEN RESUME TESTING.
I'M NOT THE ONLY ONE--AM I...?
?
THERE ARE OTHER PEOPLE HERE... WITH POWERS LIKE MINE. RIGHT?
AH... YOU MEAN THAT GIRL? SHE...
SHE TELE-PORTED! I SAW IT!!

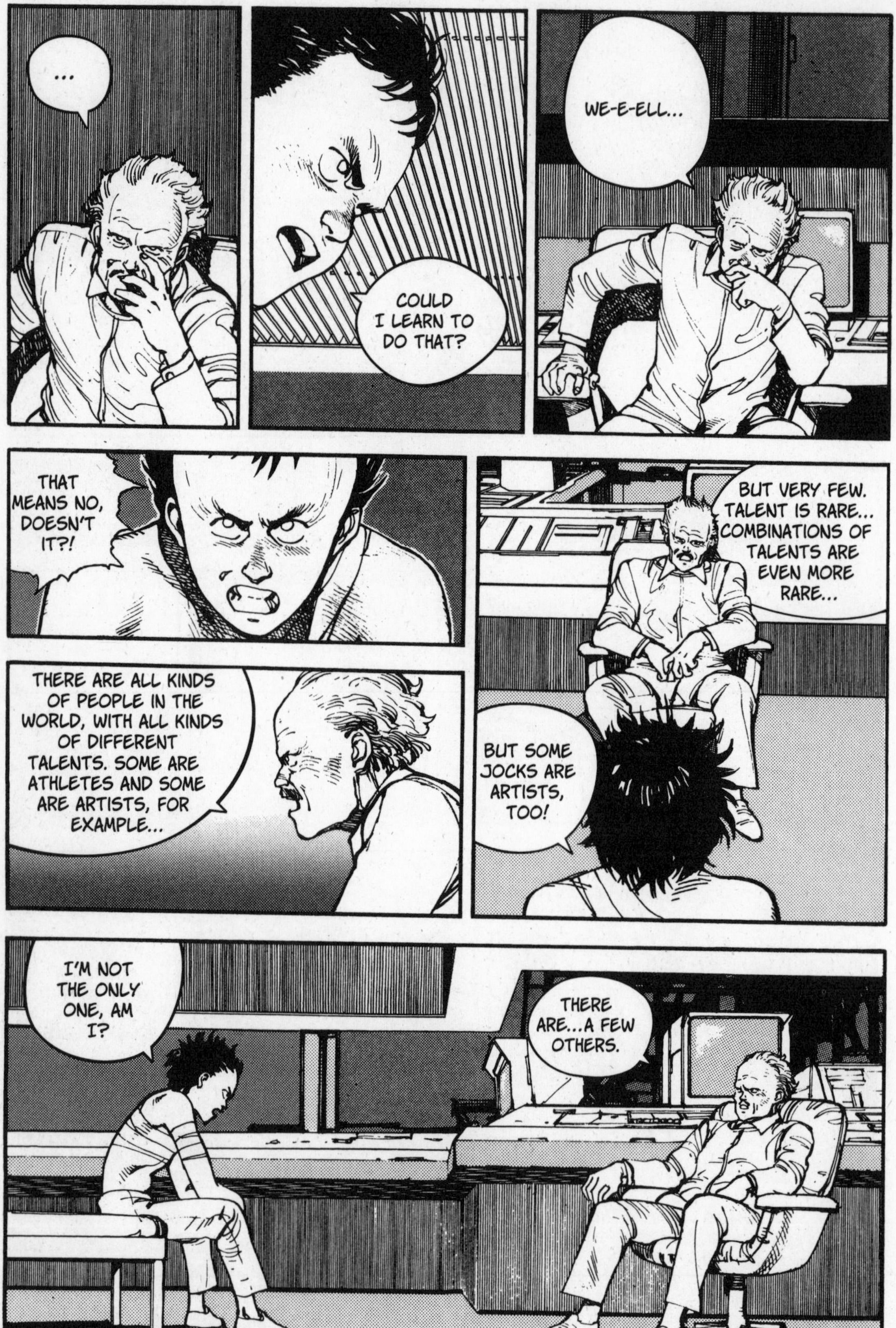
...
COULD I LEARN TO DO THAT?
WE-E-ELL...
THAT MEANS NO, DOESN'T IT?!
THERE ARE ALL KINDS OF PEOPLE IN THE WORLD, WITH ALL KINDS OF DIFFERENT TALENTS. SOME ARE ATHLETES AND SOME ARE ARTISTS, FOR EXAMPLE...
BUT SOME JOCKS ARE ARTISTS, TOO!
BUT VERY FEW. TALENT IS RARE... COMBINATIONS OF TALENTS ARE EVEN MORE RARE...
I'M NOT THE ONLY ONE, AM I?
THERE ARE...A FEW OTHERS.

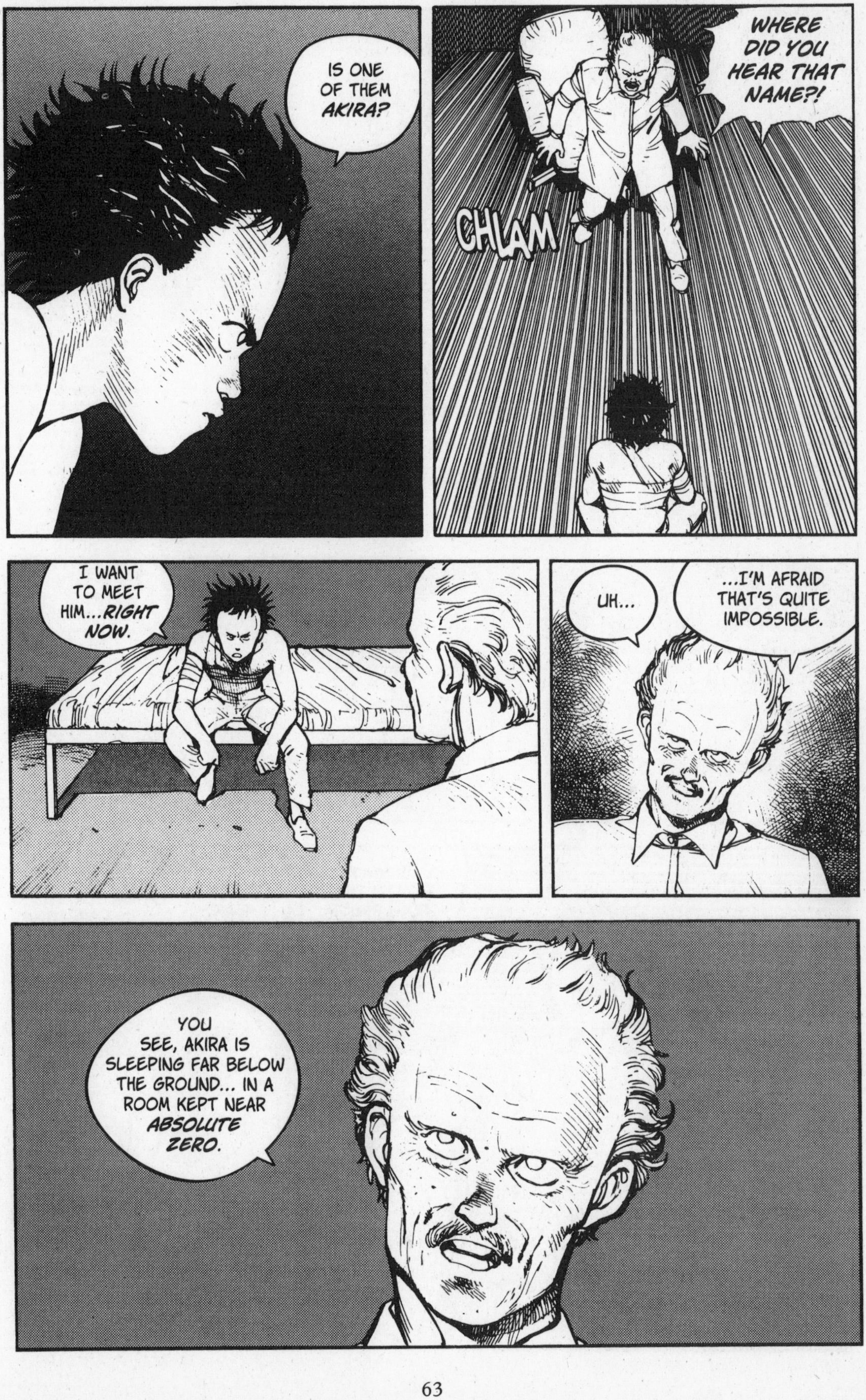
IS ONE OF THEM AKIRA?
WHERE DID YOU HEAR THAT NAME?!
CHLAM
I WANT TO MEET HIM...RIGHT NOW.
UH...
...I'M AFRAID THAT'S QUITE IMPOSSIBLE.
YOU SEE, AKIRA IS SLEEPING FAR BELOW THE GROUND... IN A ROOM KEPT NEAR ABSOLUTE ZERO.

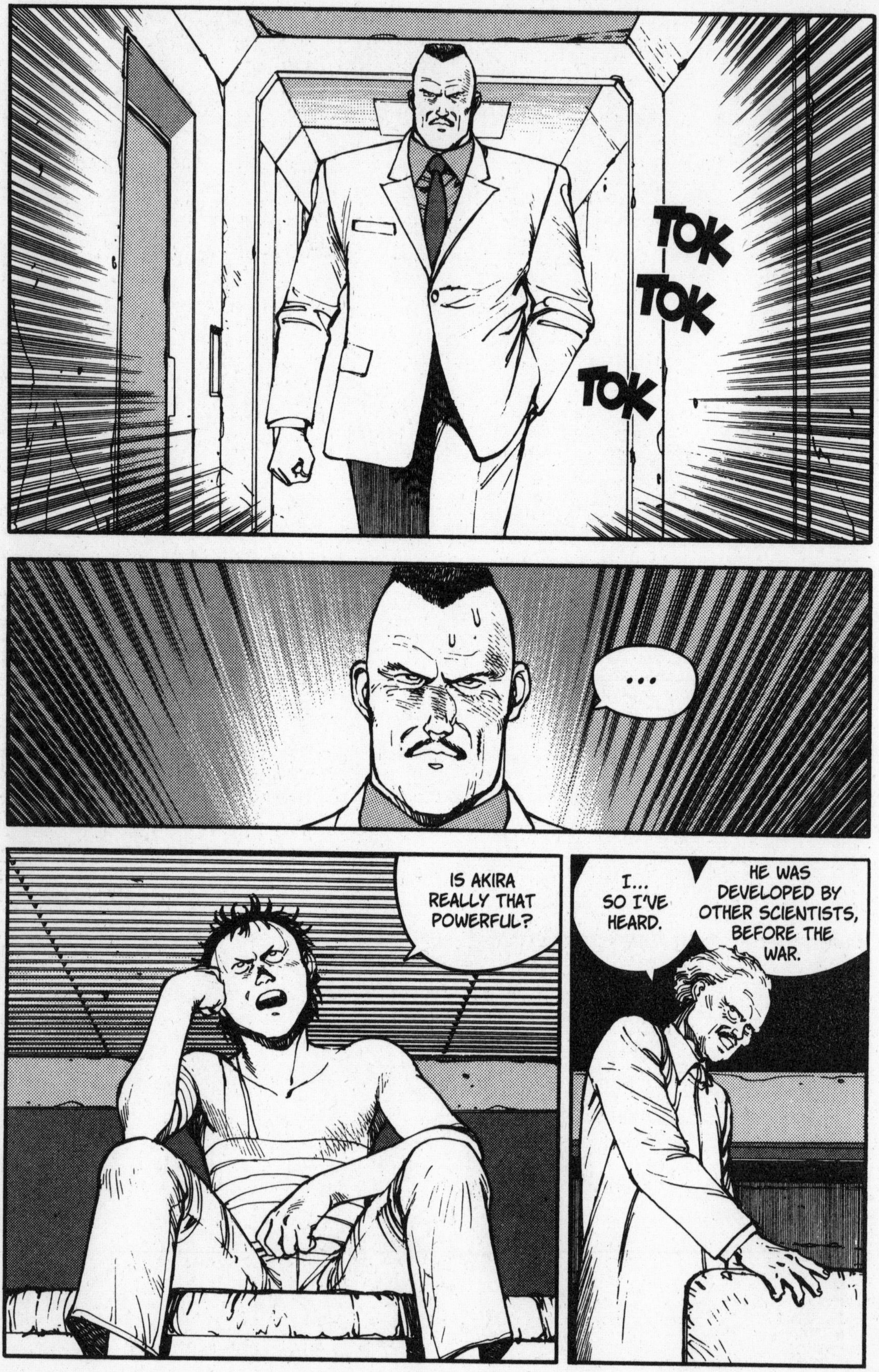
TOK
TOK
TOK
...
IS AKIRA REALLY THAT POWERFUL?
I... SO I'VE HEARD.
HE WAS DEVELOPED BY OTHER SCIENTISTS, BEFORE THE WAR.

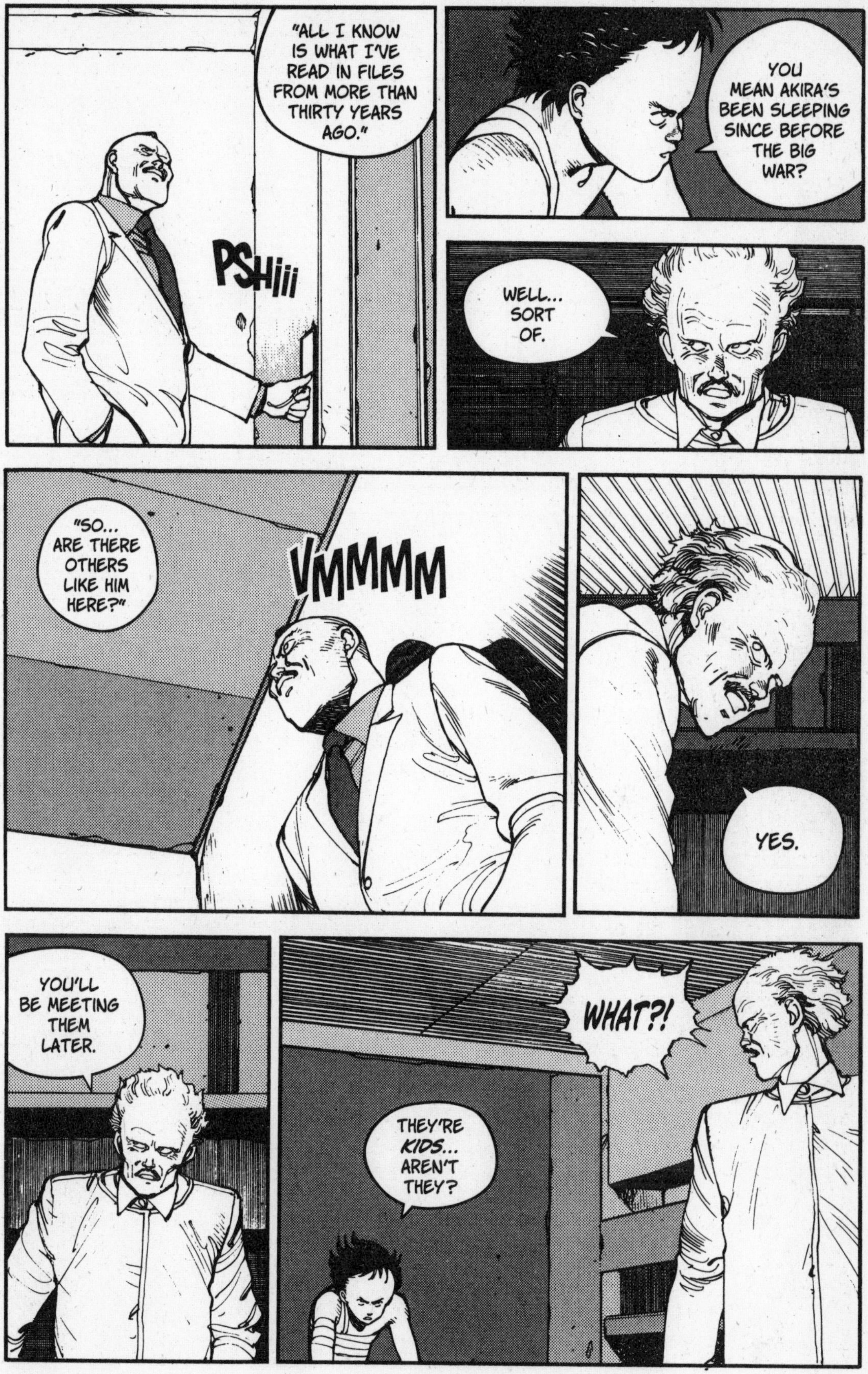
"ALL I KNOW IS WHAT I'VE READ IN FILES FROM MORE THAN THIRTY YEARS AGO."
PSHiii
YOU MEAN AKIRA'S BEEN SLEEPING SINCE BEFORE THE BIG WAR?
WELL... SORT OF.
"SO... ARE THERE OTHERS LIKE HIM HERE?"
VMMMM
YES.
YOU'LL BE MEETING THEM LATER.
WHAT?!
THEY'RE *KIDS*... AREN'T THEY?

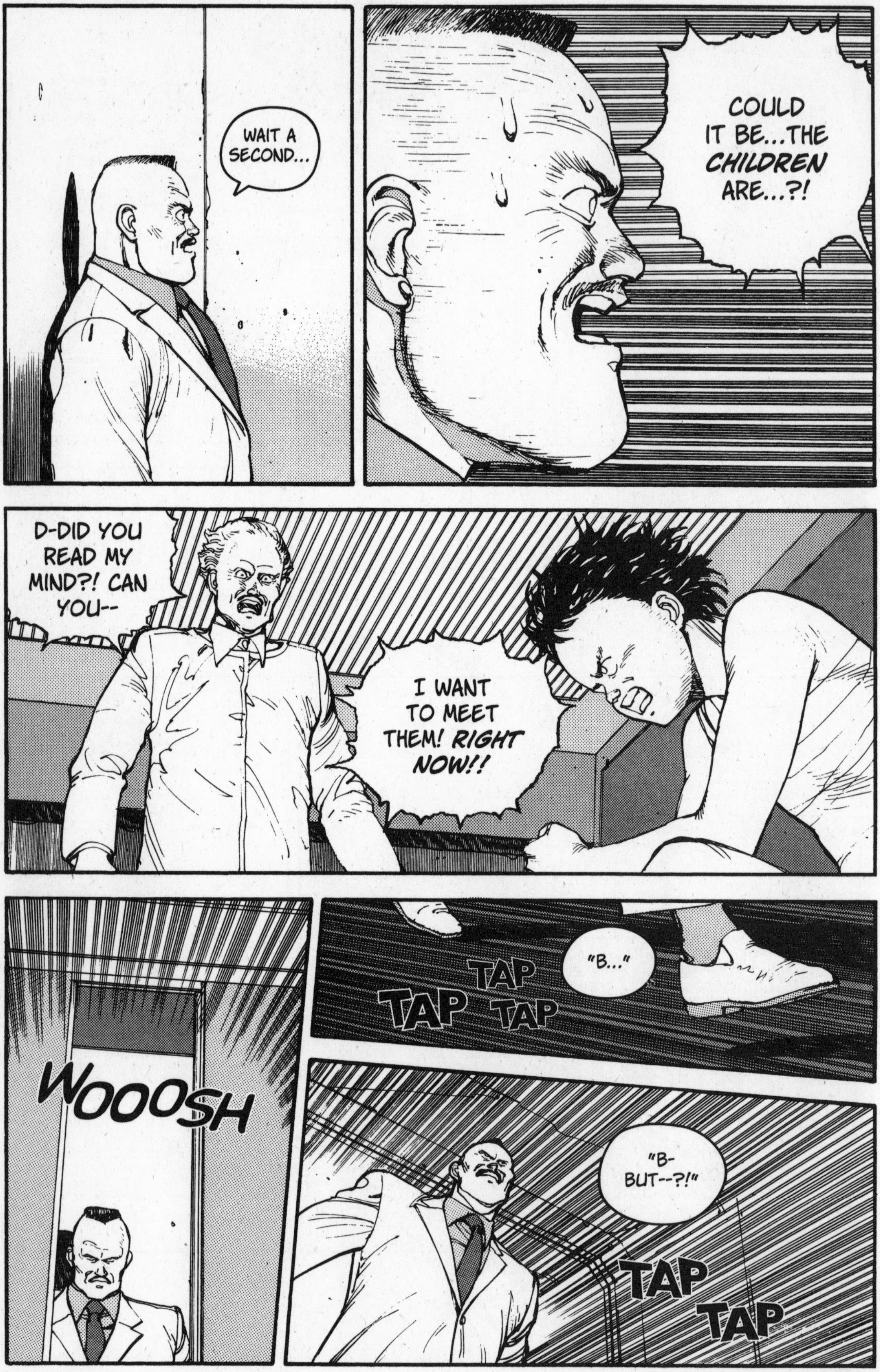
WAIT A SECOND...
COULD IT BE...THE *CHILDREN* ARE...?!
D-DID YOU READ MY MIND?! CAN YOU--
I WANT TO MEET THEM! *RIGHT NOW!!*
WOOOSH
TAP TAP
"B..."
TAP TAP
"B- BUT--?!"
TAP TAP

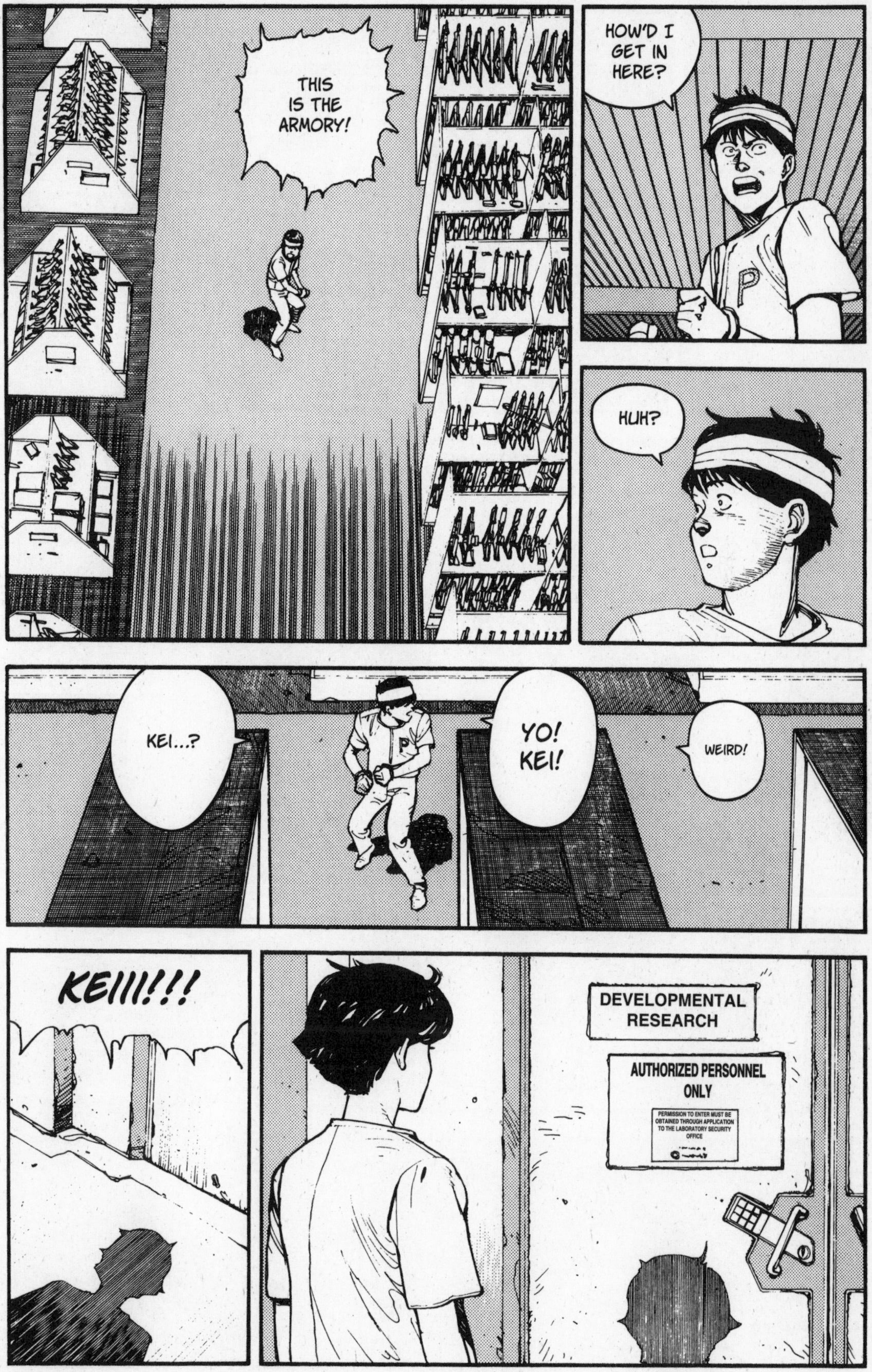
THIS IS THE ARMORY!
HOW'D I GET IN HERE?
HUH?
KEI...?
YO! KEI!
WEIRD!
KEIII!!!
DEVELOPMENTAL RESEARCH
AUTHORIZED PERSONNEL ONLY
PERMISSION TO ENTER MUST BE OBTAINED THROUGH APPLICATION TO THE LABORATORY SECURITY OFFICE

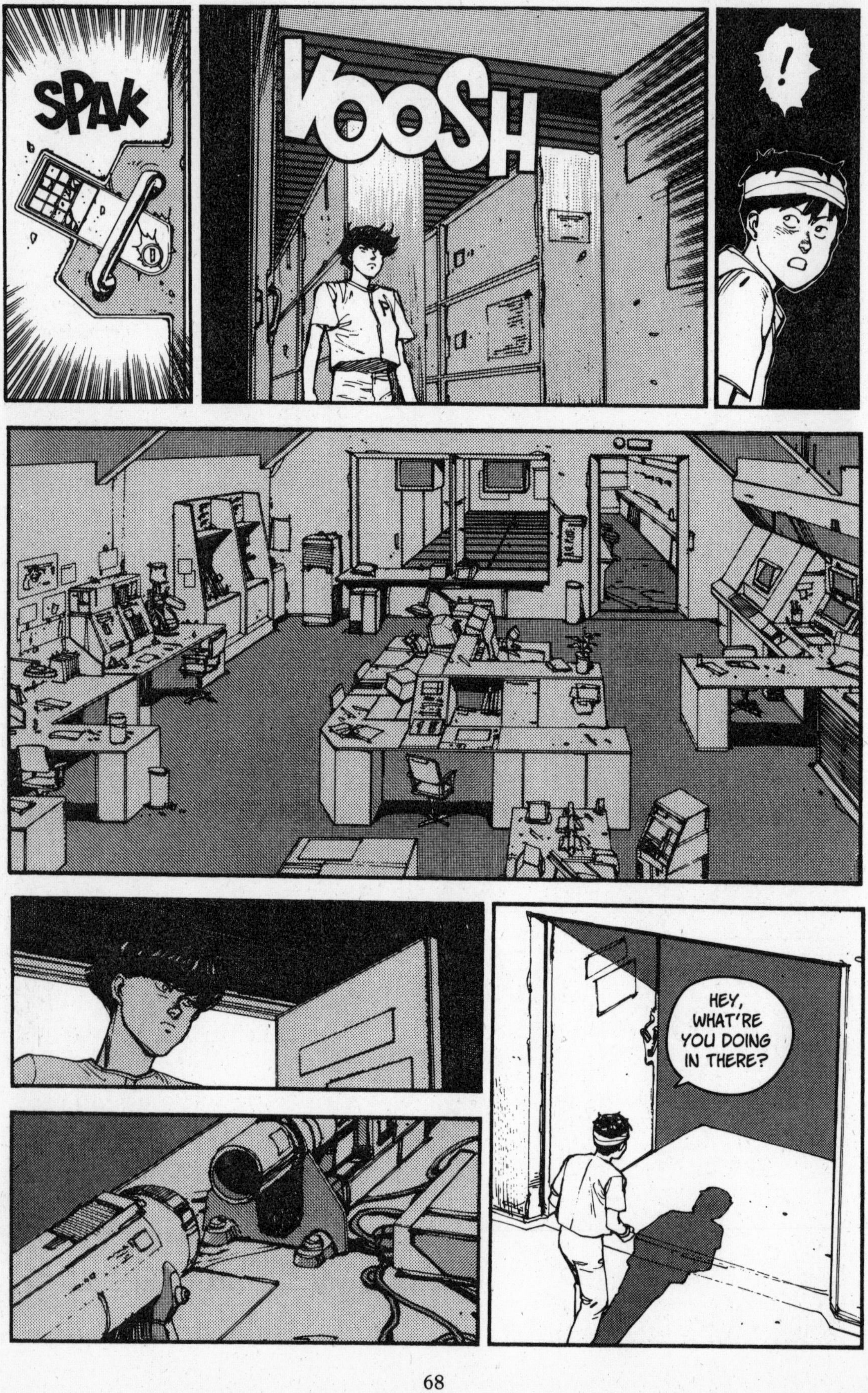
SPAK
VOOSH
!
HEY, WHAT'RE YOU DOING IN THERE?

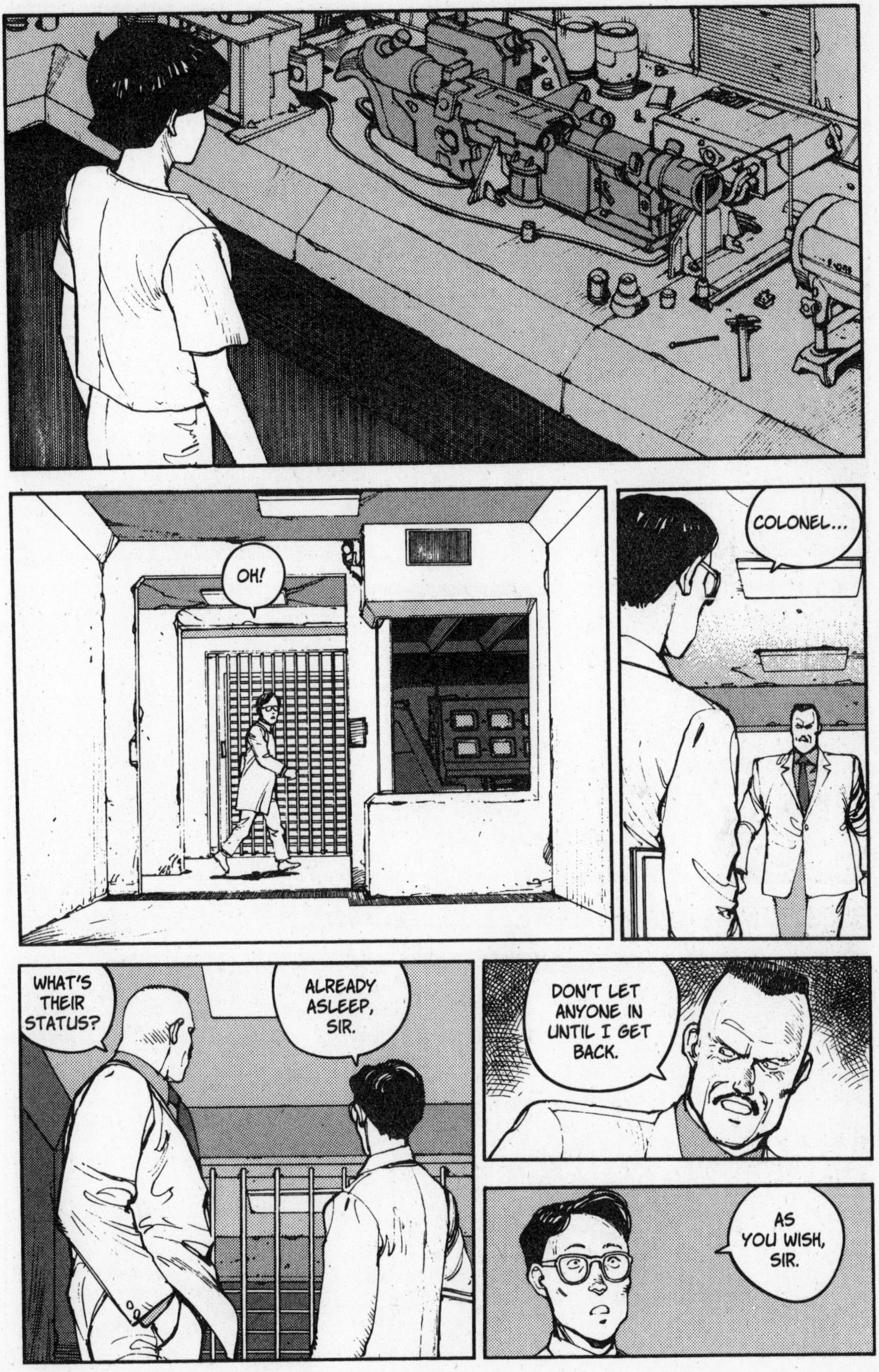
OH!
COLONEL...
WHAT'S THEIR STATUS?
ALREADY ASLEEP, SIR.
DON'T LET ANYONE IN UNTIL I GET BACK.
AS YOU WISH, SIR.

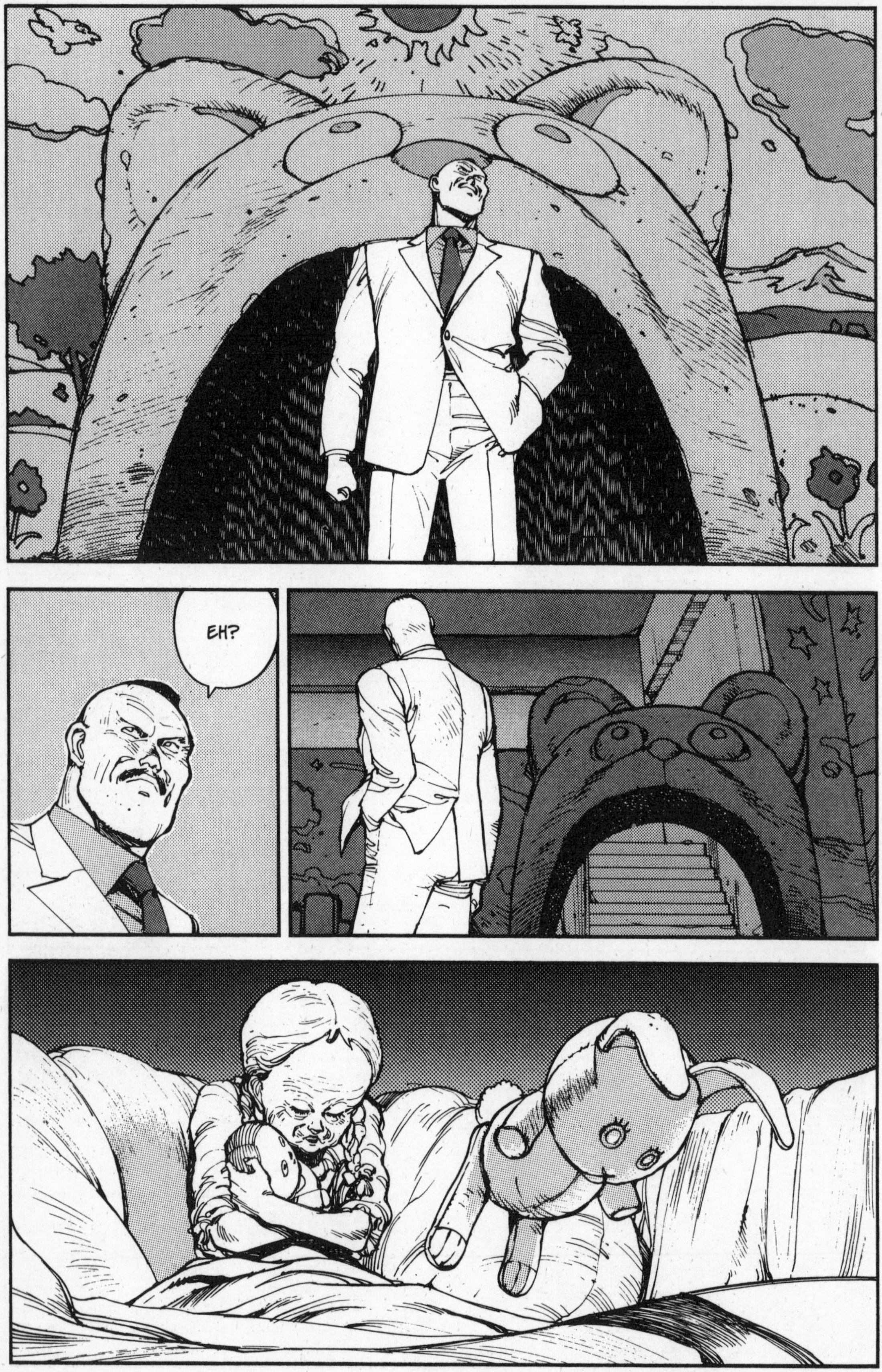
EH?

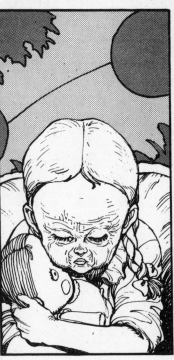

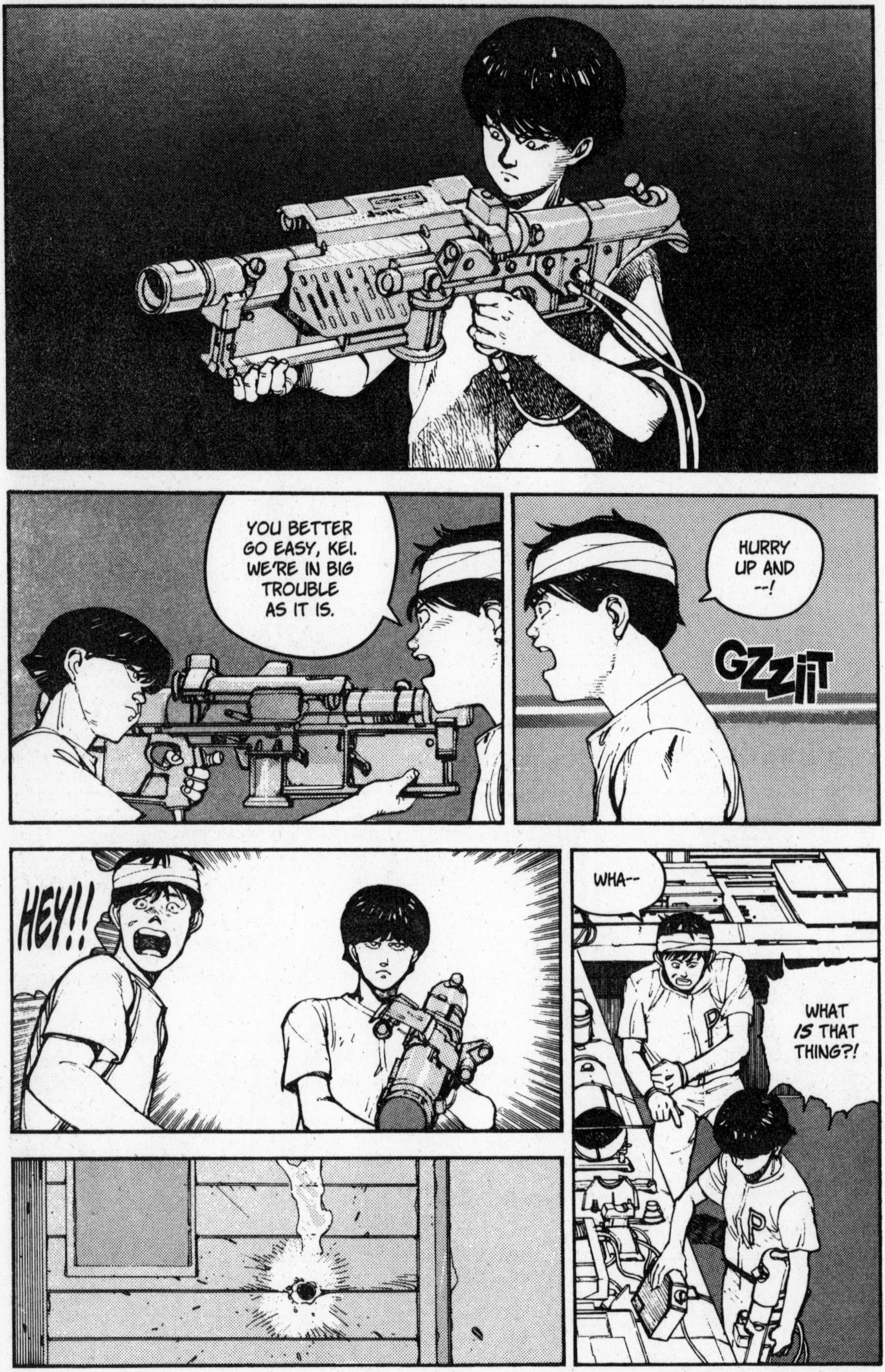

YOU BETTER GO EASY, KEI. WE'RE IN BIG TROUBLE AS IT IS.
HURRY UP AND --!
GZZIIT
HEY!!
WHA--
WHAT *IS* THAT THING?!

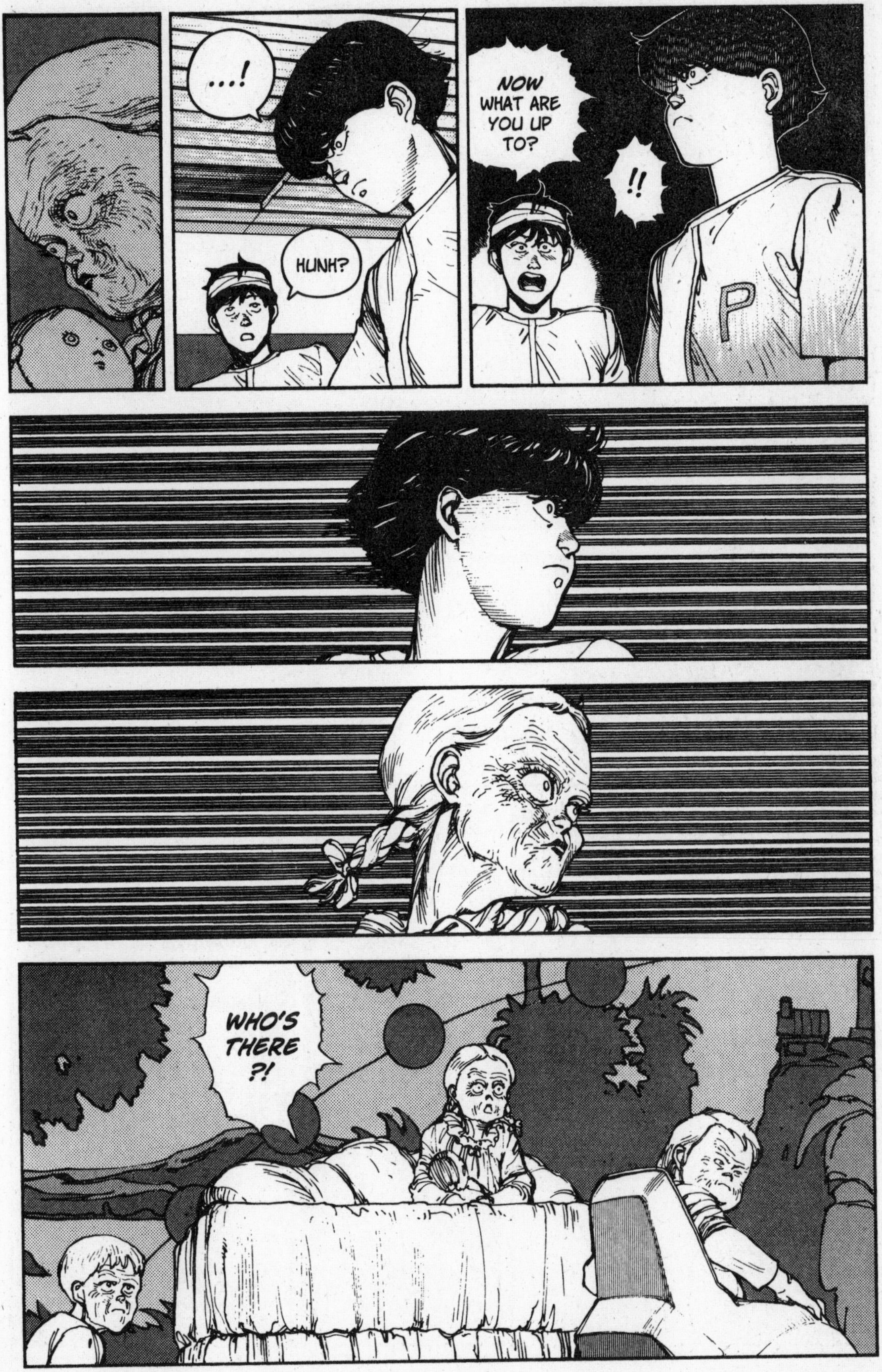
...!
HUNH?
NOW WHAT ARE YOU UP TO?
!!
WHO'S THERE ?!

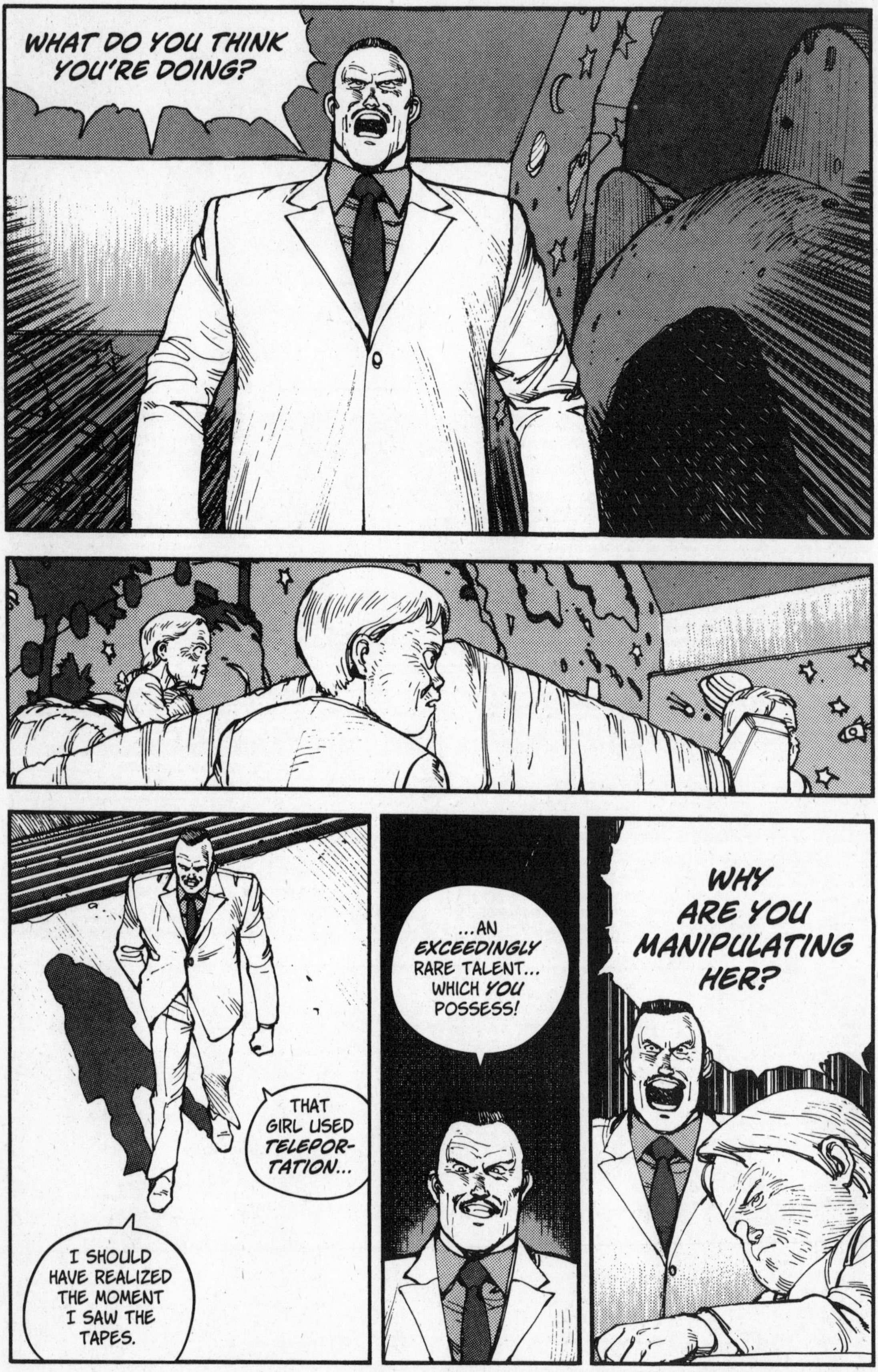
WHAT DO YOU THINK YOU'RE DOING?
THAT GIRL USED TELEPOR-TATION...
I SHOULD HAVE REALIZED THE MOMENT I SAW THE TAPES.
...AN EXCEEDINGLY RARE TALENT... WHICH YOU POSSESS!
WHY ARE YOU MANIPULATING HER?

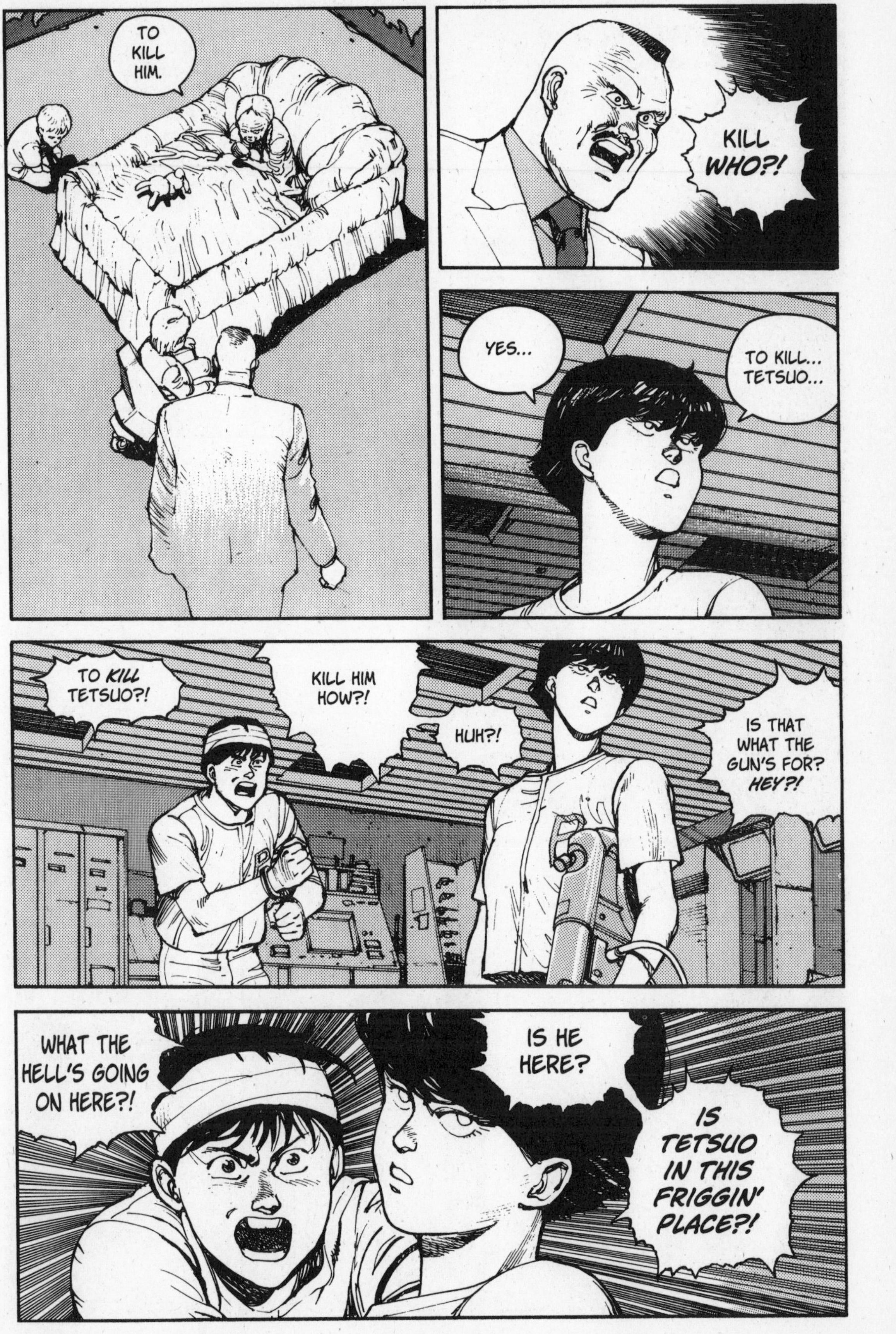
TO KILL HIM.
KILL WHO?!
YES...
TO KILL... TETSUO...
TO KILL TETSUO?!
KILL HIM HOW?!
HUH?!
IS THAT WHAT THE GUN'S FOR? HEY?!
WHAT THE HELL'S GOING ON HERE?!
IS HE HERE?
IS TETSUO IN THIS FRIGGIN' PLACE?!

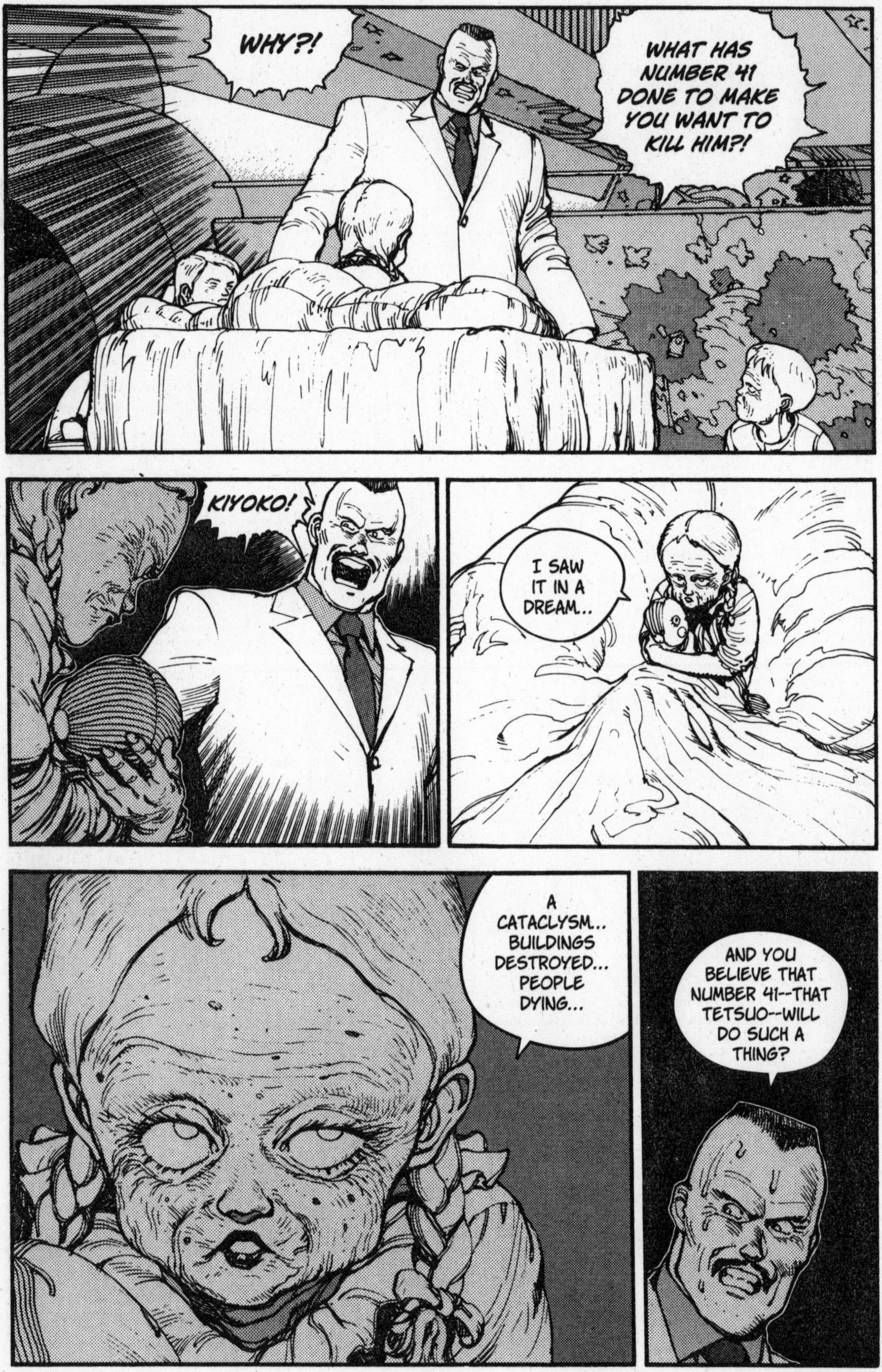
WHY?!
WHAT HAS NUMBER 41 DONE TO MAKE YOU WANT TO KILL HIM?!
KIYOKO!
I SAW IT IN A DREAM...
A CATACLYSM... BUILDINGS DESTROYED... PEOPLE DYING...
AND YOU BELIEVE THAT NUMBER 41--THAT TETSUO--WILL DO SUCH A THING?

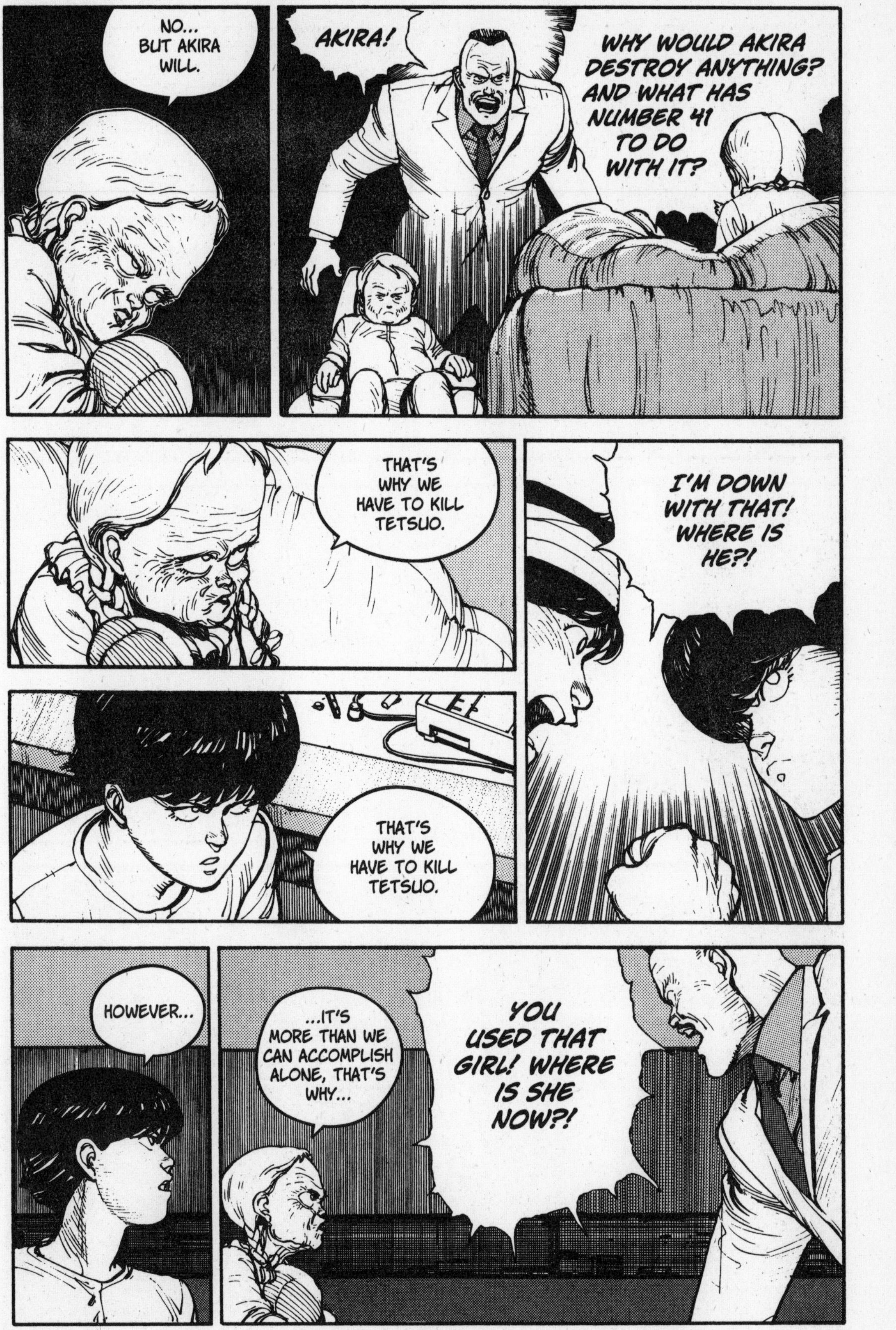

NO... BUT AKIRA WILL.
AKIRA!
WHY WOULD AKIRA DESTROY ANYTHING? AND WHAT HAS NUMBER 41 TO DO WITH IT?
THAT'S WHY WE HAVE TO KILL TETSUO.
THAT'S WHY WE HAVE TO KILL TETSUO.
I'M DOWN WITH THAT! WHERE IS HE?!
HOWEVER...
...IT'S MORE THAN WE CAN ACCOMPLISH ALONE, THAT'S WHY...
YOU USED THAT GIRL! WHERE IS SHE NOW?!

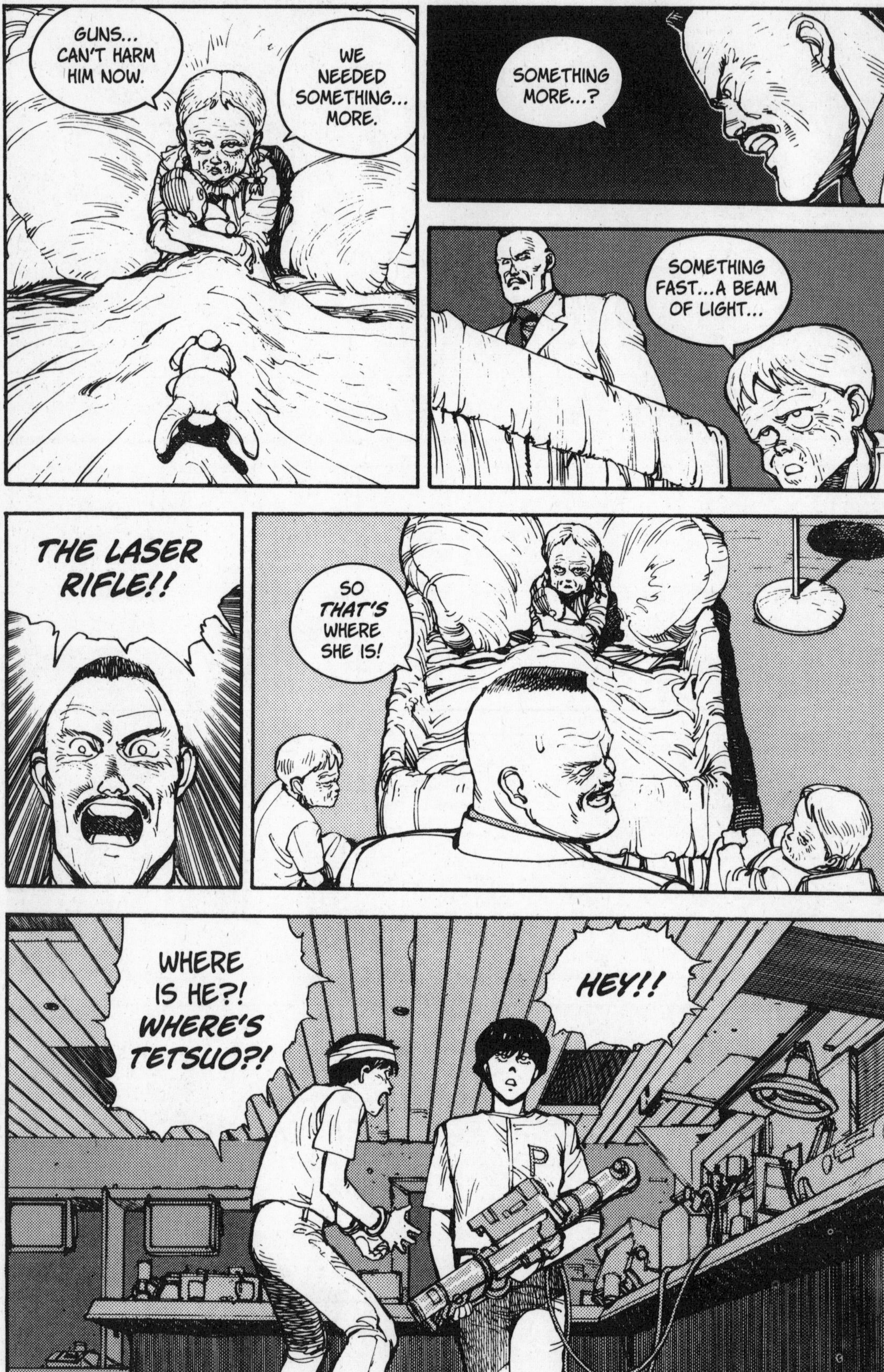
GUNS... CAN'T HARM HIM NOW.
WE NEEDED SOMETHING... MORE.
SOMETHING MORE...?
SOMETHING FAST...A BEAM OF LIGHT...
THE LASER RIFLE!!
SO *THAT'S* WHERE SHE IS!
WHERE IS HE?! *WHERE'S TETSUO?!*
*HEY!!*

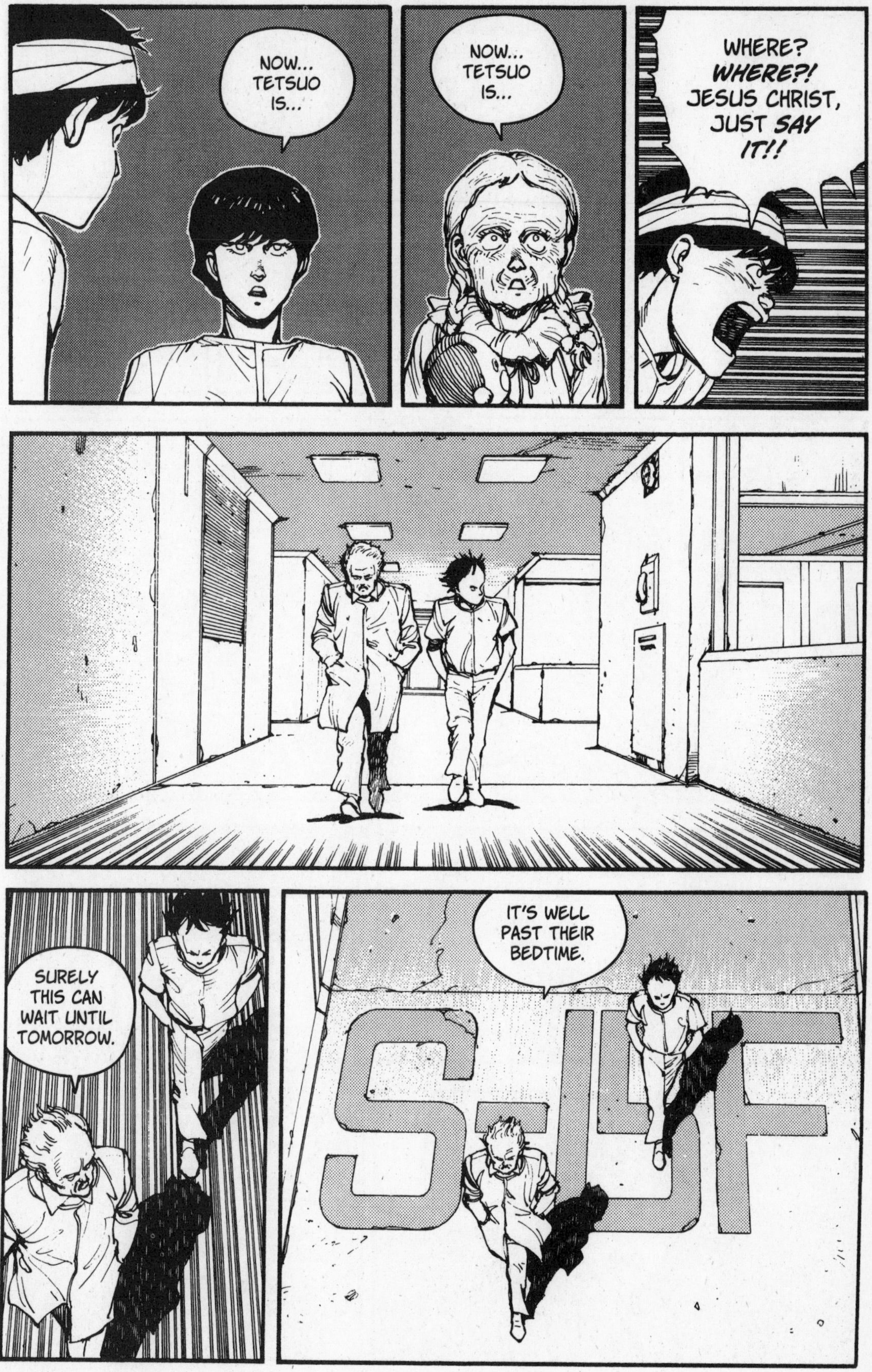
NOW... TETSUO IS...
NOW... TETSUO IS...
WHERE? *WHERE?!* JESUS CHRIST, JUST *SAY IT!!*
SURELY THIS CAN WAIT UNTIL TOMORROW.
IT'S WELL PAST THEIR BEDTIME.

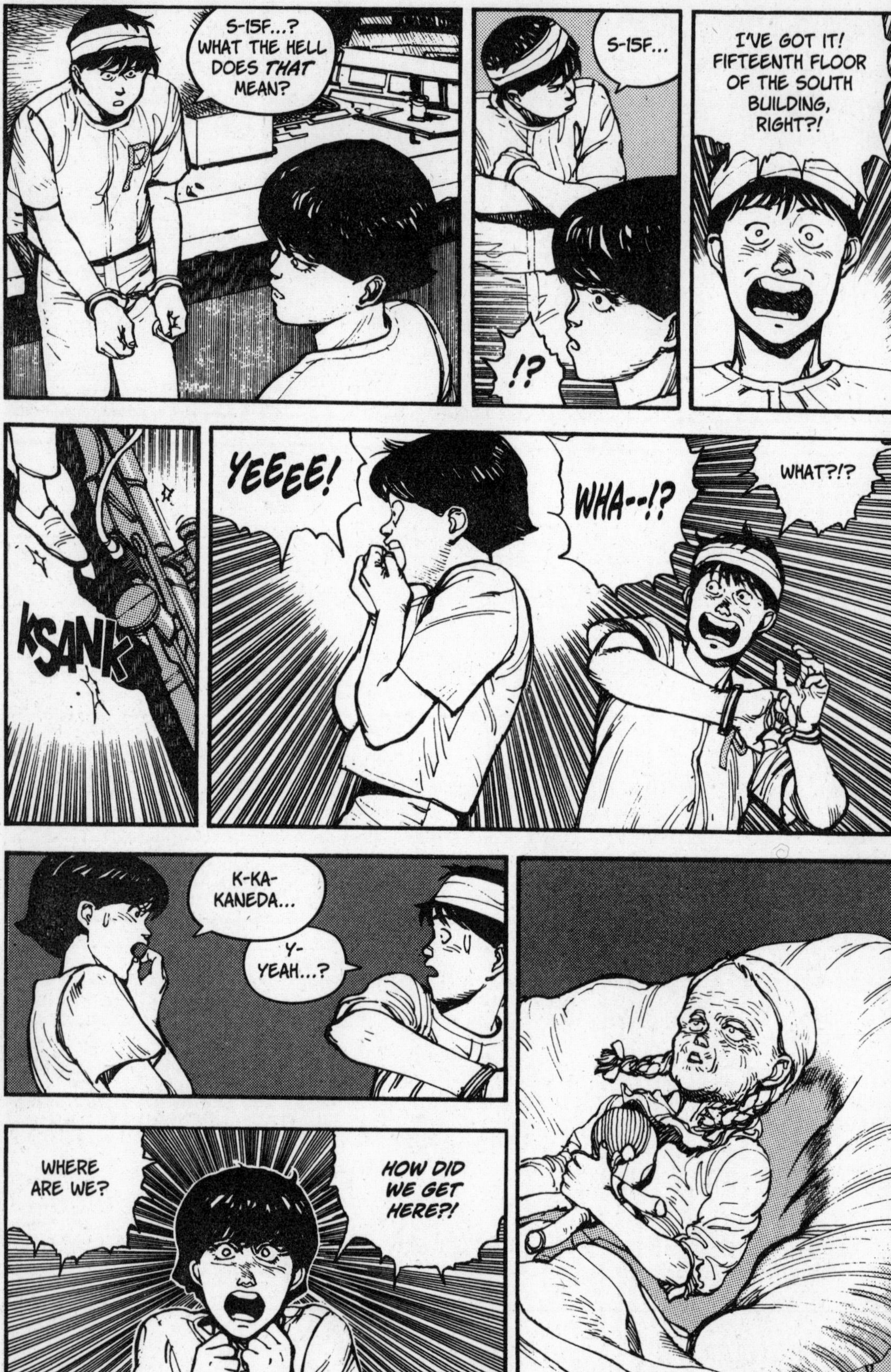
S-15F...? WHAT THE HELL DOES THAT MEAN?
S-15F...
!?
I'VE GOT IT! FIFTEENTH FLOOR OF THE SOUTH BUILDING, RIGHT?!
KSANK
YEEEEE!
WHA--!?
WHAT?!?
K-KA-KANEDA...
Y-YEAH...?
WHERE ARE WE?
HOW DID WE GET HERE?!

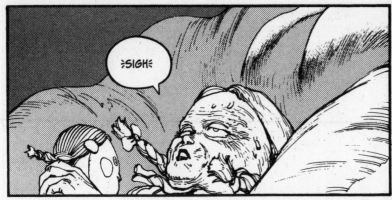

≈SIGH≈

THE GIRL IS FREE AGAIN.

WHAT?!

FREE...?! YOU MEAN UNDER HER *OWN* CONTROL?!

UH-HUNH.

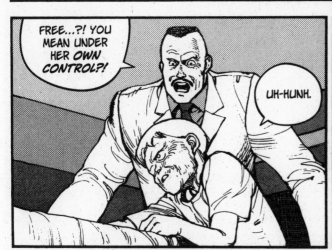

ARE YOU ALL RIGHT?

≈HUFF≈ ≈HFF≈

≈HUFF≈

ALL RIGHT!

KIYOKO, I'LL EXPECT A FULL EXPLANATION WHEN I RETURN!

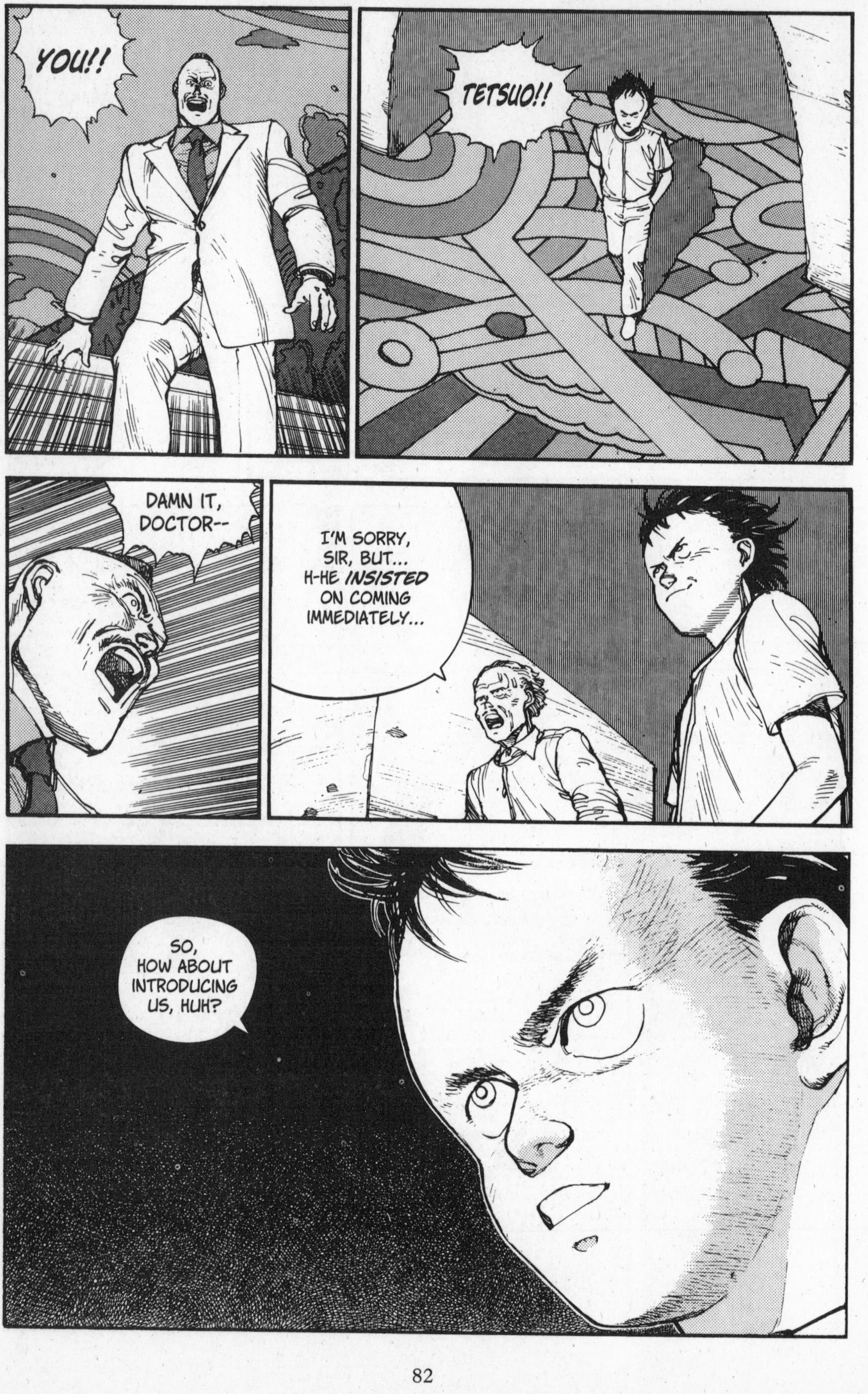
YOU!!
TETSUO!!
DAMN IT, DOCTOR--
I'M SORRY, SIR, BUT... H-HE INSISTED ON COMING IMMEDIATELY...
SO, HOW ABOUT INTRODUCING US, HUH?

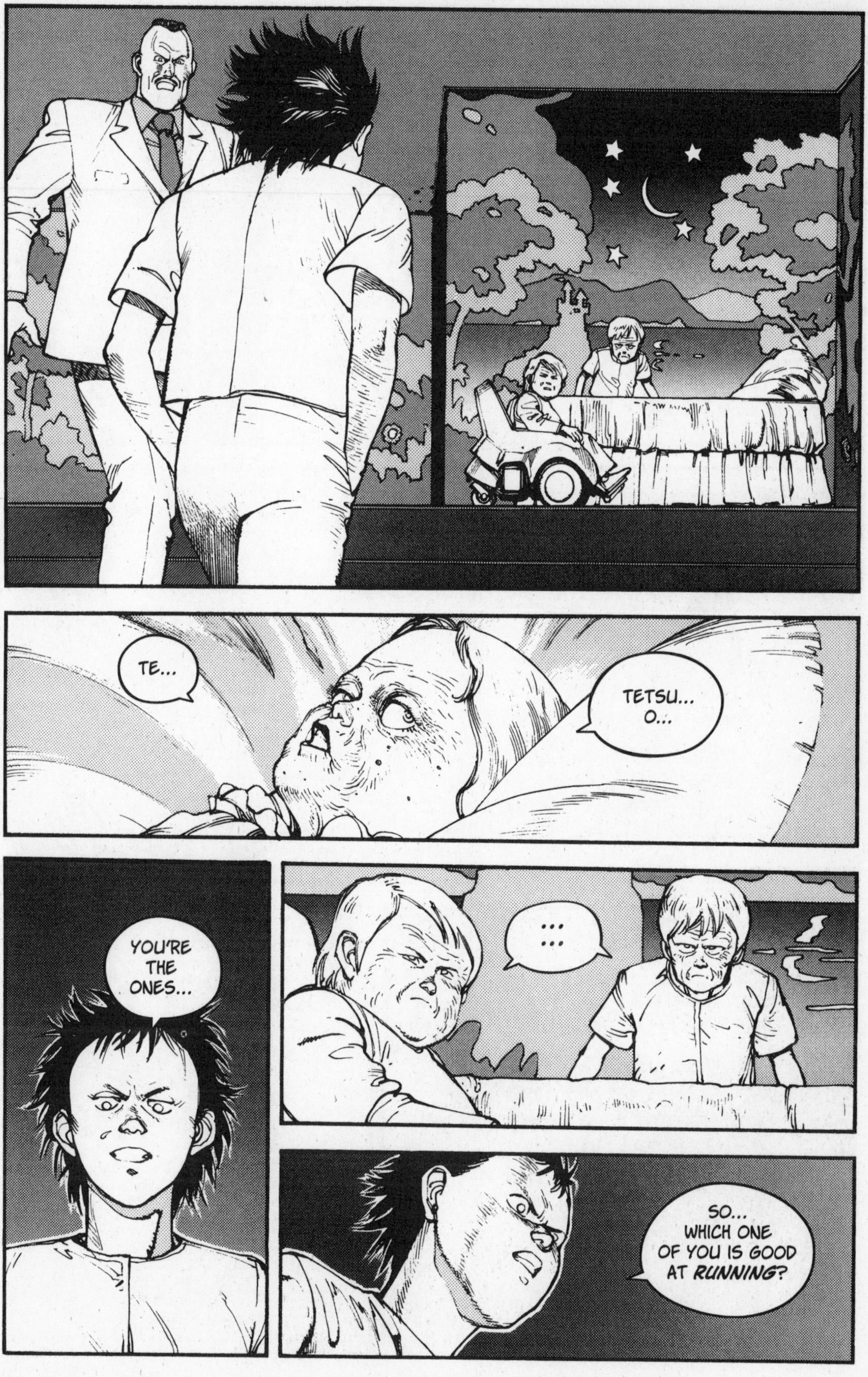
TE...
TETSU... O...
YOU'RE THE ONES...
... ...
SO... WHICH ONE OF YOU IS GOOD AT *RUNNING*?

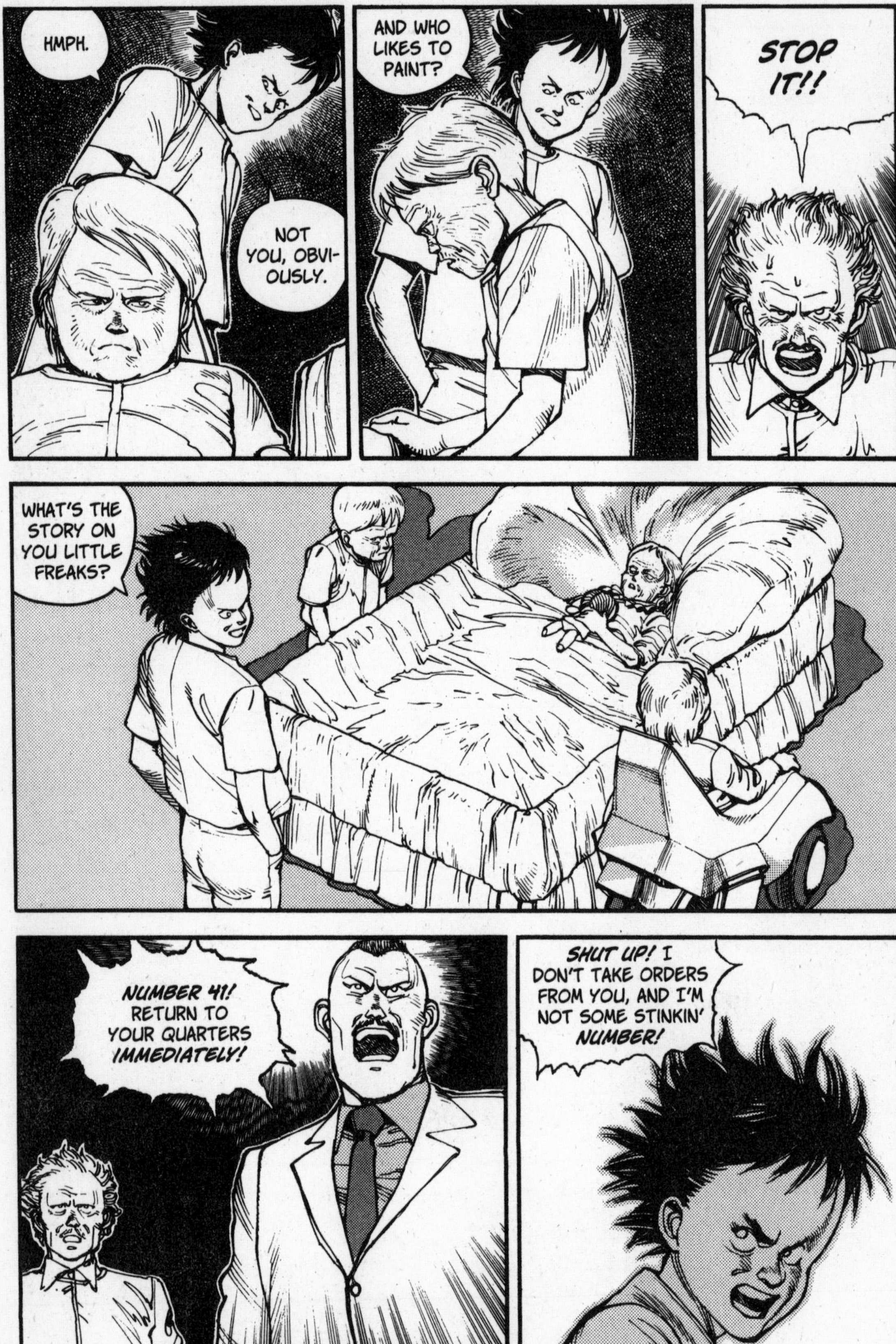
HMPH.
NOT YOU, OBVIOUSLY.
AND WHO LIKES TO PAINT?
STOP IT!!
WHAT'S THE STORY ON YOU LITTLE FREAKS?
NUMBER 41! RETURN TO YOUR QUARTERS IMMEDIATELY!
SHUT UP! I DON'T TAKE ORDERS FROM YOU, AND I'M NOT SOME STINKIN' NUMBER!

AAH...
BE CAREFUL
WITH THAT,
HUNH?

ZGWiiU

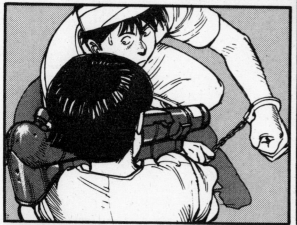

RIGHT...

WHOA! THIS
THING'S
AMAZING.

NO
SHIT.

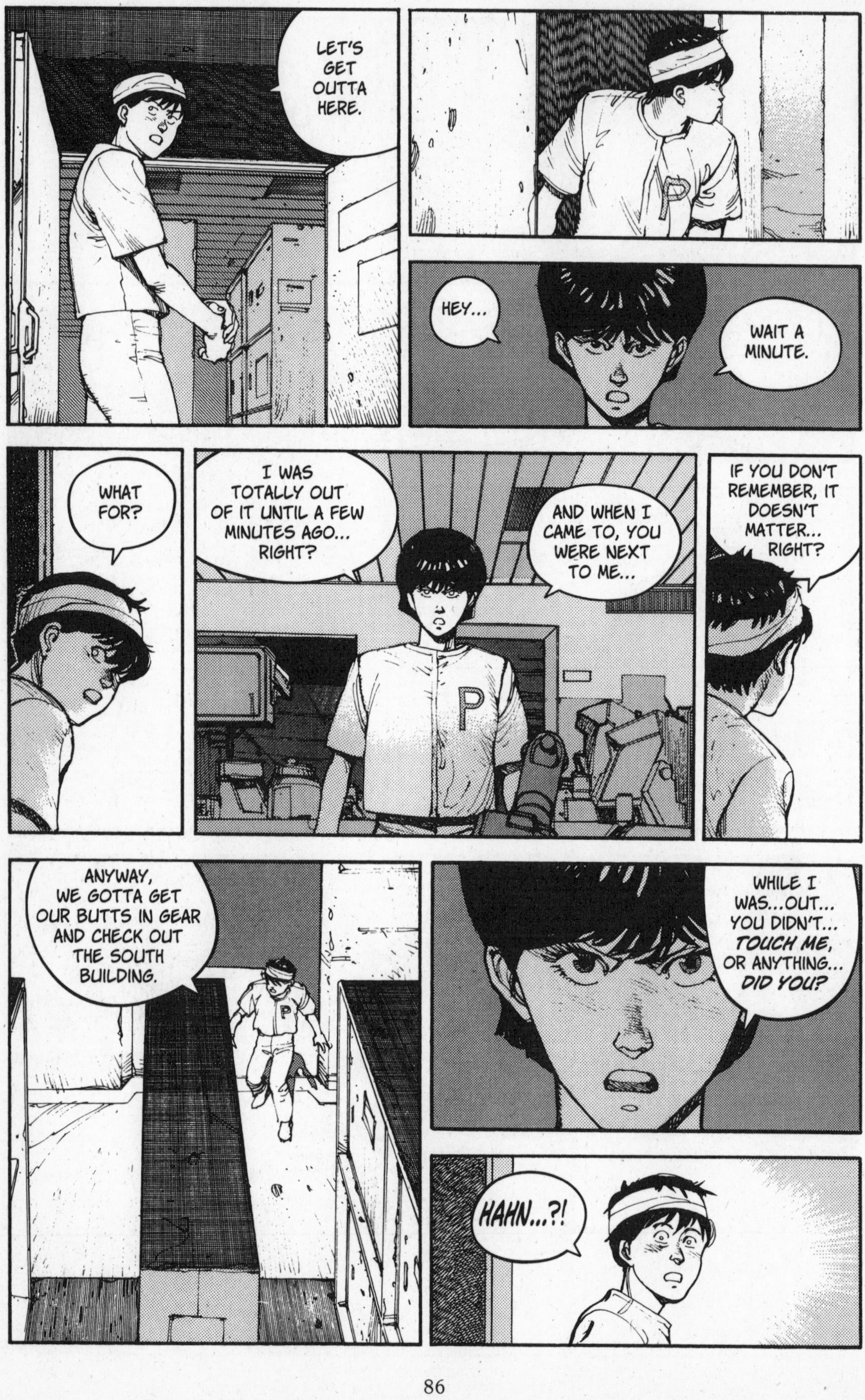
LET'S GET OUTTA HERE.
HEY...
WAIT A MINUTE.
WHAT FOR?
I WAS TOTALLY OUT OF IT UNTIL A FEW MINUTES AGO... RIGHT?
AND WHEN I CAME TO, YOU WERE NEXT TO ME...
IF YOU DON'T REMEMBER, IT DOESN'T MATTER... RIGHT?
ANYWAY, WE GOTTA GET OUR BUTTS IN GEAR AND CHECK OUT THE SOUTH BUILDING.
WHILE I WAS...OUT... YOU DIDN'T... *TOUCH ME*, OR ANYTHING... *DID YOU?*
HAHN...?!

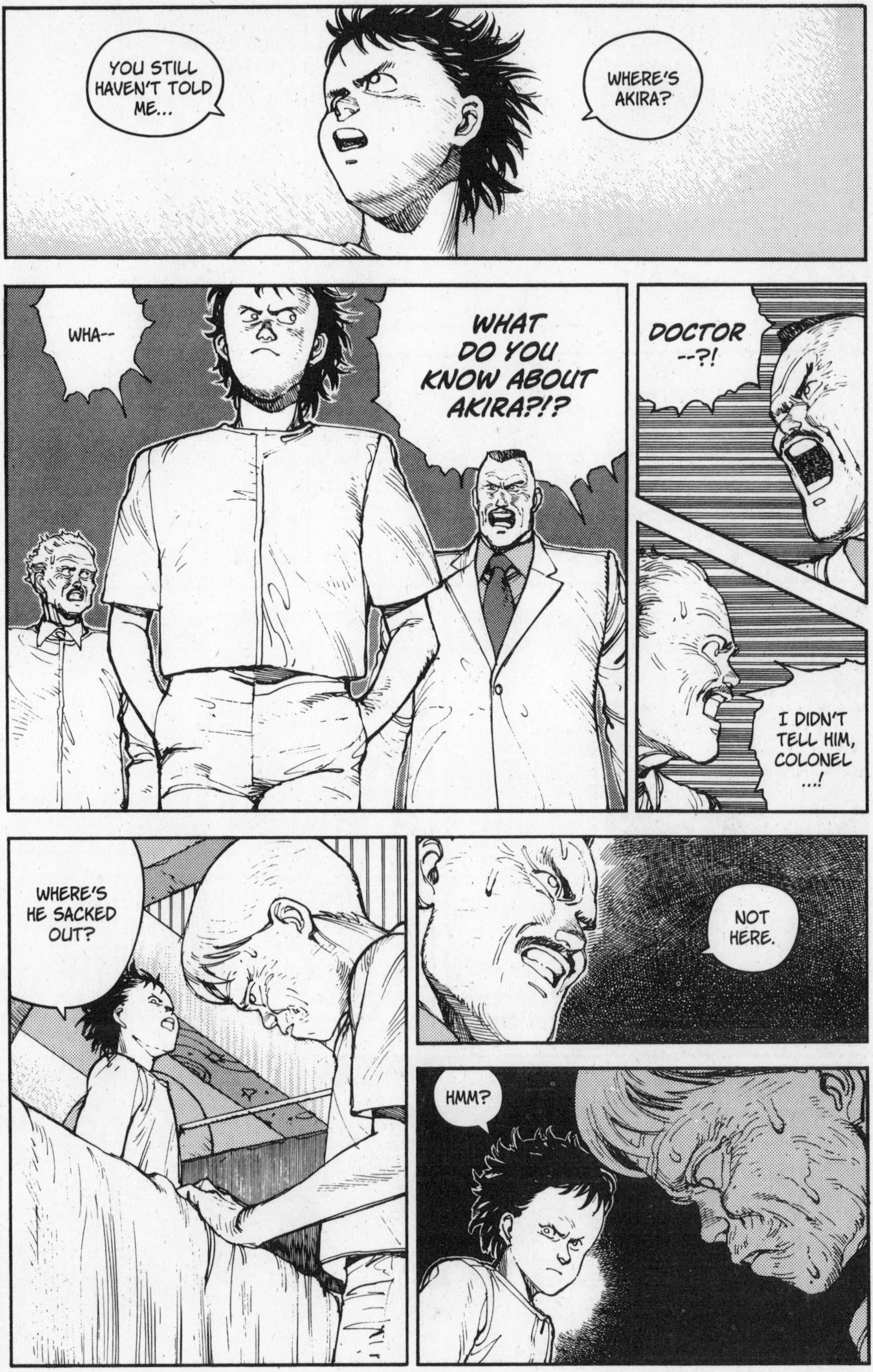
YOU STILL HAVEN'T TOLD ME...
WHERE'S AKIRA?
WHA--
WHAT DO YOU KNOW ABOUT AKIRA?!?
DOCTOR --?!
I DIDN'T TELL HIM, COLONEL ...!
WHERE'S HE SACKED OUT?
NOT HERE.
HMM?

IN ANY CASE, IT'S TIME FOR YOU TO LEAVE... TETSUO.

YES, SIR! I'M VERY SORRY, SIR!

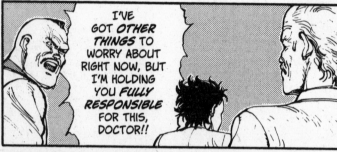

I'VE GOT *OTHER THINGS* TO WORRY ABOUT RIGHT NOW, BUT I'M HOLDING YOU *FULLY RESPONSIBLE* FOR THIS, DOCTOR!!

VVRROOM

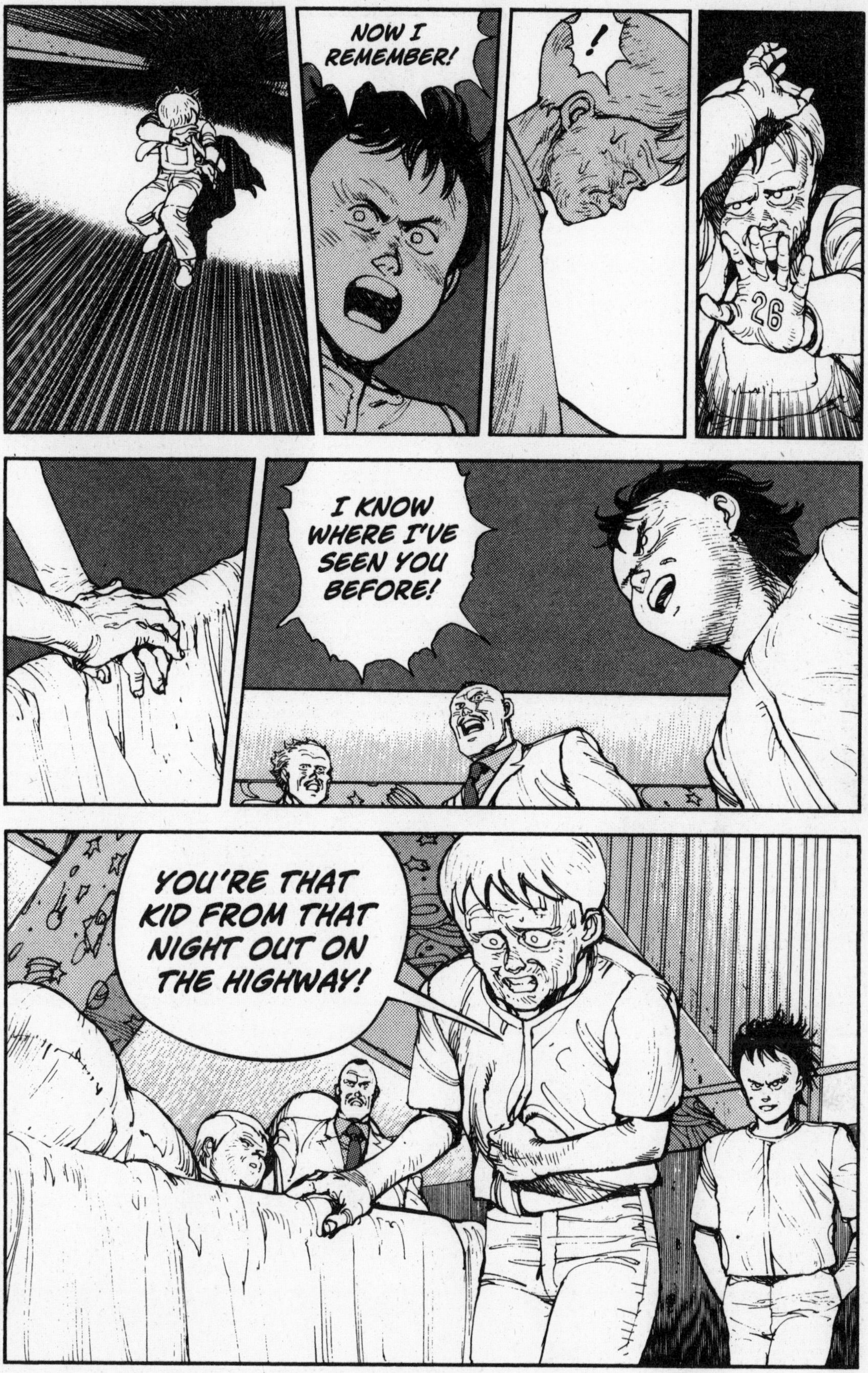
NOW I REMEMBER!
!
I KNOW WHERE I'VE SEEN YOU BEFORE!
YOU'RE THAT KID FROM THAT NIGHT OUT ON THE HIGHWAY!
26

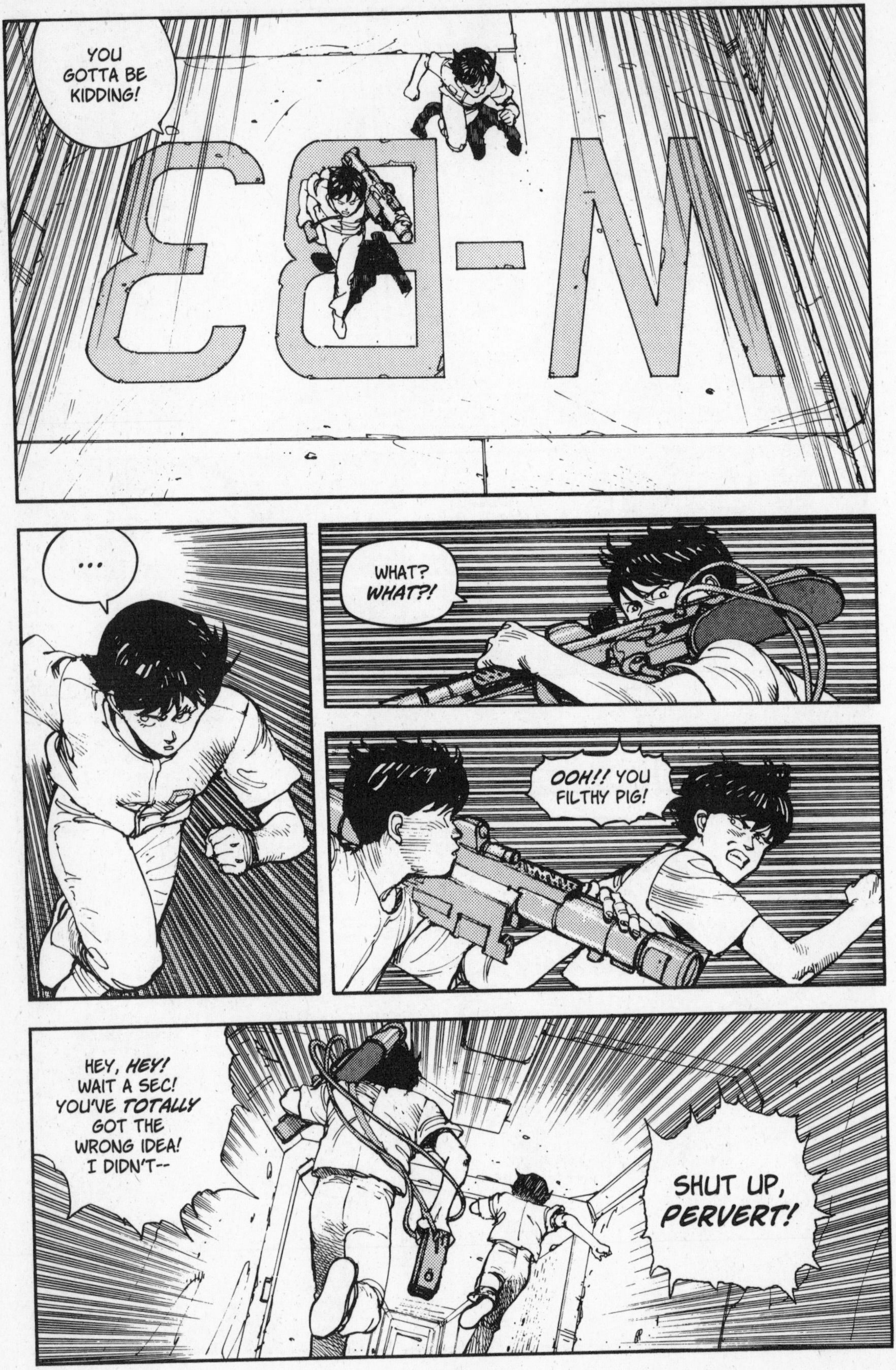

YOU GOTTA BE KIDDING!
...
WHAT? *WHAT?!*
*OOH!!* YOU FILTHY PIG!
HEY, *HEY!* WAIT A SEC! YOU'VE *TOTALLY* GOT THE WRONG IDEA! I DIDN'T--
SHUT UP, *PERVERT!*

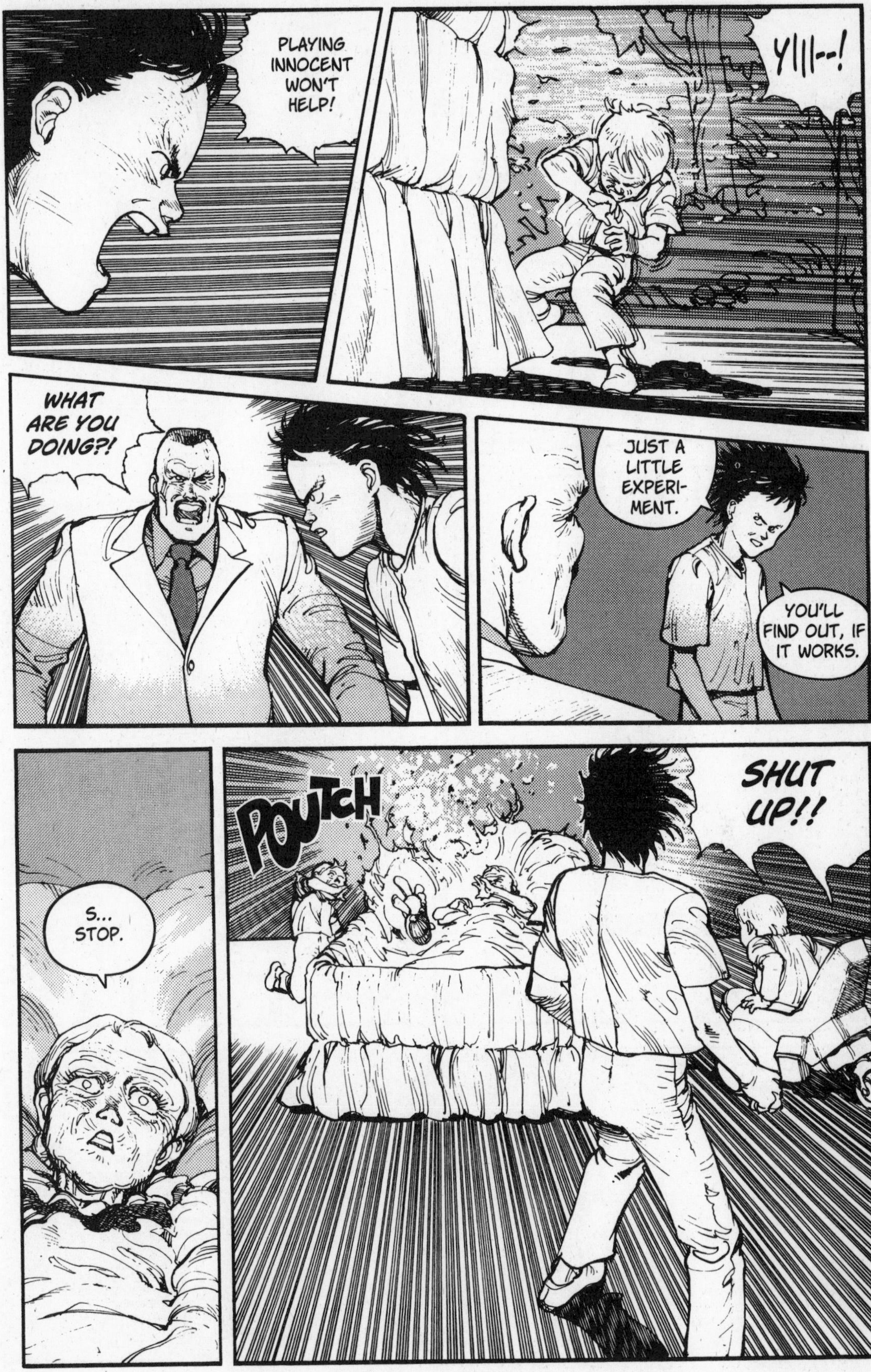

PLAYING INNOCENT WON'T HELP!
YIII--!
WHAT ARE YOU DOING?!
JUST A LITTLE EXPERI-MENT.
YOU'LL FIND OUT, IF IT WORKS.
S... STOP.
POUTCH
SHUT UP!!

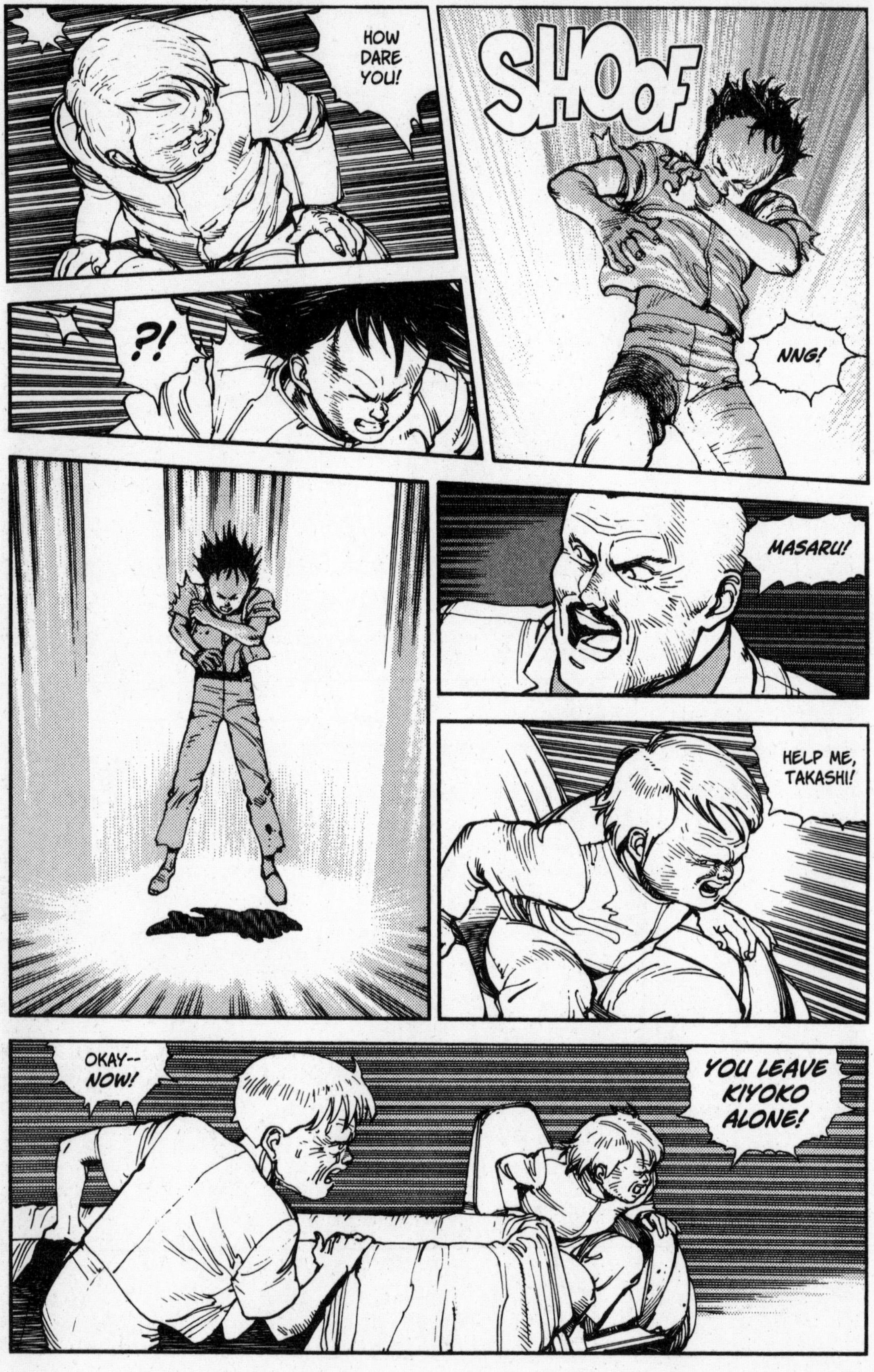
HOW DARE YOU!
?!
SHOOF
NNG!
MASARU!
HELP ME, TAKASHI!
OKAY-- NOW!
YOU LEAVE KIYOKO ALONE!

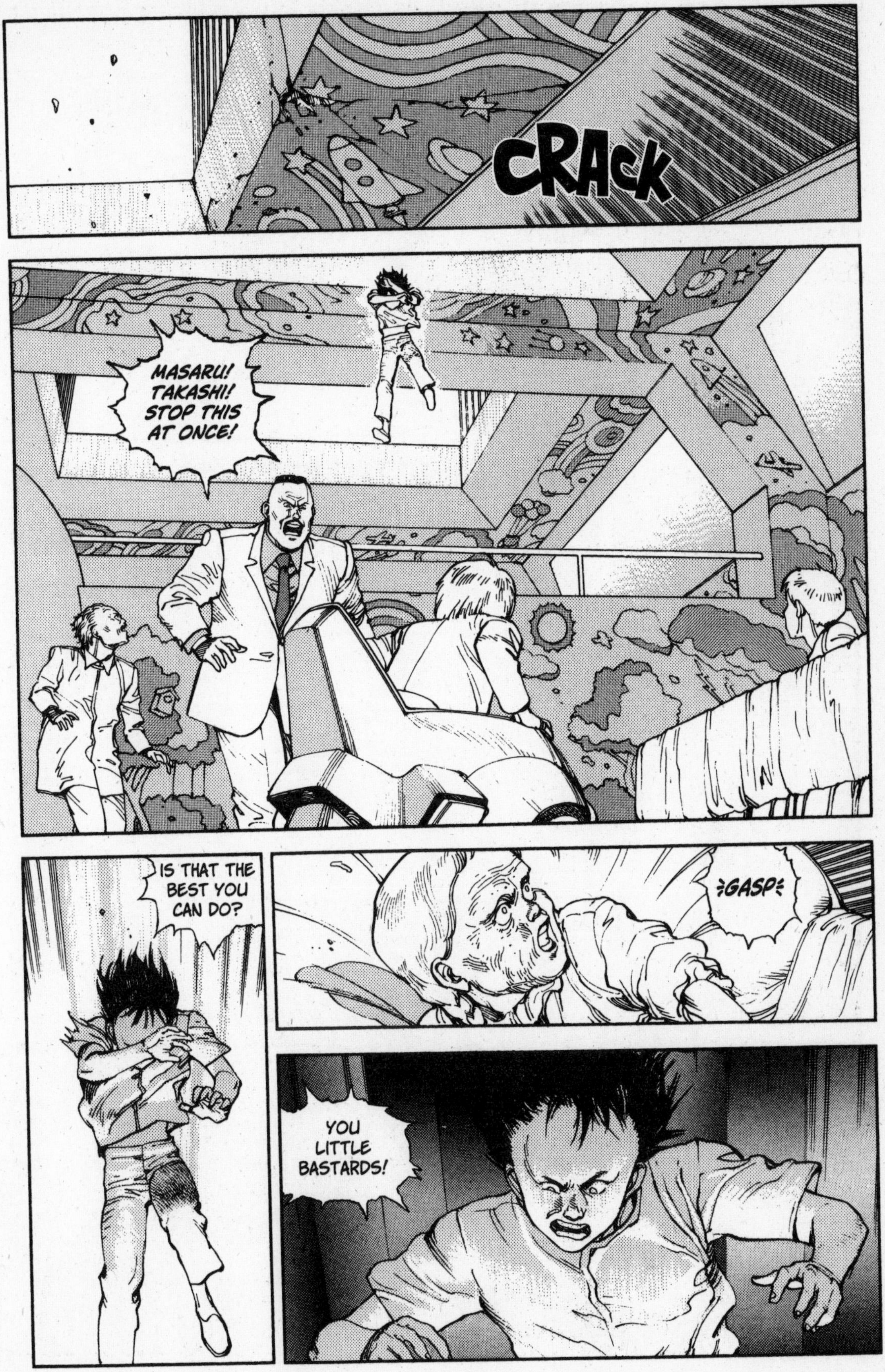
CRACK
MASARU! TAKASHI! STOP THIS AT ONCE!
IS THAT THE BEST YOU CAN DO?
GASP
YOU LITTLE BASTARDS!

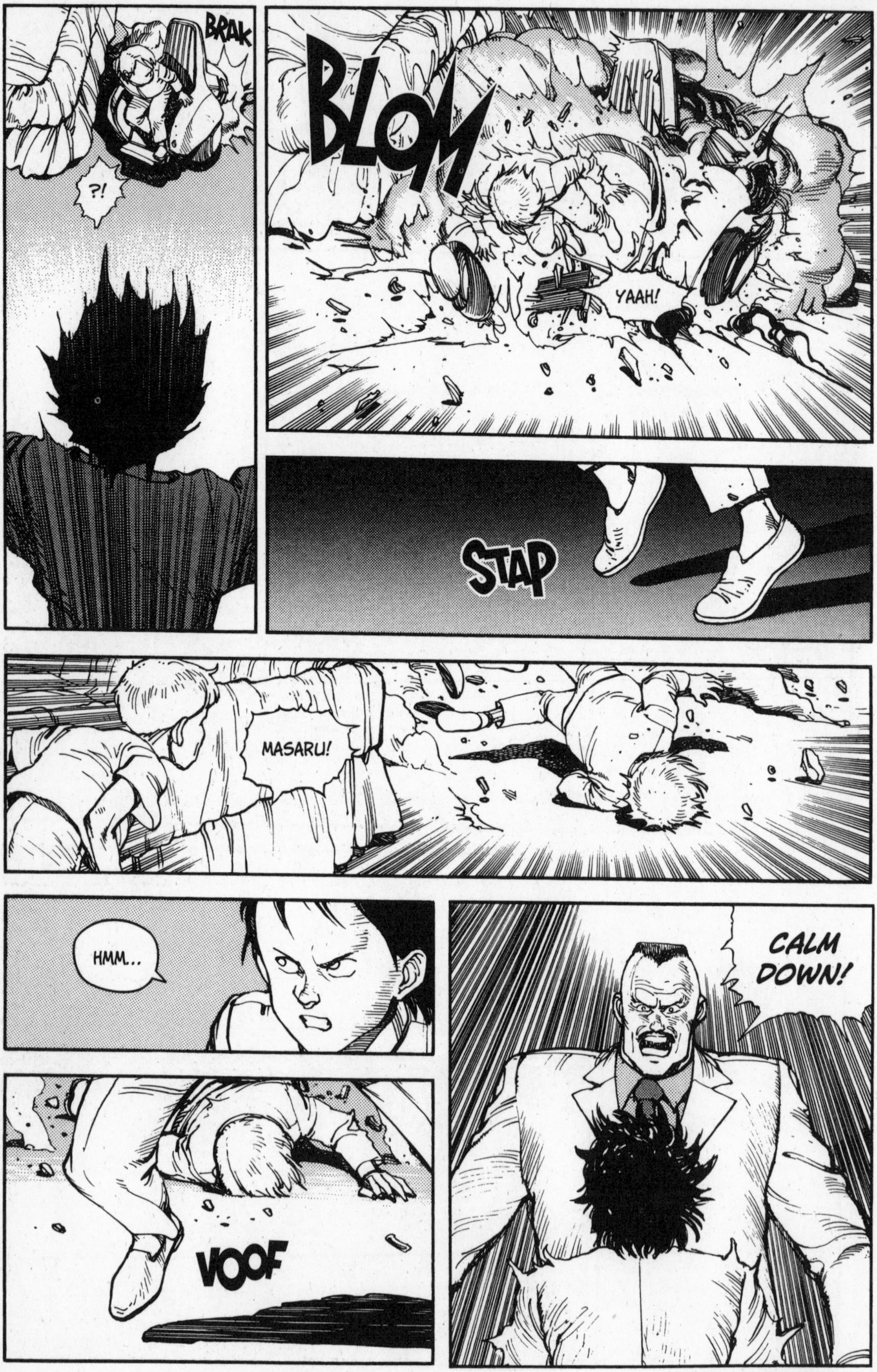

BRAK
?!
BLOM
YAAH!
STAP
MASARU!
HMM...
VOOF
CALM DOWN!

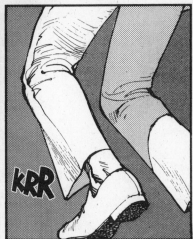

KRR

YOU GOT SOME SERIOUS *ATTITUDE...* OLD MAN.

HNNG... RRGH!

BIG GUY LIKE YOU...

ALWAYS PUSHING PEOPLE AROUND...

PLAK

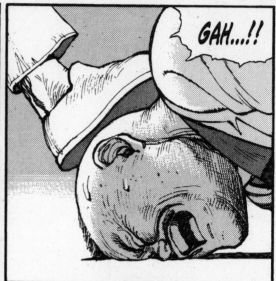

GAH...!!

THE GIRL...

SUMMON THE GIRL!

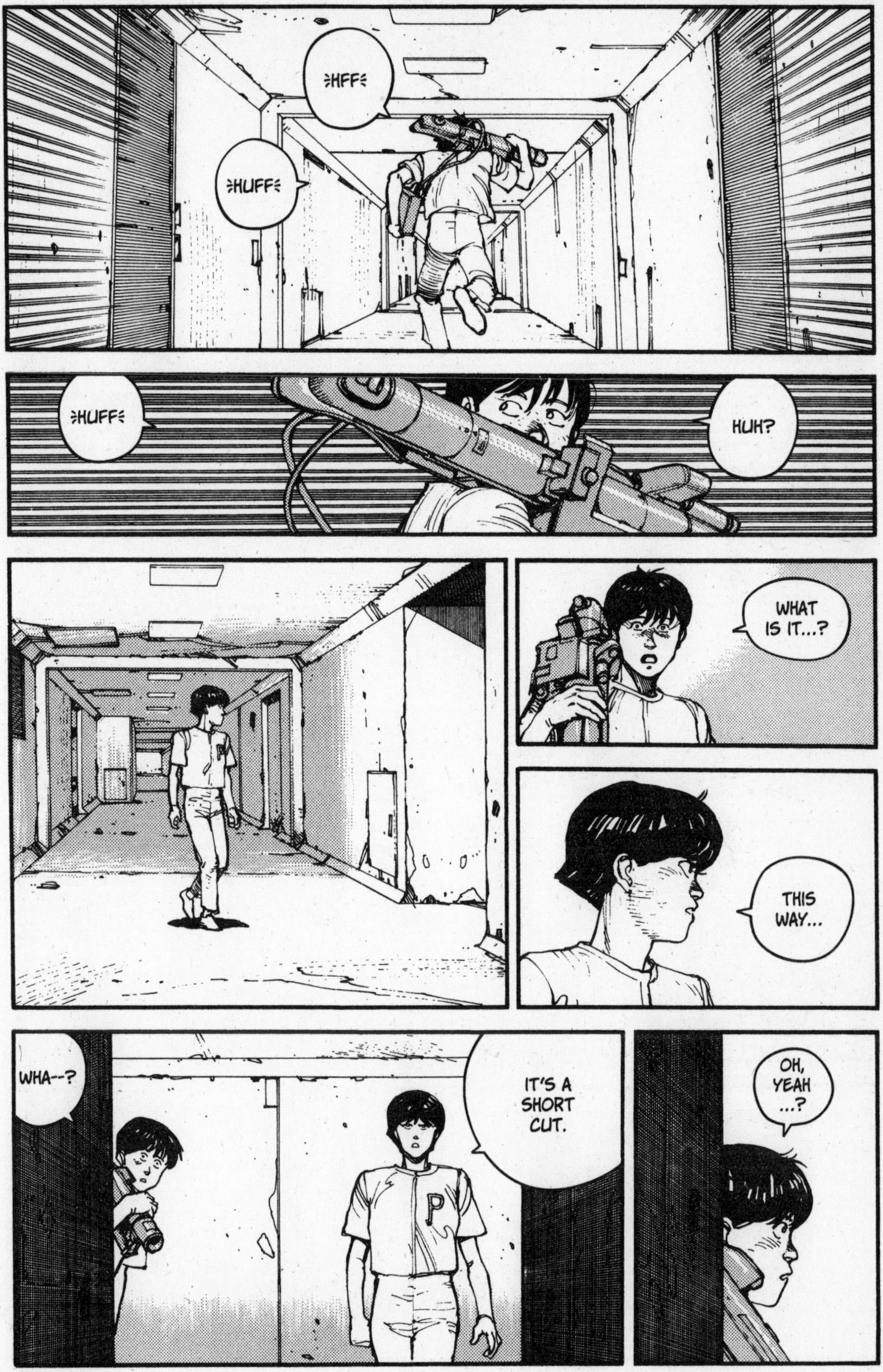
HFF
HUFF
HUFF
HUH?
WHAT IS IT...?
THIS WAY...
WHA--?
IT'S A SHORT CUT.
OH, YEAH ...?

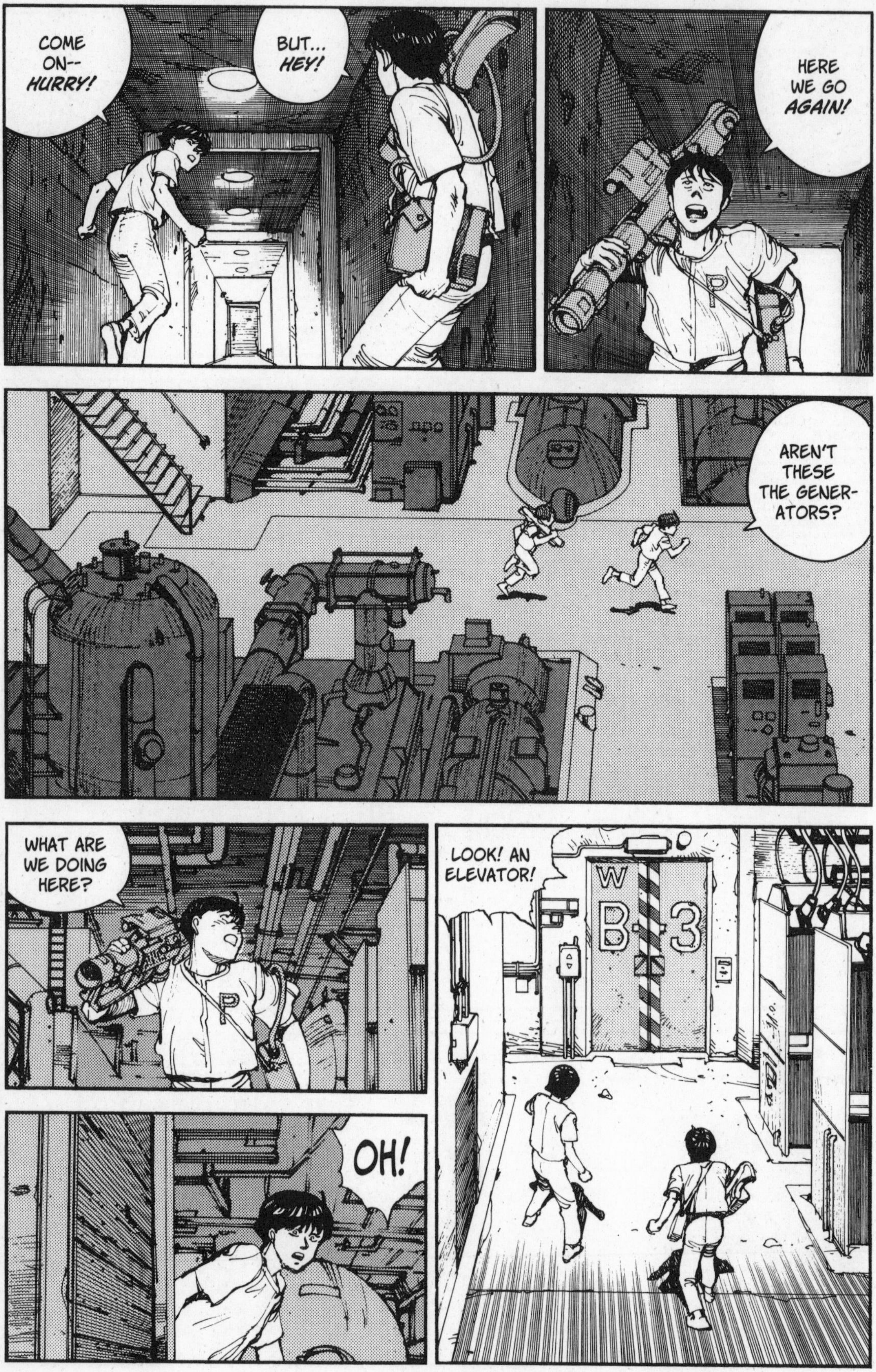
COME ON-- HURRY!
BUT... HEY!
HERE WE GO AGAIN!
AREN'T THESE THE GENERATORS?
WHAT ARE WE DOING HERE?
OH!
LOOK! AN ELEVATOR!
W
B-3

POUM

AAH...
EEH...

WHAT?
IS THAT THE
BEST YOU
GOT?!

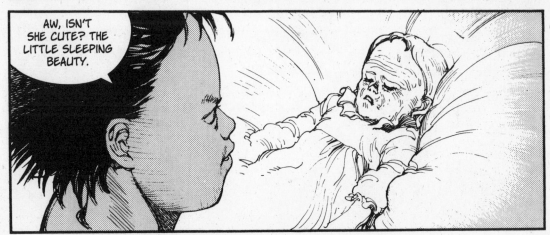

AW, ISN'T
SHE CUTE? THE
LITTLE SLEEPING
BEAUTY.

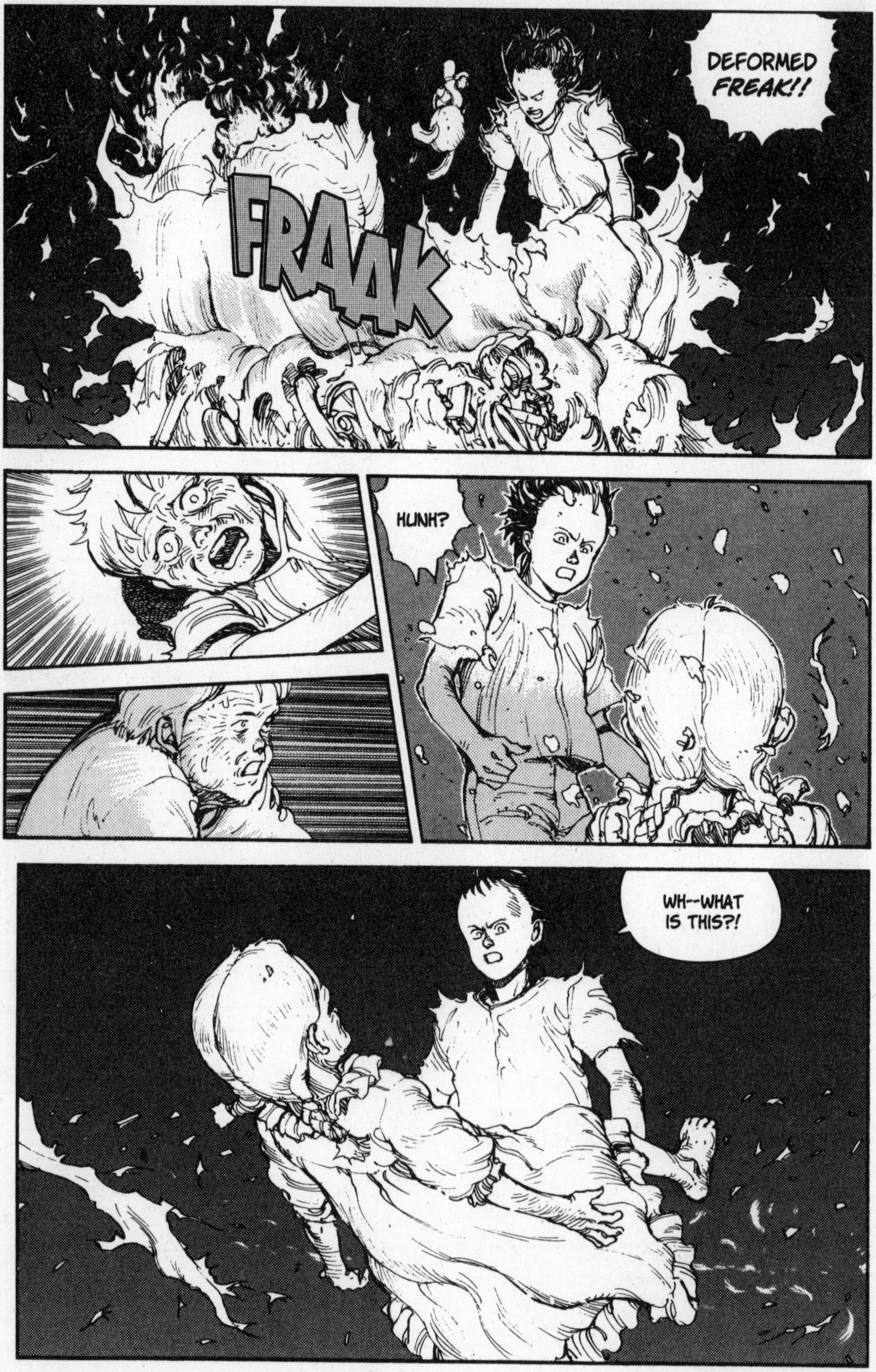
FRAAK
DEFORMED FREAK!!
HUNH?
WH--WHAT IS THIS?!

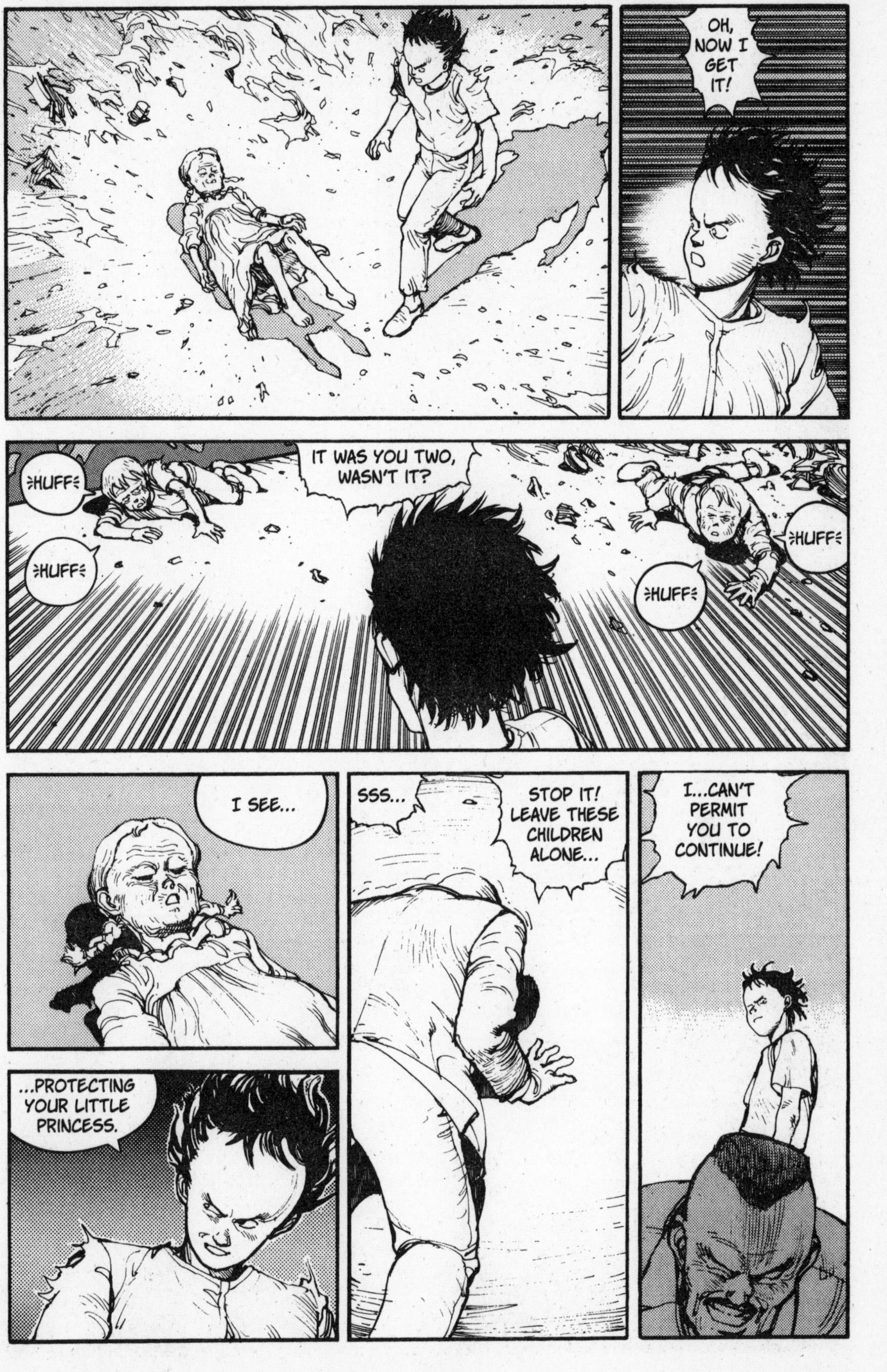
OH, NOW I GET IT!
IT WAS YOU TWO, WASN'T IT?
HUFF
HUFF
HUFF
HUFF
I SEE...
...PROTECTING YOUR LITTLE PRINCESS.
SSS...
STOP IT! LEAVE THESE CHILDREN ALONE...
I...CAN'T PERMIT YOU TO CONTINUE!

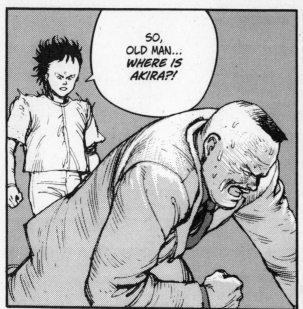

SO, OLD MAN... WHERE IS AKIRA?!

STOP! I'LL TELL YOU!

NO! DON'T!

BUT WHY NOT GIVE IT A TRY?!

DO YOU REALIZE WHAT YOU'RE SAYING?

HEAR ME OUT, COLONEL!

LET NUMBER 41 TRY TO CONTROL AKIRA!

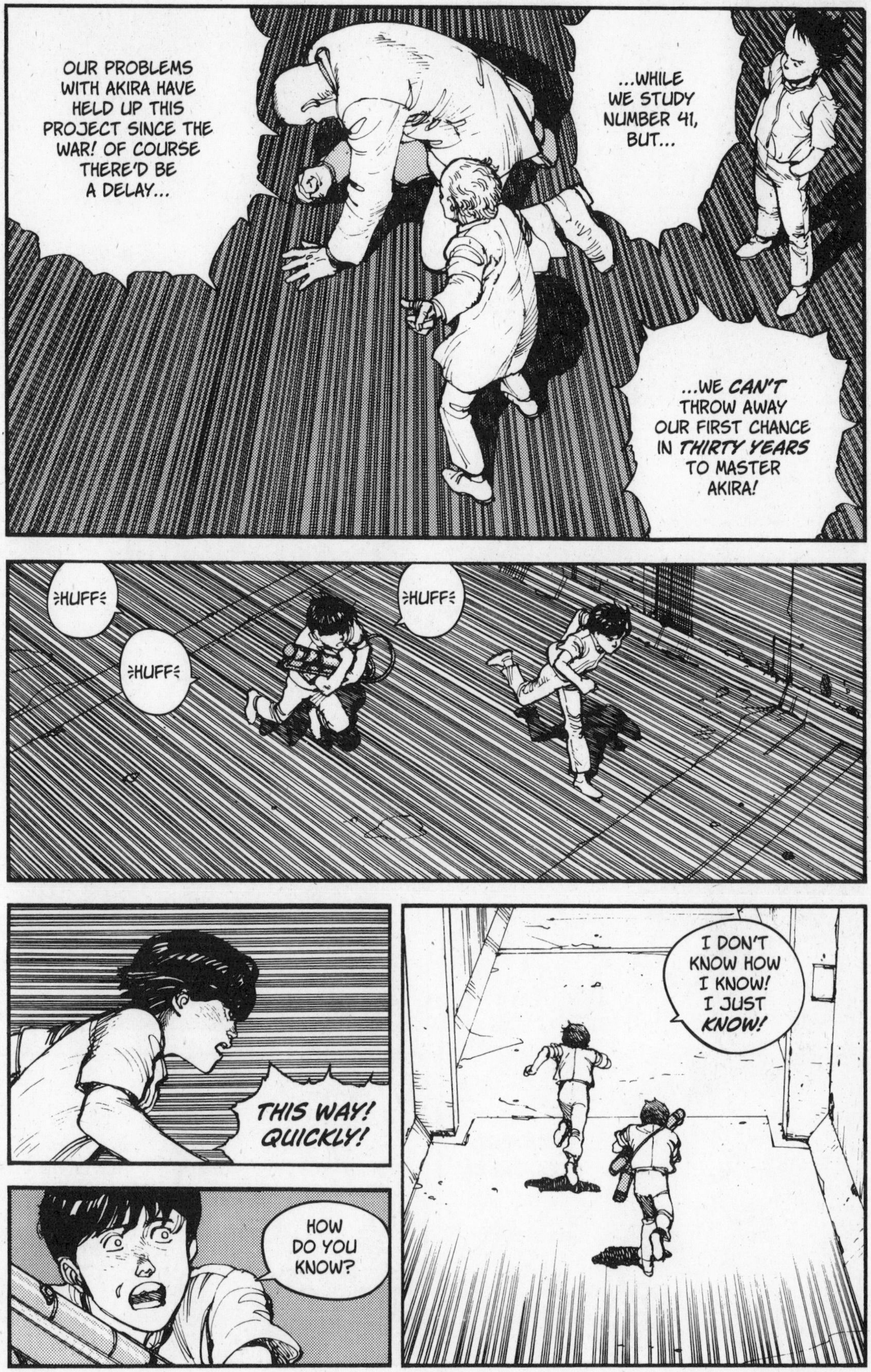
OUR PROBLEMS WITH AKIRA HAVE HELD UP THIS PROJECT SINCE THE WAR! OF COURSE THERE'D BE A DELAY...
...WHILE WE STUDY NUMBER 41, BUT...
...WE *CAN'T* THROW AWAY OUR FIRST CHANCE IN *THIRTY YEARS* TO MASTER AKIRA!
HUFF
HUFF
HUFF
*THIS WAY! QUICKLY!*
HOW DO YOU KNOW?
I DON'T KNOW HOW I KNOW! I JUST *KNOW!*

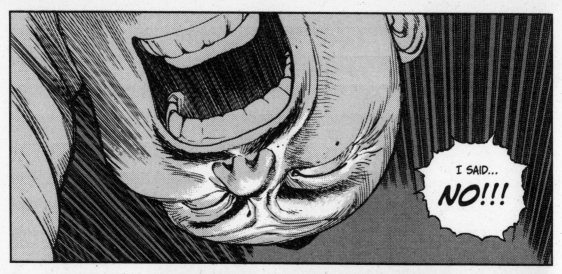

I SAID...
NO!!!

THE RISK IS TOO GREAT! WE CAN'T AWAKEN AKIRA WHILE THERE'S THE SLIGHTEST DOUBT!

BETTER HURRY IT UP...

PLEASE, COLONEL!

LET ME TRY! I'LL ASSUME FULL RESPONSIBILITY FOR THE SAFETY FACTOR!

TRUST ME!! THIS IS THE CULMINATION OF EVERYTHING I'VE WORKED AND STUDIED FOR!

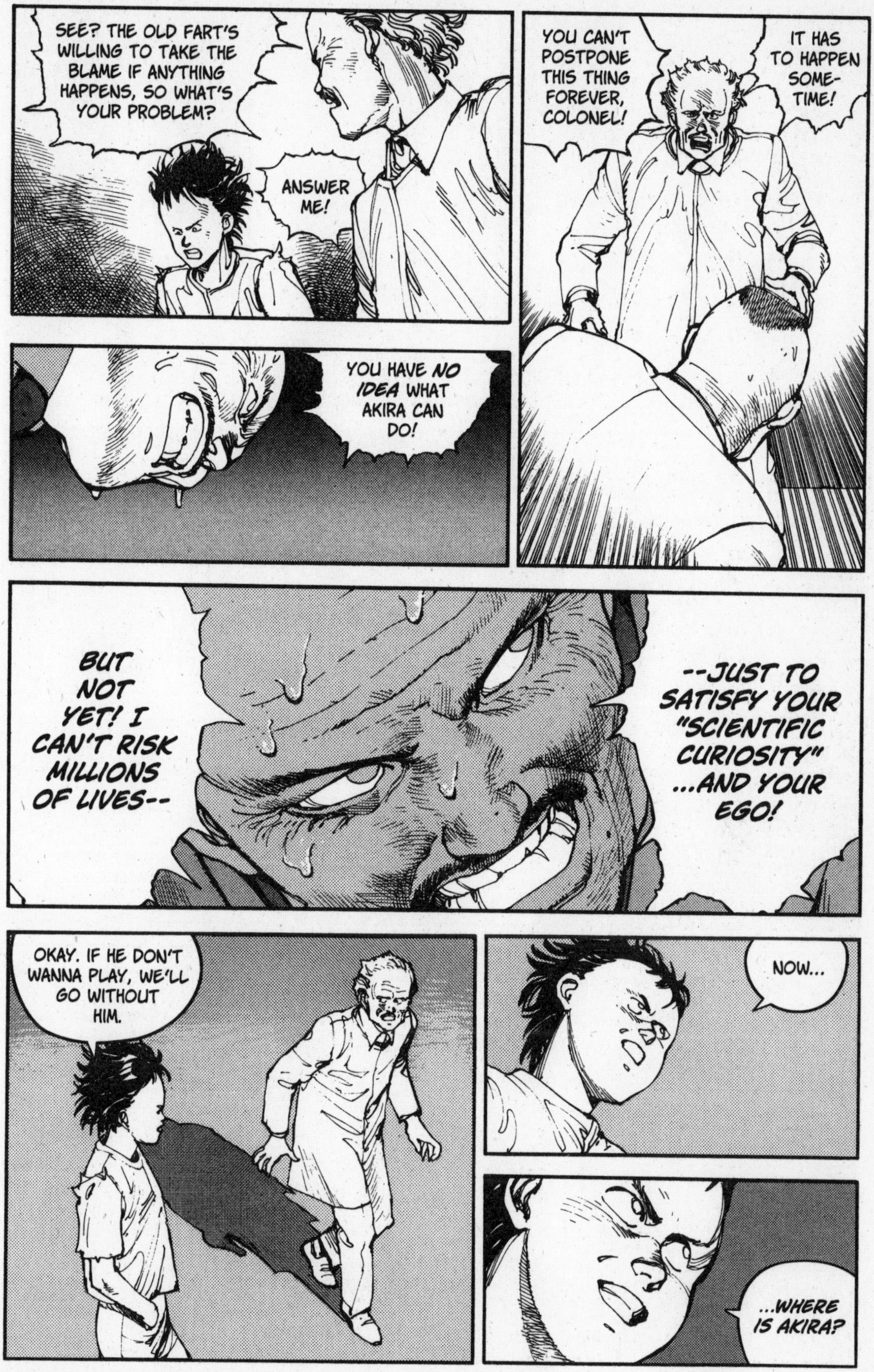
SEE? THE OLD FART'S WILLING TO TAKE THE BLAME IF ANYTHING HAPPENS, SO WHAT'S YOUR PROBLEM?
ANSWER ME!
YOU CAN'T POSTPONE THIS THING FOREVER, COLONEL!
IT HAS TO HAPPEN SOME-TIME!
YOU HAVE NO IDEA WHAT AKIRA CAN DO!
BUT NOT YET! I CAN'T RISK MILLIONS OF LIVES--
--JUST TO SATISFY YOUR "SCIENTIFIC CURIOSITY" ...AND YOUR EGO!
OKAY. IF HE DON'T WANNA PLAY, WE'LL GO WITHOUT HIM.
NOW...
...WHERE IS AKIRA?

COLONEL...?

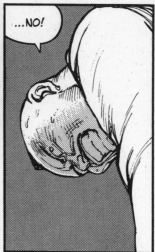

...NO!

I SAID WE DON'T NEED YOU!

! BLOK

NO... DON'T...!

≥GNNN...≤

I'M NOT STUPID, YOU KNOW. I DON'T PLAN TO TAKE ANY CHANCES WITH AKIRA.

I'M JUST LIKE YOU... INTERESTED IN *EXPERIMENTS*.

C-COLONEL...?

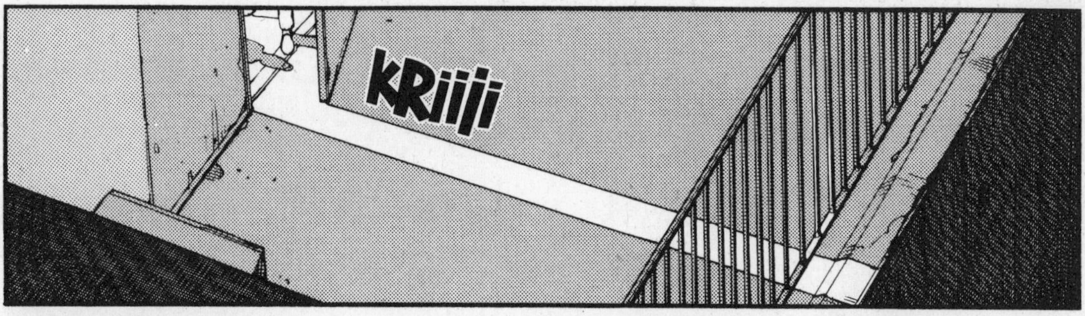
KRIIJI
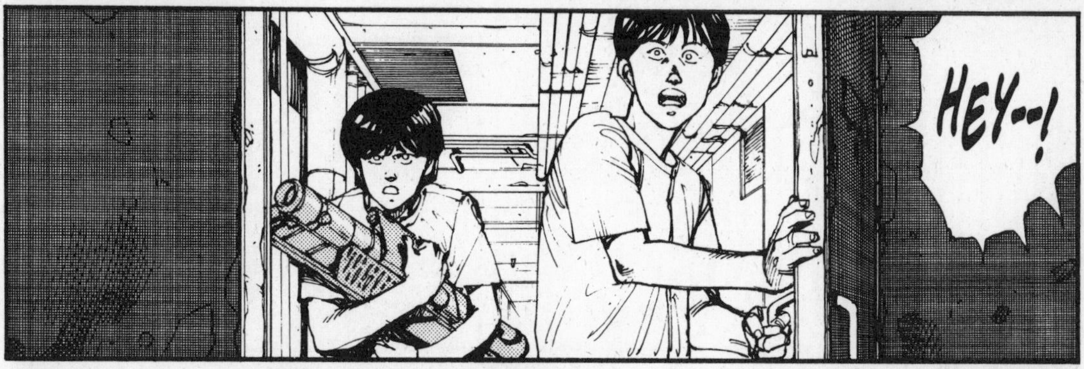
HEY--!
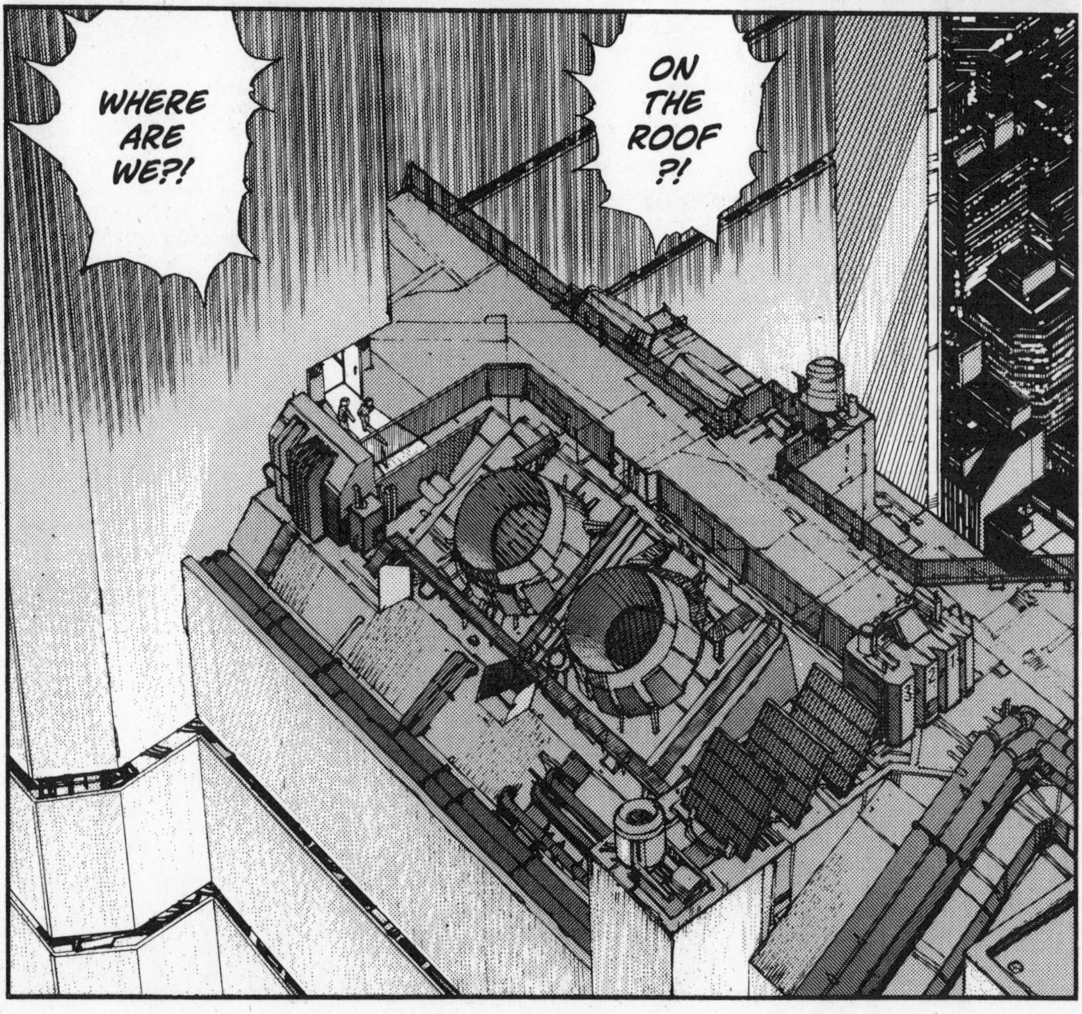
WHERE ARE WE?!
ON THE ROOF ?!

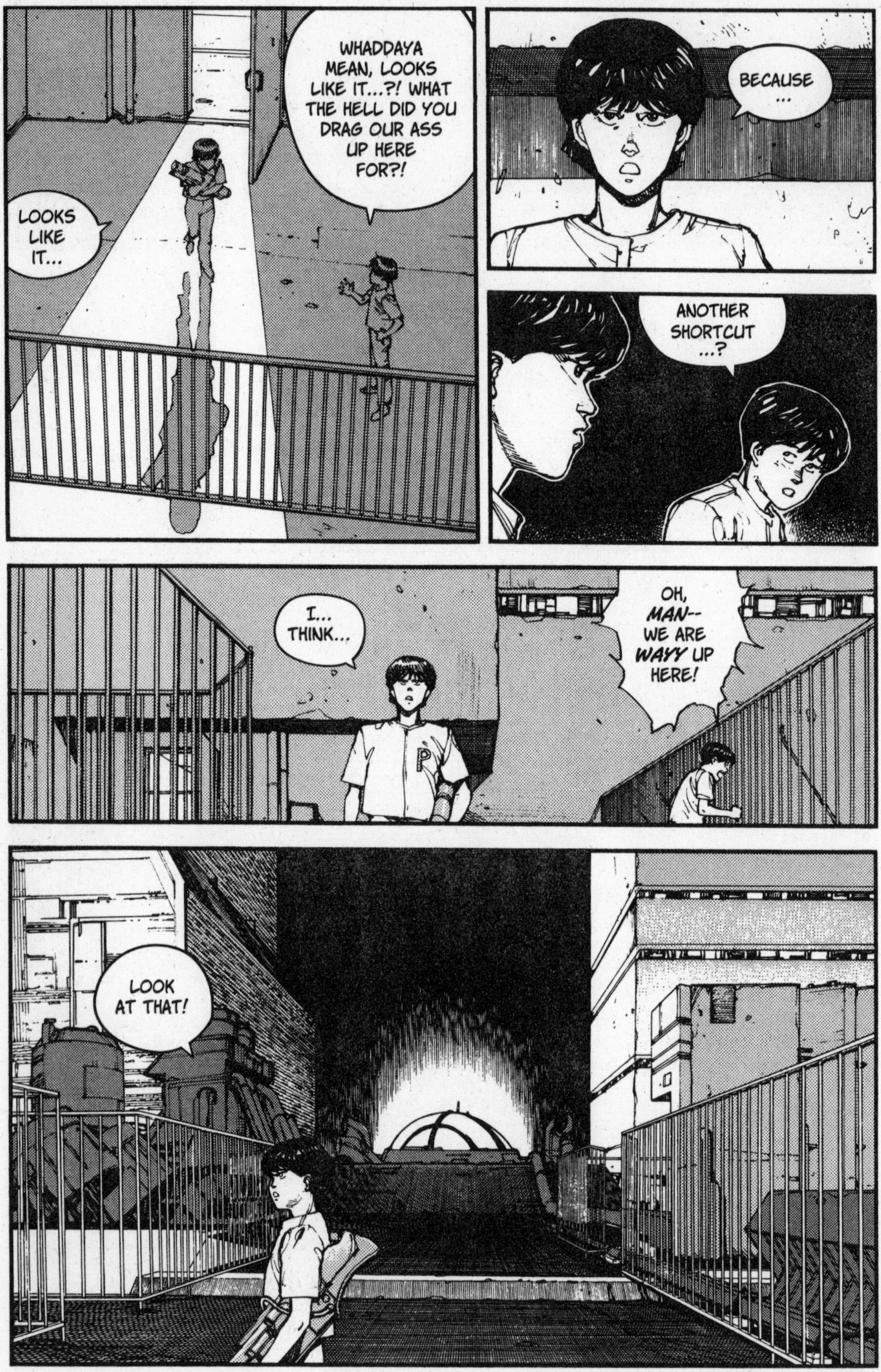
LOOKS LIKE IT...
WHADDAYA MEAN, LOOKS LIKE IT...?! WHAT THE HELL DID YOU DRAG OUR ASS UP HERE FOR?!
BECAUSE ...
ANOTHER SHORTCUT ...?
I... THINK...
OH, *MAN*-- WE ARE *WAYY* UP HERE!
LOOK AT THAT!

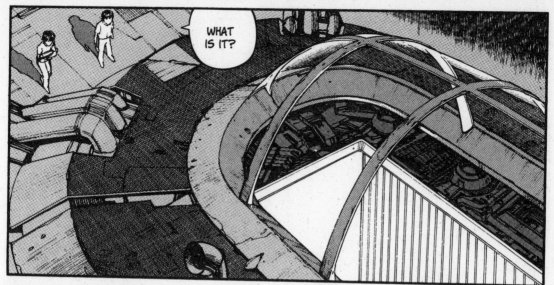

WHAT IS IT?

DO YOU THINK IT GOES ANYWHERE?

WELL...

LOOKS LIKE A BIG GREEN-HOUSE.

109

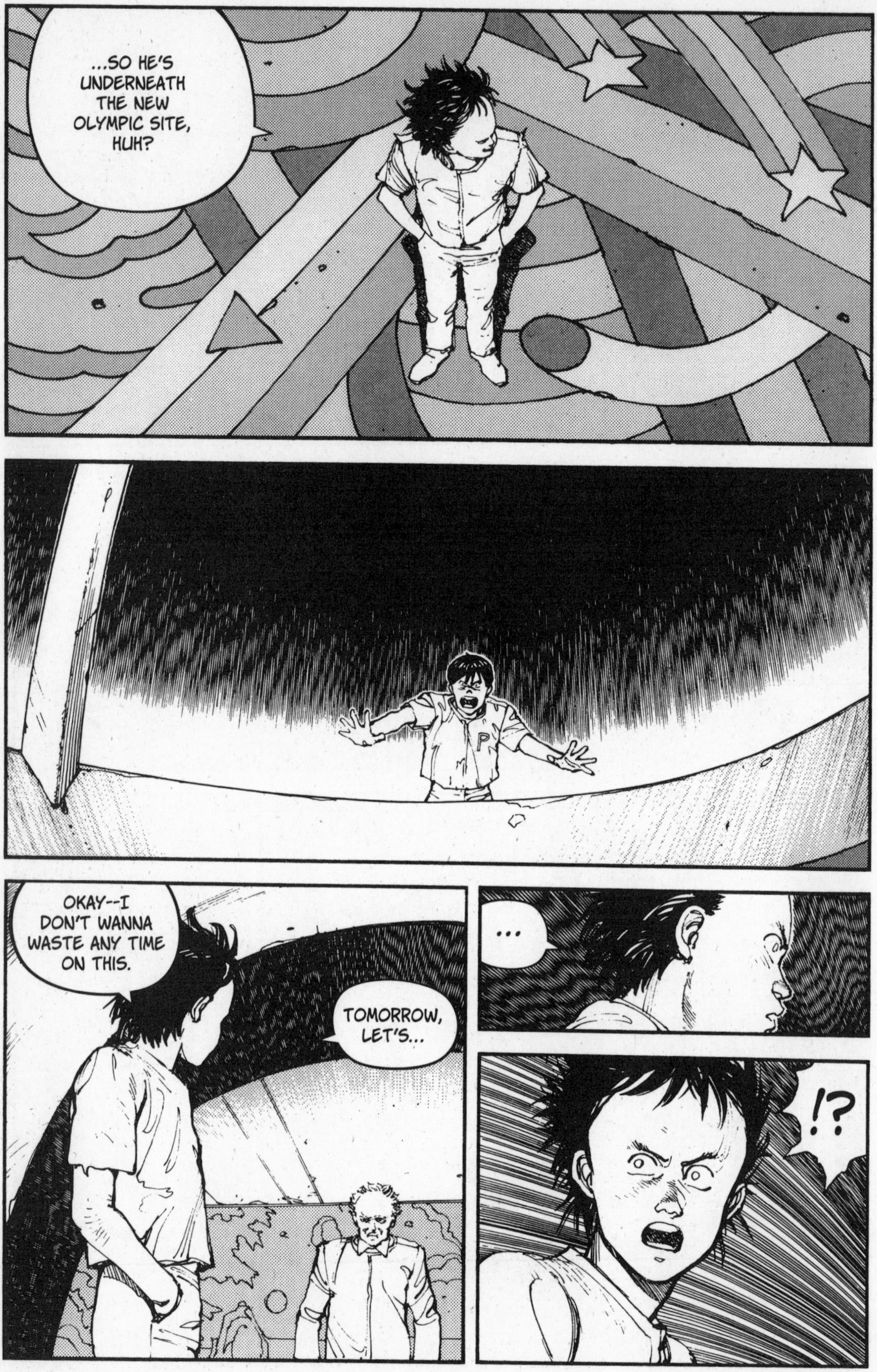
...SO HE'S UNDERNEATH THE NEW OLYMPIC SITE, HUH?
OKAY--I DON'T WANNA WASTE ANY TIME ON THIS.
TOMORROW, LET'S...
...
!?

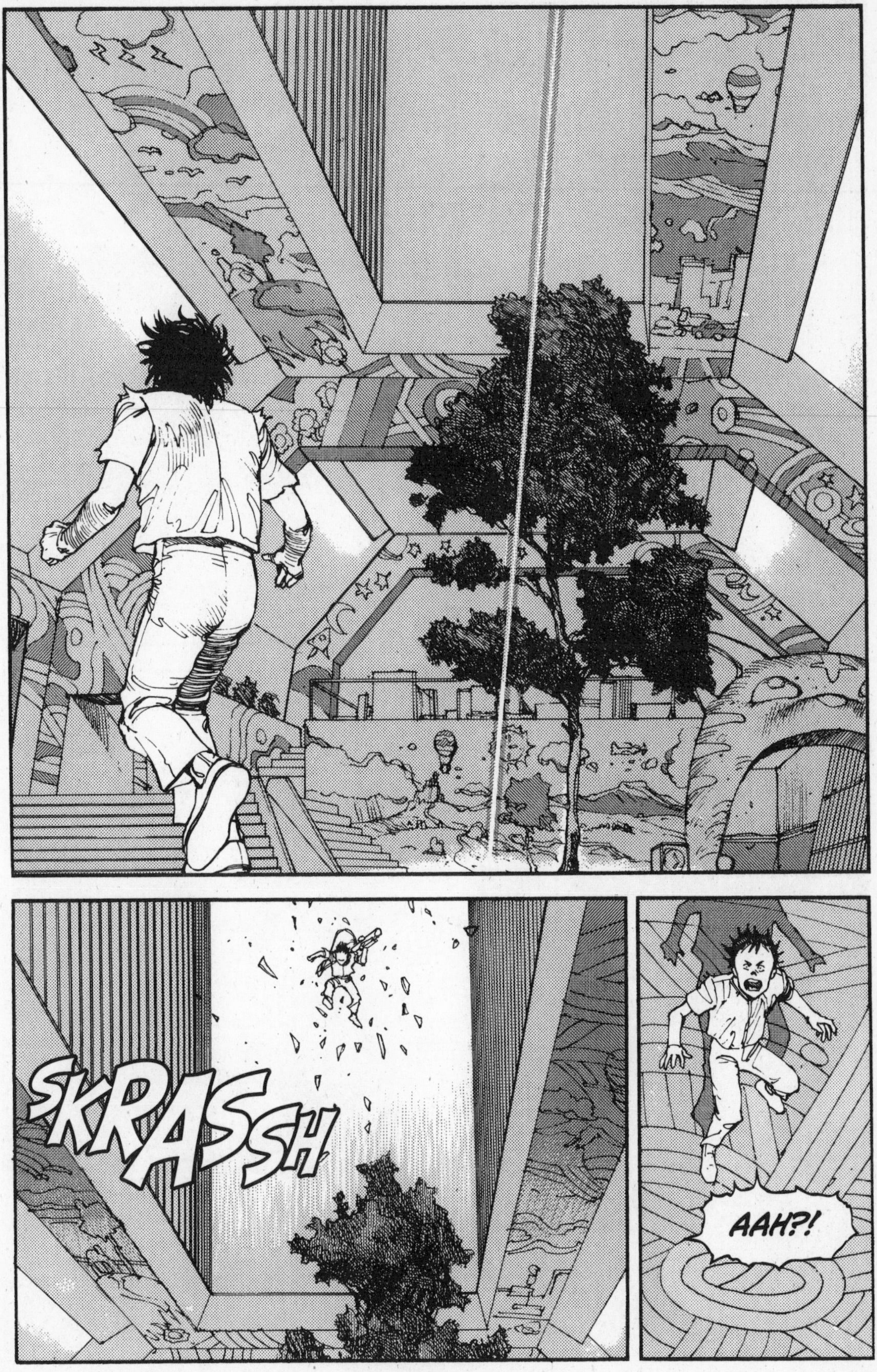
SKRASSH
AAH?!

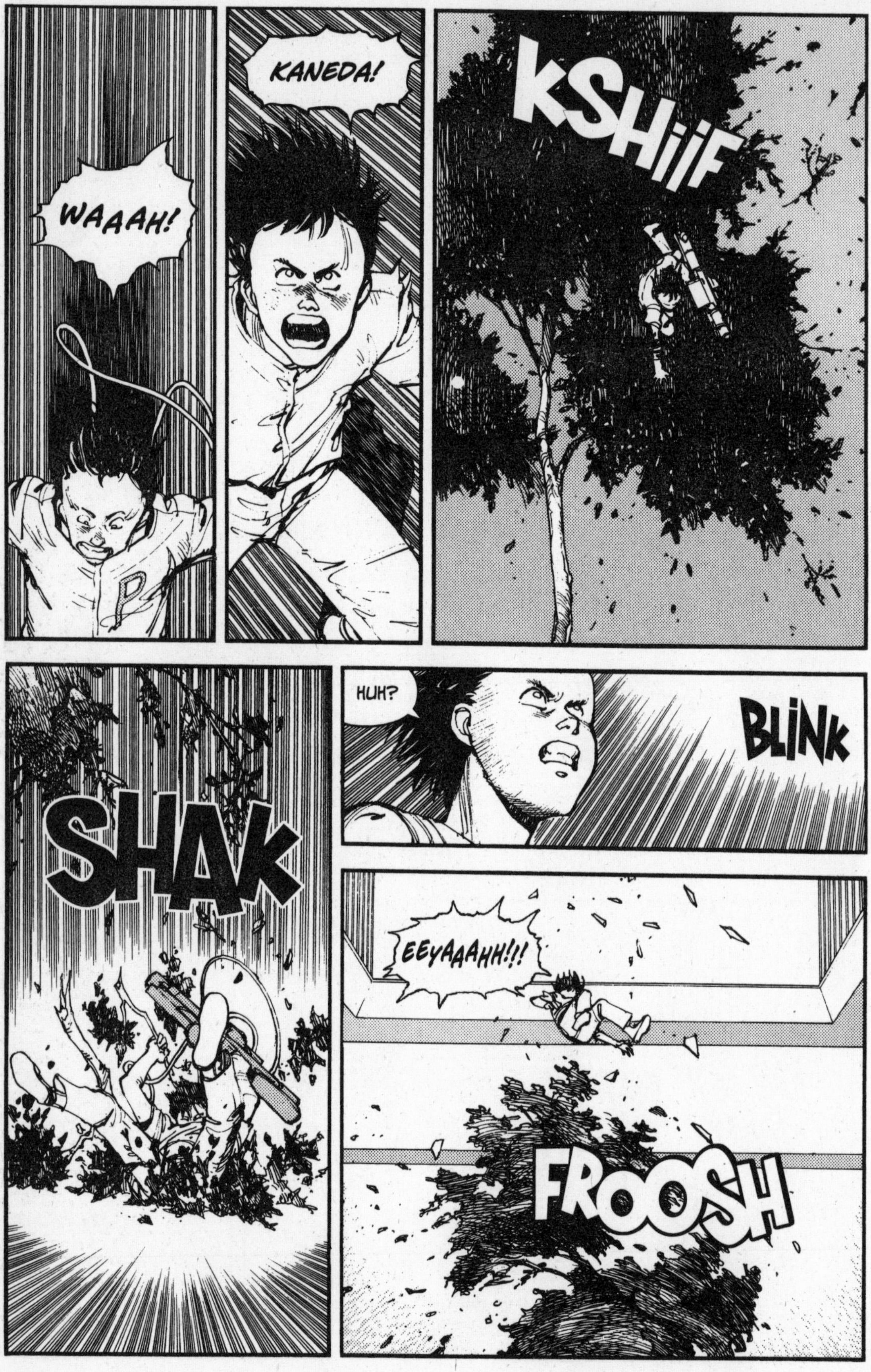
WAAAH!
KANEDA!
KSHIIF
SHAK
HUH?
BLINK
EEYAAAHH!!!
FROOSH

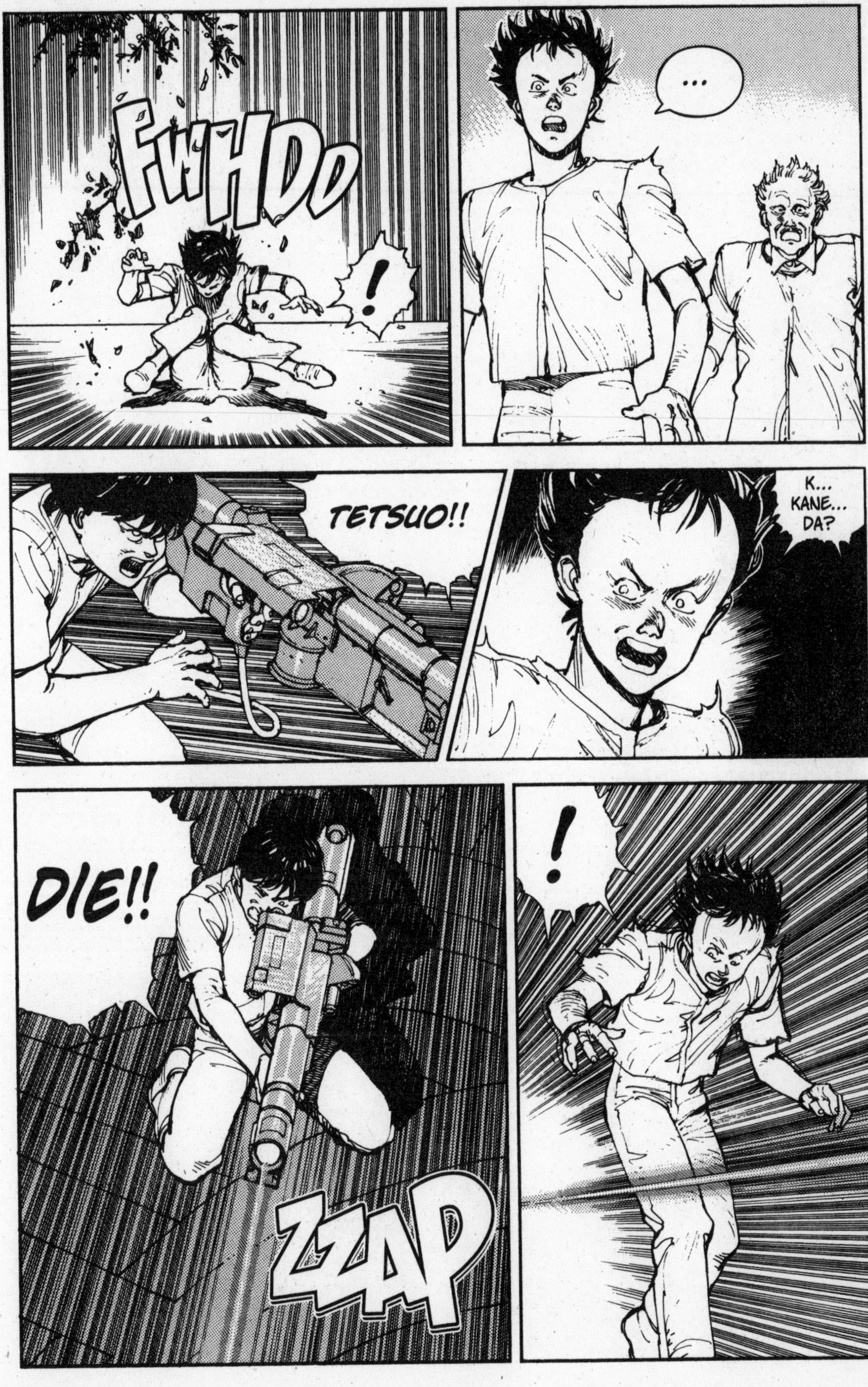
FWHDD
!
...
TETSUO!!
K... KANE... DA?
DIE!!
ZZAP
!

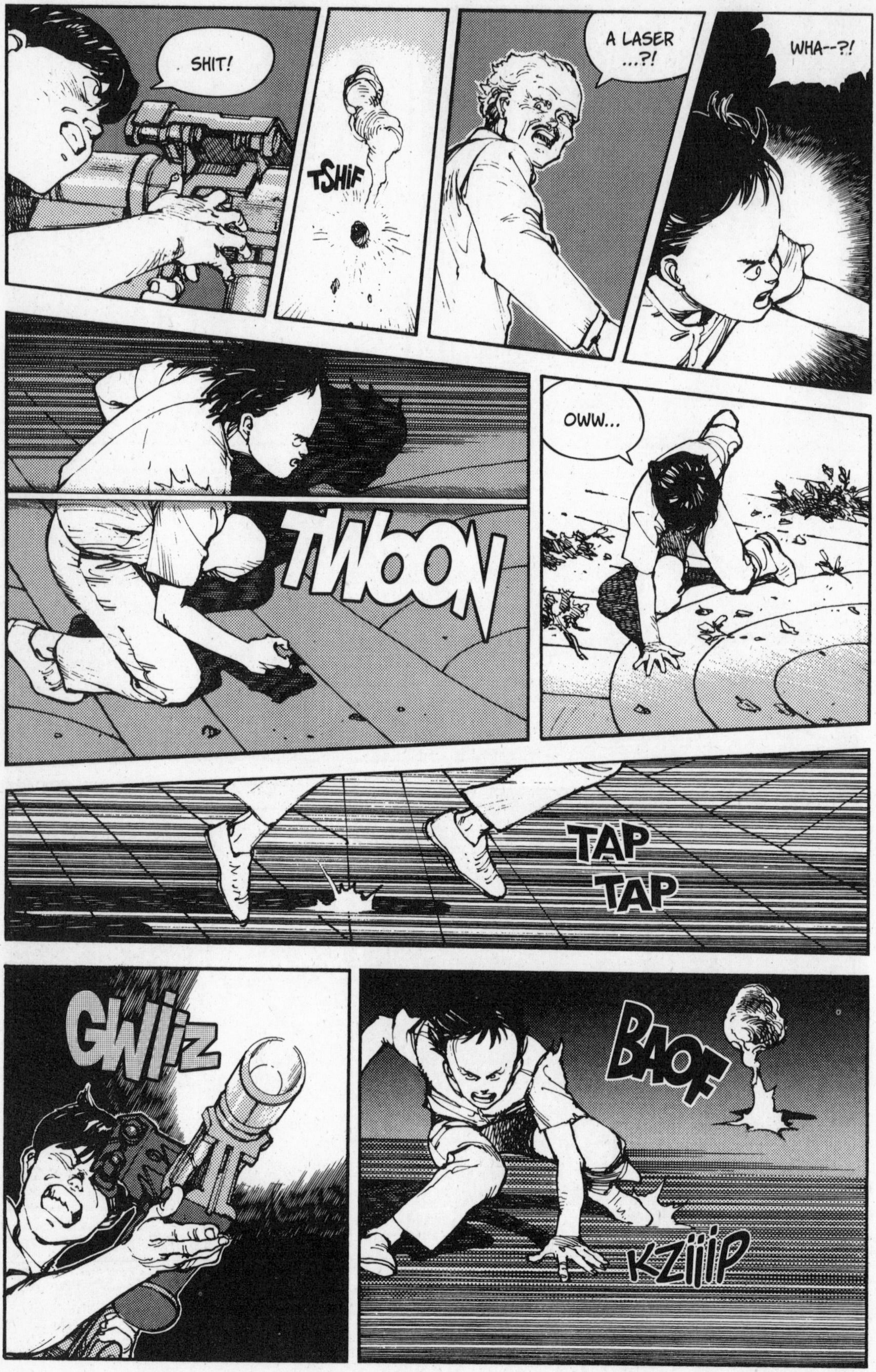
SHIT!
TSHIF
A LASER ...?!
WHA--?!
TWOON
OWW...
TAP
TAP
GWIIZ
BAOF
KZIIIP

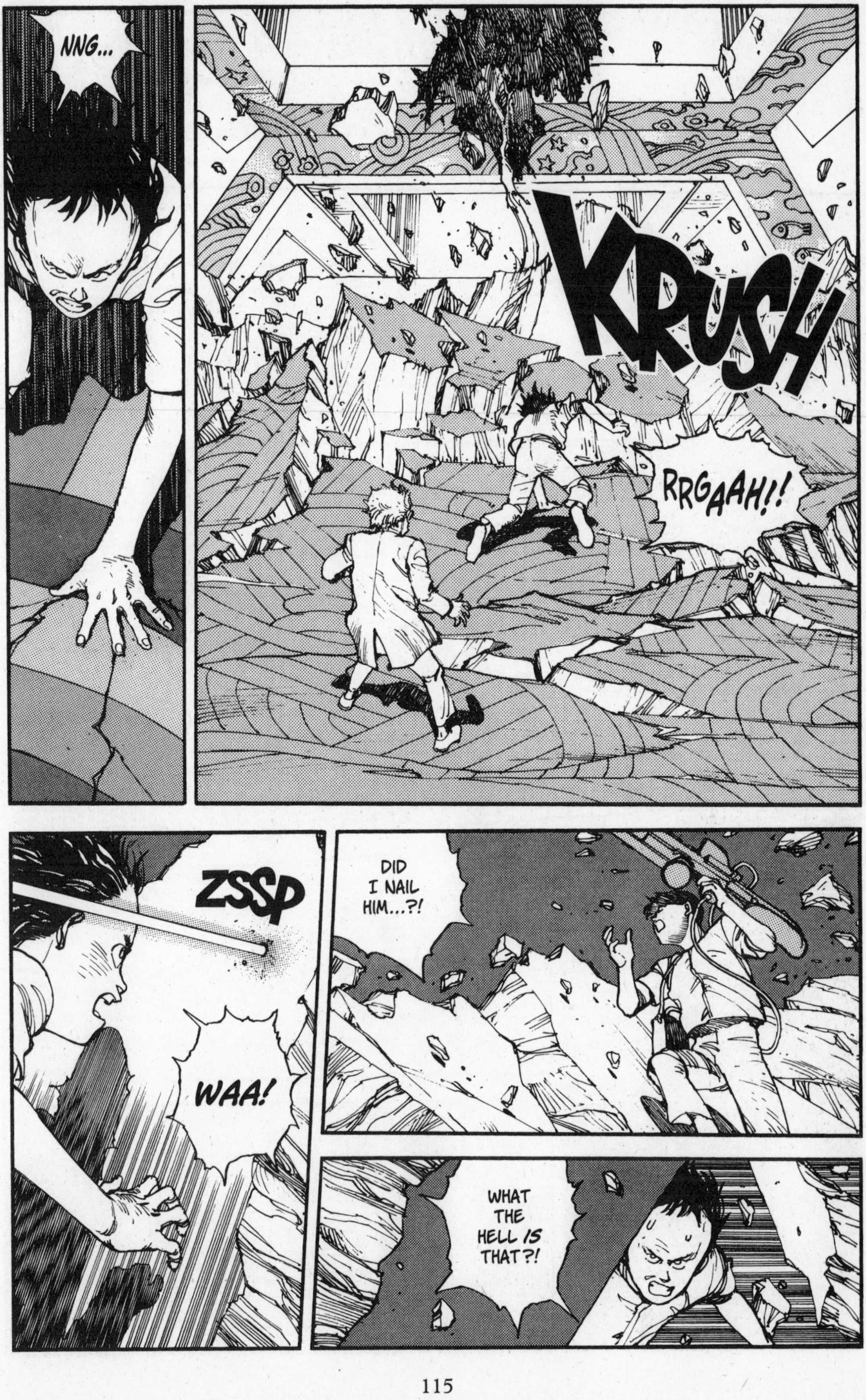
NNG...
KRUSH
RRGAAH!!
ZSSP
WAA!
DID I NAIL HIM...?!
WHAT THE HELL IS THAT?!

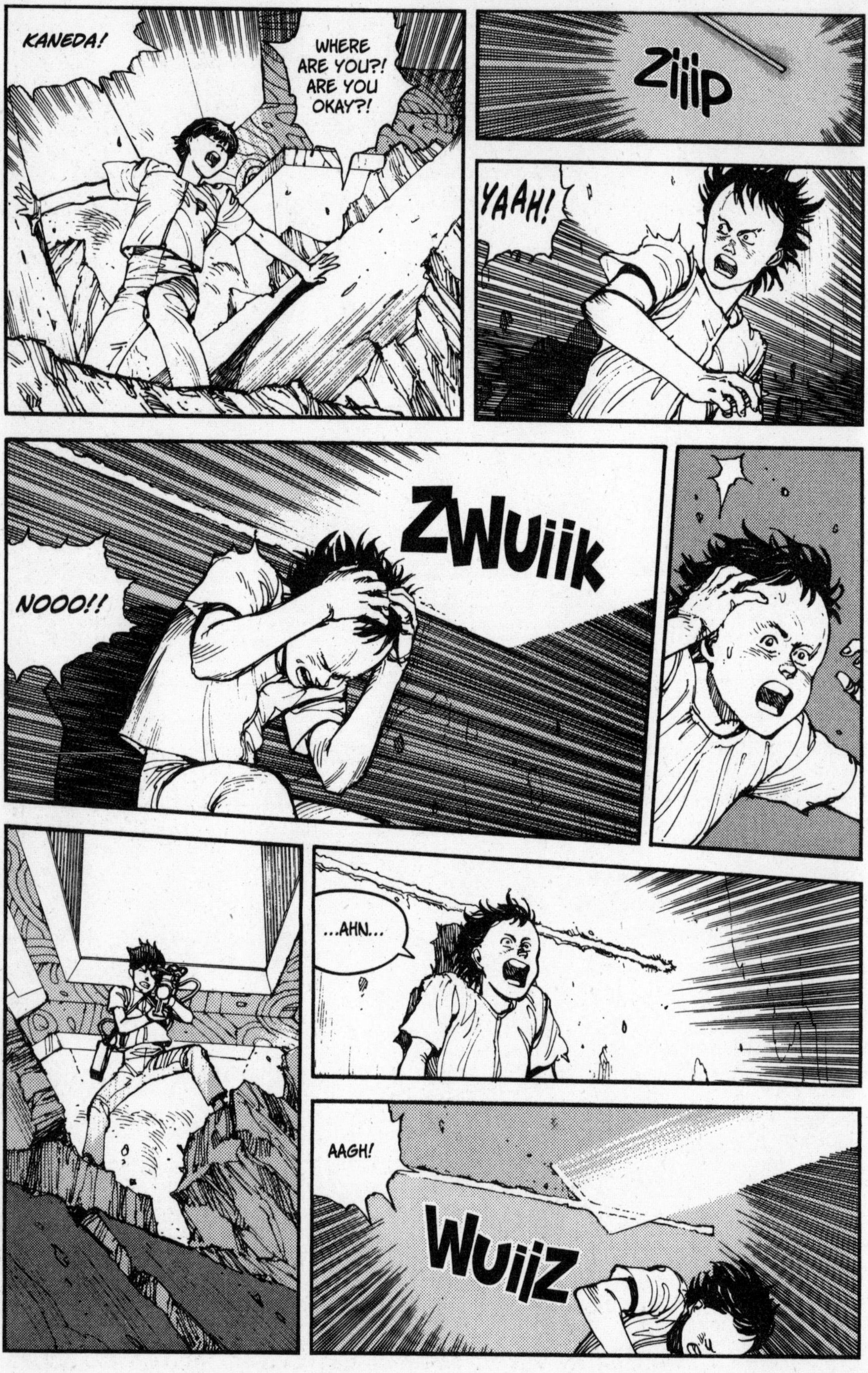
KANEDA!
WHERE ARE YOU?! ARE YOU OKAY?!
ZIIIP
YAAH!
NOOO!!
ZWUIIK
...AHN...
AAGH!
WUIIZ

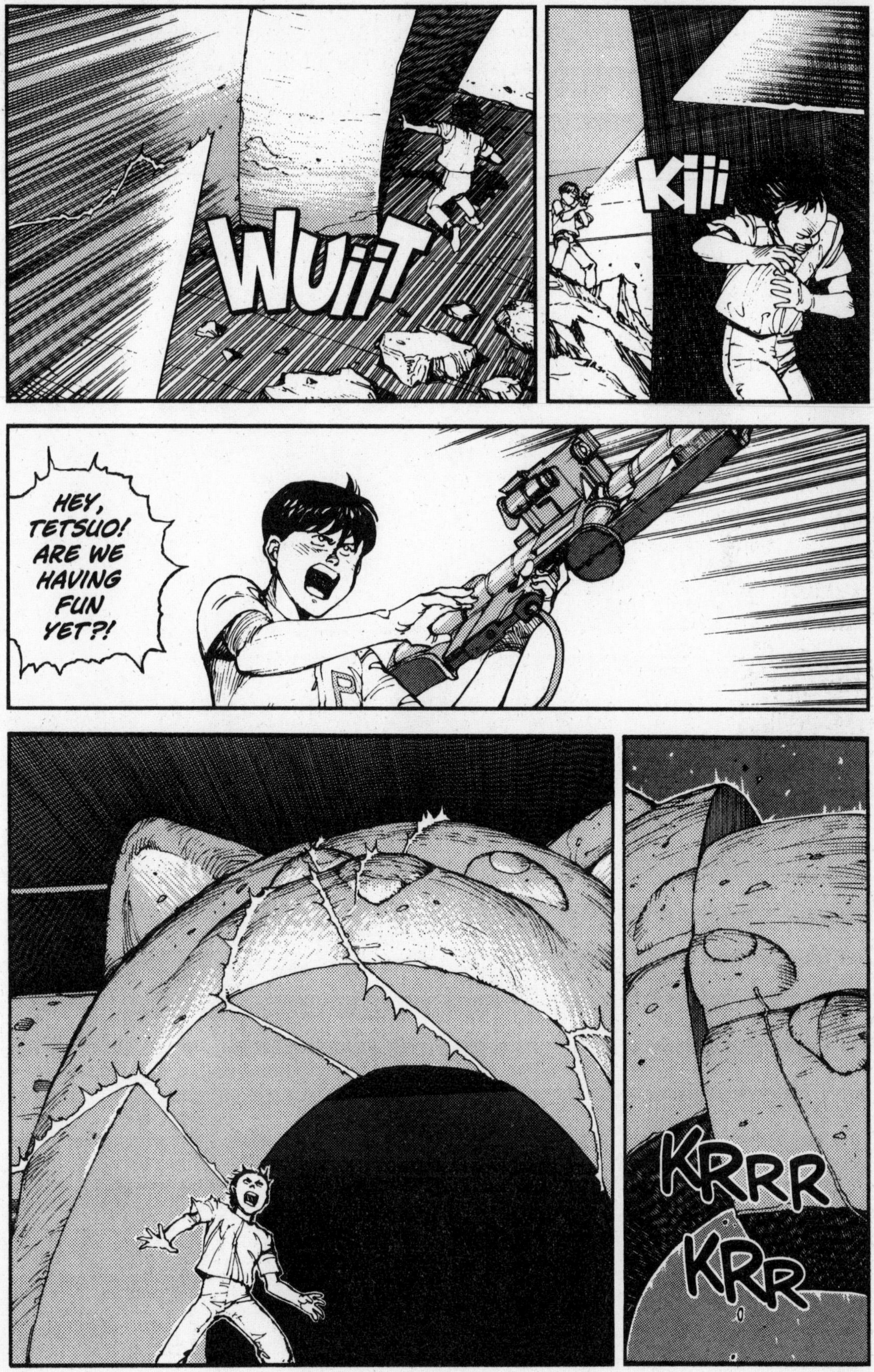
WUIIT
KIII
HEY, TETSUO! ARE WE HAVING FUN YET?!
KRRR
KRR

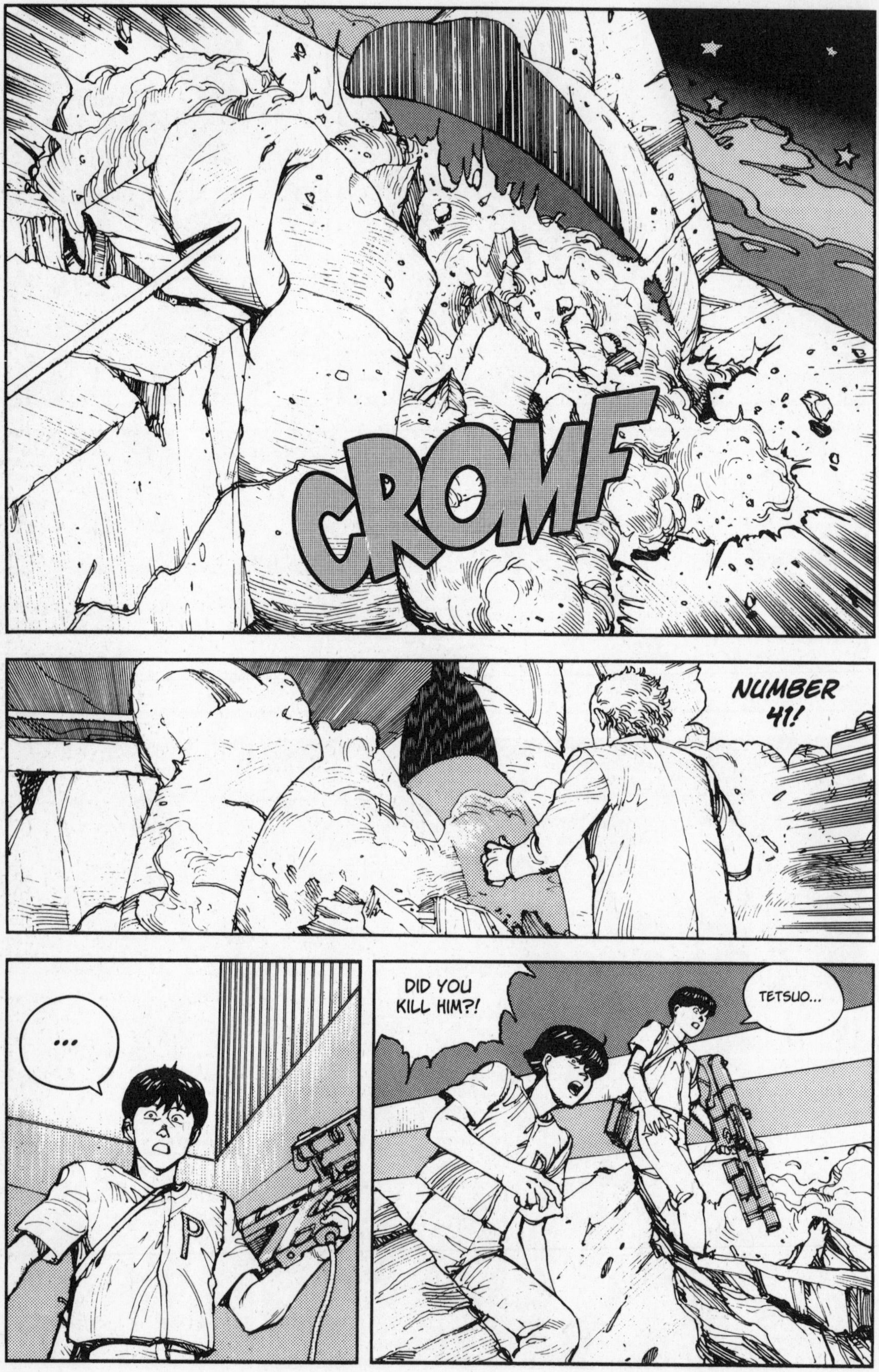
CROMF
NUMBER 41!
...
DID YOU KILL HIM?!
TETSUO...

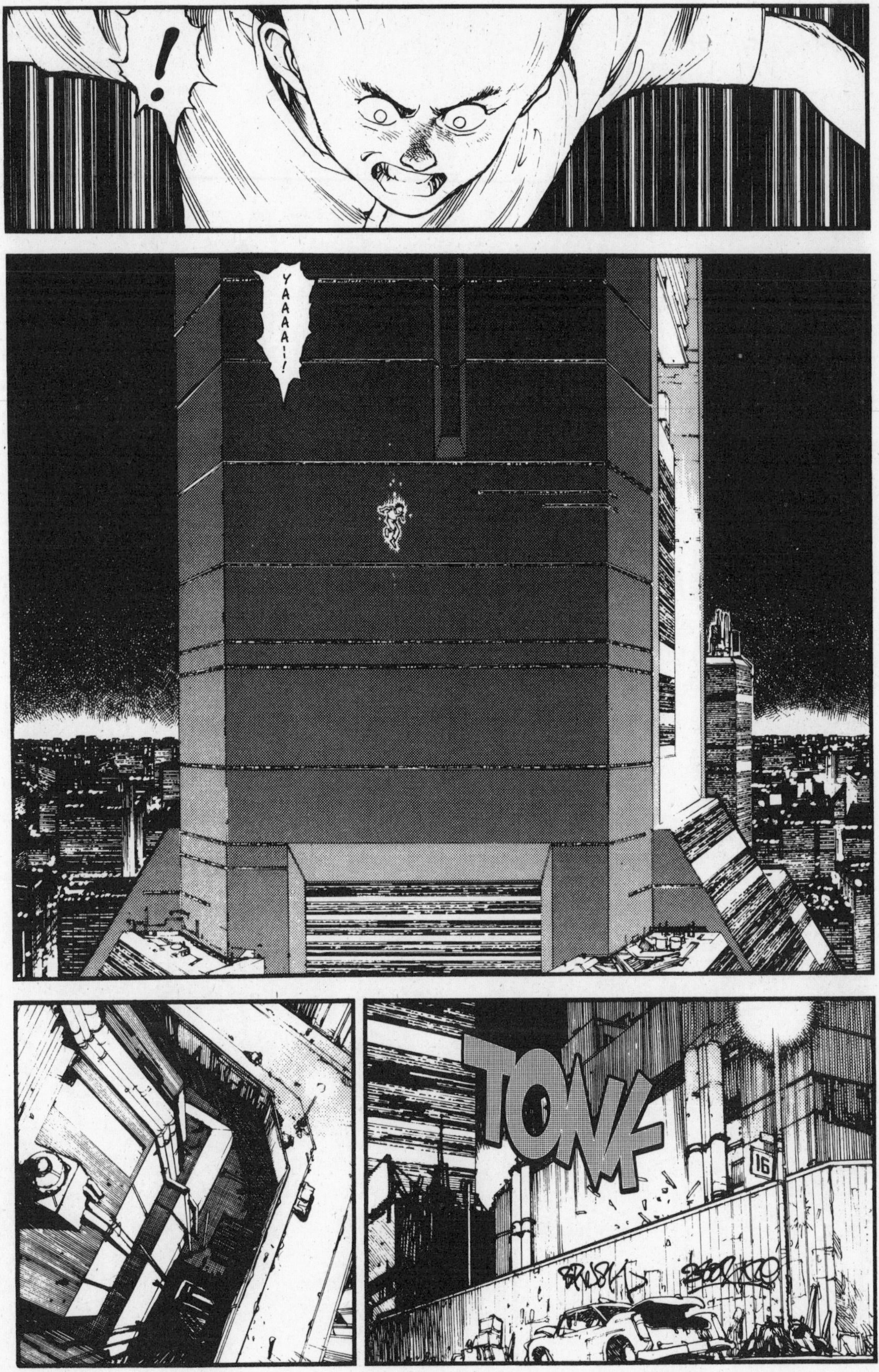
!
YAAAA!!
TOMF
16

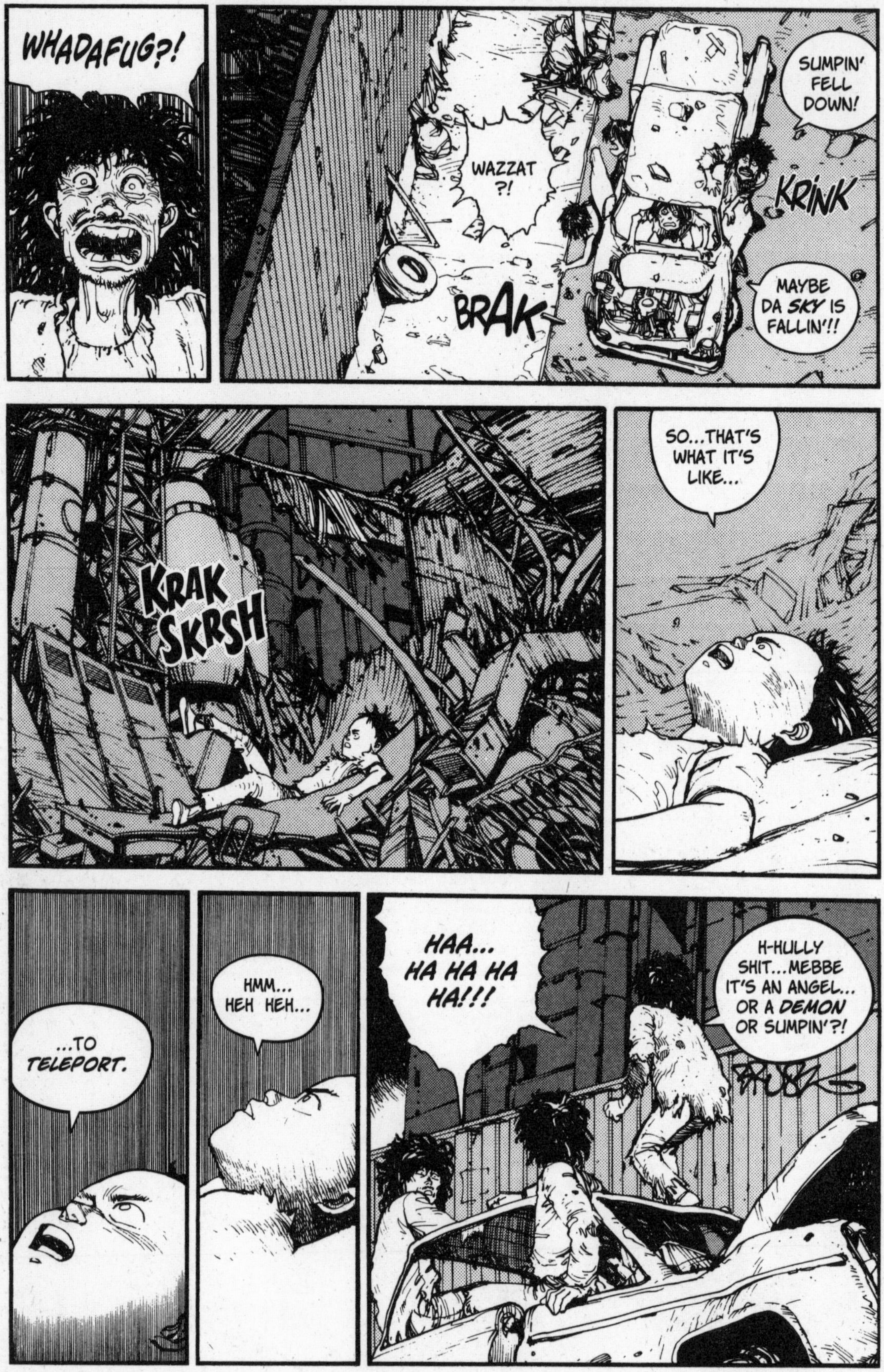
WHADAFUG?!
WAZZAT ?!
SUMPIN' FELL DOWN!
KRINK
BRAK
MAYBE DA *SKY* IS FALLIN'!!
KRAK SKRSH
SO...THAT'S WHAT IT'S LIKE...
...TO *TELEPORT.*
HMM... HEH HEH...
*HAA... HA HA HA HA!!!*
H-HULLY SHIT...MEBBE IT'S AN ANGEL... OR A *DEMON* OR SUMPIN'?!

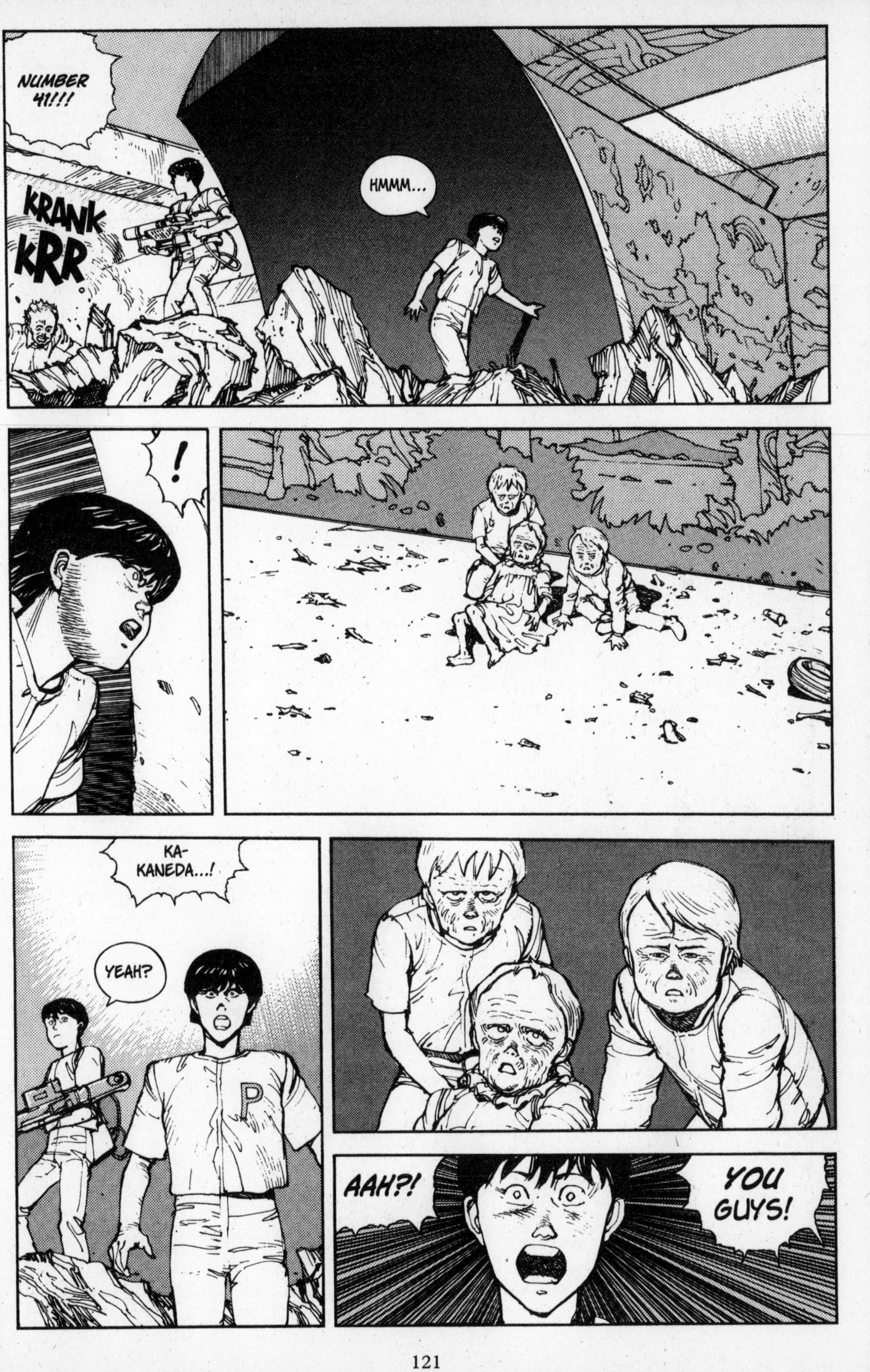
NUMBER 41!!!
KRANK KRR
HMMM...
!
KA- KANEDA...!
YEAH?
AAH?!
YOU GUYS!

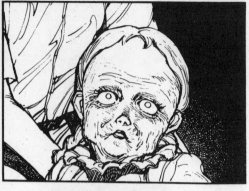

IT WAS YOU, WASN'T IT? YOU WERE GUIDING ME HERE!

UHN...

OH, *CRAP!* IT'S THAT *SKINHEAD* DUDE AGAIN!

GNNN...

HE'S *BAD NEWS*--WE GOTTA *RUN!* NOW!!

NOT YET...

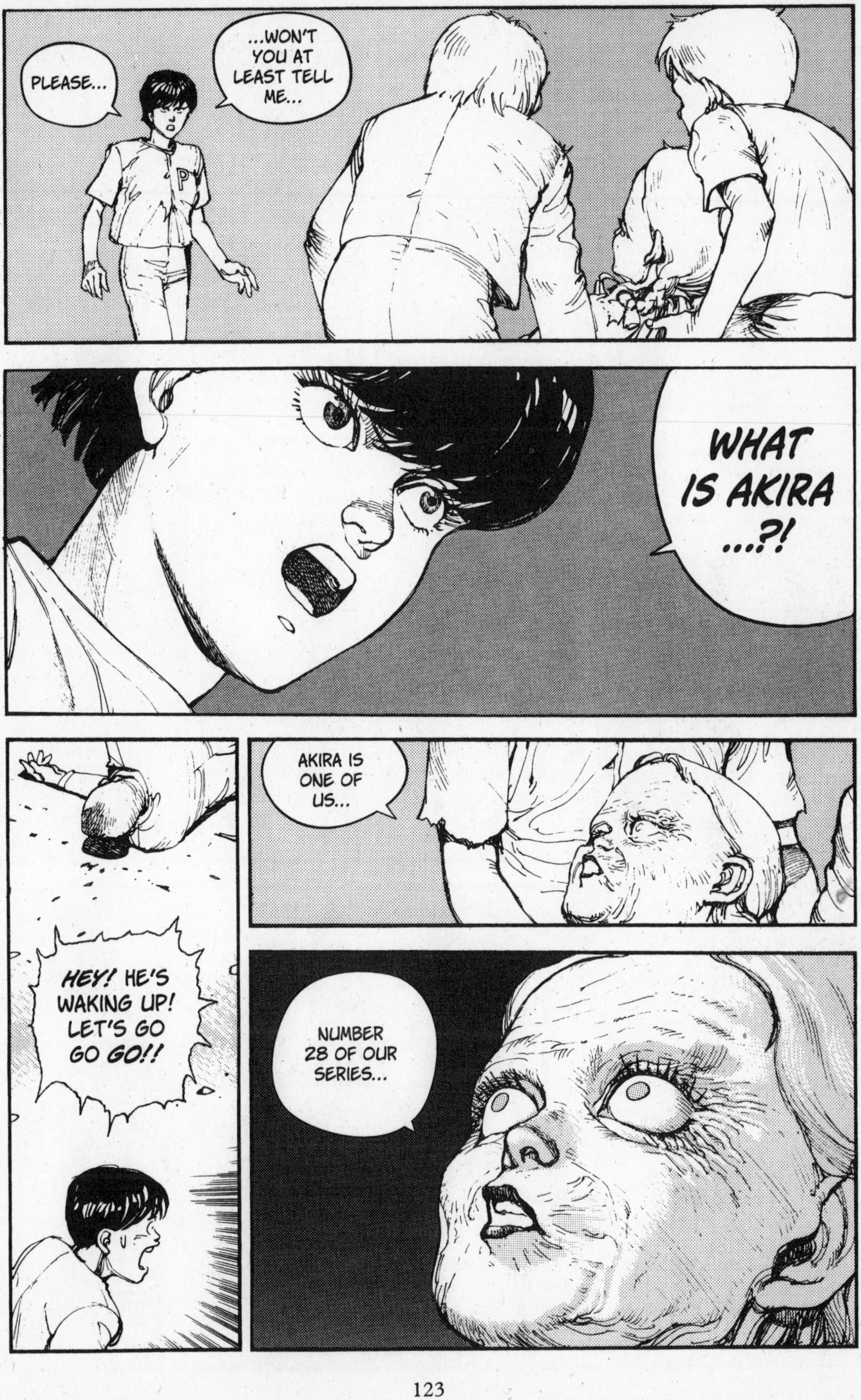
PLEASE...
...WON'T YOU AT LEAST TELL ME...
WHAT IS AKIRA ...?!
HEY! HE'S WAKING UP! LET'S GO GO GO!!
AKIRA IS ONE OF US...
NUMBER 28 OF OUR SERIES...

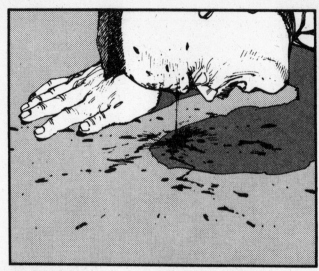

RRR...

OH, *SHIT!*

WHERE IS AKIRA NOW?

BURIED... UNDER THE OLYMPIC SITE.

UNDER--?!?

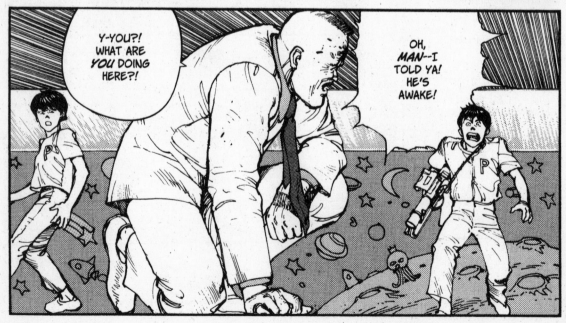

Y-YOU?! WHAT ARE *YOU* DOING HERE?!

OH, *MAN*--I TOLD YA! HE'S AWAKE!

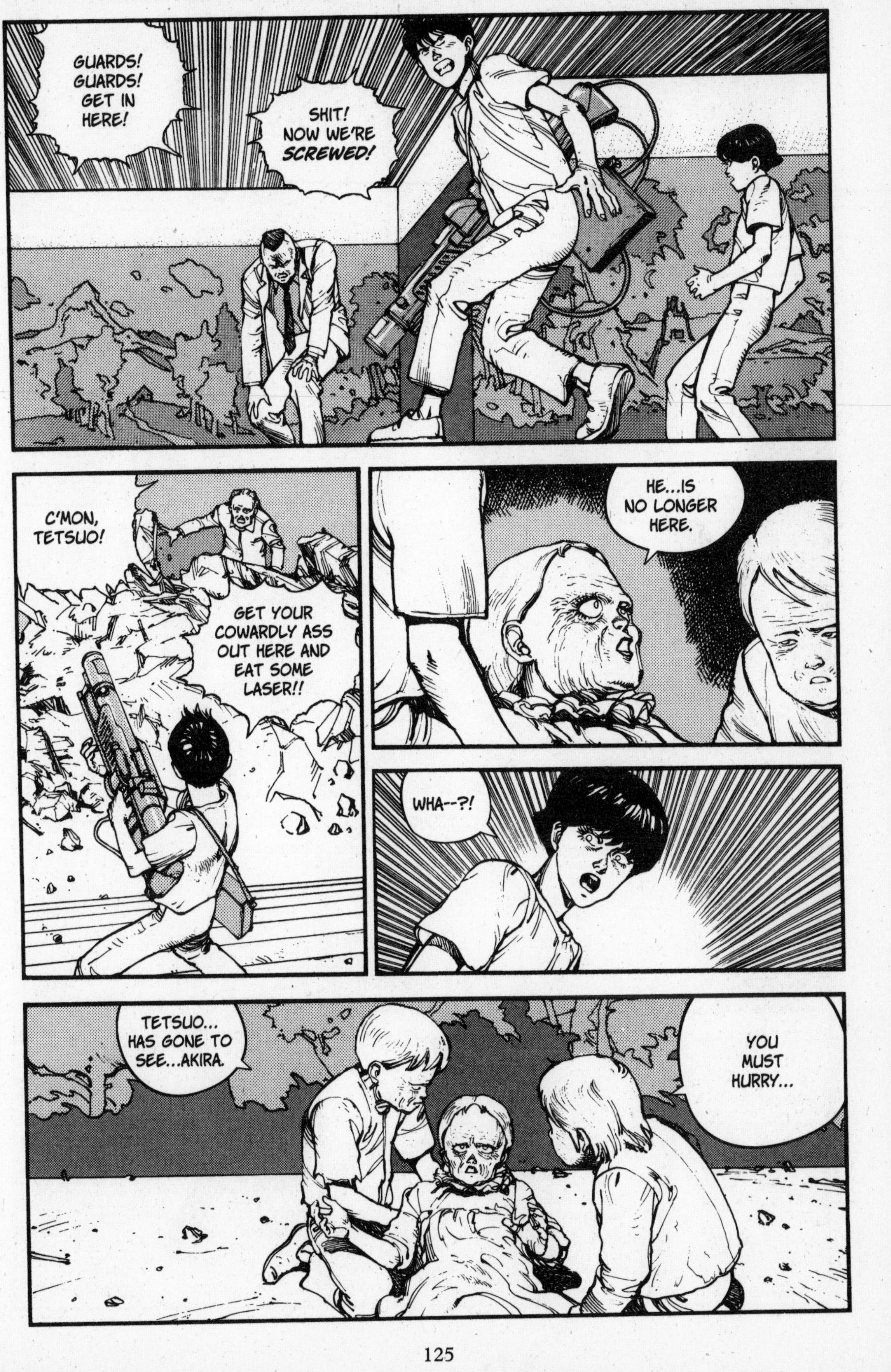
GUARDS! GUARDS! GET IN HERE!
SHIT! NOW WE'RE *SCREWED!*
C'MON, TETSUO!
GET YOUR COWARDLY ASS OUT HERE AND EAT SOME LASER!!
HE...IS NO LONGER HERE.
WHA--?!
TETSUO... HAS GONE TO SEE...AKIRA.
YOU MUST HURRY...

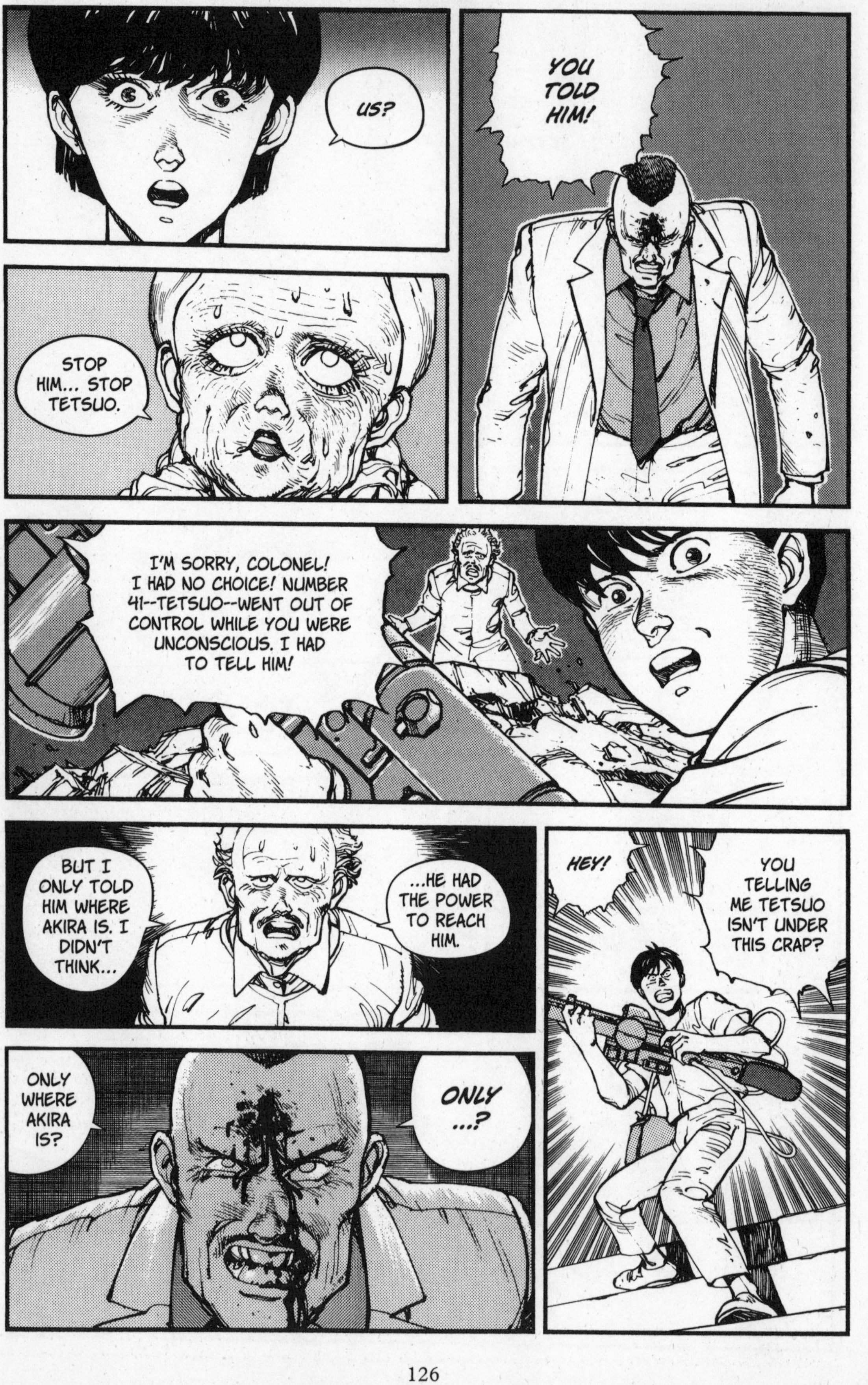
US?
STOP HIM... STOP TETSUO.
YOU TOLD HIM!
I'M SORRY, COLONEL! I HAD NO CHOICE! NUMBER 41--TETSUO--WENT OUT OF CONTROL WHILE YOU WERE UNCONSCIOUS. I HAD TO TELL HIM!
BUT I ONLY TOLD HIM WHERE AKIRA IS. I DIDN'T THINK...
...HE HAD THE POWER TO REACH HIM.
ONLY WHERE AKIRA IS?
ONLY ...?
HEY!
YOU TELLING ME TETSUO ISN'T UNDER THIS CRAP?

KANEDA!

LET'S GO!

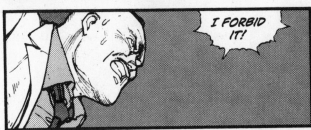

I FORBID IT!

WHY DON'T YOU JUST *DROP DEAD*, YOU UGLY BALD SKINHEAD SHAVER CUEBALL-HEADED *GOON!*

KROPF

BITE ME!

I DIDN'T THINK NUMBER 41...

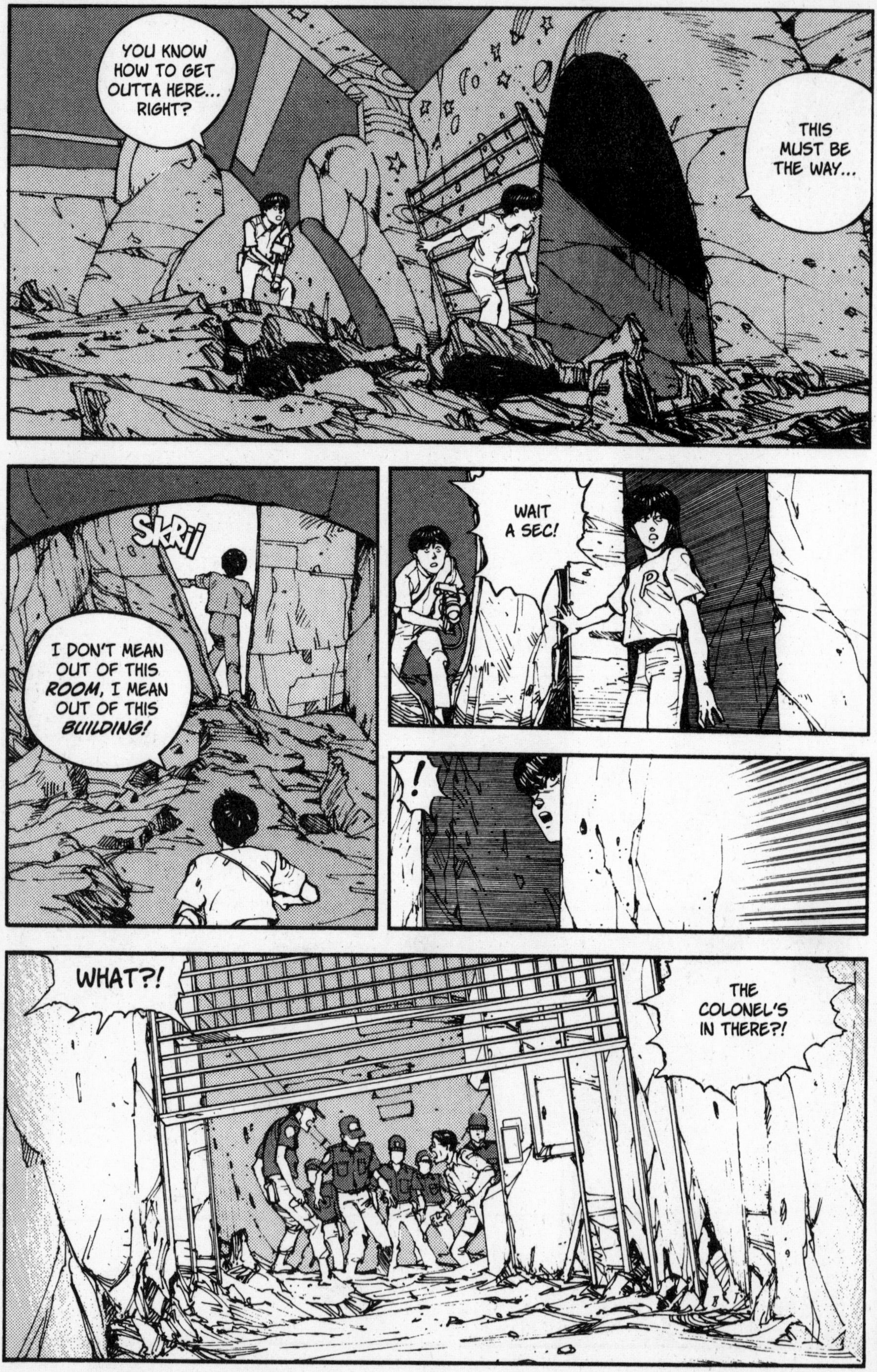
YOU KNOW HOW TO GET OUTTA HERE... RIGHT?
THIS MUST BE THE WAY...
SKRII
I DON'T MEAN OUT OF THIS *ROOM*, I MEAN OUT OF THIS *BUILDING!*
WAIT A SEC!
!
WHAT?!
THE COLONEL'S IN THERE?!

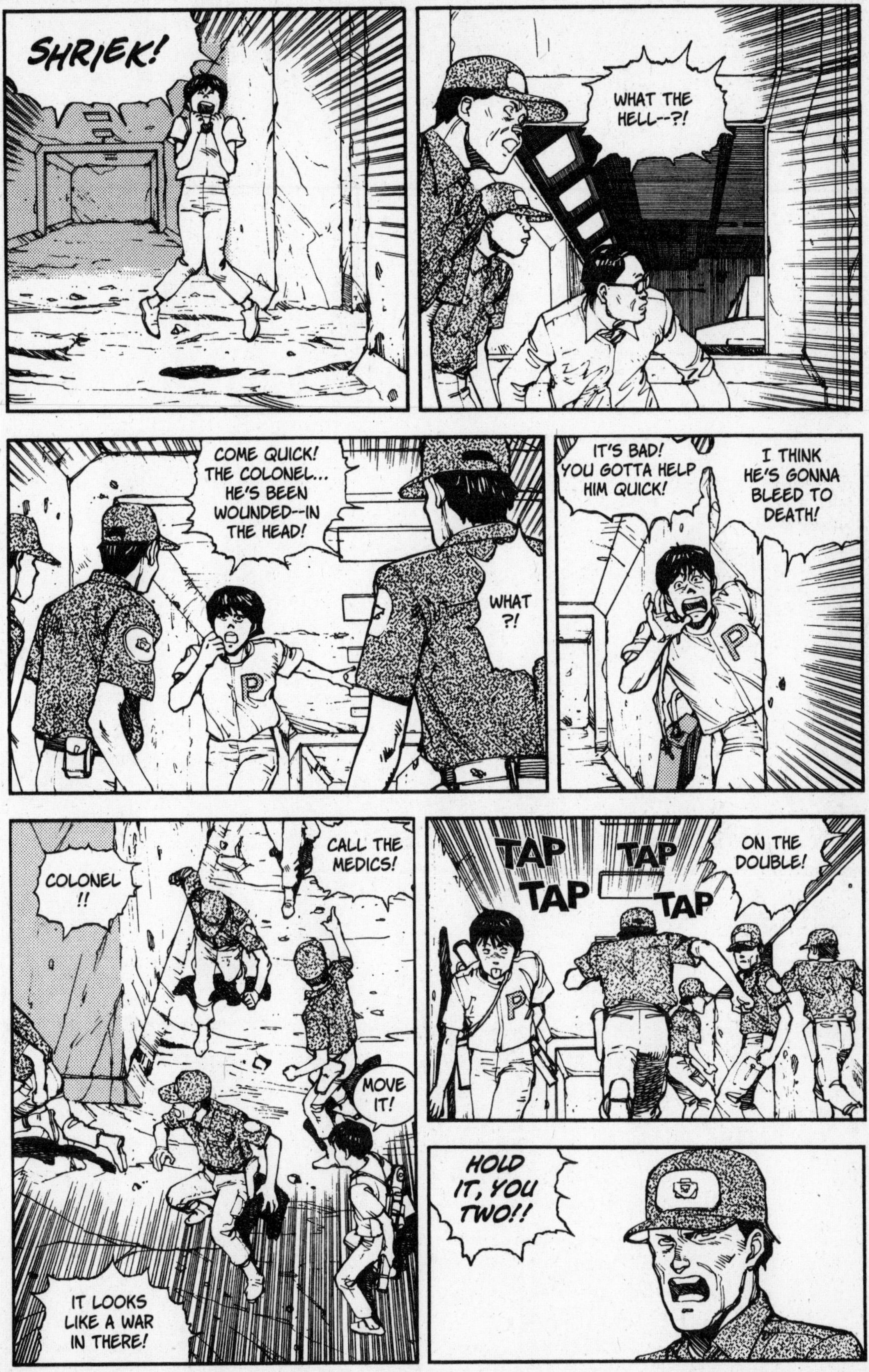
SHRIEK!
WHAT THE HELL--?!
COME QUICK! THE COLONEL... HE'S BEEN WOUNDED--IN THE HEAD!
WHAT ?!
IT'S BAD! YOU GOTTA HELP HIM QUICK!
I THINK HE'S GONNA BLEED TO DEATH!
COLONEL !!
CALL THE MEDICS!
MOVE IT!
IT LOOKS LIKE A WAR IN THERE!
TAP TAP TAP TAP
ON THE DOUBLE!
HOLD IT, YOU TWO!!

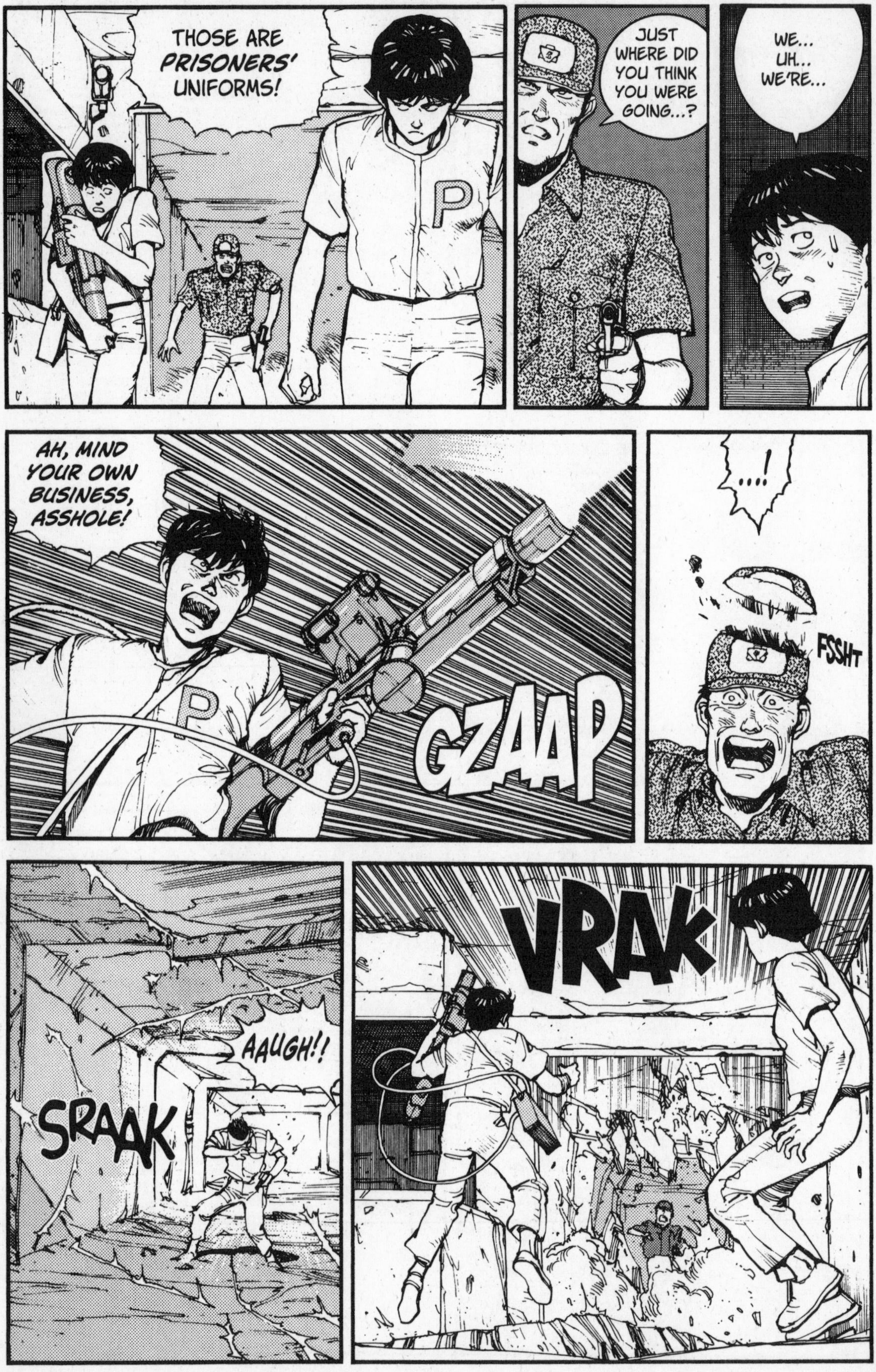

THOSE ARE PRISONERS' UNIFORMS!
JUST WHERE DID YOU THINK YOU WERE GOING...?
WE... UH... WE'RE...
AH, MIND YOUR OWN BUSINESS, ASSHOLE!
GZAAP
...!
FSSHT
AAUGH!!
SRAAK
VRAK

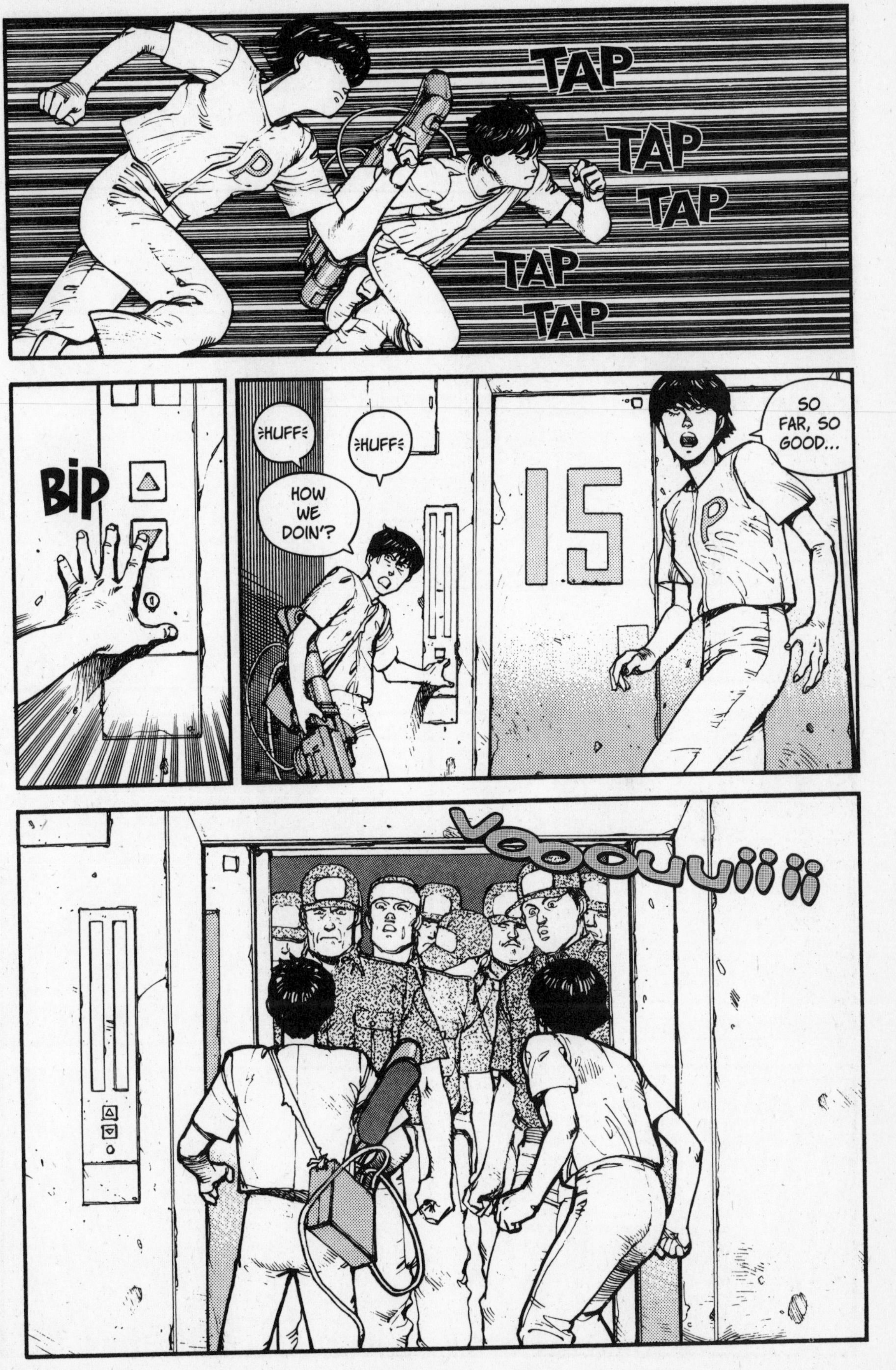
TAP
TAP
TAP
TAP
TAP
BiP
HUFF
HUFF
HOW WE DOIN'?
15
SO FAR, SO GOOD...
VOOOUUIII II

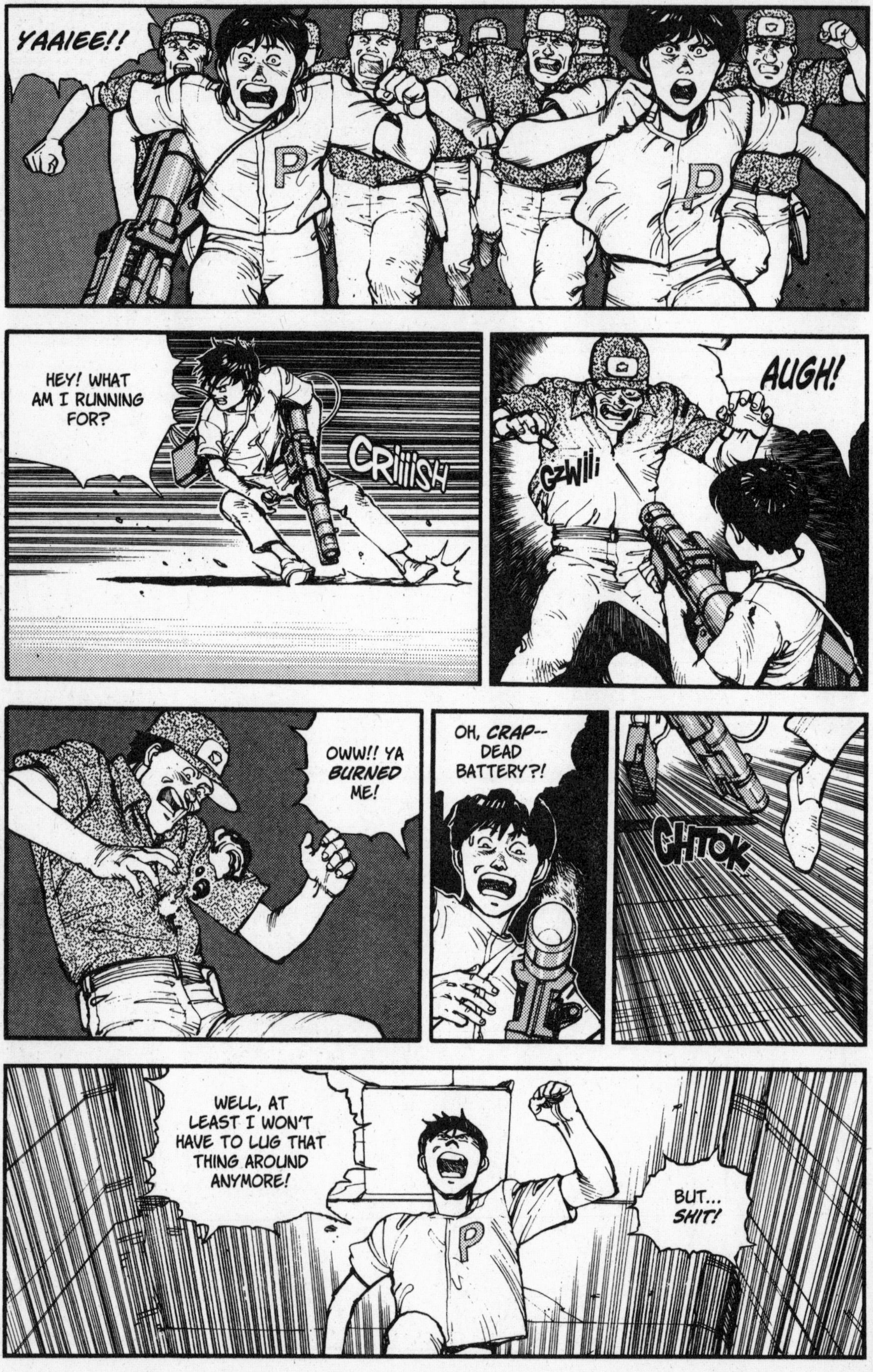
YAAIEE!!
HEY! WHAT AM I RUNNING FOR?
CRiiiiSH
AUGH!
GzWili
OWW!! YA BURNED ME!
OH, CRAP-- DEAD BATTERY?!
CHTOK
WELL, AT LEAST I WON'T HAVE TO LUG THAT THING AROUND ANYMORE!
BUT... SHIT!

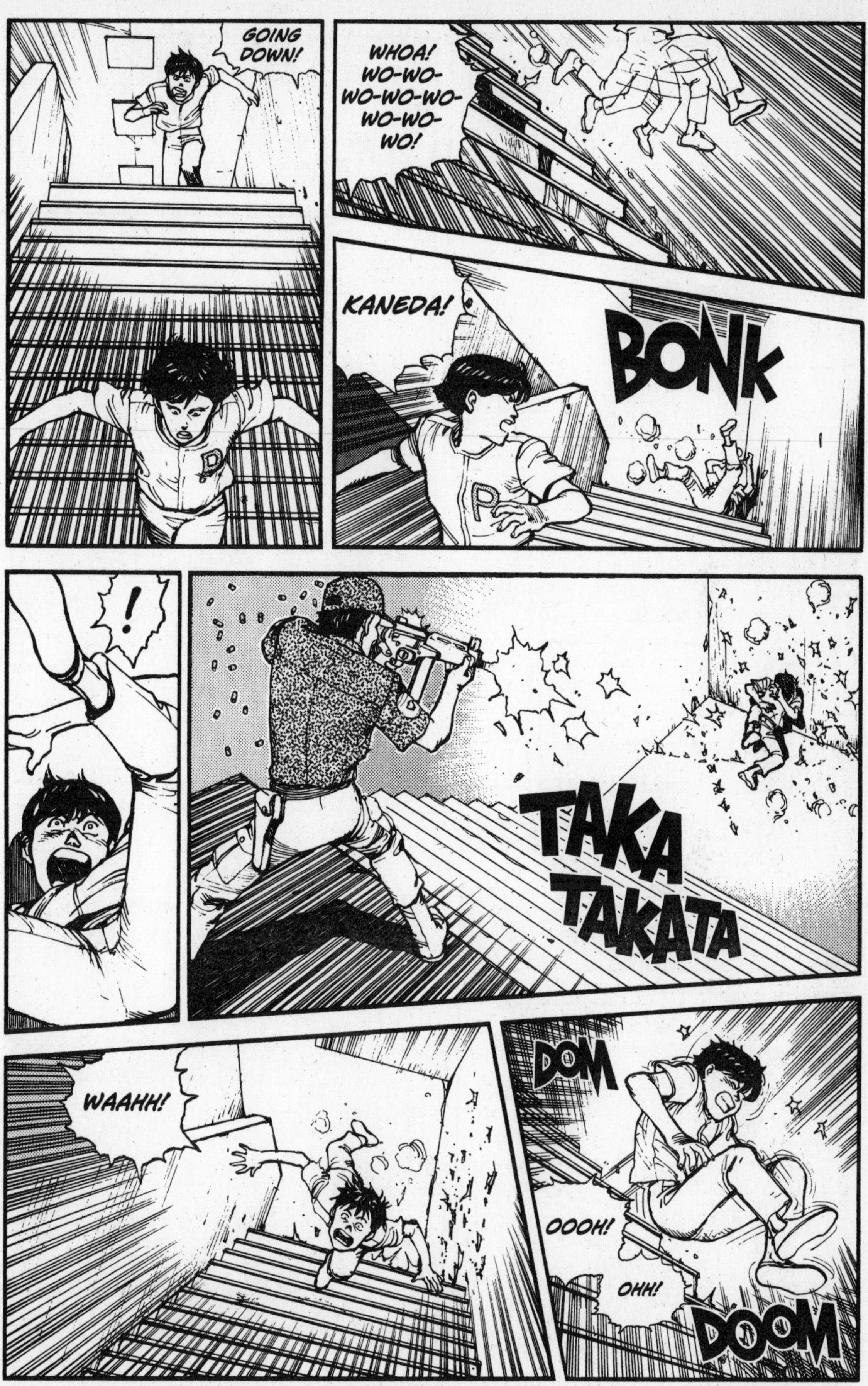
GOING DOWN!
WHOA! WO-WO-WO-WO-WO-WO-WO-WO!
KANEDA!
BONK
!
TAKA TAKATA
WAAHH!
DOM
OOOH!
OHH!
DOOM

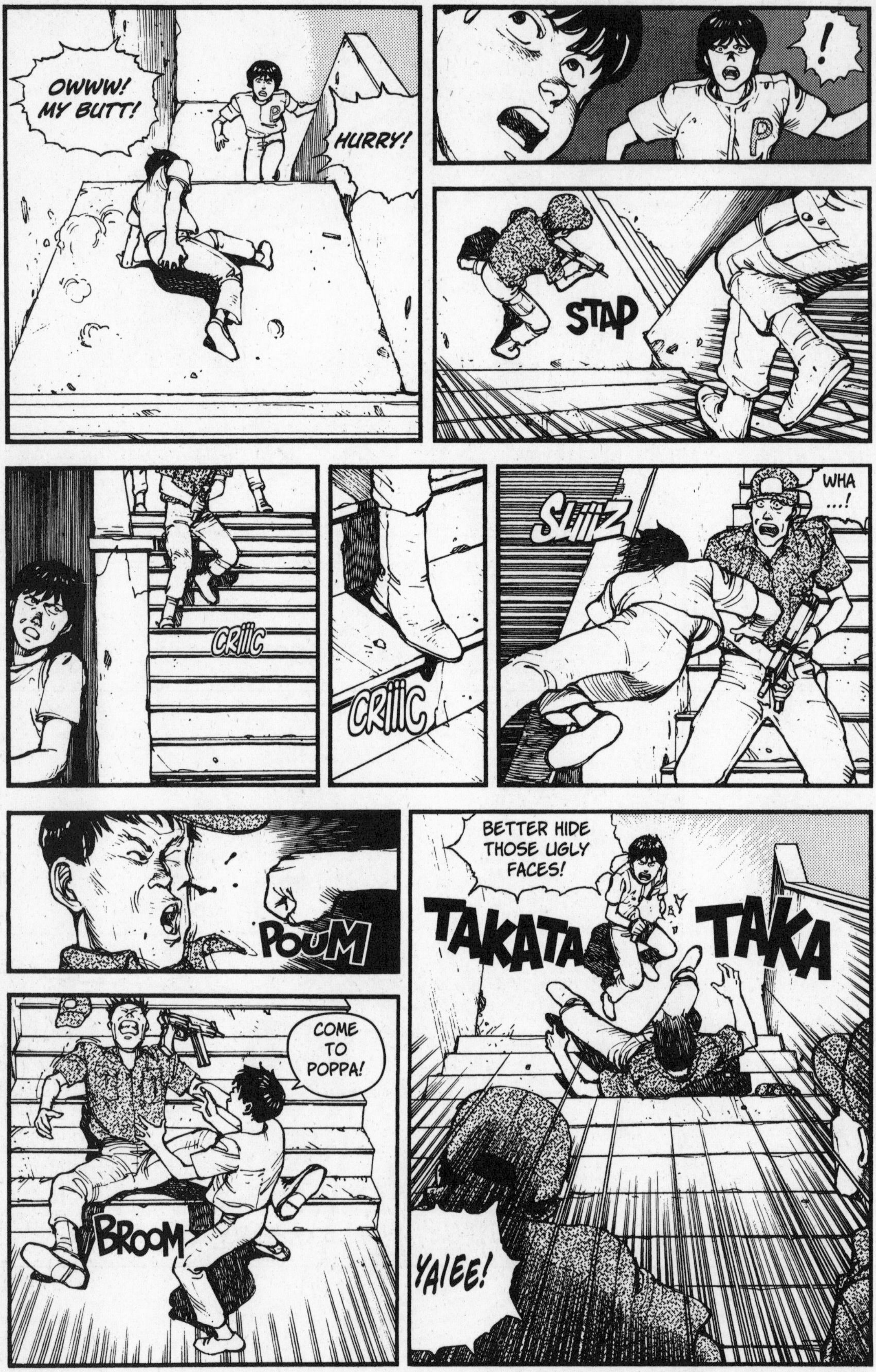
OWWW! MY BUTT!
HURRY!
!
STAP
CRIIIC
CRIIIC
SLIIIZ
WHA ...!
!
POUM
COME TO POPPA!
BROOM
BETTER HIDE THOSE UGLY FACES!
TAKATA
TAKA
YAIEE!

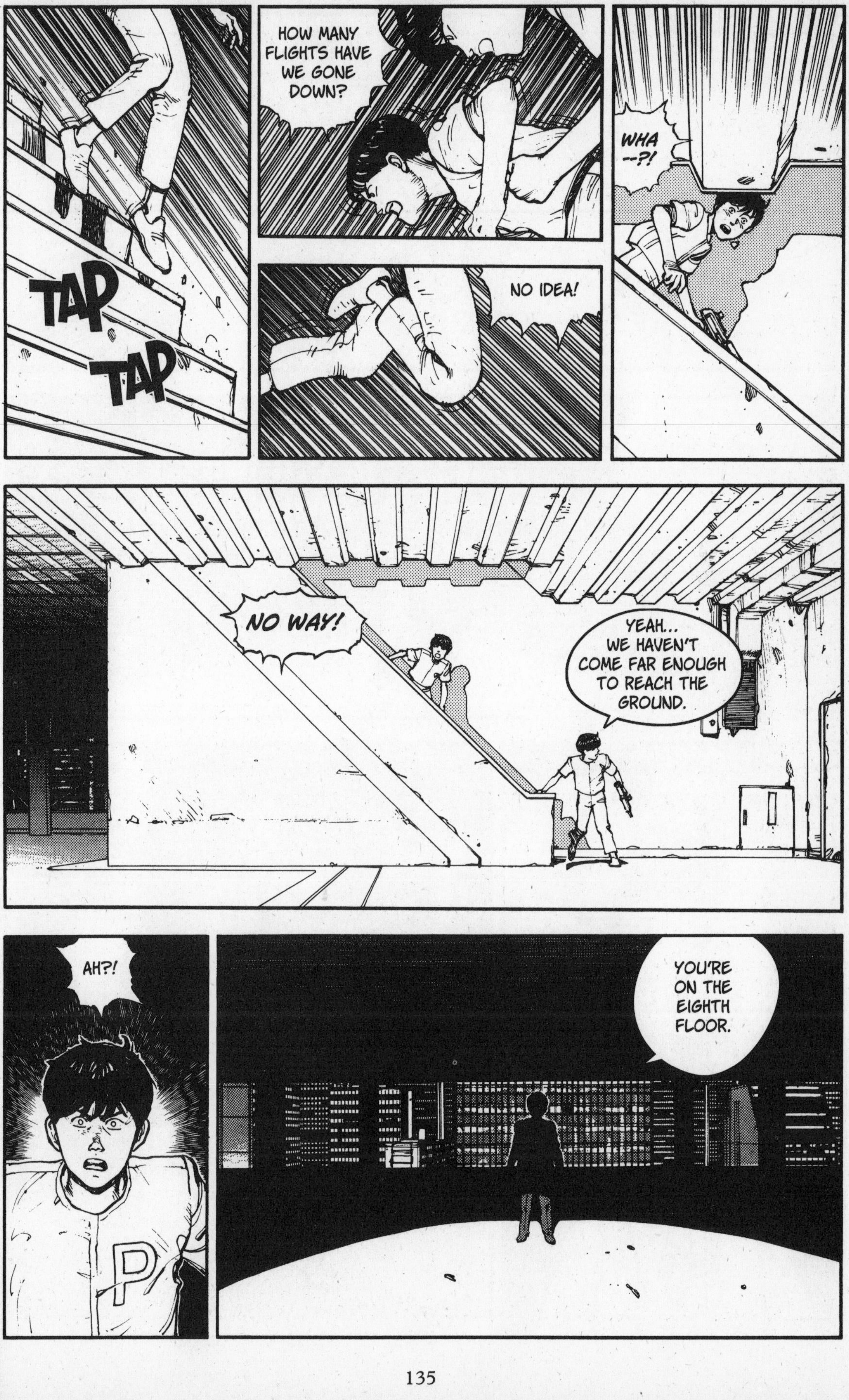
TAP
TAP
HOW MANY FLIGHTS HAVE WE GONE DOWN?
NO IDEA!
WHA --?!
NO WAY!
YEAH... WE HAVEN'T COME FAR ENOUGH TO REACH THE GROUND.
AH?!
YOU'RE ON THE EIGHTH FLOOR.

WHO THE HELL ARE YOU?!

STOP! DON'T SHOOT! WE'RE ON THE SAME SIDE!

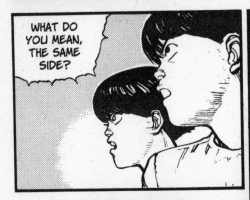

WHAT DO YOU MEAN, THE SAME SIDE?

I CAN HELP YOU GET OUT OF HERE!

WE ARE. REALLY.

I WOULDN'T LIE.

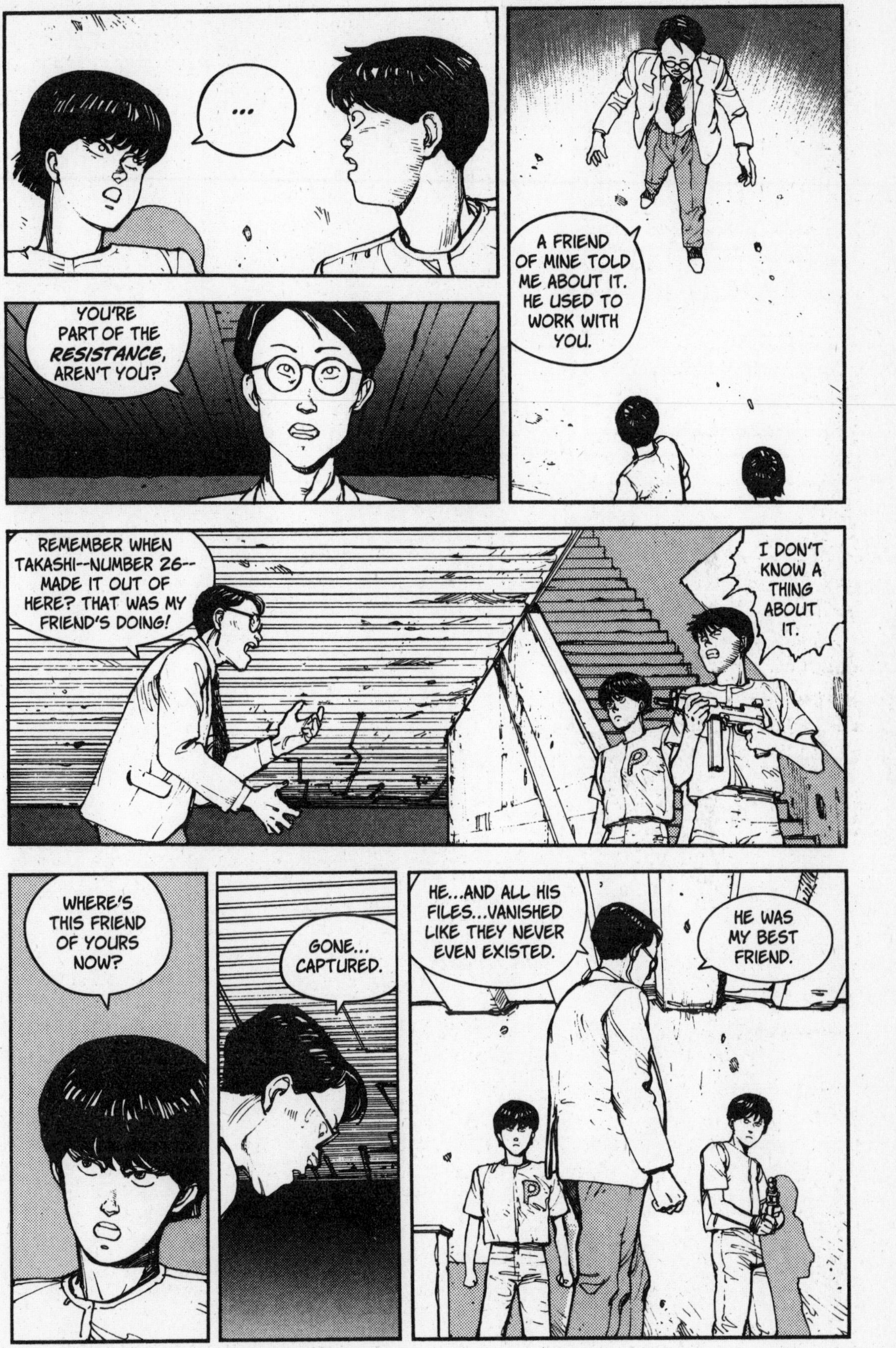
...
A FRIEND OF MINE TOLD ME ABOUT IT. HE USED TO WORK WITH YOU.
YOU'RE PART OF THE *RESISTANCE*, AREN'T YOU?
REMEMBER WHEN TAKASHI--NUMBER 26--MADE IT OUT OF HERE? THAT WAS MY FRIEND'S DOING!
I DON'T KNOW A THING ABOUT IT.
WHERE'S THIS FRIEND OF YOURS NOW?
GONE... CAPTURED.
HE...AND ALL HIS FILES...VANISHED LIKE THEY NEVER EVEN EXISTED.
HE WAS MY BEST FRIEND.

TAP

TAP
TAP

UH-OH!

NO TIME TO LOSE!

LET'S GET OUTTA HERE!

WHAT?

ARE YOU REALLY GOING TO FOLLOW HIM?

WELL, I'M NOT GONNA STICK AROUND HERE!

THIS WAY!

TOK TOK TOK TOK TOK TOK

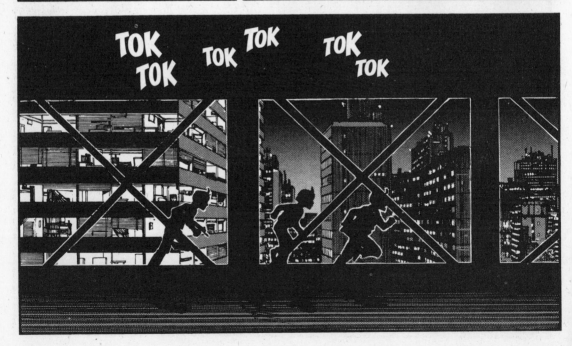

THE MAIN PANEL IS FRIED--EVERY BREAKER IS SHORTED OUT!

CLIMATE CONTROL AS WELL?

YEAH... TOTAL MELT-DOWN.

WHAT'S WITH THE EMERGENCY POWER?

IT'S ALREADY ON BUT WE GOTTA REROUTE IT!

CAN YOU BYPASS THAT BUS...?

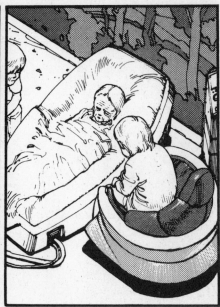

WE MUST TRY...

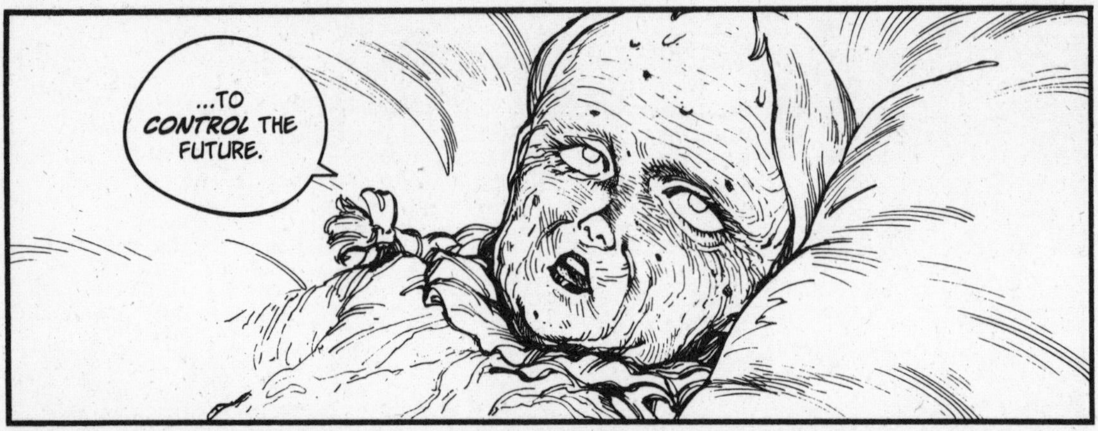
...TO CONTROL THE FUTURE.

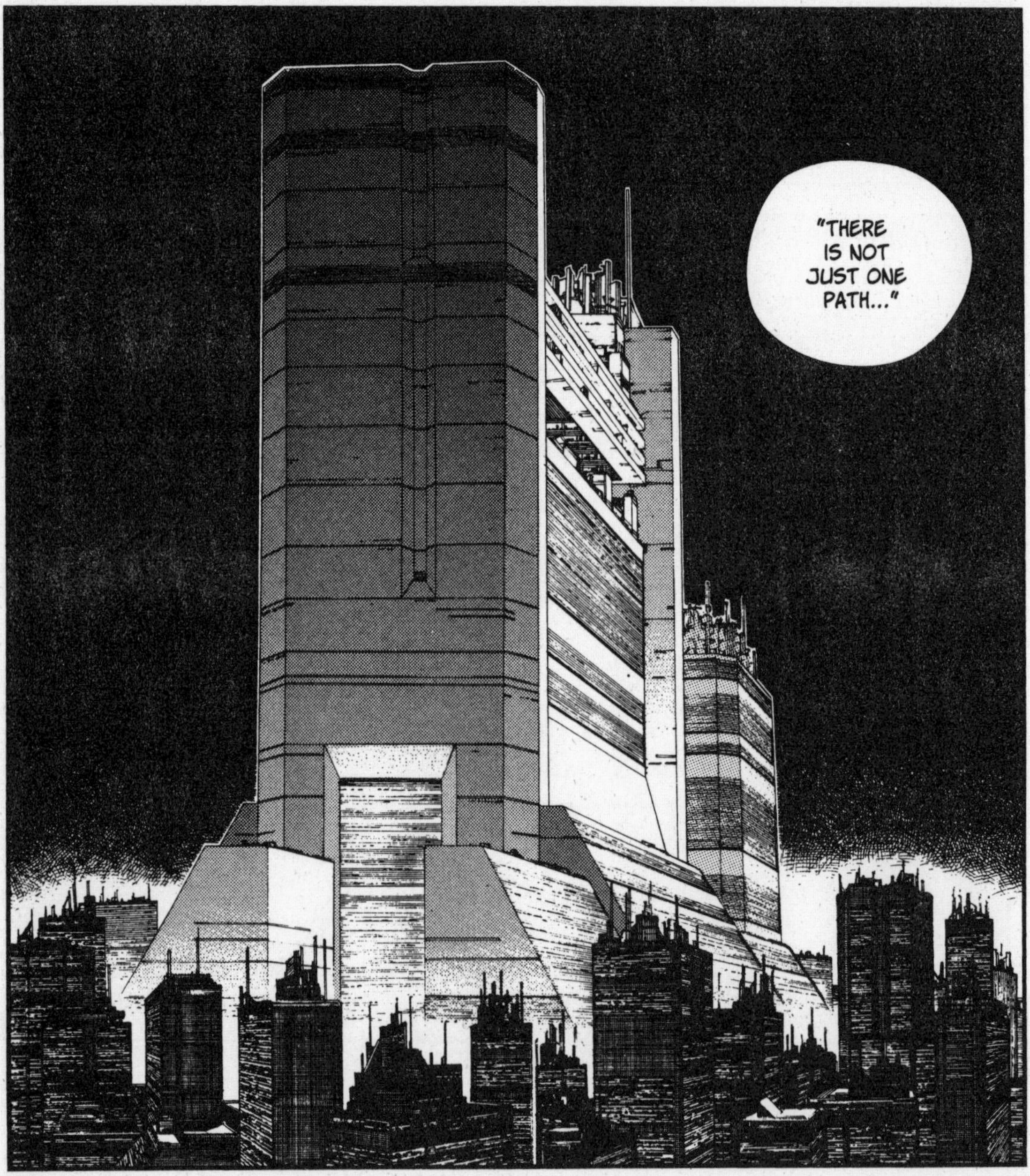
"THERE IS NOT JUST ONE PATH..."

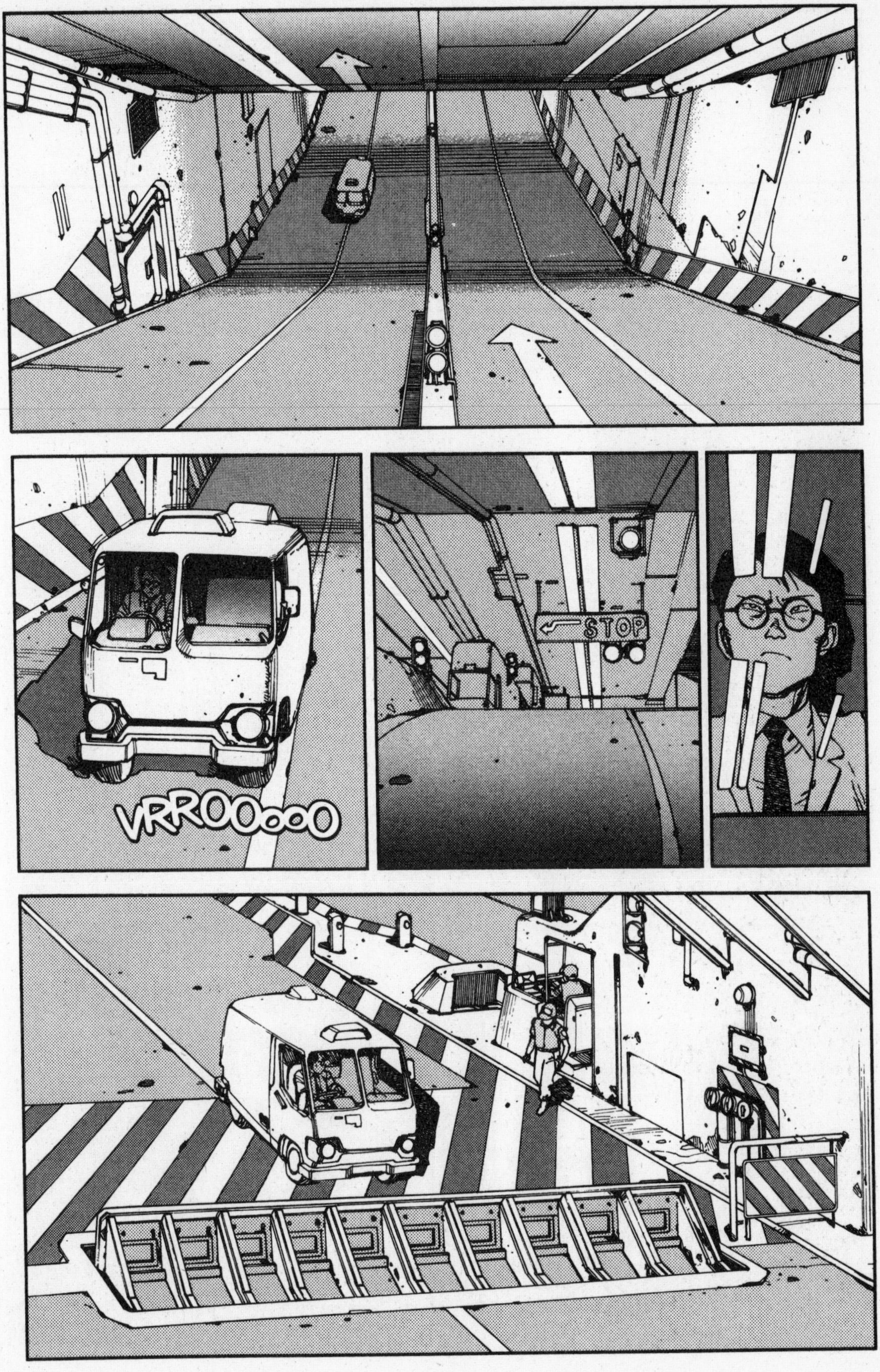
VRROOooO
STOP

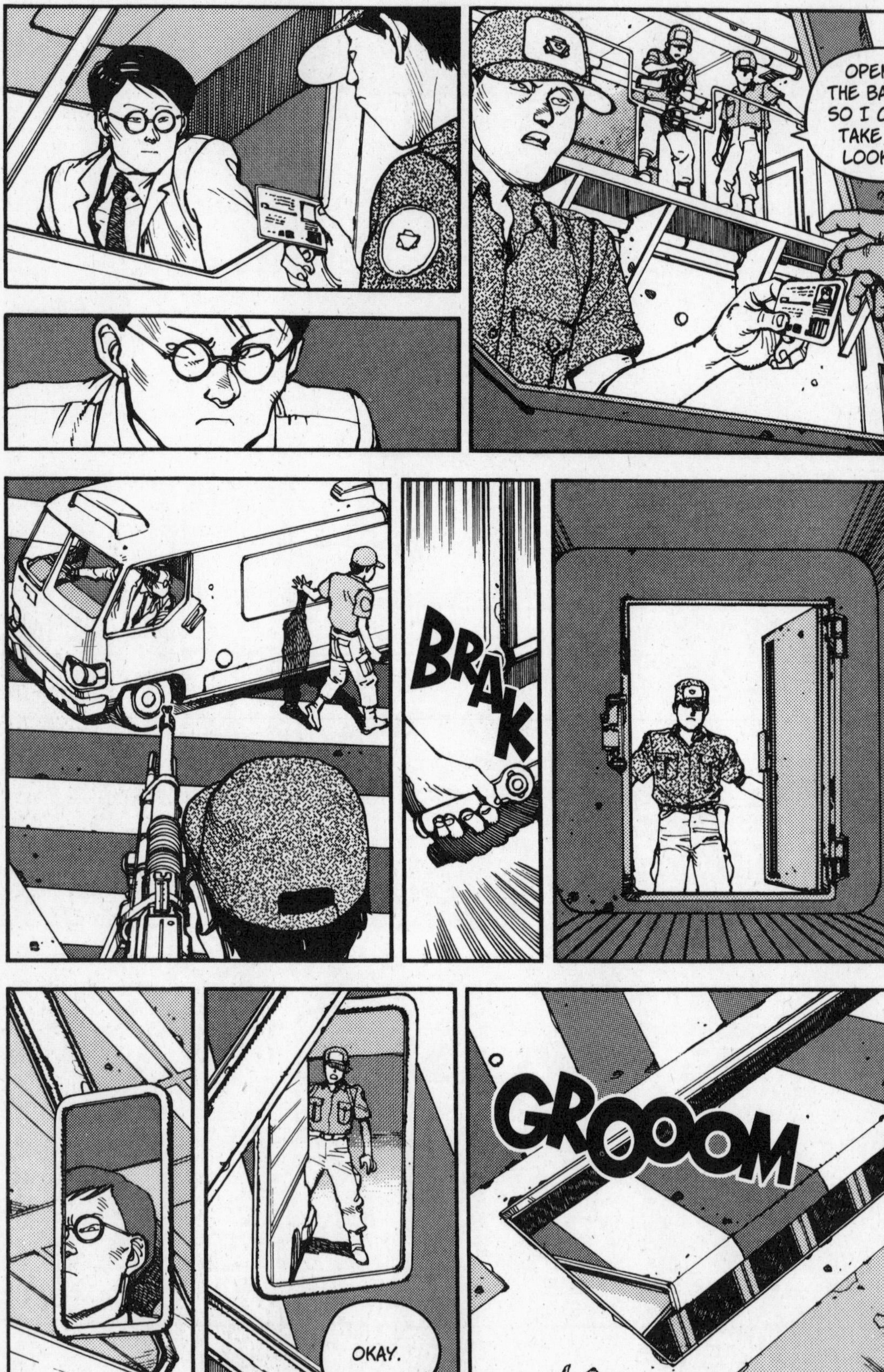
OPEN THE BACK SO I CAN TAKE A LOOK.
BRAAK
OKAY.
GROOOM

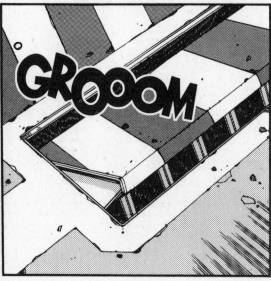

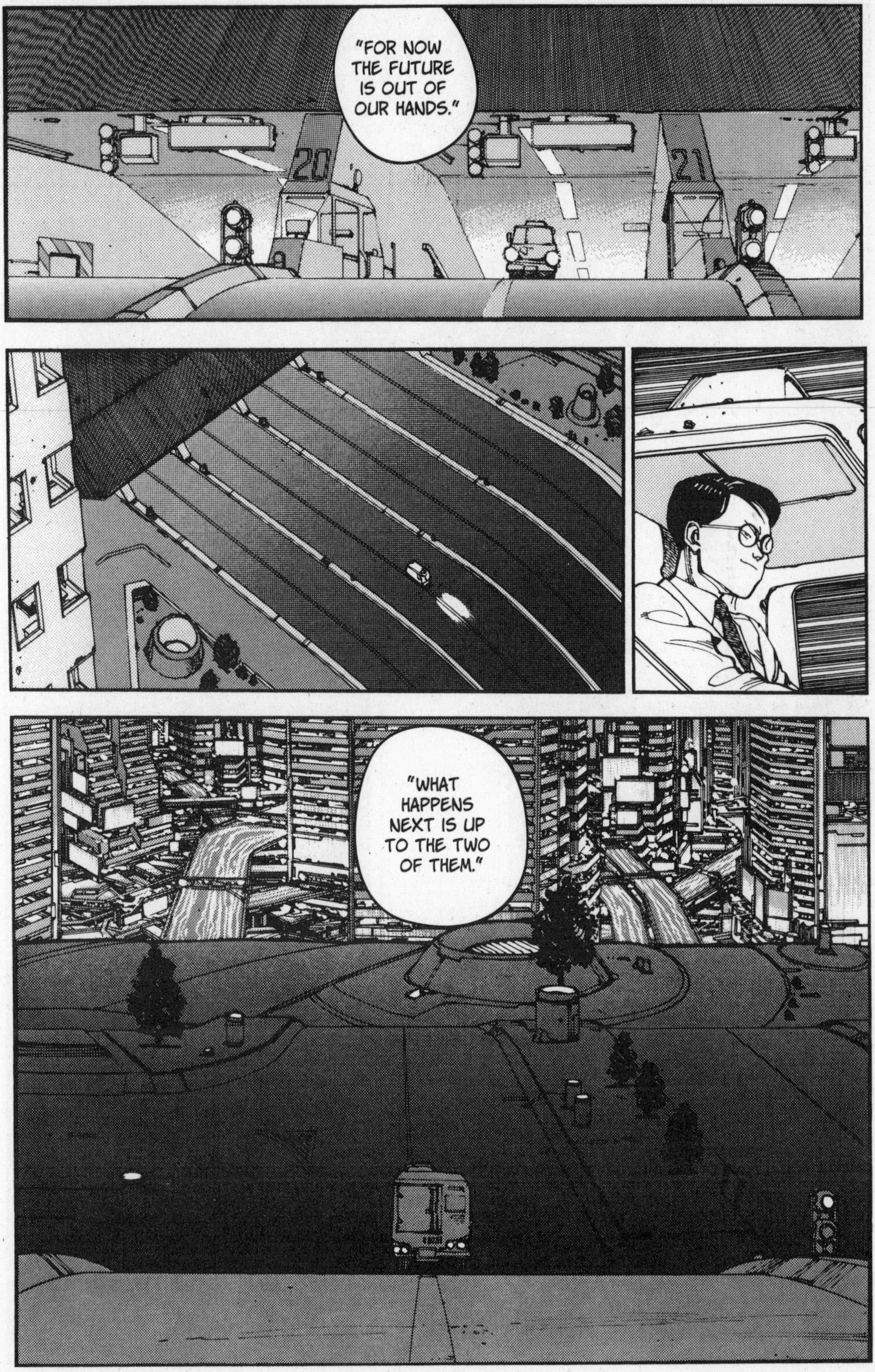
"FOR NOW THE FUTURE IS OUT OF OUR HANDS."
"WHAT HAPPENS NEXT IS UP TO THE TWO OF THEM."

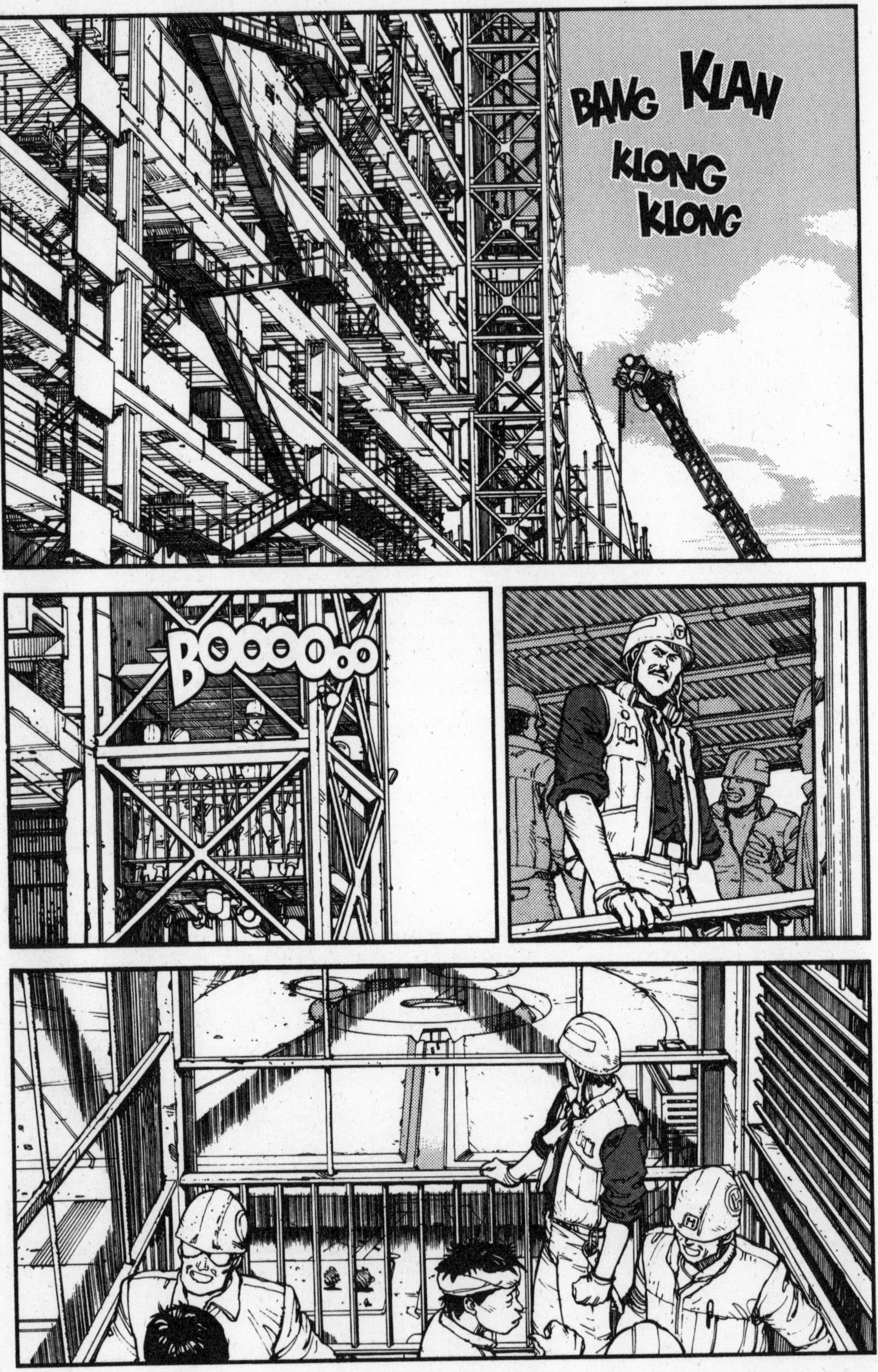
BANG KLAN
KLONG
KLONG
BOOOOO...

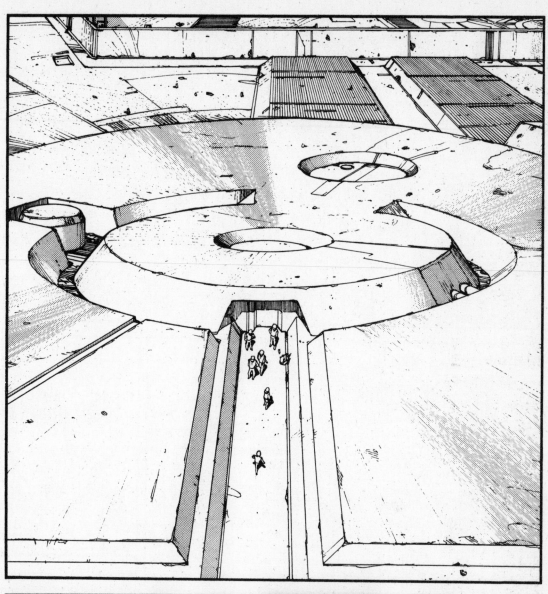

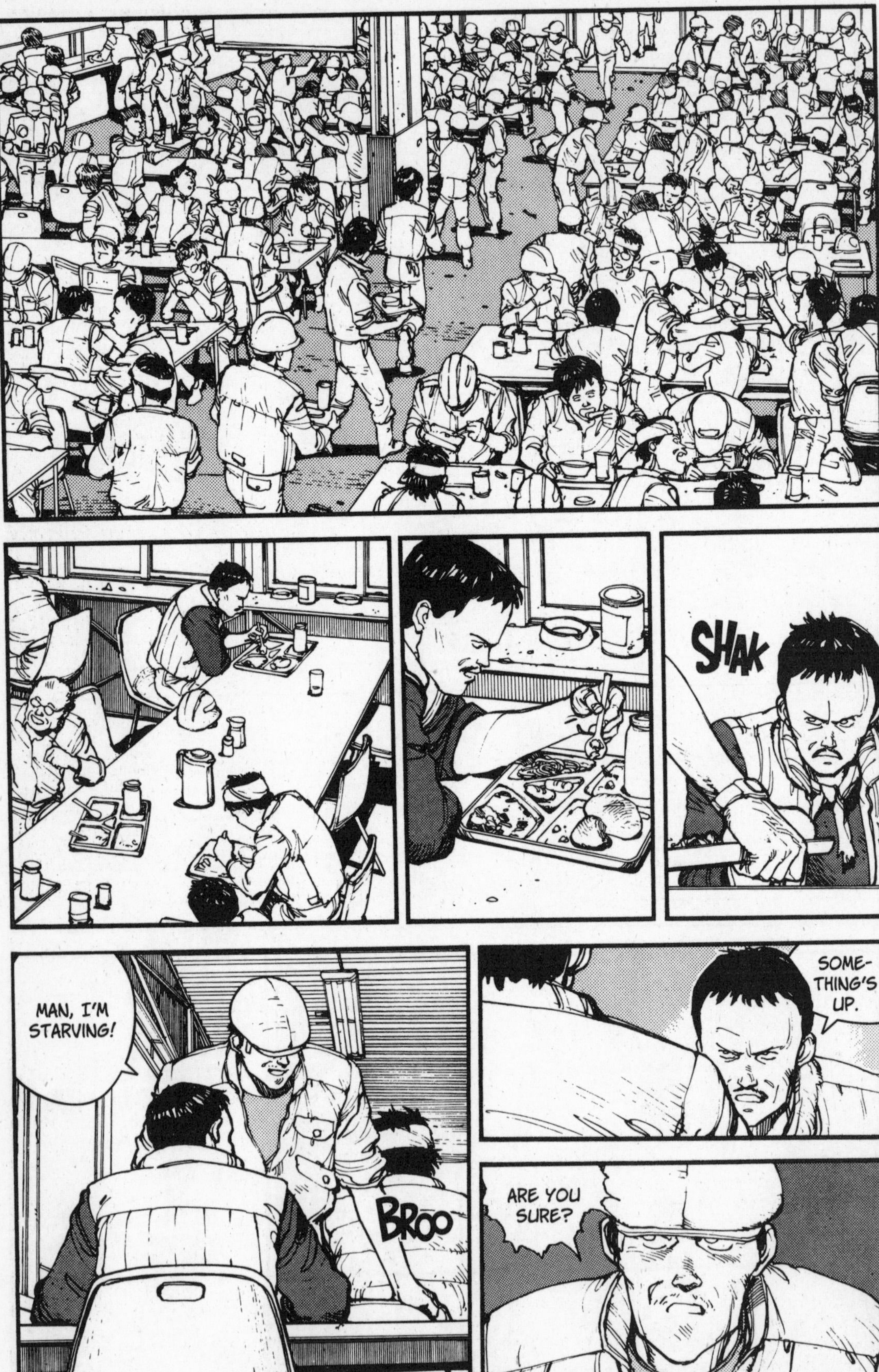
SHAK
MAN, I'M STARVING!
BROO
SOME-THING'S UP.
ARE YOU SURE?

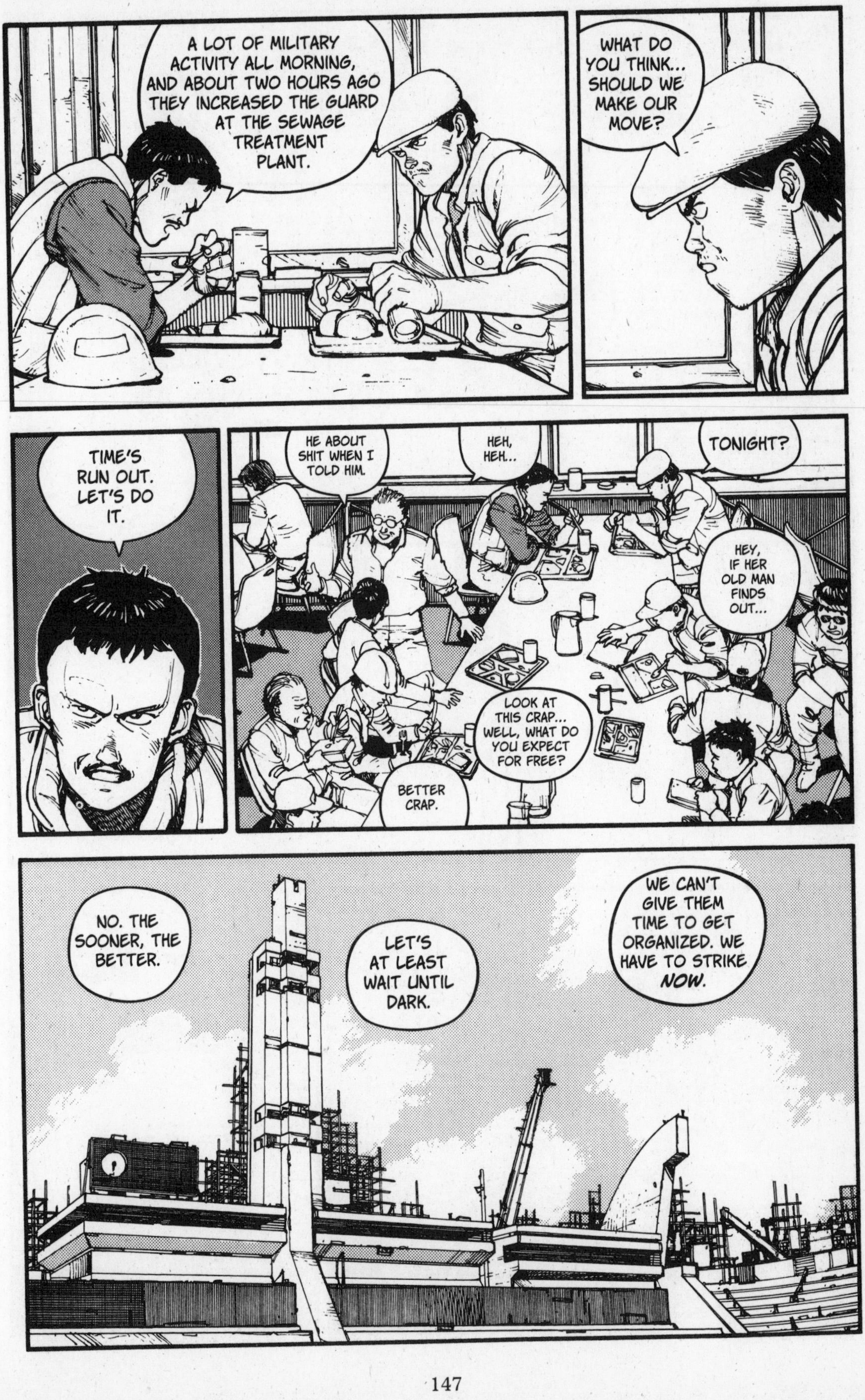
A LOT OF MILITARY ACTIVITY ALL MORNING, AND ABOUT TWO HOURS AGO THEY INCREASED THE GUARD AT THE SEWAGE TREATMENT PLANT.
WHAT DO YOU THINK... SHOULD WE MAKE OUR MOVE?
TIME'S RUN OUT. LET'S DO IT.
HE ABOUT SHIT WHEN I TOLD HIM.
HEH, HEH...
TONIGHT?
HEY, IF HER OLD MAN FINDS OUT...
LOOK AT THIS CRAP... WELL, WHAT DO YOU EXPECT FOR FREE?
BETTER CRAP.
NO. THE SOONER, THE BETTER.
LET'S AT LEAST WAIT UNTIL DARK.
WE CAN'T GIVE THEM TIME TO GET ORGANIZED. WE HAVE TO STRIKE *NOW*.

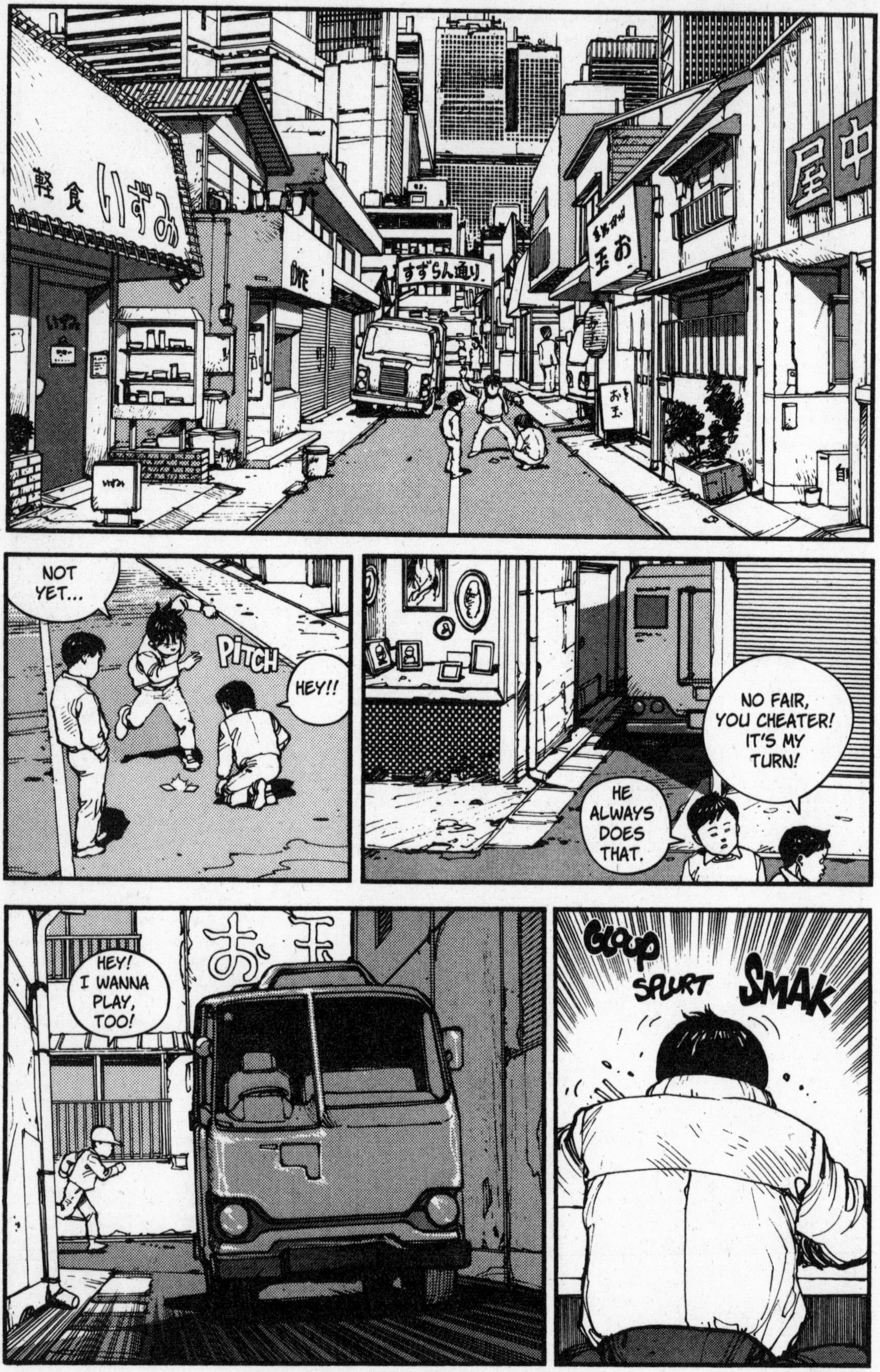
軽食 いずみ
すずらん通り
NOT YET...
PITCH
HEY!!
NO FAIR, YOU CHEATER! IT'S MY TURN!
HE ALWAYS DOES THAT.
HEY! I WANNA PLAY, TOO!
GLOOP
SPLURT
SMAK

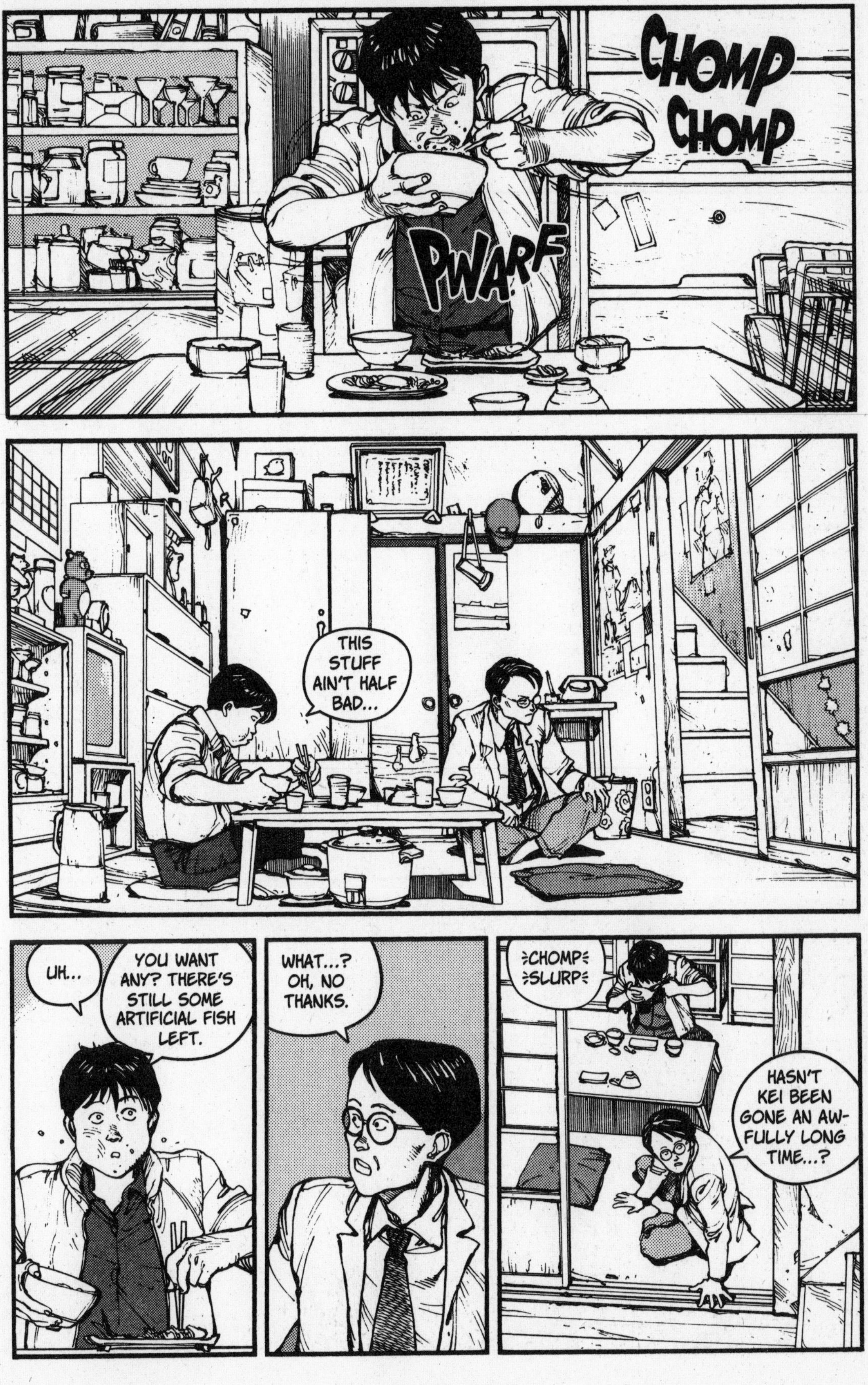
CHOMP CHOMP
PWARF
THIS STUFF AIN'T HALF BAD...
UH...
YOU WANT ANY? THERE'S STILL SOME ARTIFICIAL FISH LEFT.
WHAT...? OH, NO THANKS.
CHOMP SLURP
HASN'T KEI BEEN GONE AN AW-FULLY LONG TIME...?

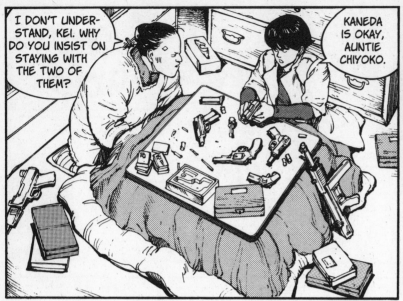

I DON'T UNDER-STAND, KEI. WHY DO YOU INSIST ON STAYING WITH THE TWO OF THEM?

KANEDA IS OKAY, AUNTIE CHIYOKO.

AS FOR THE GUY WITH THE GLASSES... I DON'T KNOW.

MMM.

THE PLAN TO FREE NUMBER 26 WAS RYUSAKU'S OPERATION...AND THIS MAN CLAIMS HE WAS IN ON THAT.

SO IF RYU COULD MEET HIM, WE'D FIND OUT FOR SURE.

IF I LEAVE HIM BEHIND AND HE TURNS OUT TO BE FAKING IT... YOU DON'T NEED THE HASSLE.

AND IF HE IS A PLANT...

...I BROUGHT HIM HERE...

...SO I'LL BE THE ONE WHO TAKES CARE OF IT.

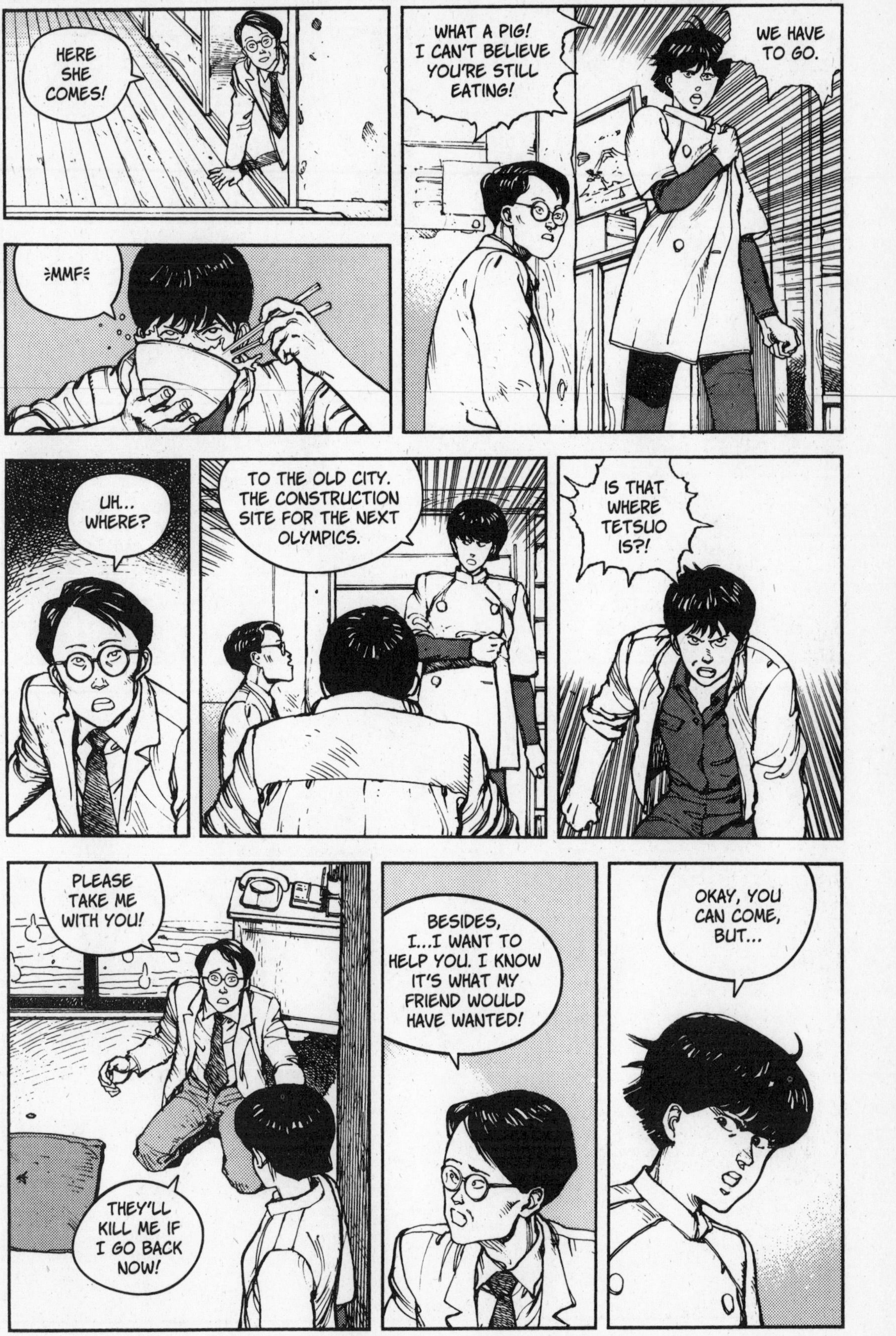
HERE SHE COMES!
WHAT A PIG! I CAN'T BELIEVE YOU'RE STILL EATING!
WE HAVE TO GO.
≶MMF≶
UH... WHERE?
TO THE OLD CITY. THE CONSTRUCTION SITE FOR THE NEXT OLYMPICS.
IS THAT WHERE TETSUO IS?!
PLEASE TAKE ME WITH YOU!
THEY'LL KILL ME IF I GO BACK NOW!
BESIDES, I...I WANT TO HELP YOU. I KNOW IT'S WHAT MY FRIEND WOULD HAVE WANTED!
OKAY, YOU CAN COME, BUT...

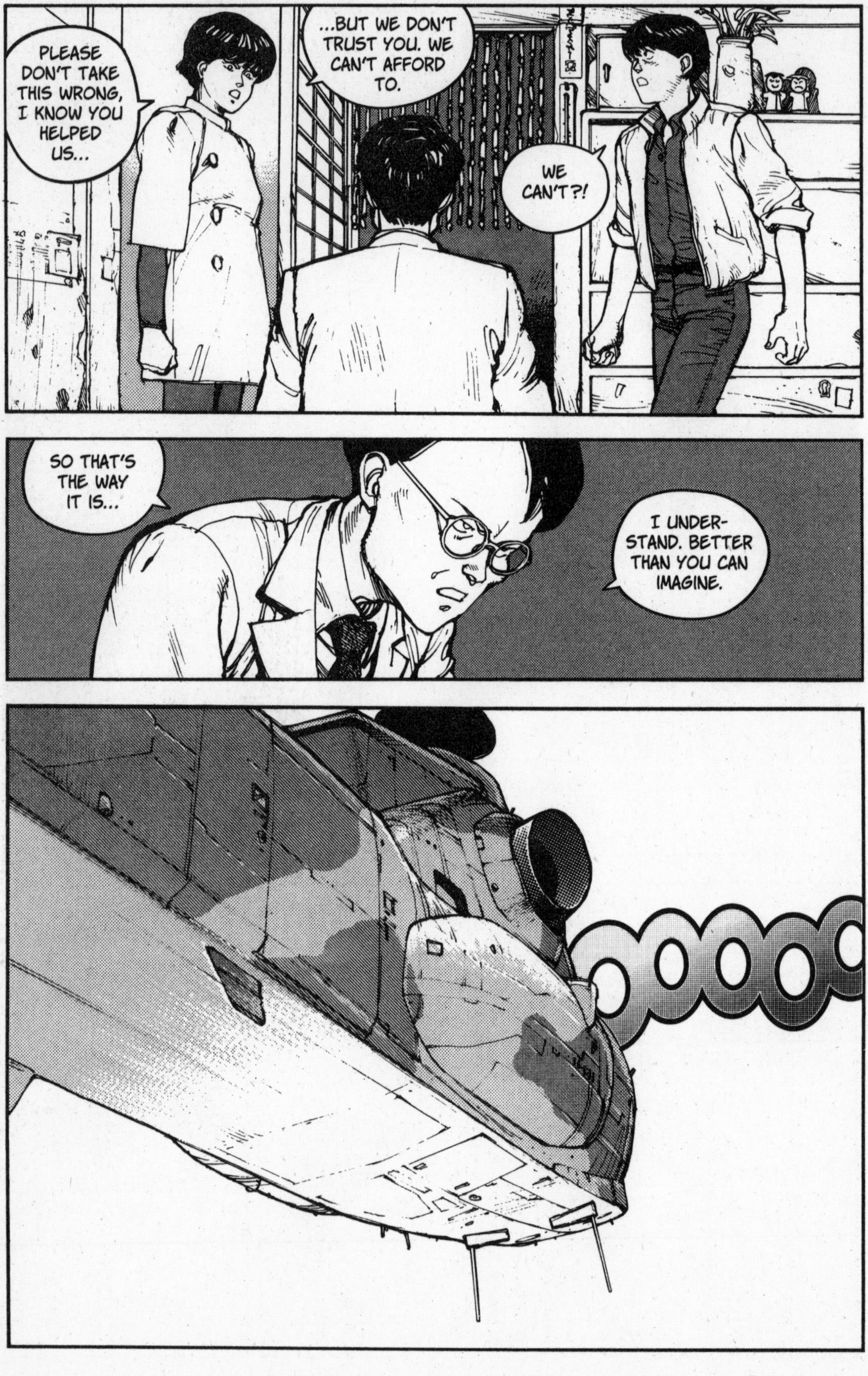
PLEASE DON'T TAKE THIS WRONG, I KNOW YOU HELPED US...
...BUT WE DON'T TRUST YOU. WE CAN'T AFFORD TO.
WE CAN'T?!
SO THAT'S THE WAY IT IS...
I UNDER-STAND. BETTER THAN YOU CAN IMAGINE.

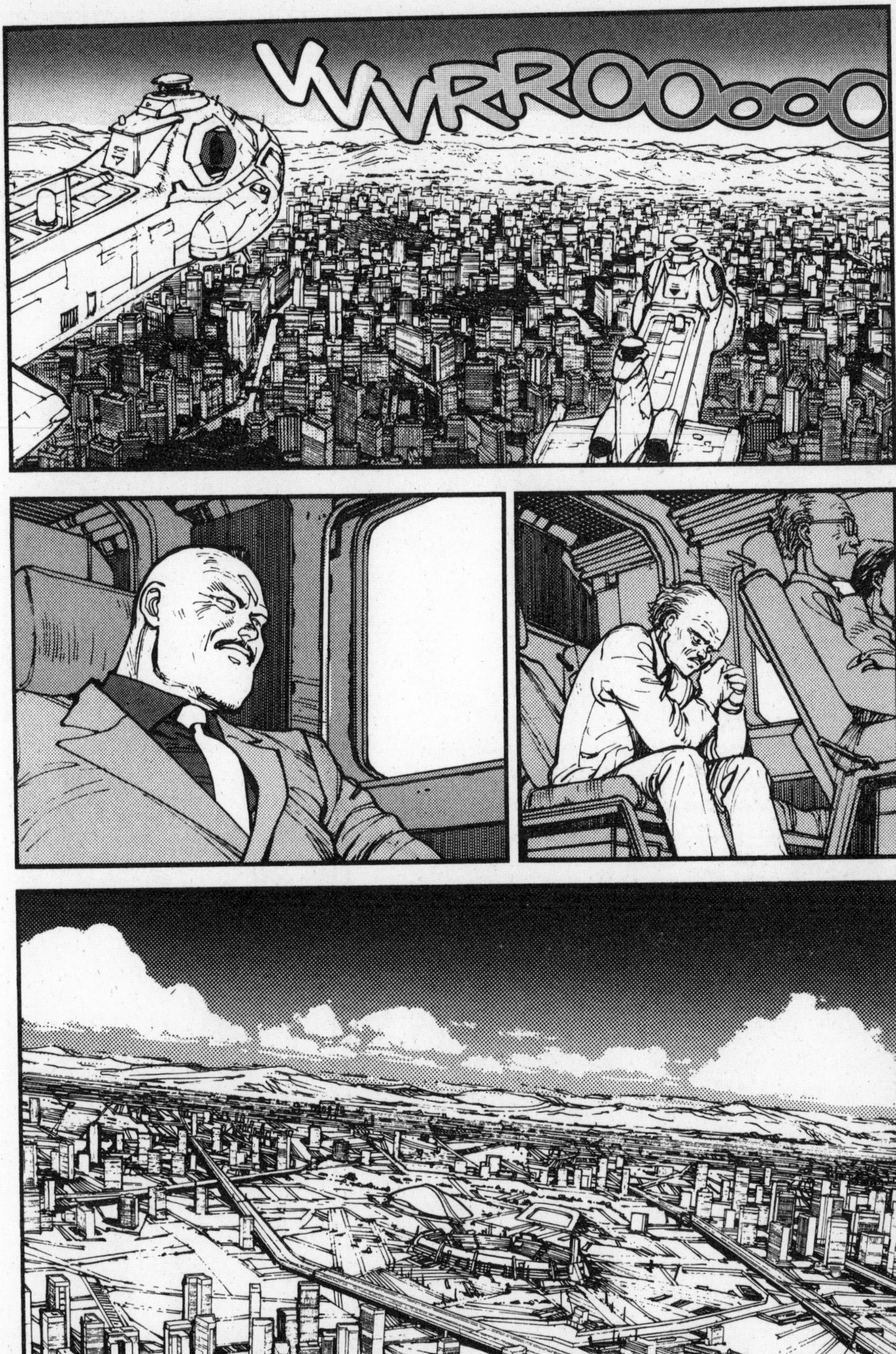
WVRROOooo

HMM...

WHO GOES THERE?

WE'RE PART OF THE NEW SUPPORT STAFF.

WE JUST GOT REASSIGNED HERE.

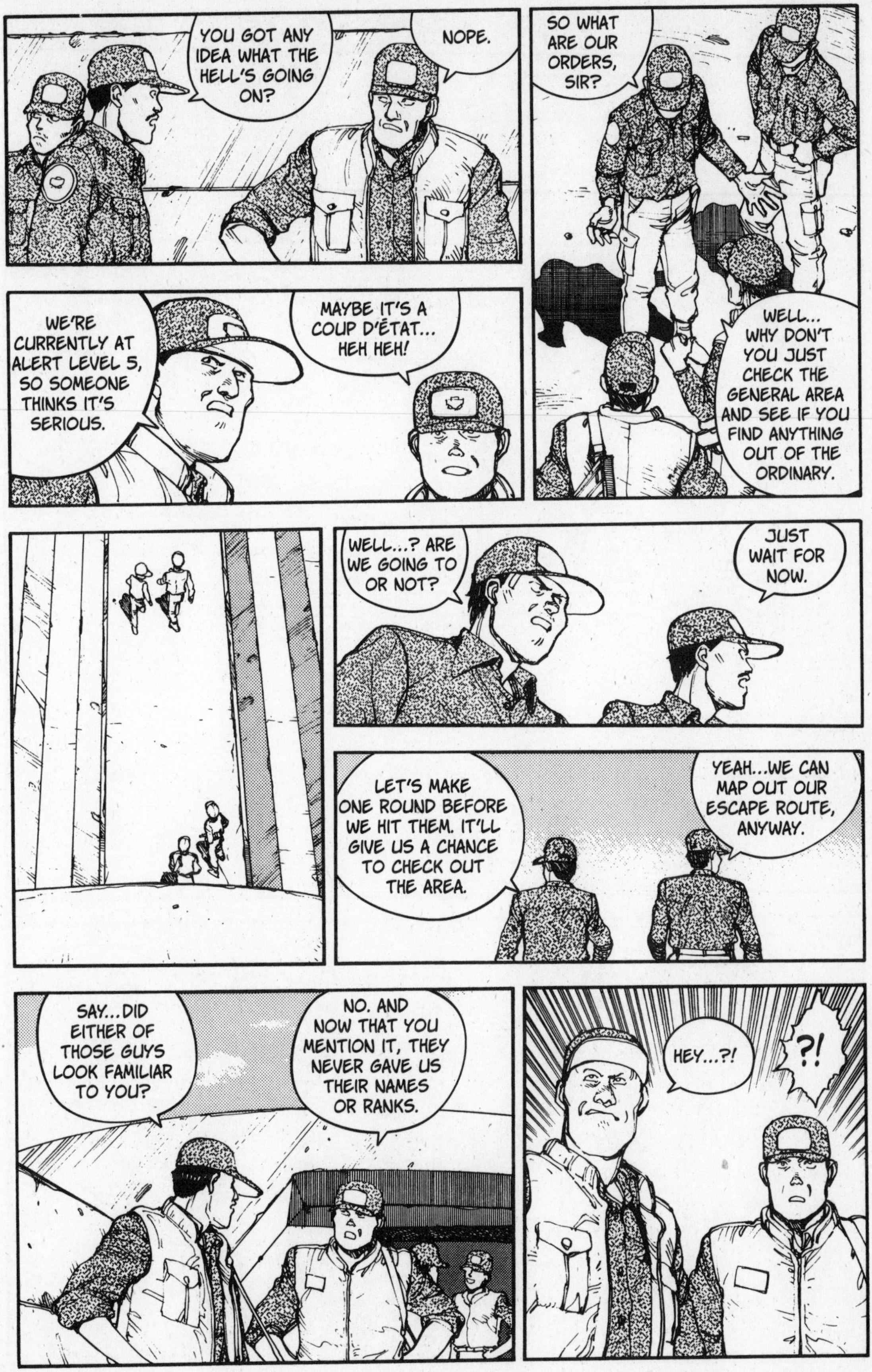
YOU GOT ANY IDEA WHAT THE HELL'S GOING ON?
NOPE.
SO WHAT ARE OUR ORDERS, SIR?
WE'RE CURRENTLY AT ALERT LEVEL 5, SO SOMEONE THINKS IT'S SERIOUS.
MAYBE IT'S A COUP D'ÉTAT... HEH HEH!
WELL... WHY DON'T YOU JUST CHECK THE GENERAL AREA AND SEE IF YOU FIND ANYTHING OUT OF THE ORDINARY.
WELL...? ARE WE GOING TO OR NOT?
JUST WAIT FOR NOW.
LET'S MAKE ONE ROUND BEFORE WE HIT THEM. IT'LL GIVE US A CHANCE TO CHECK OUT THE AREA.
YEAH...WE CAN MAP OUT OUR ESCAPE ROUTE, ANYWAY.
SAY...DID EITHER OF THOSE GUYS LOOK FAMILIAR TO YOU?
NO. AND NOW THAT YOU MENTION IT, THEY NEVER GAVE US THEIR NAMES OR RANKS.
HEY...?!
?!

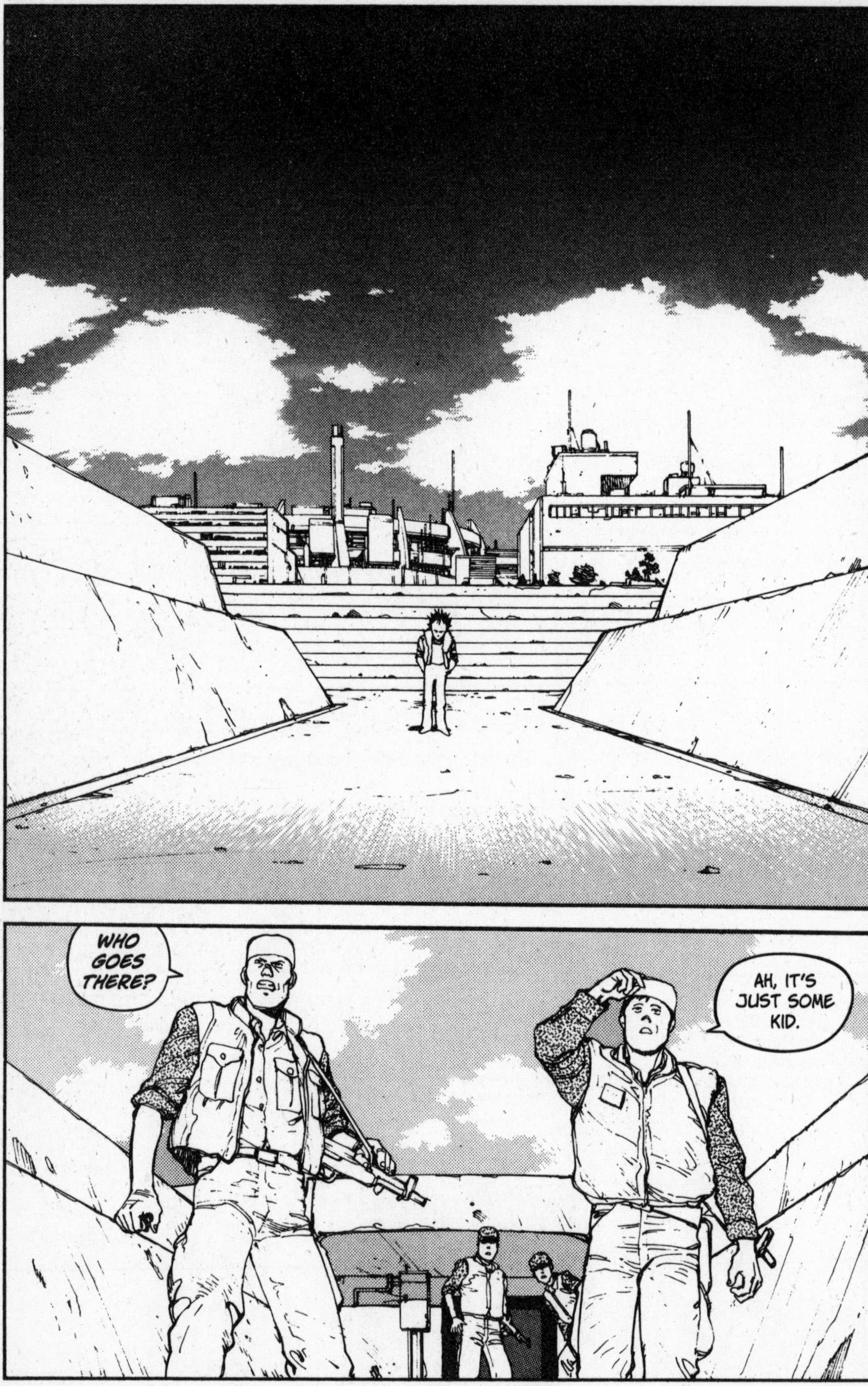
WHO GOES THERE?
AH, IT'S JUST SOME KID.

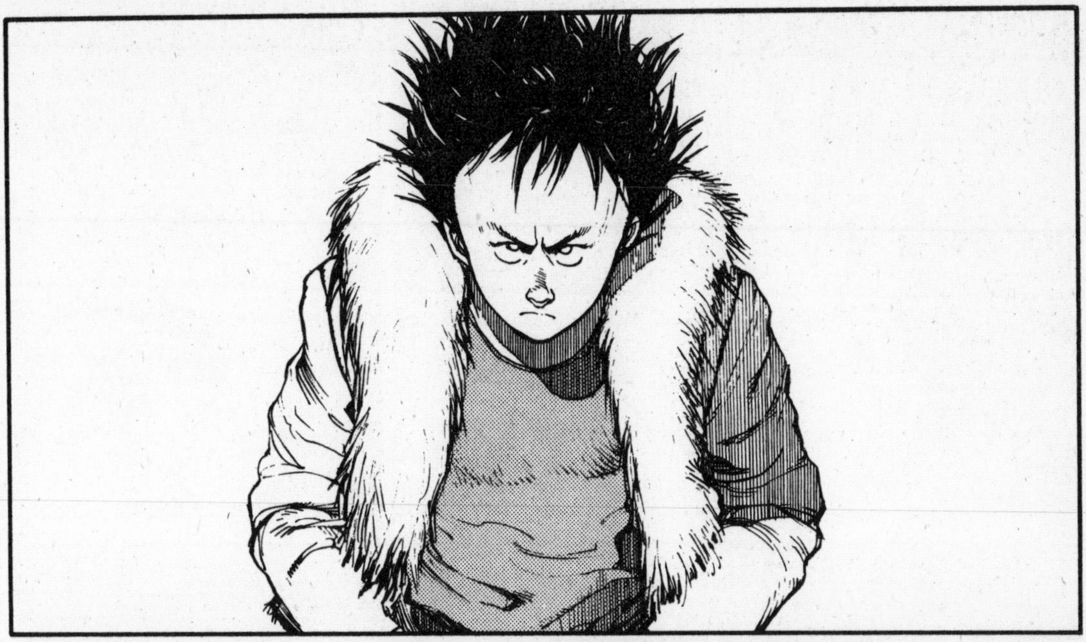

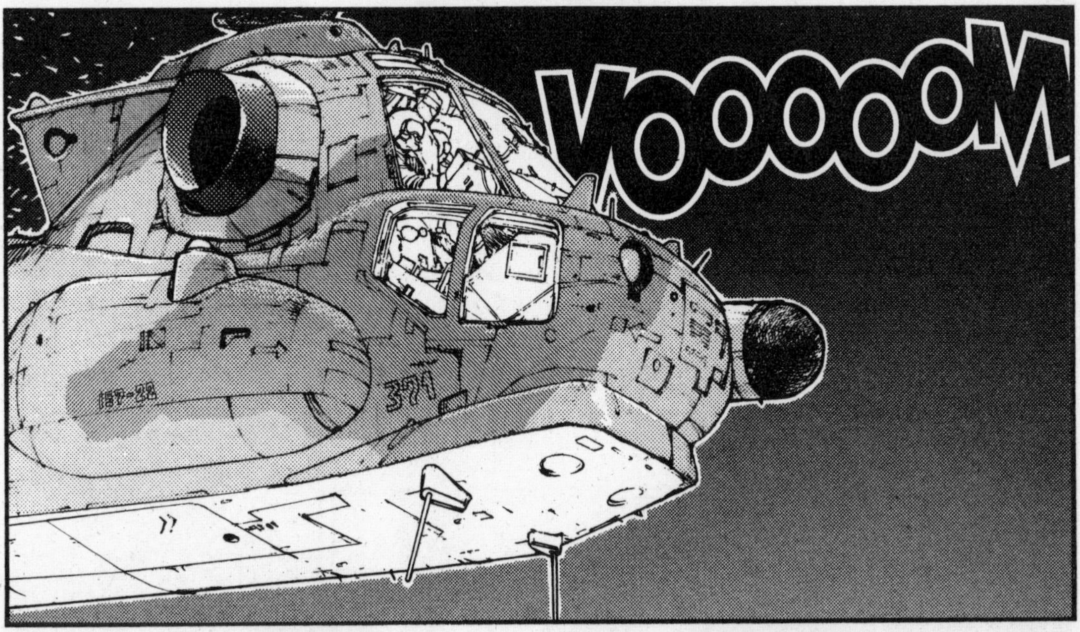
VOOOOOM

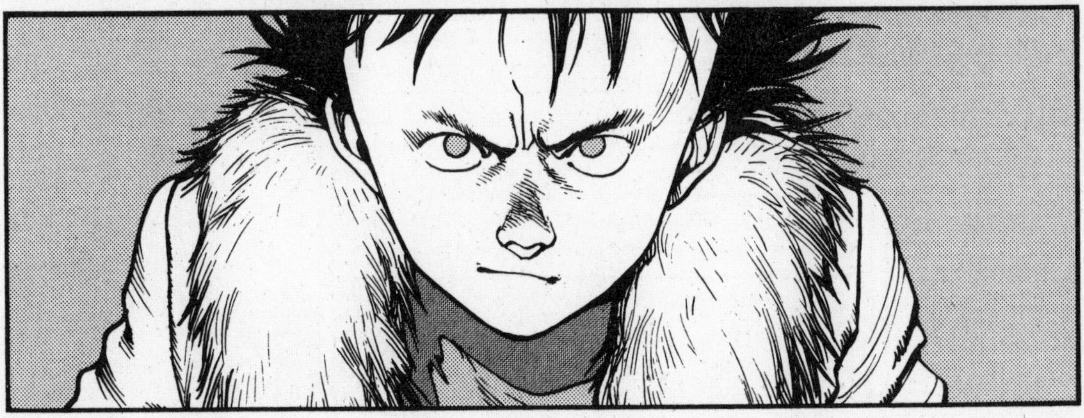

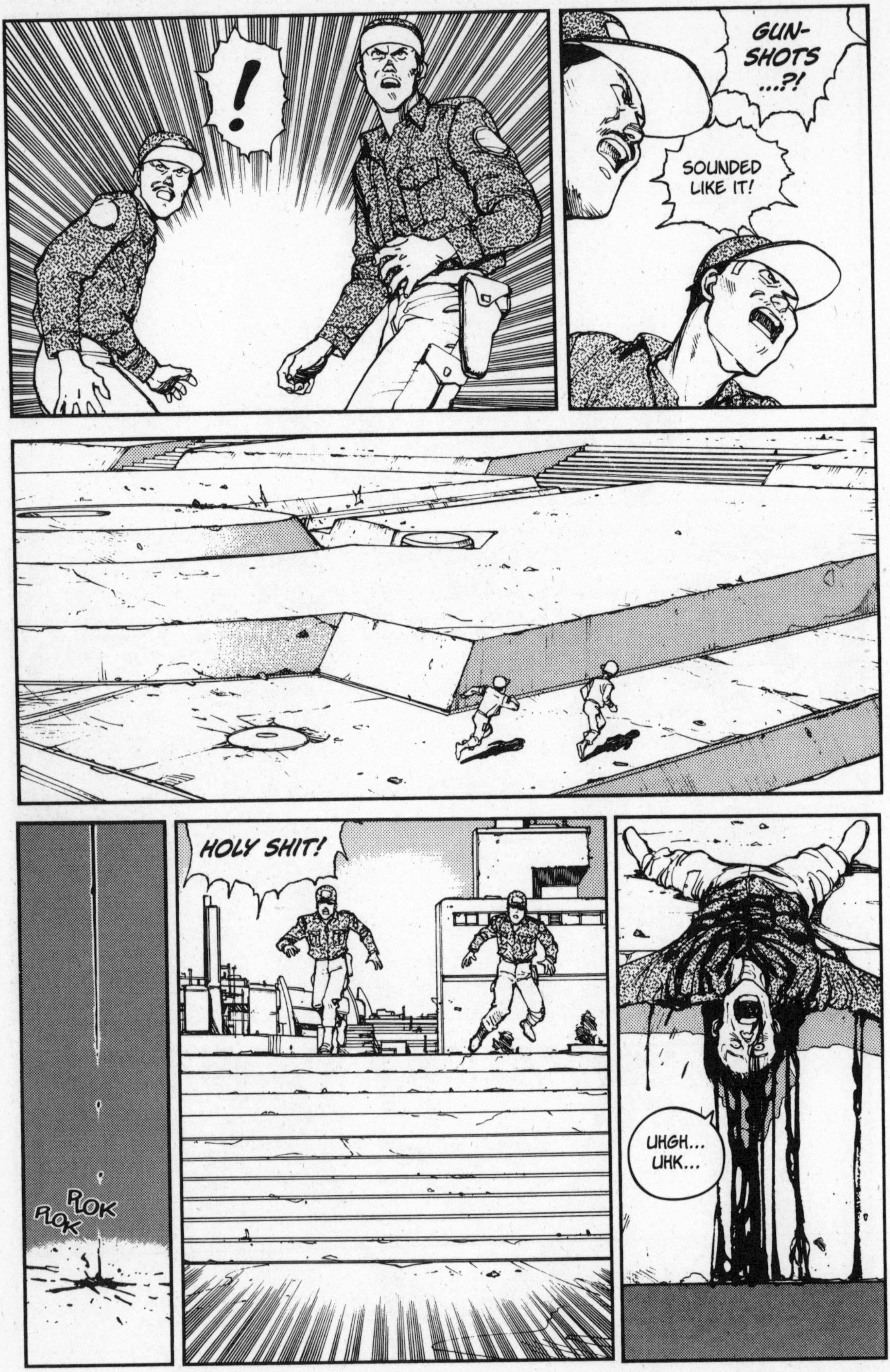
!
GUN-SHOTS ...?!
SOUNDED LIKE IT!
PLOK PLOK
HOLY SHIT!
UHGH... UHK...

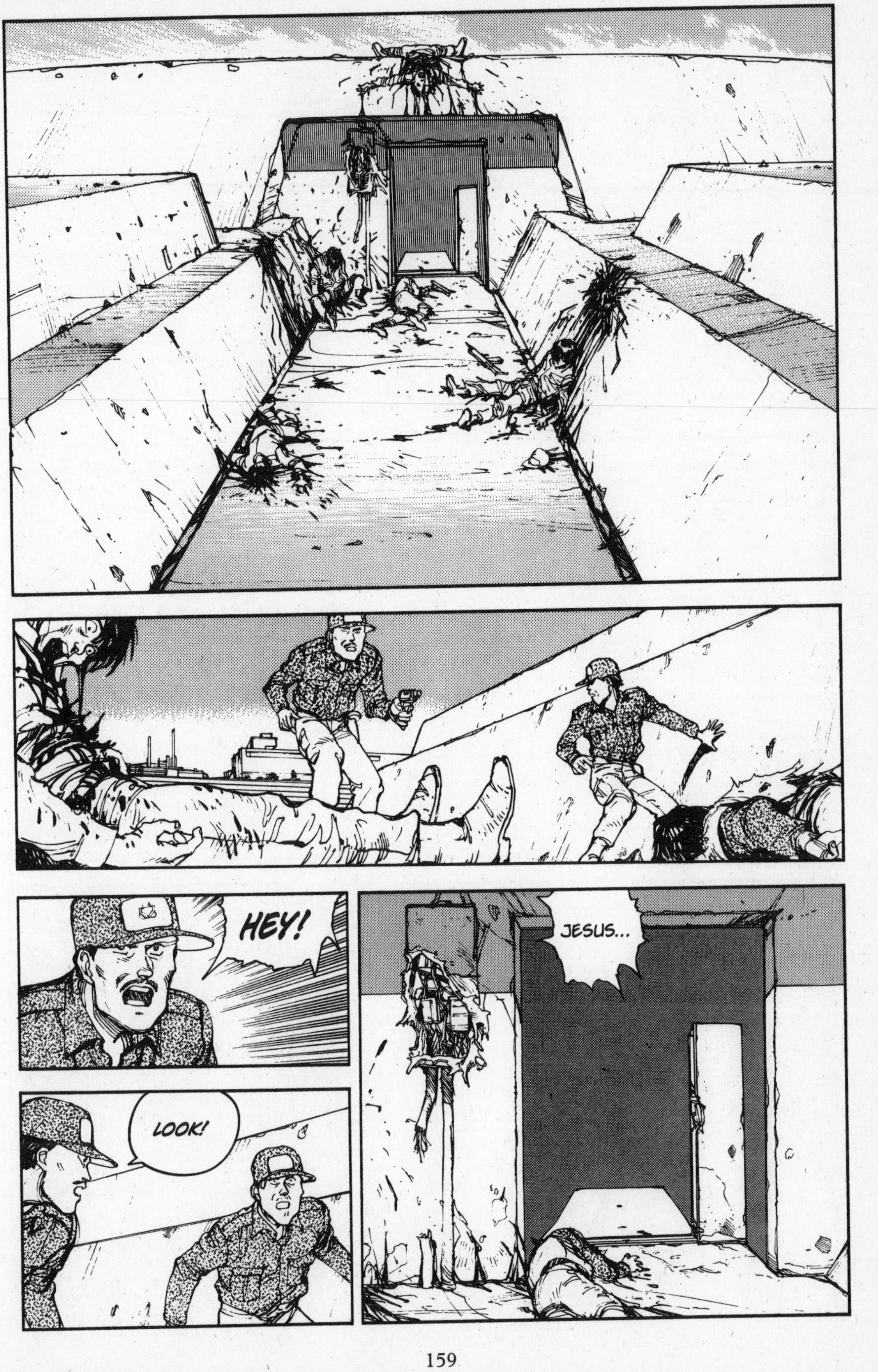
HEY!
LOOK!
JESUS...

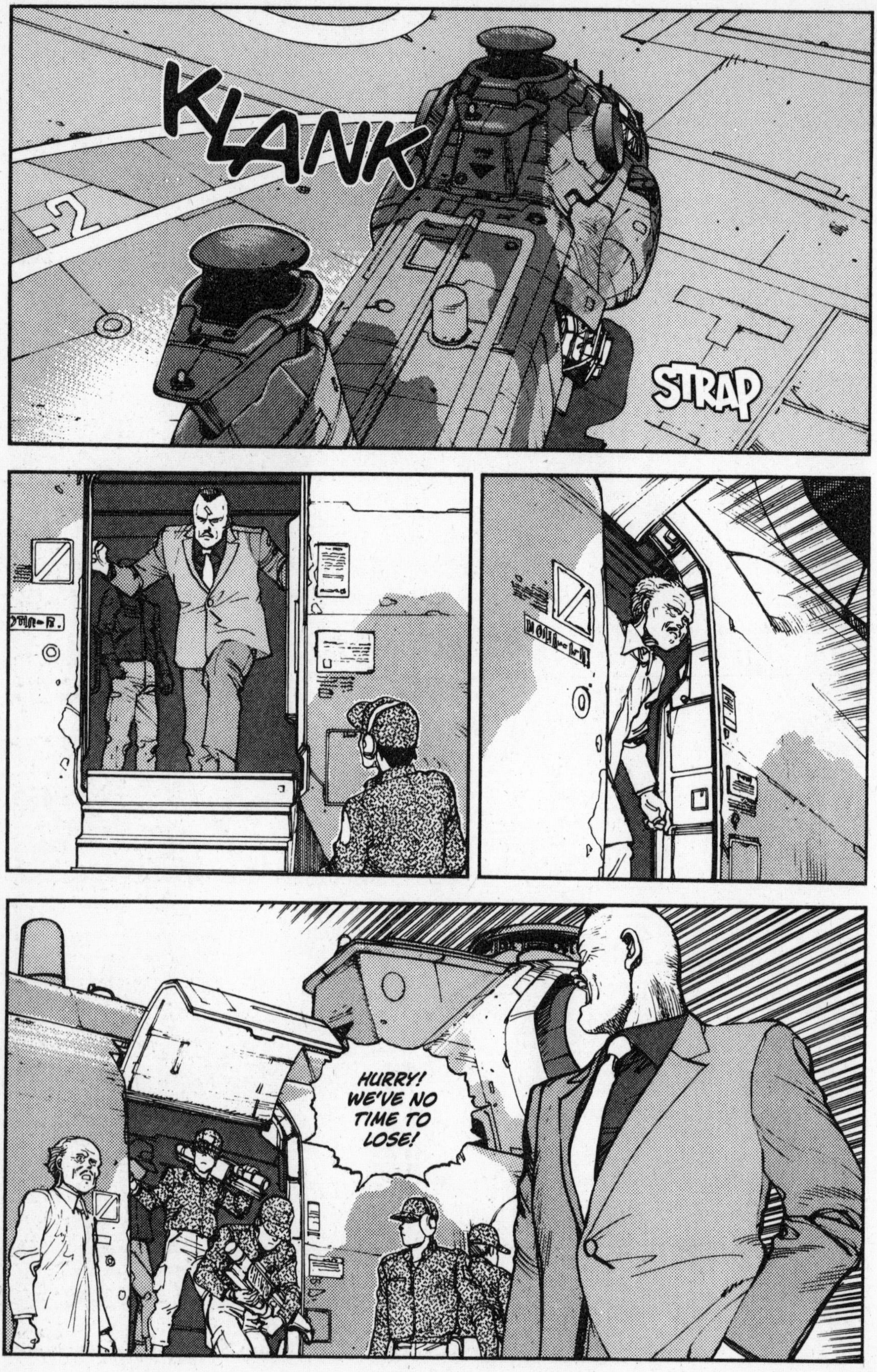
KLANK
STRAP
HURRY! WE'VE NO TIME TO LOSE!

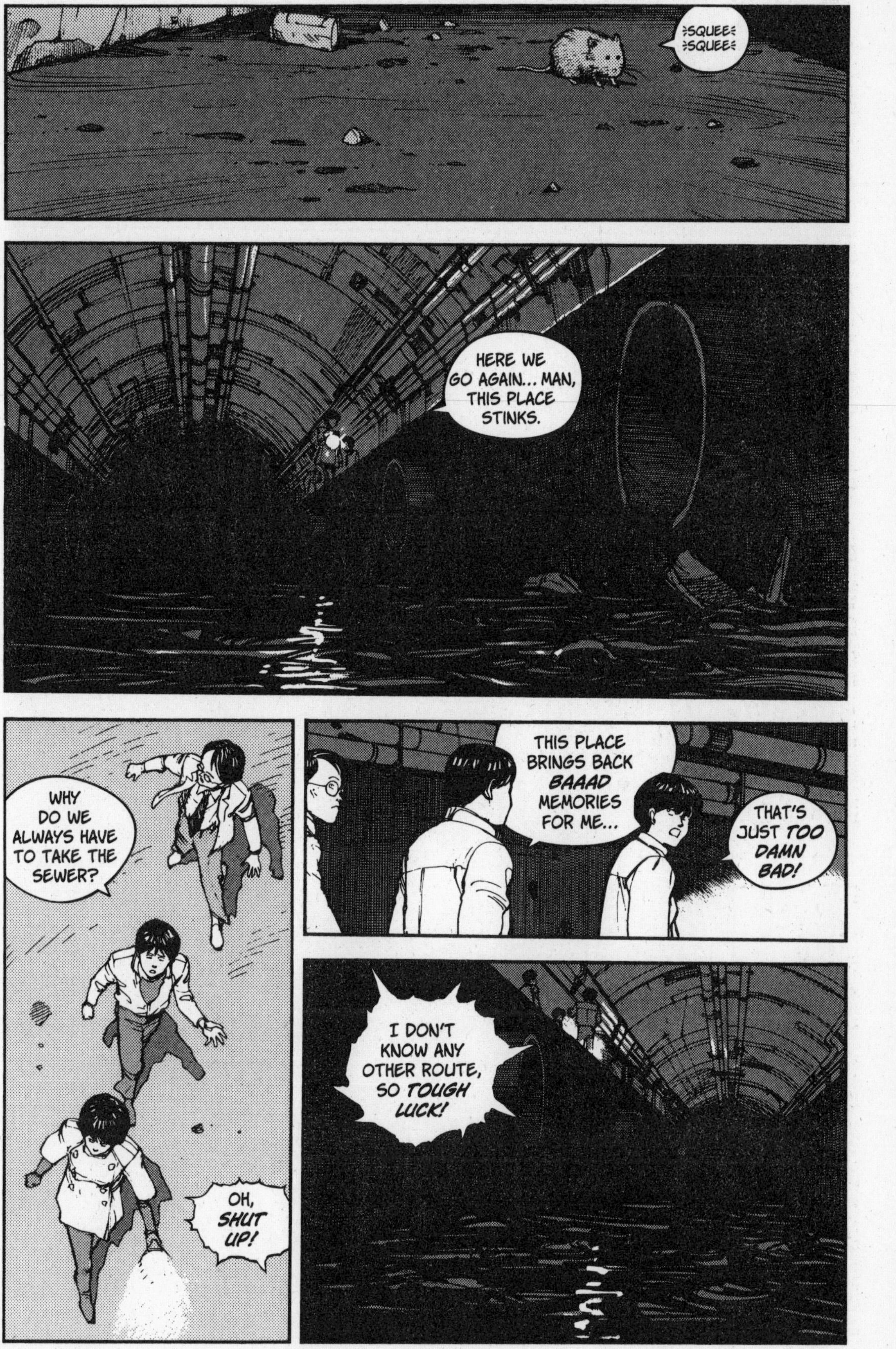
SQUEE SQUEE
HERE WE GO AGAIN... MAN, THIS PLACE STINKS.
WHY DO WE ALWAYS HAVE TO TAKE THE SEWER?
OH, *SHUT UP!*
THIS PLACE BRINGS BACK *BAAAD* MEMORIES FOR ME...
THAT'S JUST *TOO DAMN BAD!*
I DON'T KNOW ANY OTHER ROUTE, SO *TOUGH LUCK!*

TAP

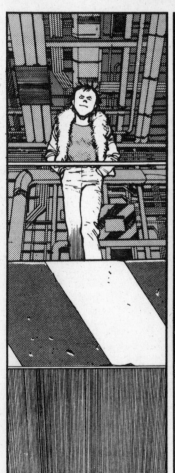

HERE AT LAST.

BE CAREFUL.

NO GUN DID THAT TO THOSE GUYS, RYU.

YEAH.

I DUNNO...WE MIGHT BE BITING OFF MORE THAN WE CAN CHEW, HERE...

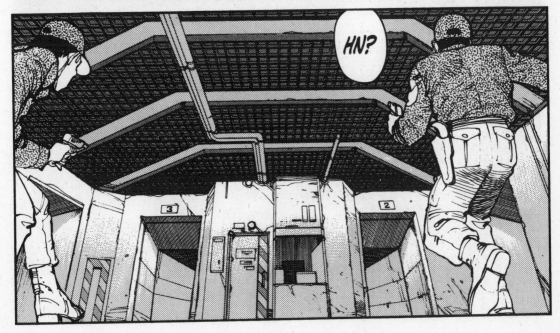

HN?

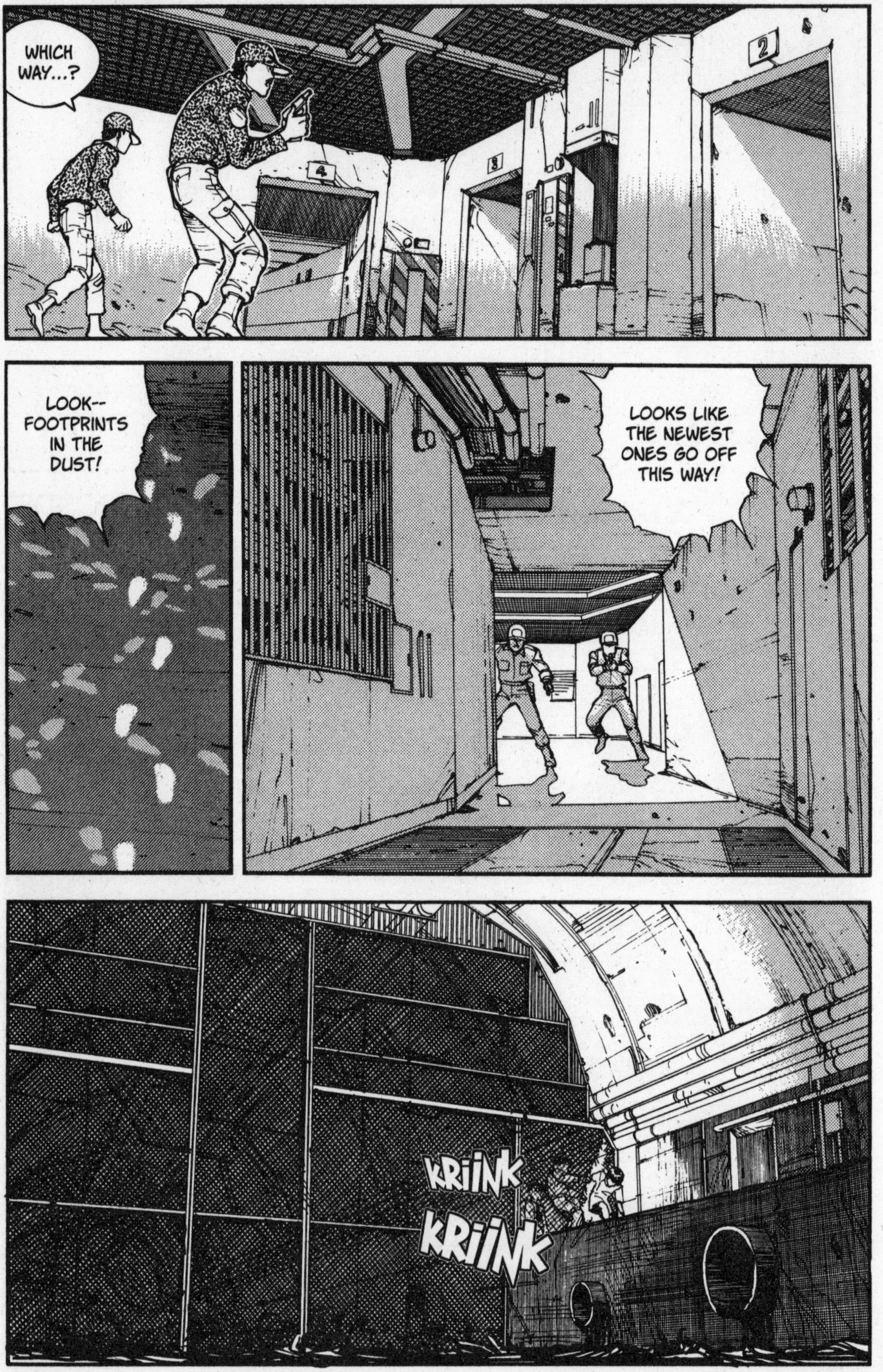
WHICH WAY...?
LOOK-- FOOTPRINTS IN THE DUST!
LOOKS LIKE THE NEWEST ONES GO OFF THIS WAY!
KRIINK
KRIINK

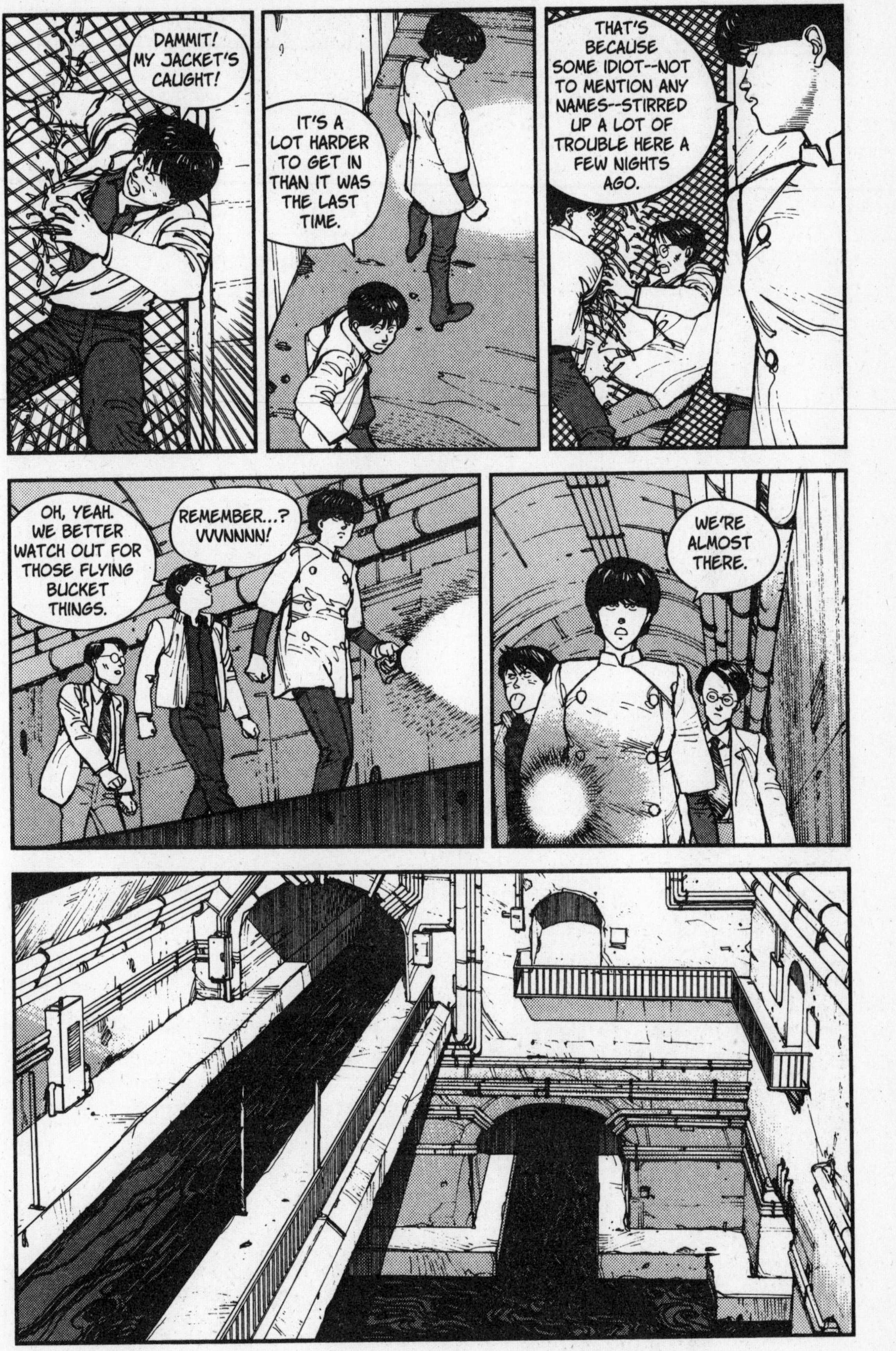
DAMMIT! MY JACKET'S CAUGHT!
IT'S A LOT HARDER TO GET IN THAN IT WAS THE LAST TIME.
THAT'S BECAUSE SOME IDIOT--NOT TO MENTION ANY NAMES--STIRRED UP A LOT OF TROUBLE HERE A FEW NIGHTS AGO.
OH, YEAH. WE BETTER WATCH OUT FOR THOSE FLYING BUCKET THINGS.
REMEMBER...? VVVNNNN!
WE'RE ALMOST THERE.

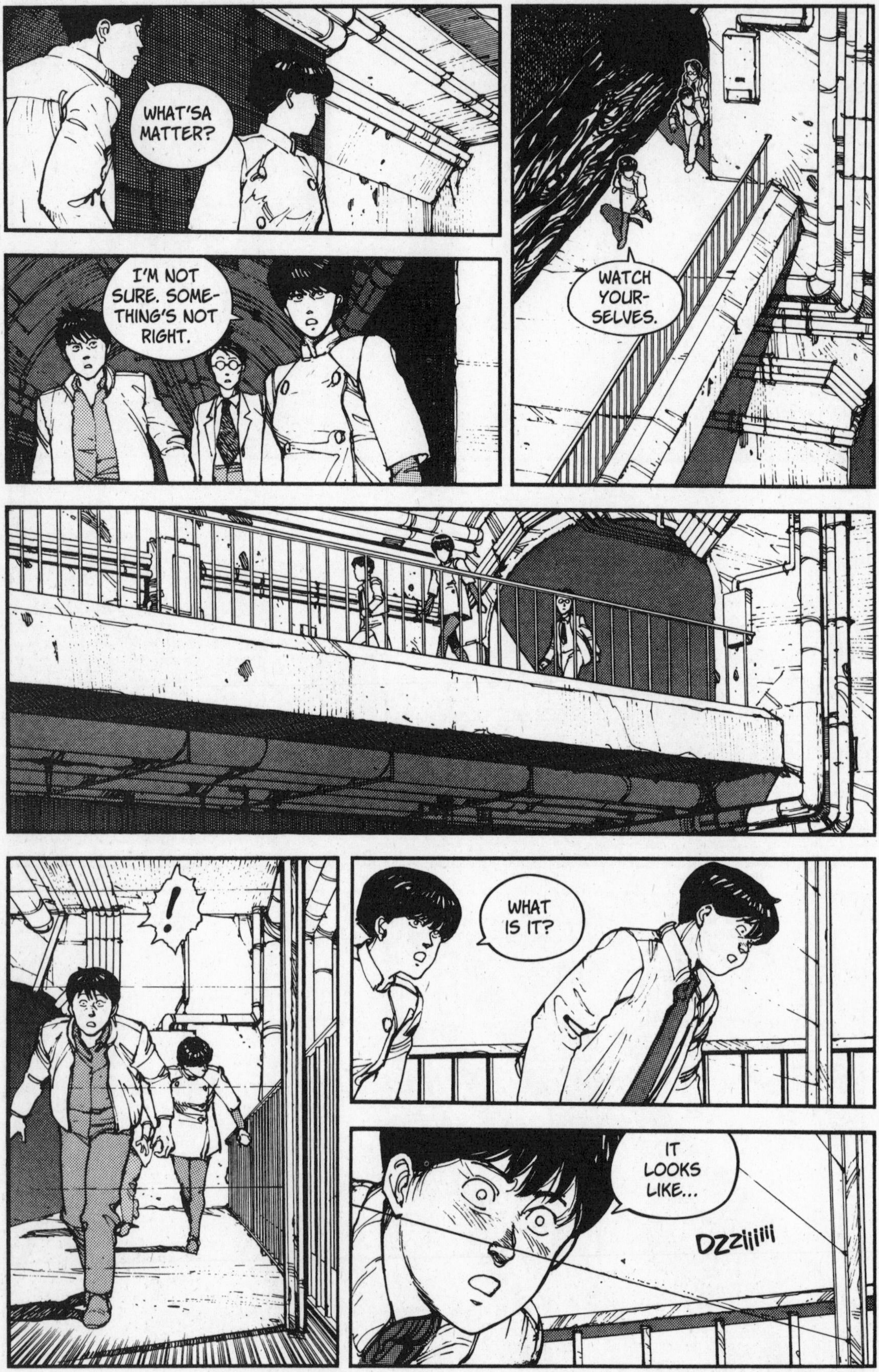
WHAT'SA MATTER?
I'M NOT SURE. SOME-THING'S NOT RIGHT.
WATCH YOUR-SELVES.
!
WHAT IS IT?
IT LOOKS LIKE...
DZZIIIIII

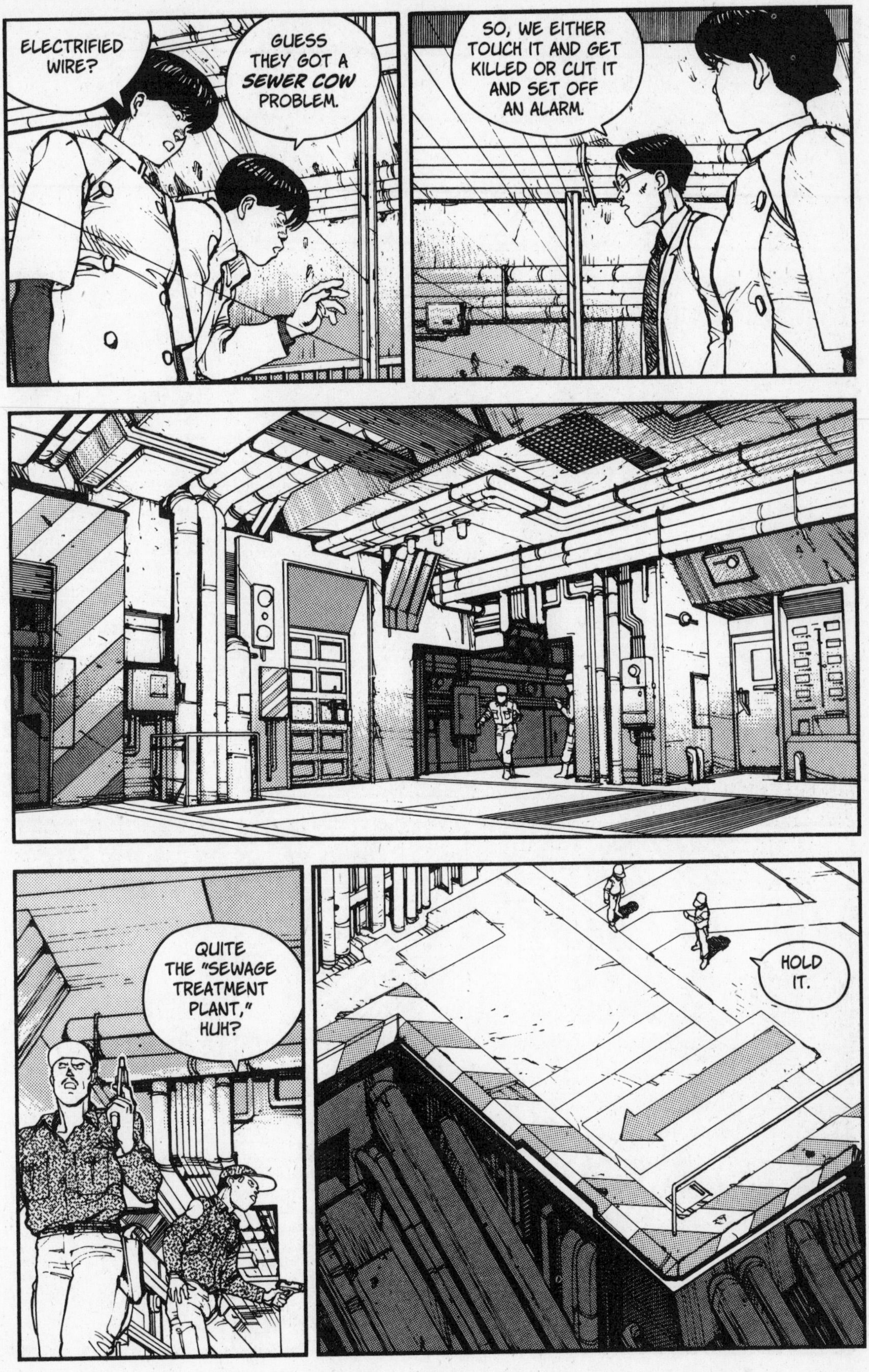
ELECTRIFIED WIRE?
GUESS THEY GOT A *SEWER COW* PROBLEM.
SO, WE EITHER TOUCH IT AND GET KILLED OR CUT IT AND SET OFF AN ALARM.
QUITE THE "SEWAGE TREATMENT PLANT," HUH?
HOLD IT.

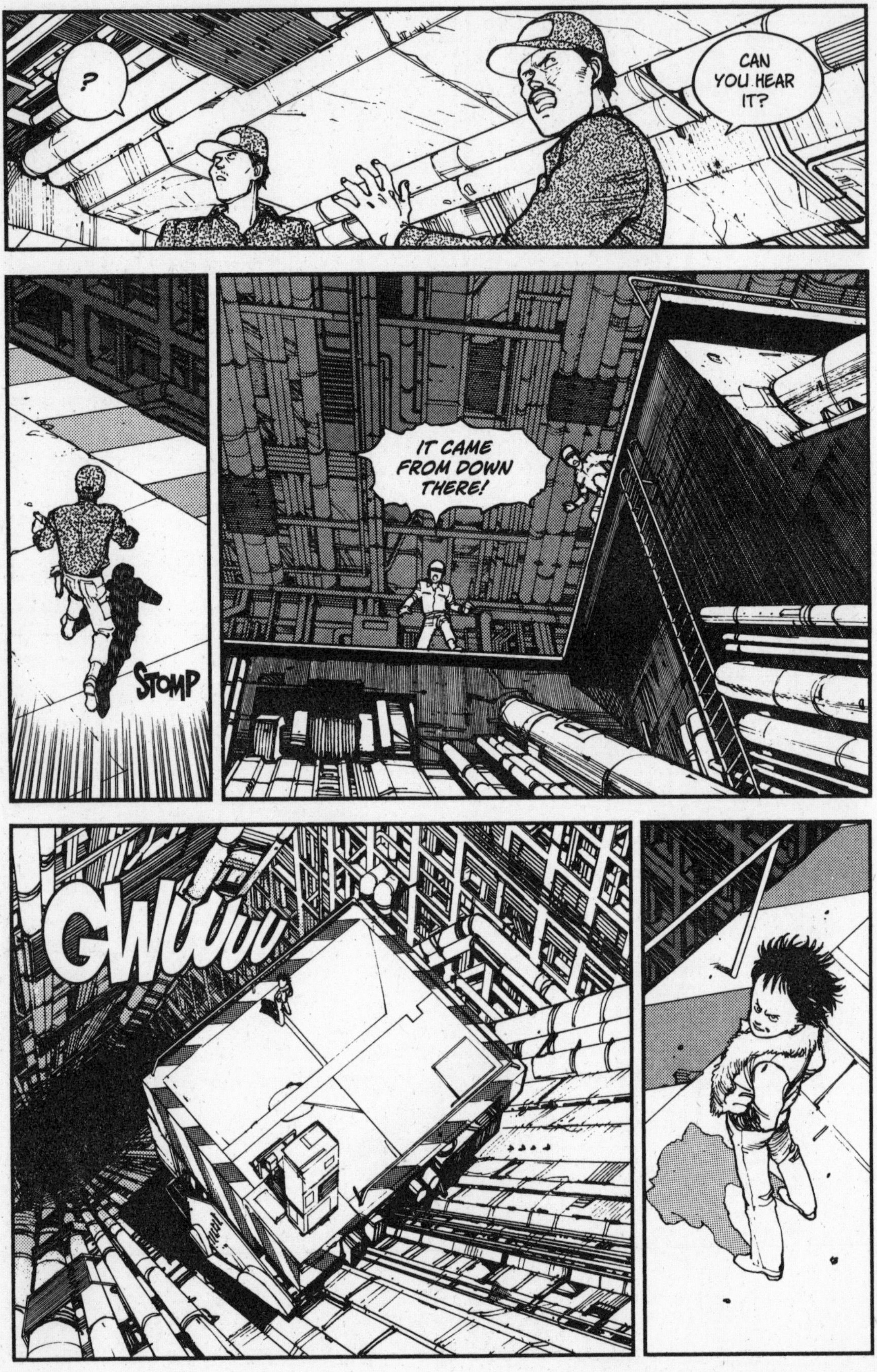
?
CAN YOU HEAR IT?
STOMP
IT CAME FROM DOWN THERE!
GWUUU

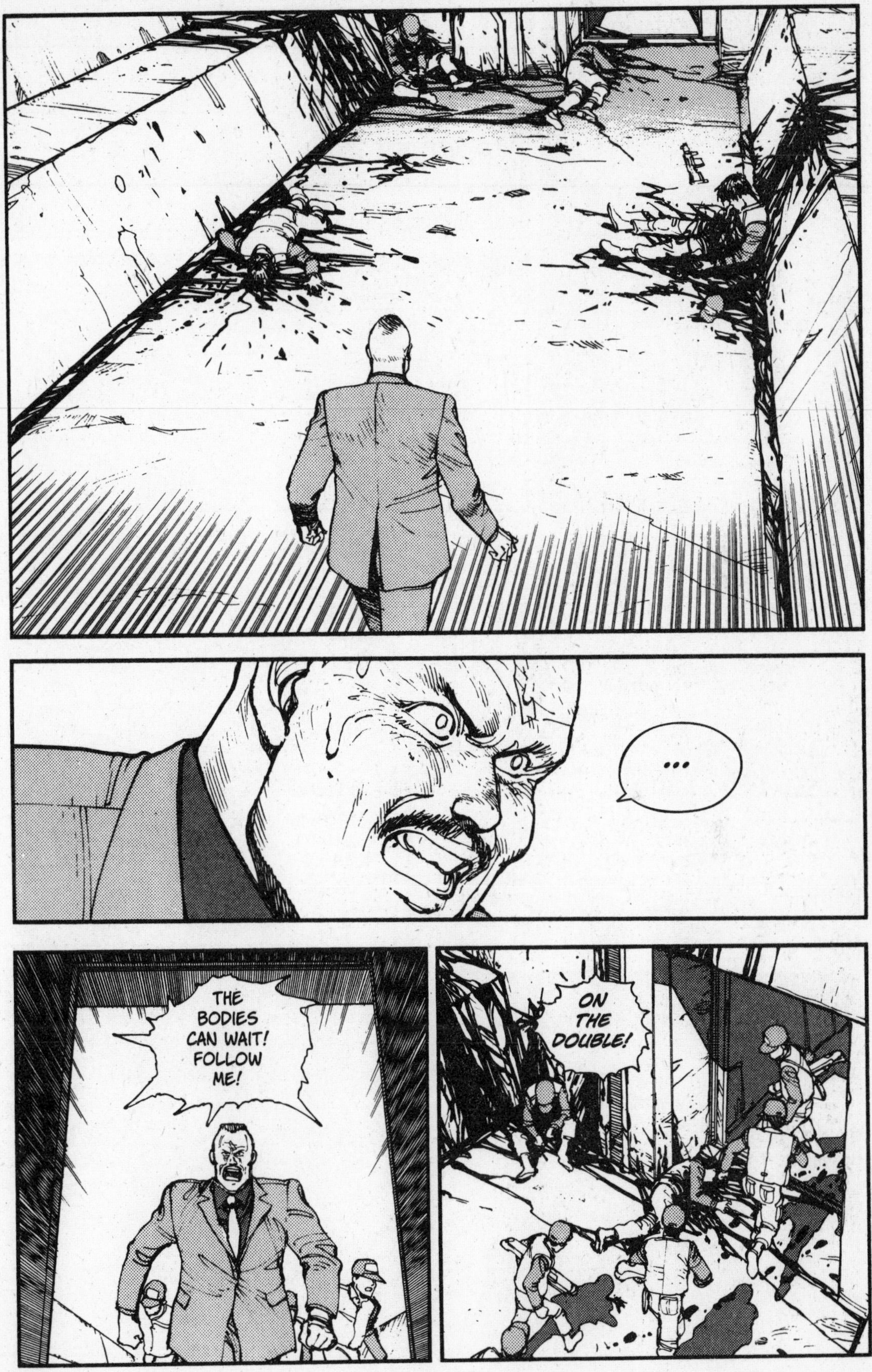
...
THE BODIES CAN WAIT! FOLLOW ME!
ON THE DOUBLE!

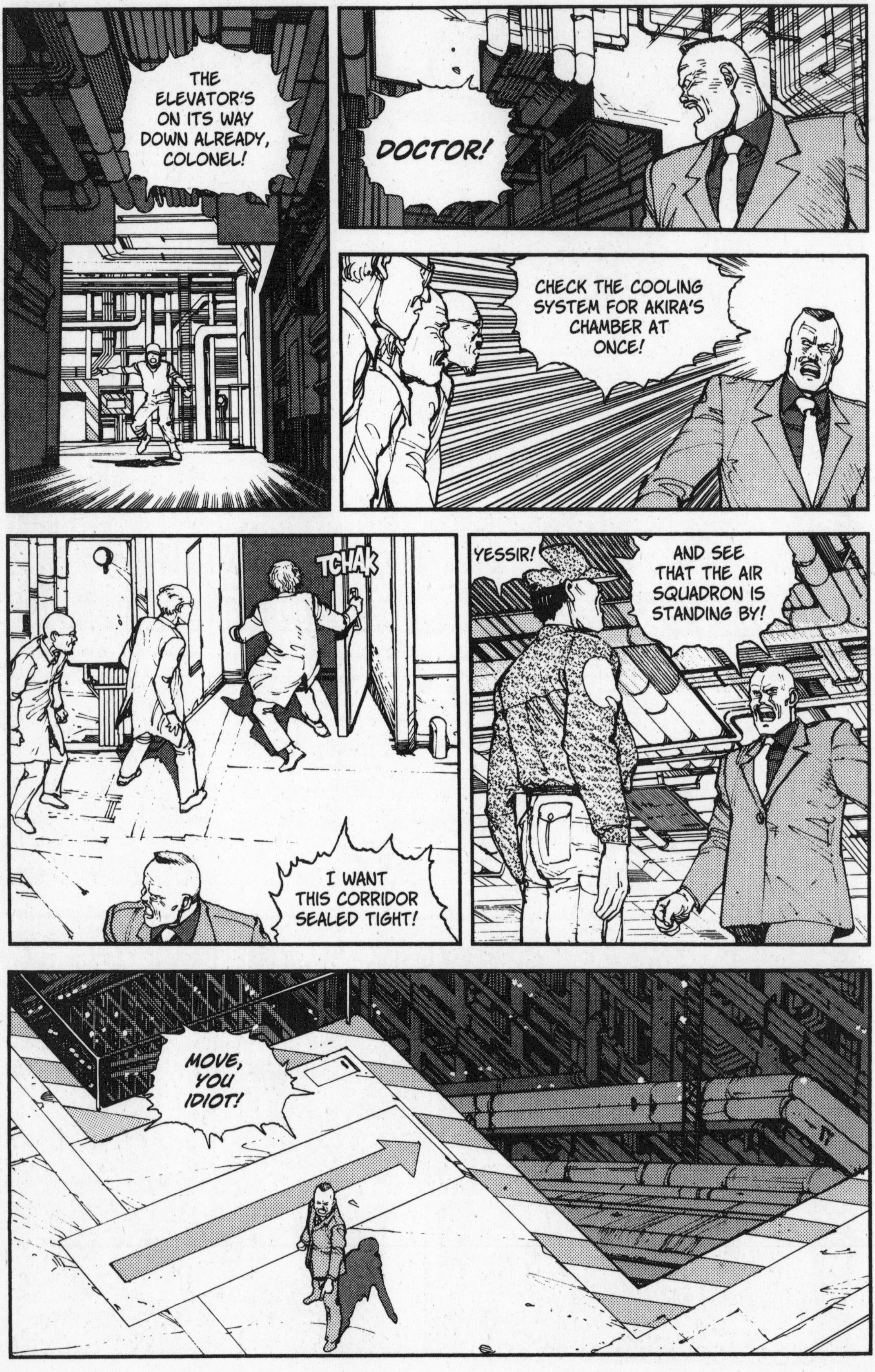
THE ELEVATOR'S ON ITS WAY DOWN ALREADY, COLONEL!
DOCTOR!
CHECK THE COOLING SYSTEM FOR AKIRA'S CHAMBER AT ONCE!
TCHAK
I WANT THIS CORRIDOR SEALED TIGHT!
YESSIR!
AND SEE THAT THE AIR SQUADRON IS STANDING BY!
MOVE, YOU IDIOT!

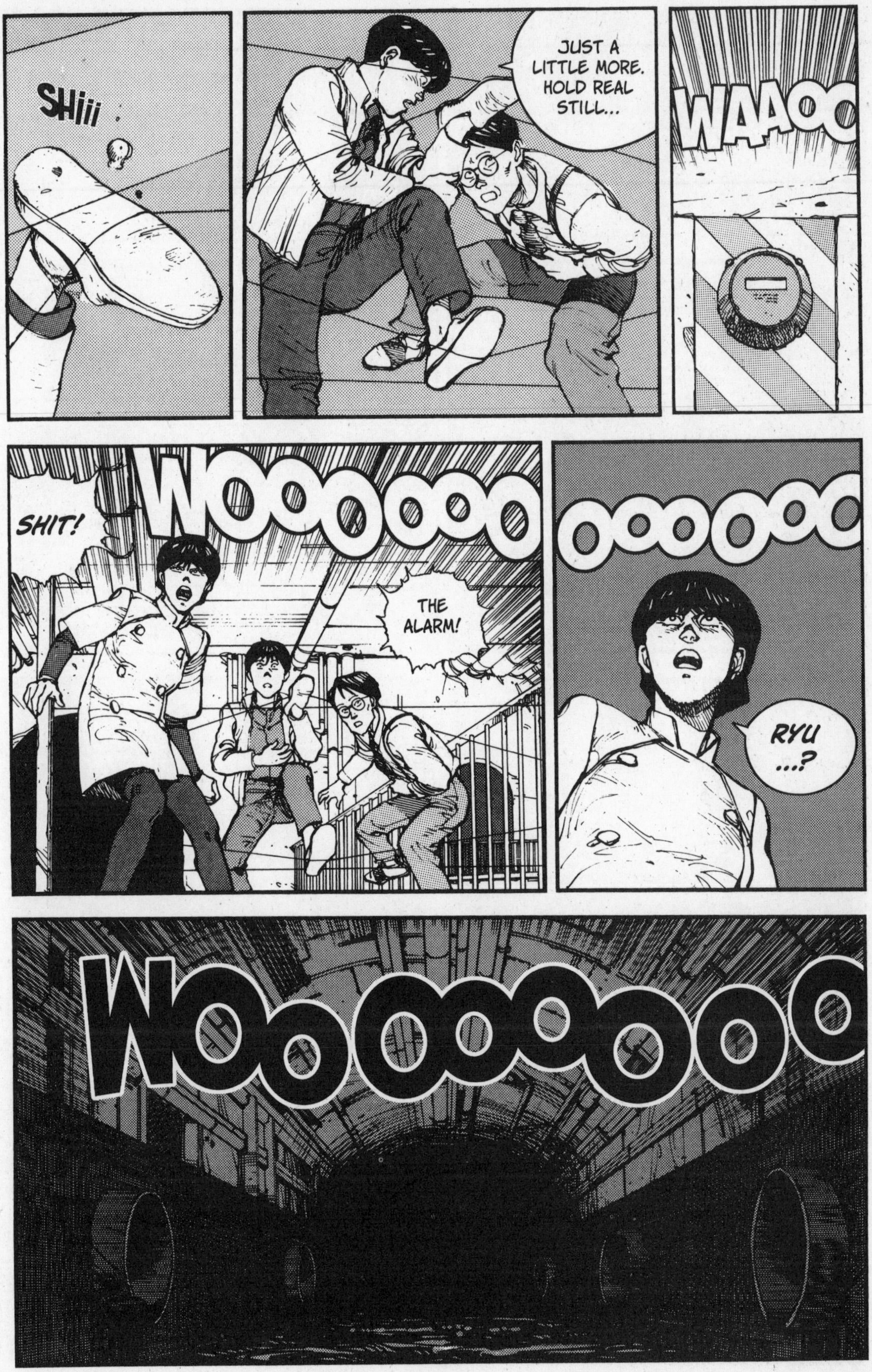
SHiii
JUST A LITTLE MORE. HOLD REAL STILL...
WAAOO
WOOOOOO
SHIT!
THE ALARM!
OOOOOO
RYU ...?
WOOOOOOO

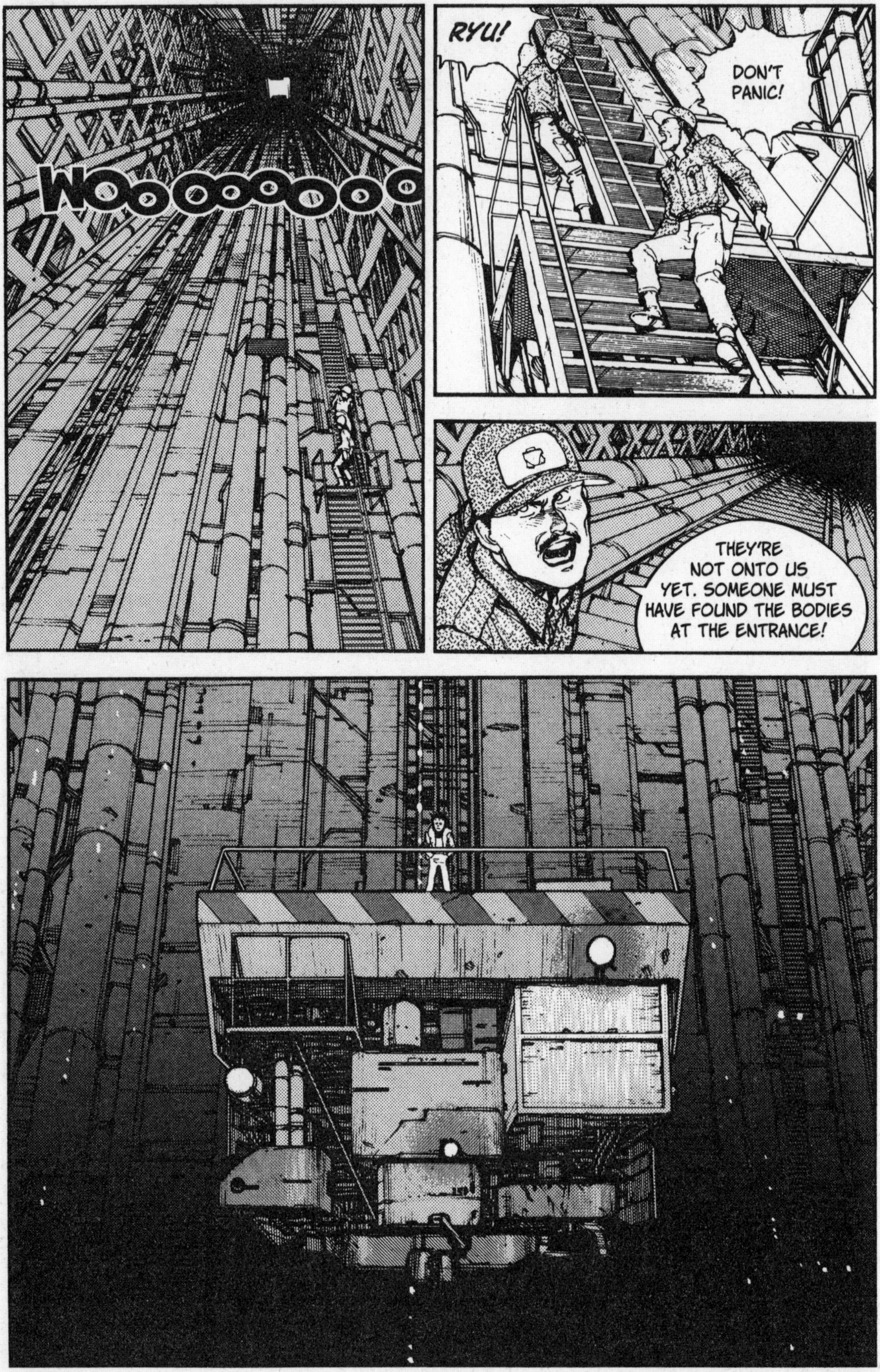
WOOOOOOOOO
RYU!
DON'T PANIC!
THEY'RE NOT ONTO US YET. SOMEONE MUST HAVE FOUND THE BODIES AT THE ENTRANCE!

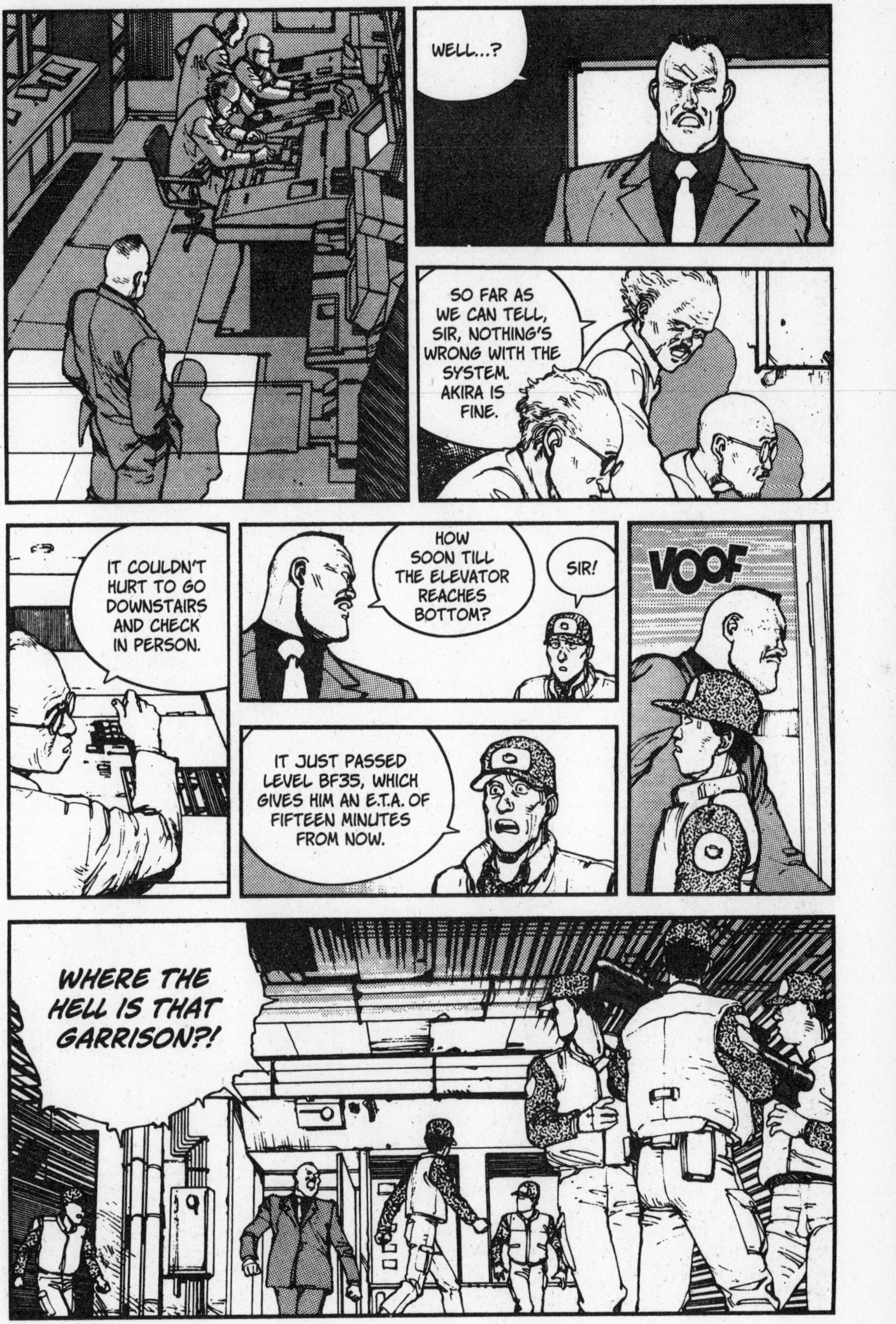

WELL...?
SO FAR AS WE CAN TELL, SIR, NOTHING'S WRONG WITH THE SYSTEM. AKIRA IS FINE.
IT COULDN'T HURT TO GO DOWNSTAIRS AND CHECK IN PERSON.
HOW SOON TILL THE ELEVATOR REACHES BOTTOM?
SIR!
IT JUST PASSED LEVEL BF35, WHICH GIVES HIM AN E.T.A. OF FIFTEEN MINUTES FROM NOW.
VOOF
WHERE THE HELL IS THAT GARRISON?!

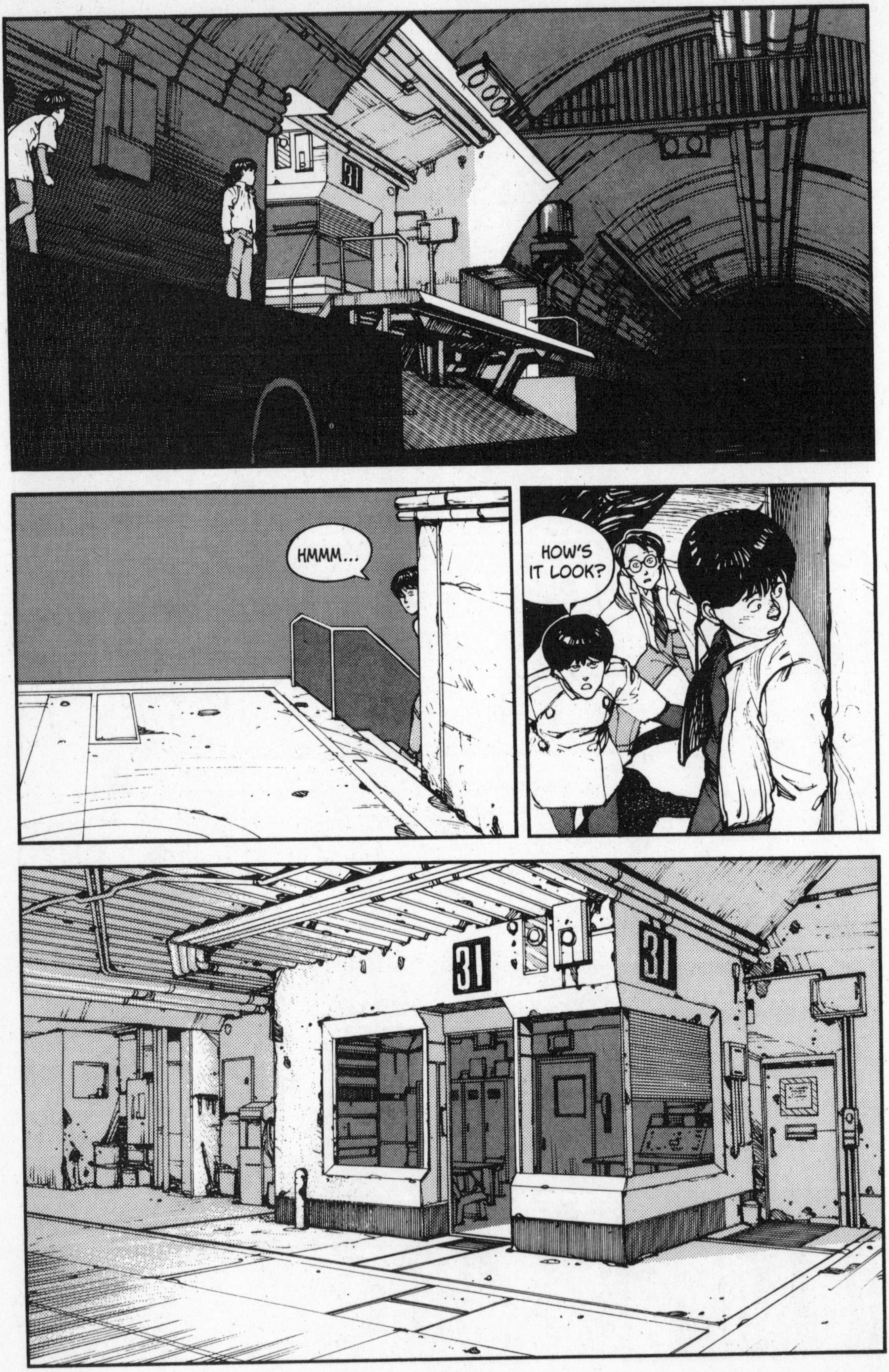
31
HMMM...
HOW'S IT LOOK?
31
31

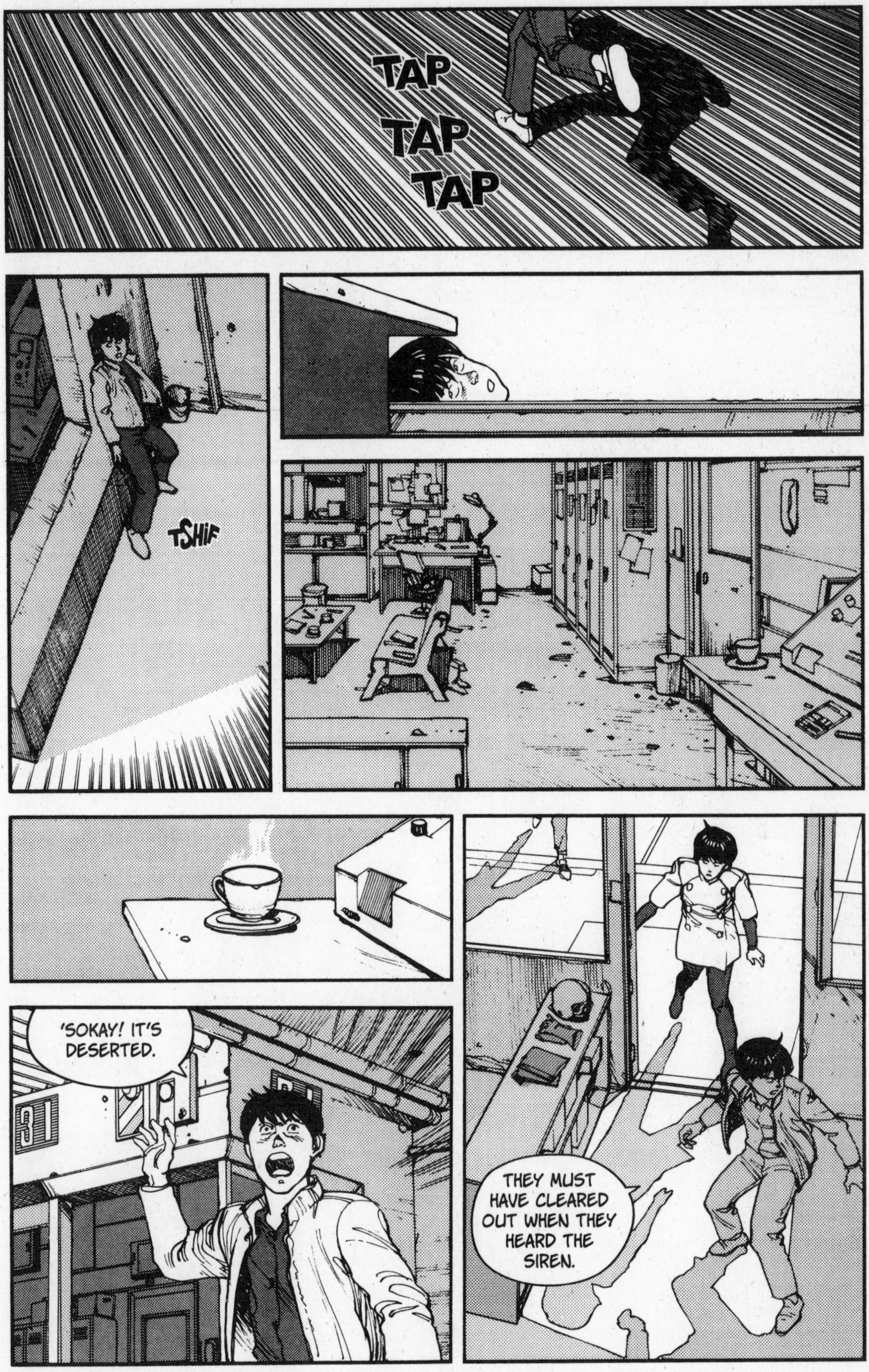
TAP
TAP
TAP
TSHIF
'SOKAY! IT'S DESERTED.
THEY MUST HAVE CLEARED OUT WHEN THEY HEARD THE SIREN.

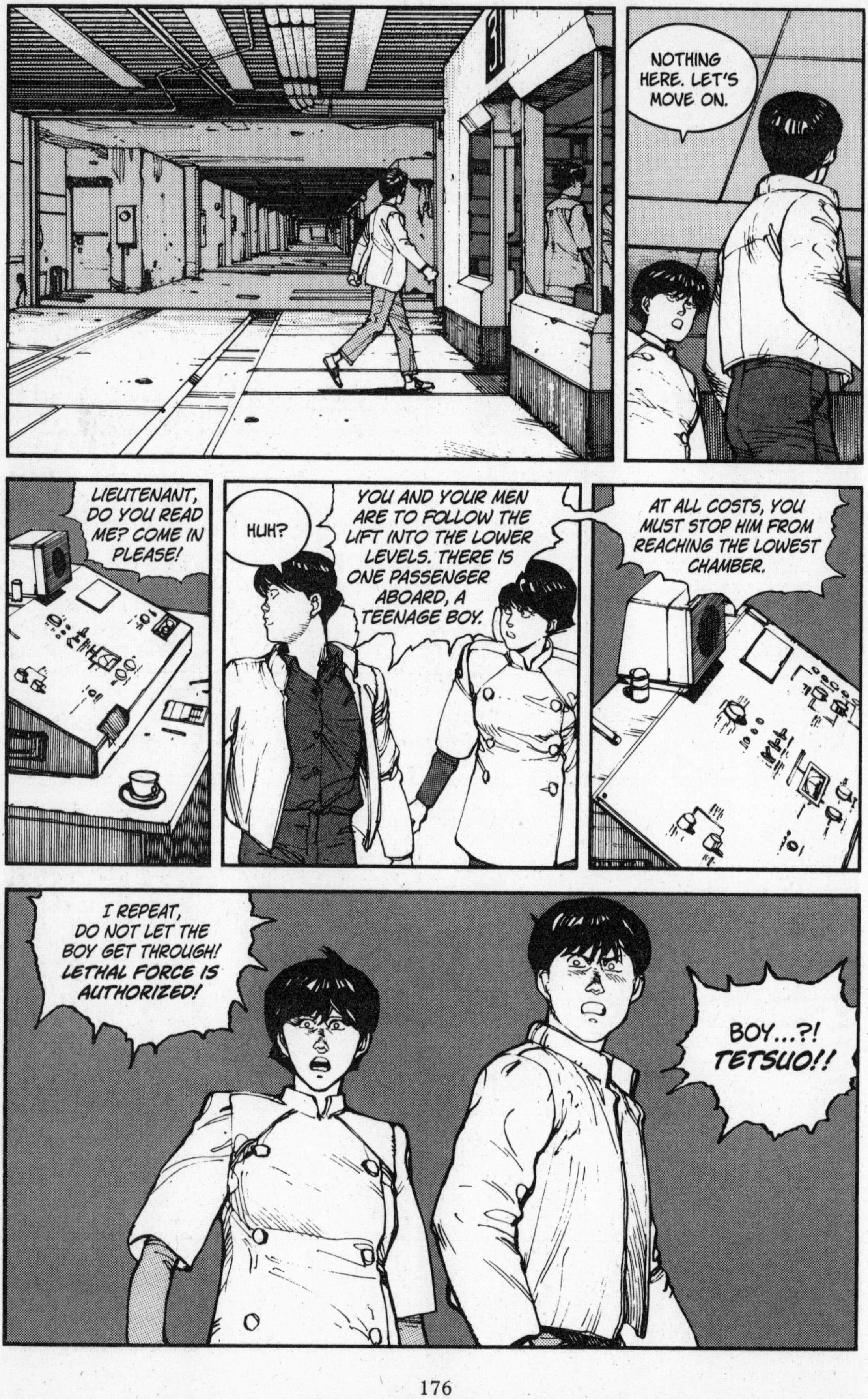
NOTHING HERE. LET'S MOVE ON.
LIEUTENANT, DO YOU READ ME? COME IN PLEASE!
HUH?
YOU AND YOUR MEN ARE TO FOLLOW THE LIFT INTO THE LOWER LEVELS. THERE IS ONE PASSENGER ABOARD, A TEENAGE BOY.
AT ALL COSTS, YOU MUST STOP HIM FROM REACHING THE LOWEST CHAMBER.
I REPEAT, DO NOT LET THE BOY GET THROUGH! LETHAL FORCE IS AUTHORIZED!
BOY...?! TETSUO!!

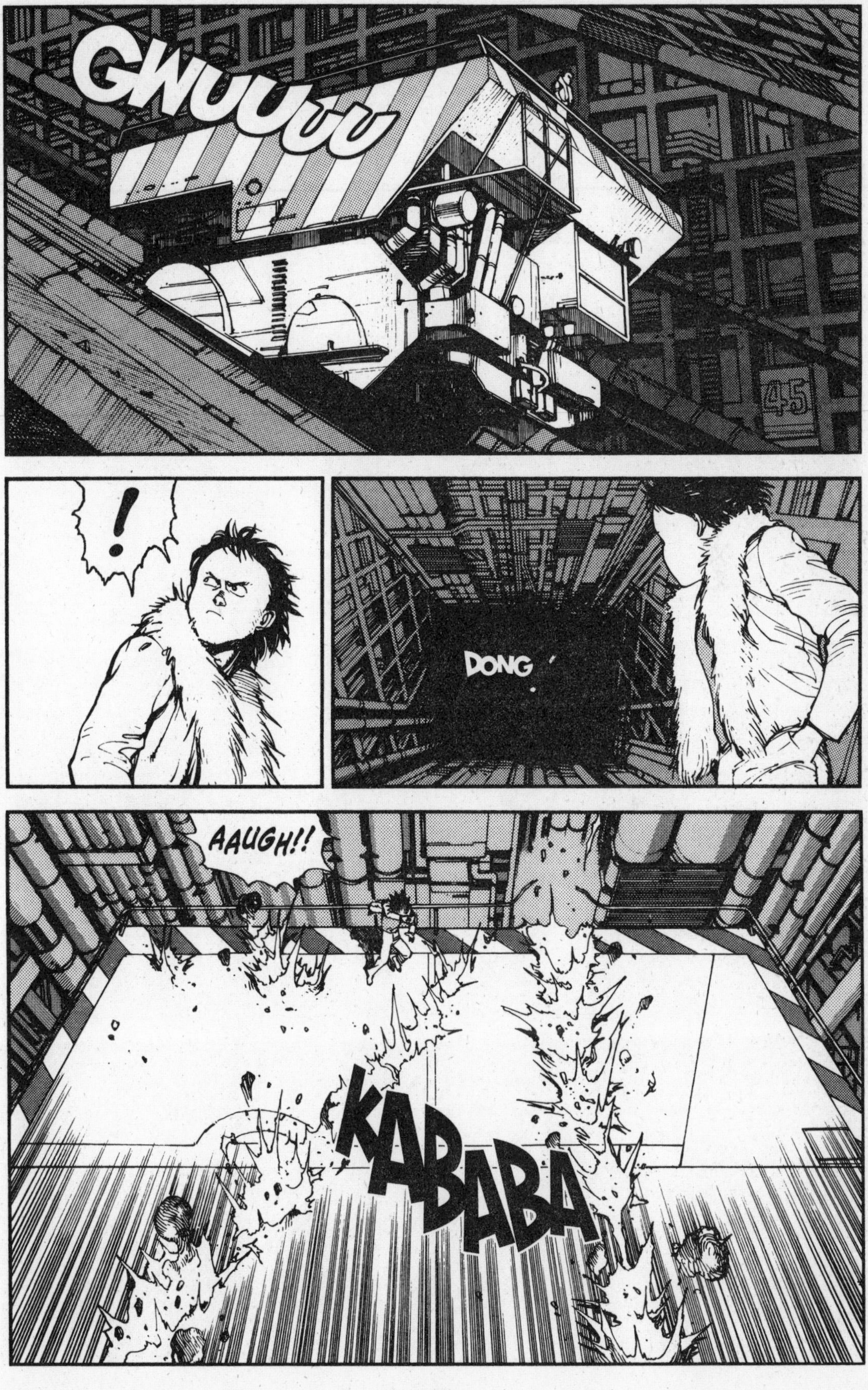
GWUUUU
!
DONG
AAUGH!!
KABABA

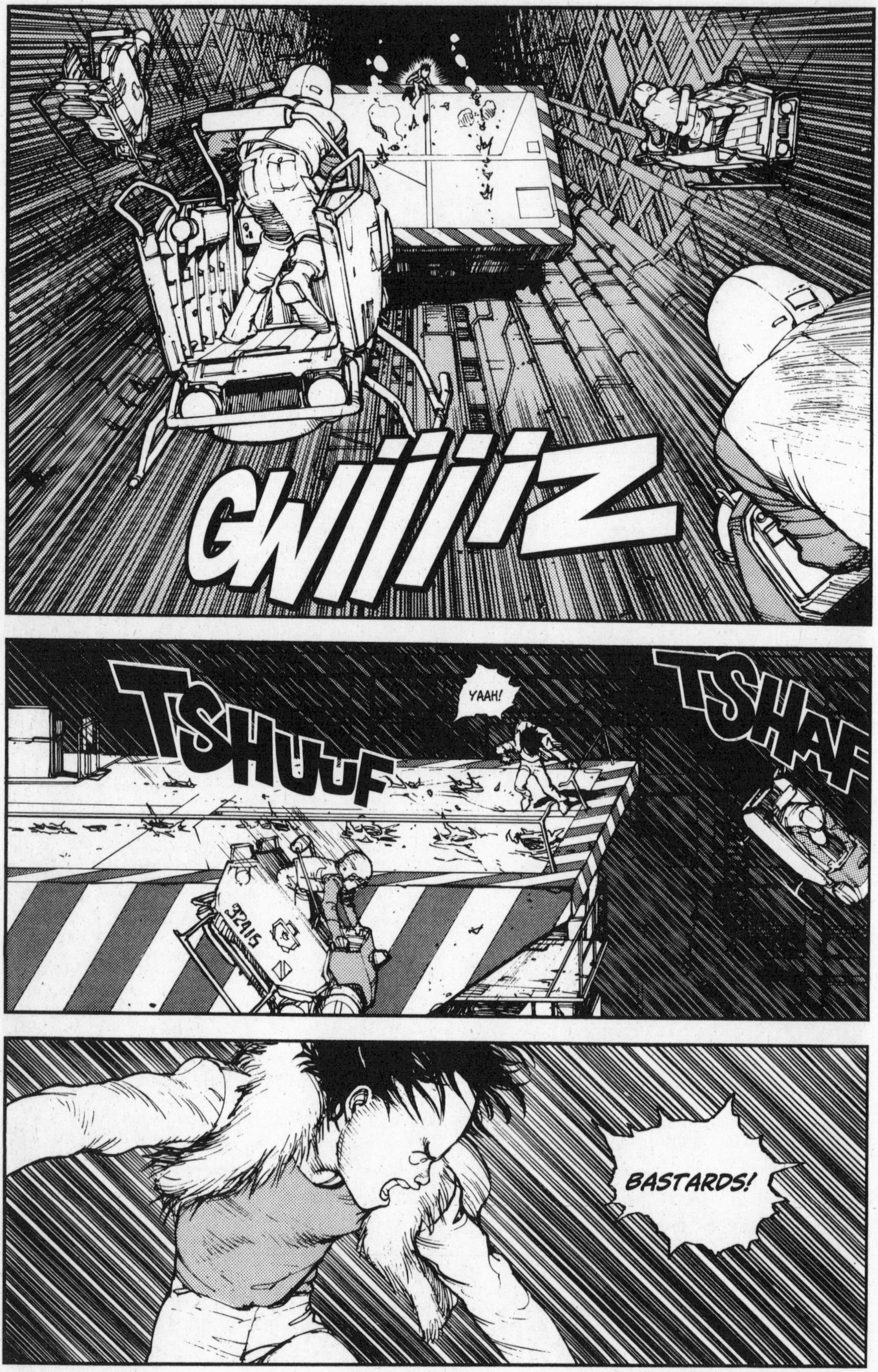
GWIIIIZ
TSHUUF
YAAH!
TSHAF
BASTARDS!

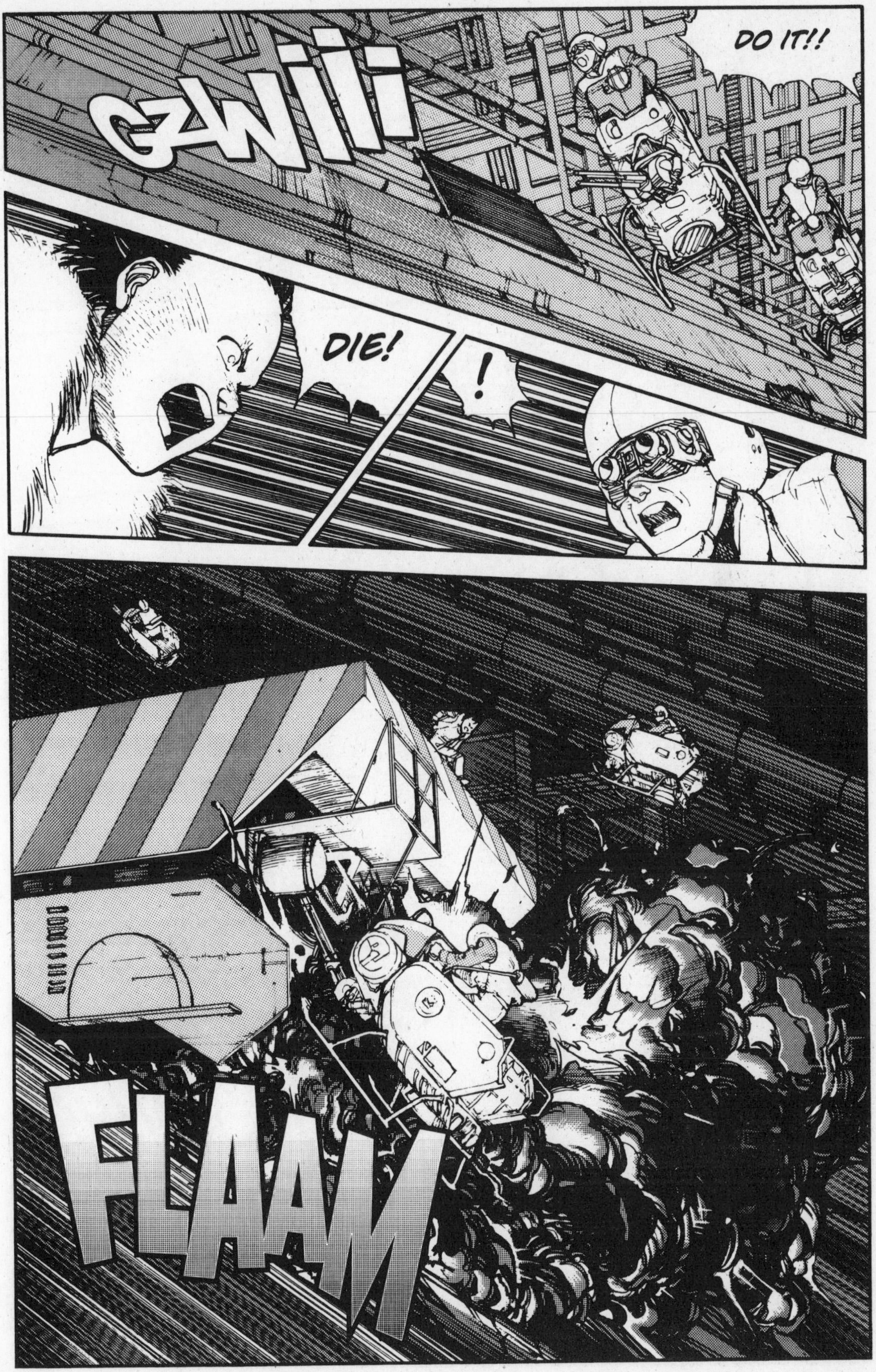
GZWIII
DO IT!!
DIE!
!
FLAAM

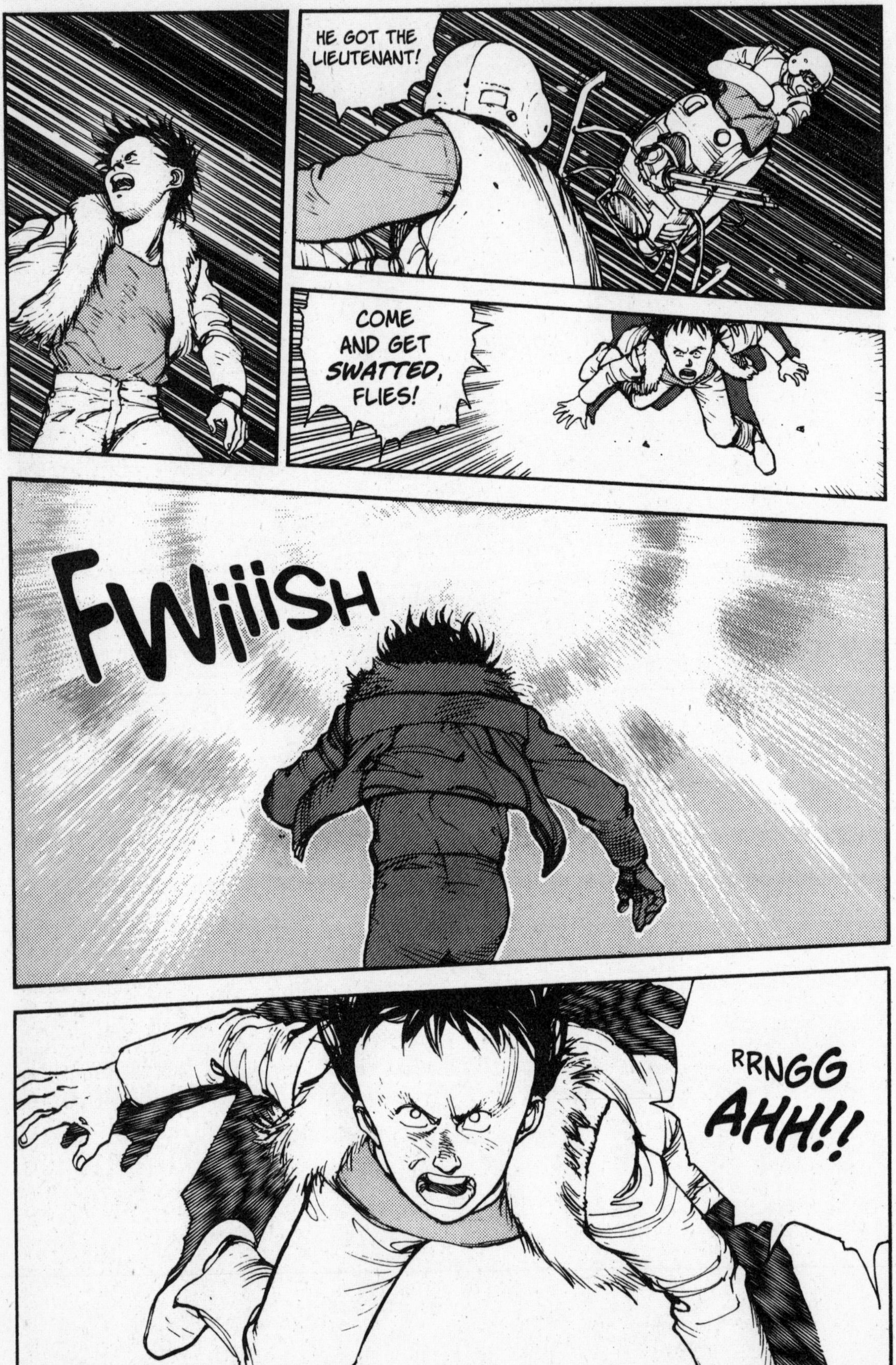
HE GOT THE LIEUTENANT!
COME AND GET SWATTED, FLIES!
FWiiiSH
RRNGG AHH!!

OF COURSE I READ THE RESULTS OF HIS APTITUDE TESTS, BUT I DON'T SEE WHAT...

THEN YOU MUST UNDER-STAND THAT HE'S BEYOND OUR CONTROL!

WHAT WOULD YOU SUG-GEST?

EH...?

.....

IS THERE A PROBLEM?

THERE...THERE'S BEEN AN INCREASE IN TEMPERATURE IN THE CENTRAL CHAMBER.

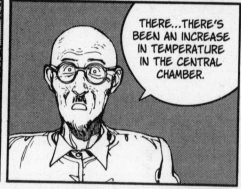

IT'S UP TO 0.00051° KELVIN! VACUUM READINGS FOR THE DEWAR FLASK ARE NORMAL.

WHAT ABOUT THE SECOND CHAMBER? AND THE THIRD...?

WHAT?!

THERE'S BEEN NO CHANGE... SO FAR.

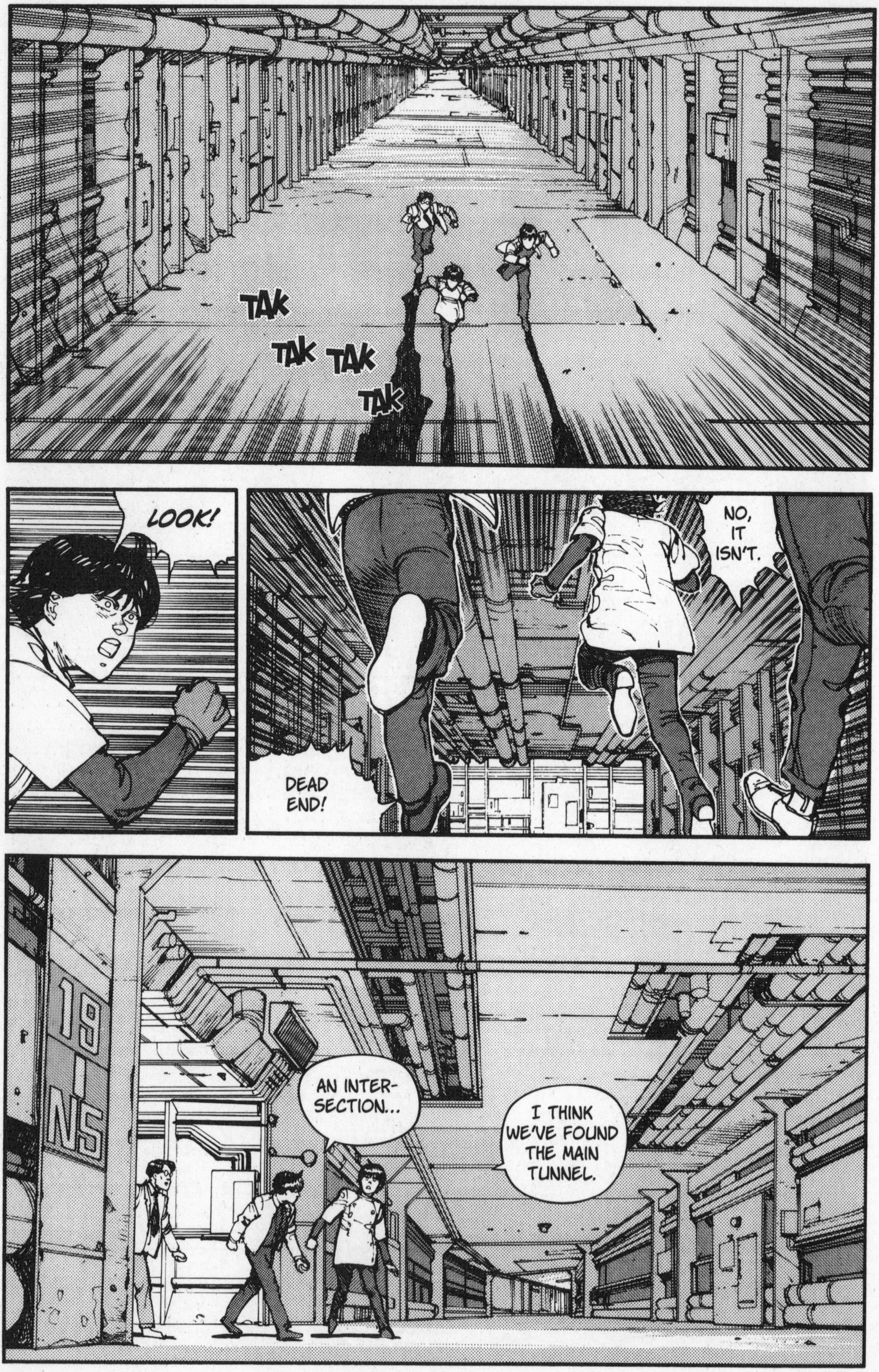
TAK
TAK TAK
TAK
LOOK!
DEAD END!
NO, IT ISN'T.
19
NS
AN INTER-SECTION...
I THINK WE'VE FOUND THE MAIN TUNNEL.

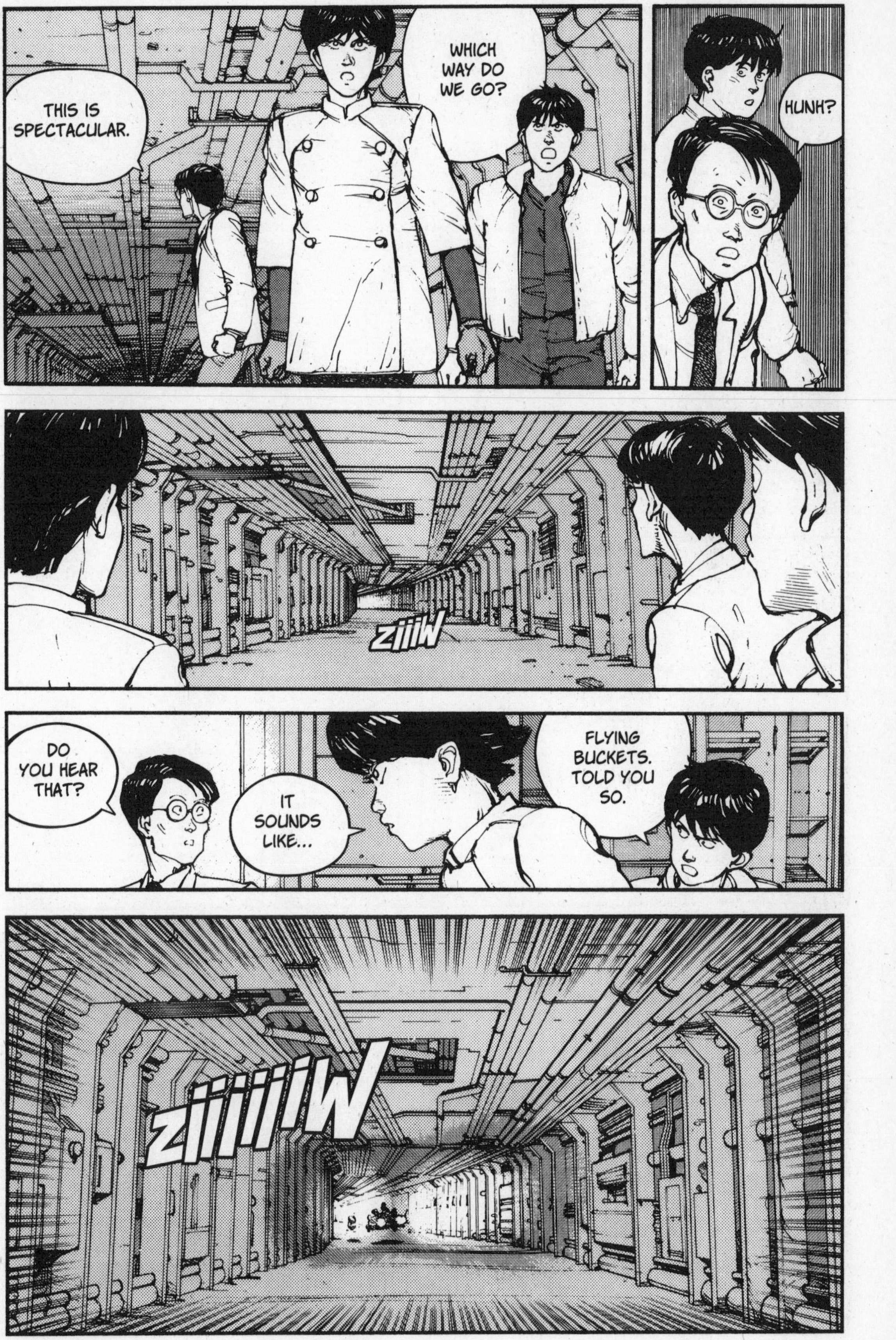
THIS IS SPECTACULAR.
WHICH WAY DO WE GO?
HUNH?
ZIIIW
DO YOU HEAR THAT?
IT SOUNDS LIKE...
FLYING BUCKETS. TOLD YOU SO.
ZIIIIIW

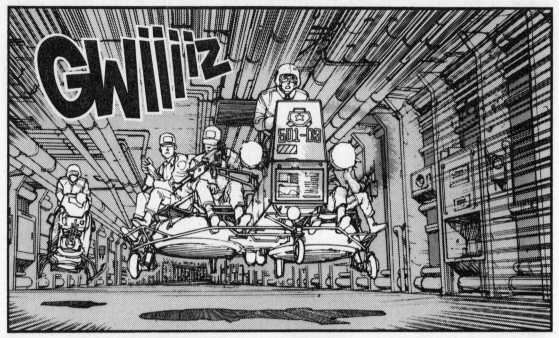

GWIIIZ

HERE THEY COME.

!

NOTHING PERSONAL. JUST DON'T TRY ANYTHING.

WIIIIZGWII

WHOA, CHECK IT OUT... ONE OF THOSE WAS A "SIX-PIECE BUCKET."

THE PARTY MUST BE OFF THAT WAY.

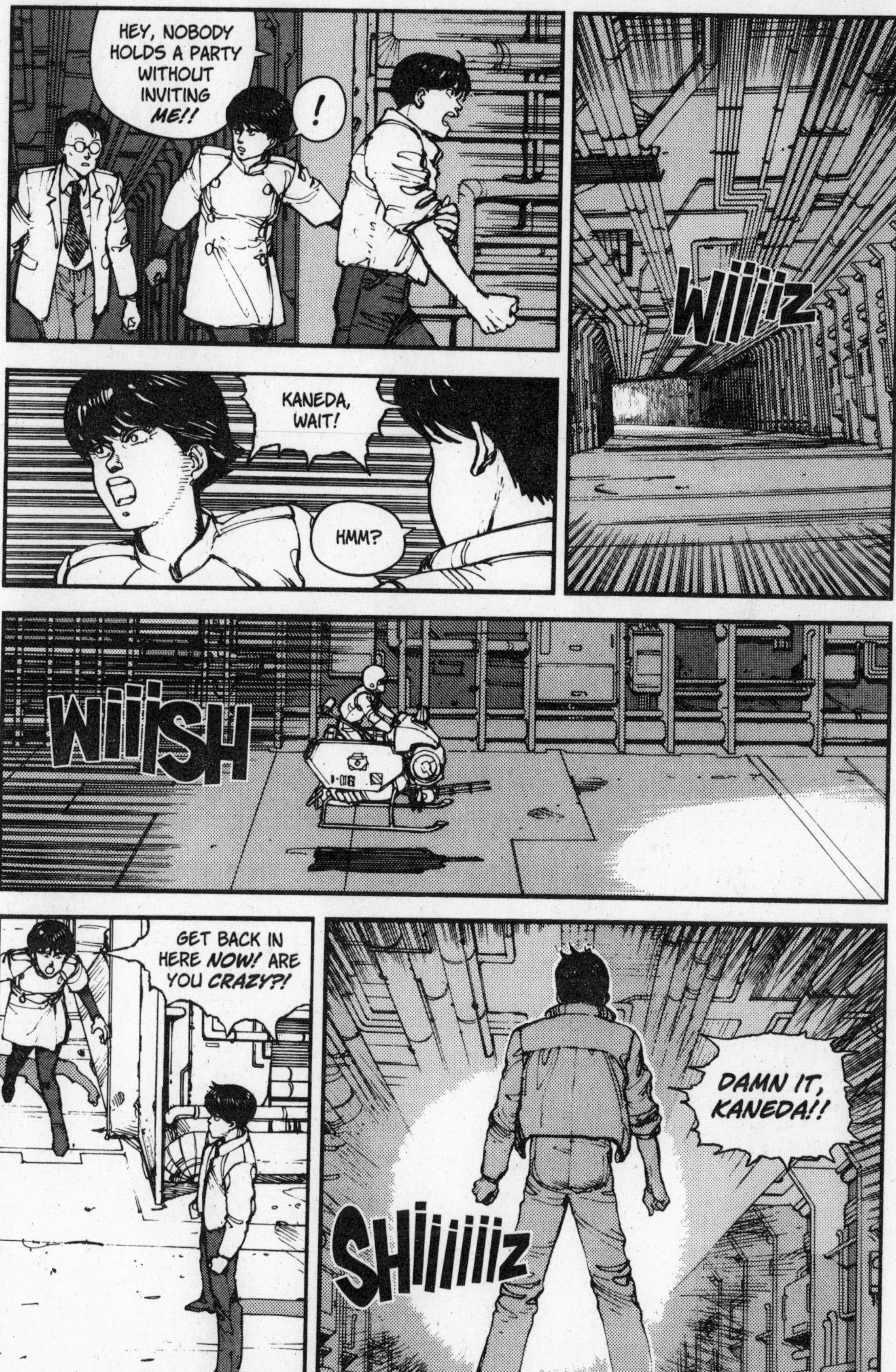
HEY, NOBODY HOLDS A PARTY WITHOUT INVITING *ME!!*
!
KANEDA, WAIT!
HMM?
WIIIIZ
WIIISH
GET BACK IN HERE *NOW!* ARE YOU *CRAZY?!*
DAMN IT, KANEDA!!
SHIIIIIIZ

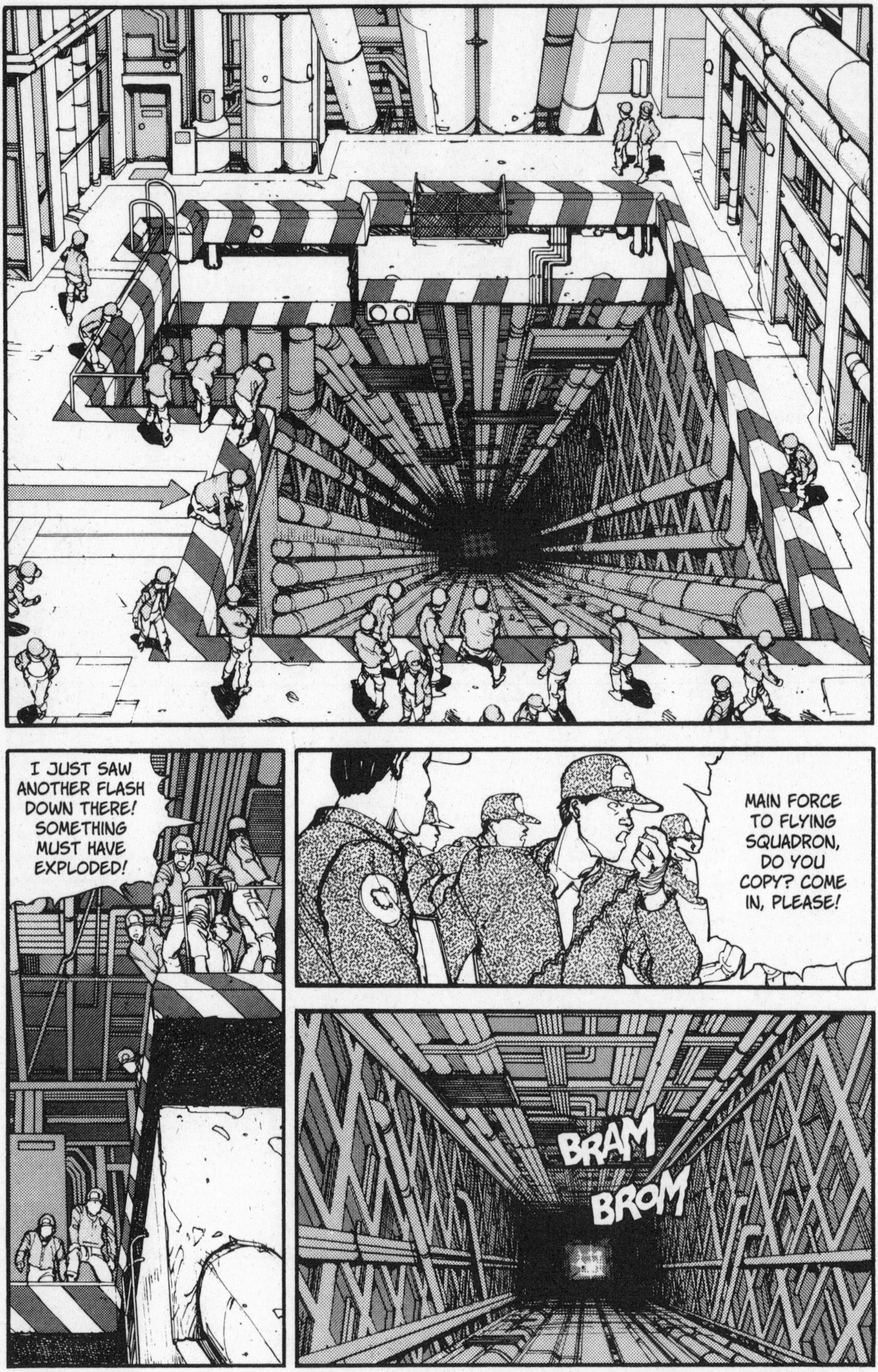
I JUST SAW ANOTHER FLASH DOWN THERE! SOMETHING MUST HAVE EXPLODED!
MAIN FORCE TO FLYING SQUADRON, DO YOU COPY? COME IN, PLEASE!
BRAM
BROM

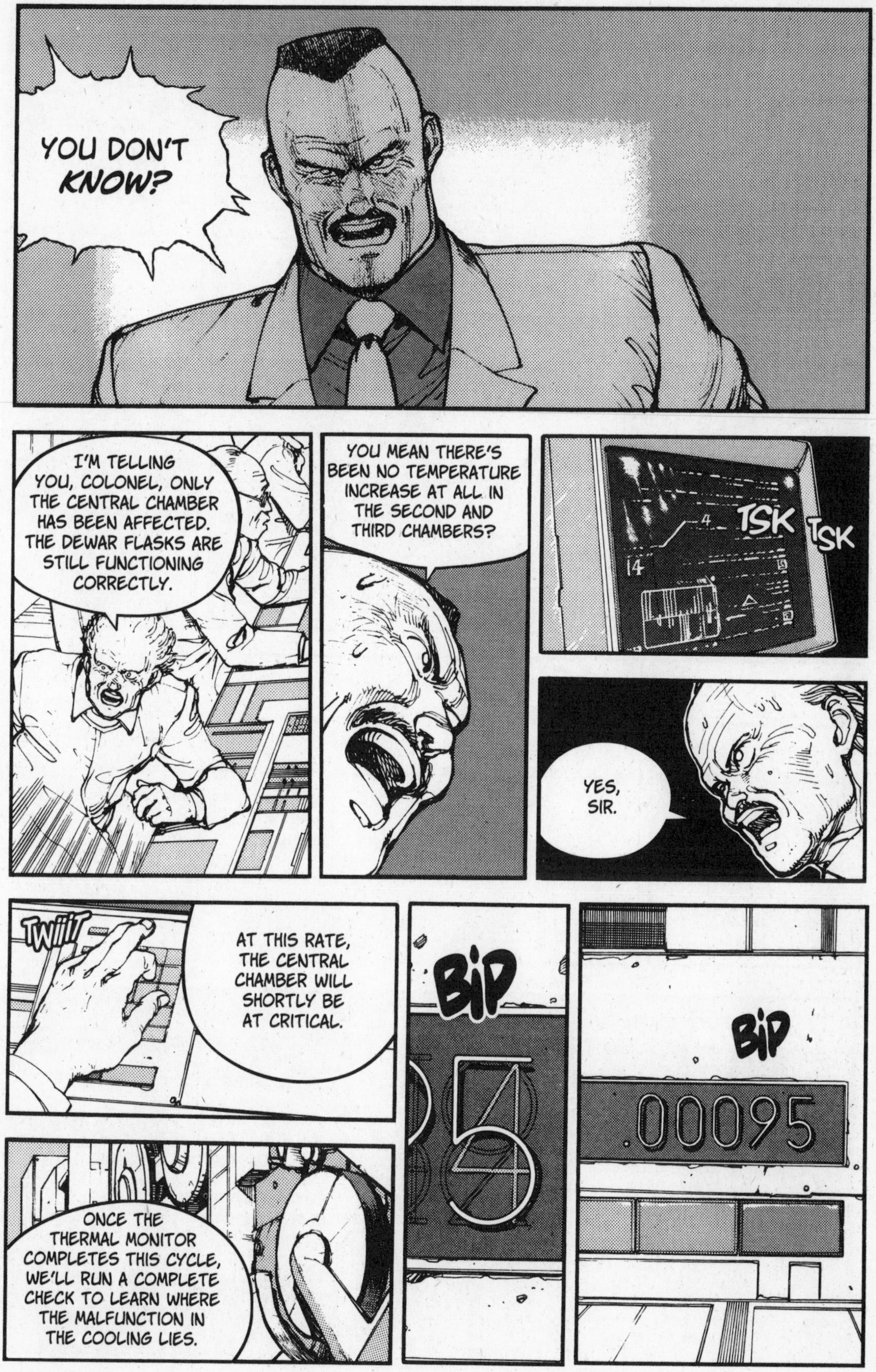
YOU DON'T KNOW?
I'M TELLING YOU, COLONEL, ONLY THE CENTRAL CHAMBER HAS BEEN AFFECTED. THE DEWAR FLASKS ARE STILL FUNCTIONING CORRECTLY.
YOU MEAN THERE'S BEEN NO TEMPERATURE INCREASE AT ALL IN THE SECOND AND THIRD CHAMBERS?
TSK TSK
YES, SIR.
TWIIIT
AT THIS RATE, THE CENTRAL CHAMBER WILL SHORTLY BE AT CRITICAL.
ONCE THE THERMAL MONITOR COMPLETES THIS CYCLE, WE'LL RUN A COMPLETE CHECK TO LEARN WHERE THE MALFUNCTION IN THE COOLING LIES.
BIP
BIP
.00095

BROMF

HA HA HA HA HA HA HA!

097 BIP

WARNING

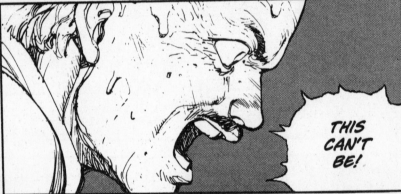

THIS CAN'T BE!

WHAT DO YOU MEAN, DOCTOR?

THERE IS NO MALFUNCTION! THE COOLING SYSTEM FOR THE CENTRAL CHAMBER IS FUNCTIONING PERFECTLY!

WHAT?!

TSHIF
HUH?
BRAK
SKIIZ
BRAAAOO

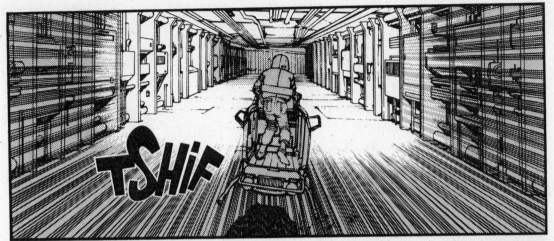

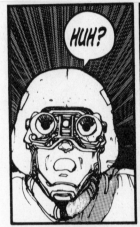

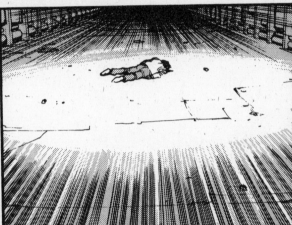

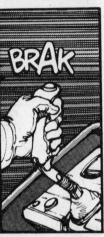

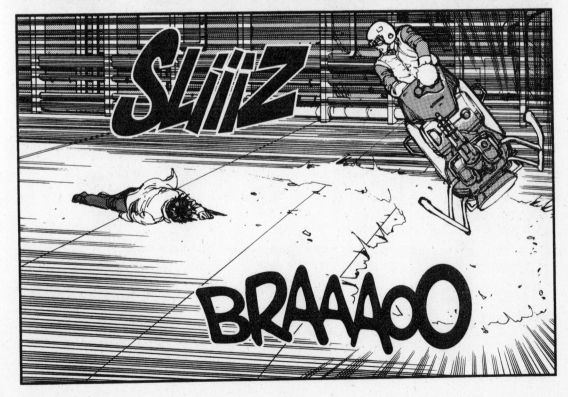

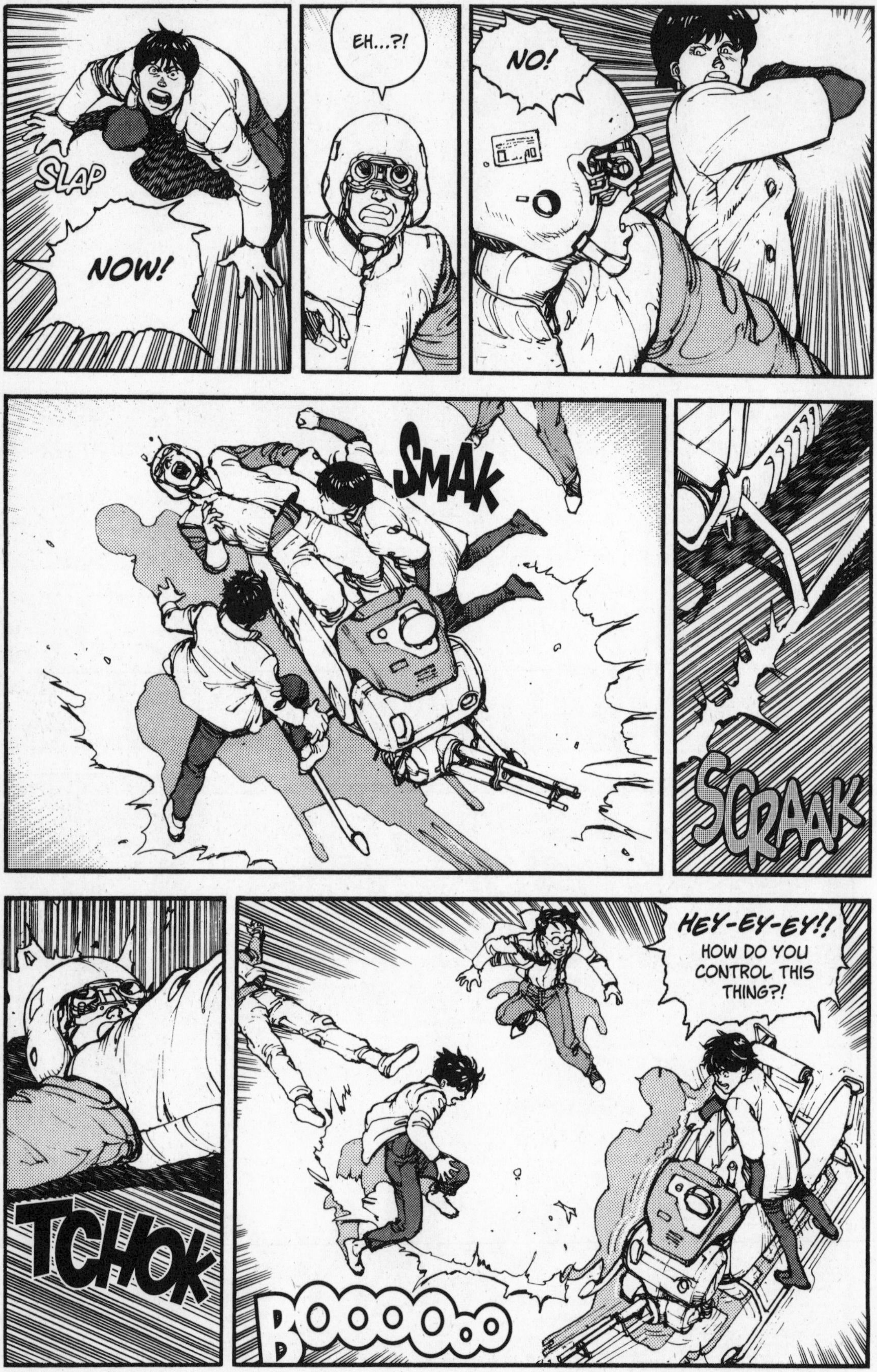
SLAP
NOW!
EH...?!
NO!
SMAK
SCRAAK
TCHOK
BOOOO..
HEY-EY-EY!!
HOW DO YOU CONTROL THIS THING?!

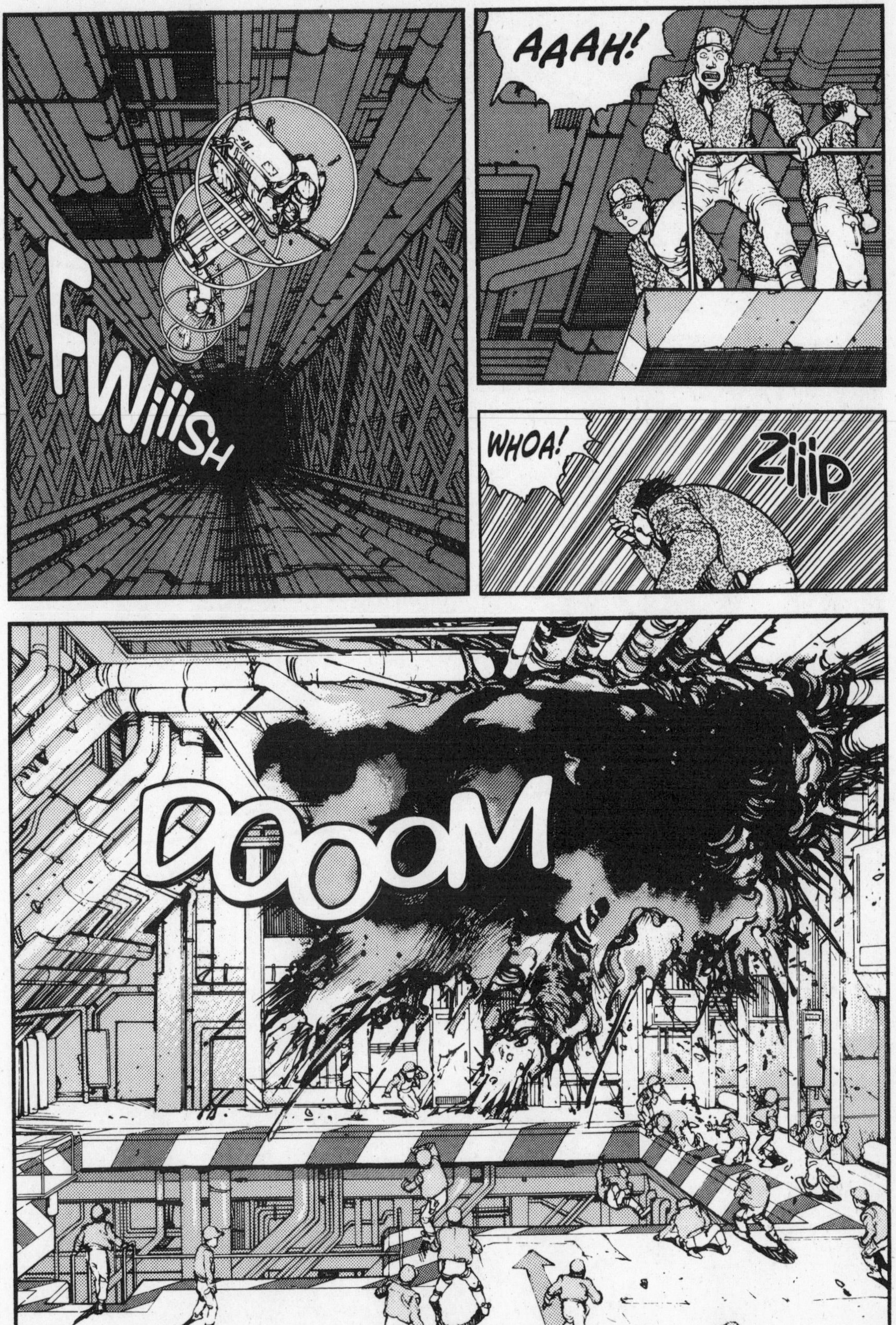
FWiiiSH
AAAH!
WHOA!
Ziiip
DOOOM

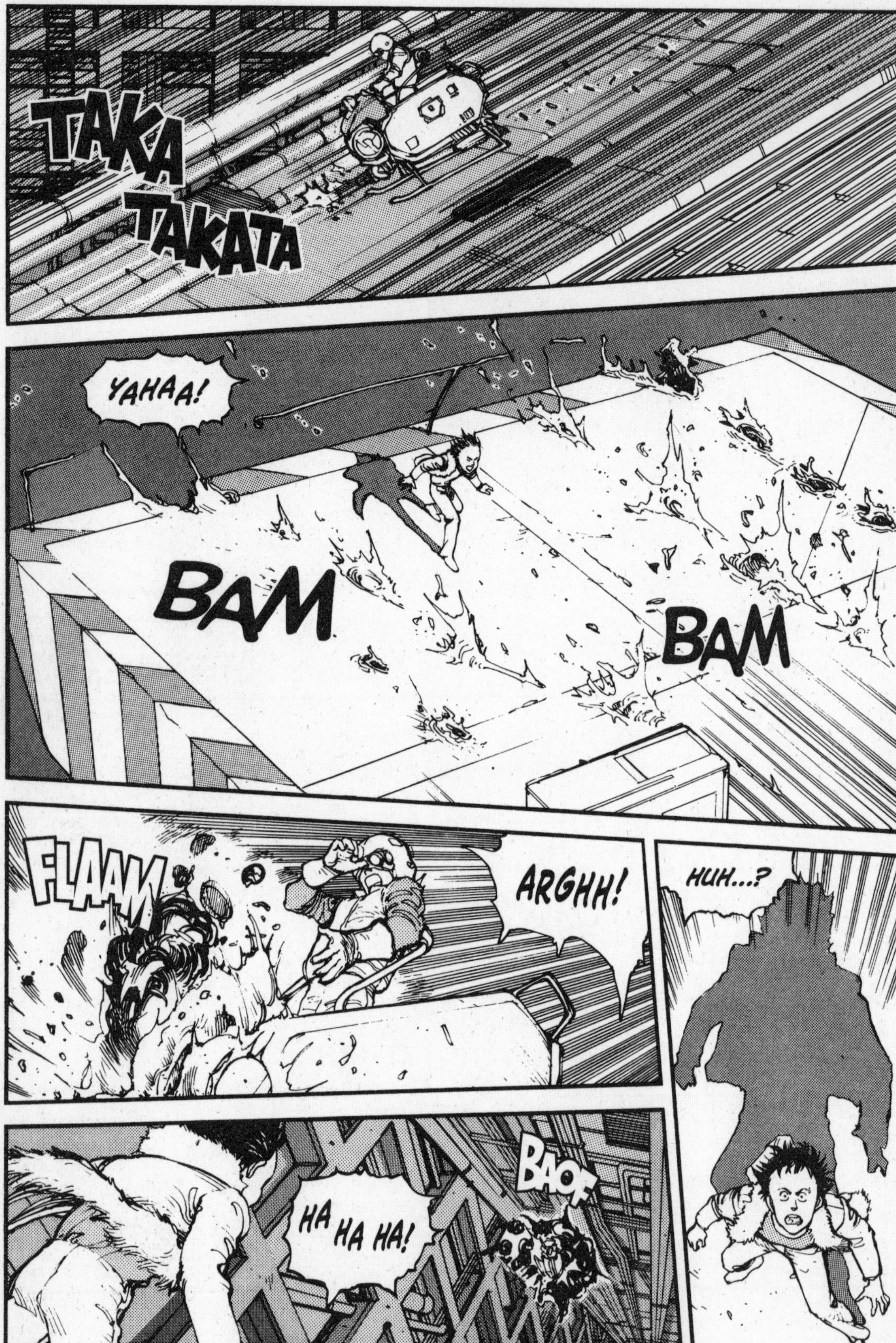
TAKA
TAKATA
YAHAA!
BAM
BAM
FLAAM
ARGHH!
HA HA HA!
BAOF
HUH...?

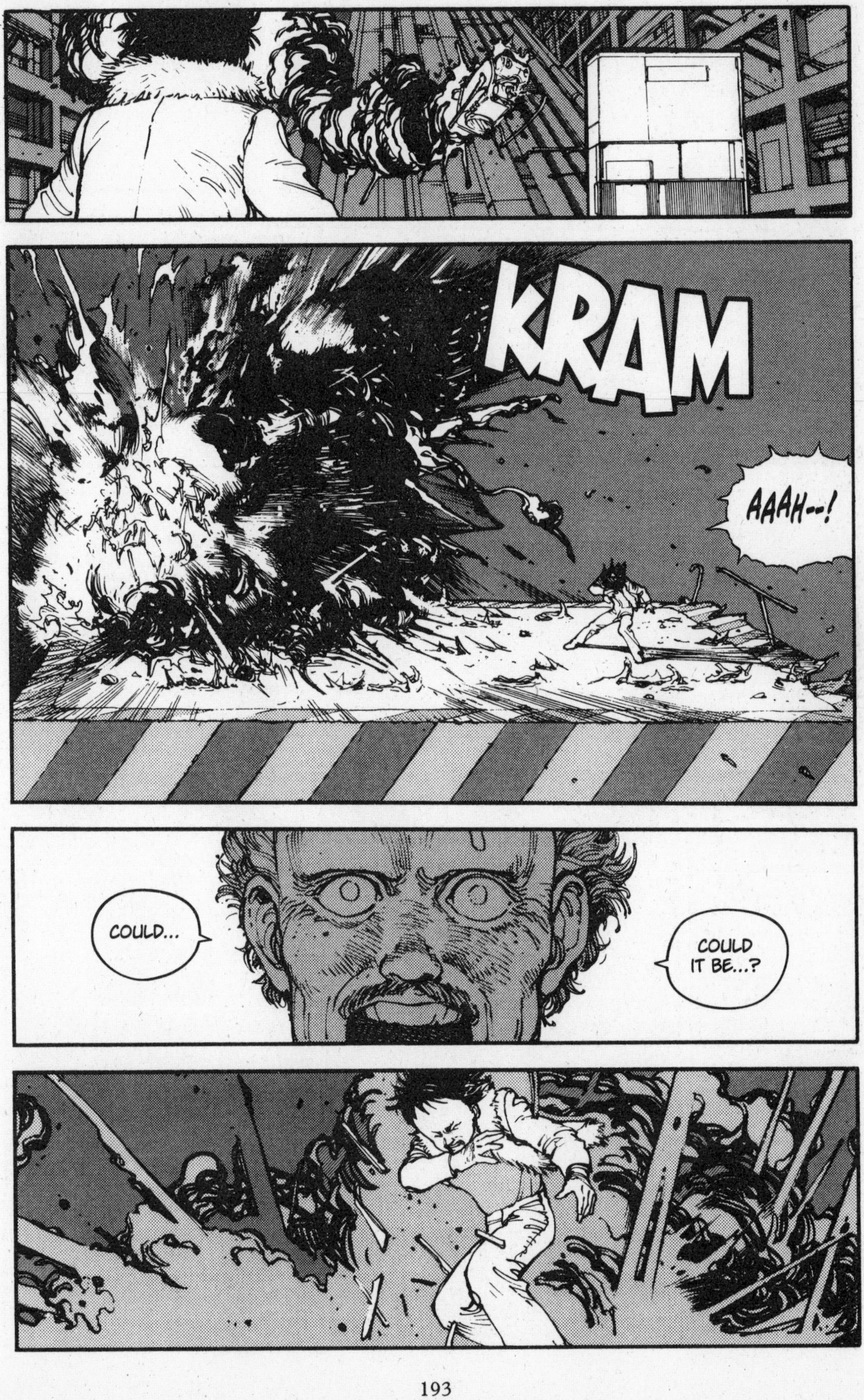
KRAM
AAAH--!
COULD...
COULD IT BE...?

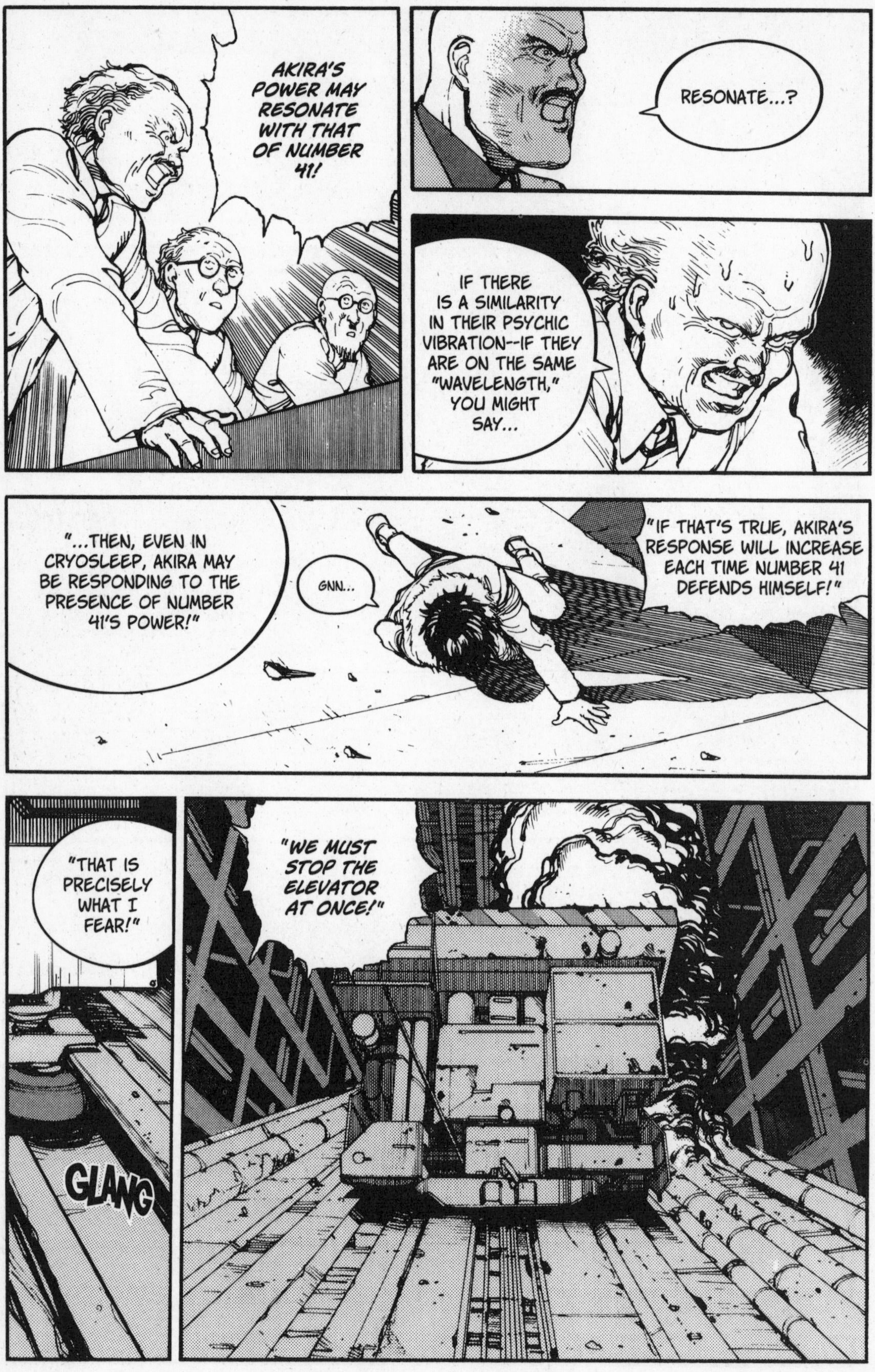
AKIRA'S POWER MAY RESONATE WITH THAT OF NUMBER 41!
RESONATE...?
IF THERE IS A SIMILARITY IN THEIR PSYCHIC VIBRATION--IF THEY ARE ON THE SAME "WAVELENGTH," YOU MIGHT SAY...
"...THEN, EVEN IN CRYOSLEEP, AKIRA MAY BE RESPONDING TO THE PRESENCE OF NUMBER 41'S POWER!"
GNN...
"IF THAT'S TRUE, AKIRA'S RESPONSE WILL INCREASE EACH TIME NUMBER 41 DEFENDS HIMSELF!"
"THAT IS PRECISELY WHAT I FEAR!"
GLANG
"WE MUST STOP THE ELEVATOR AT ONCE!"

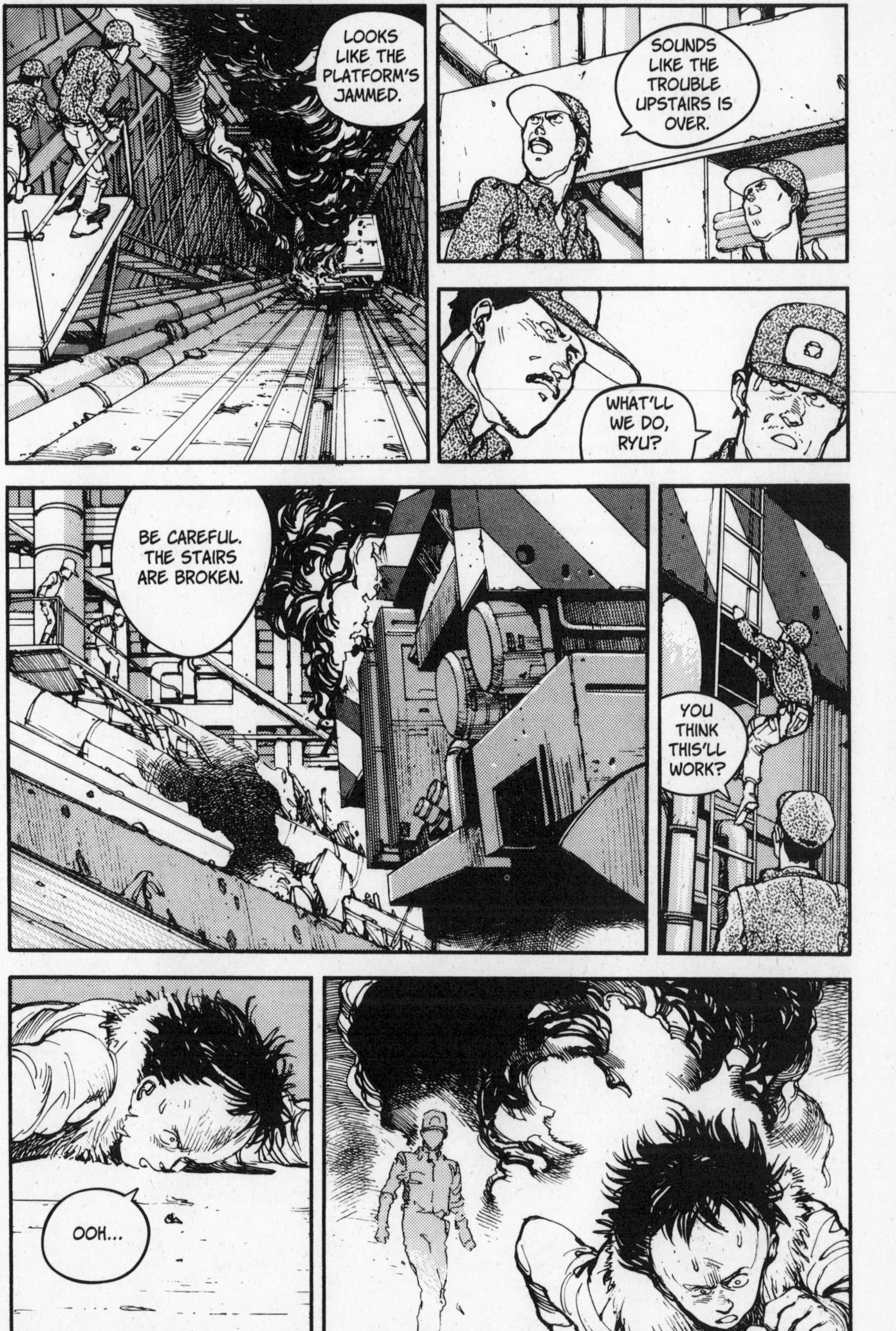
LOOKS LIKE THE PLATFORM'S JAMMED.
SOUNDS LIKE THE TROUBLE UPSTAIRS IS OVER.
WHAT'LL WE DO, RYU?
BE CAREFUL. THE STAIRS ARE BROKEN.
YOU THINK THIS'LL WORK?
OOH...

IT'S A KID!

HEY, ARE YOU OKAY?

DOESN'T LOOK LIKE YOU'RE HURT ANYWHERE. CAN YOU GET UP?

WHAT A JOKE... I CAN'T BELIEVE THIS SHIT.

YOU MEAN, YOU WERE ON THE ELEVATOR?

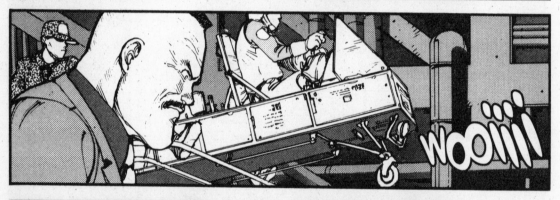

WOOiiii

YOU HEARD THE ORDER! HOLD YOUR FIRE!

DON'T DO ANYTHING TO GET NUMBER 41 UPSET!

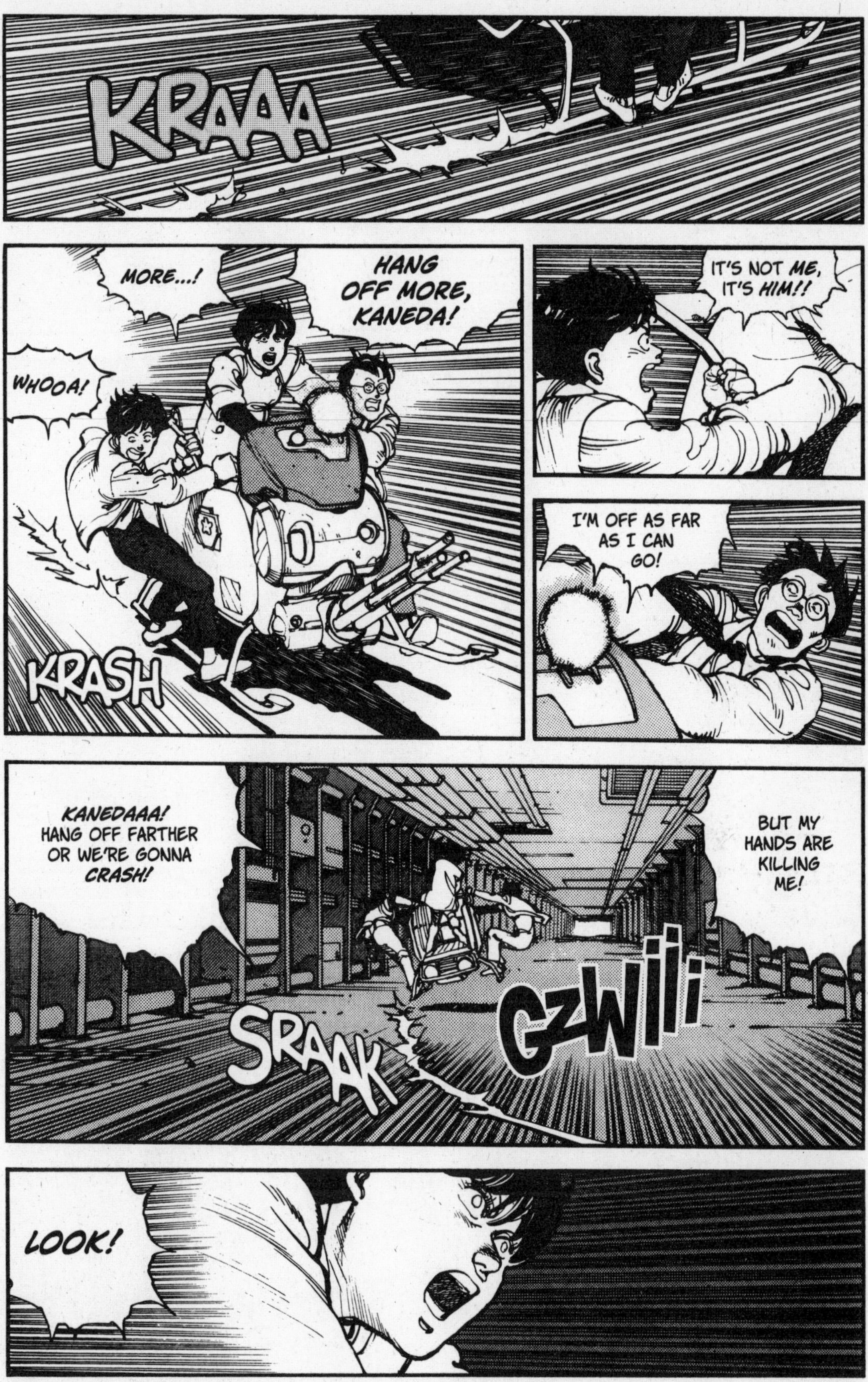
KRAAA
MORE...!
HANG OFF MORE, KANEDA!
WHOOA!
KRASH
IT'S NOT ME, IT'S HIM!!
I'M OFF AS FAR AS I CAN GO!
KANEDAAA! HANG OFF FARTHER OR WE'RE GONNA CRASH!
BUT MY HANDS ARE KILLING ME!
SRAAK
GZWIII
LOOK!

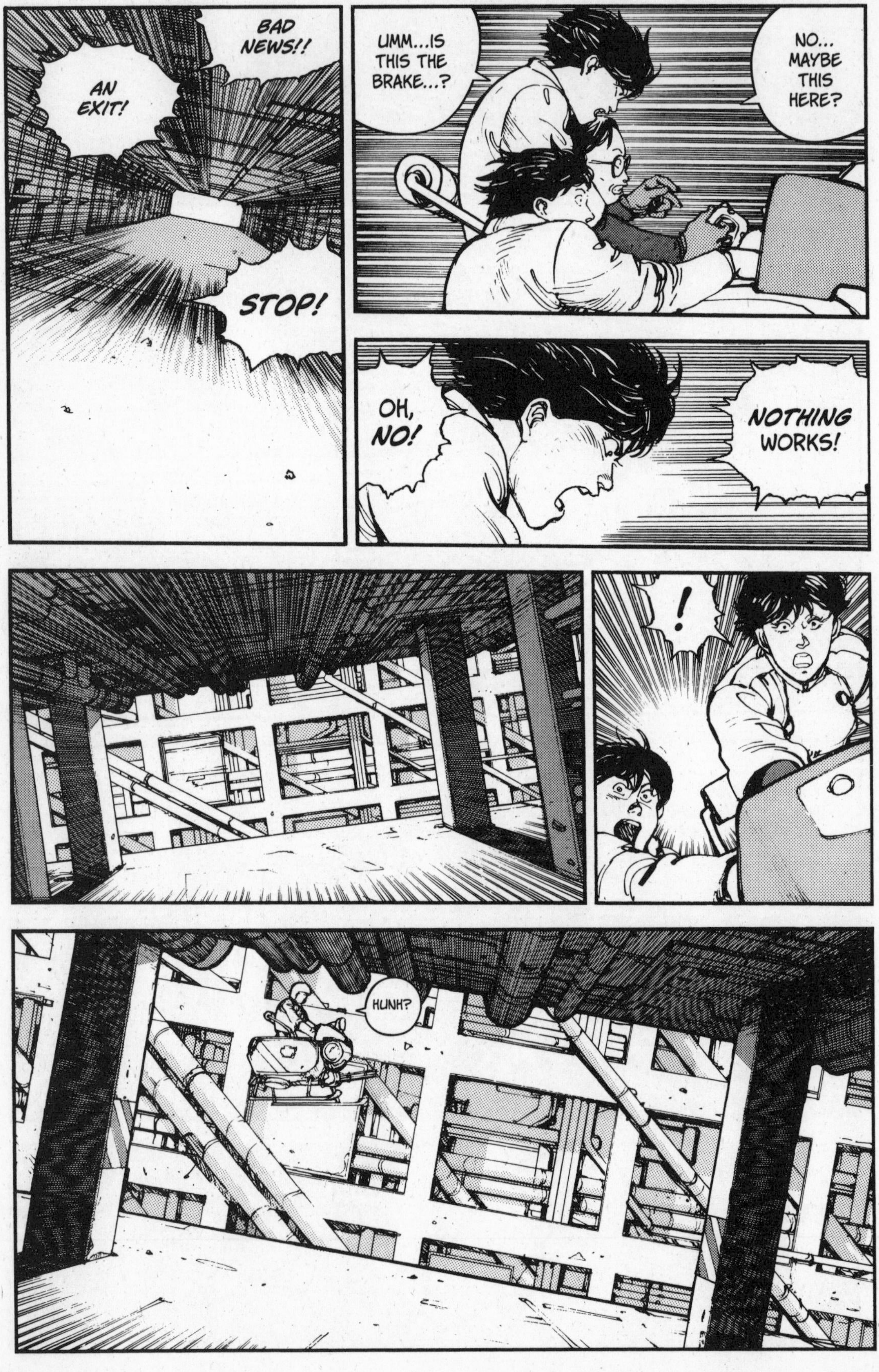
BAD NEWS!!
AN EXIT!
STOP!
UMM...IS THIS THE BRAKE...?
NO... MAYBE THIS HERE?
OH, NO!
NOTHING WORKS!
!
HUNH?

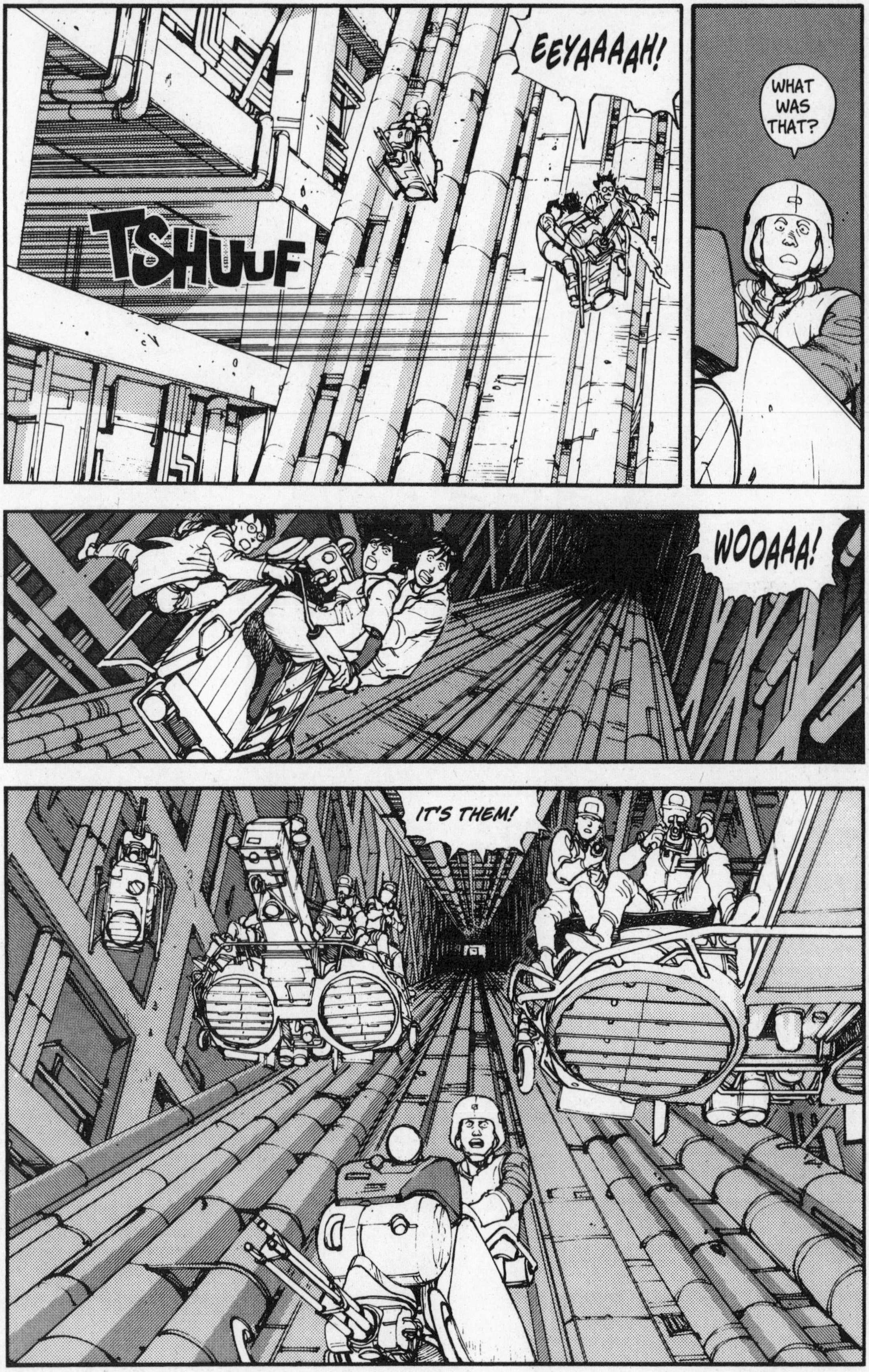
EEYAAAAH!
TSHUUF
WHAT WAS THAT?
WOOAAA!
IT'S THEM!

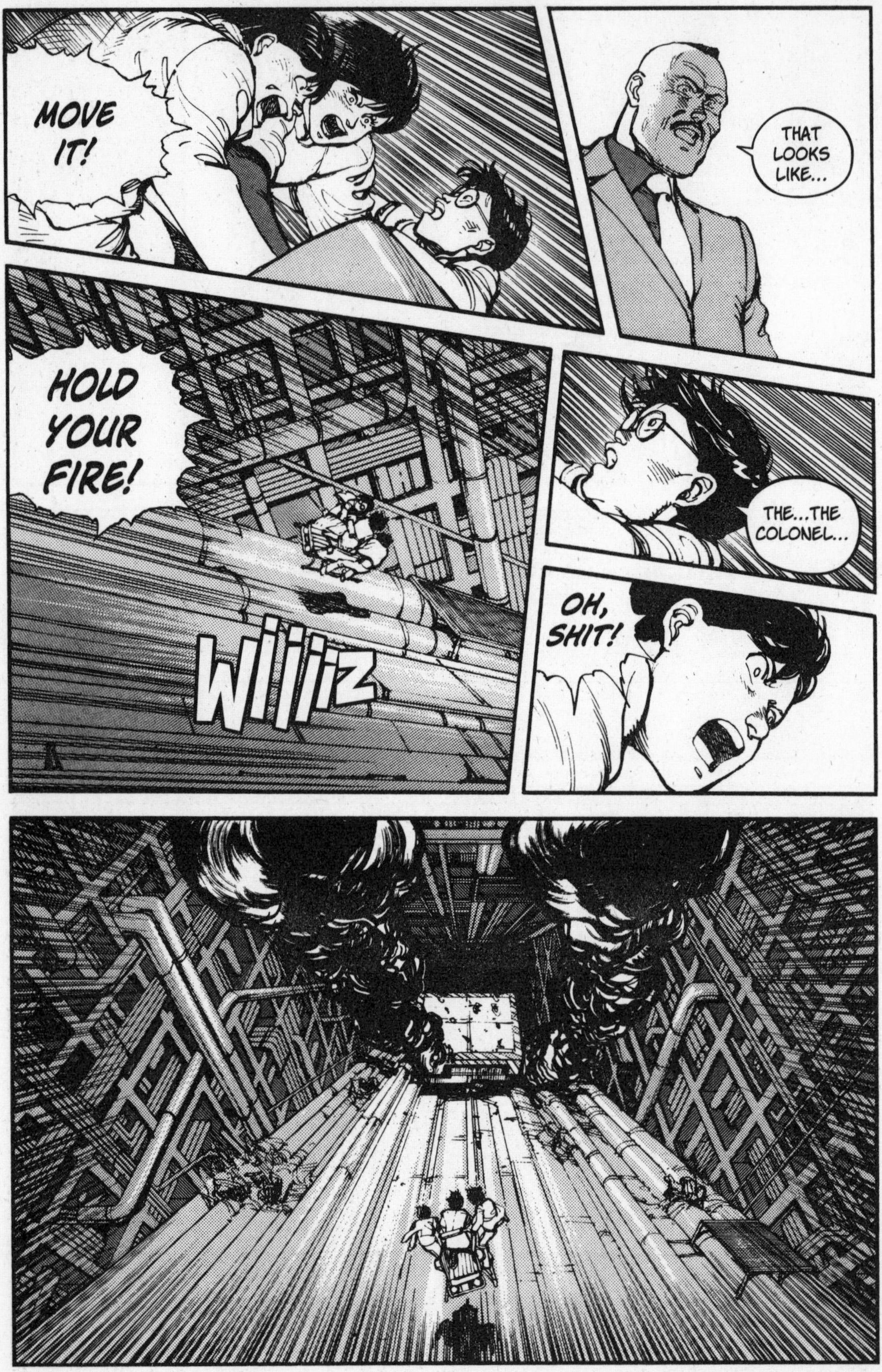
MOVE IT!
THAT LOOKS LIKE...
HOLD YOUR FIRE!
WIIIIZ
THE...THE COLONEL...
OH, SHIT!

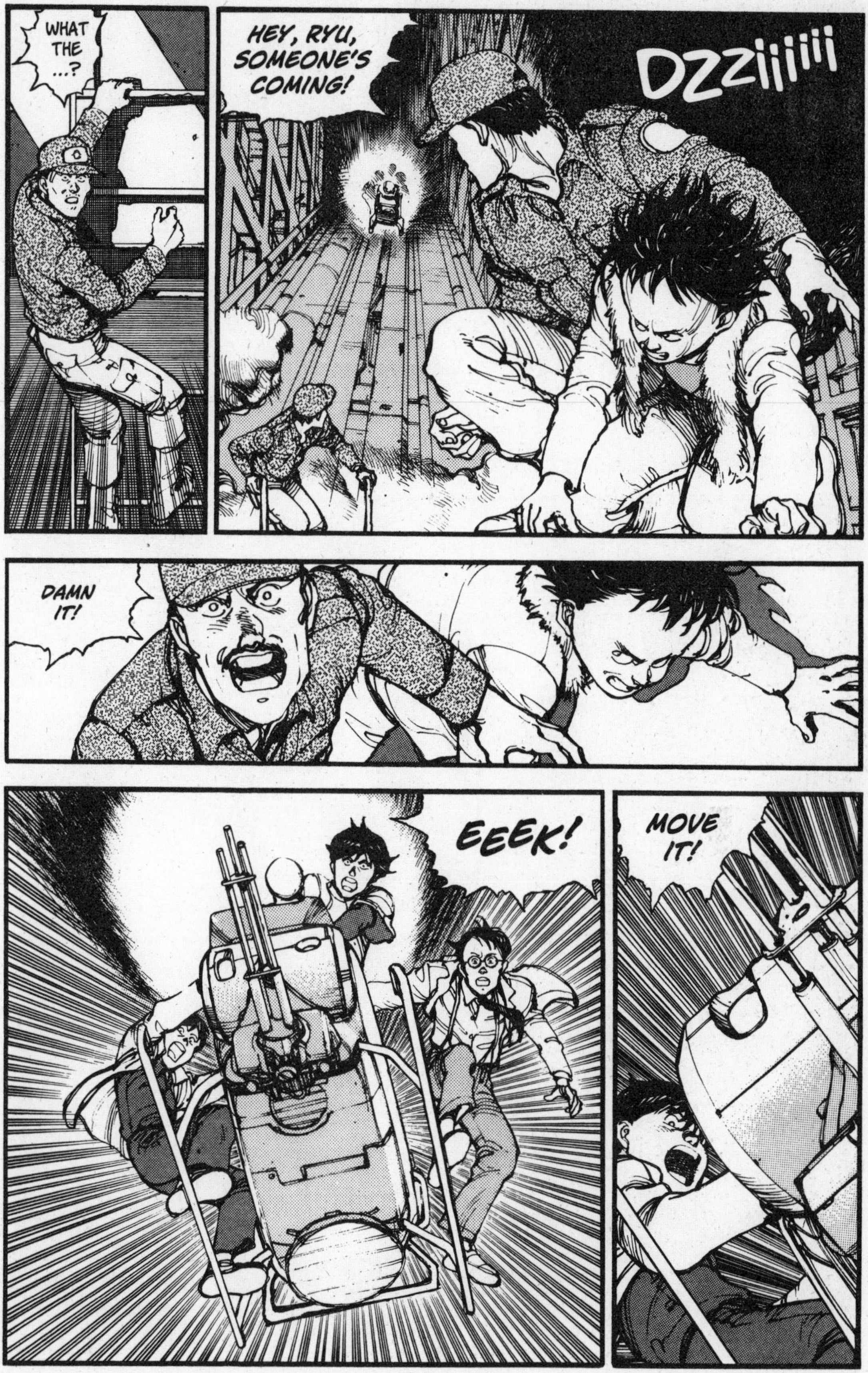
WHAT THE ...?
HEY, RYU, SOMEONE'S COMING!
DZZiiiiii
DAMN IT!
EEEK!
MOVE IT!

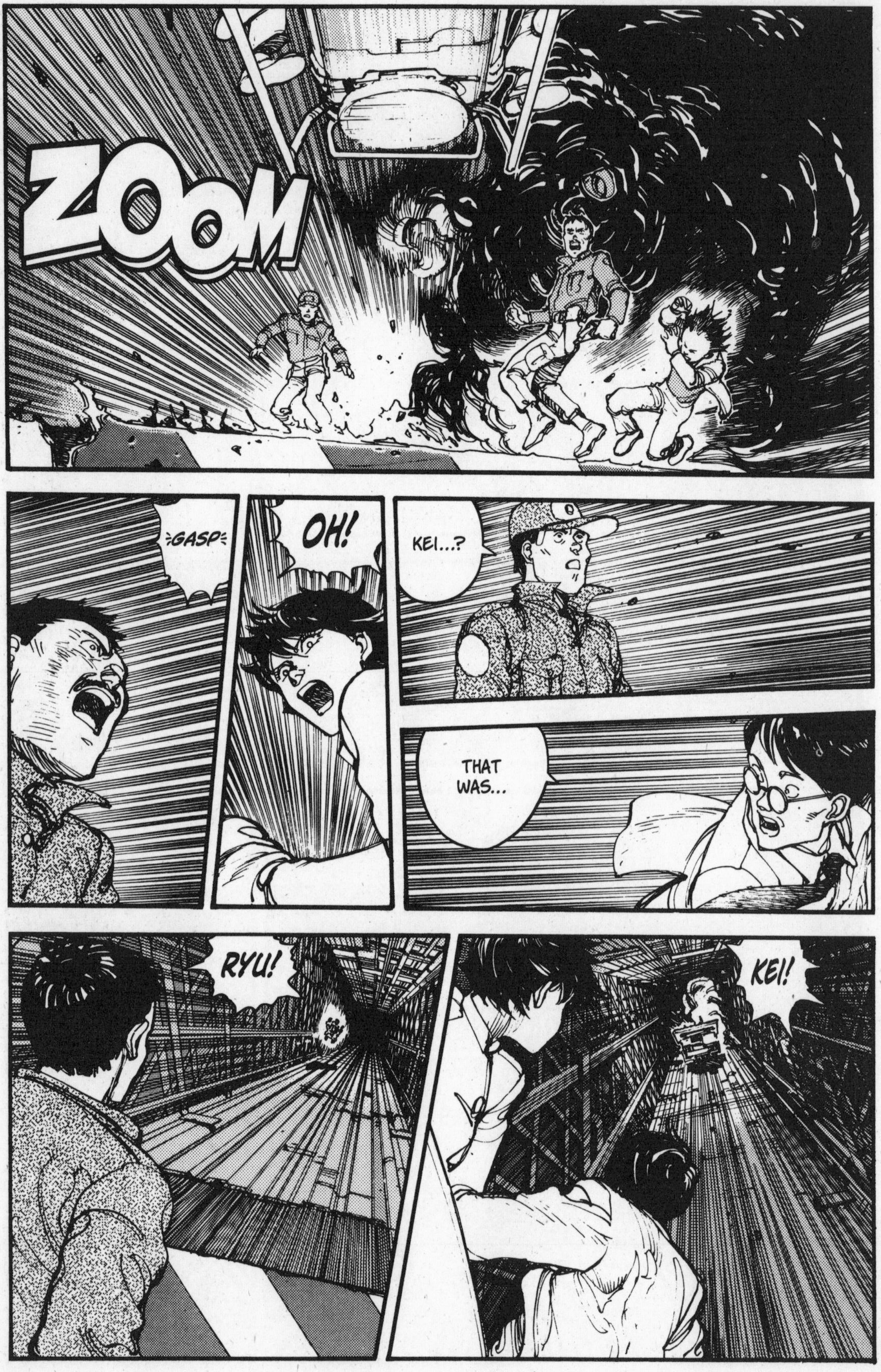
ZOOM
GASP
OH!
KEI...?
THAT WAS...
RYU!
KEI!

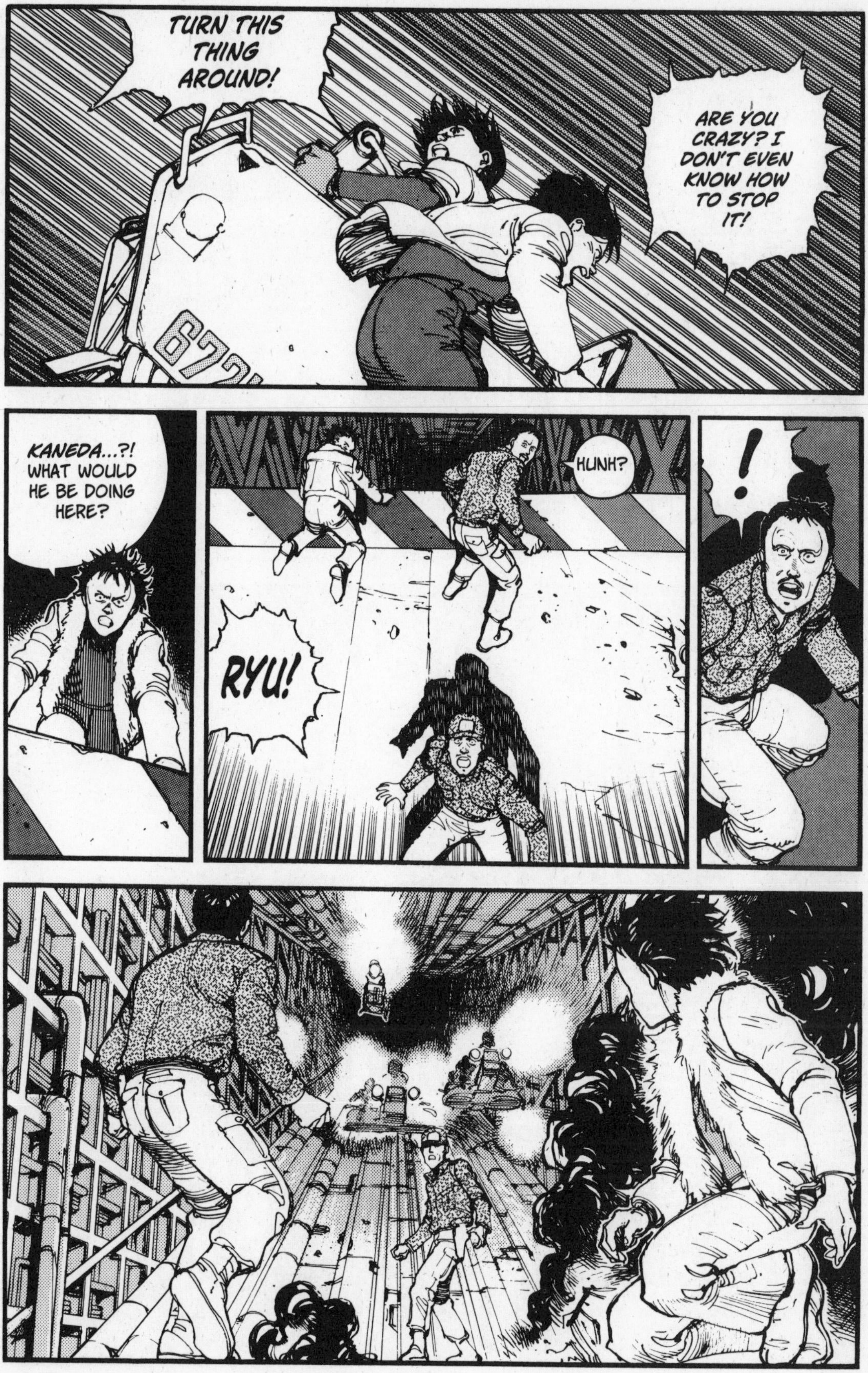
TURN THIS THING AROUND!
ARE YOU CRAZY? I DON'T EVEN KNOW HOW TO STOP IT!
KANEDA...?! WHAT WOULD HE BE DOING HERE?
HUNH?
RYU!
!

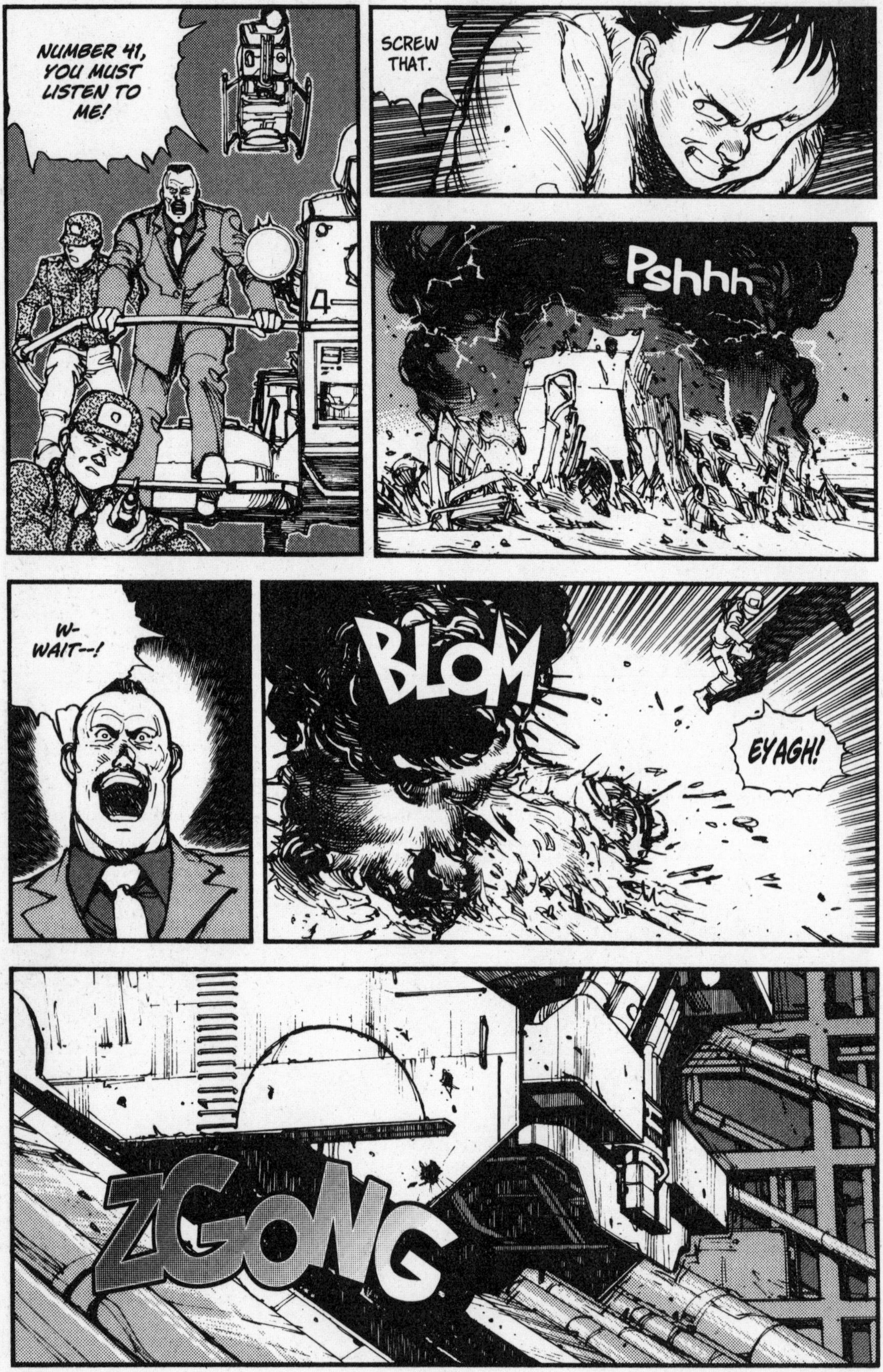
NUMBER 41, YOU MUST LISTEN TO ME!
SCREW THAT.
Pshhh
W-WAIT--!
BLOM
EYAGH!
ZGONG

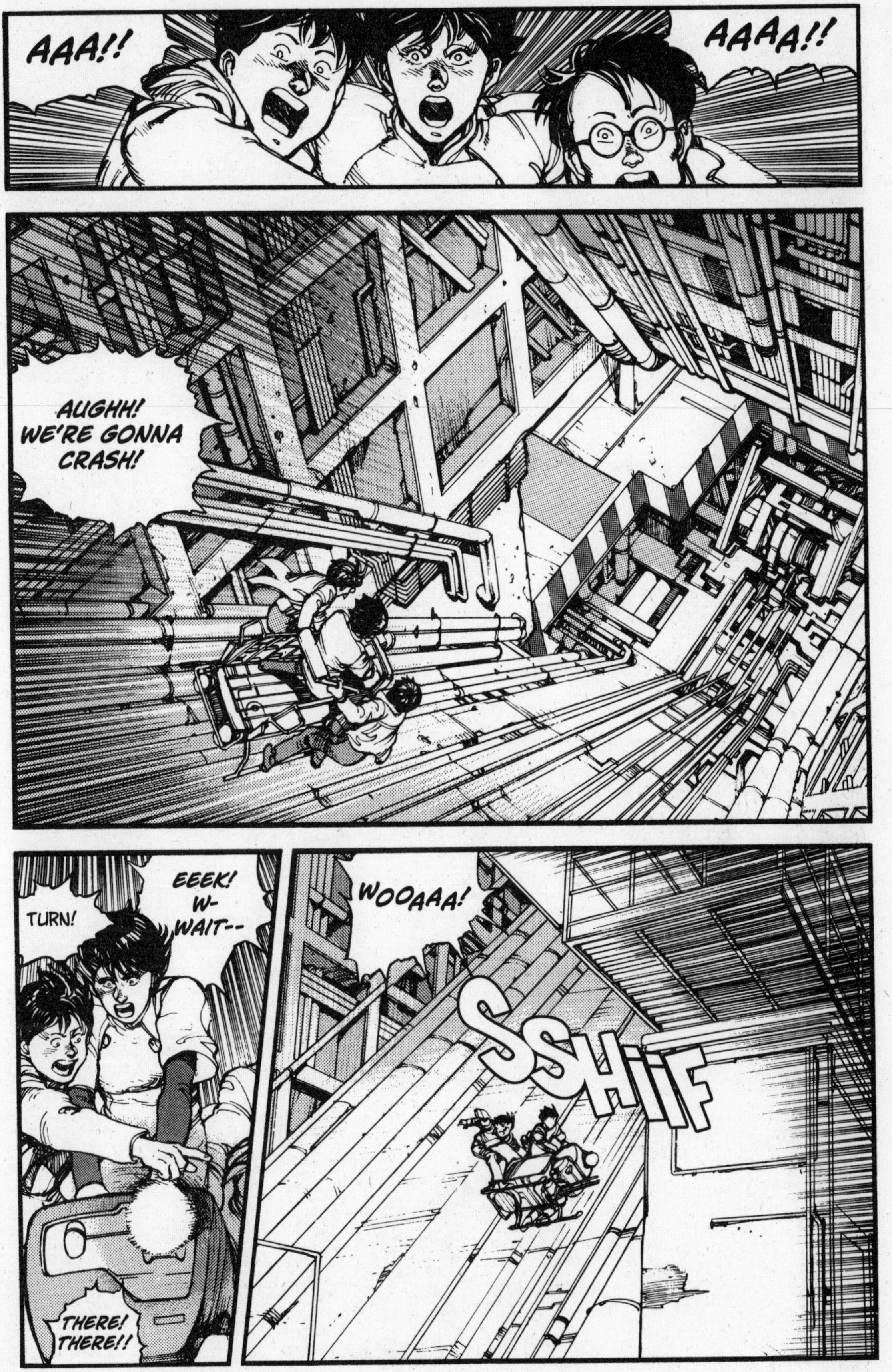
AAA!!
AAAA!!
AUGHH! WE'RE GONNA CRASH!
TURN!
EEEK! W-WAIT--
THERE! THERE!!
WOOAAA!
SSHiiF

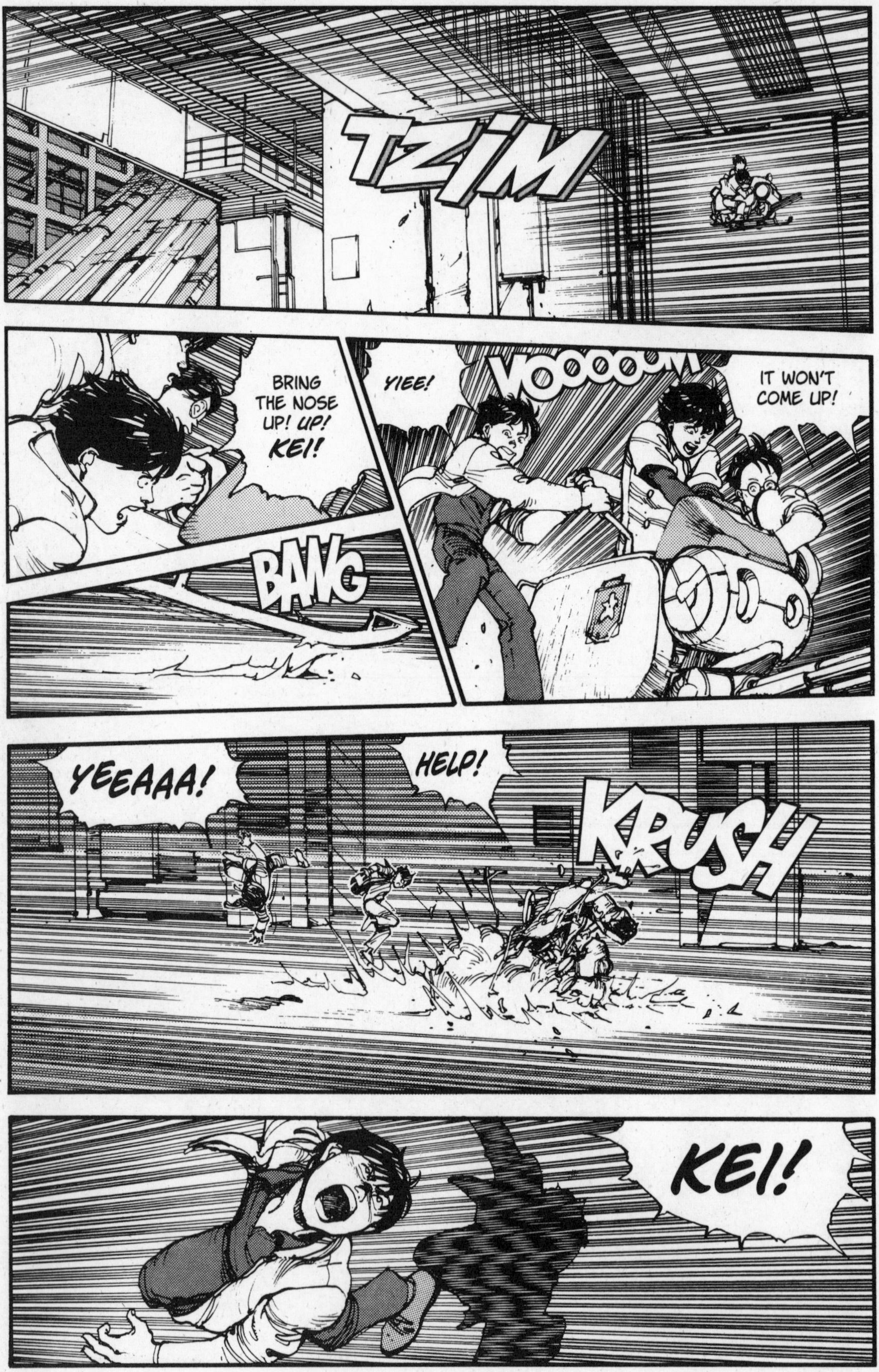
TZIM
BRING THE NOSE UP! UP! KEI!
BANG
YIEE!
VOOOOOM
IT WON'T COME UP!
YEEAAA!
HELP!
KRUSH
KEI!

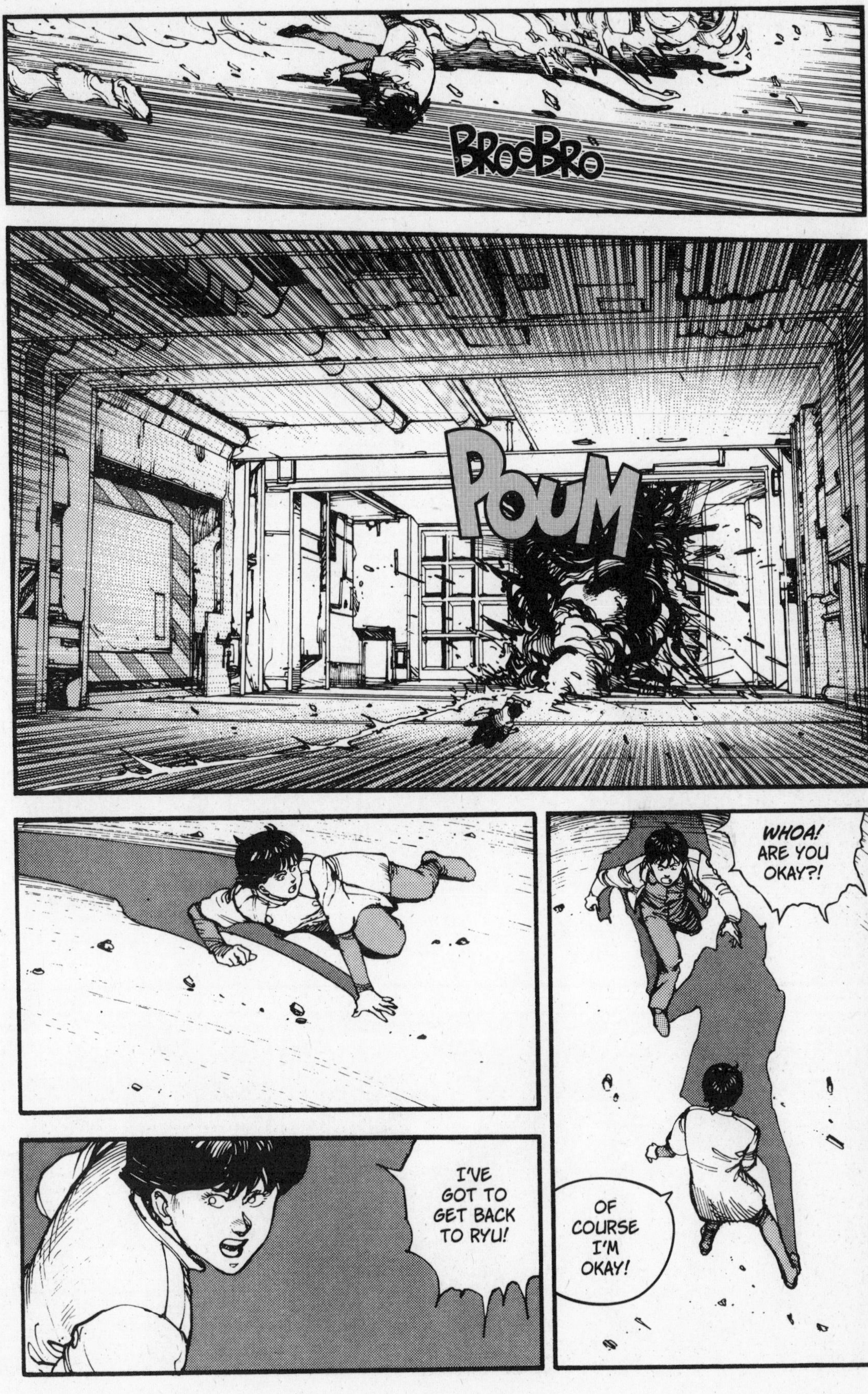
BROOBRO
POUM
I'VE GOT TO GET BACK TO RYU!
WHOA! ARE YOU OKAY?!
OF COURSE I'M OKAY!

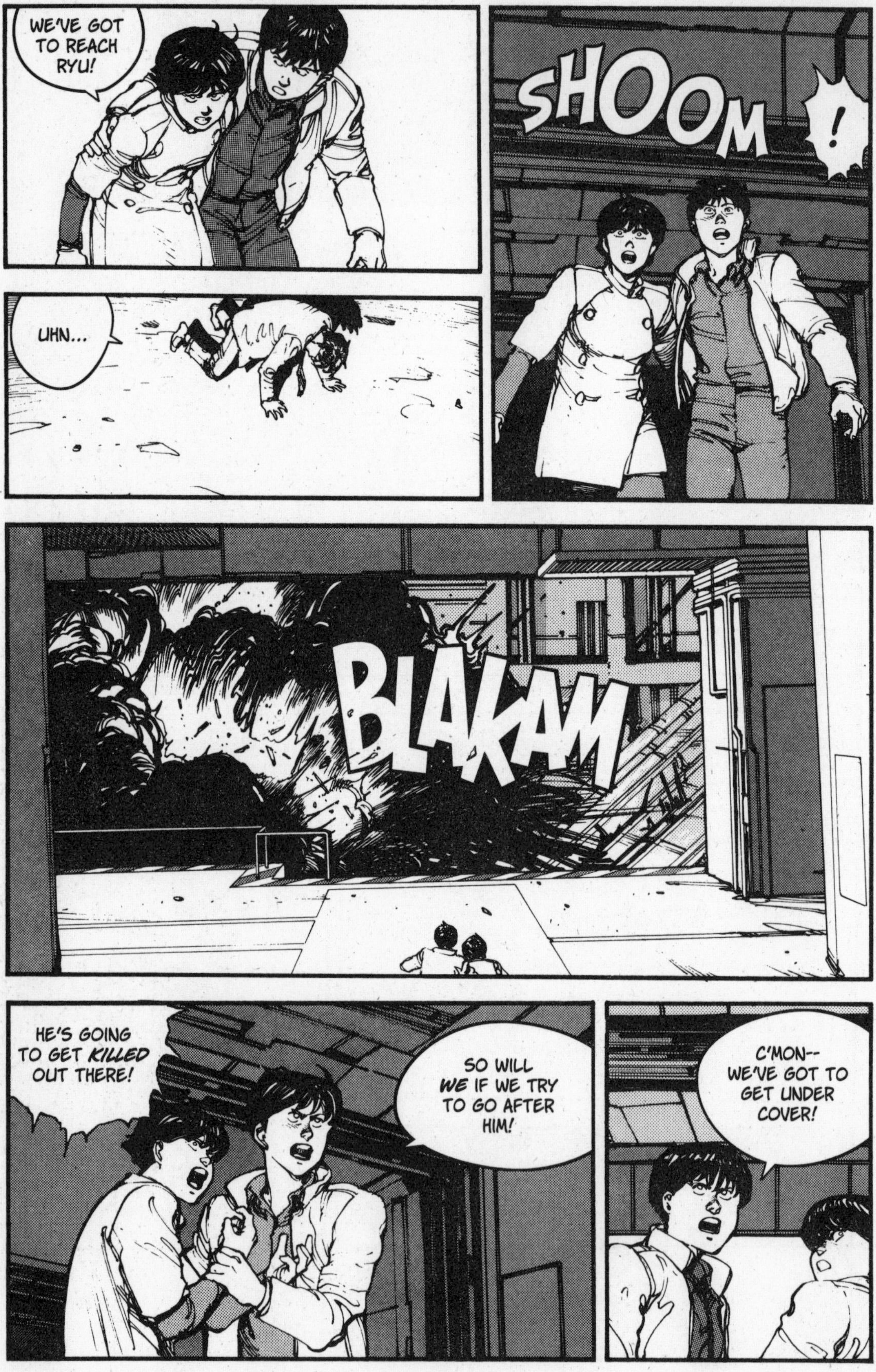
WE'VE GOT TO REACH RYU!
SHOOM !
UHN...
BLAKAM
HE'S GOING TO GET KILLED OUT THERE!
SO WILL WE IF WE TRY TO GO AFTER HIM!
C'MON-- WE'VE GOT TO GET UNDER COVER!

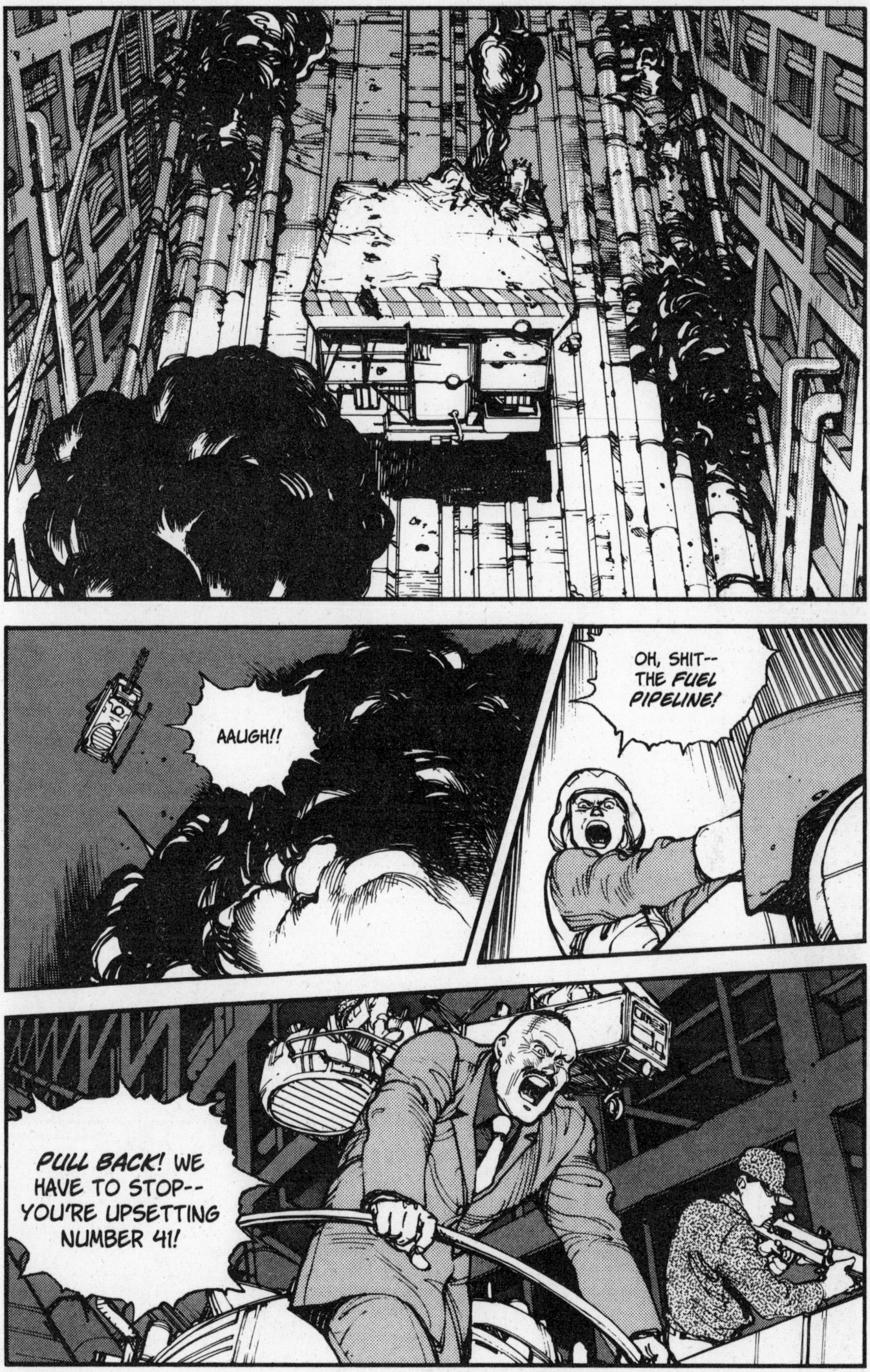
AAUGH!!
OH, SHIT--
THE *FUEL PIPELINE!*
*PULL BACK!* WE HAVE TO STOP--
YOU'RE UPSETTING NUMBER 41!

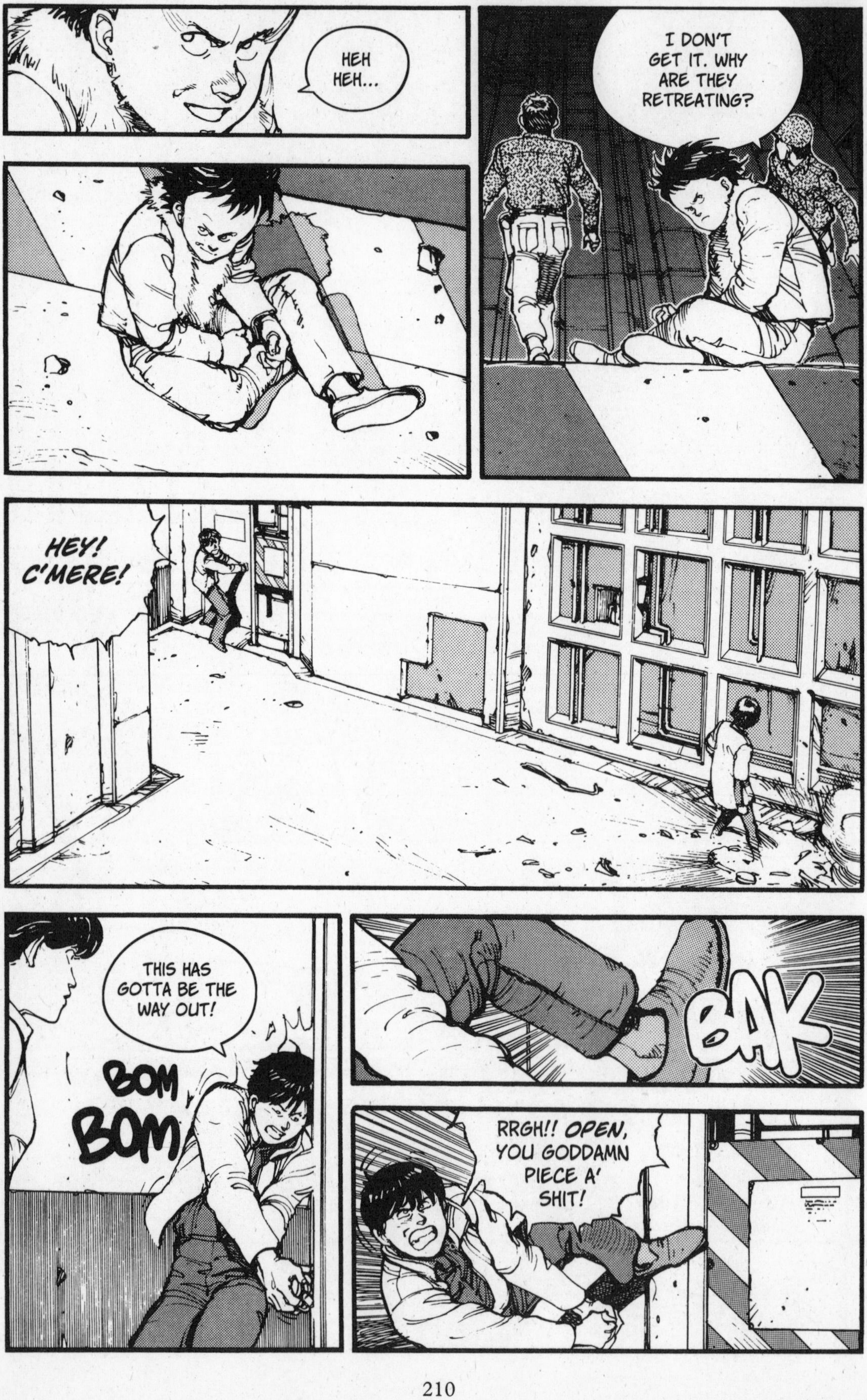
HEH HEH...
I DON'T GET IT. WHY ARE THEY RETREATING?
HEY! C'MERE!
THIS HAS GOTTA BE THE WAY OUT!
BOM BOM
BAK
RRGH!! OPEN, YOU GODDAMN PIECE A' SHIT!

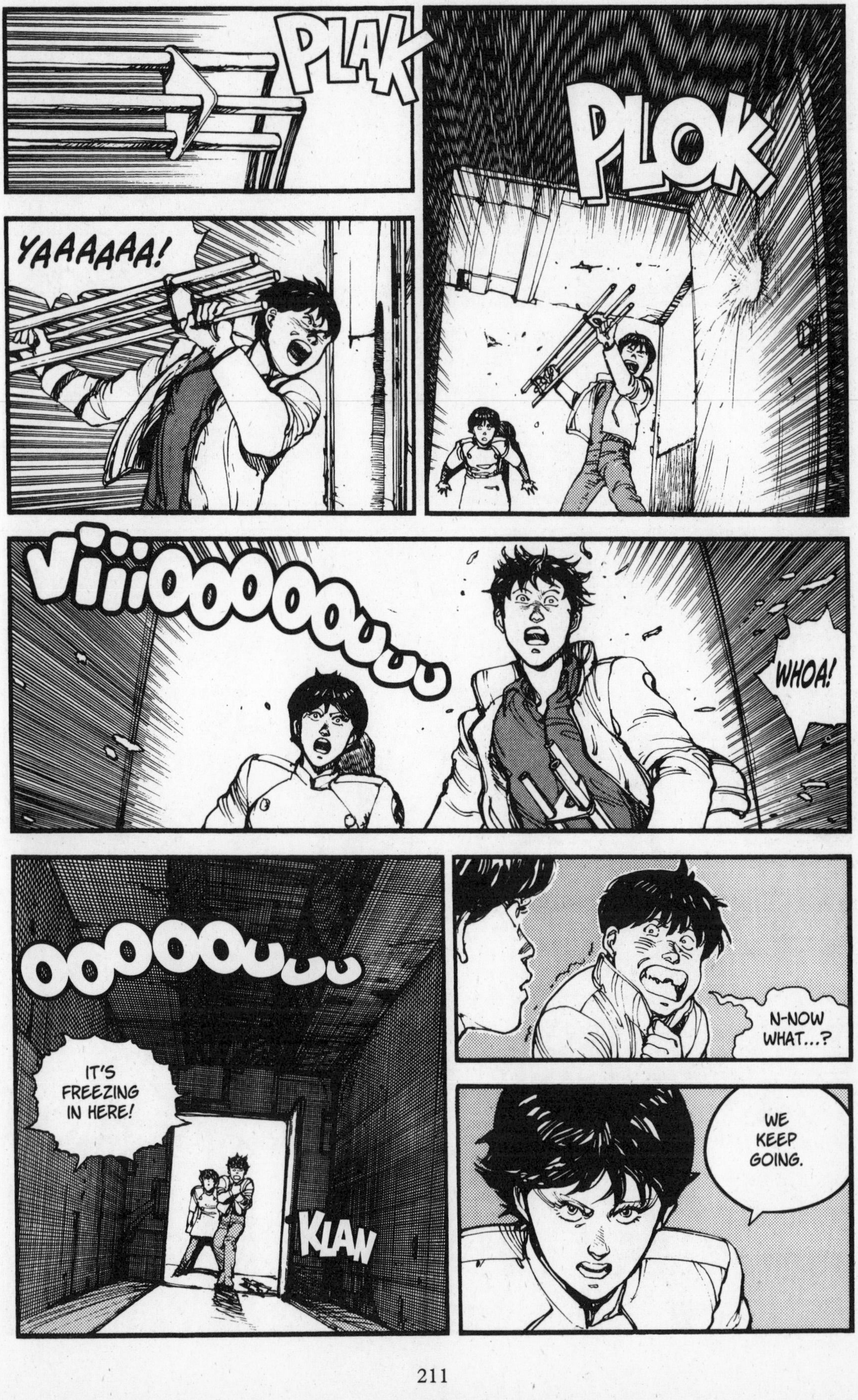
PLAK
PLOK
YAAAAAA!
VIIIOOOOOOUUU
WHOA!
OOOOOUUU
IT'S FREEZING IN HERE!
KLAN
N-NOW WHAT...?
WE KEEP GOING.

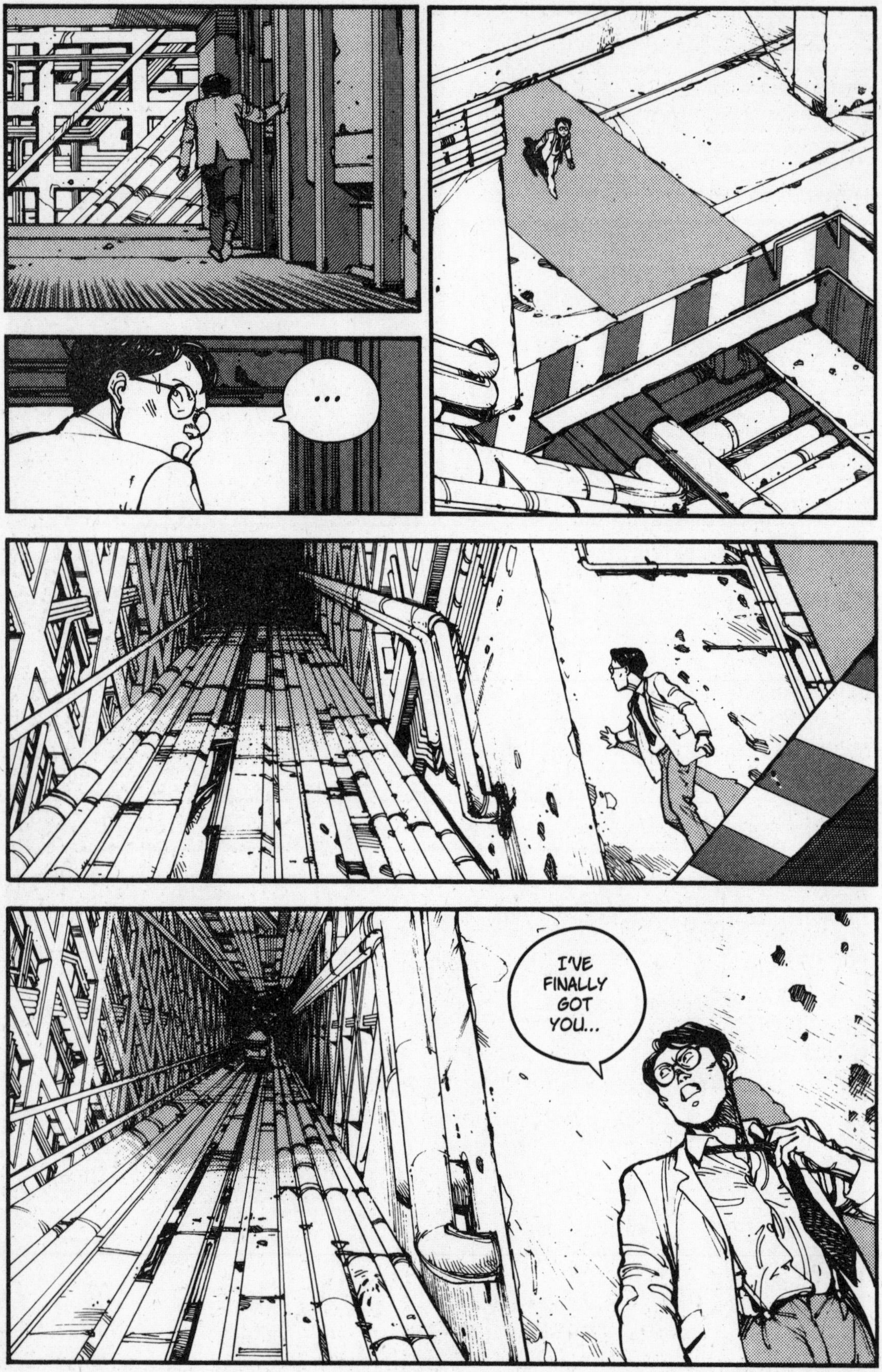
...
I'VE FINALLY GOT YOU...

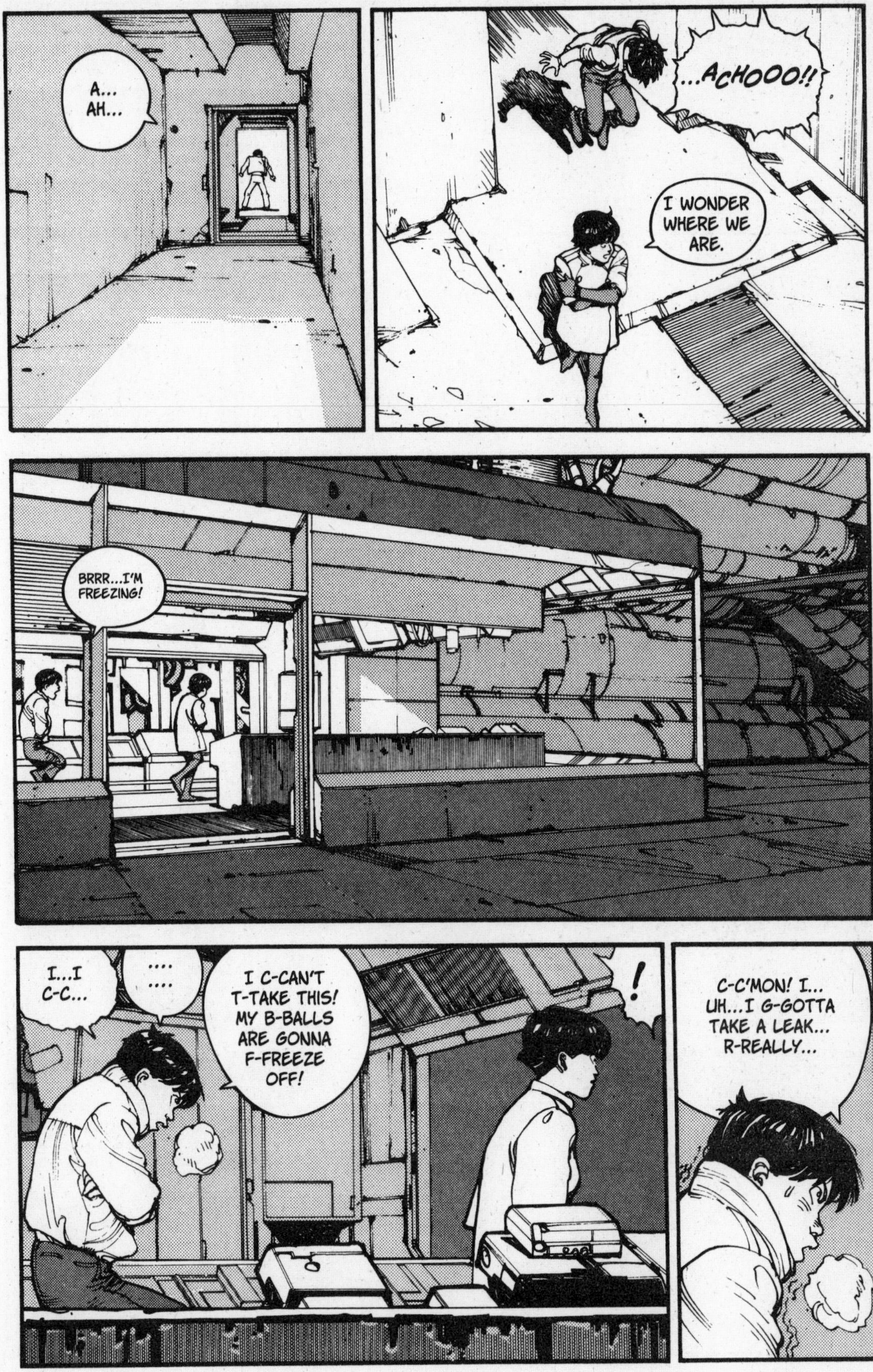
A...
AH...
...ACHOOO!!
I WONDER WHERE WE ARE.
BRRR...I'M FREEZING!
I...I C-C...
....
....
I C-CAN'T T-TAKE THIS! MY B-BALLS ARE GONNA F-FREEZE OFF!
!
C-C'MON! I... UH...I G-GOTTA TAKE A LEAK... R-REALLY...

AH? AAH!!

KANEDA, LOOK!

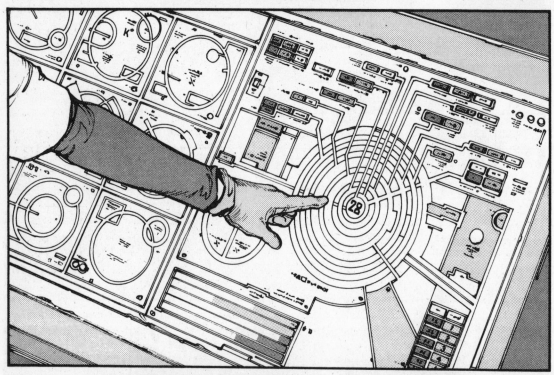

S-SO WHAT...?

THAT'S WHERE WE'LL FIND NUMBER 28!

214

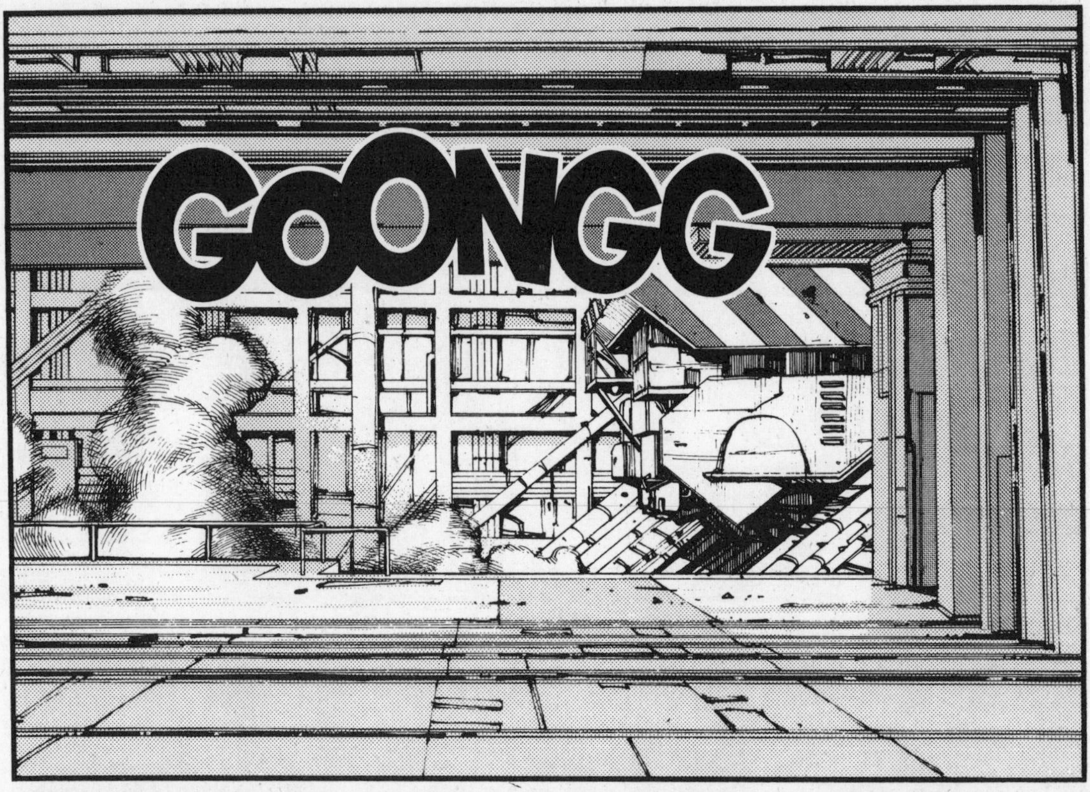
GOONGG
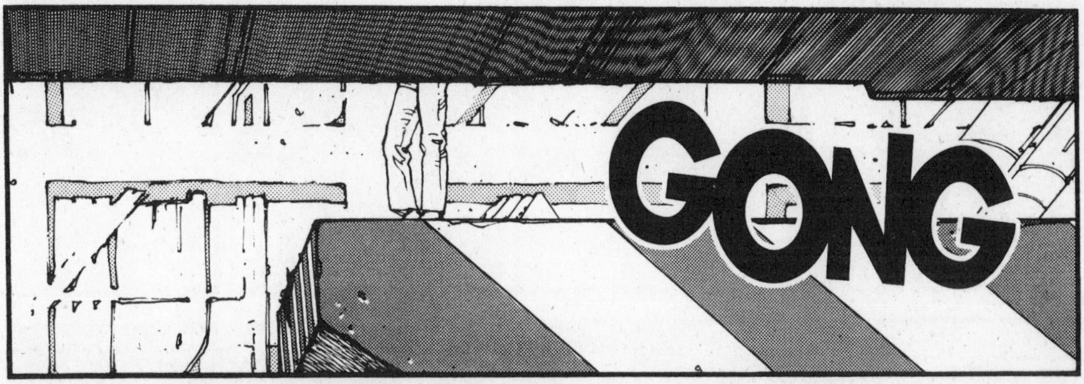
GONG
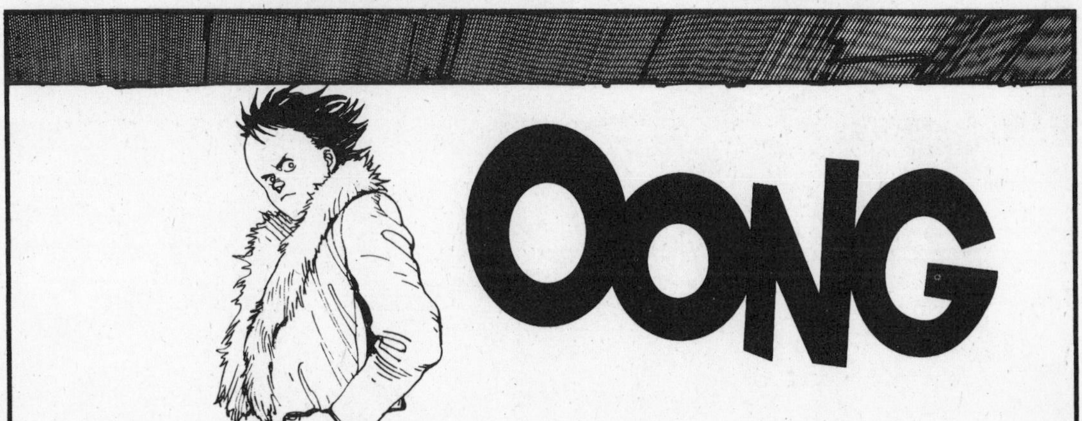
OONG

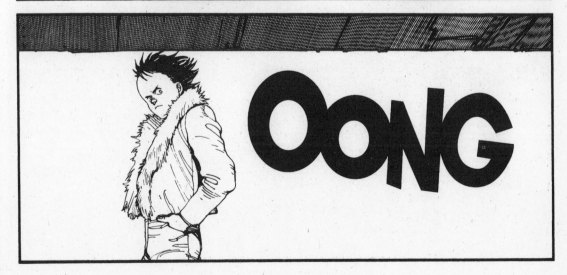

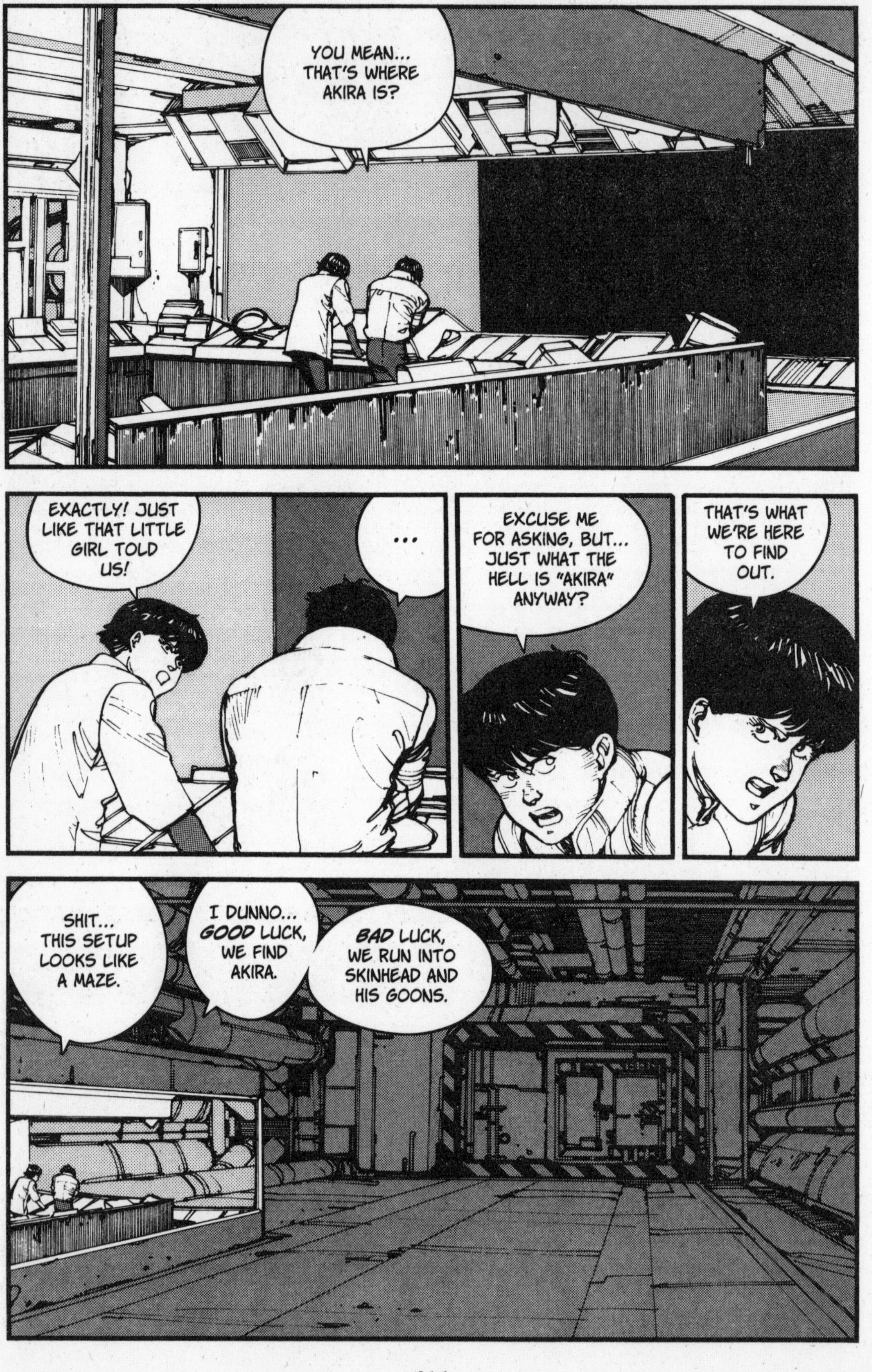
YOU MEAN... THAT'S WHERE AKIRA IS?
EXACTLY! JUST LIKE THAT LITTLE GIRL TOLD US!
...
EXCUSE ME FOR ASKING, BUT... JUST WHAT THE HELL IS "AKIRA" ANYWAY?
THAT'S WHAT WE'RE HERE TO FIND OUT.
SHIT... THIS SETUP LOOKS LIKE A MAZE.
I DUNNO... GOOD LUCK, WE FIND AKIRA.
BAD LUCK, WE RUN INTO SKINHEAD AND HIS GOONS.

WHILE I'M ALIVE, NO ONE IS TO SHOOT WITHOUT MY DIRECT ORDER.

AND IF YOU ARE FORCED TO FIRE...

...YOU MUST KILL HIM WITH THE FIRST SHOT!

THERE WILL BE NO SECOND CHANCES WITH NUMBER 41!

UNDER-STOOD, SIR!

217

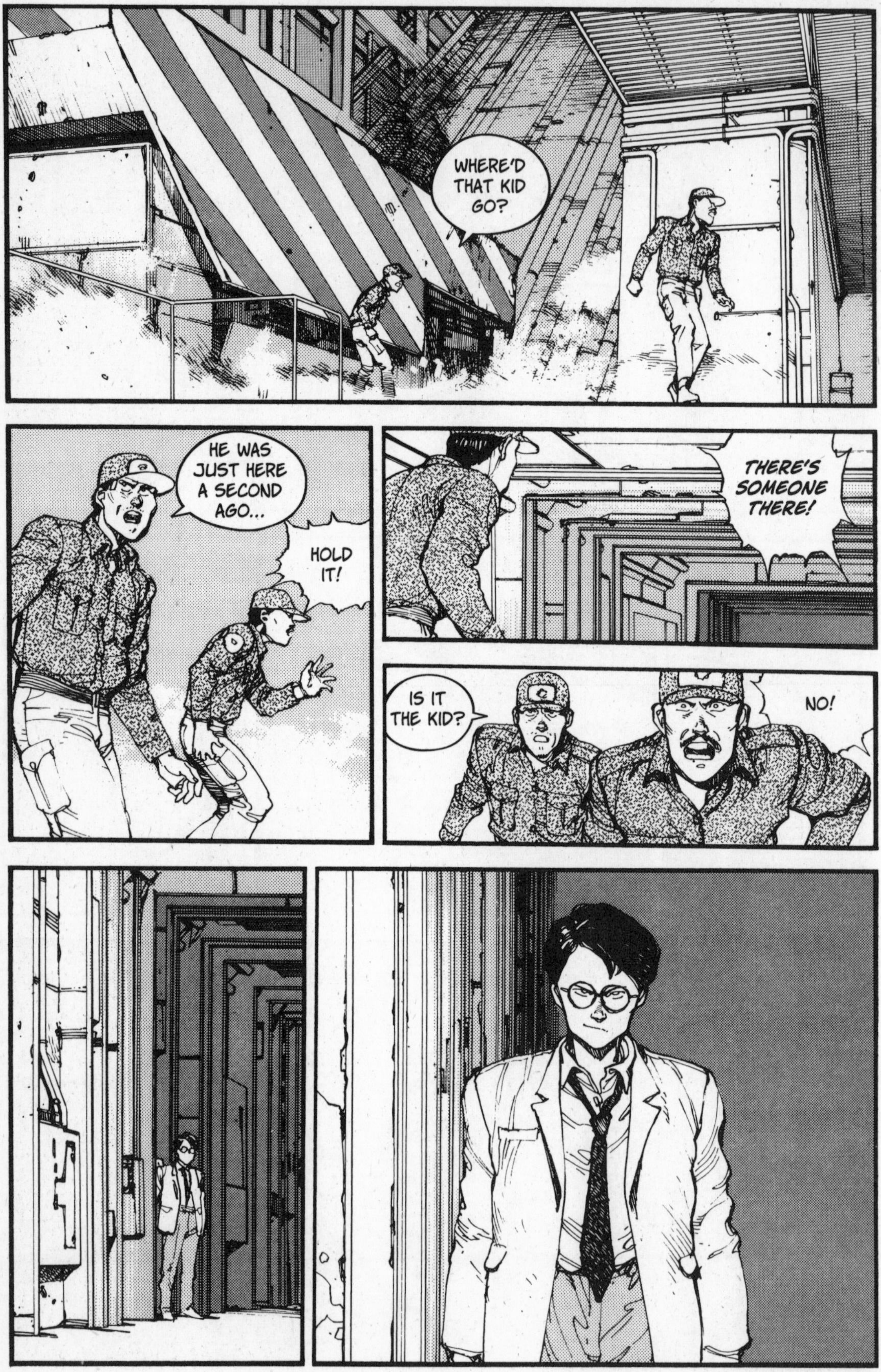
WHERE'D THAT KID GO?
HE WAS JUST HERE A SECOND AGO...
HOLD IT!
THERE'S SOMEONE THERE!
IS IT THE KID?
NO!

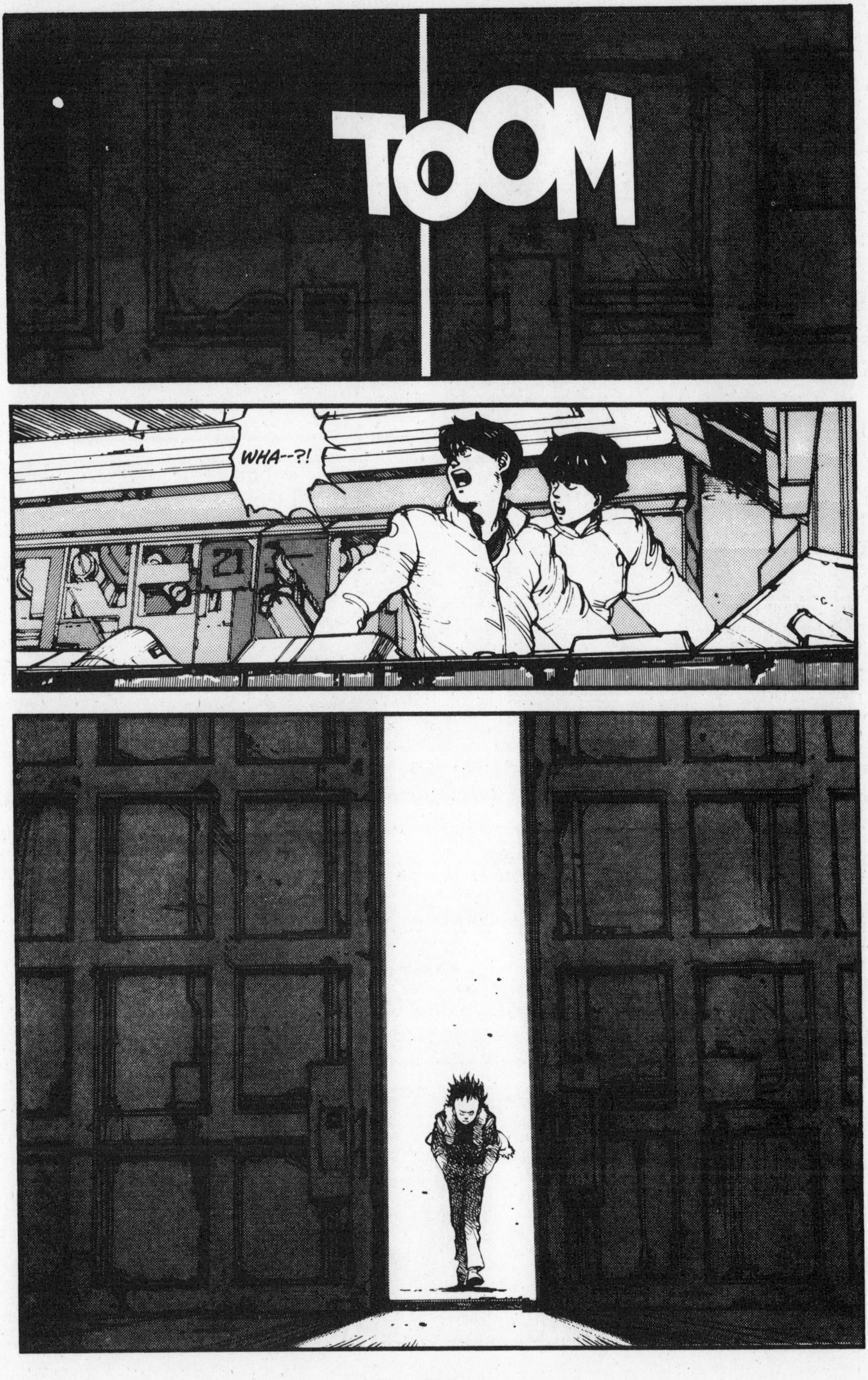
TOOM
WHA--?!

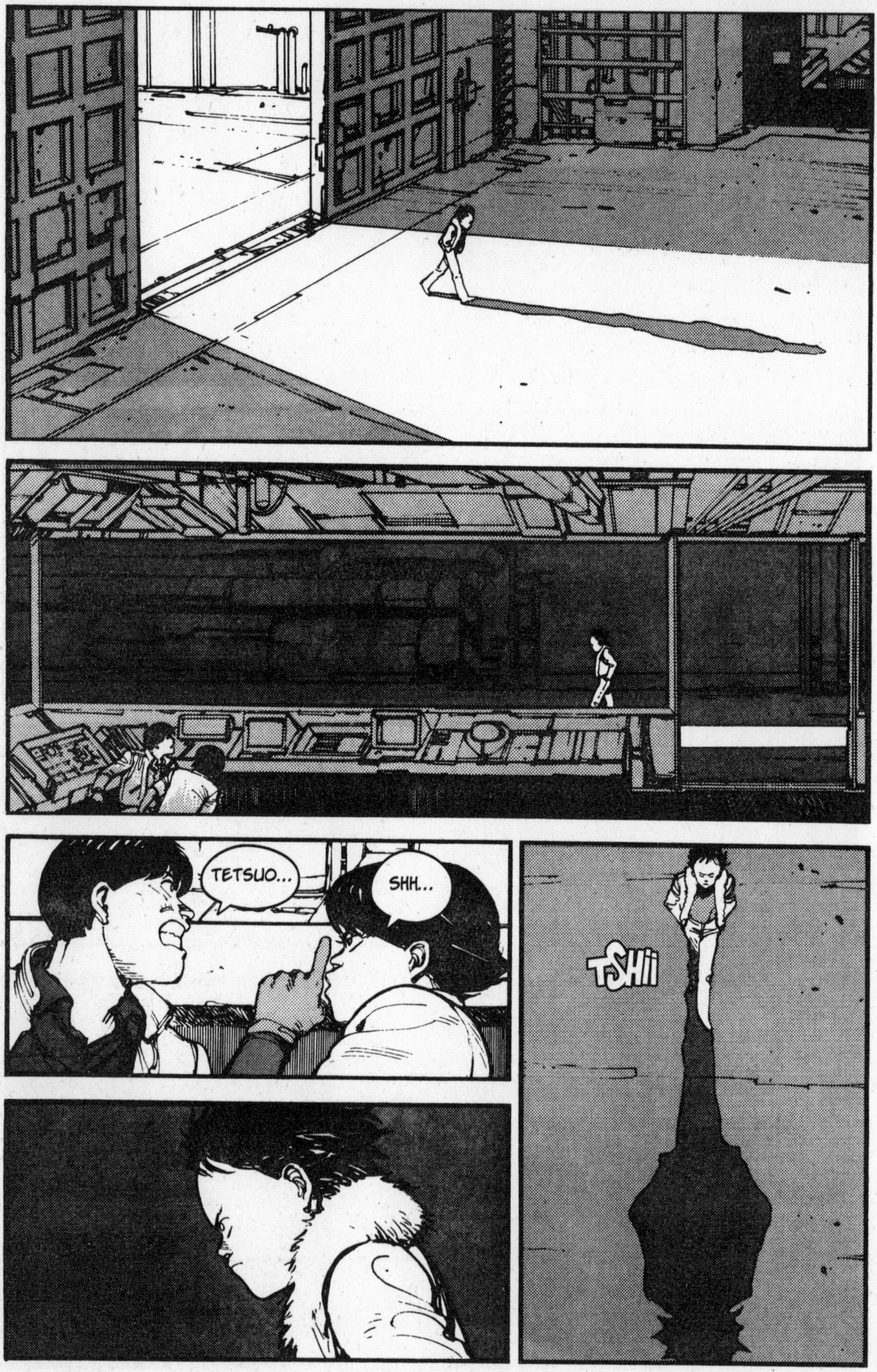
TETSUO...
SHH...
TSHii

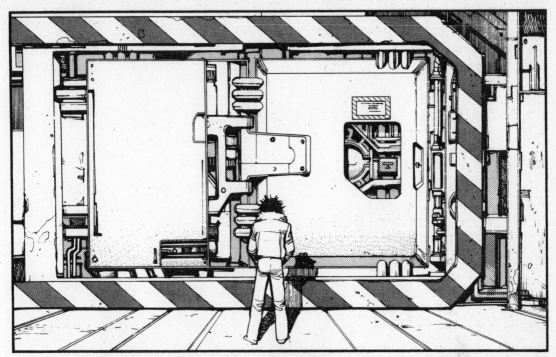

DAMN...

THERE'S NOTHING WE CAN DO RIGHT NOW BUT WAIT...

BUT...I WONDER IF...

...THAT DOOR...?

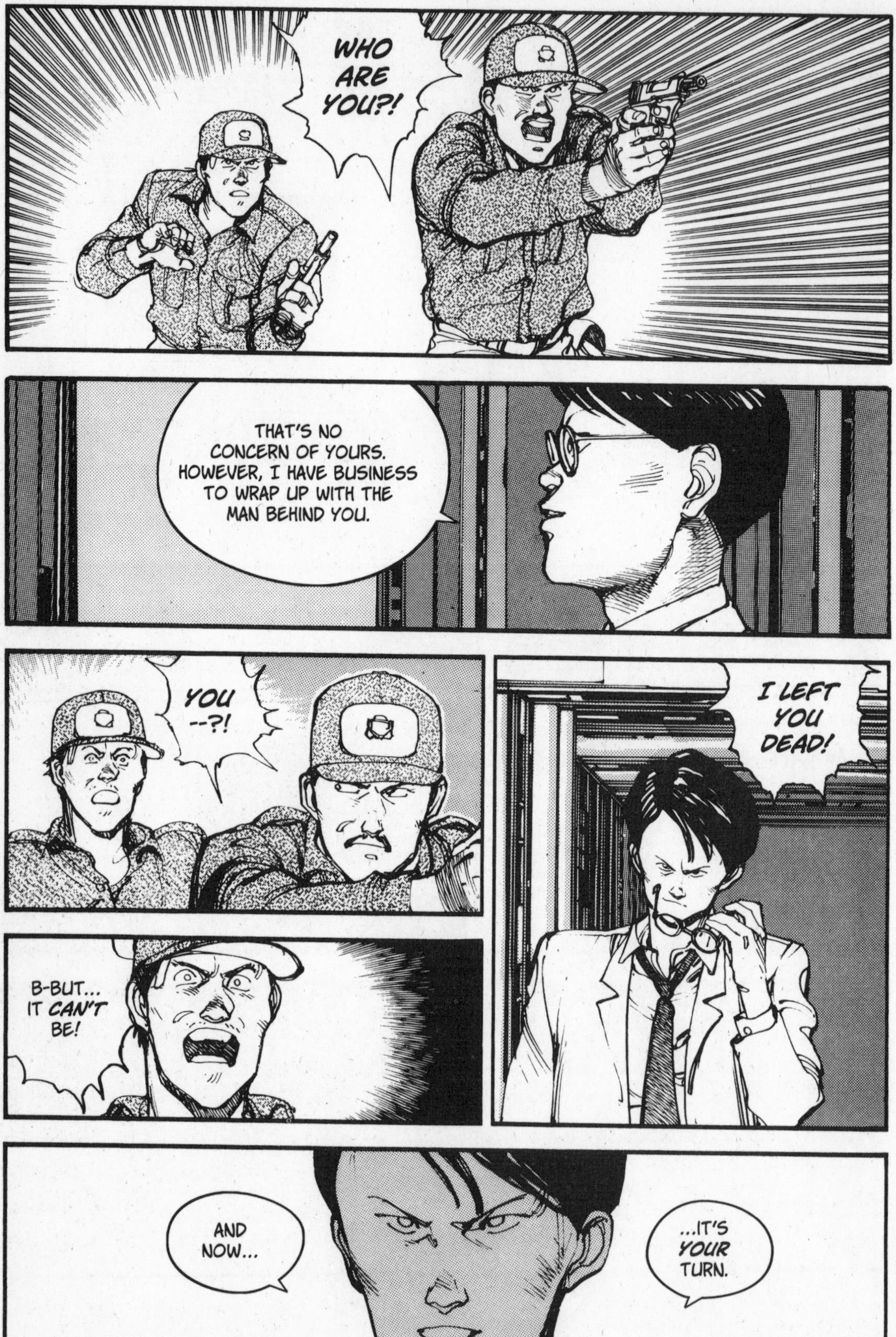
WHO ARE YOU?!
THAT'S NO CONCERN OF YOURS. HOWEVER, I HAVE BUSINESS TO WRAP UP WITH THE MAN BEHIND YOU.
YOU --?!
B-BUT... IT *CAN'T* BE!
I LEFT YOU DEAD!
AND NOW...
...IT'S *YOUR* TURN.

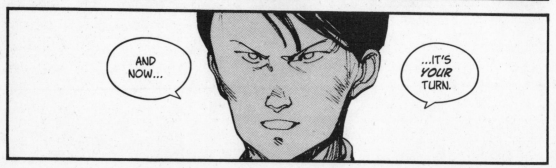

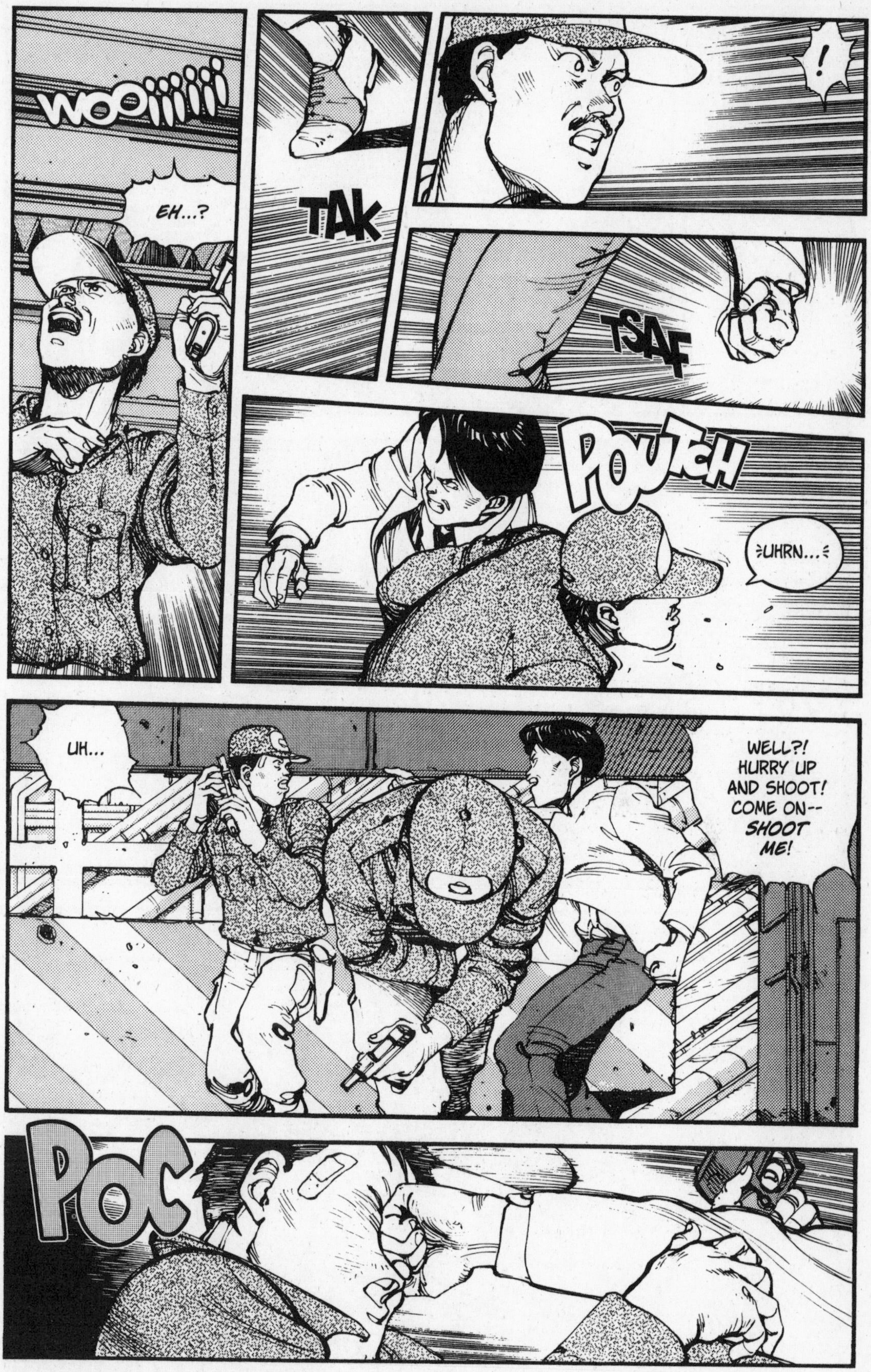
WOOiiiiiii
EH...?
TAK
!
TSAF
POUTCH
UHRN...
UH...
WELL?! HURRY UP AND SHOOT! COME ON-- SHOOT ME!
POC

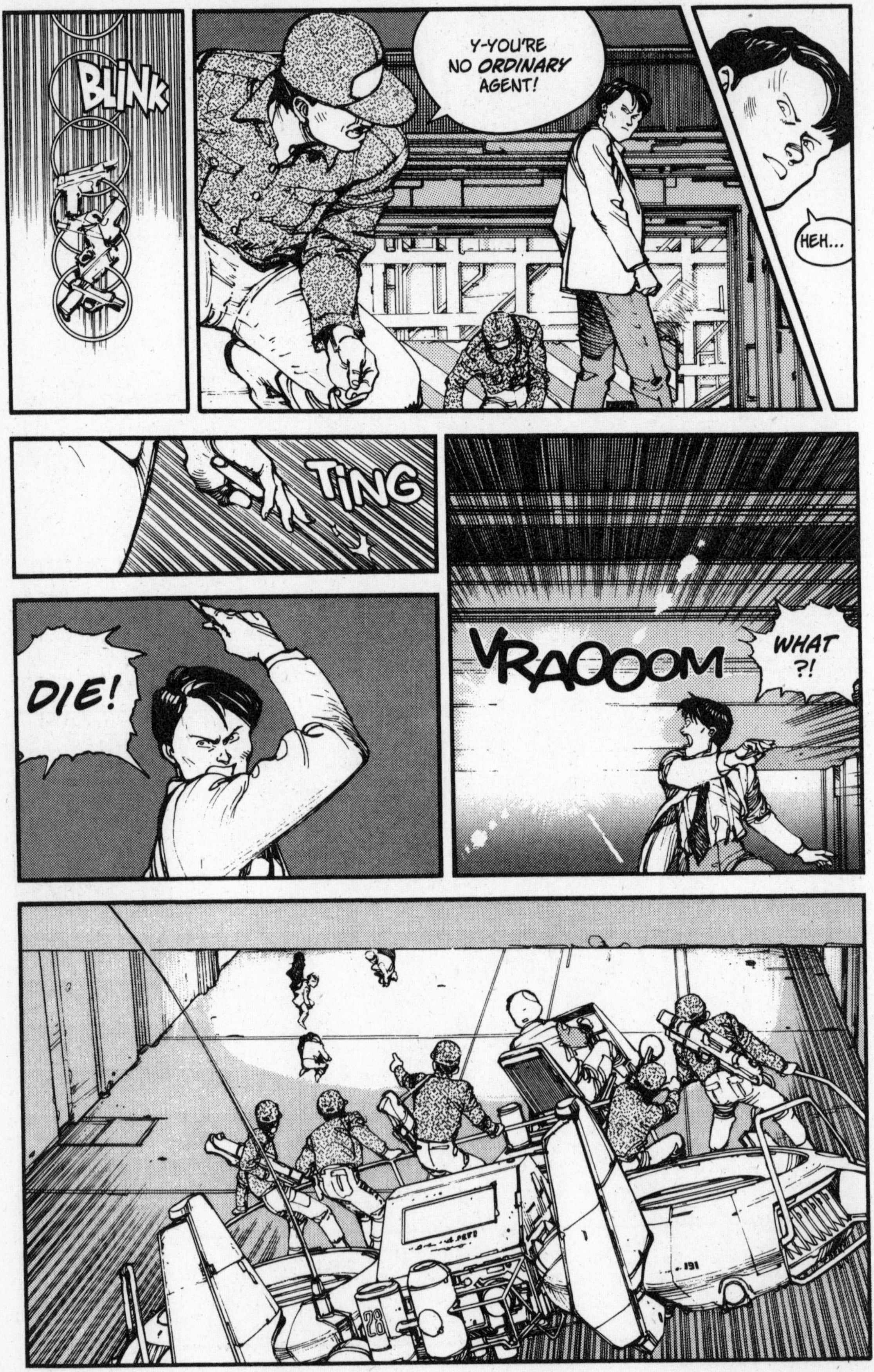
BLINK
Y-YOU'RE NO ORDINARY AGENT!
HEH...
TING
VRAOOOM
WHAT ?!
DIE!

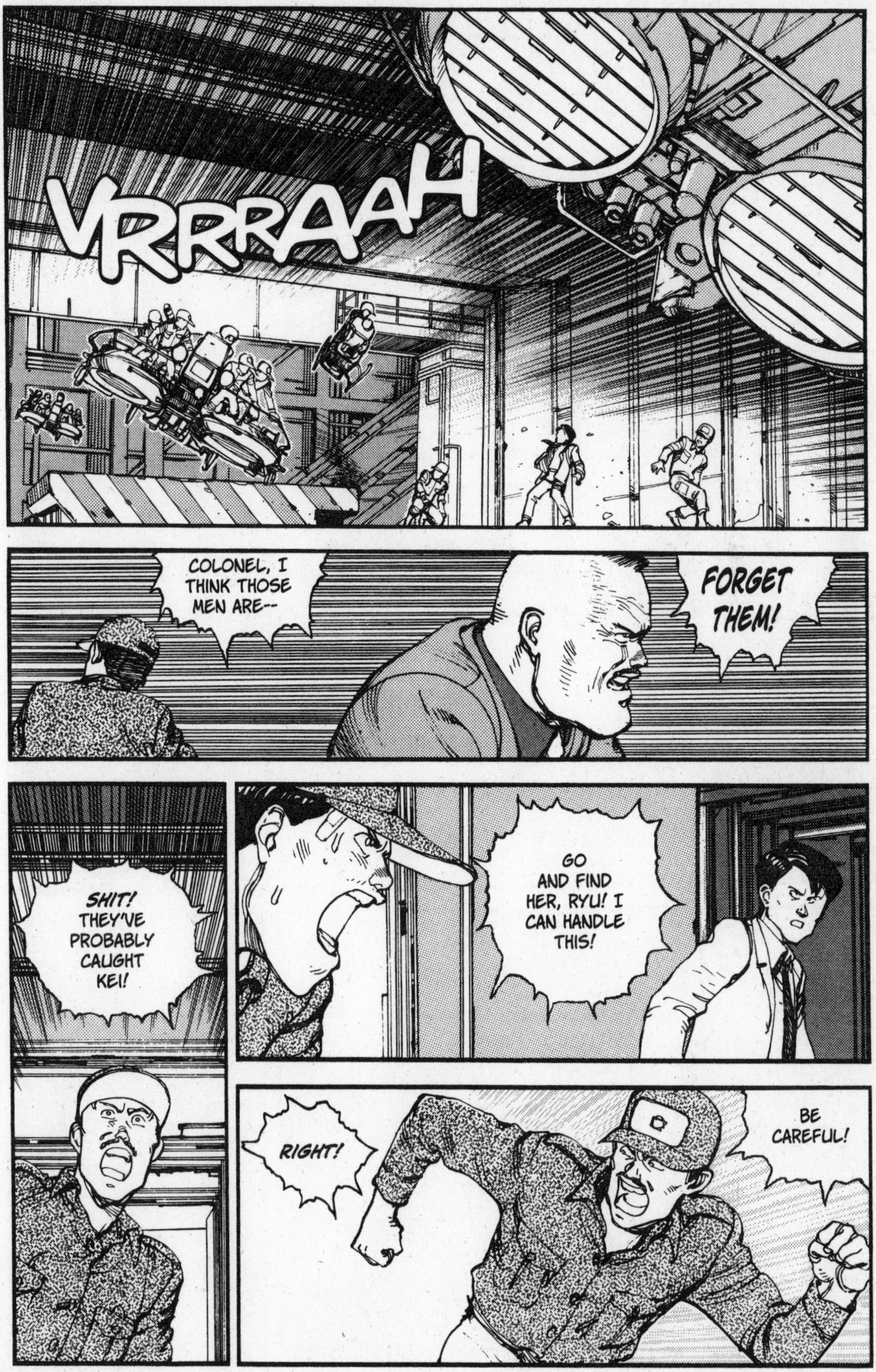

VRRRAAH
COLONEL, I THINK THOSE MEN ARE--
FORGET THEM!
SHIT! THEY'VE PROBABLY CAUGHT KEI!
GO AND FIND HER, RYU! I CAN HANDLE THIS!
RIGHT!
BE CAREFUL!

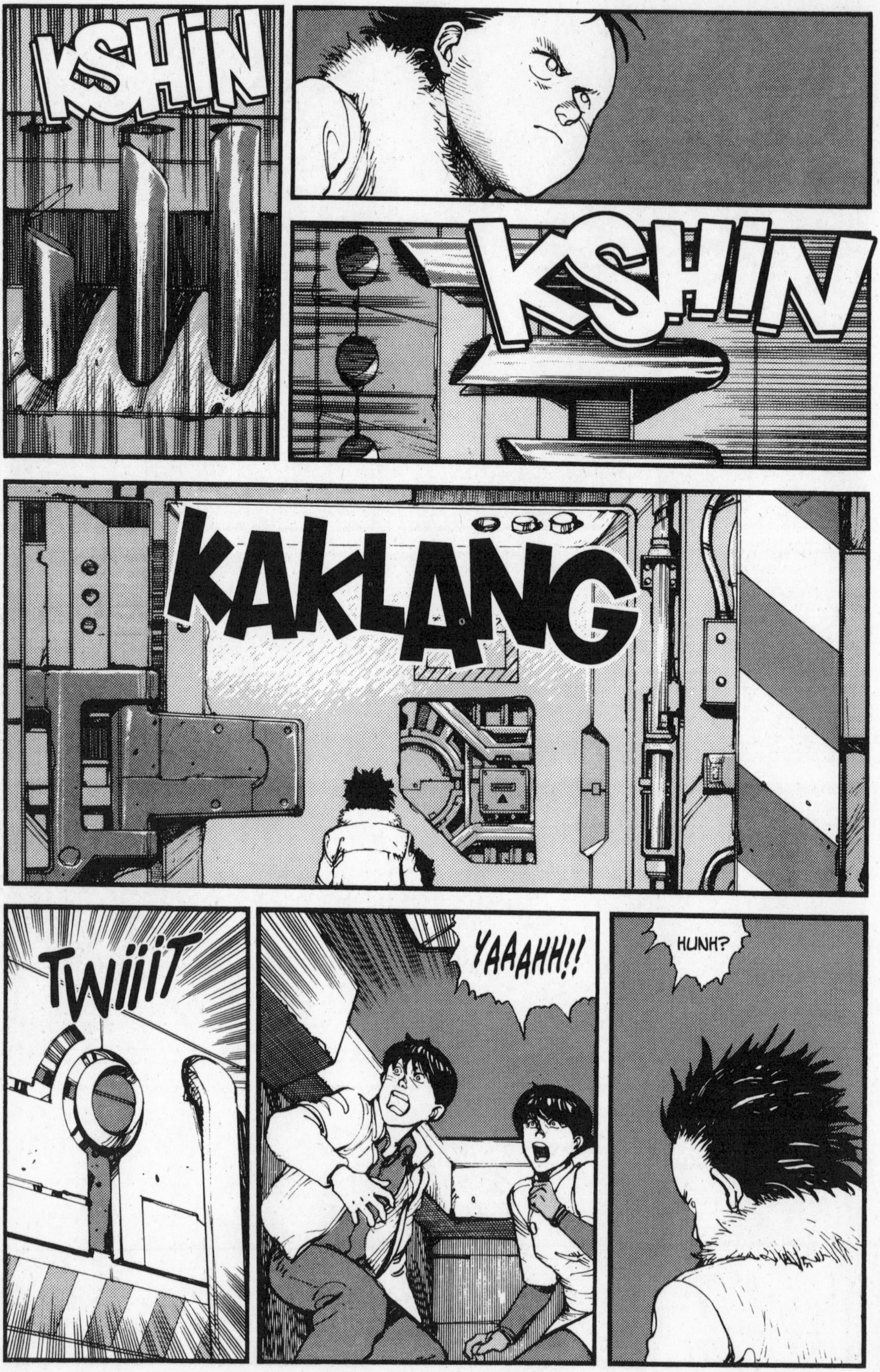
KSHIN
KSHIN
KAKLANG
TWIIIT
YAAAHH!!
HUNH?

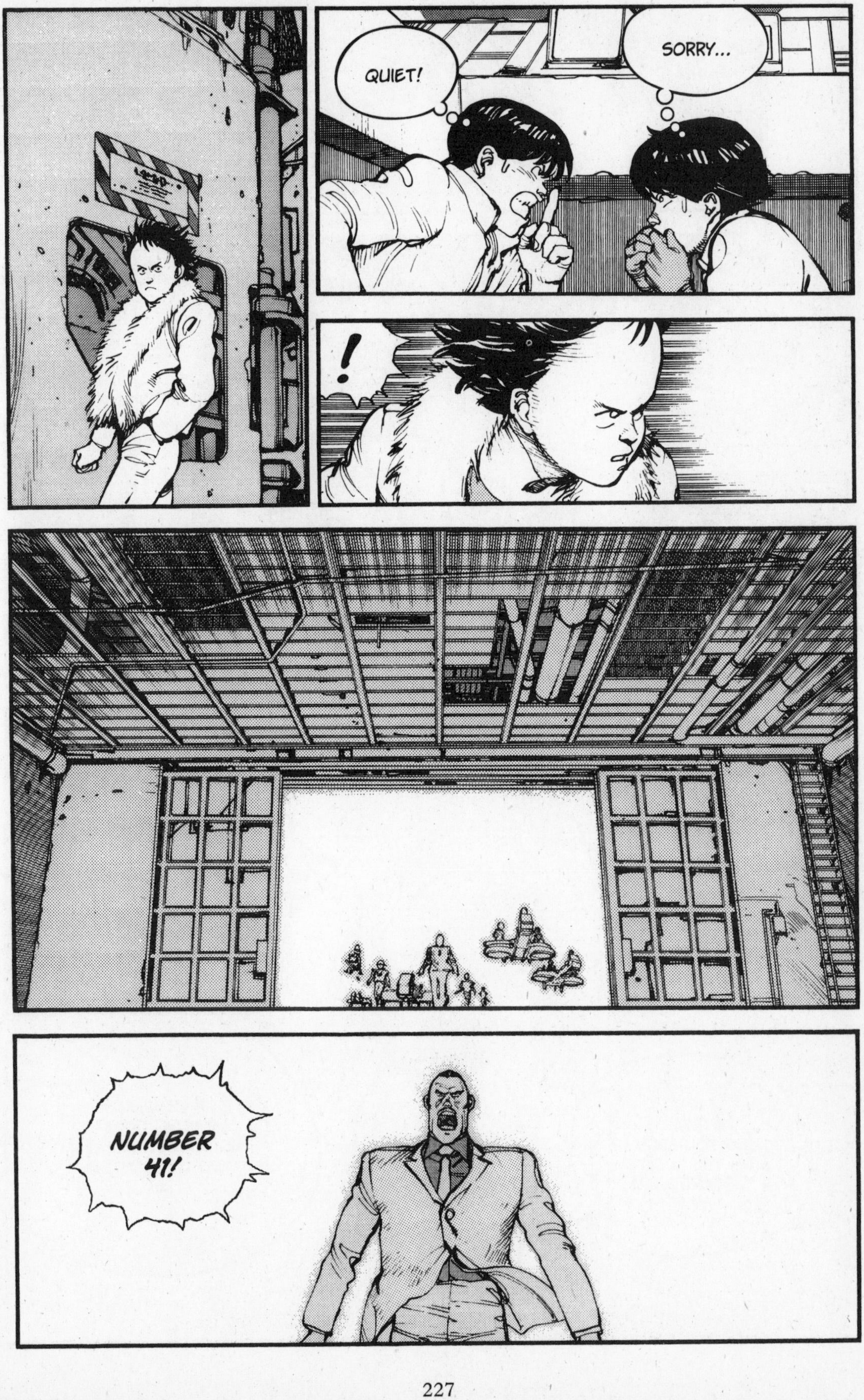
QUIET!
SORRY...
!
NUMBER 41!

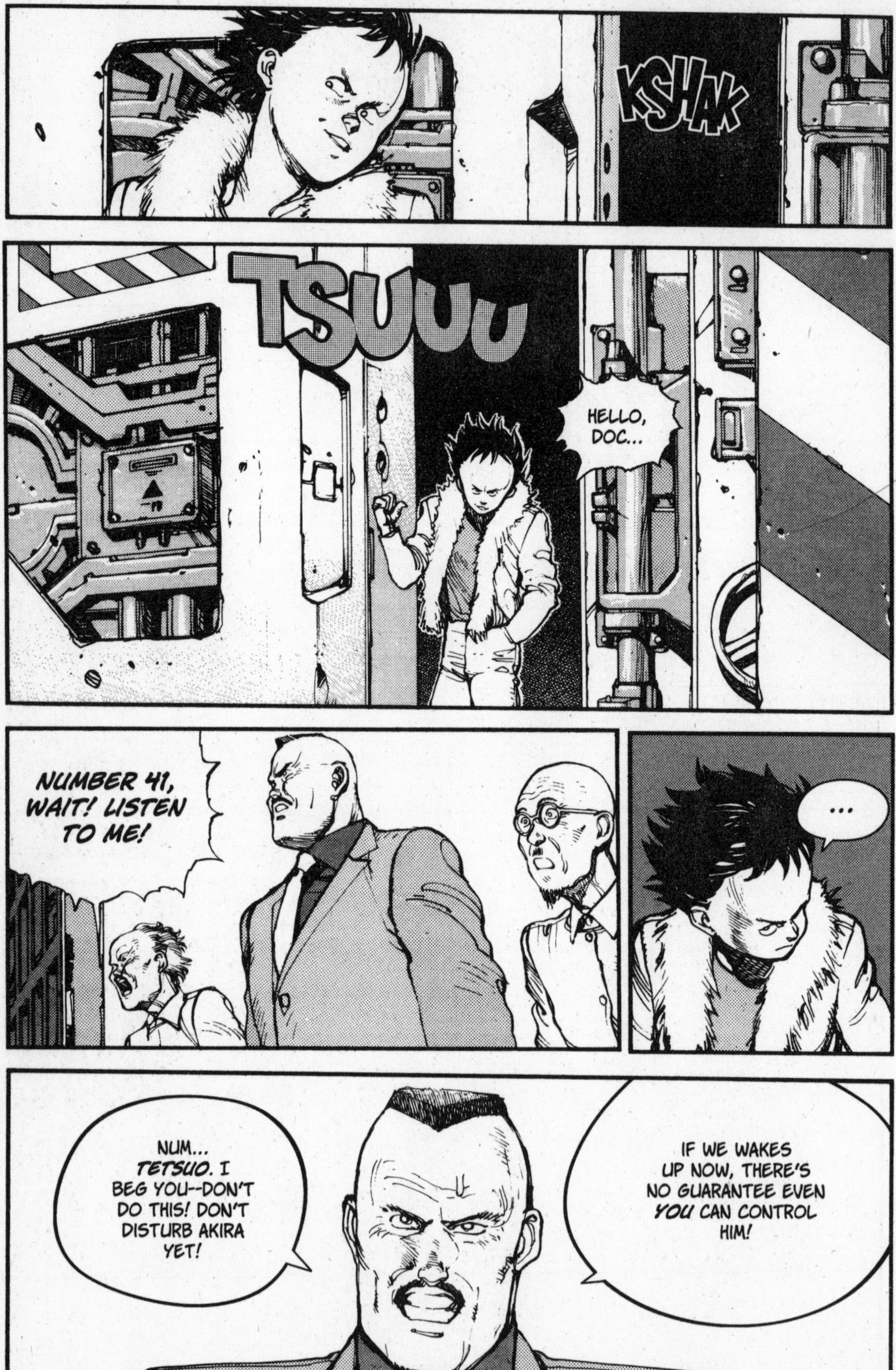
KSHAK
TSUUU
HELLO, DOC...
NUMBER 41, WAIT! LISTEN TO ME!
...
NUM... TETSUO. I BEG YOU--DON'T DO THIS! DON'T DISTURB AKIRA YET!
IF WE WAKES UP NOW, THERE'S NO GUARANTEE EVEN YOU CAN CONTROL HIM!

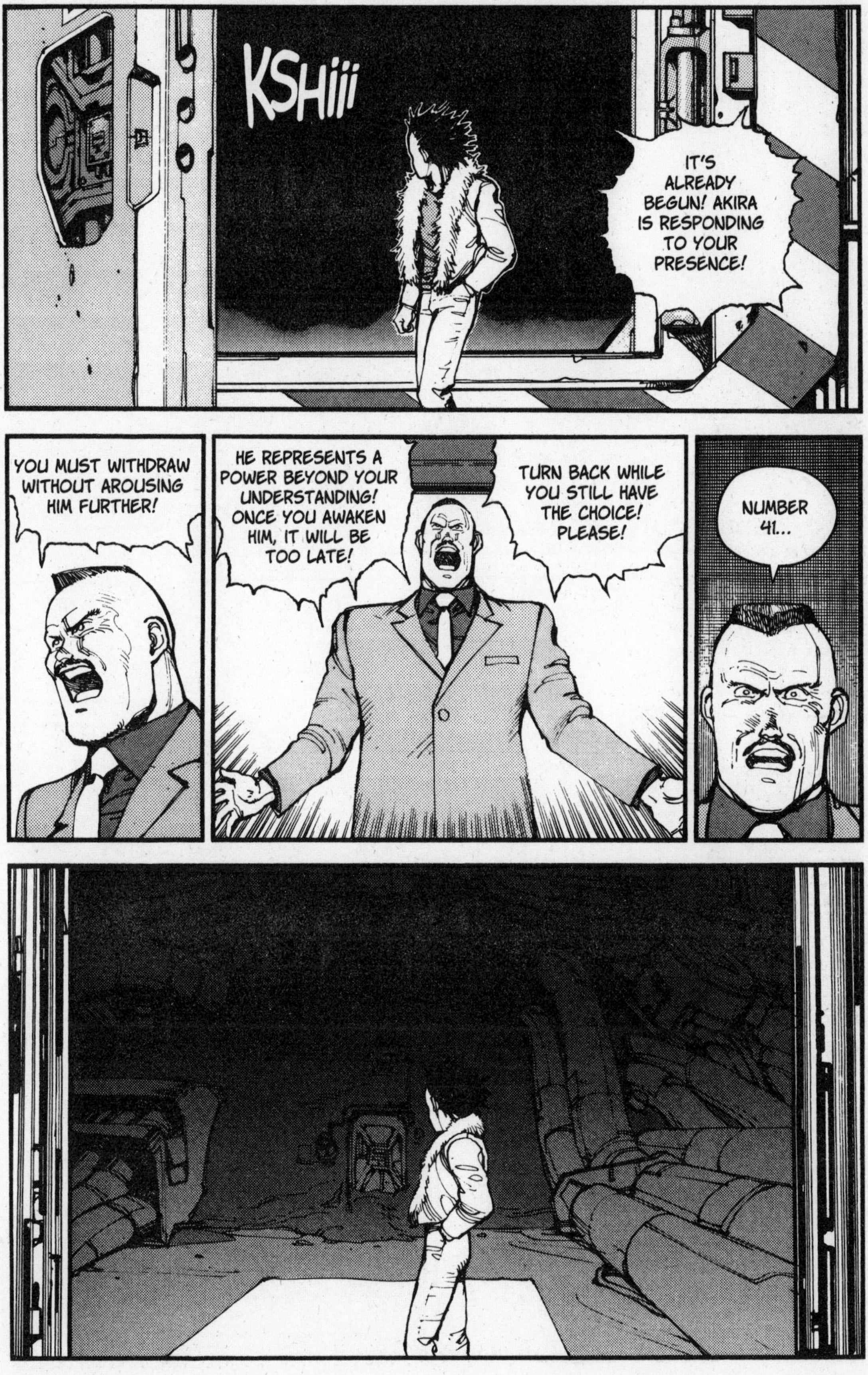
KSHiii
IT'S ALREADY BEGUN! AKIRA IS RESPONDING TO YOUR PRESENCE!
YOU MUST WITHDRAW WITHOUT AROUSING HIM FURTHER!
HE REPRESENTS A POWER BEYOND YOUR UNDERSTANDING! ONCE YOU AWAKEN HIM, IT WILL BE TOO LATE!
TURN BACK WHILE YOU STILL HAVE THE CHOICE! PLEASE!
NUMBER 41...

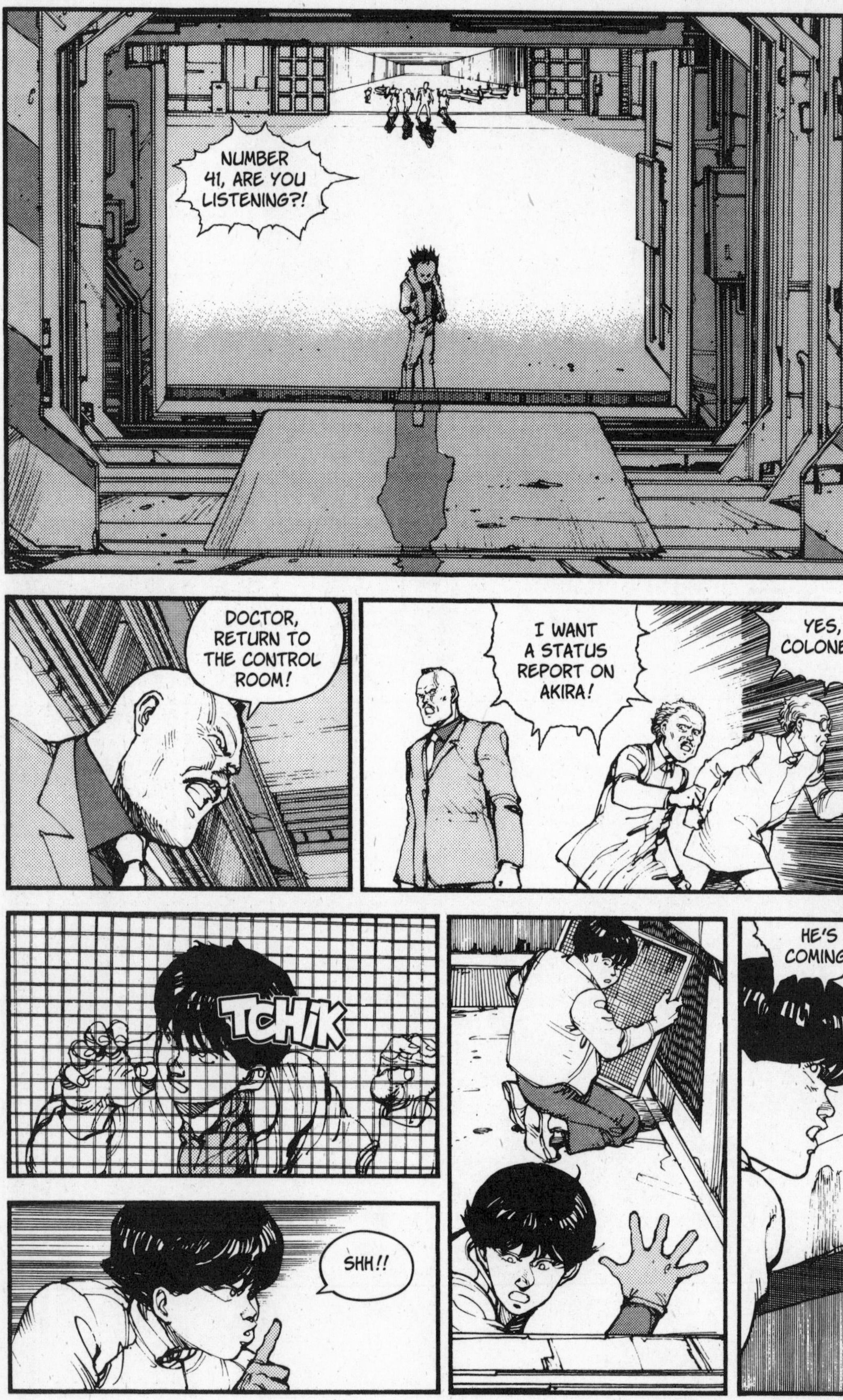
NUMBER 41, ARE YOU LISTENING?!
DOCTOR, RETURN TO THE CONTROL ROOM!
I WANT A STATUS REPORT ON AKIRA!
YES, COLONEL!
TCHIK
HE'S COMING!
SHH!!

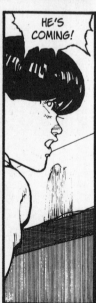

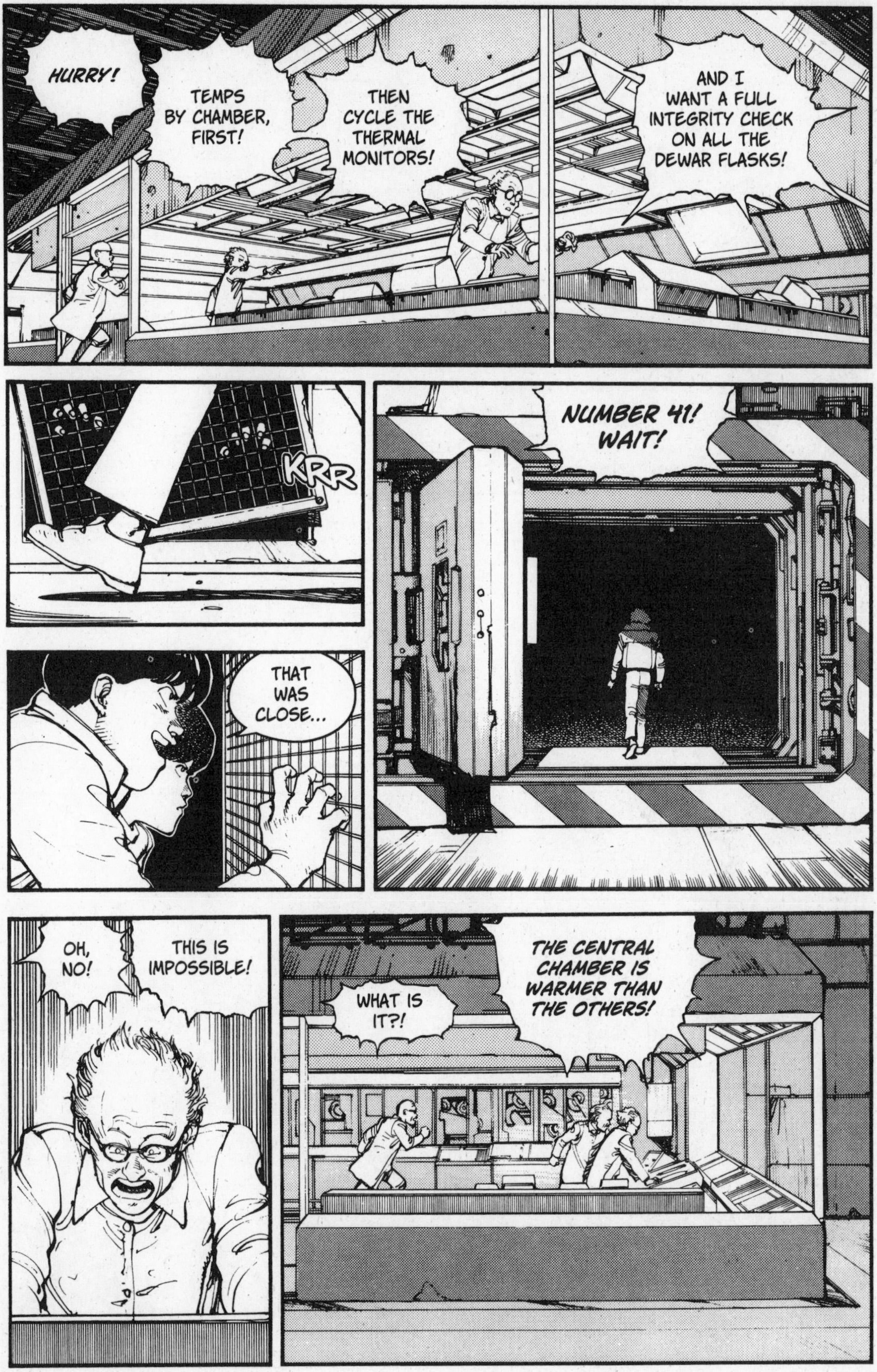
HURRY!
TEMPS BY CHAMBER, FIRST!
THEN CYCLE THE THERMAL MONITORS!
AND I WANT A FULL INTEGRITY CHECK ON ALL THE DEWAR FLASKS!
KRR
NUMBER 41! WAIT!
THAT WAS CLOSE...
OH, NO!
THIS IS IMPOSSIBLE!
WHAT IS IT?!
THE CENTRAL CHAMBER IS WARMER THAN THE OTHERS!

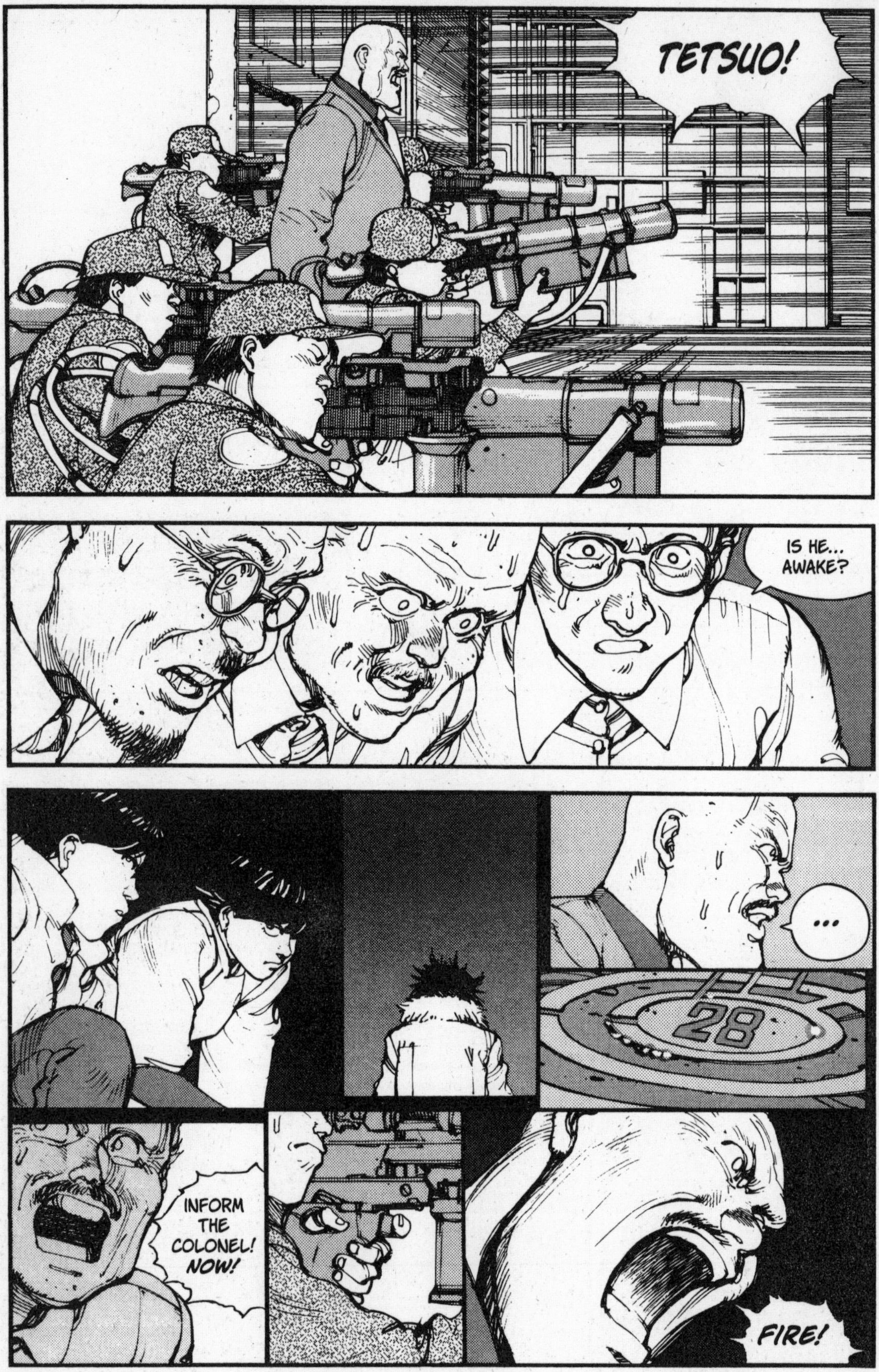
TETSUO!
IS HE... AWAKE?
...
INFORM THE COLONEL! NOW!
FIRE!

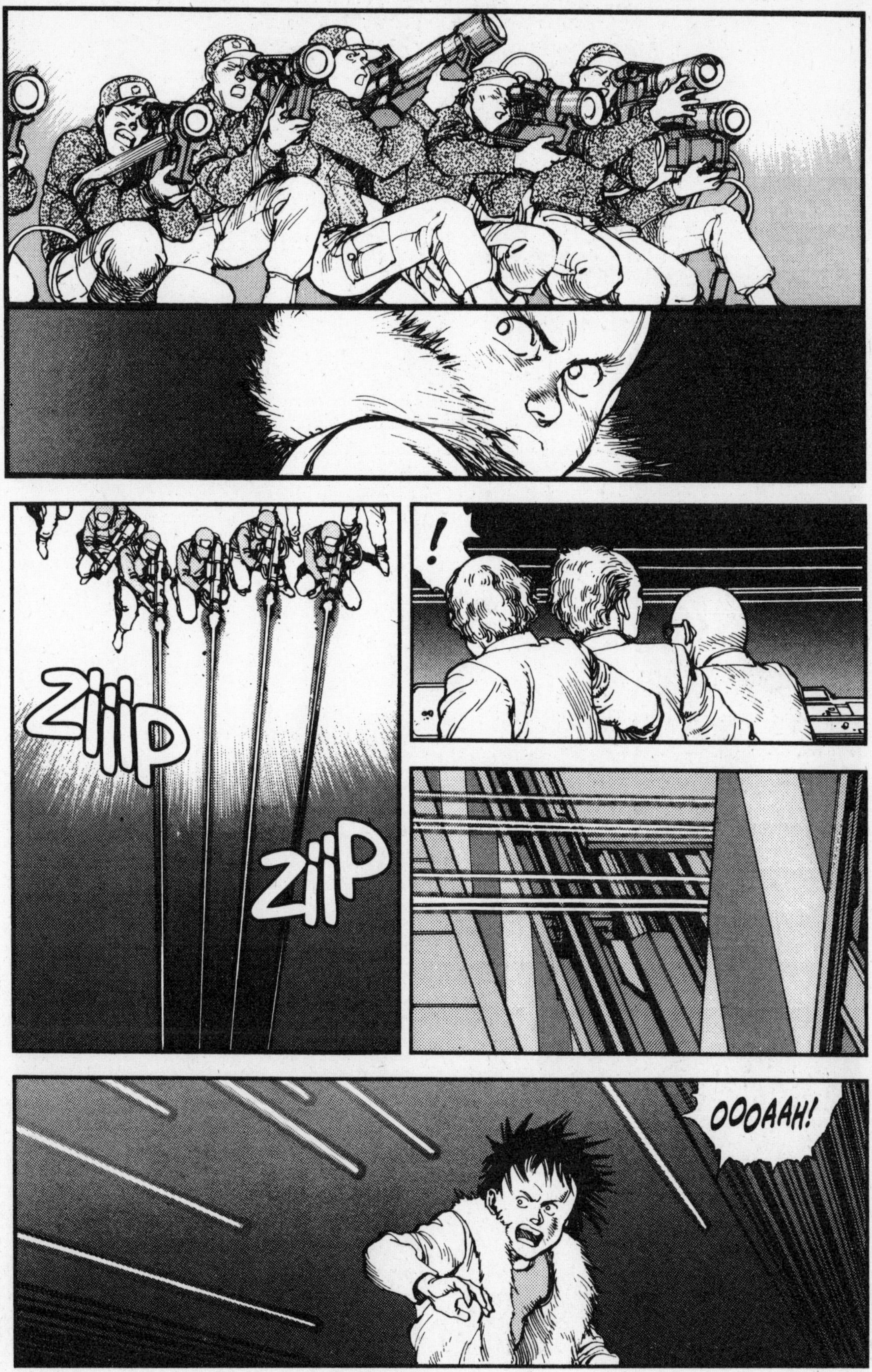
ZiiiP
ZiiP
!
OOOAAH!

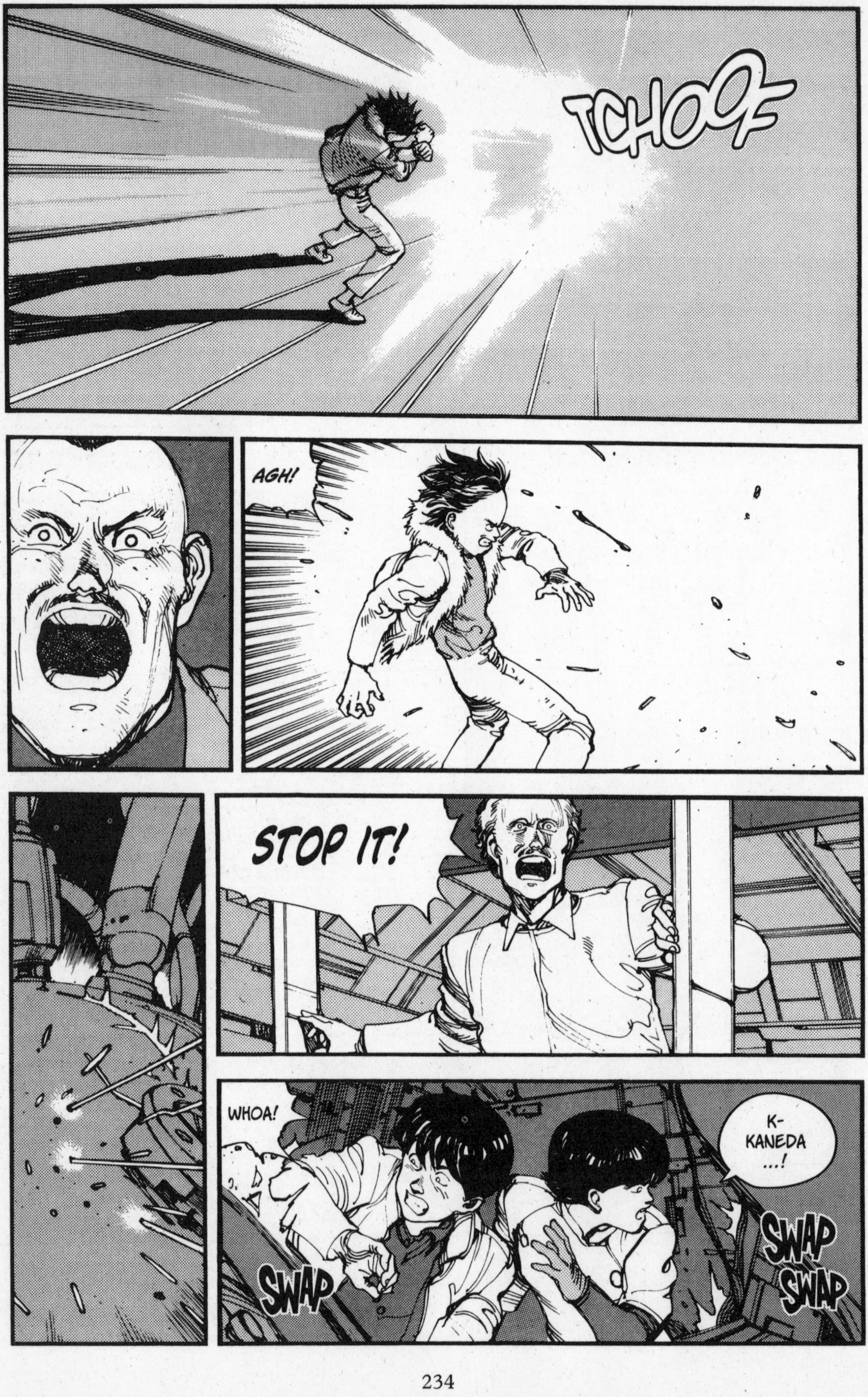
TCHOOF
AGH!
STOP IT!
WHOA!
K-
KANEDA
...!
SWAP
SWAP
SWAP

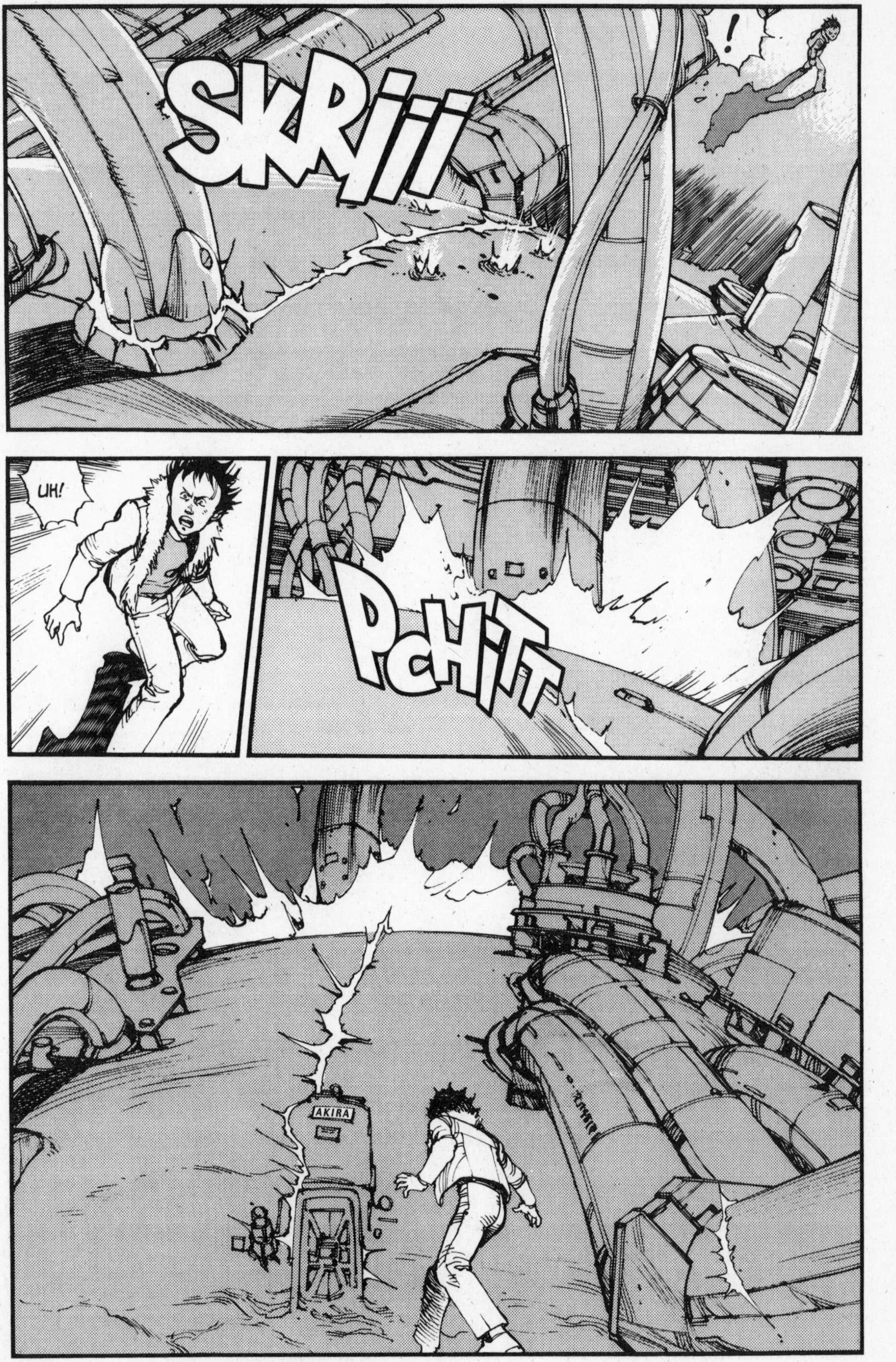
SKRIII
!
UH!
PCHITT
AKIRA

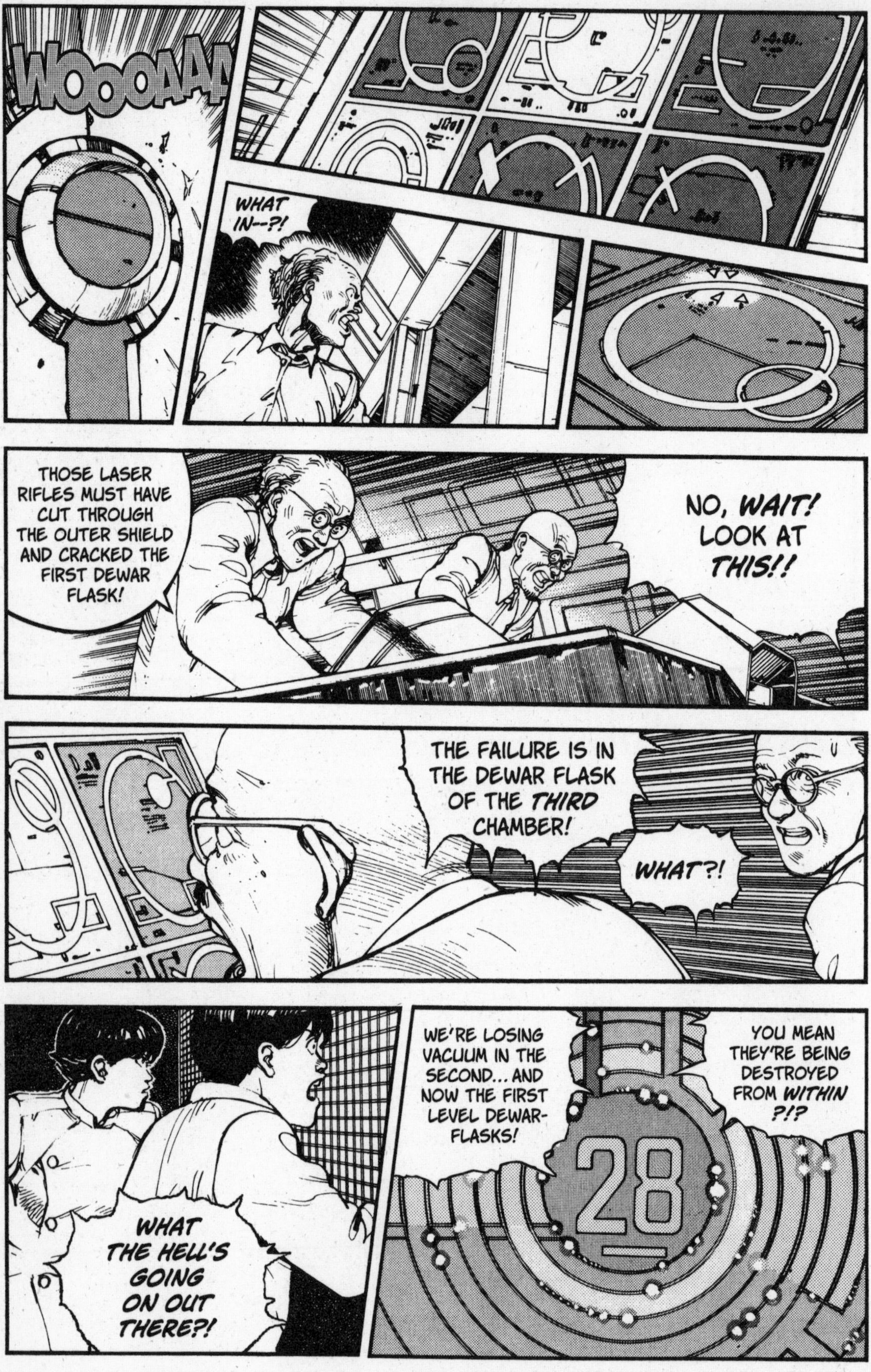
WOOOAAAA
WHAT IN--?!
THOSE LASER RIFLES MUST HAVE CUT THROUGH THE OUTER SHIELD AND CRACKED THE FIRST DEWAR FLASK!
NO, WAIT! LOOK AT THIS!!
THE FAILURE IS IN THE DEWAR FLASK OF THE THIRD CHAMBER!
WHAT?!
WHAT THE HELL'S GOING ON OUT THERE?!
WE'RE LOSING VACUUM IN THE SECOND... AND NOW THE FIRST LEVEL DEWAR-FLASKS!
YOU MEAN THEY'RE BEING DESTROYED FROM WITHIN ?!?
28

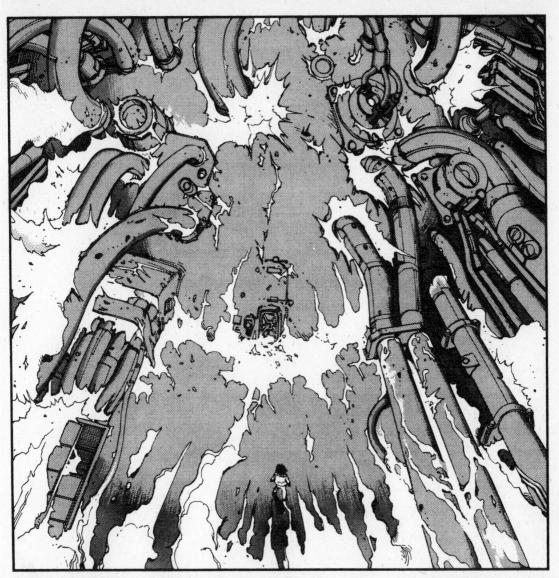

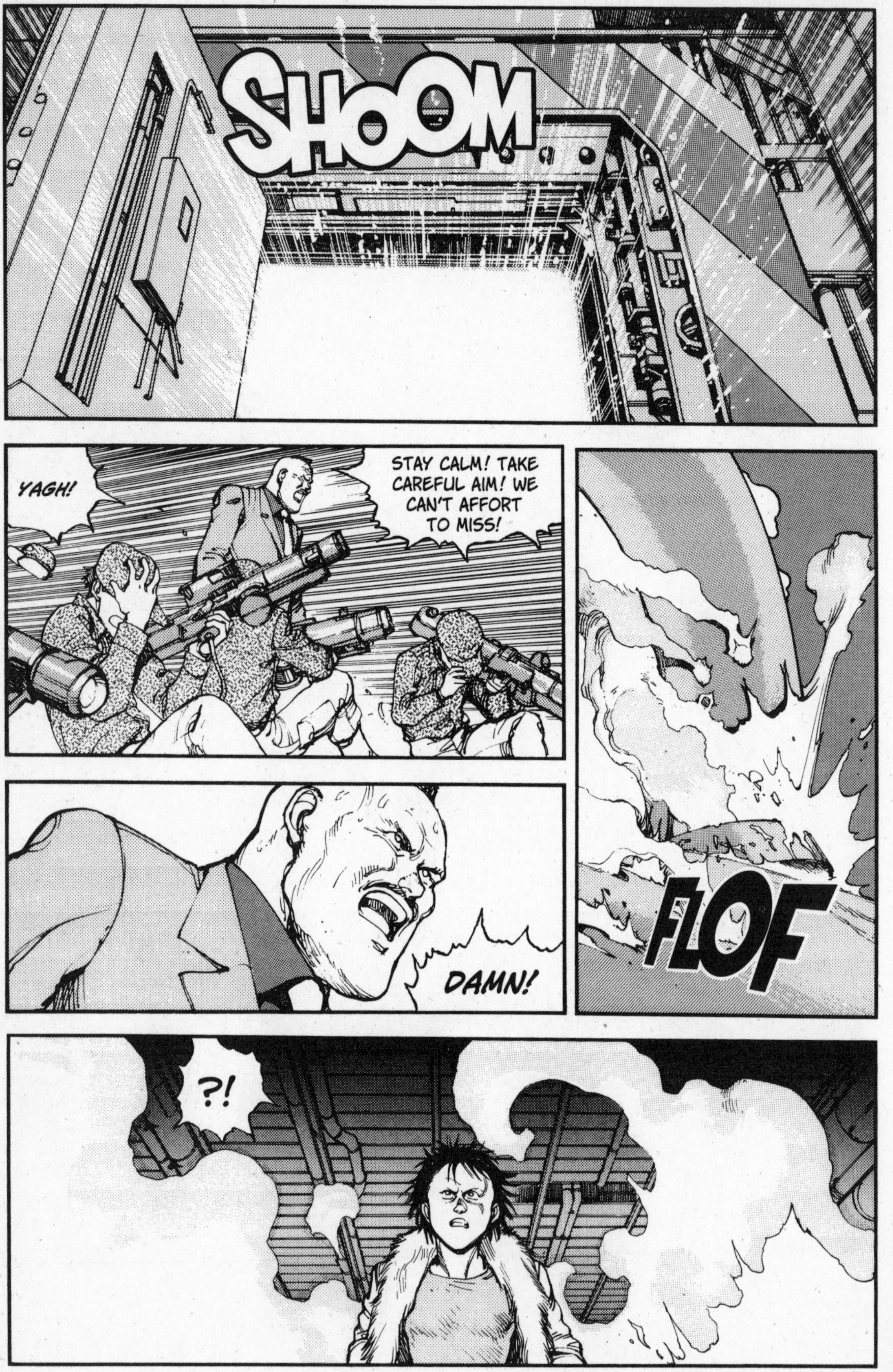
SHOOM
YAGH!
STAY CALM! TAKE CAREFUL AIM! WE CAN'T AFFORT TO MISS!
FLOF
DAMN!
?!

KSHHH

GAME OVER...

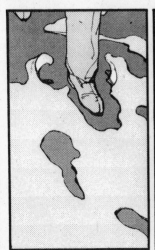

...
...

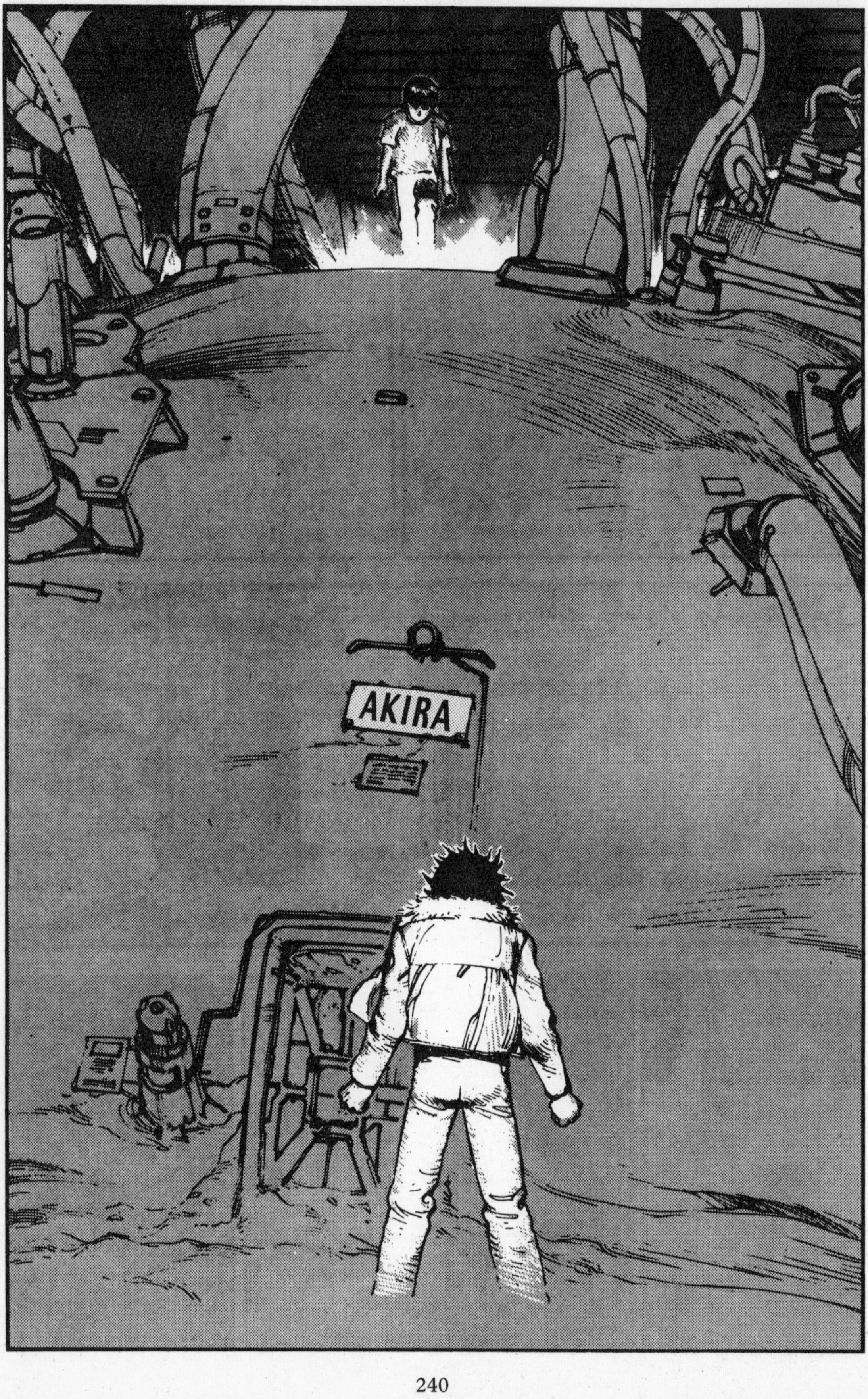
AKIRA

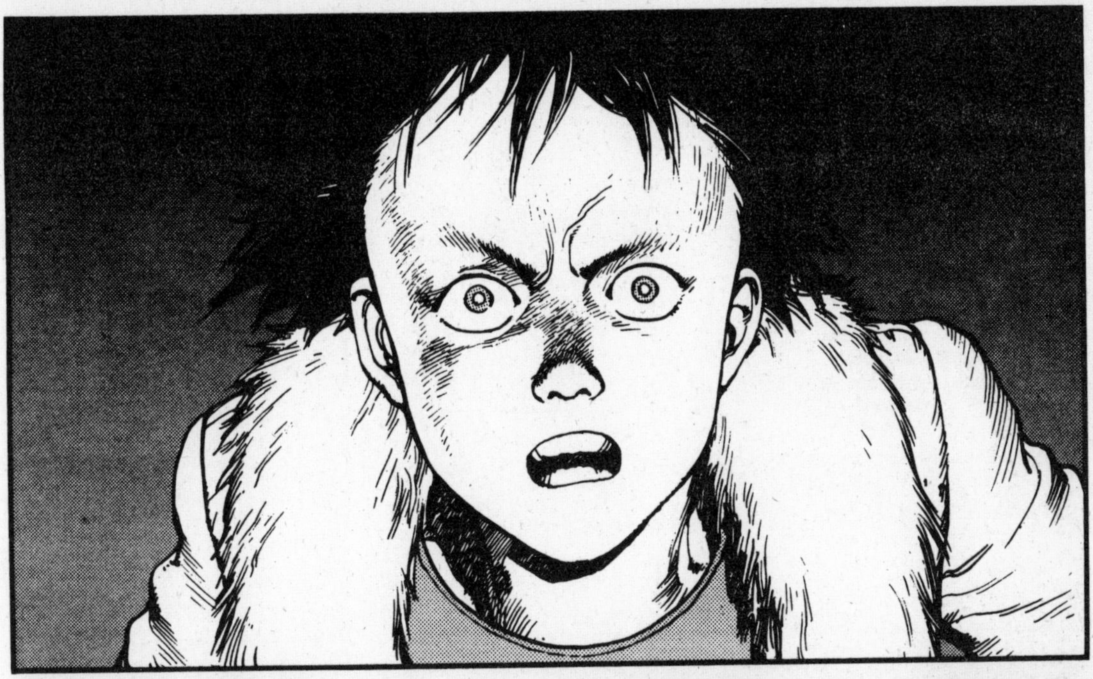
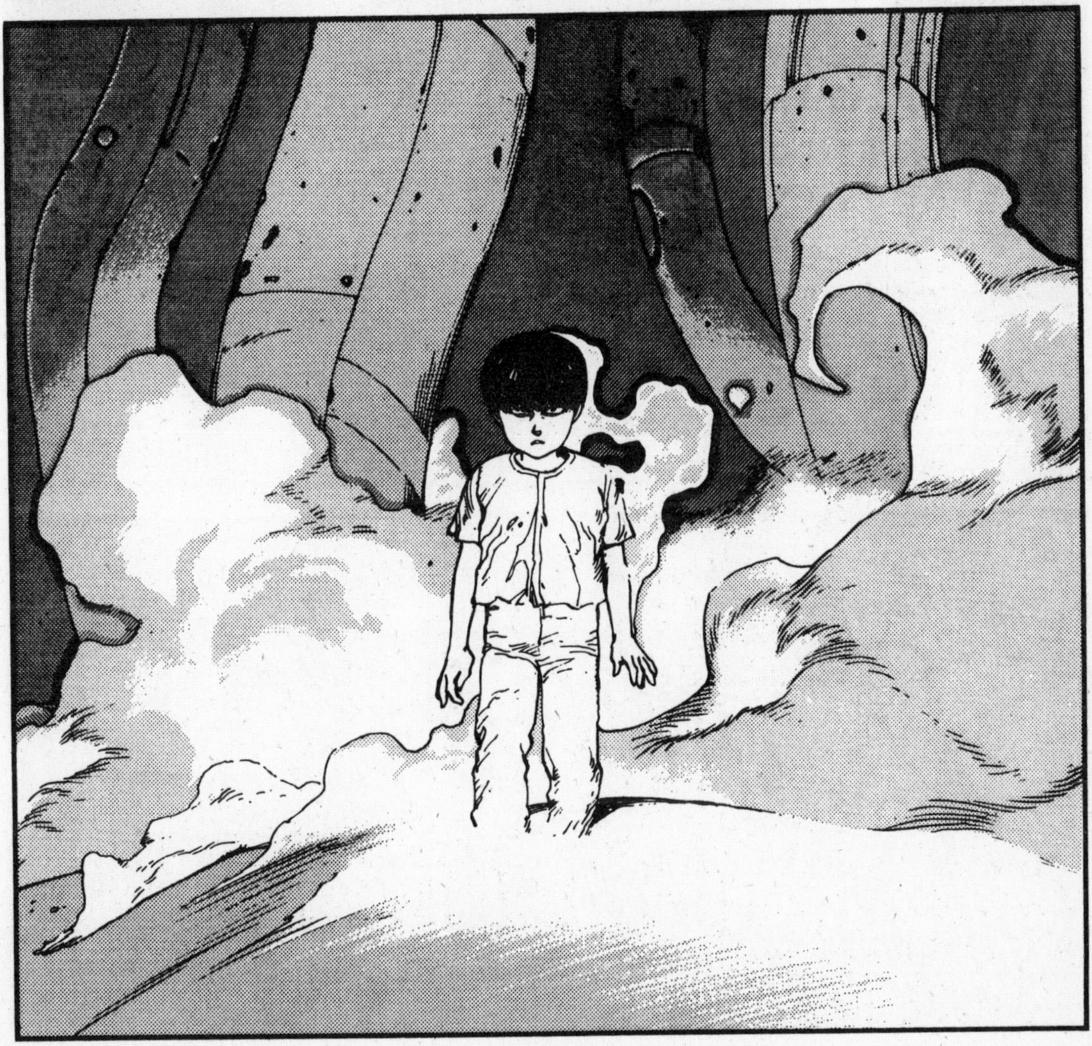

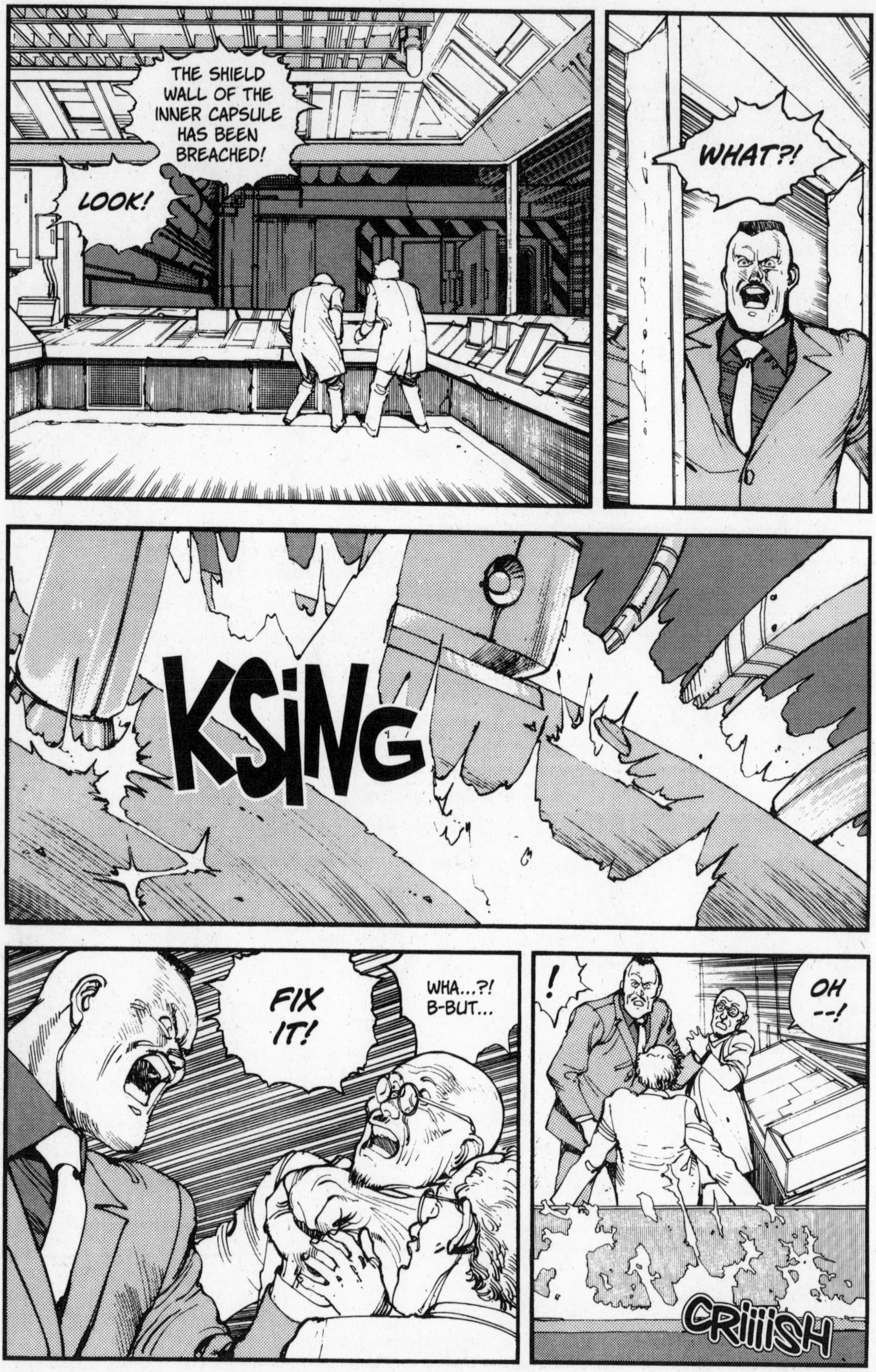
THE SHIELD WALL OF THE INNER CAPSULE HAS BEEN BREACHED!
LOOK!
WHAT?!
KSiNG
FIX IT!
WHA...?! B-BUT...
!
OH --!
CRiiiiSH

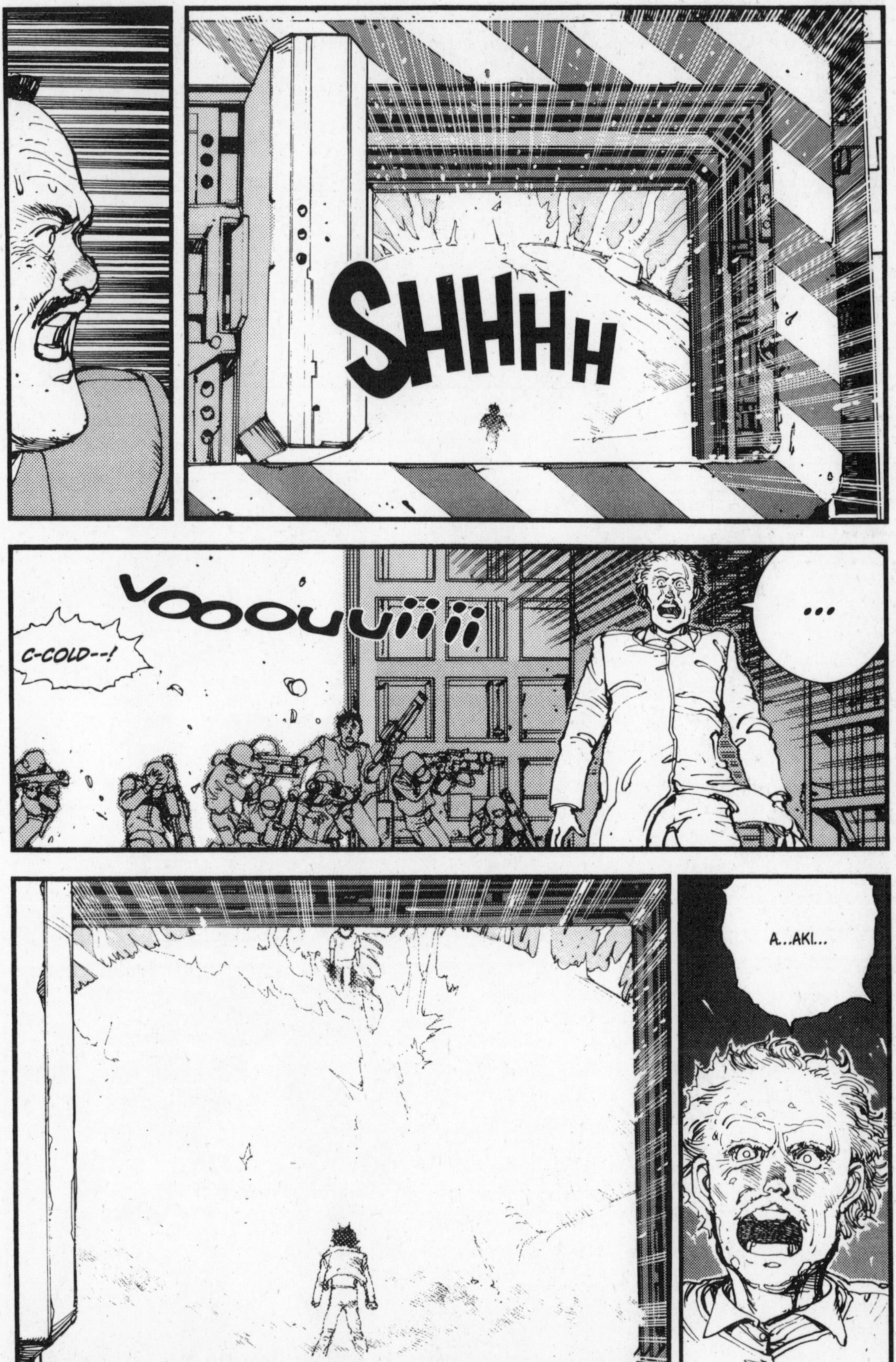
SHHHH
C-COLD--!
VOOOUUIIII
...
A...AKI...

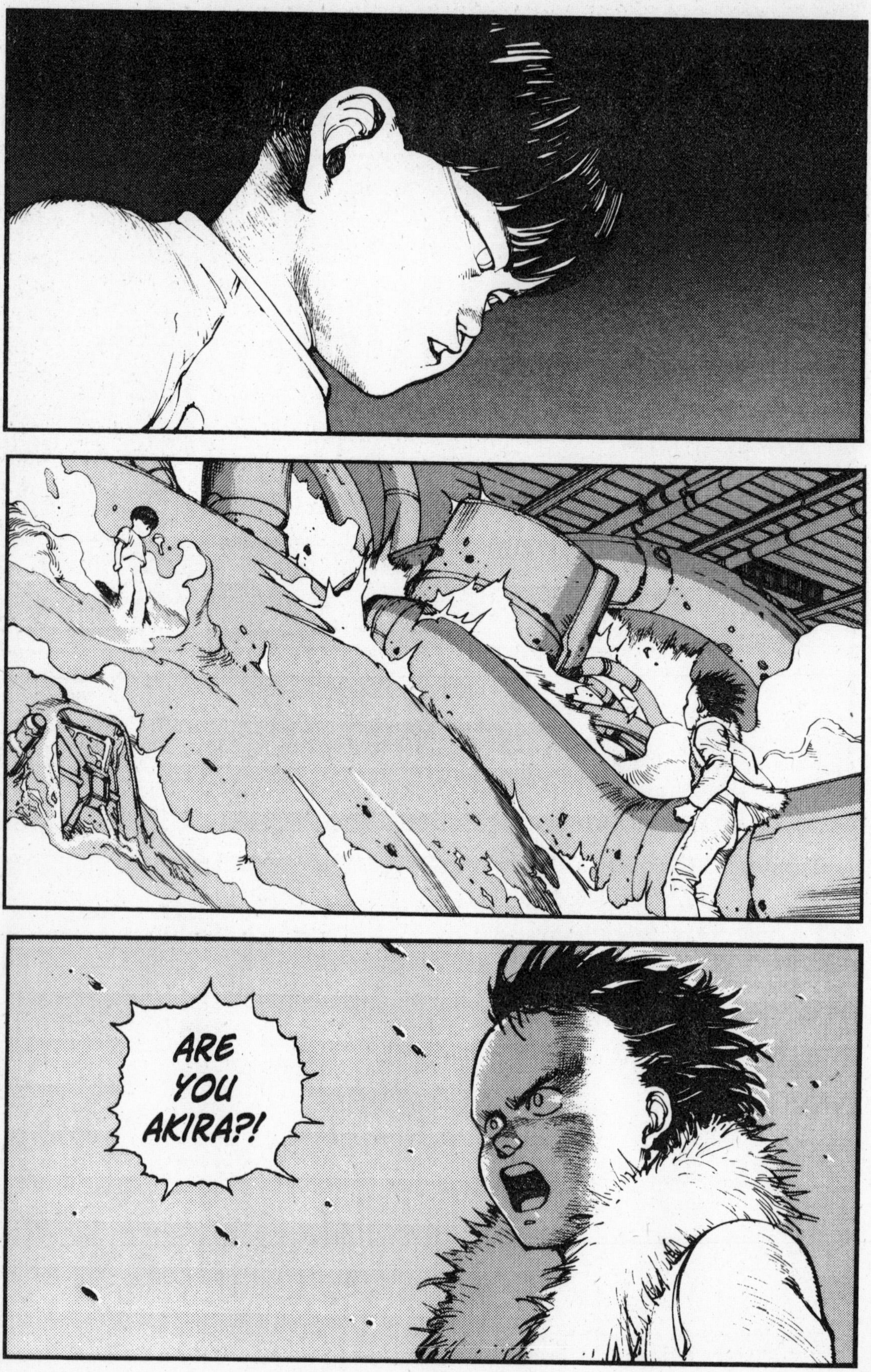
ARE YOU AKIRA?!

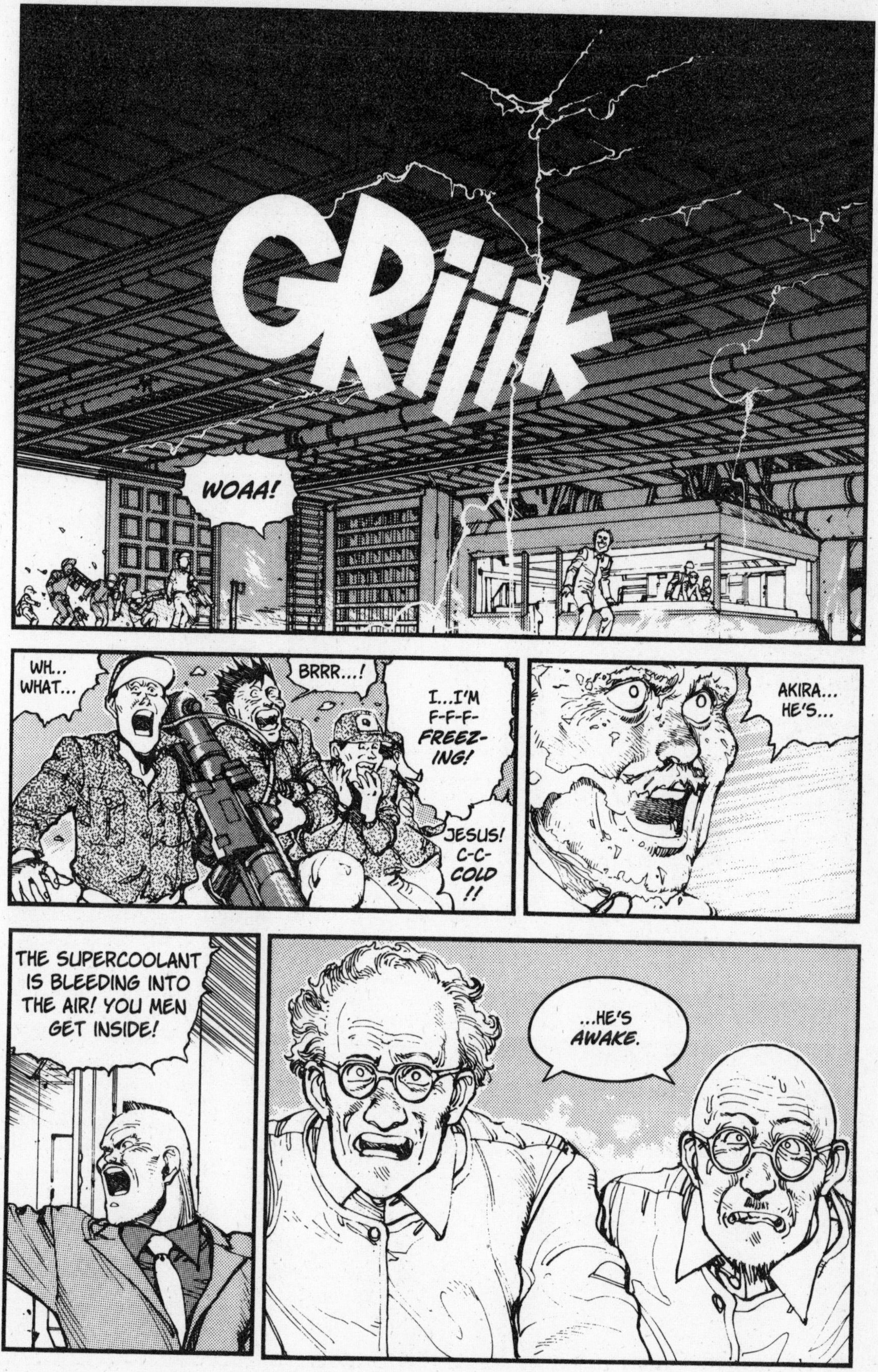
GRiiik
WOAA!
WH... WHAT...
BRRR...!
I...I'M F-F-F-FREEZ-ING!
JESUS! C-C-COLD !!
AKIRA... HE'S...
THE SUPERCOOLANT IS BLEEDING INTO THE AIR! YOU MEN GET INSIDE!
...HE'S AWAKE.

AM I NUTS OR IS IT GETTING GODDAMN COLD IN HERE?

HE'S AWAKE...? MEANING... NO WAY!

GZiiT

SHIT!

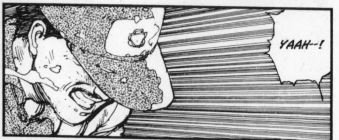

YAAH--!

SHiiiiiz

WHAT IS THIS?!

SHHHH

WHAT ARE YOU WAITING FOR?! COME ON!!

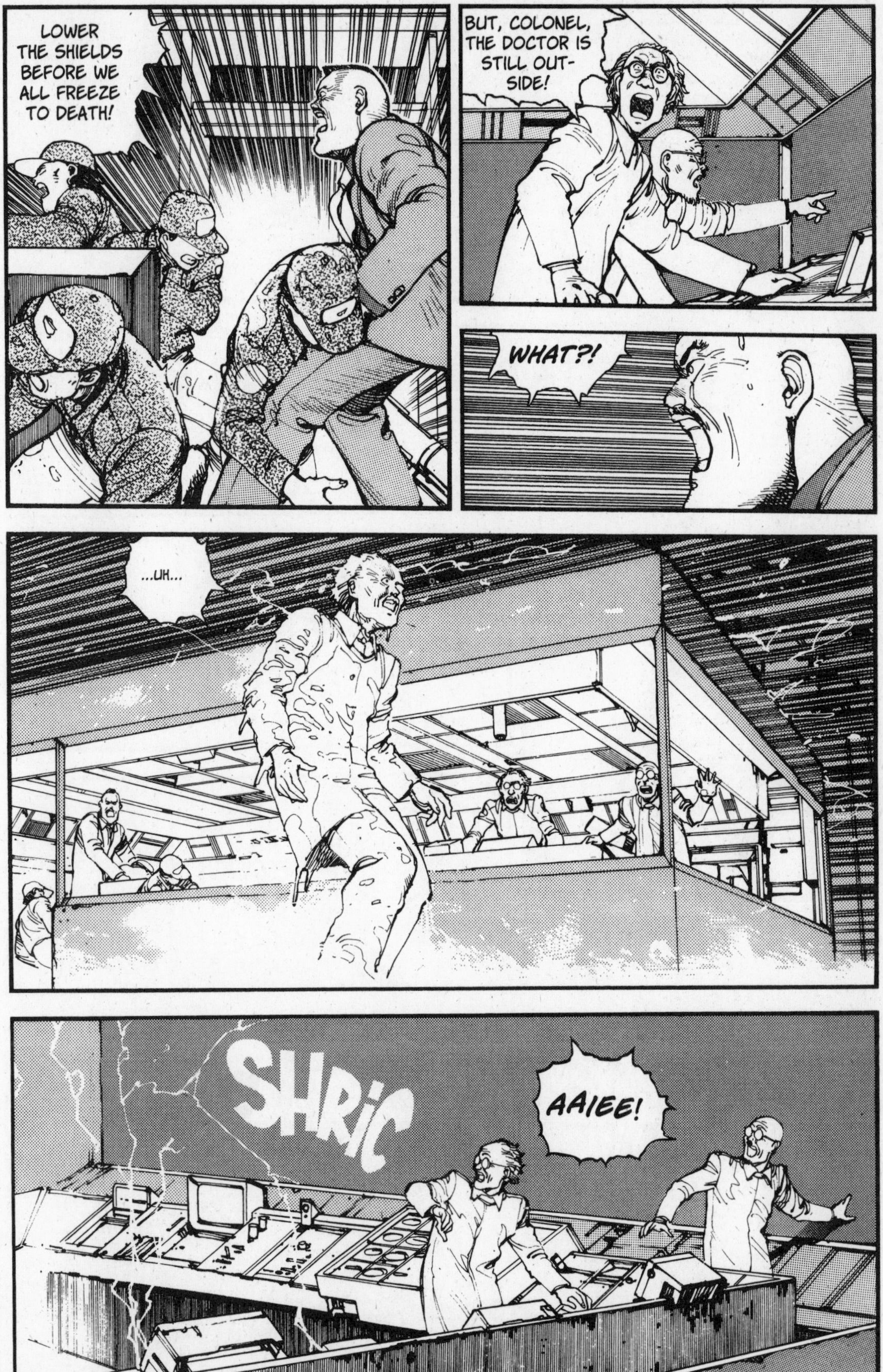
LOWER THE SHIELDS BEFORE WE ALL FREEZE TO DEATH!
BUT, COLONEL, THE DOCTOR IS STILL OUT-SIDE!
WHAT?!
...UH...
SHRIC
AAIEE!

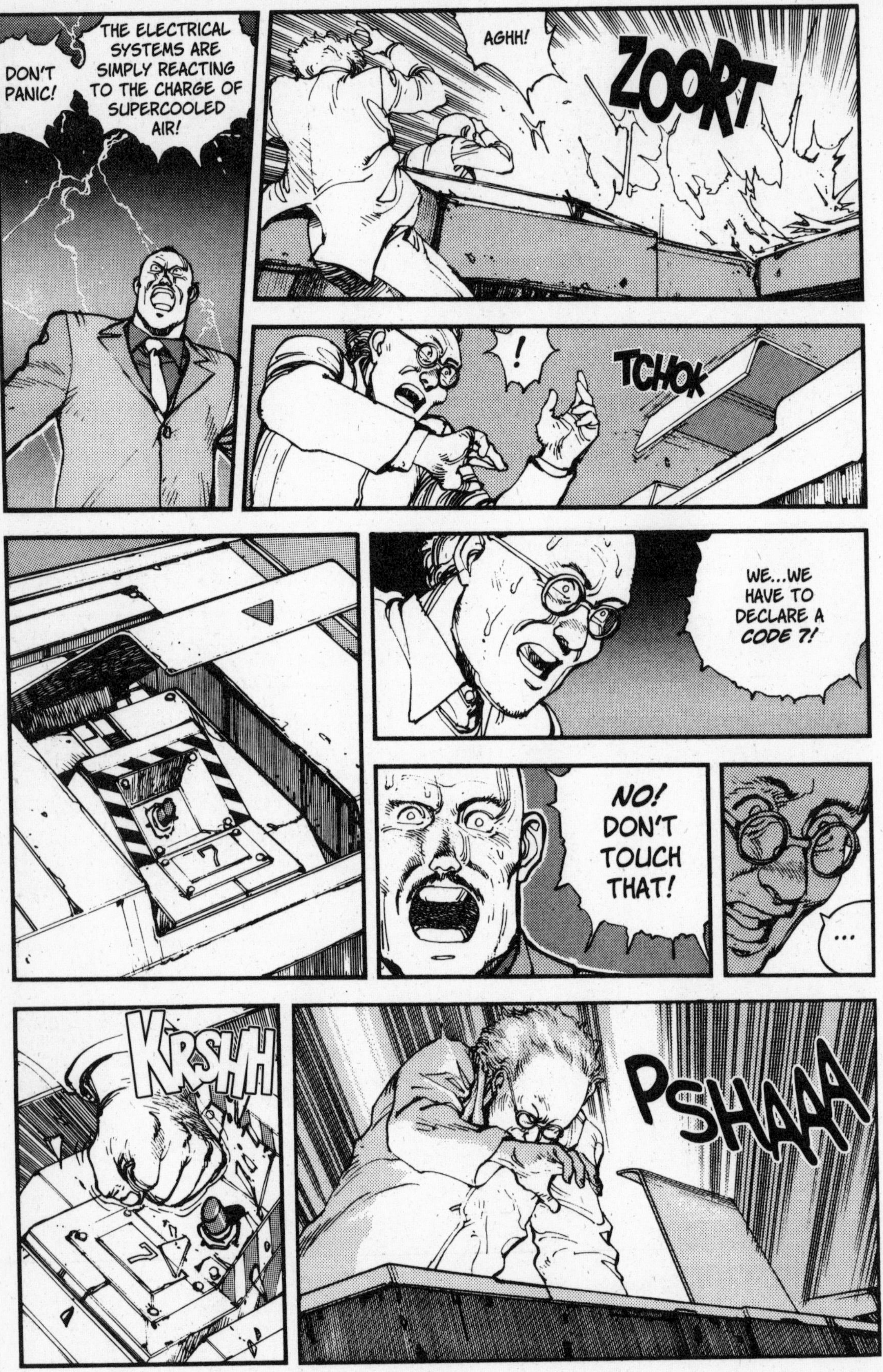
DON'T PANIC!
THE ELECTRICAL SYSTEMS ARE SIMPLY REACTING TO THE CHARGE OF SUPERCOOLED AIR!
AGHH!
ZOORT
!
TCHOK
WE...WE HAVE TO DECLARE A *CODE 7!*
*NO!* DON'T TOUCH THAT!
...
KRSHH
PSHAAA

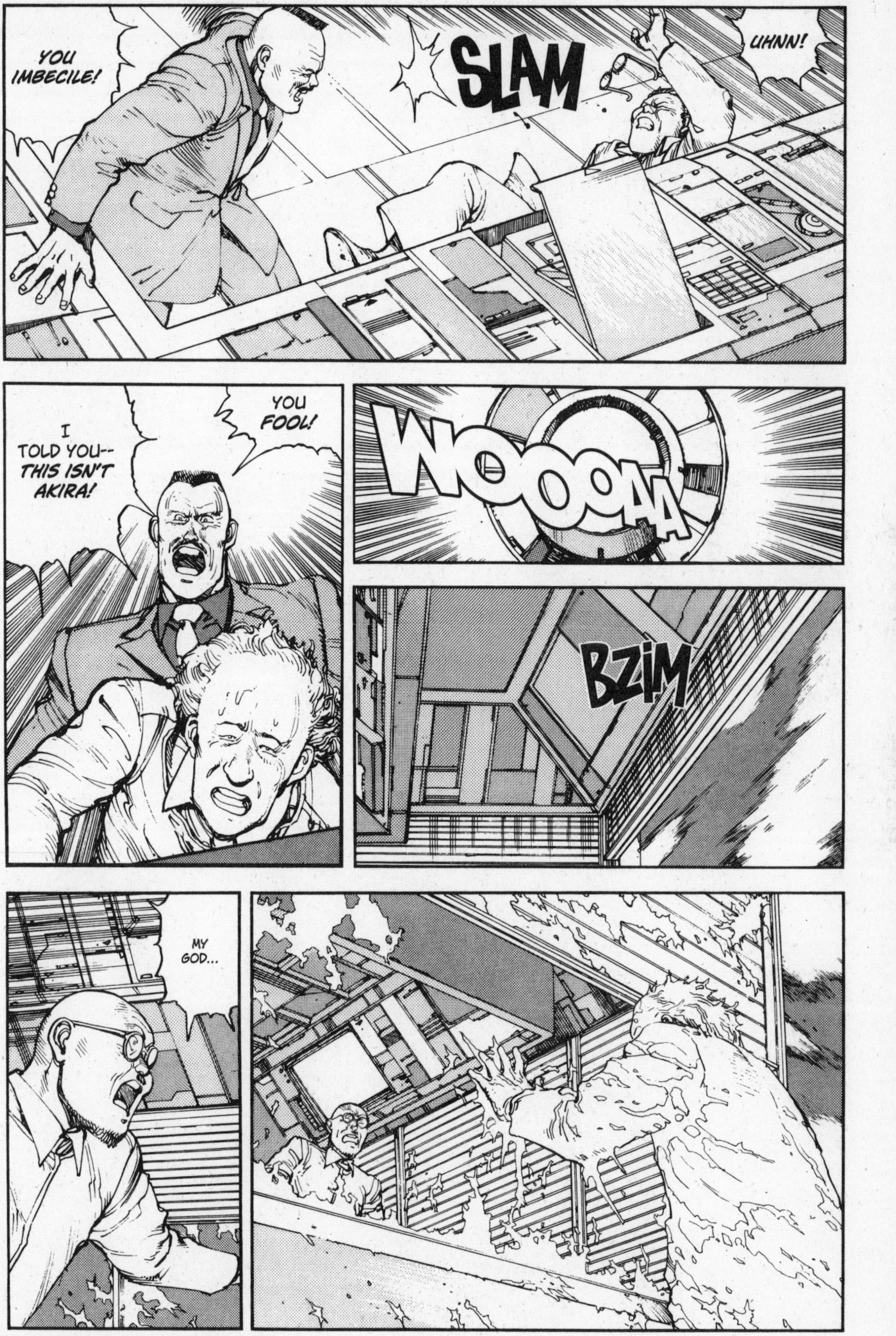
YOU IMBECILE!
SLAM
UHNN!
I TOLD YOU-- THIS ISN'T AKIRA!
YOU FOOL!
WOOOAA
BZIM
MY GOD...

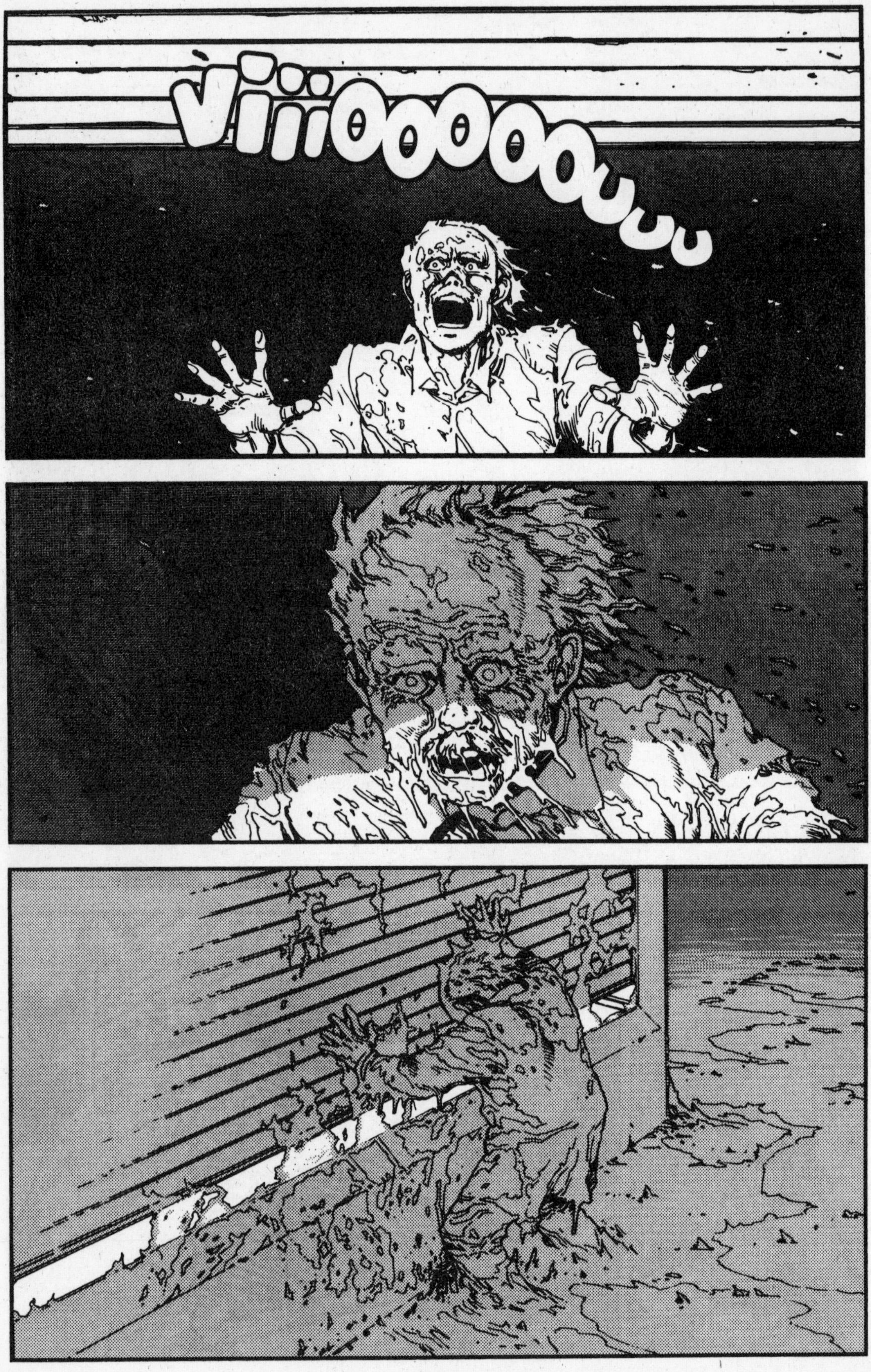
ViiiOOOOouuu

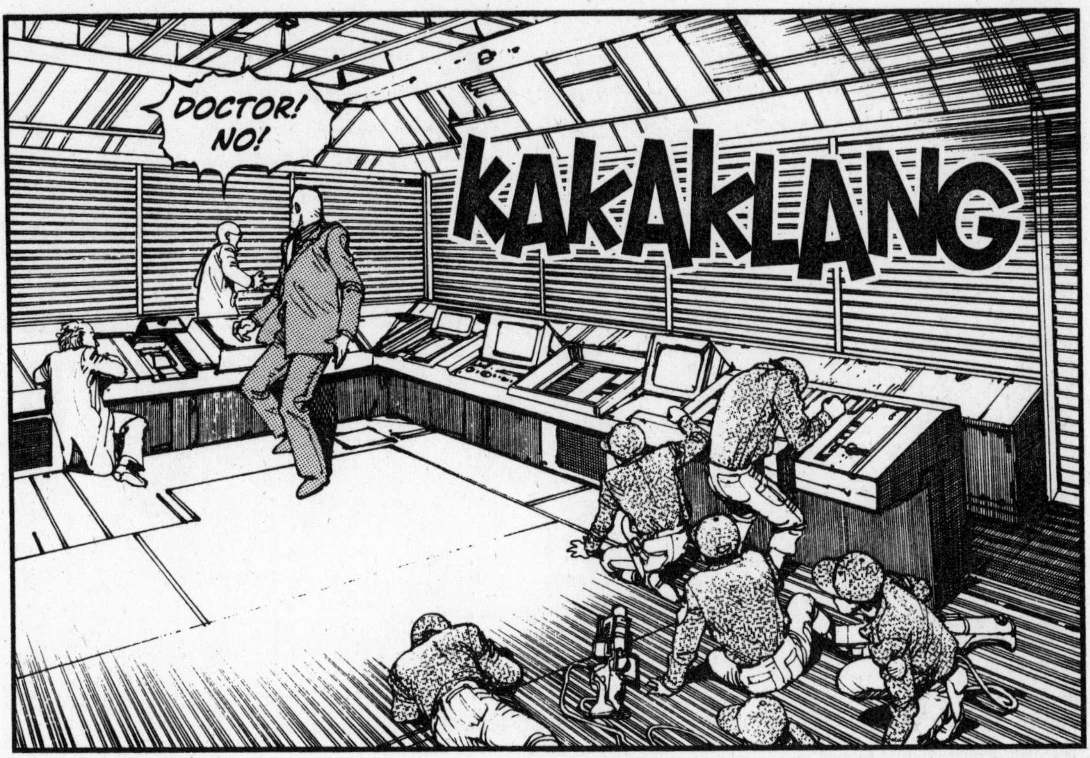
DOCTOR! NO!
KAKAKLANG

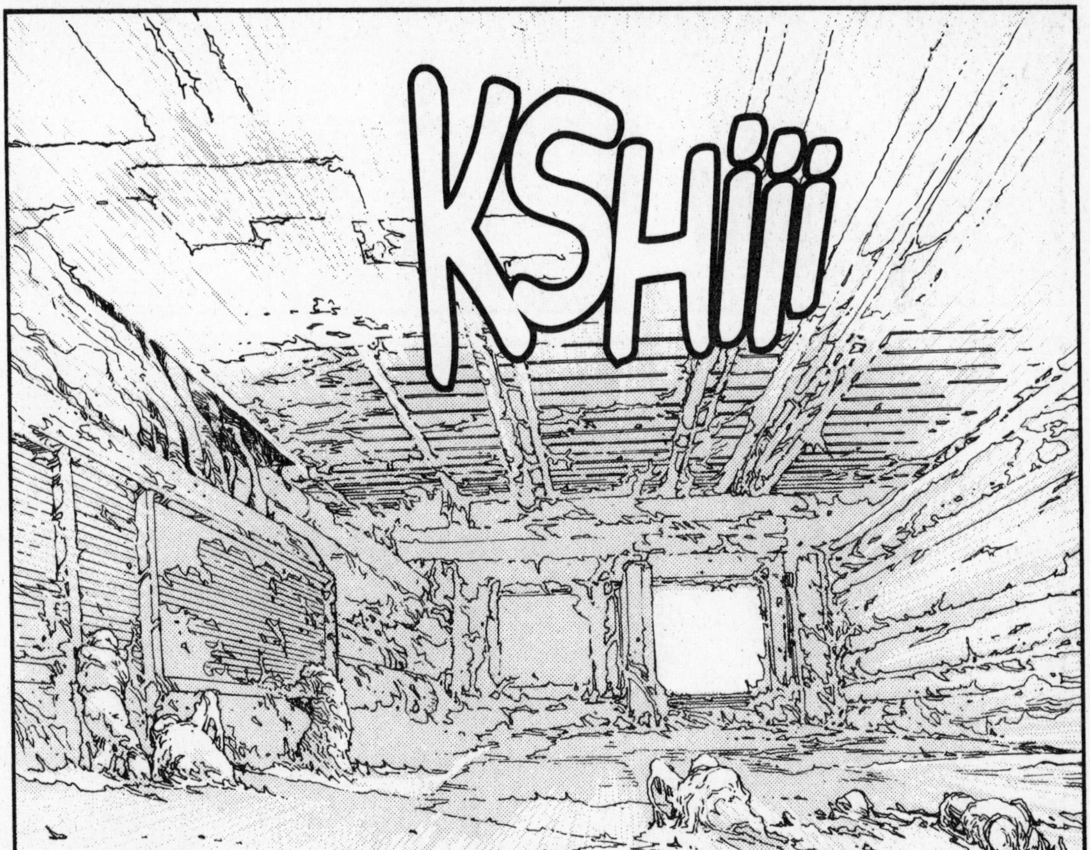
KSHiii

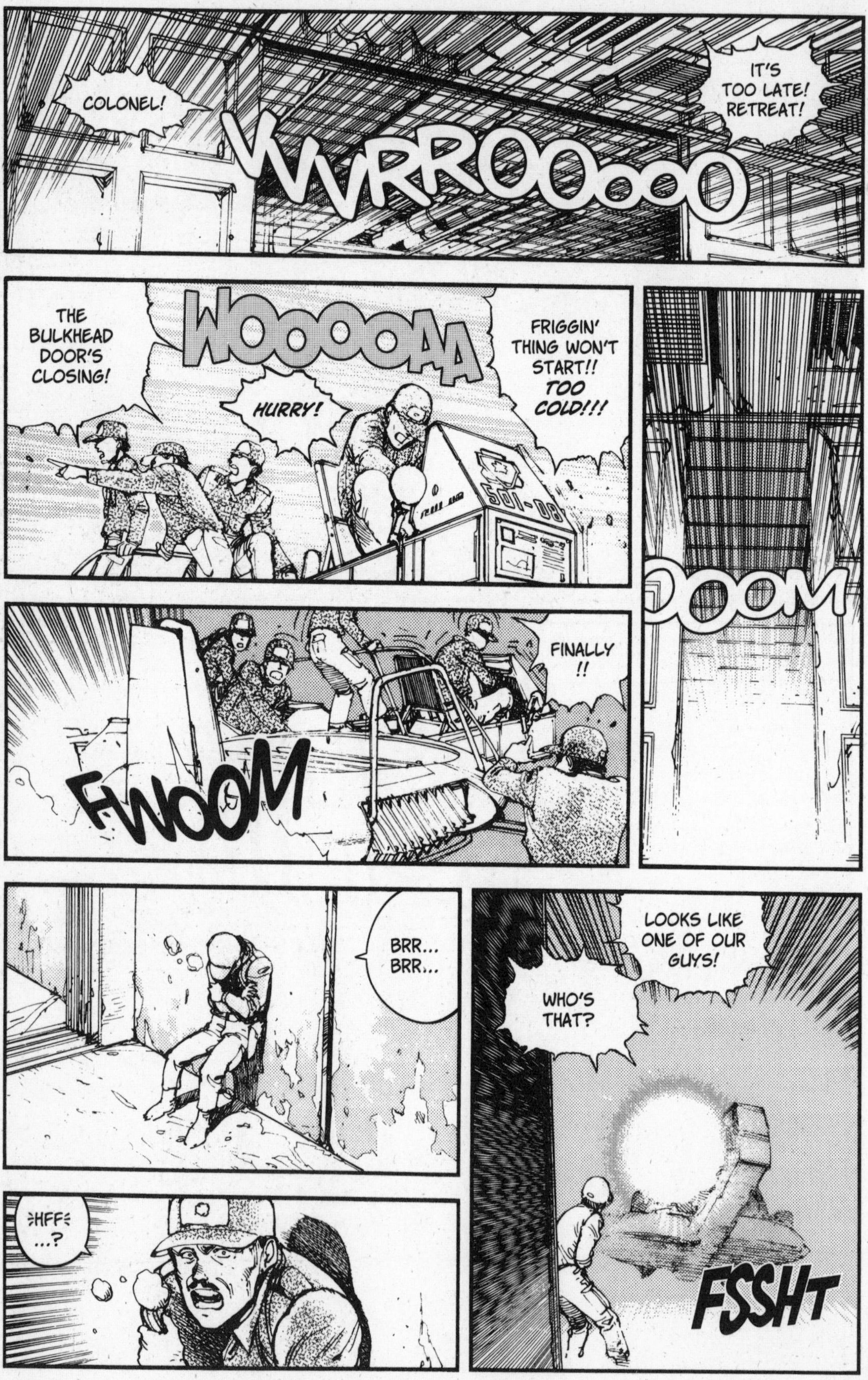

COLONEL!
WVRROOooOO
IT'S TOO LATE! RETREAT!
THE BULKHEAD DOOR'S CLOSING!
WOOOOAA
HURRY!
FRIGGIN' THING WON'T START!! *TOO COLD!!!*
FINALLY !!
FWOOM
OOOM
BRR... BRR...
HFF ...?
LOOKS LIKE ONE OF OUR GUYS!
WHO'S THAT?
FSSHT

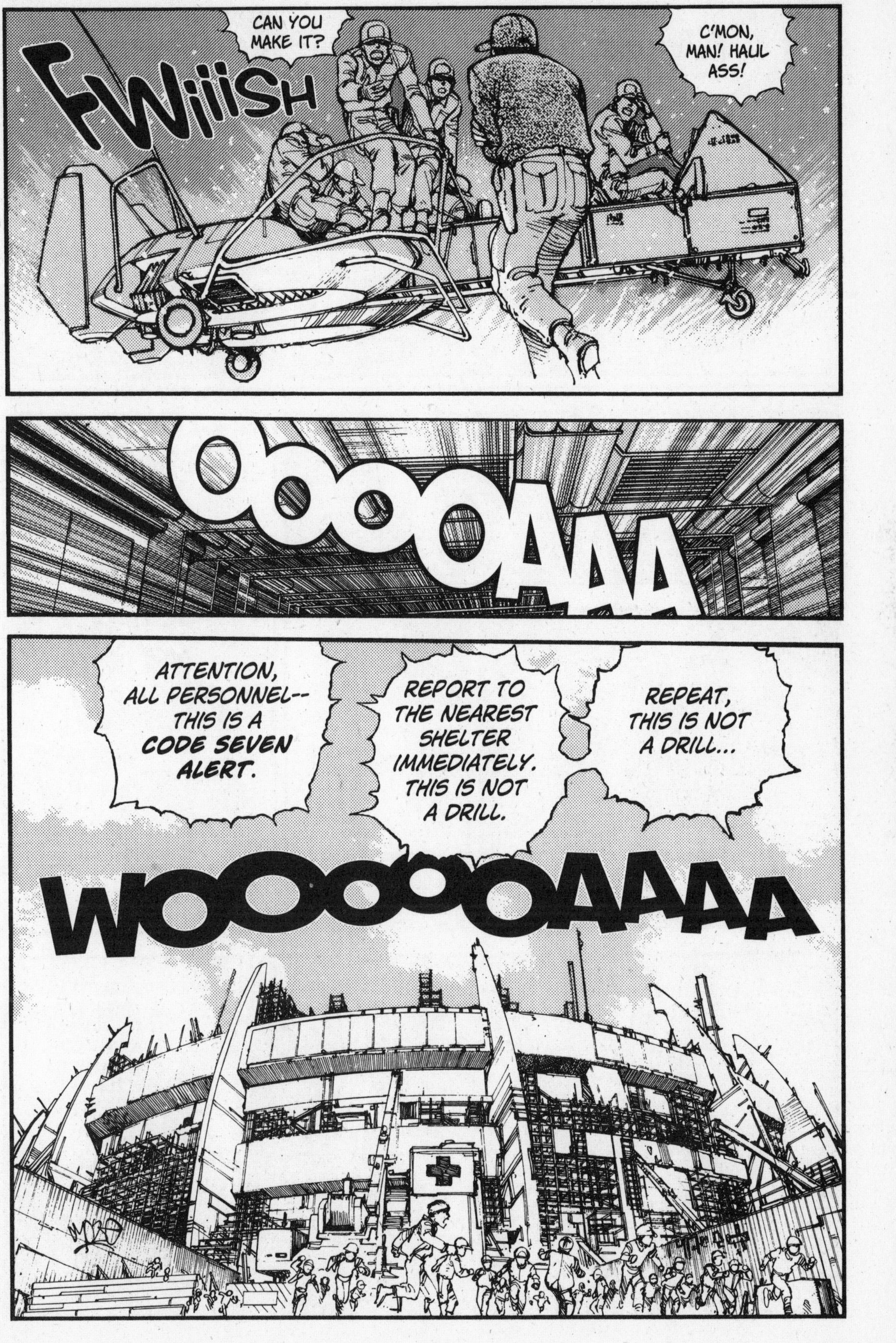
FWIIISH
CAN YOU MAKE IT?
C'MON, MAN! HAUL ASS!
OOOOAAA
ATTENTION, ALL PERSONNEL-- THIS IS A CODE SEVEN ALERT.
REPORT TO THE NEAREST SHELTER IMMEDIATELY. THIS IS NOT A DRILL.
REPEAT, THIS IS NOT A DRILL...
WOOOOOAAAA

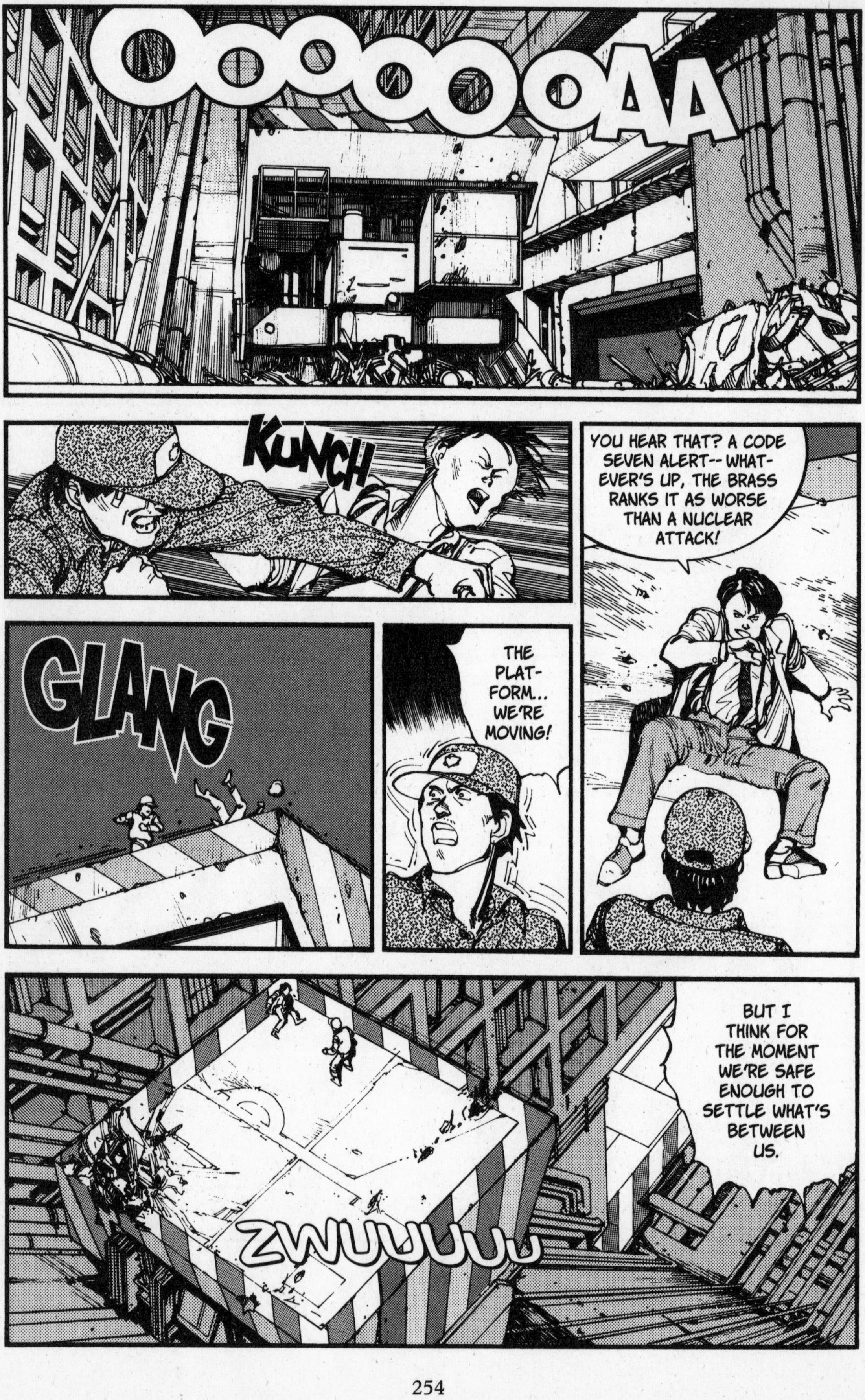

OOOOOOAA
KUNCH
YOU HEAR THAT? A CODE SEVEN ALERT-- WHAT-EVER'S UP, THE BRASS RANKS IT AS WORSE THAN A NUCLEAR ATTACK!
GLANG
THE PLAT-FORM... WE'RE MOVING!
BUT I THINK FOR THE MOMENT WE'RE SAFE ENOUGH TO SETTLE WHAT'S BETWEEN US.
ZWUUUUUU

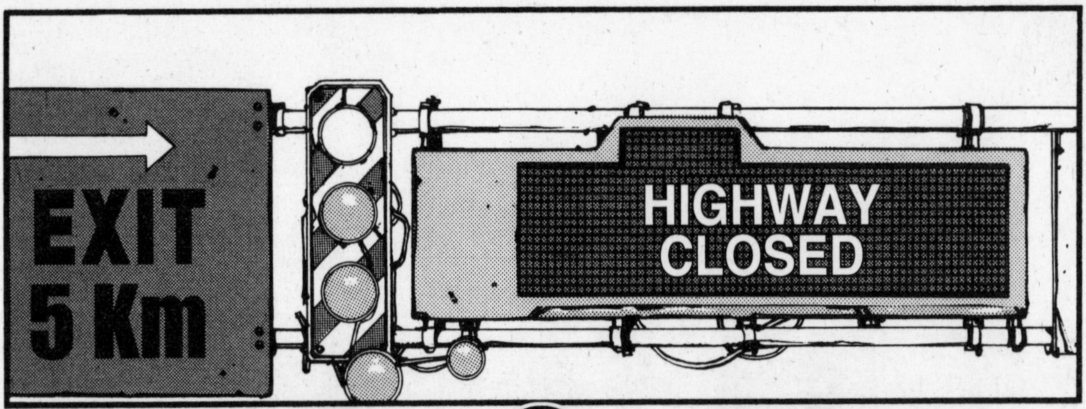
EXIT
5 Km
HIGHWAY
CLOSED

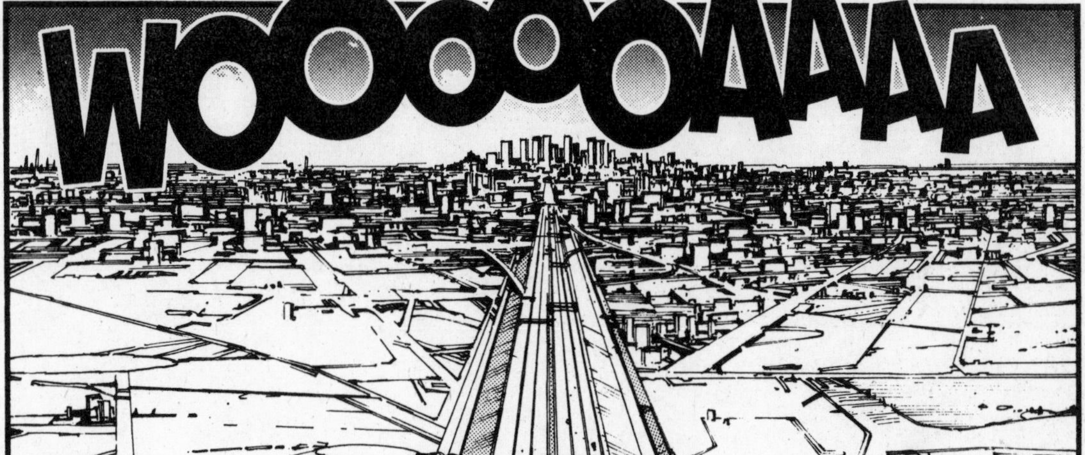
WOOOOOAAAA

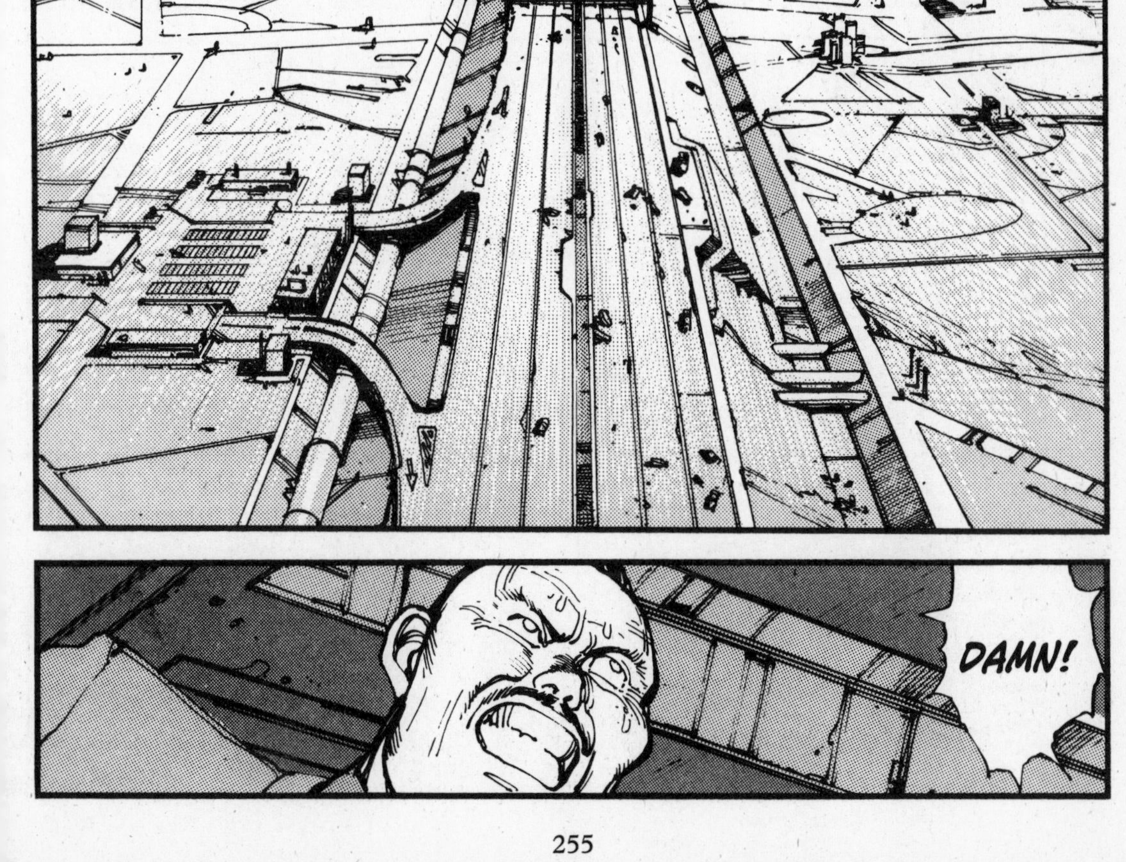
DAMN!

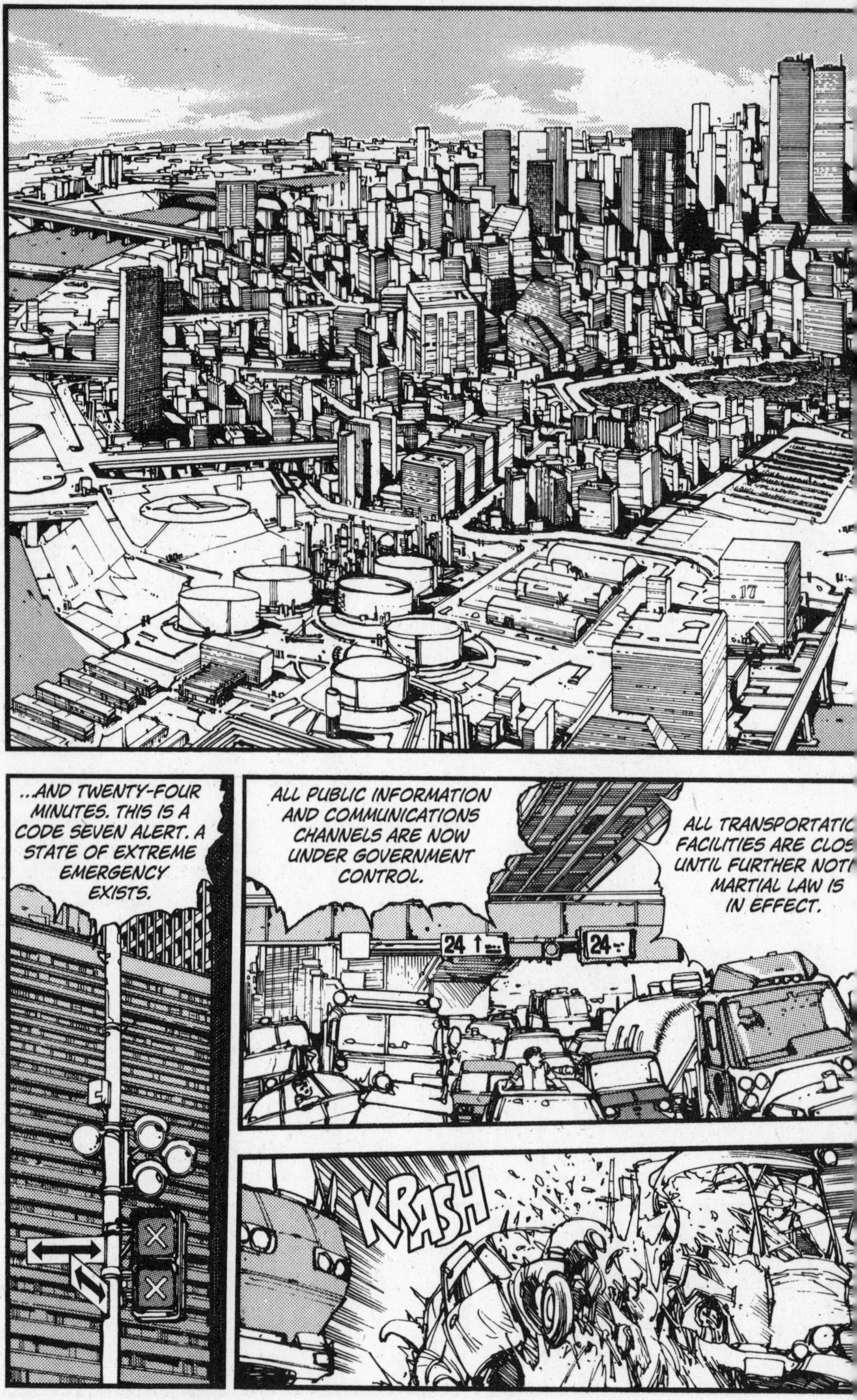
.17
...AND TWENTY-FOUR MINUTES. THIS IS A CODE SEVEN ALERT. A STATE OF EXTREME EMERGENCY EXISTS.
ALL PUBLIC INFORMATION AND COMMUNICATIONS CHANNELS ARE NOW UNDER GOVERNMENT CONTROL.
ALL TRANSPORTATIC FACILITIES ARE CLOS UNTIL FURTHER NOTI MARTIAL LAW IS IN EFFECT.
24
24
KRASH

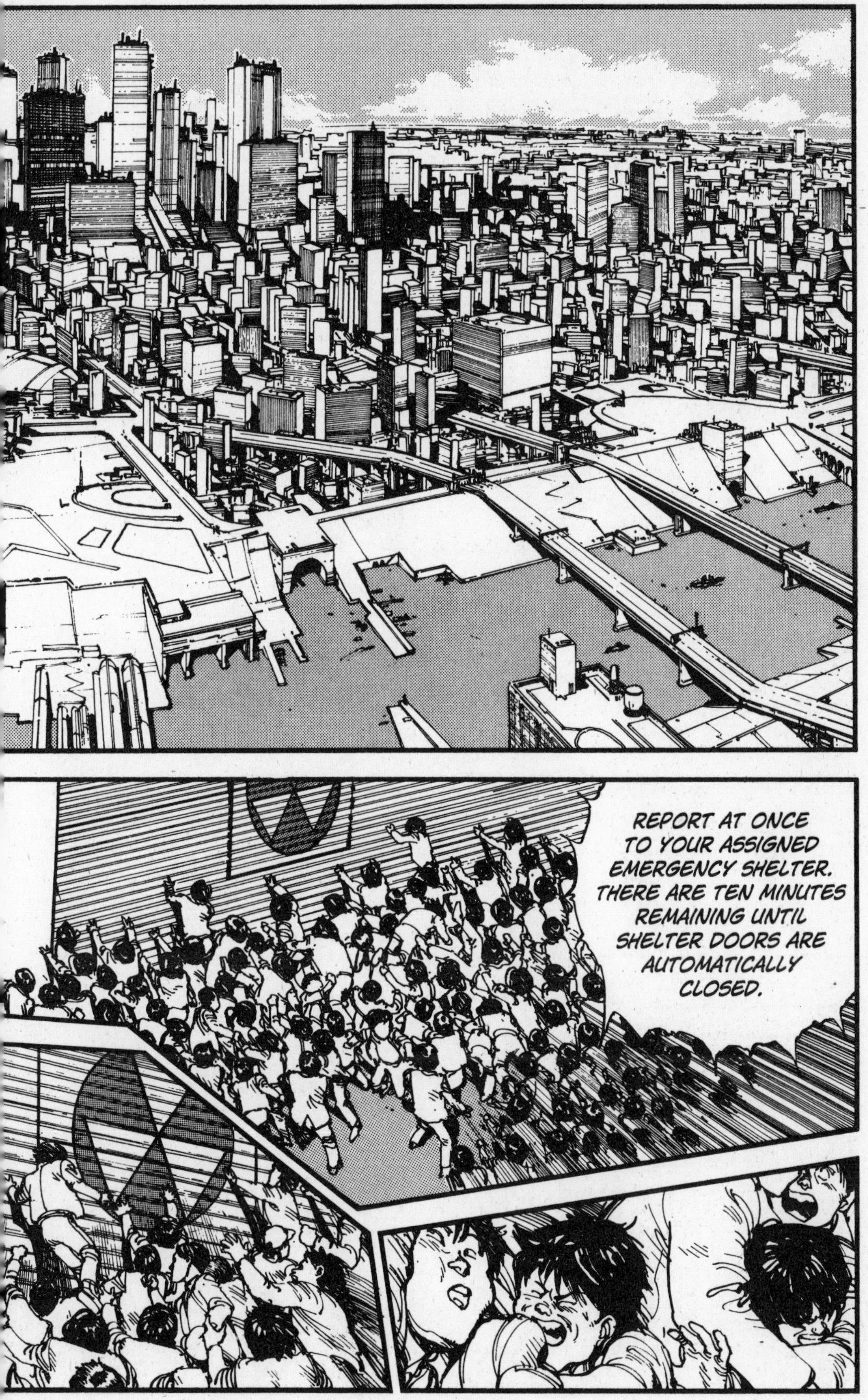
REPORT AT ONCE TO YOUR ASSIGNED EMERGENCY SHELTER. THERE ARE TEN MINUTES REMAINING UNTIL SHELTER DOORS ARE AUTOMATICALLY CLOSED.

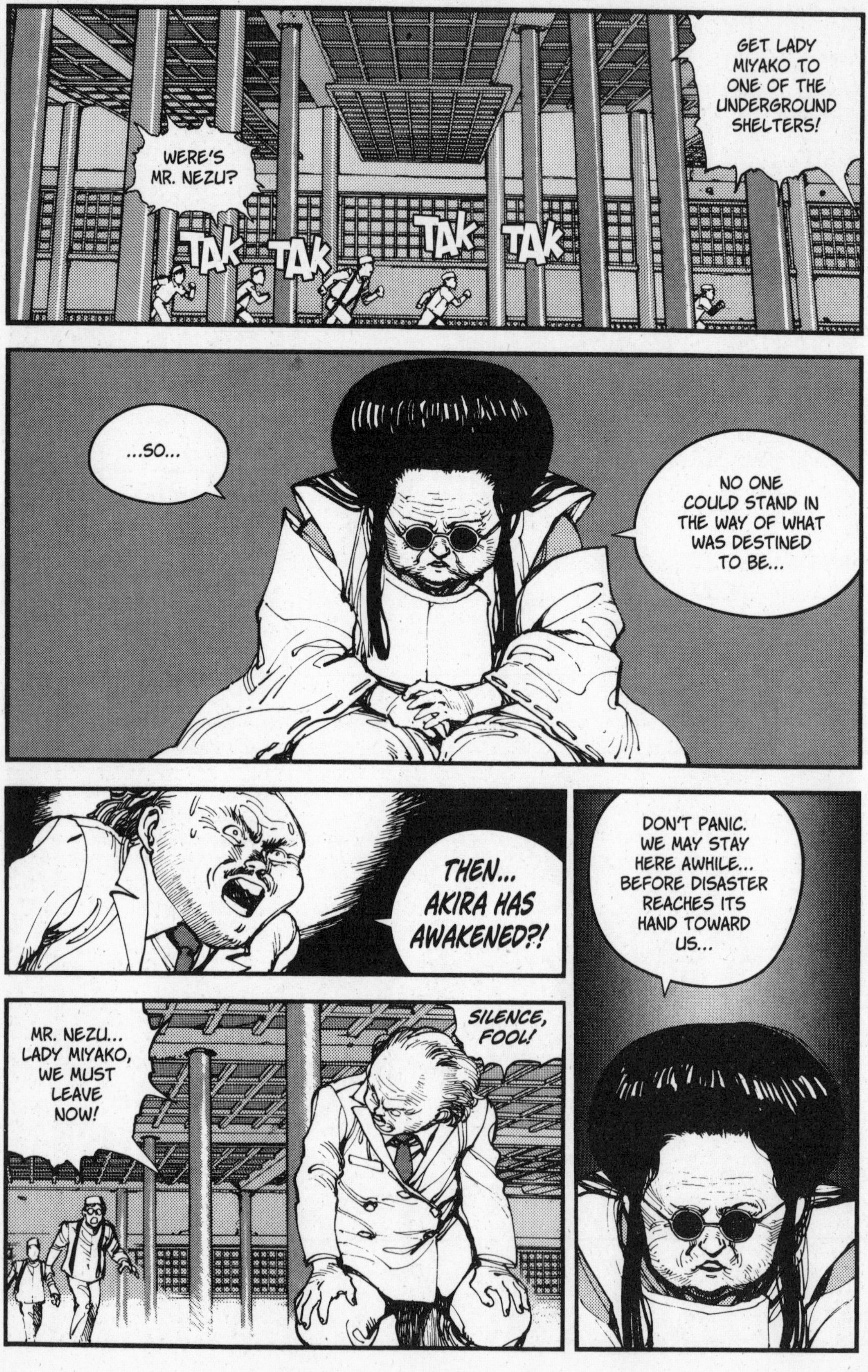
WERE'S MR. NEZU?
TAK TAK TAK TAK
GET LADY MIYAKO TO ONE OF THE UNDERGROUND SHELTERS!
...SO...
NO ONE COULD STAND IN THE WAY OF WHAT WAS DESTINED TO BE...
THEN... AKIRA HAS AWAKENED?!
DON'T PANIC. WE MAY STAY HERE AWHILE... BEFORE DISASTER REACHES ITS HAND TOWARD US...
MR. NEZU... LADY MIYAKO, WE MUST LEAVE NOW!
SILENCE, FOOL!

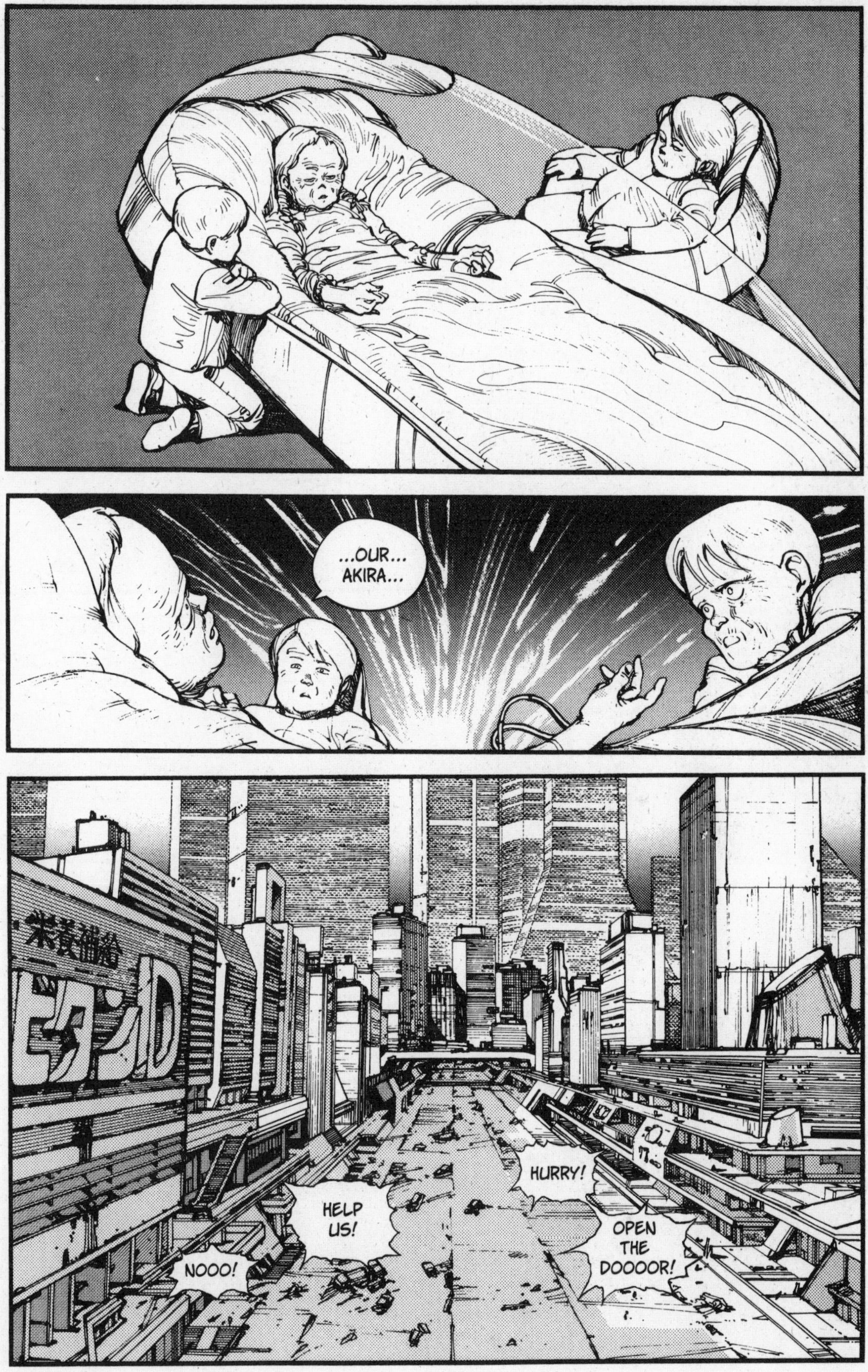
...OUR... AKIRA...
栄養補給
HURRY!
HELP US!
OPEN THE DOOOOR!
NOOO!

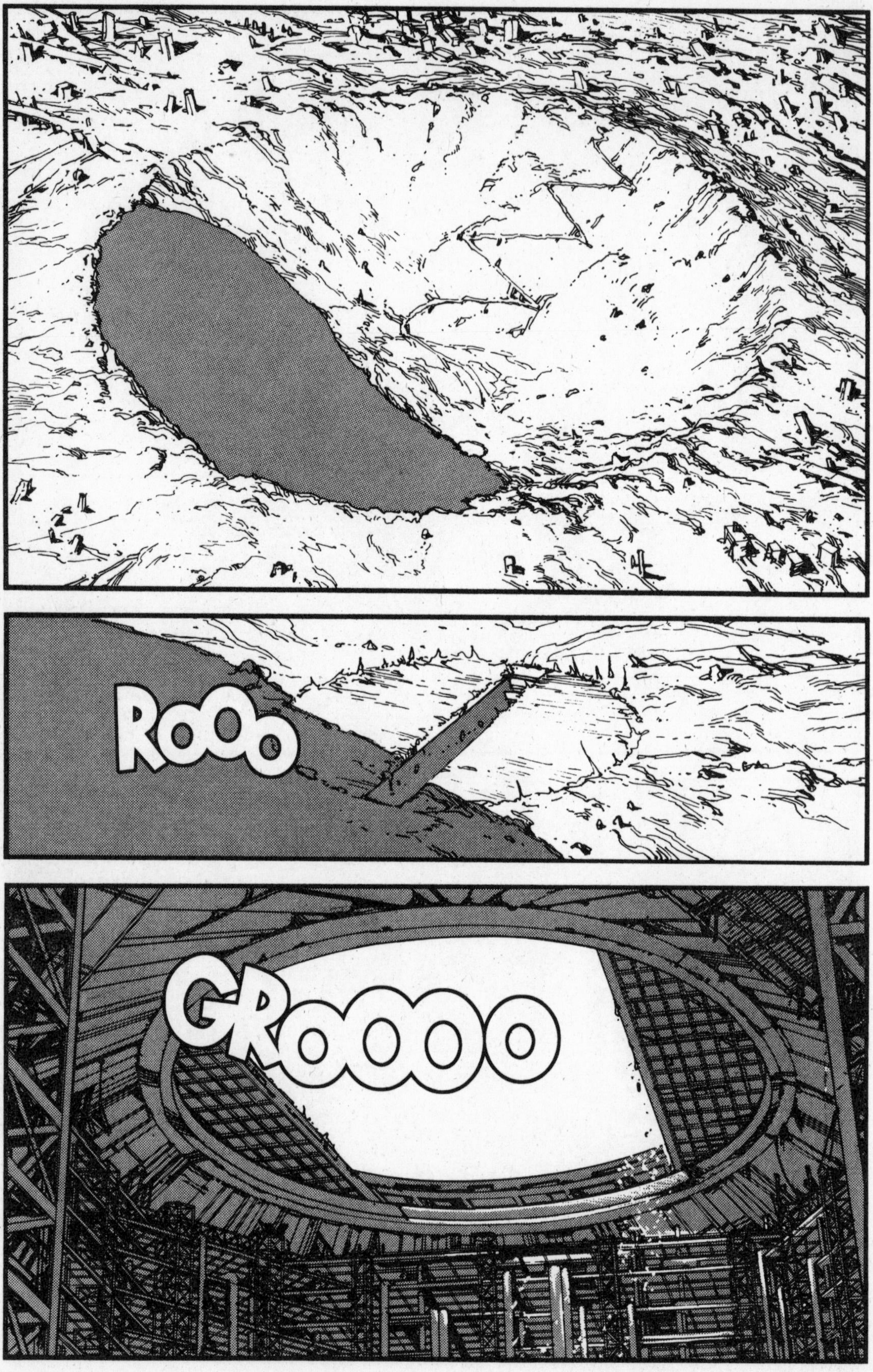
ROOO
GROOOOO

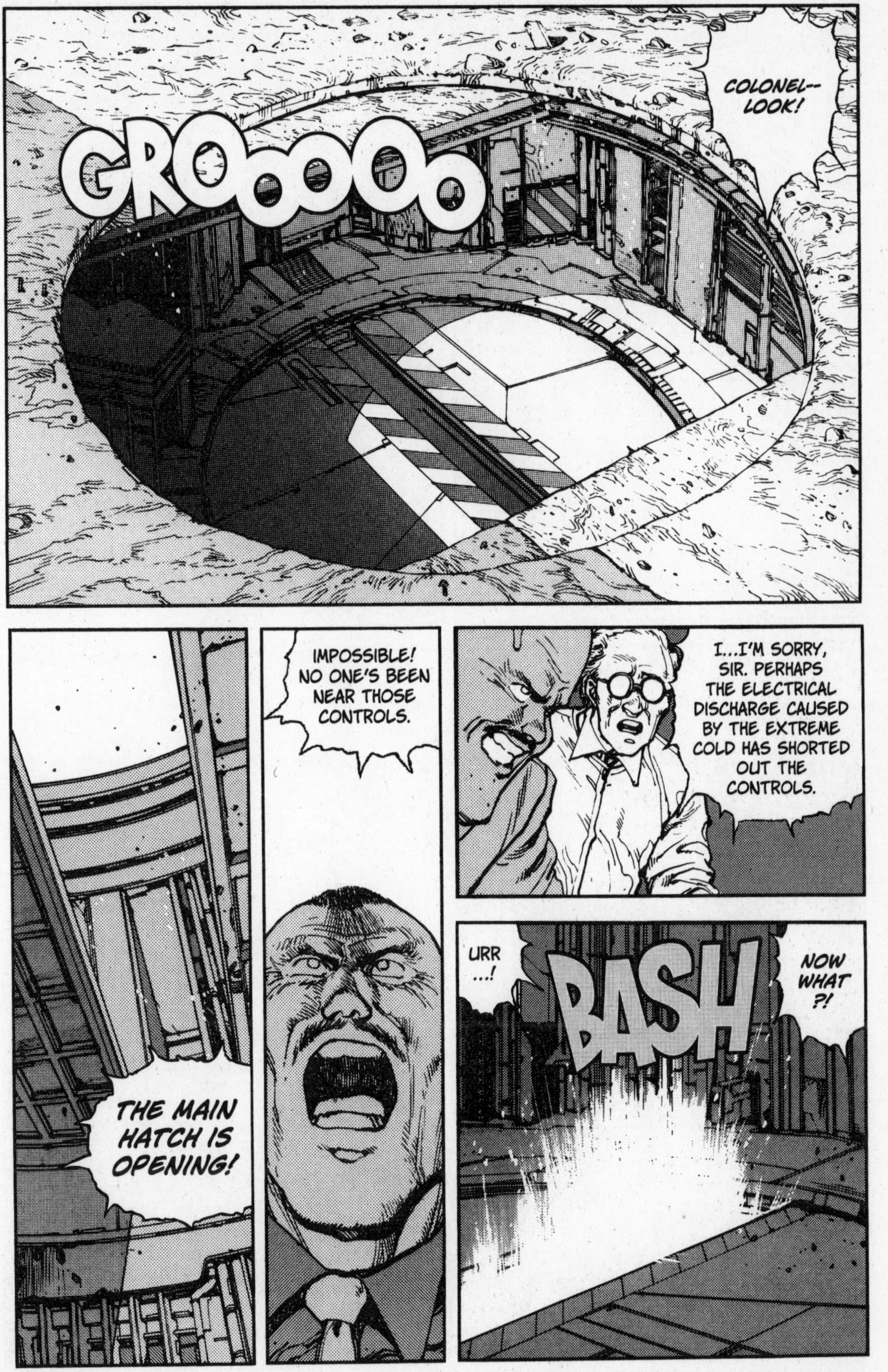
GROOOOOO
COLONEL--
LOOK!
THE MAIN
HATCH IS
OPENING!
IMPOSSIBLE!
NO ONE'S BEEN
NEAR THOSE
CONTROLS.
I...I'M SORRY,
SIR. PERHAPS
THE ELECTRICAL
DISCHARGE CAUSED
BY THE EXTREME
COLD HAS SHORTED
OUT THE
CONTROLS.
URR
...!
BASH
NOW
WHAT
?!

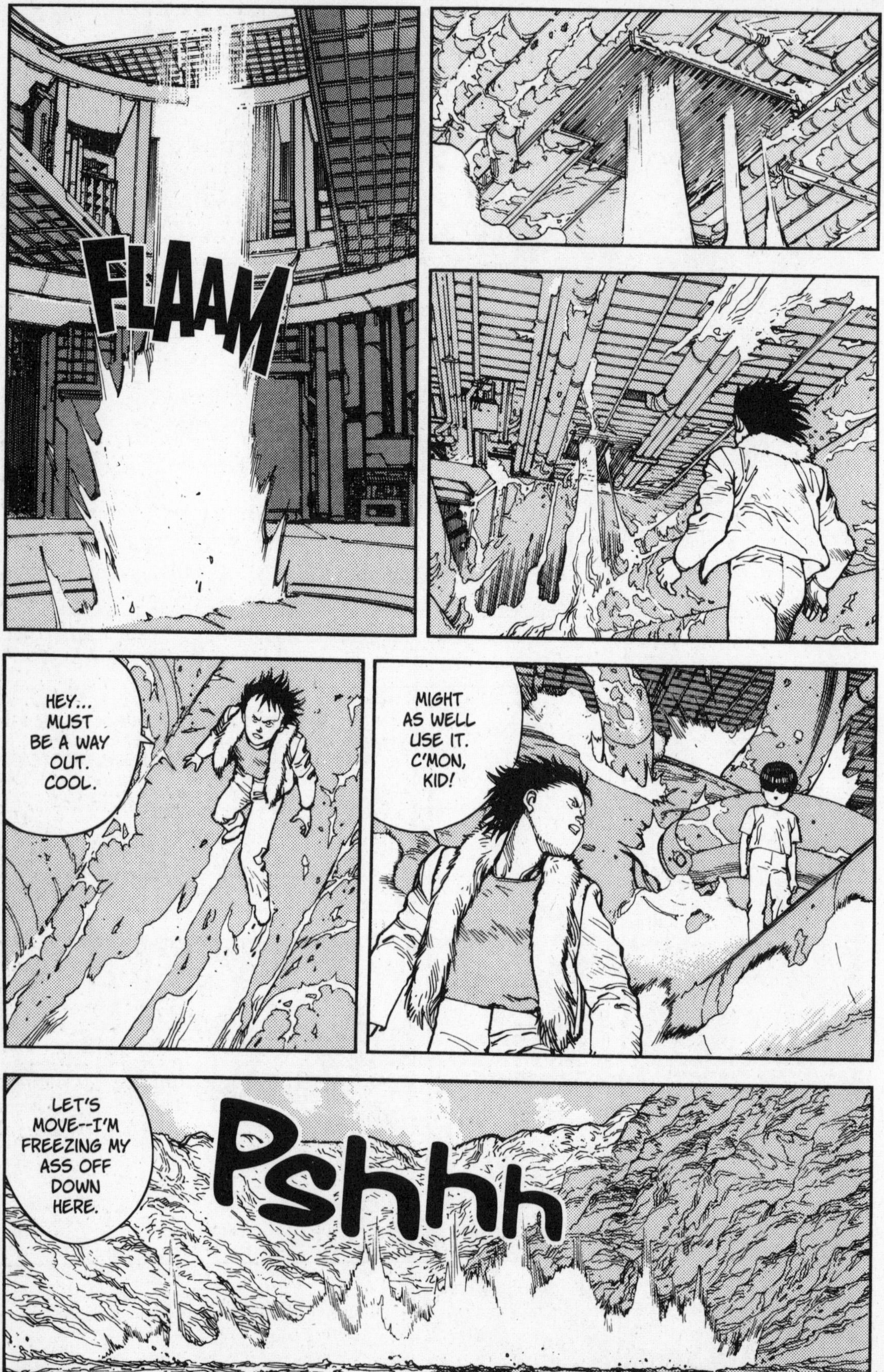
FLAAM
HEY... MUST BE A WAY OUT. COOL.
MIGHT AS WELL USE IT. C'MON, KID!
LET'S MOVE--I'M FREEZING MY ASS OFF DOWN HERE.
Pshhh

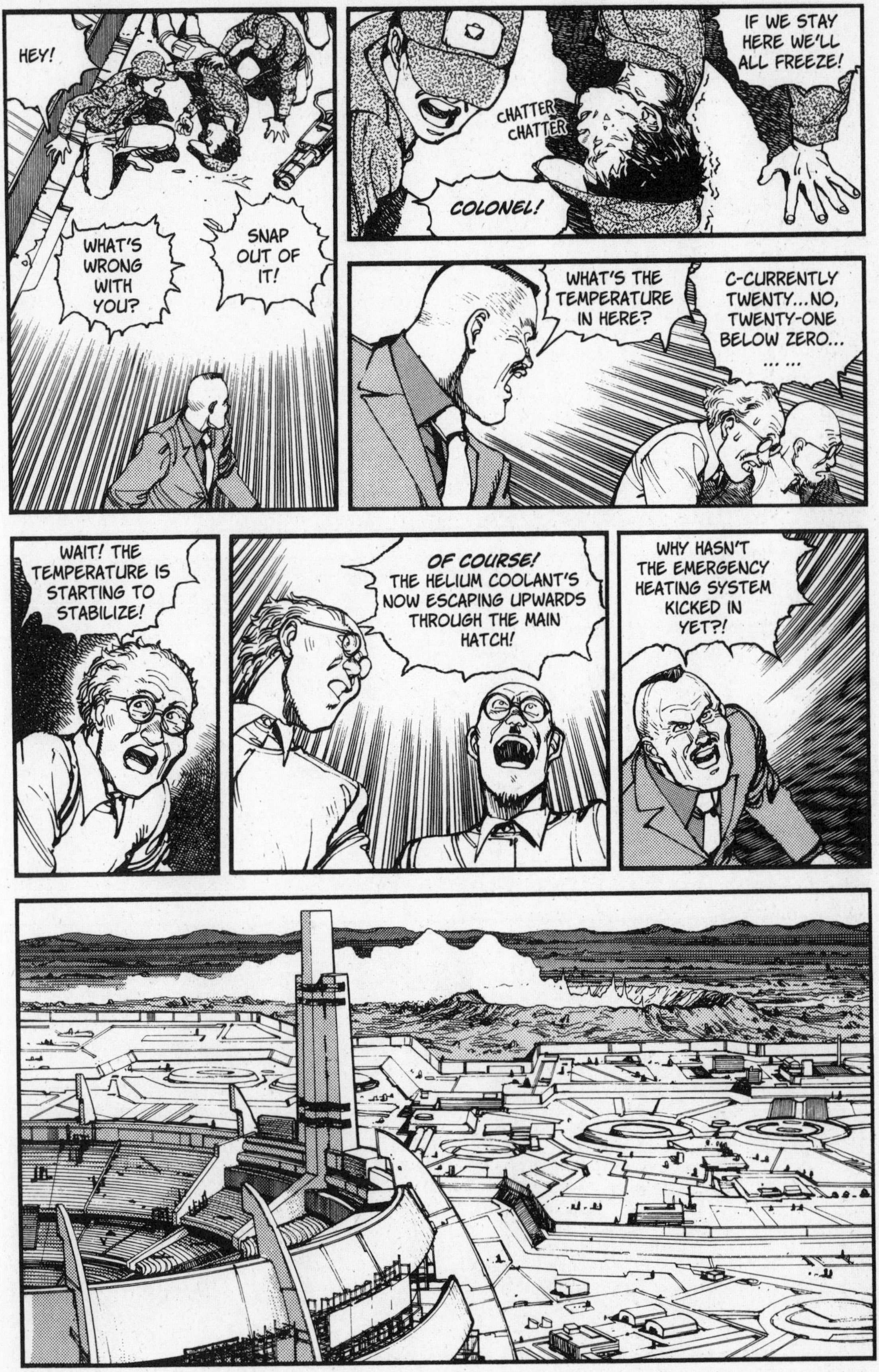
HEY!
WHAT'S WRONG WITH YOU?
SNAP OUT OF IT!
CHATTER CHATTER
COLONEL!
IF WE STAY HERE WE'LL ALL FREEZE!
WHAT'S THE TEMPERATURE IN HERE?
C-CURRENTLY TWENTY...NO, TWENTY-ONE BELOW ZERO...
... ...
WAIT! THE TEMPERATURE IS STARTING TO STABILIZE!
OF COURSE! THE HELIUM COOLANT'S NOW ESCAPING UPWARDS THROUGH THE MAIN HATCH!
WHY HASN'T THE EMERGENCY HEATING SYSTEM KICKED IN YET?!

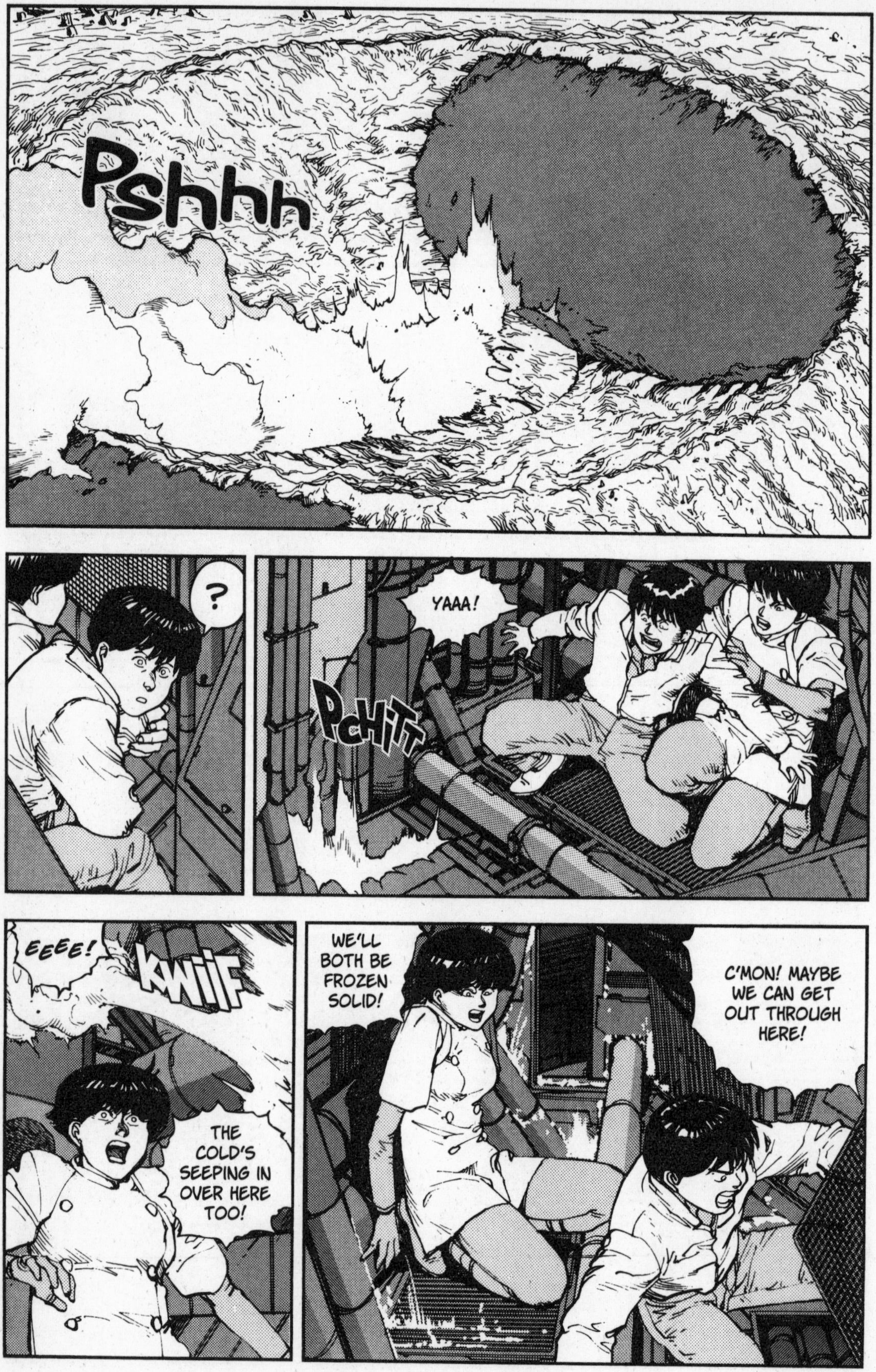
Pshhh
?
YAAA!
PCHITT
EEEE!
KWIIF
THE COLD'S SEEPING IN OVER HERE TOO!
WE'LL BOTH BE FROZEN SOLID!
C'MON! MAYBE WE CAN GET OUT THROUGH HERE!

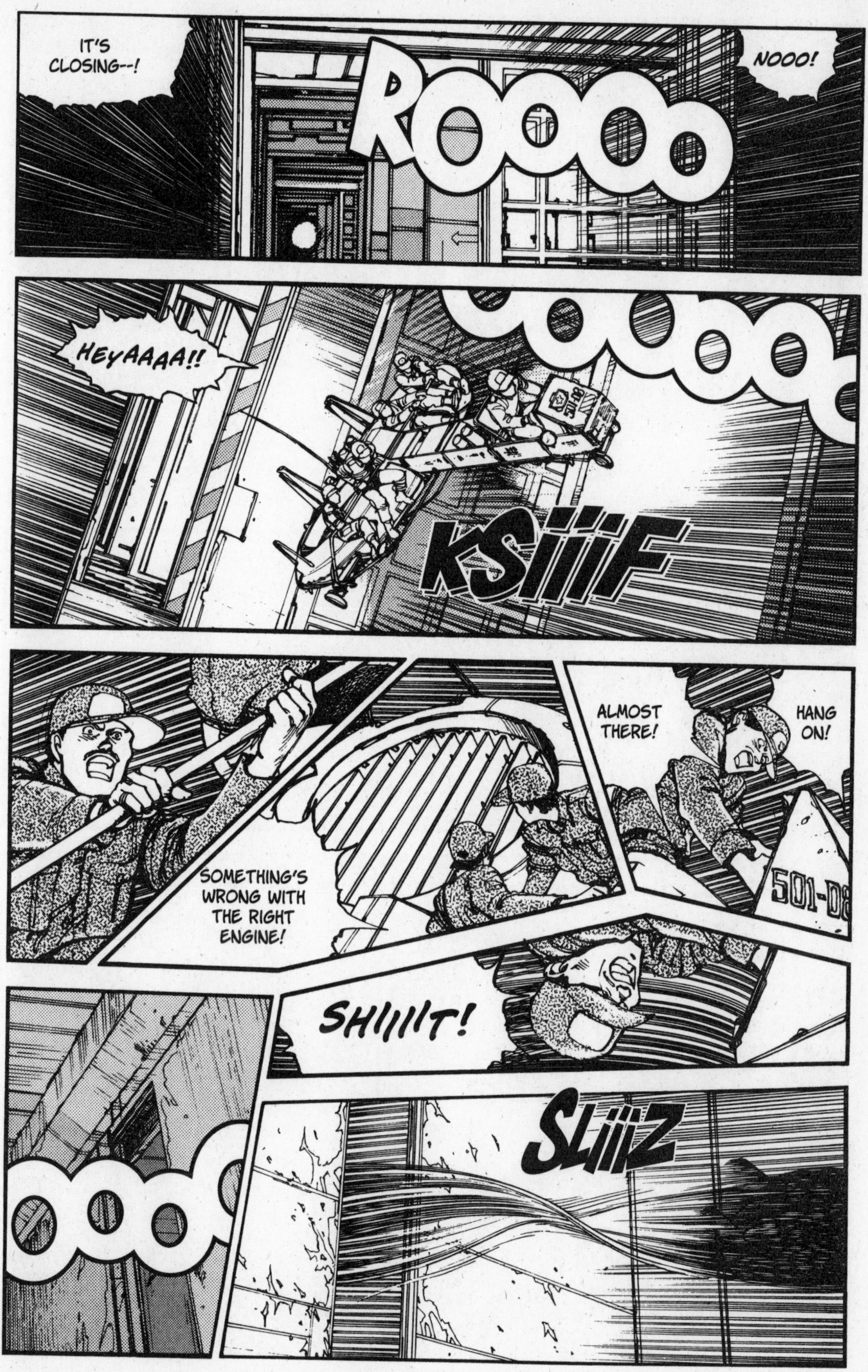
IT'S CLOSING--!
ROOOO
NOOO!
HEYAAAA!!
OOOOOO
KSIIIF
SOMETHING'S WRONG WITH THE RIGHT ENGINE!
ALMOST THERE!
HANG ON!
501-D8
SHIIIIT!
OOOO
SLIIIZ

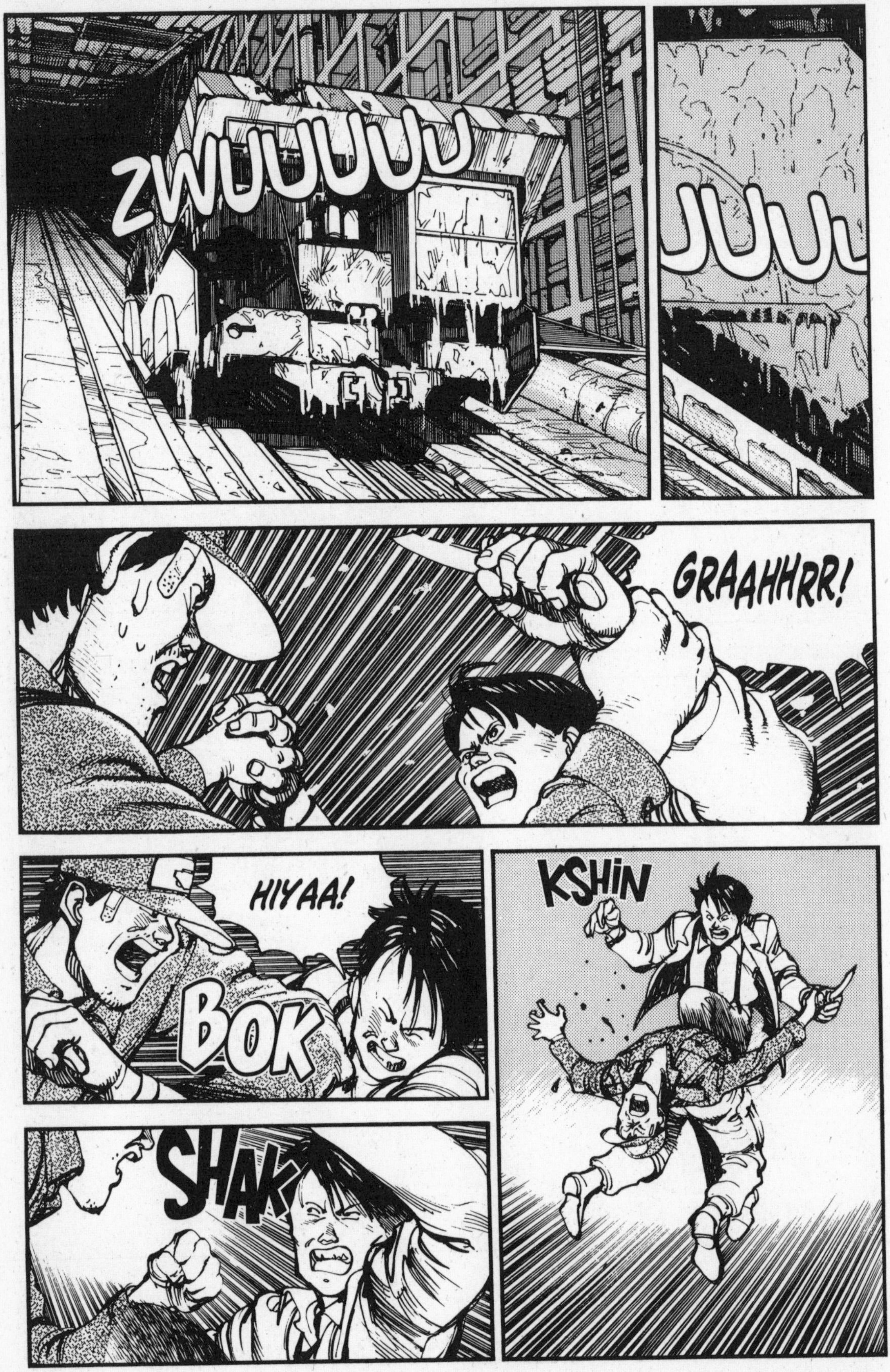
ZWUUUUU
UUUU
GRAAHHRR!
HIYAA!
BOK
SHAK
KSHIN

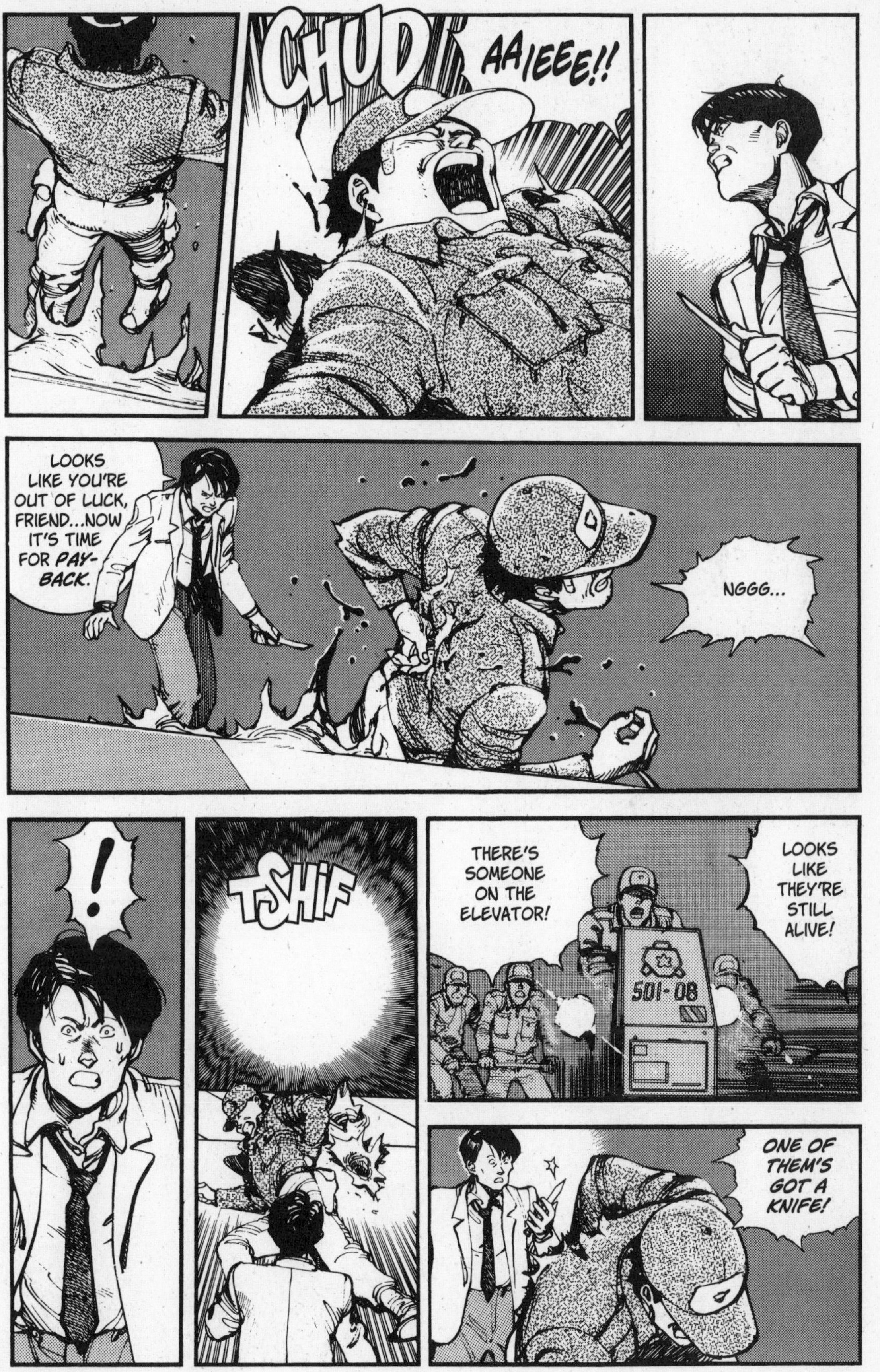
CHUD
AAIEEE!!
LOOKS LIKE YOU'RE OUT OF LUCK, FRIEND...NOW IT'S TIME FOR PAY-BACK.
NGGG...
!
TSHIF
THERE'S SOMEONE ON THE ELEVATOR!
LOOKS LIKE THEY'RE STILL ALIVE!
501-08
ONE OF THEM'S GOT A KNIFE!

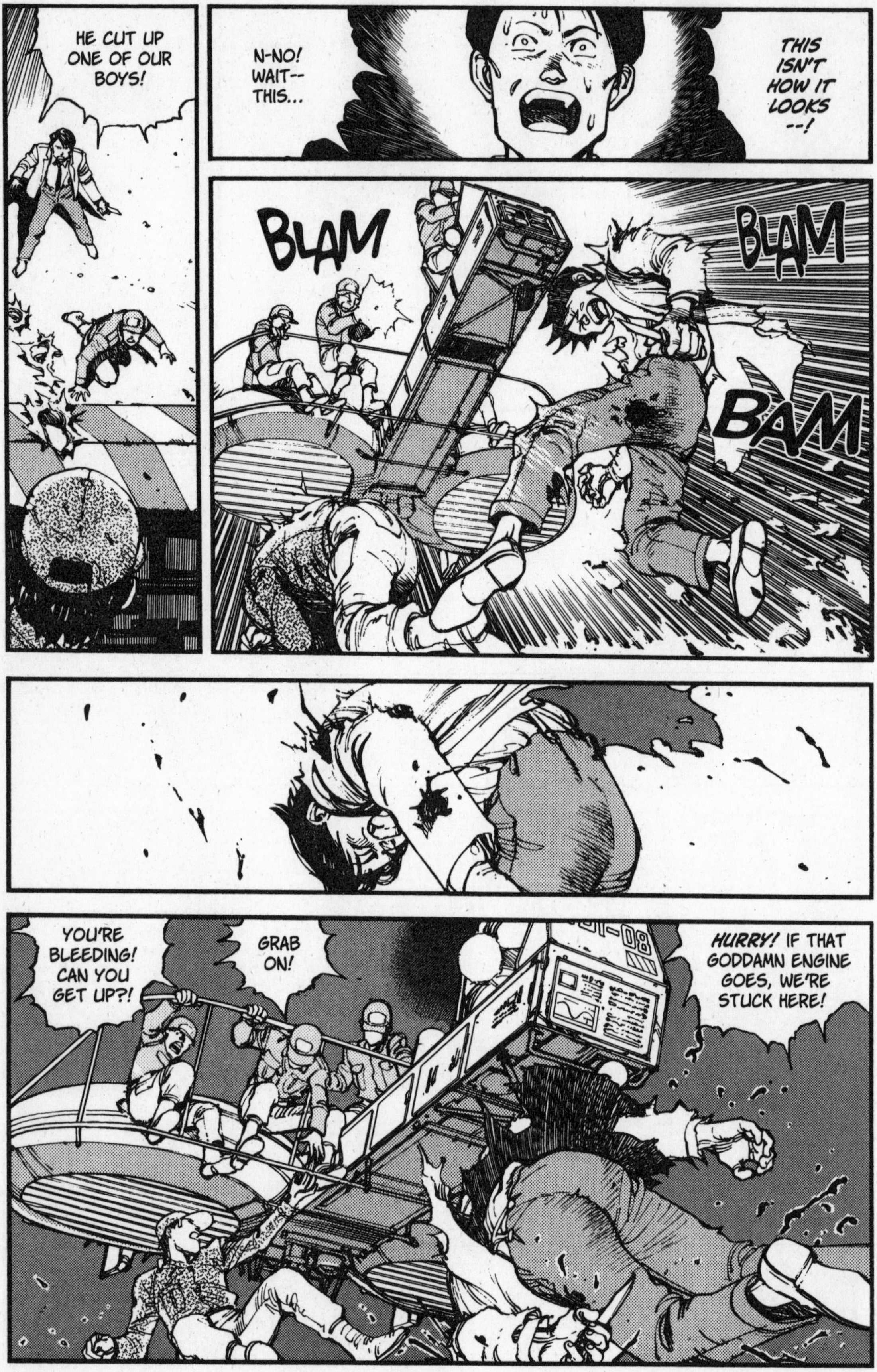
HE CUT UP ONE OF OUR BOYS!
N-NO! WAIT-- THIS...
THIS ISN'T HOW IT LOOKS --!
BLAM
BLAM
BAM
YOU'RE BLEEDING! CAN YOU GET UP?!
GRAB ON!
HURRY! IF THAT GODDAMN ENGINE GOES, WE'RE STUCK HERE!

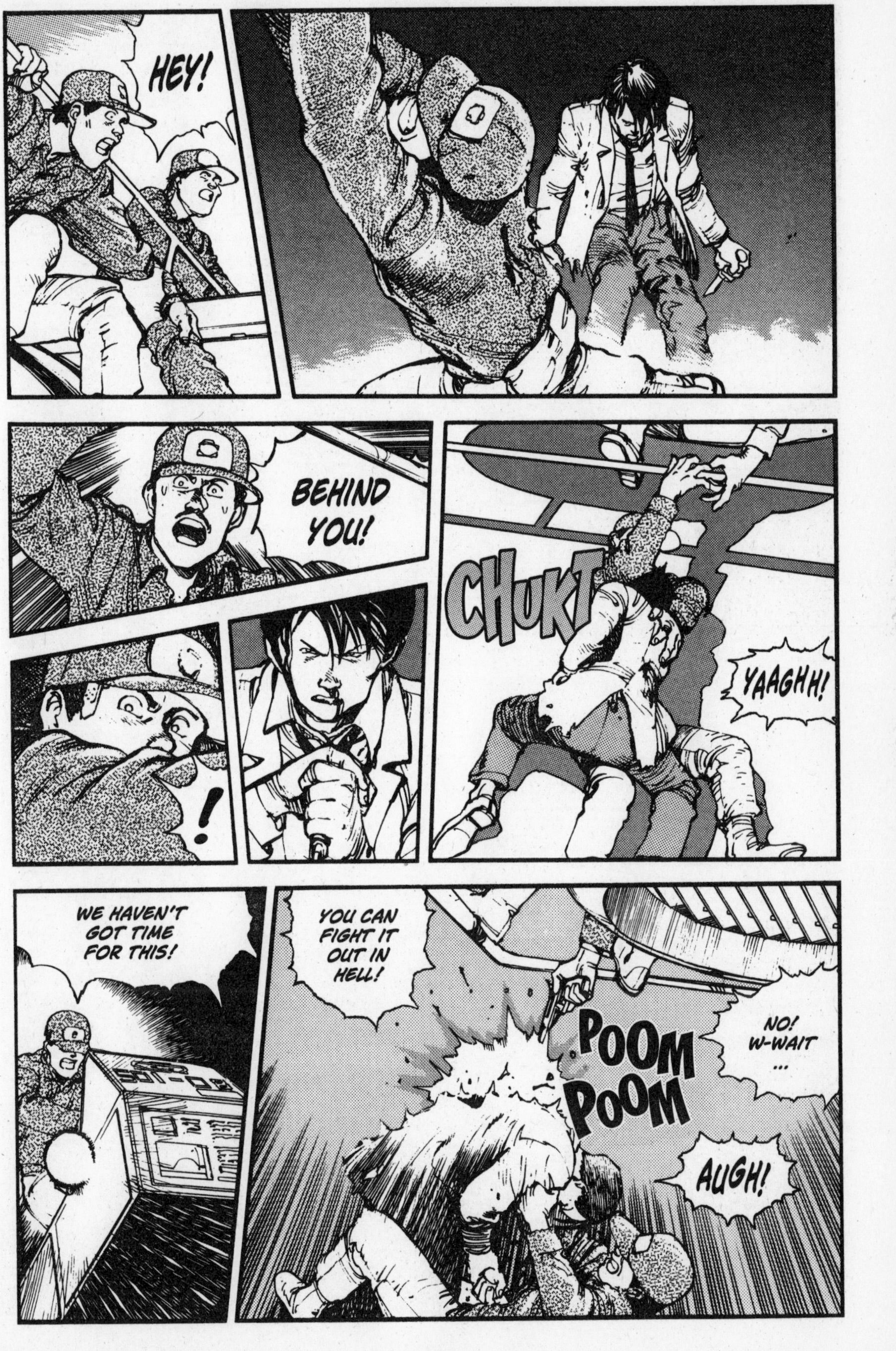
HEY!
BEHIND YOU!
CHUKT
YAAGHH!
!
WE HAVEN'T GOT TIME FOR THIS!
YOU CAN FIGHT IT OUT IN HELL!
POOM POOM
NO! W-WAIT ...
AUGH!

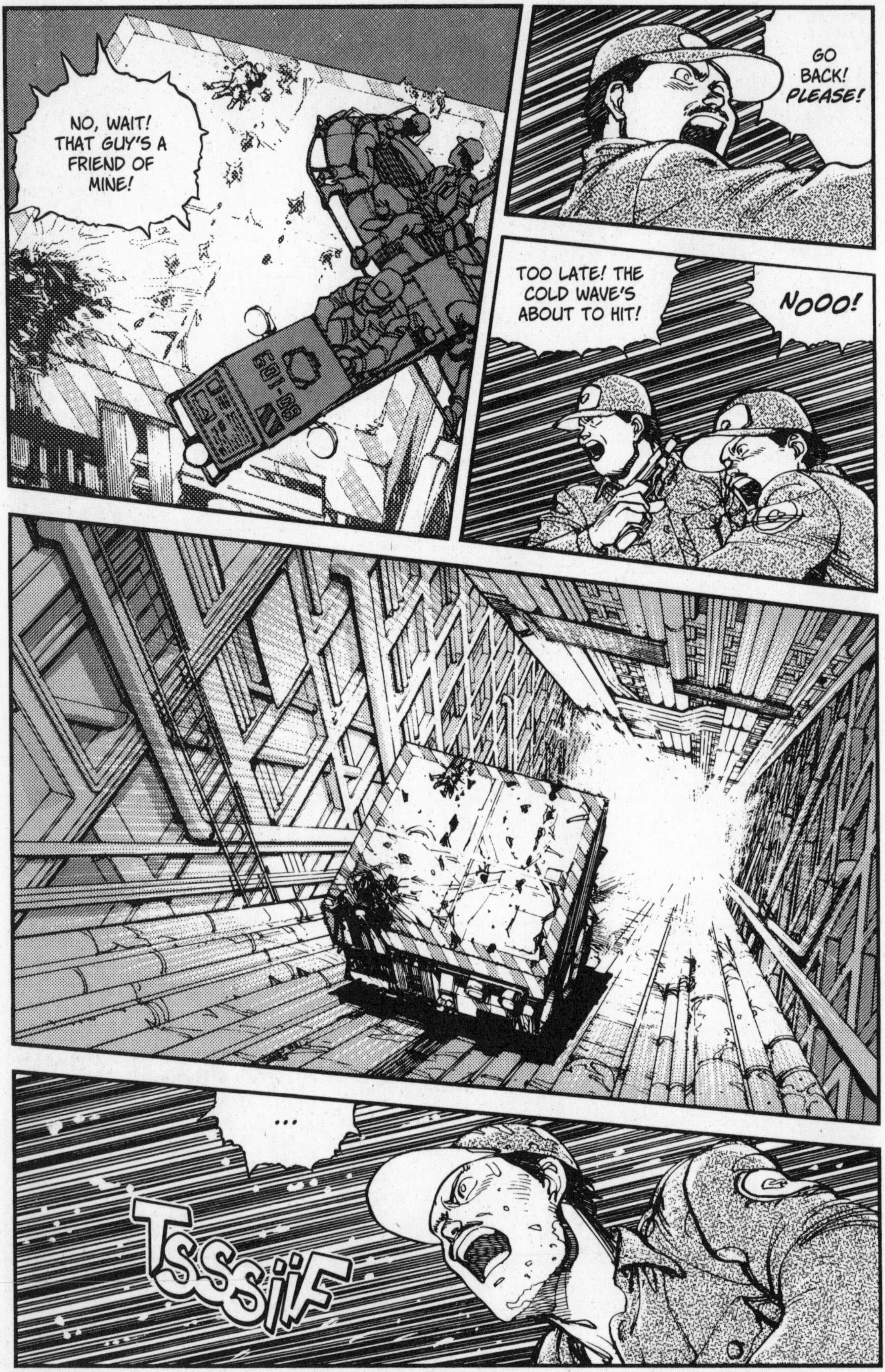
NO, WAIT! THAT GUY'S A FRIEND OF MINE!
GO BACK! PLEASE!
TOO LATE! THE COLD WAVE'S ABOUT TO HIT!
NOOO!
...
TSSSIIF

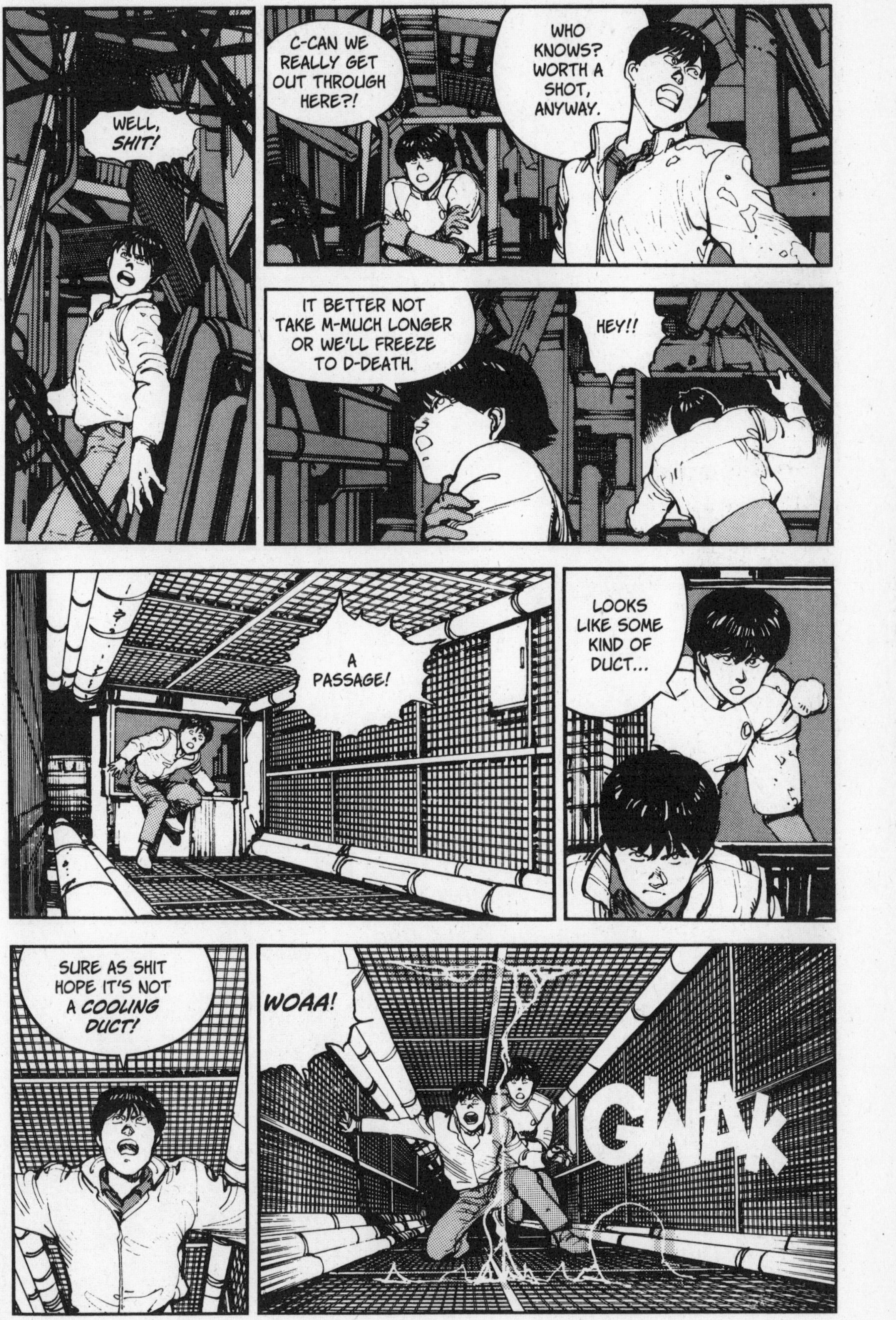
WELL, SHIT!
C-CAN WE REALLY GET OUT THROUGH HERE?!
WHO KNOWS? WORTH A SHOT, ANYWAY.
IT BETTER NOT TAKE M-MUCH LONGER OR WE'LL FREEZE TO D-DEATH.
HEY!!
A PASSAGE!
LOOKS LIKE SOME KIND OF DUCT...
SURE AS SHIT HOPE IT'S NOT A COOLING DUCT!
WOAA!
GWAK

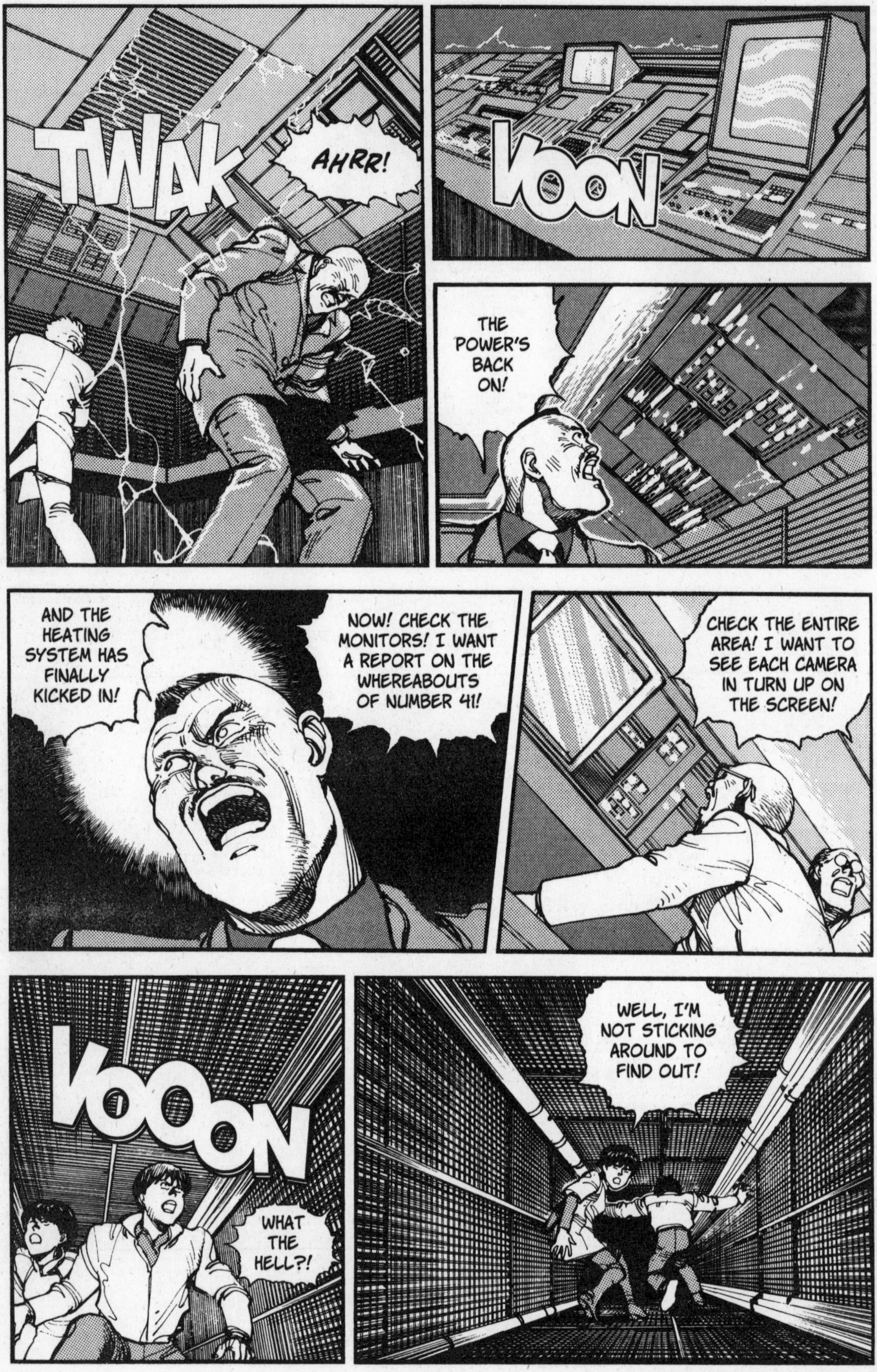
TWAK
AHRR!
VOON
THE POWER'S BACK ON!
AND THE HEATING SYSTEM HAS FINALLY KICKED IN!
NOW! CHECK THE MONITORS! I WANT A REPORT ON THE WHEREABOUTS OF NUMBER 41!
CHECK THE ENTIRE AREA! I WANT TO SEE EACH CAMERA IN TURN UP ON THE SCREEN!
VOOON
WHAT THE HELL?!
WELL, I'M NOT STICKING AROUND TO FIND OUT!

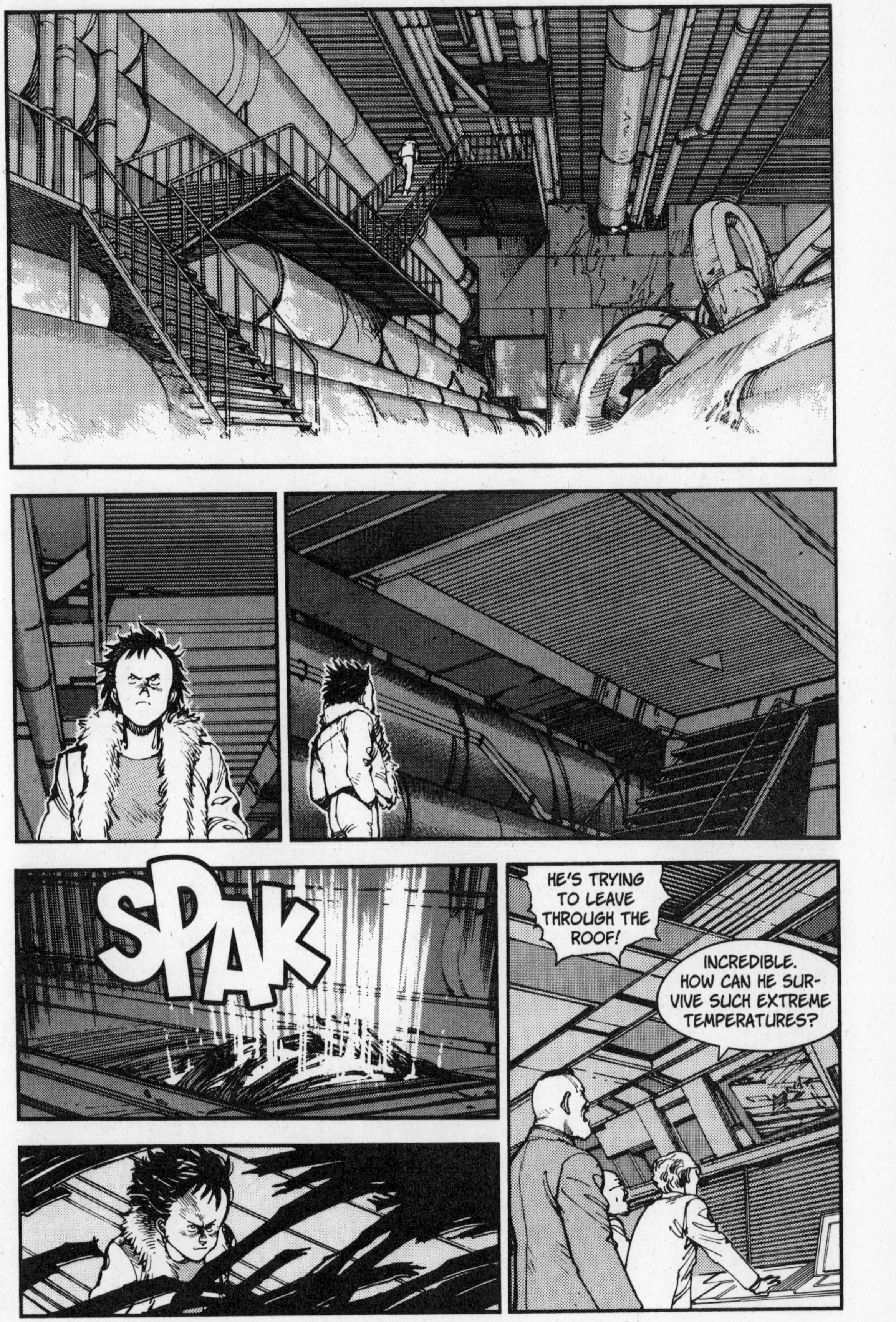
SPAK
HE'S TRYING TO LEAVE THROUGH THE ROOF!
INCREDIBLE. HOW CAN HE SURVIVE SUCH EXTREME TEMPERATURES?

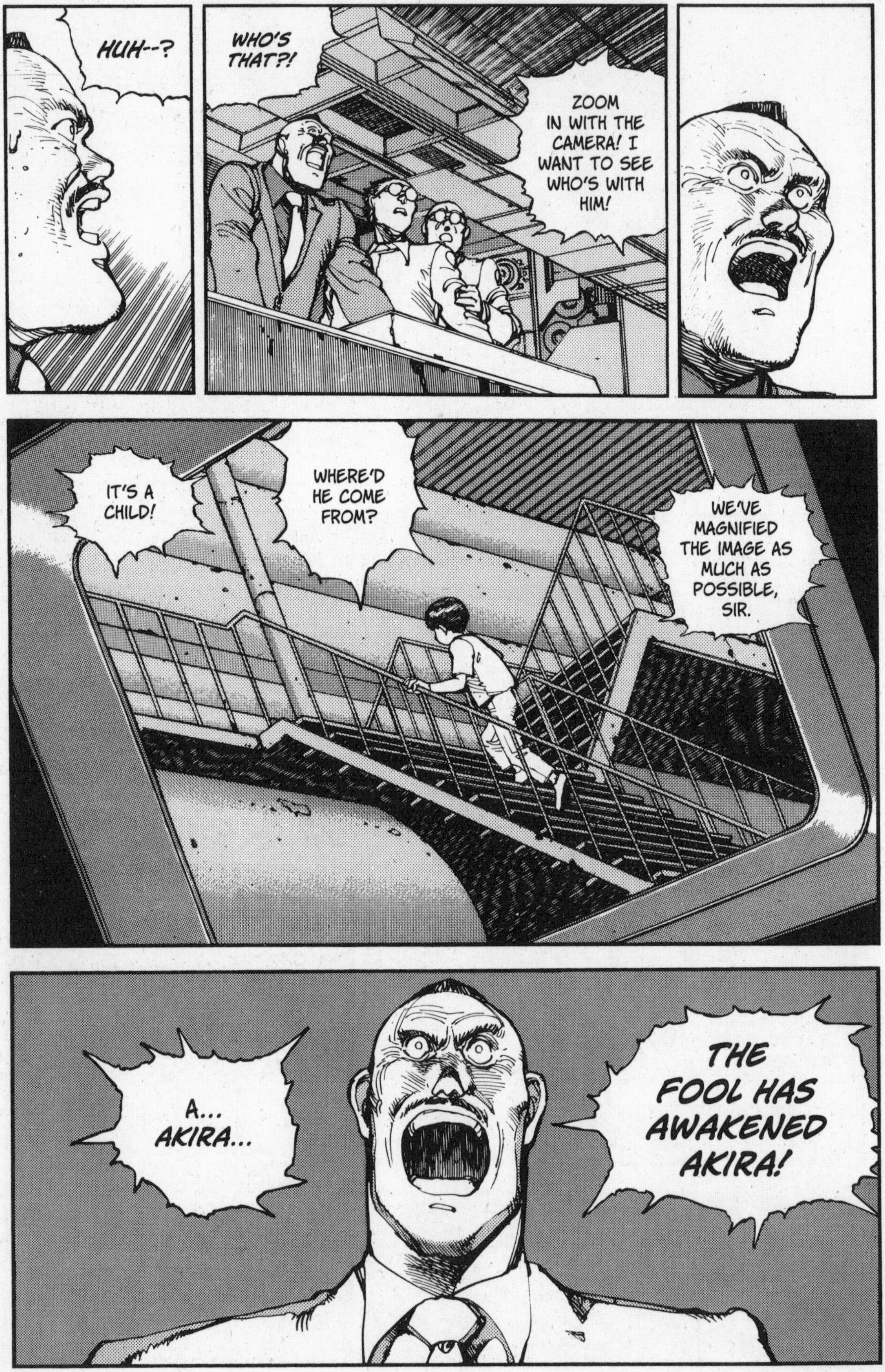
HUH--?
WHO'S THAT?!
ZOOM IN WITH THE CAMERA! I WANT TO SEE WHO'S WITH HIM!
IT'S A CHILD!
WHERE'D HE COME FROM?
WE'VE MAGNIFIED THE IMAGE AS MUCH AS POSSIBLE, SIR.
A... AKIRA...
THE FOOL HAS AWAKENED AKIRA!

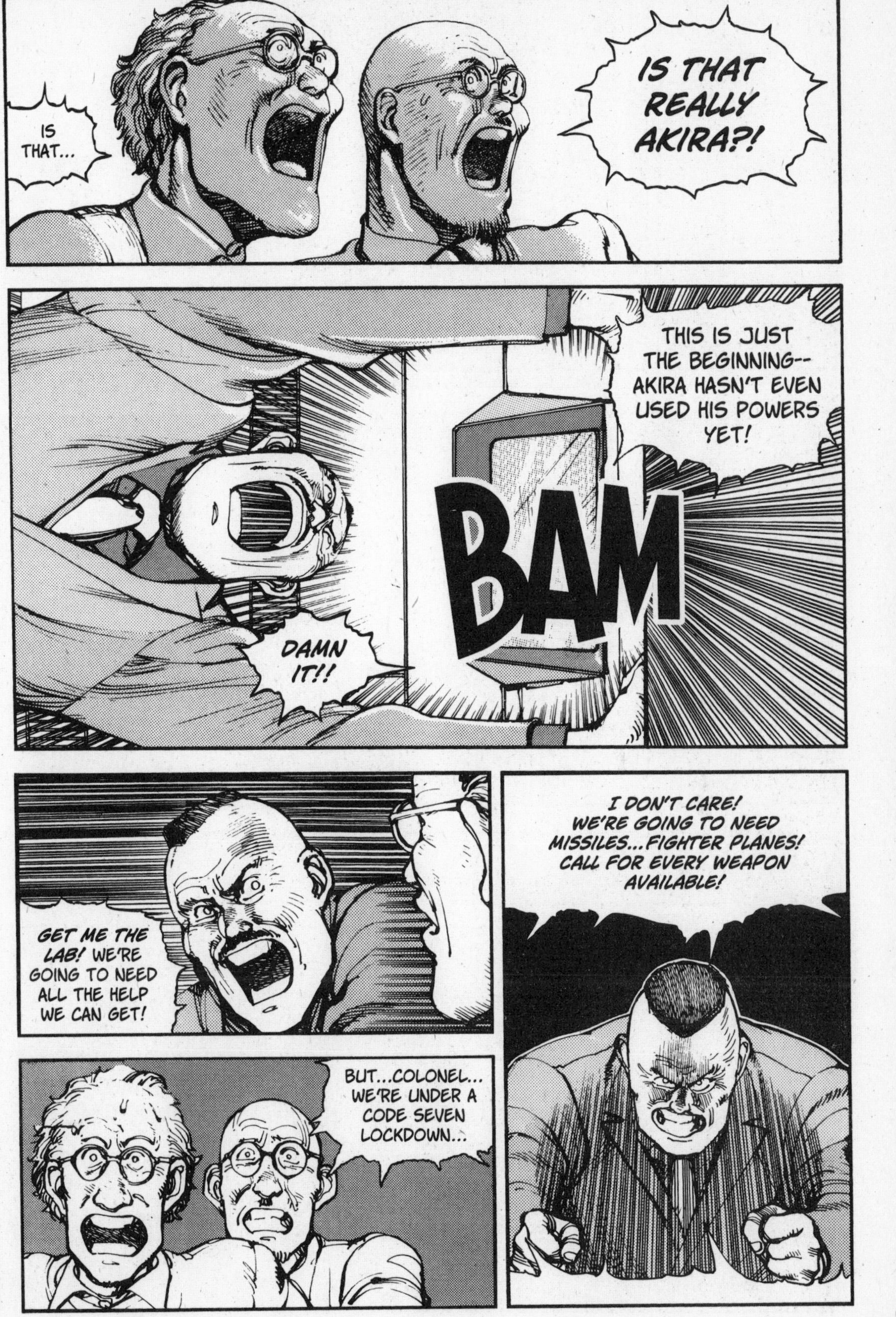
IS THAT...
IS THAT REALLY AKIRA?!
THIS IS JUST THE BEGINNING-- AKIRA HASN'T EVEN USED HIS POWERS YET!
BAM
DAMN IT!!
GET ME THE LAB! WE'RE GOING TO NEED ALL THE HELP WE CAN GET!
BUT...COLONEL... WE'RE UNDER A CODE SEVEN LOCKDOWN...
I DON'T CARE! WE'RE GOING TO NEED MISSILES...FIGHTER PLANES! CALL FOR EVERY WEAPON AVAILABLE!

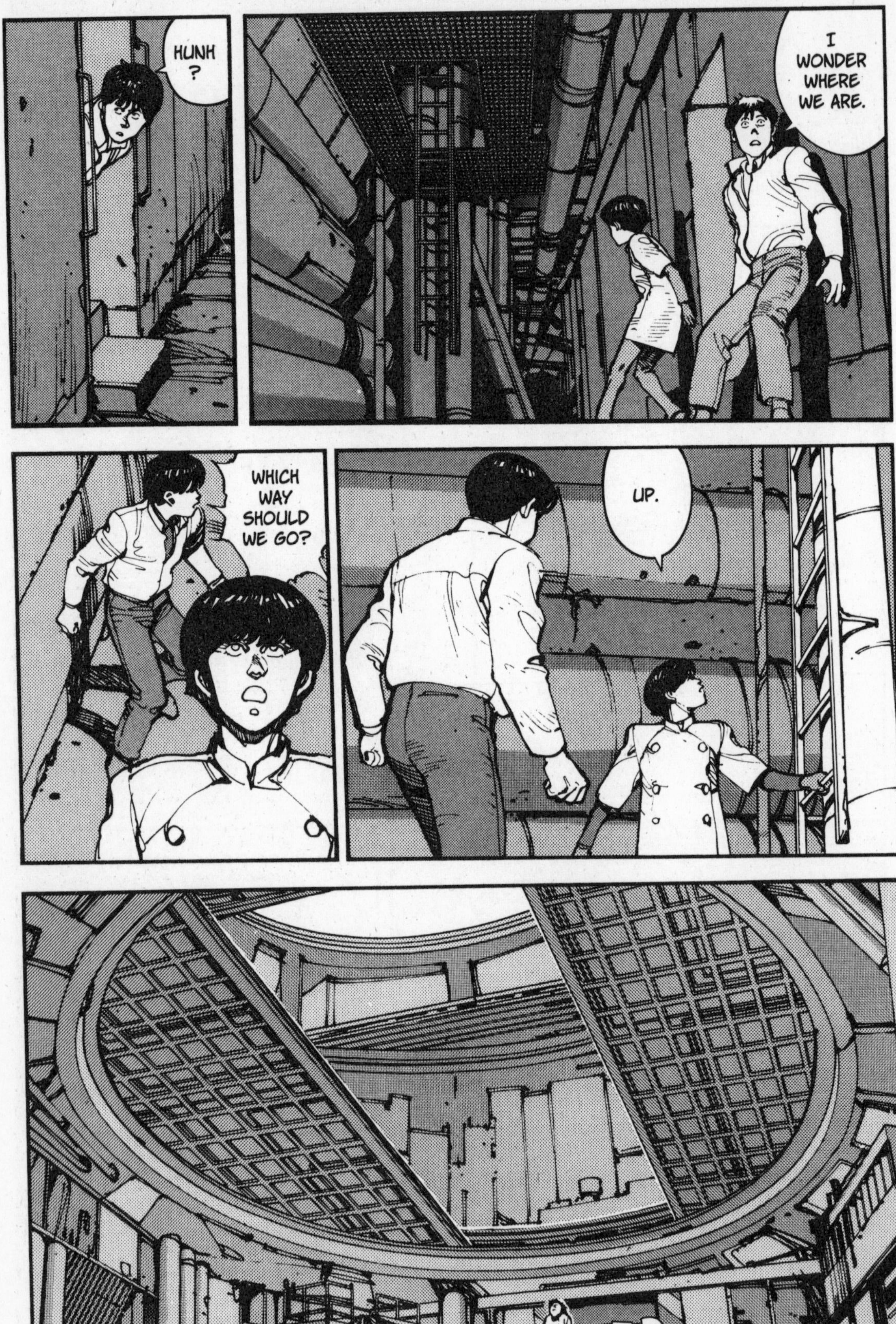
HUNH ?
I WONDER WHERE WE ARE.
WHICH WAY SHOULD WE GO?
UP.
STAP

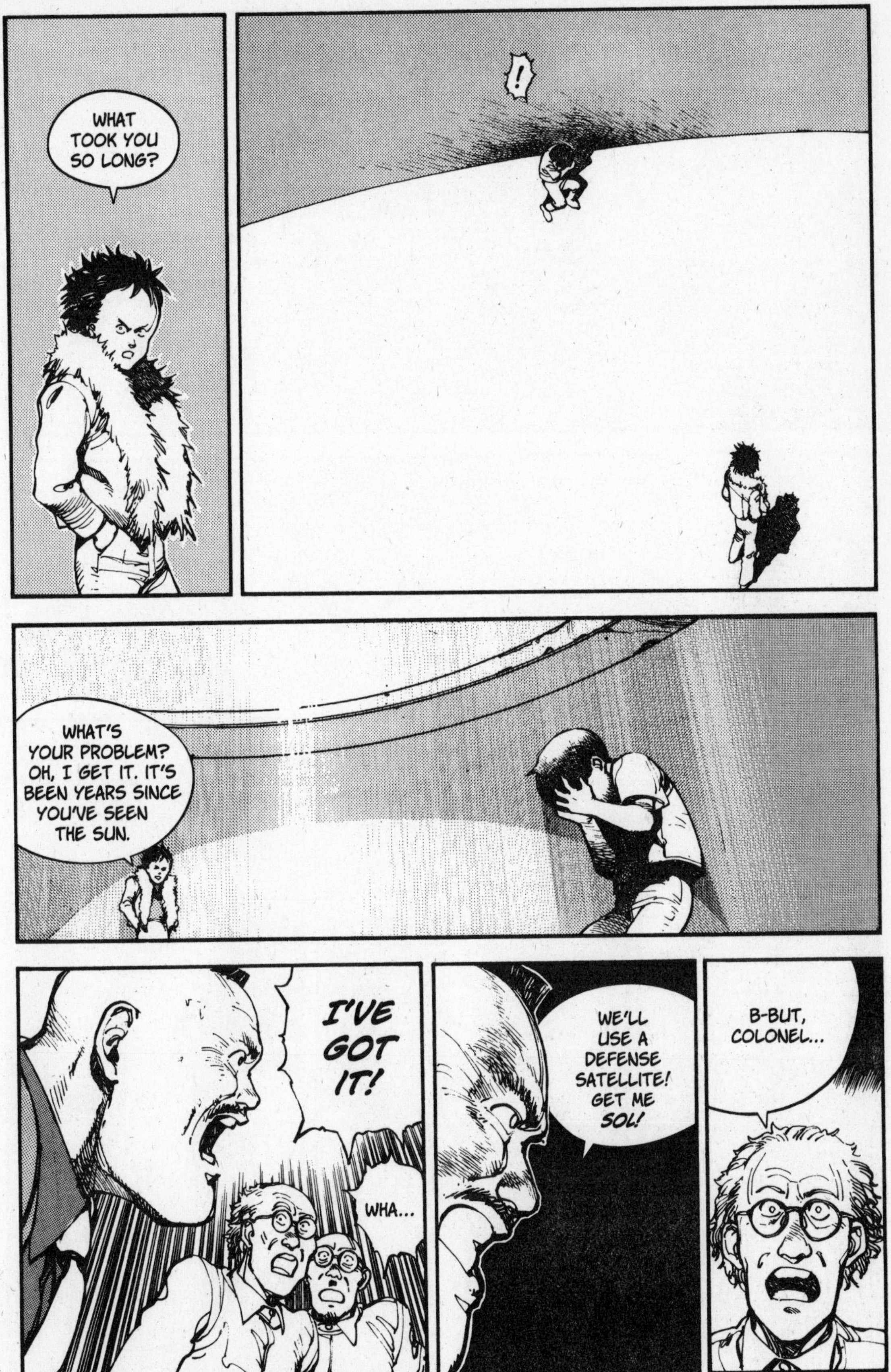
WHAT TOOK YOU SO LONG?
!
WHAT'S YOUR PROBLEM? OH, I GET IT. IT'S BEEN YEARS SINCE YOU'VE SEEN THE SUN.
I'VE GOT IT!
WHA...
WE'LL USE A DEFENSE SATELLITE! GET ME SOL!
B-BUT, COLONEL...

CAN SOL BE CONTROLLED FROM HERE?

IT-IT'S POSSIBLE...

...BUT ONLY IF THE CONTROL CENTER PATCHES US THROUGH!

DO IT! WE MUST KILL THEM BOTH... DESTROY THEM WHILE WE STILL HAVE A CHANCE!

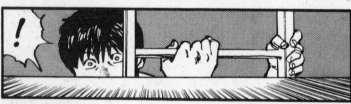

!

SUNLIGHT!

TAKE A LOOK!

AT WHAT?

OH!

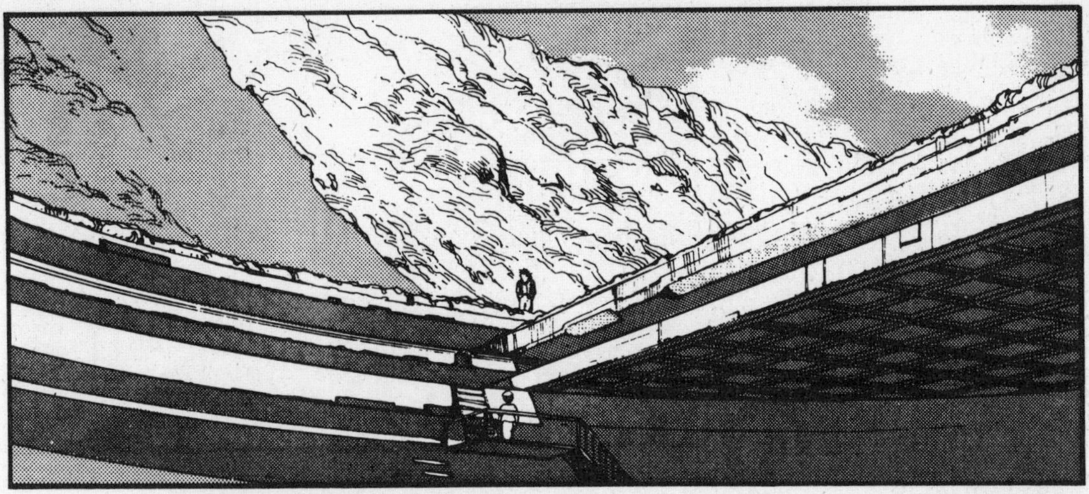

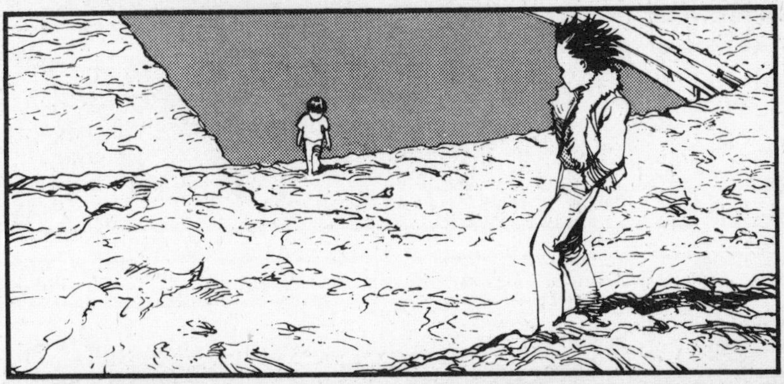

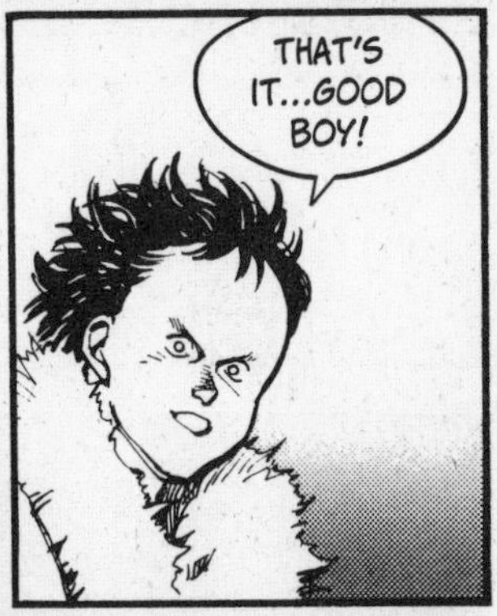
THAT'S IT...GOOD BOY!

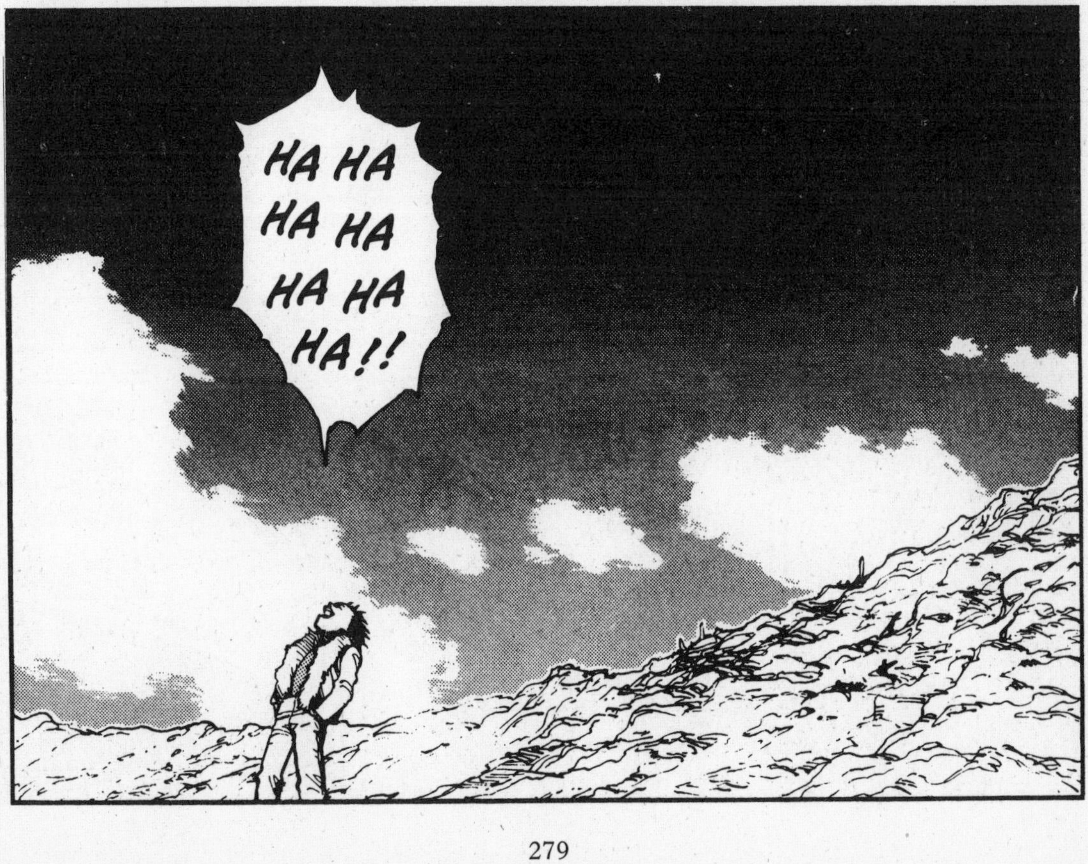
HA HA HA HA HA HA HA!!

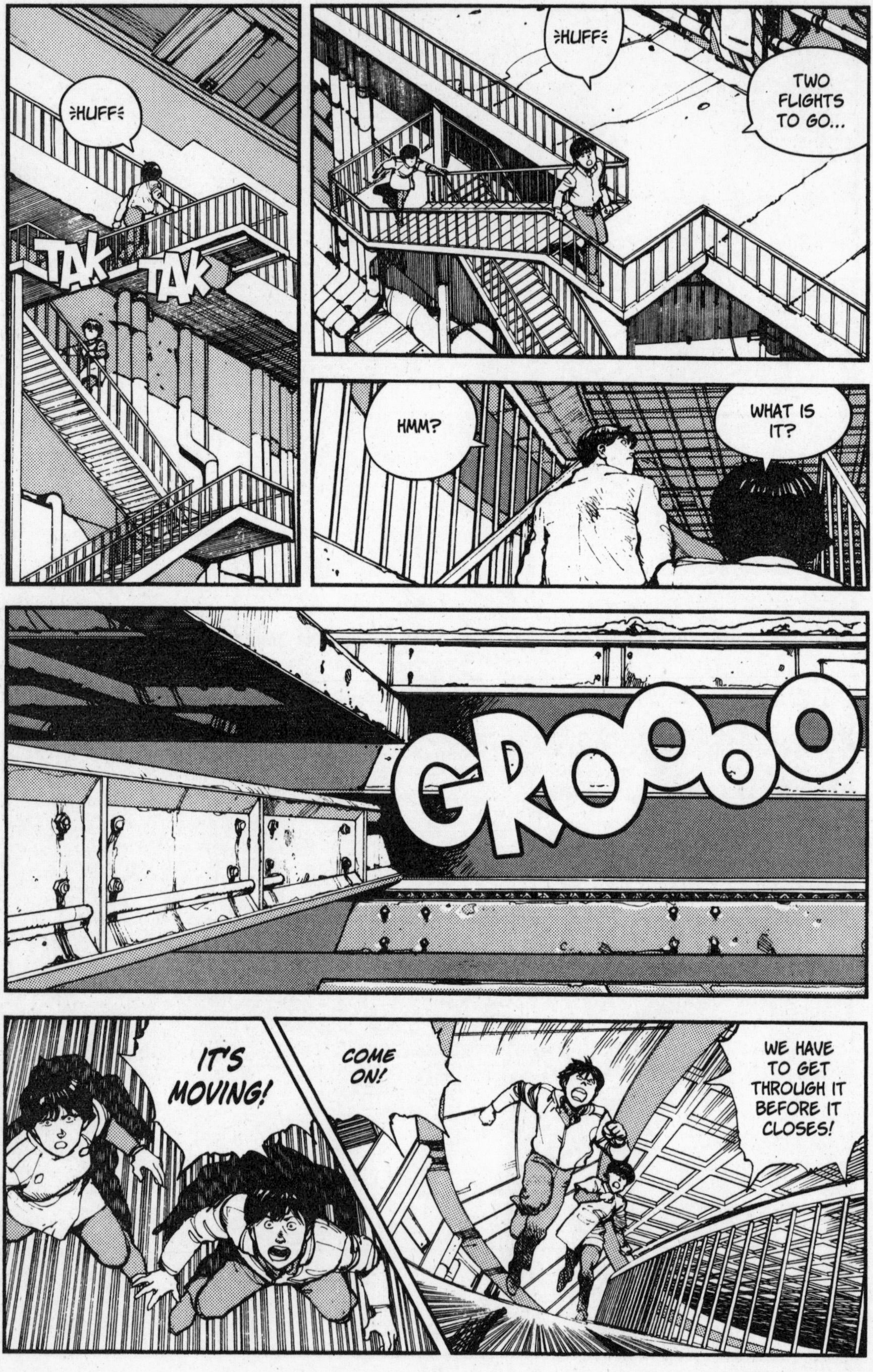

HUFF
TAK TAK
HUFF
TWO FLIGHTS TO GO...
HMM?
WHAT IS IT?
GROOOOO
IT'S MOVING!
COME ON!
WE HAVE TO GET THROUGH IT BEFORE IT CLOSES!

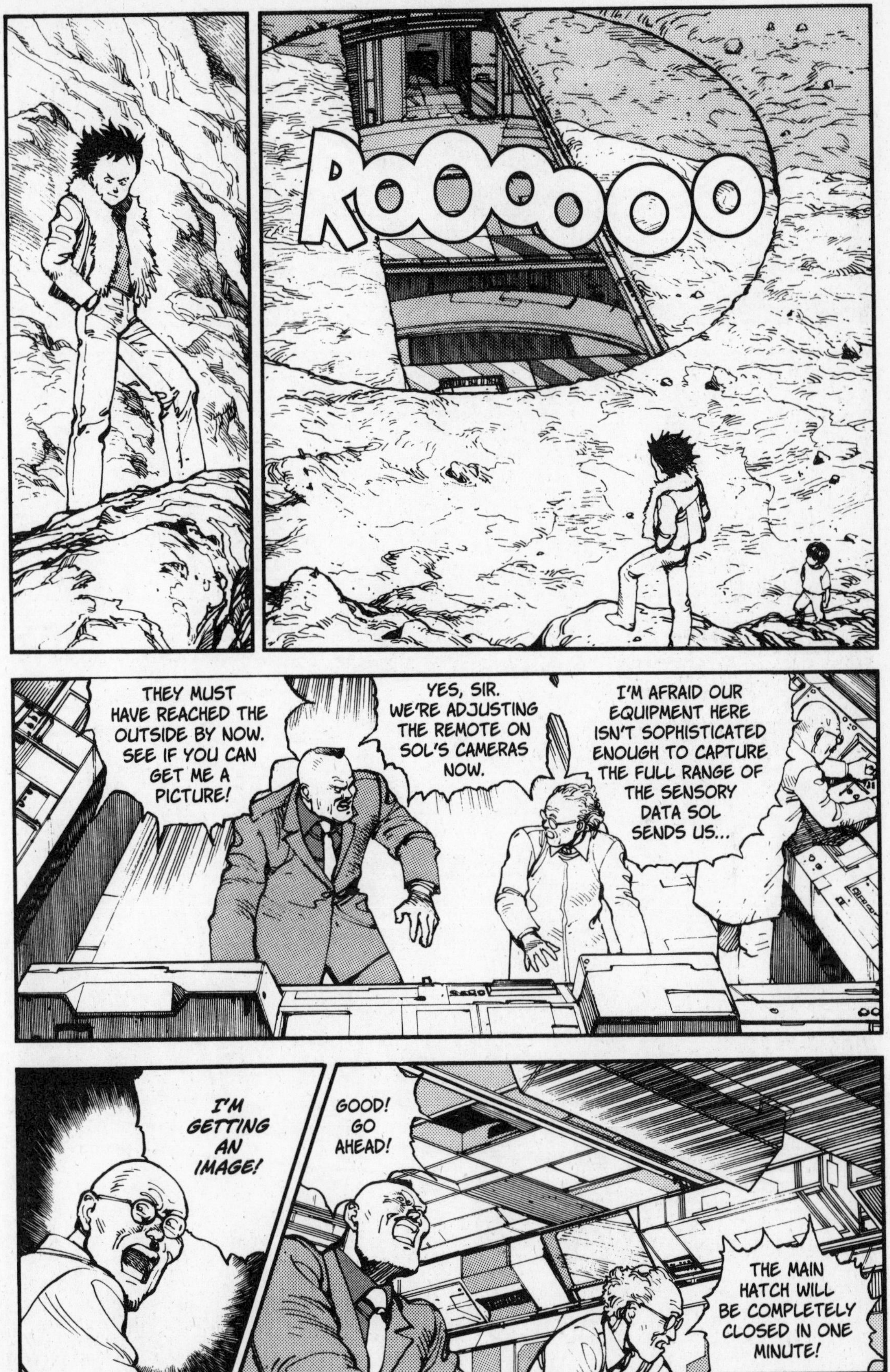
ROOOOOO
THEY MUST HAVE REACHED THE OUTSIDE BY NOW. SEE IF YOU CAN GET ME A PICTURE!
YES, SIR. WE'RE ADJUSTING THE REMOTE ON SOL'S CAMERAS NOW.
I'M AFRAID OUR EQUIPMENT HERE ISN'T SOPHISTICATED ENOUGH TO CAPTURE THE FULL RANGE OF THE SENSORY DATA SOL SENDS US...
I'M GETTING AN IMAGE!
GOOD! GO AHEAD!
THE MAIN HATCH WILL BE COMPLETELY CLOSED IN ONE MINUTE!

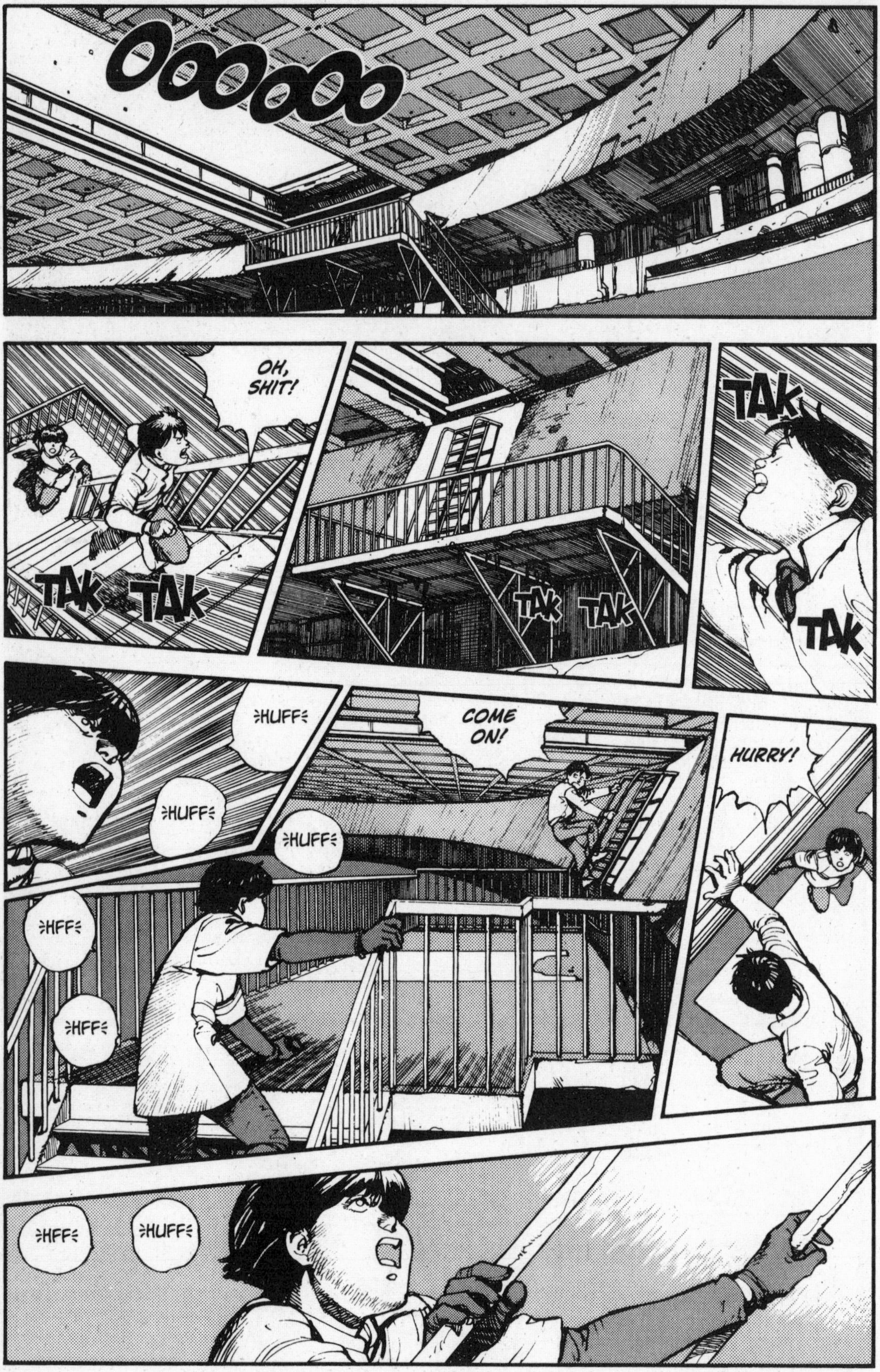
OOOOOO
OH, SHIT!
TAK TAK
TAK TAK
TAK
TAK
HUFF
HUFF
HUFF
COME ON!
HFF
HFF
HURRY!
HFF
HUFF

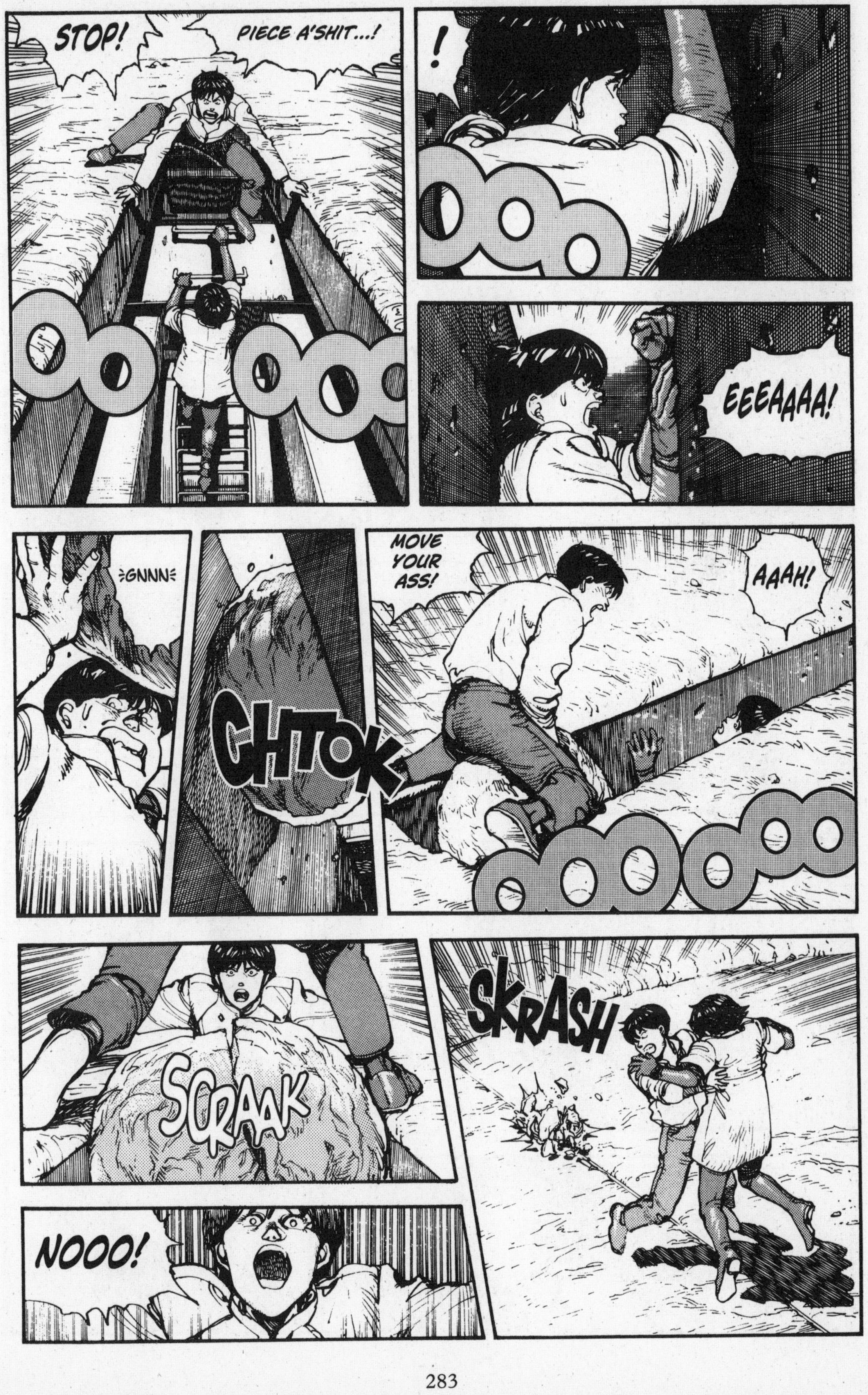
STOP!
PIECE A'SHIT...!
!
EEEAAAA!
GNNN
CHTOK
MOVE YOUR ASS!
AAAH!
SCRAAK
NOOO!
SKRASH

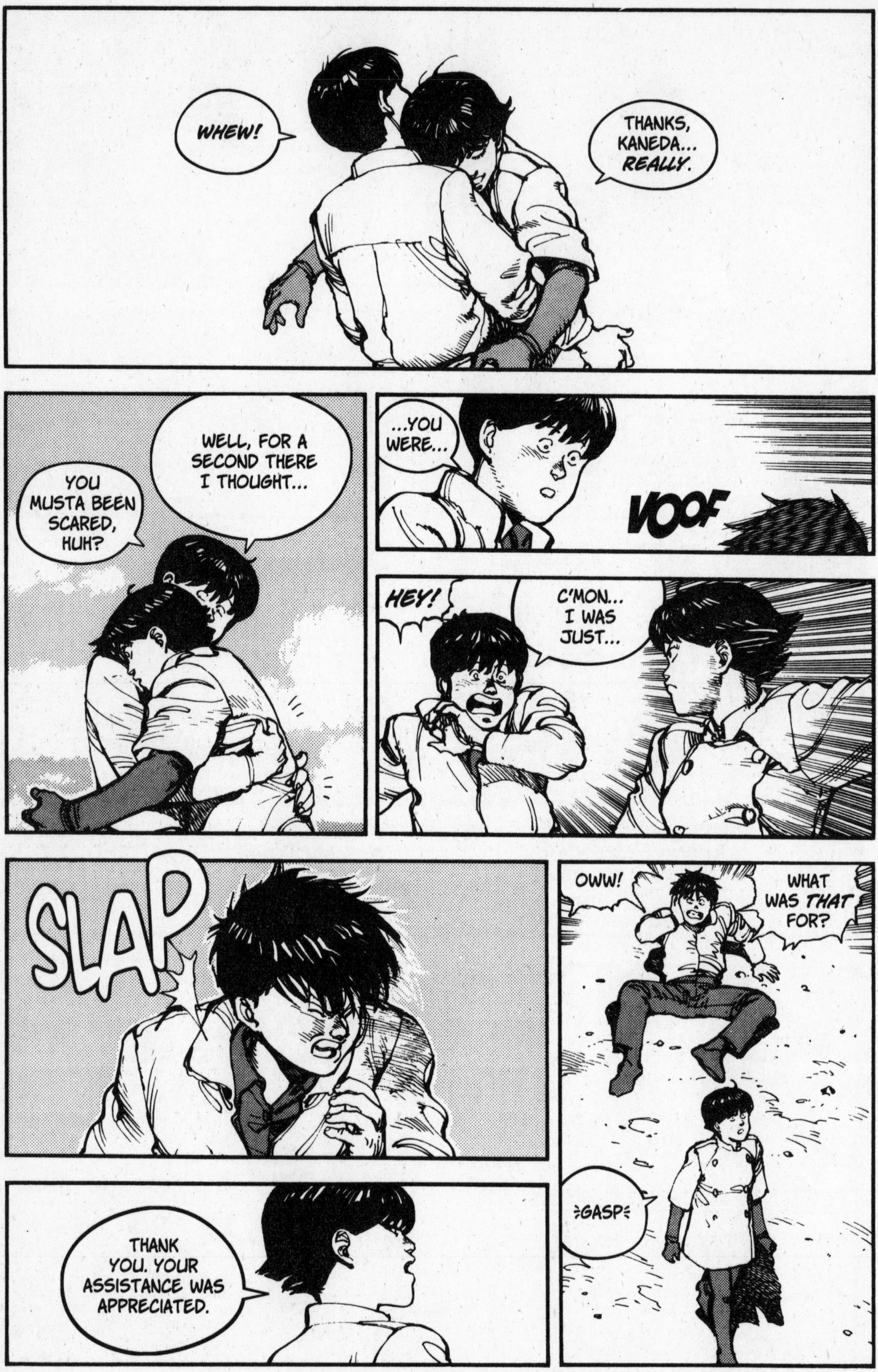
WHEW!
THANKS, KANEDA... REALLY.
YOU MUSTA BEEN SCARED, HUH?
WELL, FOR A SECOND THERE I THOUGHT...
...YOU WERE...
VOOF
HEY!
C'MON... I WAS JUST...
SLAP
THANK YOU. YOUR ASSISTANCE WAS APPRECIATED.
OWW!
WHAT WAS THAT FOR?
GASP

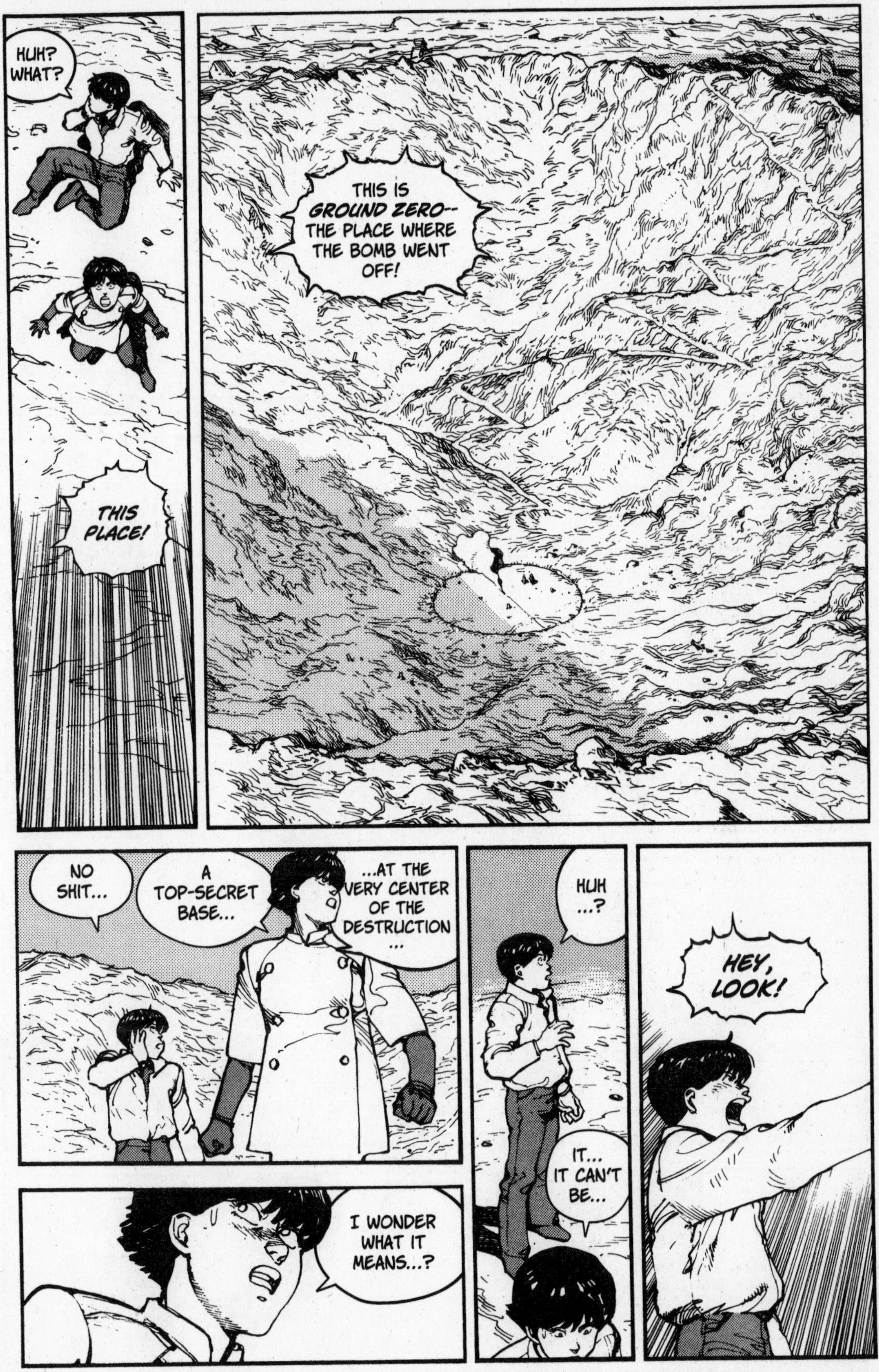
HUH? WHAT?
THIS PLACE!
THIS IS GROUND ZERO-- THE PLACE WHERE THE BOMB WENT OFF!
NO SHIT...
A TOP-SECRET BASE...
...AT THE VERY CENTER OF THE DESTRUCTION ...
I WONDER WHAT IT MEANS...?
HUH ...?
IT... IT CAN'T BE...
HEY, LOOK!

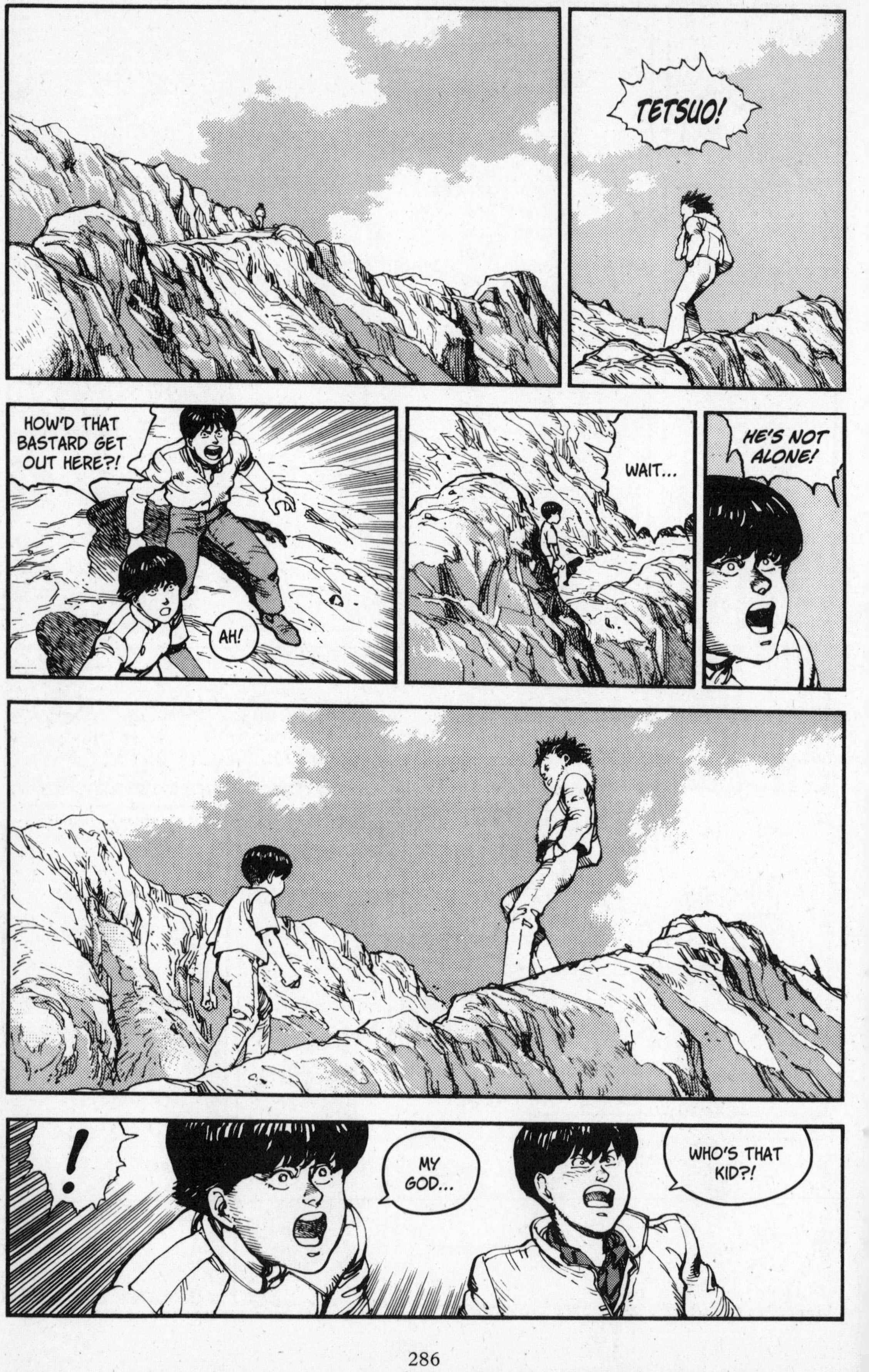
TETSUO!
HOW'D THAT BASTARD GET OUT HERE?!
AH!
WAIT...
HE'S NOT ALONE!
!
MY GOD...
WHO'S THAT KID?!

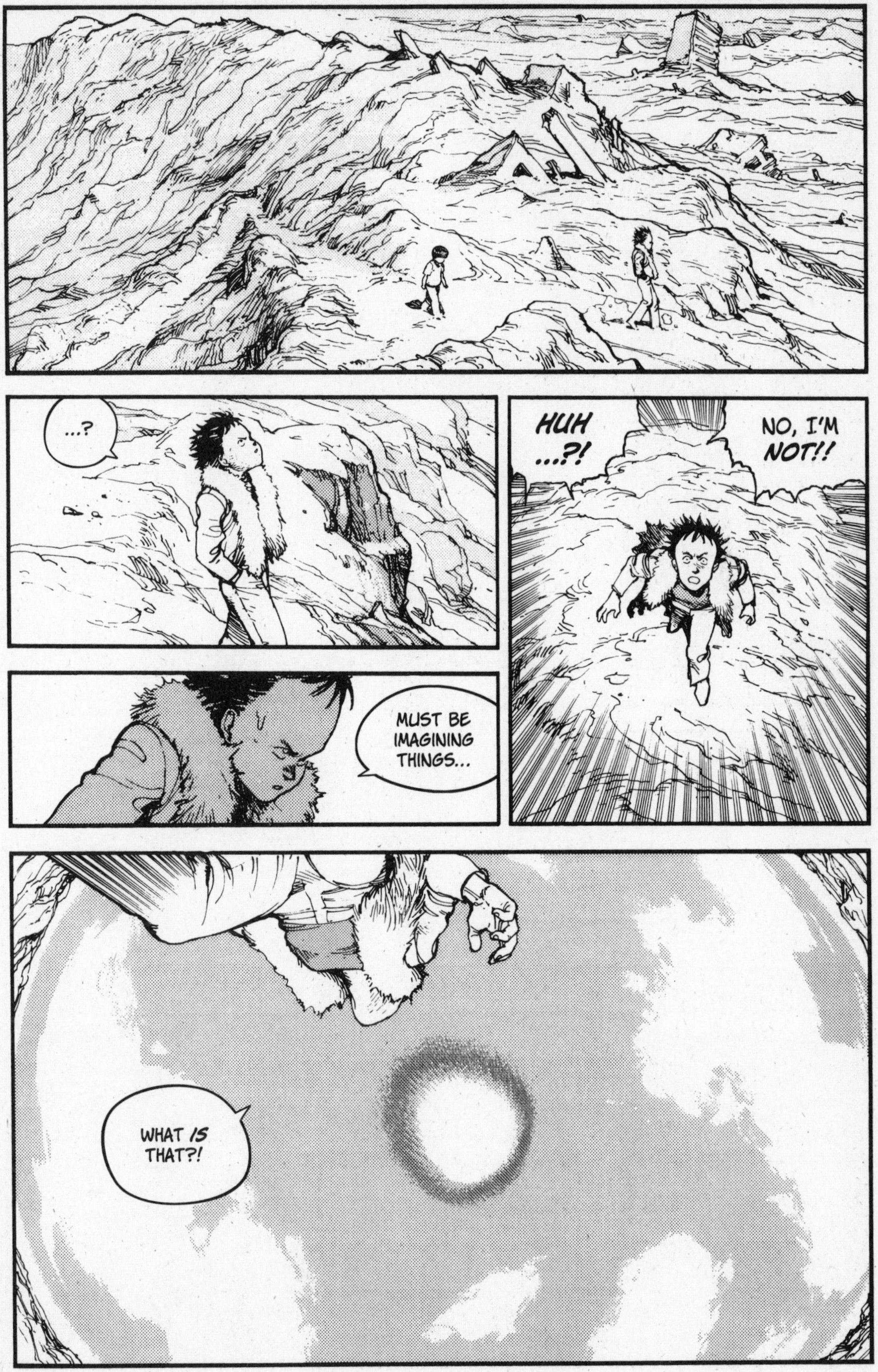

...?
HUH ...?!
NO, I'M NOT!!
MUST BE IMAGINING THINGS...
WHAT IS THAT?!

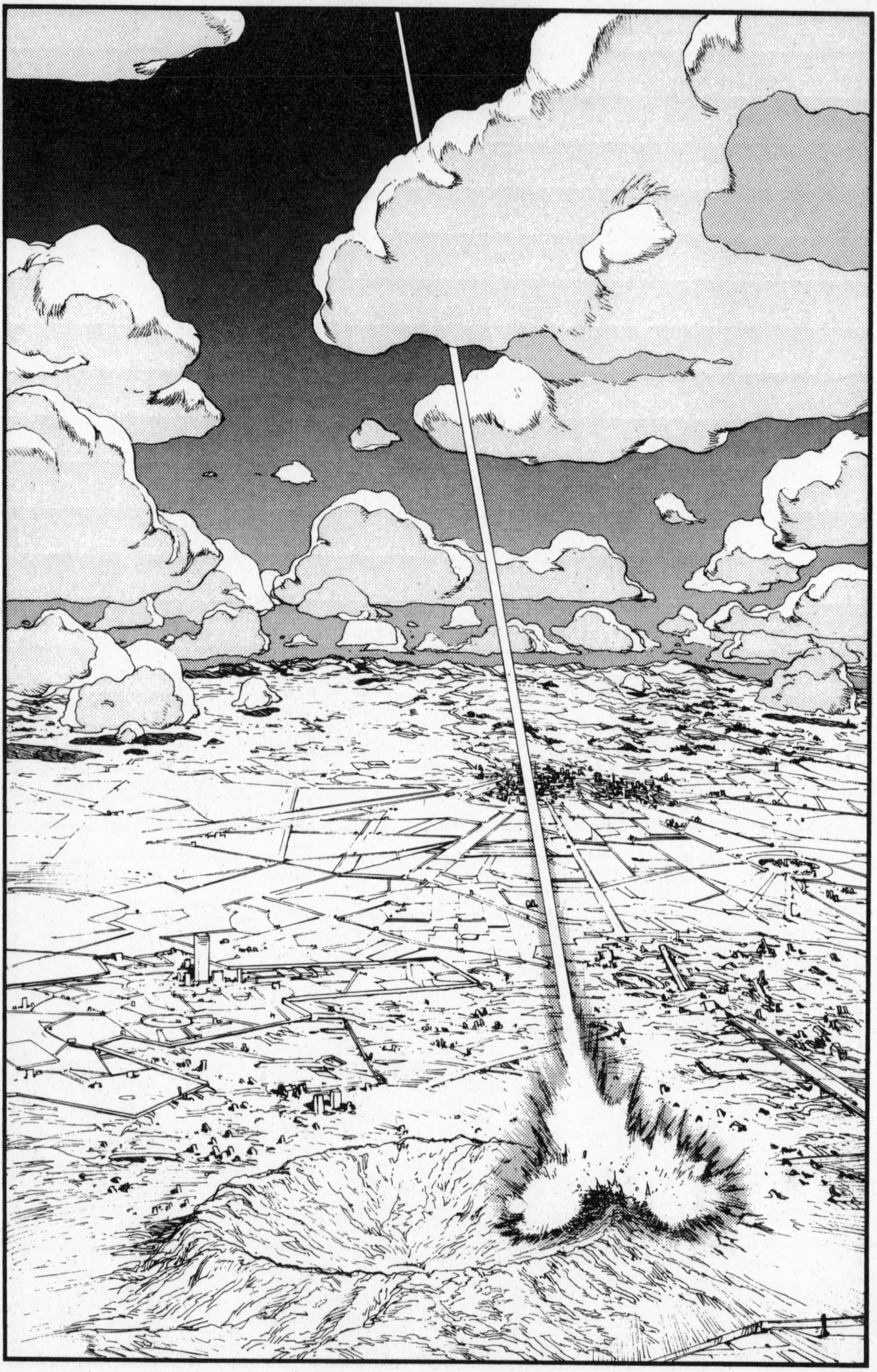

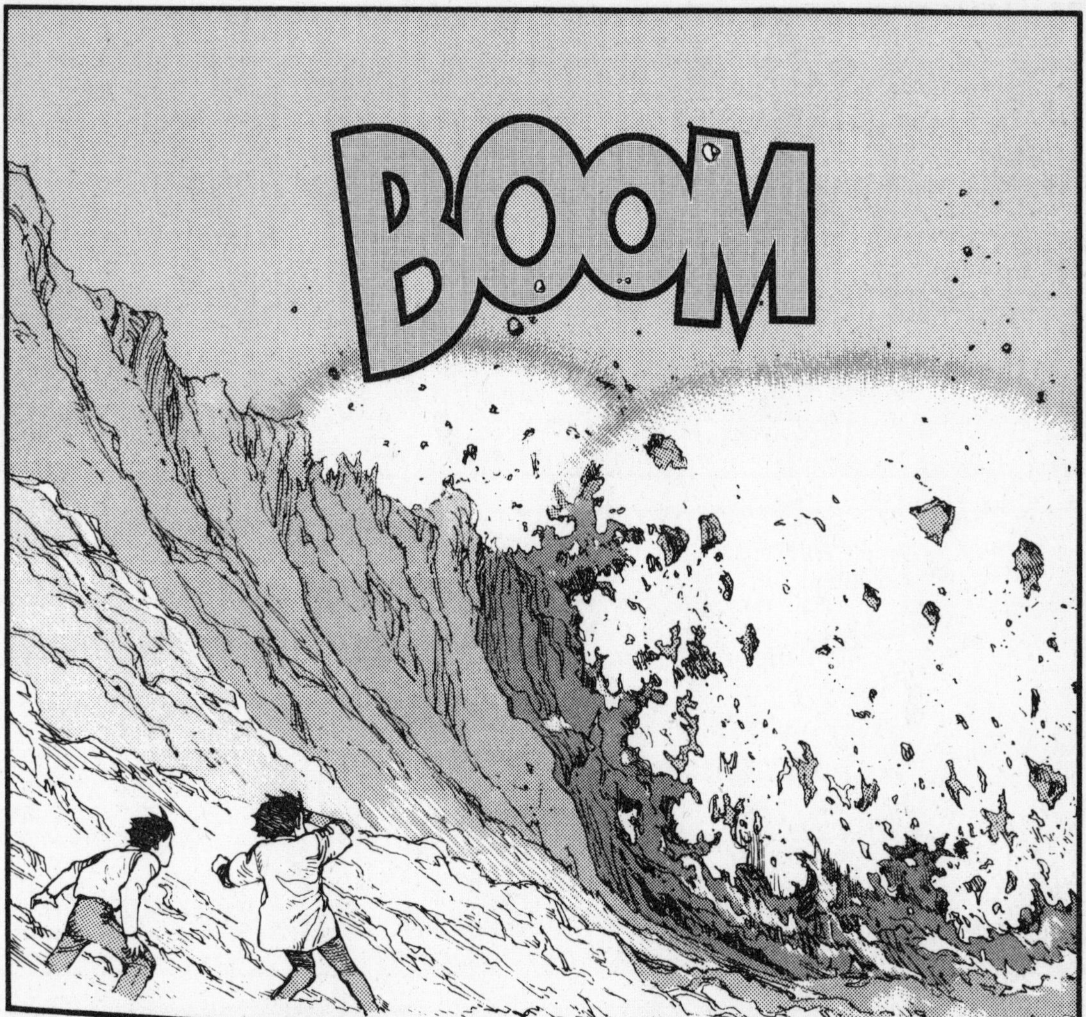
BOOM
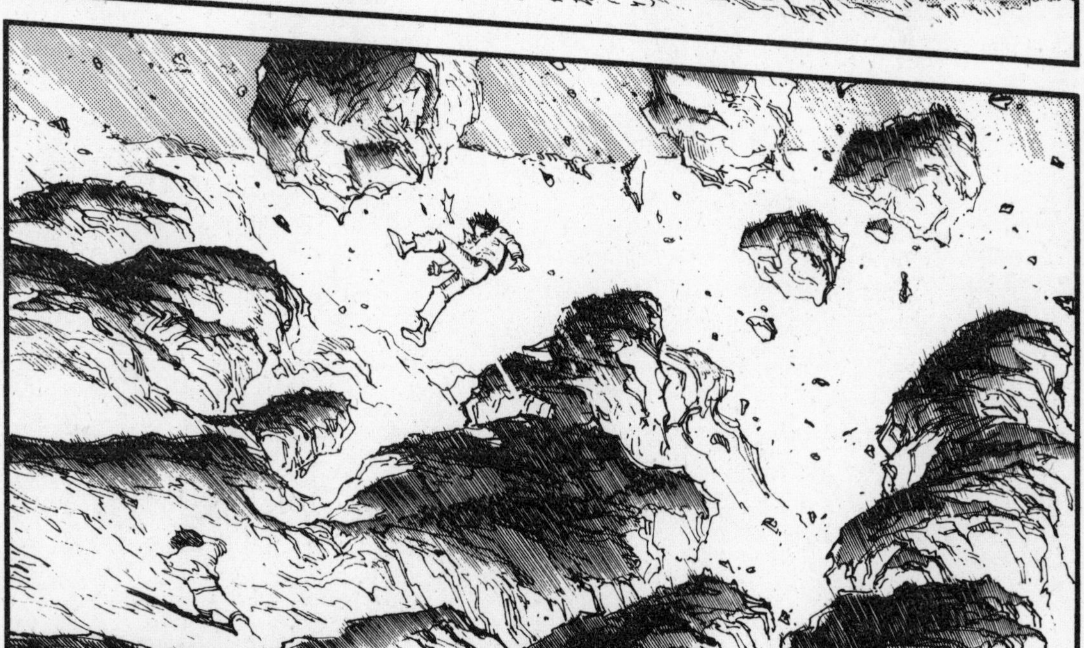

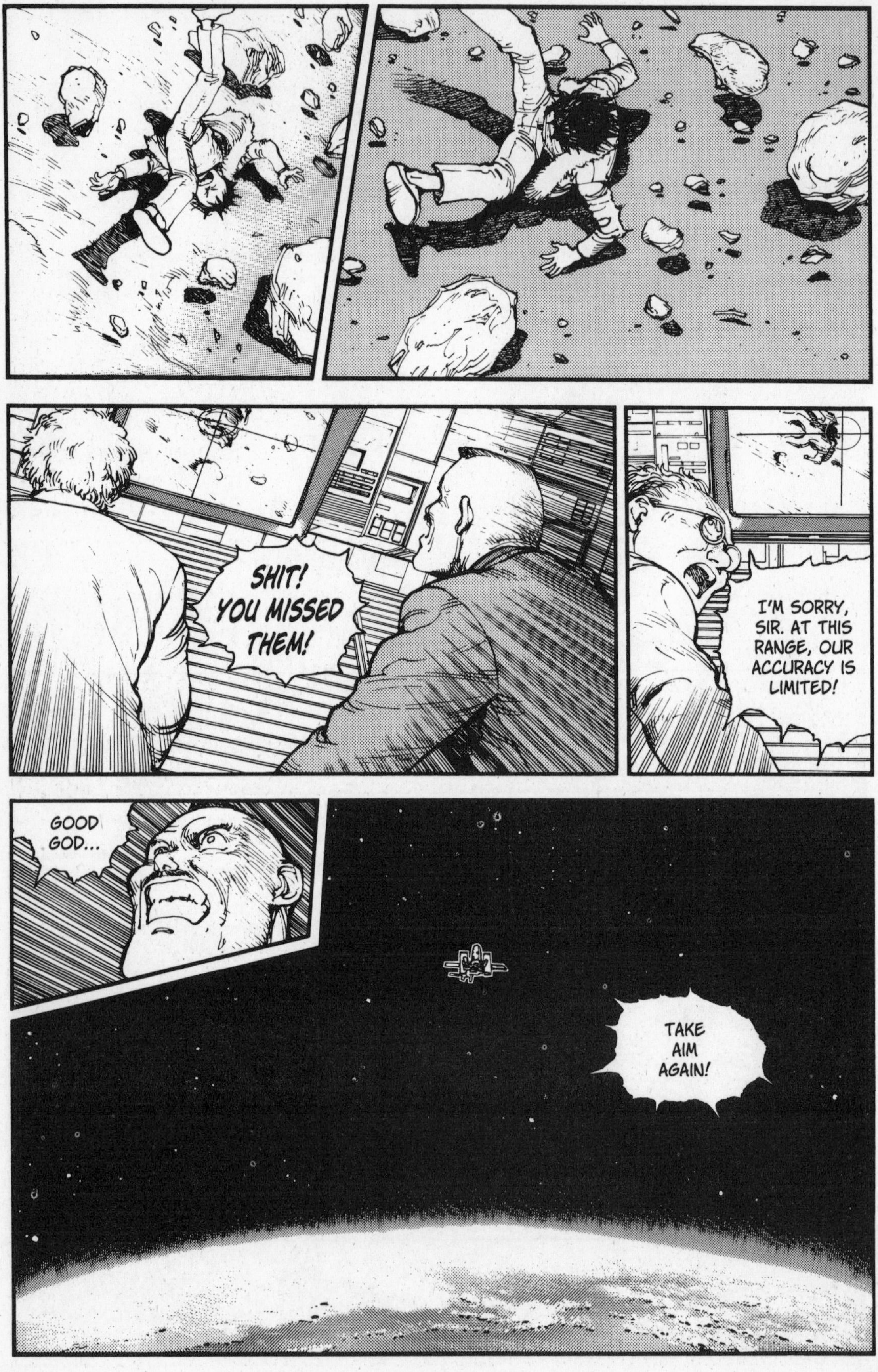
SHIT! YOU MISSED THEM!
I'M SORRY, SIR. AT THIS RANGE, OUR ACCURACY IS LIMITED!
GOOD GOD...
TAKE AIM AGAIN!

ERROR-CORRECTION DATA COMPILED! TRACKING CONTROL ADJUSTMENTS COMPLETE!

LOCKED ON...*FIRE!*

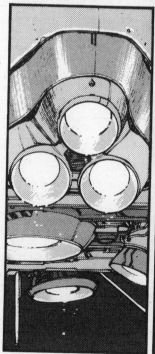

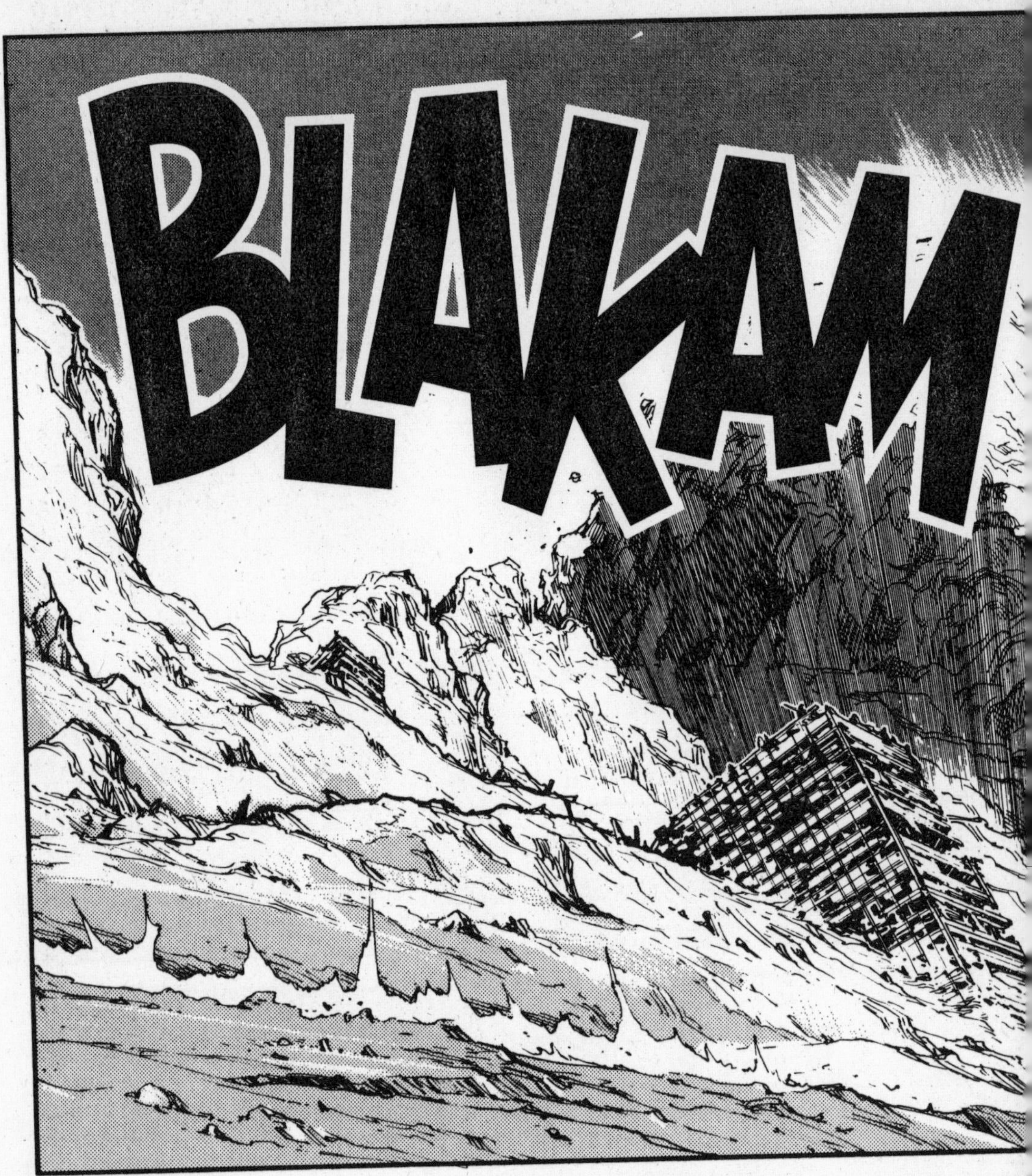
BLAKAM
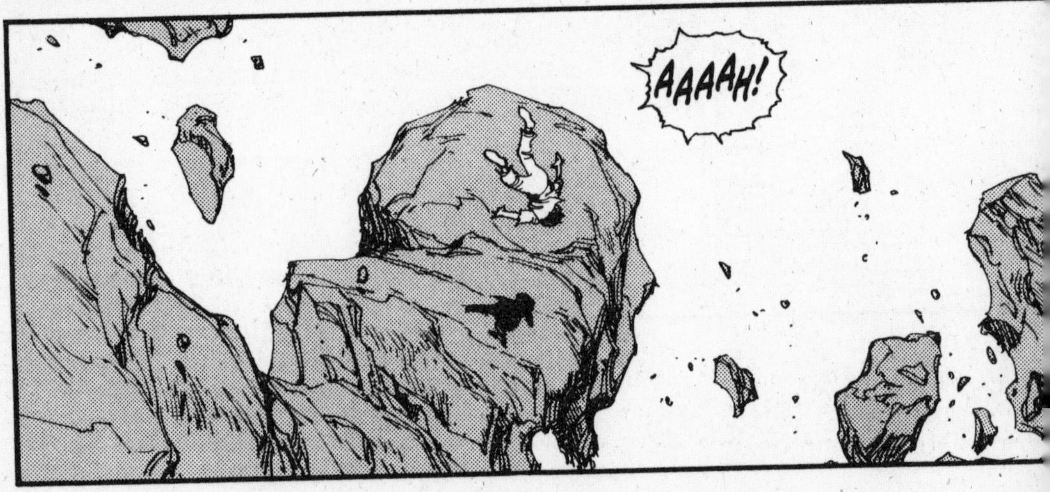
AAAAH!

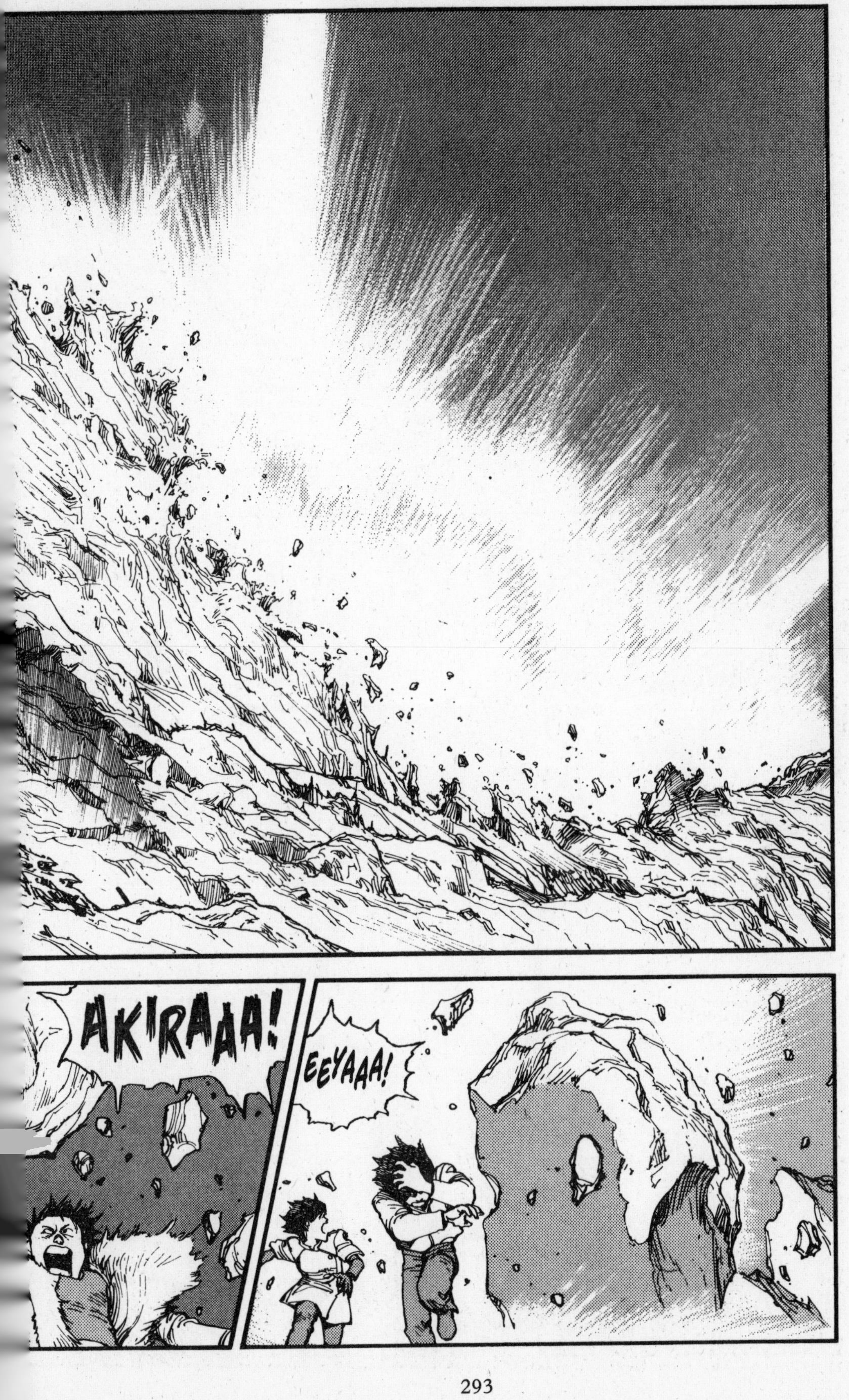
AKIRAAA!
EEYAAA!

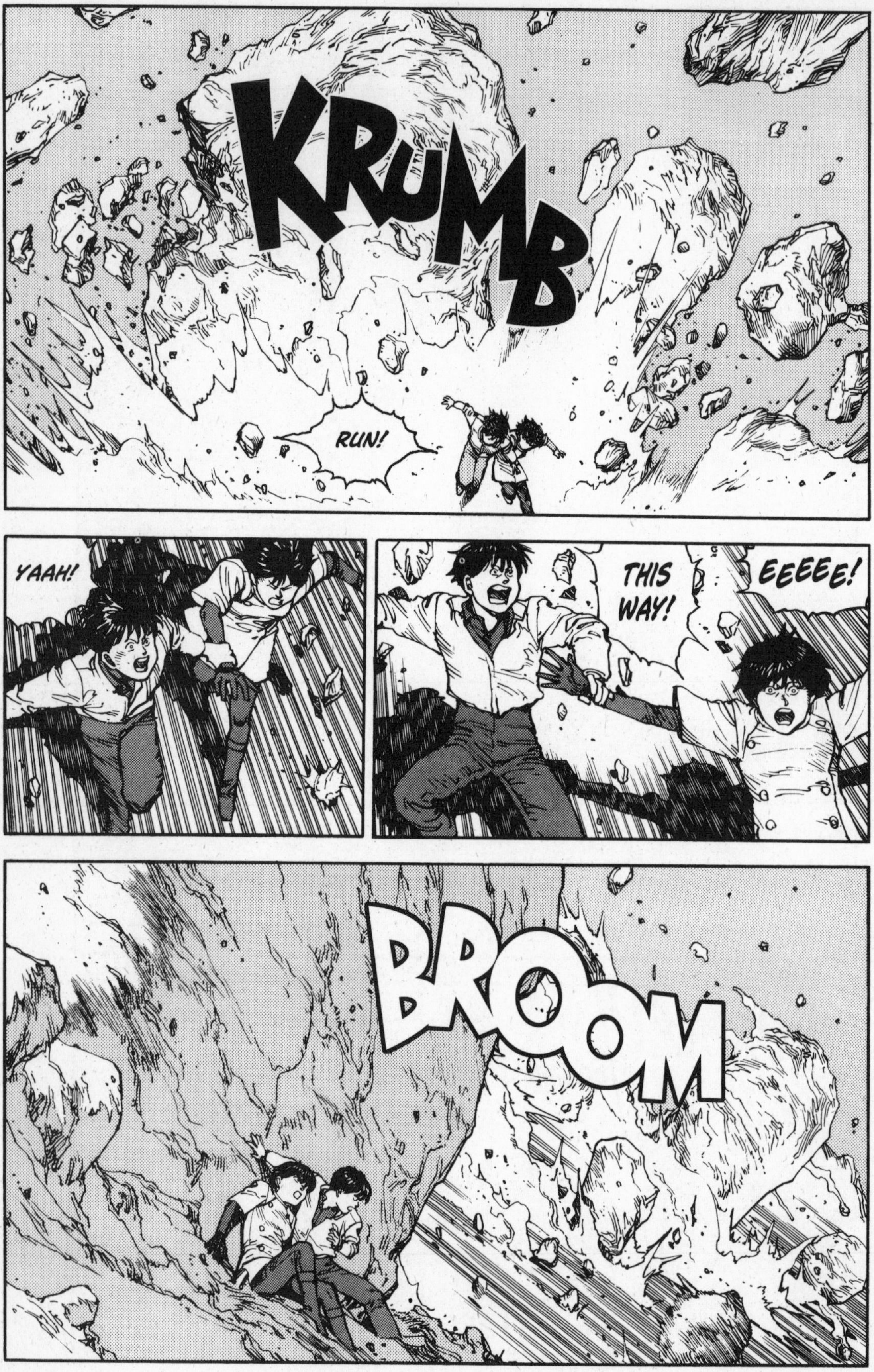
KRUMB
RUN!
YAAH!
THIS WAY!
EEEEE!
BROOM

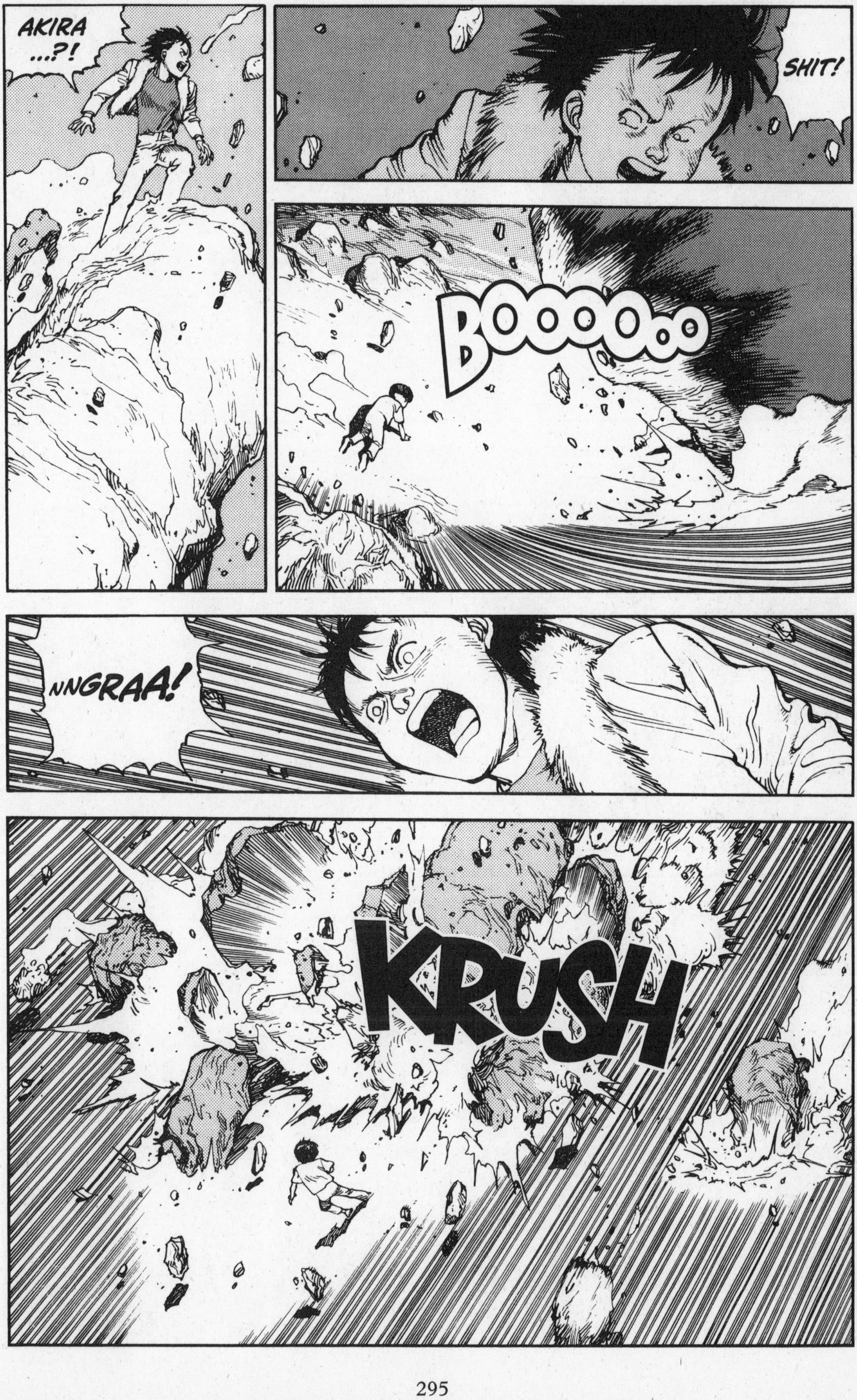

AKIRA ...?!
SHIT!
BOOOOoo
NNGRAA!
KRUSH

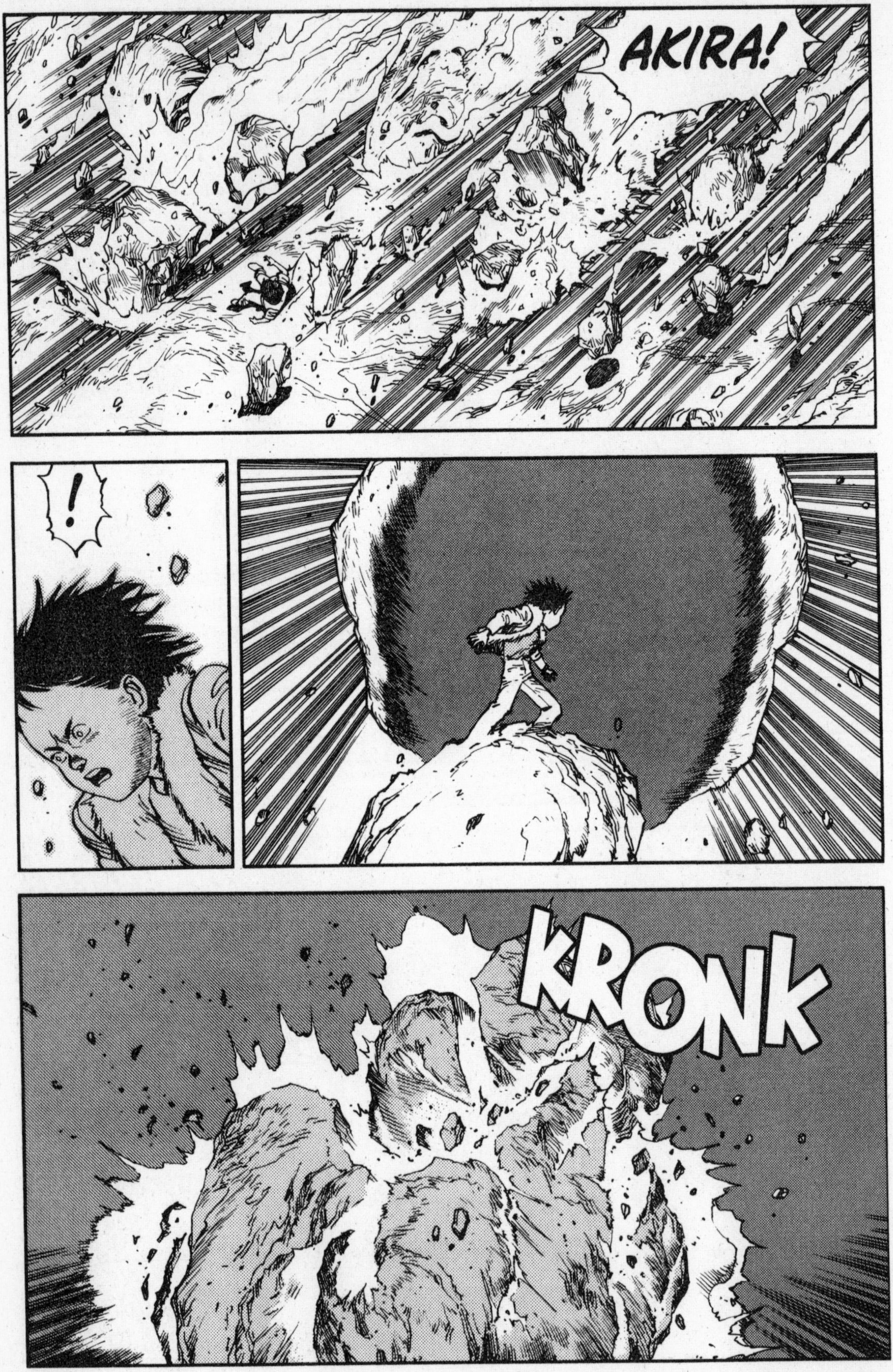
AKIRA!
!
KRONK

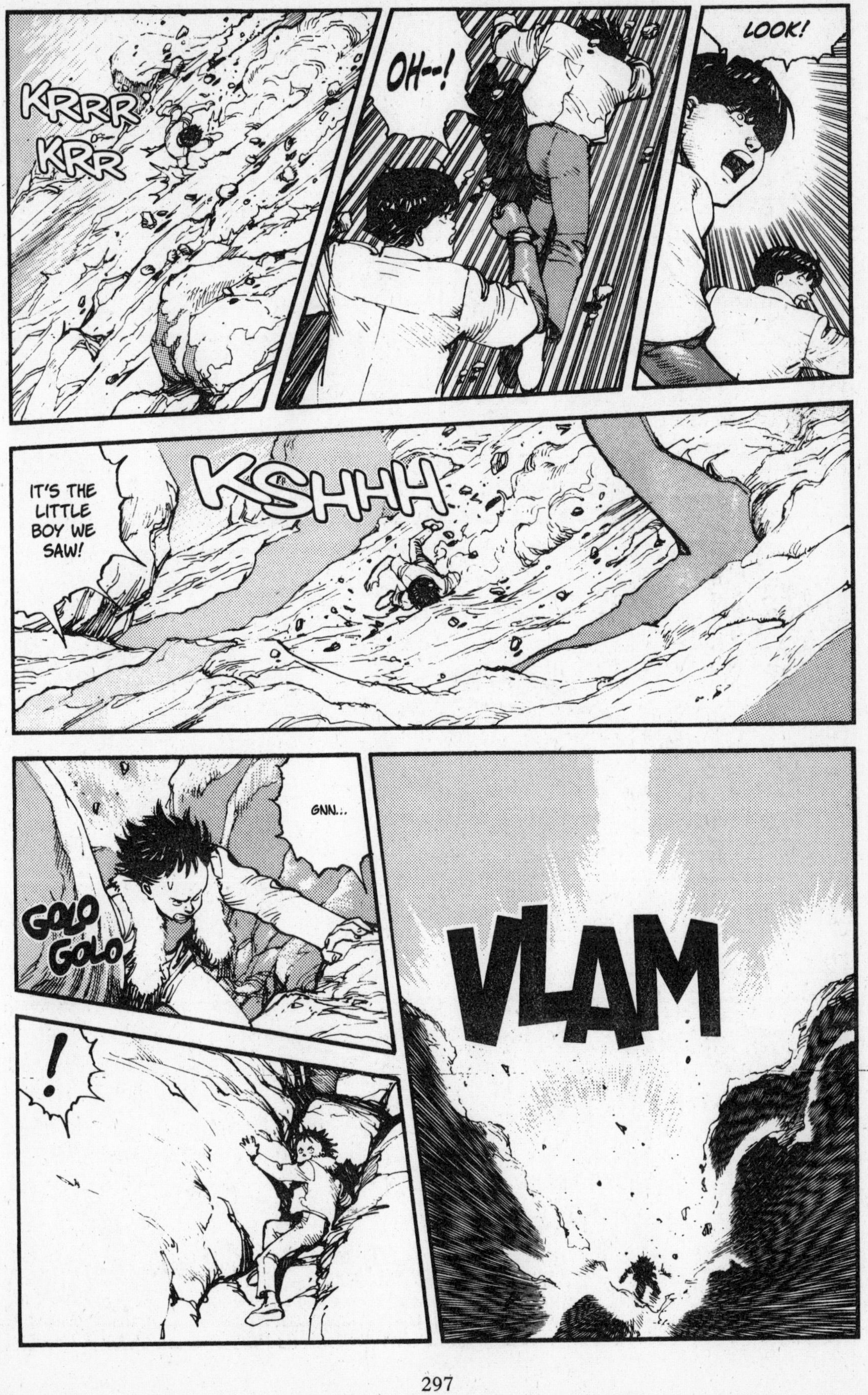
KRRR
KRR
OH--!
LOOK!
IT'S THE LITTLE BOY WE SAW!
KSHHH
GOLO GOLO
GNN...
!
VLAM

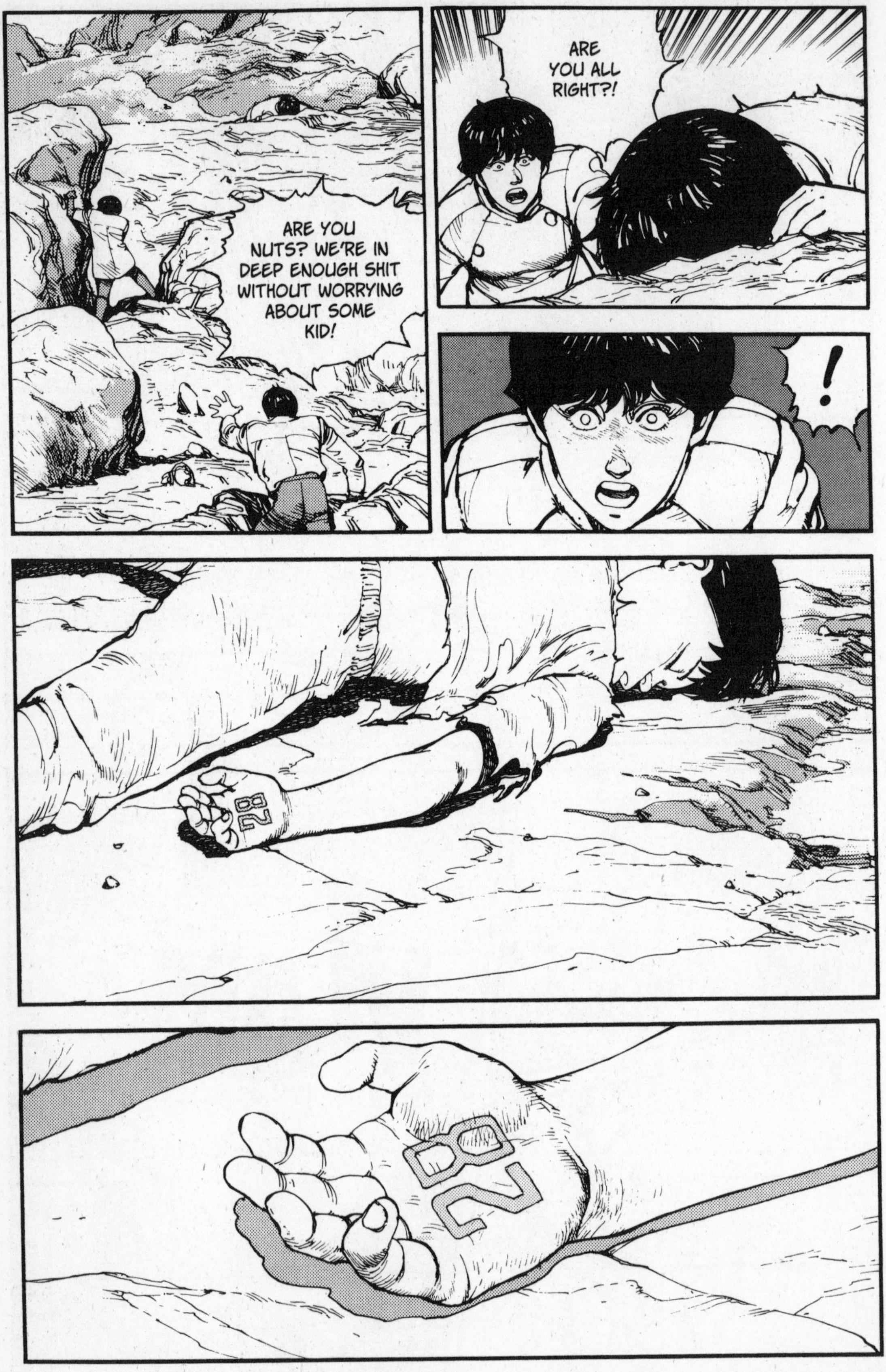
ARE YOU NUTS? WE'RE IN DEEP ENOUGH SHIT WITHOUT WORRYING ABOUT SOME KID!
ARE YOU ALL RIGHT?!
!
82
82

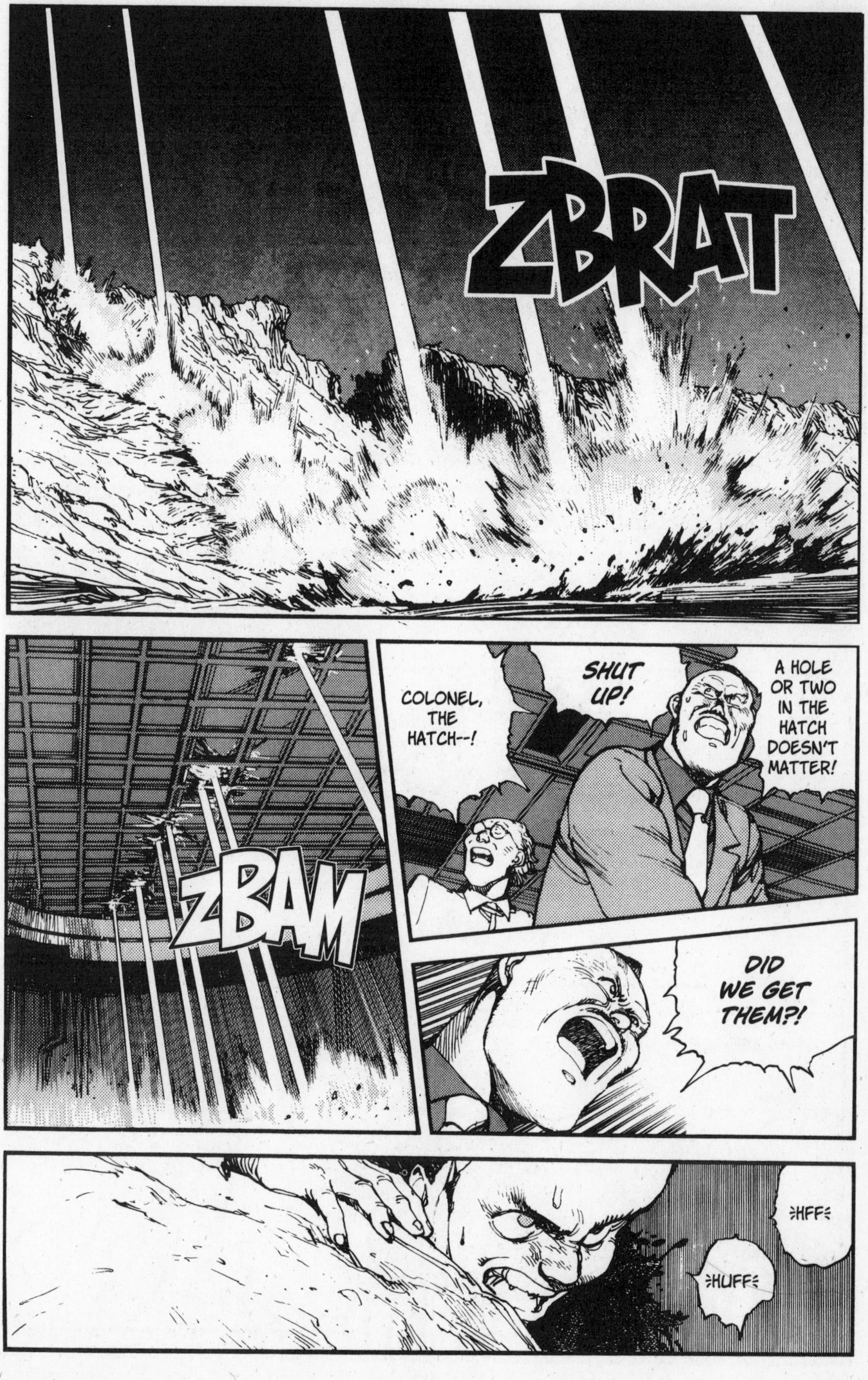
ZBRAT
ZBAM
COLONEL, THE HATCH--!
SHUT UP!
A HOLE OR TWO IN THE HATCH DOESN'T MATTER!
DID WE GET THEM?!
HFF
HUFF

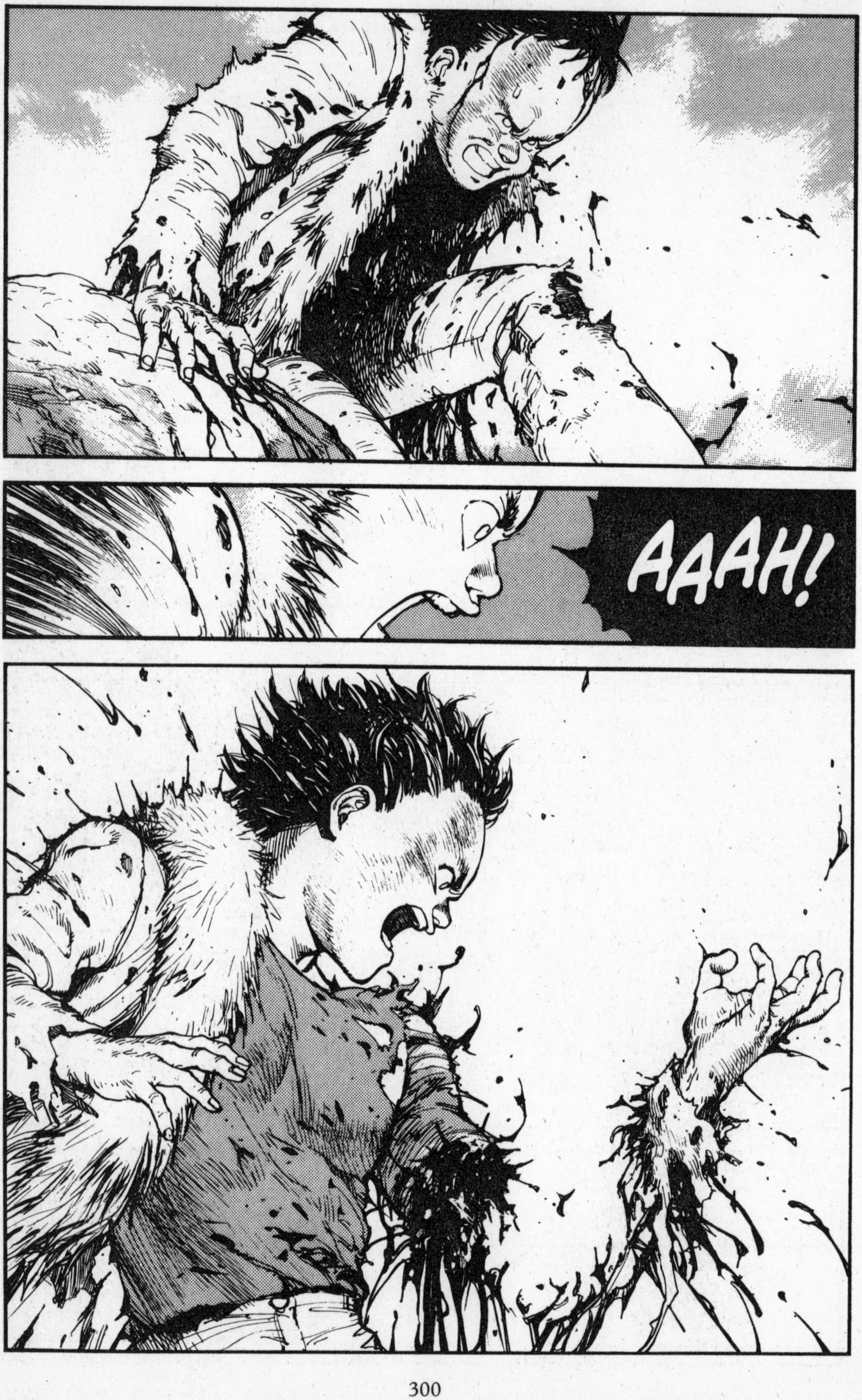
AAAH!

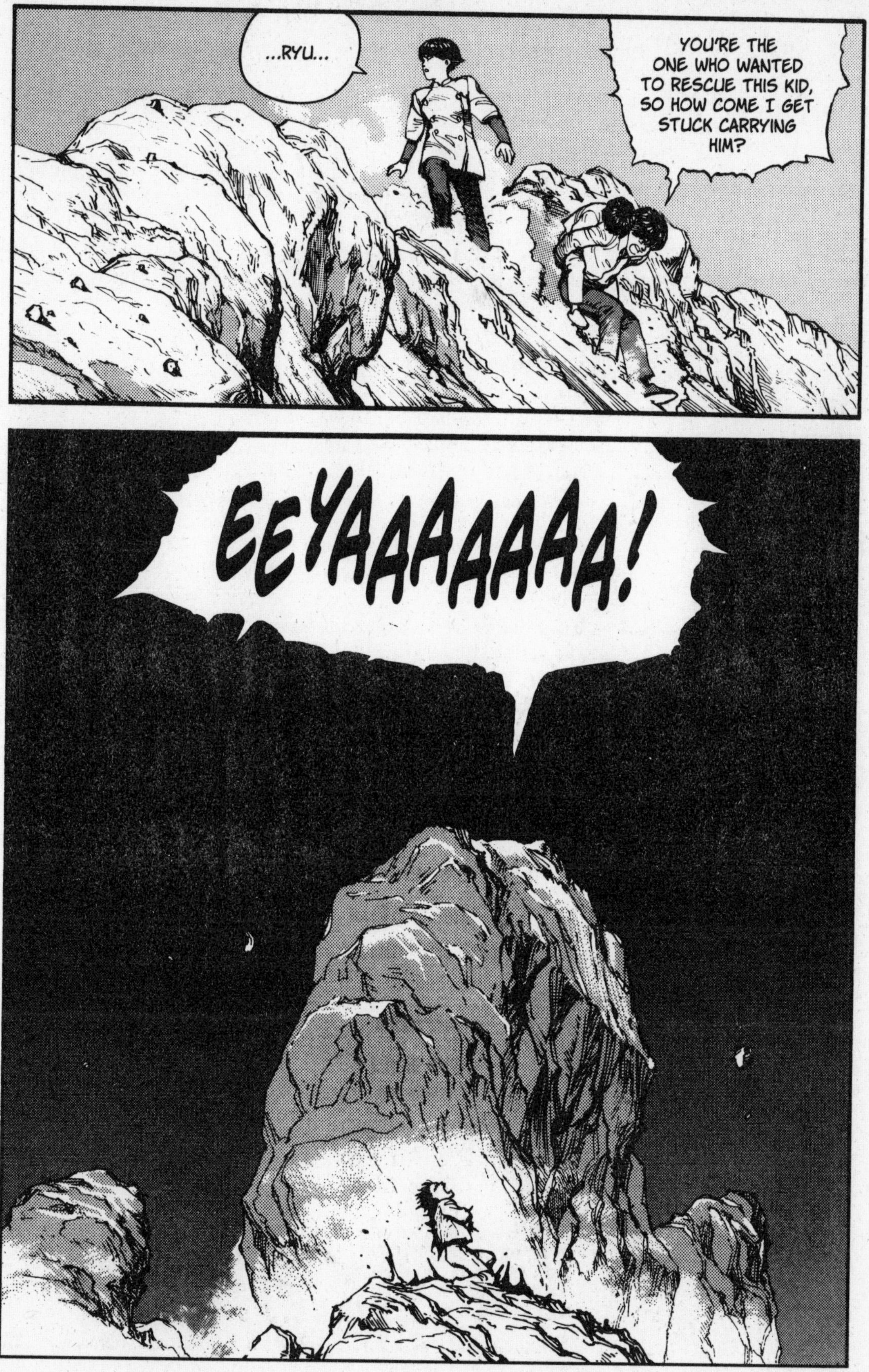
...RYU...
YOU'RE THE ONE WHO WANTED TO RESCUE THIS KID, SO HOW COME I GET STUCK CARRYING HIM?
EEYAAAAAAAA!

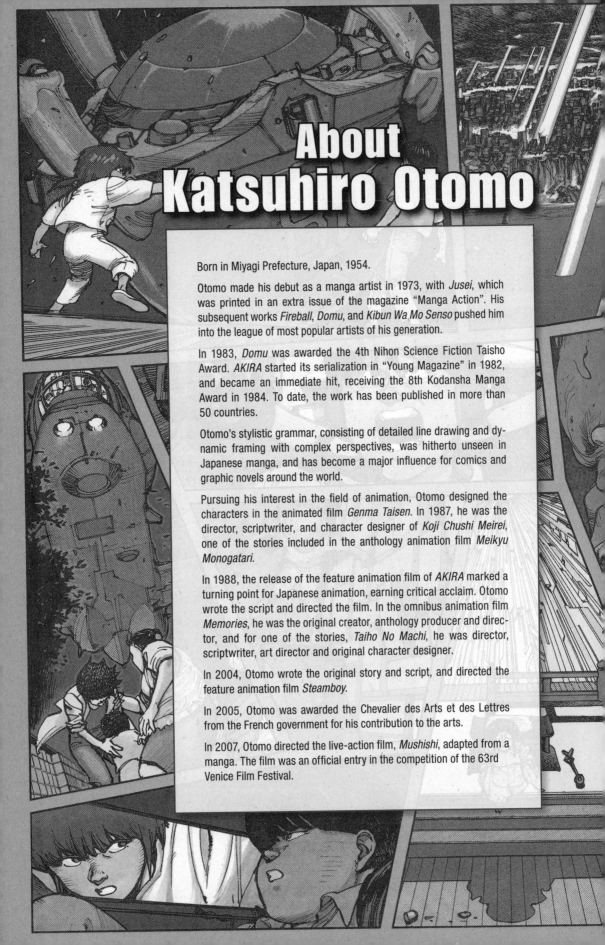

# About Katsuhiro Otomo

Born in Miyagi Prefecture, Japan, 1954.

Otomo made his debut as a manga artist in 1973, with *Jusei*, which was printed in an extra issue of the magazine "Manga Action". His subsequent works *Fireball*, *Domu*, and *Kibun Wa Mo Senso* pushed him into the league of most popular artists of his generation.

In 1983, *Domu* was awarded the 4th Nihon Science Fiction Taisho Award. *AKIRA* started its serialization in "Young Magazine" in 1982, and became an immediate hit, receiving the 8th Kodansha Manga Award in 1984. To date, the work has been published in more than 50 countries.

Otomo's stylistic grammar, consisting of detailed line drawing and dynamic framing with complex perspectives, was hitherto unseen in Japanese manga, and has become a major influence for comics and graphic novels around the world.

Pursuing his interest in the field of animation, Otomo designed the characters in the animated film *Genma Taisen*. In 1987, he was the director, scriptwriter, and character designer of *Koji Chushi Meirei*, one of the stories included in the anthology animation film *Meikyu Monogatari*.

In 1988, the release of the feature animation film of *AKIRA* marked a turning point for Japanese animation, earning critical acclaim. Otomo wrote the script and directed the film. In the omnibus animation film *Memories*, he was the original creator, anthology producer and director, and for one of the stories, *Taiho No Machi*, he was director, scriptwriter, art director and original character designer.

In 2004, Otomo wrote the original story and script, and directed the feature animation film *Steamboy*.

In 2005, Otomo was awarded the Chevalier des Arts et des Lettres from the French government for his contribution to the arts.

In 2007, Otomo directed the live-action film, *Mushishi*, adapted from a manga. The film was an official entry in the competition of the 63rd Venice Film Festival.

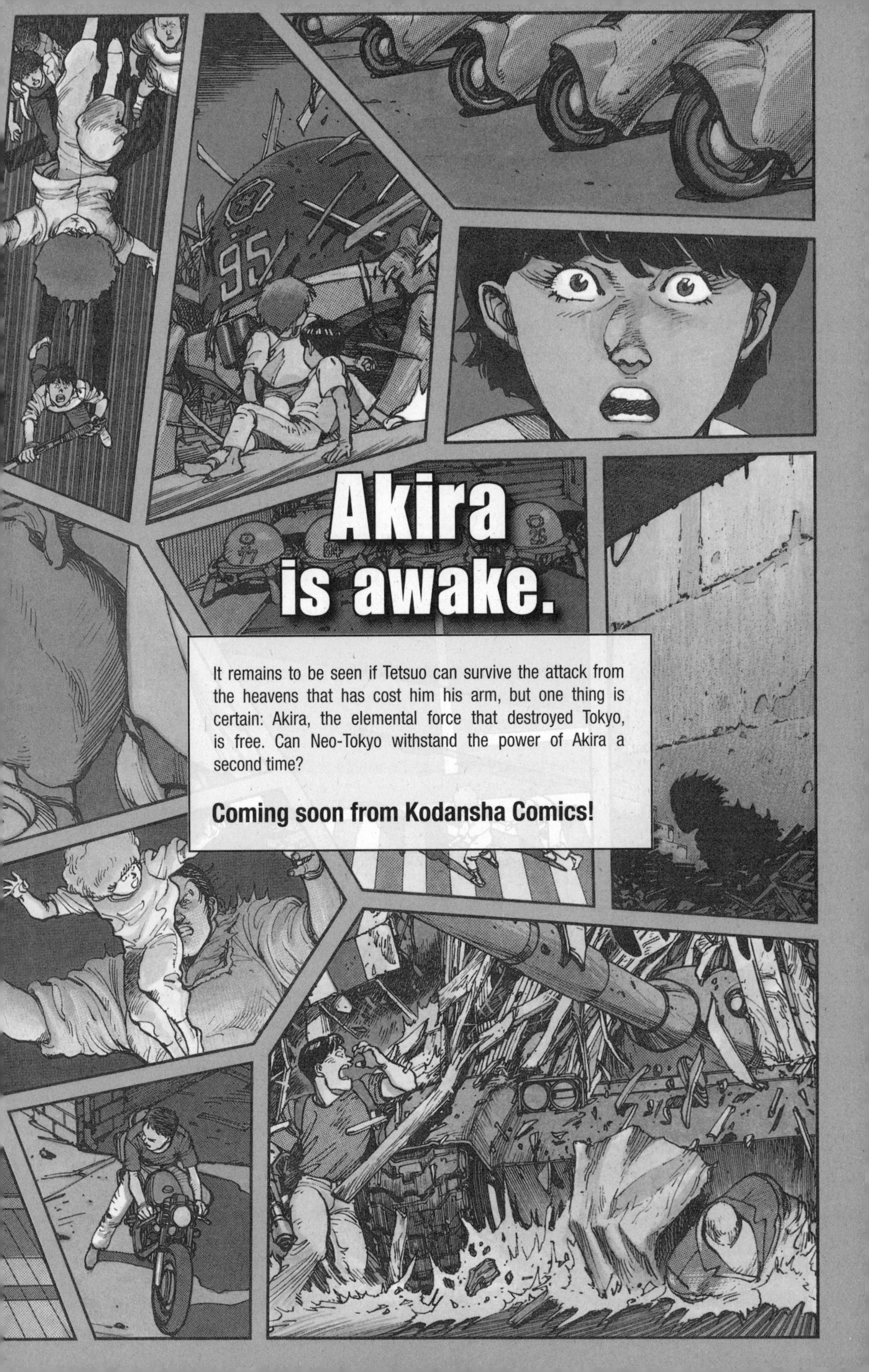
Akira
is awake.
It remains to be seen if Tetsuo can survive the attack from the heavens that has cost him his arm, but one thing is certain: Akira, the elemental force that destroyed Tokyo, is free. Can Neo-Tokyo withstand the power of Akira a second time?
Coming soon from Kodansha Comics!

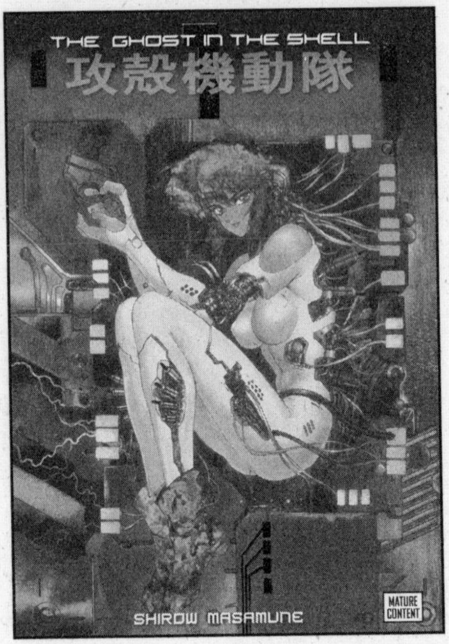
THE GHOST IN THE SHELL
攻殻機動隊
SHIROW MASAMUNE
MATURE CONTENT
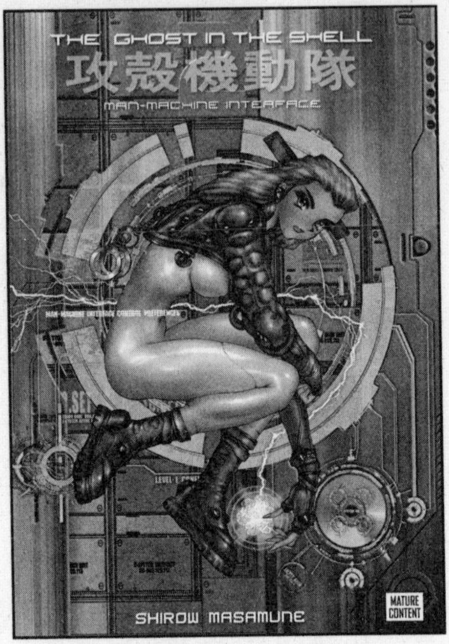
THE GHOST IN THE SHELL
攻殻機動隊
MAN-MACHINE INTERFACE
SHIROW MASAMUNE
MATURE CONTENT

**The Ghost in the Shell series:**

**The Graphic Novels That Inspired a Generation of Filmmakers**

**In a futuristic world where society has become highly information intensive, and the human mind can dive directly into the computer network through neural devices, the thin line that defines the conscious self is referred to as one's "ghost." Major Motoko Kusanagi, leading Public Security Bureau Section 9, is human—but with an entirely cybernetic body. As her team solves one case after another of network crime and terrorism, she encounters a highly intelligent being that is not organic in origin.**

**#1 The Ghost in the Shell**

**#2 Man-Machine Interface**

**#1.5 Human Error Processor**

KC KODANSHA COMICS